EDITORS
Arnold P. Goldstein, Syracu
Leonard Krasner, Stanford University &

RESEARCH DESIGN IN
CLINICAL PSYCHOLOGY

RESEARCH DESIGN IN CLINICAL PSYCHOLOGY

Second Edition

ALAN E. KAZDIN
Yale University

Allyn and Bacon
Boston • London • Toronto • Sydney • Tokyo • Singapore

ISBN 0-205-14587-6

Printed in the United States of America

98 97 96 95 94   10 9 8 7 6 5 4

Library of Congress Cataloging-in-Publication Data

Kazdin, Alan E.
     Research design in clinical psychology / by Alan E. Kazdin.—2nd
        p.   cm.—(general psychology series ; 169)
     Includes bibliographical references and indexes.

     1. Clinical psychology—Research—Methodology. I. Title.
II. Series.
     [DNLM: 1. Psychology, CLinical. 2. Research Design. WM 105
K23r]
RC467.8.K39   1991
616.89'0072—dc20
DNLM/DLC
for Library of Congress   91-4603
                                                                                          CIP

To Nicole & Michelle

CONTENTS

PREFACE

The purpose of the present book is to describe and discuss methodology and research design in clinical psychology. The focus is on clinical psychology but the issues and methods are relevant to other areas as well, such as counseling, education, psychiatry, and social work, to mention a few. The topics within each of these areas span theory, research, and application. Consequently, many of the methodological challenges are shared. The book elaborates the methods of conducting research and the broad range of practices, procedures, and designs for developing a sound knowledge base.

Many available texts on methodology elaborate fundamental practices and methods of research design. Often research methods are presented by describing idealized conditions of laboratory studies or in abstract discussions removed from investigations within the field. In clinical psychology as well as related areas a great deal of research is conducted outside of the laboratory. Essentials of research design are no less important. Indeed, an in-depth understanding of research design is of even greater importance in clinical research than in areas where laboratory controls and procedures are routinely available. In clinical research, the range of influences that can obscure the relations among variables is vast. These influences cannot be used as an excuse for poorly designed research. On the contrary, the subject matter requires grasp of the nuances of design so that special experimental arrangements, novel control conditions, and methods of statistical evaluation can be deployed to maximize clarity of our results. Research design in clinical work requires rigor and creativity as a defense against the multitude of influences that can hide the relations among variables.

The scope of the areas researched and the challenging obstacles that can arise have made research design in clinical psychology a rich topic. Traditionally, clinical psychology has embraced a variety of topics including the study of personality, assessment and prediction of psychological functioning and adjustment, etiology, course, and outcome of various forms of psychopathology, processes and outcomes of psychotherapy and other forms of intervention, and cross-cultural differences in personality and behavior, among others. Many issues of contemporary life have added to the range of topics, as witnessed by the strong role that clinical psychology plays in health psychology, rehabilitation, and prevention, and the understanding of violence, crime, homelessness, substance abuse, alternative family constellation patterns in child rearing, treatment and care of children and the elderly, and child and adult development. The complexion of current social living and the broad range of social and cultural issues contribute to the richness of the field.

The topical breadth also has been accompanied by a diversity of research methods. Consider a few of the dimensions that convey the methodological diversity of the field. Research in clinical psychology encompasses large-scale investigations as well as experiments with individual subjects; methods of data evaluation include inferential statistical techniques as well as nonstatistical and clinical criteria to assess change; experiments are conducted not only in laboratory settings, but also in hospitals, clinics, schools, and in the community. The diversity of topics and types of research requires coverage and appreciation of the full range of methodological weapons that can be deployed to combat ambiguity.

The present book is designed to address methodology in the contexts in which clinical psychologists are called upon to work with the special demands that these contexts impose. Although specific methodological practices and procedures are covered in detail, the book focuses on their underpinnings and raison d'être. After all, methodology is not merely a compilation of practices and procedures. Rather, it is an approach toward problem solving, thinking, and acquiring knowledge. An investigator in clinical psychology frequently is called upon to resolve questions related to evaluation when the usual practices cannot be used and to maximize the knowledge yield from the demonstration.

The content of the book encompasses diverse topics, including experimental design, assessment, sources of artifact and bias, data analyses and interpretation, and ethical issues raised by research. Issues are traced as they emerge in planning and executing research including developing the research idea, selecting methods, procedures, and assessment devices, analyzing and interpreting the data, and preparing the written report of the results. At each stage of research, principles, pitfalls, artifacts, and biases, alternative strategies, and guidelines are presented. Attention also is devoted to quasi-experiments, subject-selection studies, case studies and single-case experiments for clinical use, criteria for evaluating clinical interventions, and other issues as they interface with clinical research.

The topics of the book represent an expansion over those included in the first edition. Since the prior version, the substantive topics and methodological strategies in clinical psychology have continued to proliferate. The revised text has been designed to reflect methods, issues, and topics of contemporary research. The revised edition elaborates a broad range of experimental and quasi-experimental designs for research and clinical application, alternative statistical considerations that relate to design of the study and evaluation of the results, ethical responsibilities of the investigator, and integration of methodology and the decision-making process to augment the preparation of manuscripts for publication. New chapters and variations in chapter organization have been required to convey contemporary methods of clinical research. Several topics of the prior edition have been retained, including many of the basic design and assessment alternatives and the rationale for basic practices.

Examples draw upon classic studies as well as from recent research to illustrate points; the examples largely have been updated in the present edition.

The present edition includes didactic aids for the reader. First, outlines are provided at the beginning of each chapter. The purpose is to help organize the content and scope of the issues that each topic entails. Second, at the end of each chapter, a short list of readings is provided. These readings refer to more specialized presentations of topics within the chapter for the interested reader. Finally, a Glossary is included at the end of the book to centralize and briefly define terms introduced throughout the chapters. Although the book is not overabundant in terminology, there is value to providing a quick reference to terms and practices.

Several people have contributed to the thrust and focus of this book over the last several years. The list of mentors, colleagues, and students would be lengthy; the net effect would be to diffuse the gratitude I feel to each individual. Opportunities to interact with several editors of the American Psychological Association journals and to work closely with associate editors, consulting editors, and reviewers for journals within clinical psychology were invaluable. These contacts were very helpful in placing many methodological issues in the context of the broader research base of the field and common methodological shortcomings of all of our work. The manuscript benefited by able assistance throughout. Mary Dulgeroff and Claudia Wolfson played central roles in bringing this manuscript to fruition. I am grateful for their assistance. Jerome Frank, Vice-President of Pergamon Press, provided support and advice throughout preparation of this book. His untimely death is a personal and professional loss to those of us fortunate to share a portion of his life.

Several sources of research support were provided during the period in which this book was written. I am especially grateful to the National Institute of Mental Health for the support of a Research Scientist Award (MH00353), which provided research, educational, and training opportunities directly related to assessment, methodology, and design. Also, support for research projects from the National Institute of Mental Health (MH35408), The Robert Wood Johnson Foundation, and The Rivendell Foundation of America during preparation of this book is gratefully acknowledged.

INTRODUCTION

The general purpose of science is to establish knowledge. Many areas of scientific investigation, such as the study of the stars, weather, plants, and animals, are familiar to us. Although the general subject matter of these areas is generally familiar, the systematic methods of investigation in scientific research and how these methods improve upon casual observation are not widely appreciated. Indeed, occasionally the public is skeptical about scientific research and what it yields. For example, the seemingly frequent findings that various foods or food additives may cause cancer in animals has raised public disenchantment with scientific research. New products and by-products and materials or elements present in everyday life (e.g., asbestos, radon) continue to be shown in research to contribute to cancer risk in humans. The disenchantment is reflected in the quip that "the only thing that causes cancer is scientific research!"

Scientific research is essential for understanding natural phenomena. Although a number of research methods are available, they have in common careful observation and systematic evaluation of the subject matter under varying conditions. The diverse methods constitute special arrangements and plans of observation that are designed to uncover relations between variables in a relatively unambiguous fashion. The relations may seem apparent in nature when a particular phenomenon is observed casually. Yet many relations are obscured by the complex interrelations and combinations of many variables as they normally appear. The task of identifying relations is compounded by the characteristics and limits of our perception. Among complex relations, it is easy and natural for us to connect variables perceptually and conceptually and to then integrate these into our belief systems. The relations can be firmly entrenched independently of whether the variables genuinely go together or are related in fact.

Scientific research attempts to simplify the complexity of nature and to isolate a particular phenomenon for careful scrutiny. The relation is examined by manipulating or varying values of the variable of interest while controlling extraneous factors that might otherwise influence the results. By controlling or holding constant sources of influence that might vary under ordinary circumstances, the relation between the variables of interest can be examined. In addition to arranging features of nature, science also provides a method to aid perception. The methods consist of diverse practices, procedures, and decision rules to aid in drawing conclusions and in reaching a consensus about relations observed in research.

In the present book, we shall discuss the several methods of research within clinical psychology. More central than the individual methods of research is the logic and underlying issues that the research methods are designed to address. Research methods are implemented to address specific concerns, potential problems, artifacts, and biases that serve as impediments to knowledge. It is important to understand these impediments, especially so in clinical, counseling, educational psychology, and other areas where research spans theory and application. Outside of the laboratory, it is usually the case that rigors of research methods and experimentation are challenged. Understanding the underlying obstacles to knowledge is critical because of the need to apply methodology to draw valid inferences.

METHODOLOGY AND RESEARCH DESIGN

Methodology refers to the diverse principles, procedures, and practices that govern research. Within that general domain is the concept of *research design,* which refers to the plan or arrangement that is used to examine the question of interest. These terms tend to focus on the specific practices and options that characterize research. The focus of the present book is on methodology and research design and hence will cover diverse practices and procedures. Yet, the focus on concrete methods and practices has the danger of emphasizing ingredients of research and perhaps conjuring up a cookbook for the design of experiments. Research design is not a matter of including specific practices or ingredients. Even highly revered practices (e.g., random assignment of subjects, use of large sample sizes) may be unnecessary to reach valid inferences in a given study. The issue is one of understanding the rationale for methodological practices as well as the practices themselves.

Methodology refers to a way of thinking and as such it is beneficial to avoid over concretization of the research process. Design and methodology alert us to the issues that affect how we examine and interpret phenomena. Consider an example of the type of thinking that methodology fosters. Sir Francis Galton (1822–1911), the British scientist, examined the extent to which prayer increases longevity (see Galton, 1872). Specifically, he was interested in whether praying for the health and longevity of other people in fact added years to the lives of those people. The hypothesis would be one of great theoretical and applied interest to say the least. Galton reasoned that if prayer were effective, then kings, queens, and other royalty would live longer than others. After all, their health and longevity are consistently the objects of prayer (as attested to by frequent exhortations, "Long live the Queen," in contrast to the vastly less familiar, "Long live the beggar").

Galton reported data from different groups who were presumed to vary in the extent to which people prayed for their health and longevity. The groups and the data they generated are noteworthy (see Galton, 1872). The results indicated that royalty died at an earlier age than nonroyalty. Specifically, the results indicated that the mean (average) age at the time of death of royalty was 64.0 years, a number *lower* than other groups, including lawyers (68.1 years), naval officers (68.4 years), men of literature and science (67.6 years), the gentry (70.2 years), and other groups. Thus, royalty died at a younger age. Does this study show that prayer was *in*effective in increasing the longevity of royalty? Of course not.

Methodology teaches us ways to think about the relations among variables, about causes and effects, and about conclusions drawn from theory, research, and experience. In the specific case of Galton's study, methodology draws our attention to the hypothesis, findings, how the phenomenon was studied, and alternative explanations of the data. It might well be that at the time of Galton, royalty without the benefit of other people's prayers would have died at an earlier age than the mean of 64.0 years. Perhaps the sedentary schedule, rich food, weighty responsibility, frequent guest appearances, and tight fitting, heavy, and jewel-laden clothes of royalty would have conspired to produce a much earlier death. Let us say, for hypothetical purposes, that royalty during the time of Galton would normally live to be 55 years of age, on average. This figure contrasts with the mean of 64 years found by Galton. It is quite possible that prayer did in fact increase longevity from, say, 55 to 64 years of the royalty included in Galton's study. The data only show that royalty died at a younger age than comparison samples. Yet the hypothesis is not that royalty will live longer than nonroyalty but whether prayer increases longevity. It is quite possible that prayer increases longevity (number of years of living) without making one group of people actually live longer than another group. The original hypothesis remains unscathed and in need of further testing.

All sorts of research possibilities might be generated to clarify the results. We might, for example, wish to examine the longevity of royalty and the extent to which royalty are prayed for. Presumably "more might be better" and all royalty are not prayed for equally. Groups within the overall "royalty class" might be matched on health characteristics related to longevity (e.g., age, sex, blood pressure, family history of disease and longevity) but who vary in the extent to which they are the objects of prayer. To ensure that they differed in the extent to which they were prayed for, perhaps we could survey the public to identify the persons for whom their prayers are directed. Also, it is possible that members of royalty themselves engage in more (or less) praying than do others. Perhaps *praying* rather than *being prayed for* is critical. In general, we would wish to control for or assess several variables that plausibly relate to longevity to ensure that these did not vary between groups or were taken into account when comparing groups.

It is important not to belabor the example. At the same time, how a study is conducted very much determines the extent to which the conclusions can be interpreted. Methodology is a way of thinking about phenomena because it alerts us to the types of questions to ask and, equally important, to the practices designed to obtain enlightened answers.

Designing experimental research often is presented as a straightforward enterprise. At the most rudimentary level, the design includes an experimental and a control group. The experimental group receives some form of the experimental condition or intervention; the control group does not receive the intervention. Differences between groups are considered to reflect the effect of the experimental manipulation. Although the basic comparison is well intentioned in principle, it greatly oversimplifies the bulk of contemporary research and the type of control procedures required in most studies in clinical psychology. Research design is a fascinating topic because of the many different ways in which experiments can be completed, the advantages and disadvantages associated with the available design options, and the contribution of different designs to the results.

Scientific hypotheses are attempts to explain, predict, and explore specific relations. When hypotheses are formulated, they represent "if–then" statements about a particular phenomenon. The "if" portion of the hypothesis often refers to the independent variable that is manipulated or varied in some other way, whereas the "then" portion refers to the dependent variable or resulting data. Findings consistent with an experimental hypothesis do not necessarily prove that hypothesis. Data could only be taken as proof of a hypothesis if no conceivable alternative hypothesis could account for the results or if the predicted relations would be obtained if and only if the hypothesis were true. Yet these requirements are more likely to be met in logic and deductive reasoning than in scientific research. Whether another hypothesis conceivably could account for the results may be a matter for future investigators to elaborate. Also, whether a finding would only result from a particular hypothesis cannot be known with any certainty. The confidence of certainty provided in logical deductions is not available in science. Of course, this fact refers to the logical bases of scientific conclusions. As scientists, we often feel quite certain about our conclusions. The experience or feeling of certainty is separate from the logical status and truth value of scientific propositions.

Not all experiments are conducted to test a particular prediction or "if–then" relation. Many experiments explore the relations of variables and are not formulated as tests of hypotheses. Yet the tenuous nature of the conclusions still applies. The findings, however systematic, do not necessarily reflect the effects of the manipulated variables. The findings may be a function of unspecified factors extraneous to the manipulation itself. A number of these factors may be uncontrolled variables within or outside of the experiment and serve as explanations of the findings.

Although many extraneous factors can be recognized and controlled in advance of an experiment, others cannot. It may even take years of research to recognize that something in the experiment other than the variable of interest contributed to the original findings. For example, in human drug research, a routine practice is to keep the hospital staff or experimenters naive so that they do not know who is receiving the experimental (treatment) drug and who is receiving a placebo. Keeping staff naive is now recognized to be important because their beliefs and expectancies can influence patients' behavior independently of the drugs. In years past, many drug studies lacking this precaution were completed and can now be only regarded as inconclusive.

Methodology is directed at planning an experiment in such a way as to rule out competing explanations of the results. The better an experiment is designed, the fewer the alternative plausible explanations that can be advanced to account for the findings. Ideally, only the effects of the independent variable could be advanced as the basis for the results. Several methodological features we shall discuss are designed to maximize clarity of the findings.

PHILOSOPHY OF SCIENCE, RESEARCH METHODOLOGY, AND STATISTICAL INFERENCE

Experimentation encompasses three broad interrelated topics: philosophy of science, research methodology, and statistical inference. Philosophy of science considers the logical and epistemological underpinnings of the scientific method in general. Historically, experimentation has been closely tied to philosophical thought. Topics such as the basis of knowledge, the organization and limitations of perception, the nature of "causal" relations, methods and limitations of inductive reasoning, the conditions required for testing and verifying predictions, and indeed the very notion of a "hypothesis" all revert to philosophy. The philosophy of science reveals, among other things, that there may be fundamental limitations from a logical standpoint in what experiments can provide in the way of knowing. Experimental methods rely upon several presuppositions and assumptions about the nature of the world and how information about natural phenomena can be elaborated. Even to speak of experimentation glosses over a host of assumptions about the legitimacy of empirical knowledge and the methods through which it is obtained.

The philosophy of science can cogently challenge the assumptions about the basis of empirical knowledge. The philosophical challenge points to the tenuous nature of empirical knowledge and its logical limits. Yet the challenge has not deterred research from progressing to elaborate natural phenomena. The day-to-day business of the researcher requires planning investigations so that conceptual, interpretive, and practical problems are minimized. Research methodology, rather than philosophy of science, enters at this point to provide options that maximize the clarity of the results.

Broadly conceived, methodology encompasses the procedures and practices of conducting and designing research so that lawful relations can be identified. Results of research by their very nature are ambiguous because any particular finding may depend on unique features of the setting and experimental arrangement in which the finding was obtained. Because ambiguity can never be eliminated, *minimizing ambiguity* is the primary task of research methods and the goal of a given experiment.

Statistical inference is integrally related to experimentation because of the extensive reliance upon statistical tests in research to draw conclusions from the data. Also, statistical techniques can be used to focus the interpretation of the findings of a particular study. Statistical controls or analyses of variables within the study that might contribute to or be confounded with the independent variable can help to reduce the plausibility of alternative interpretations of the results. Thus statistical analyses often work in concert with methodology.

Statistical evaluation provides agreed-upon decision rules so that there is some uniformity in the criteria used to draw conclusions. Ironically, the criteria for making statistical inferences themselves often are based on arbitrary decisions. For example, the precise point that a finding is called statistically reliable or "significant" is purely a matter of convention rather than being a statistically or logically justifiable criterion or, in a given situation, even well advised. The manner in which experimental data should be analyzed statistically and the advantages and disadvantages of different types of analyses are widely discussed and debated. Theoretical developments in mathematics and statistics have made the area of statistical inference extremely important in its own right in understanding how data are to be interpreted and how experiments are to be designed to maximize interpretability.

The philosophy of science, research methodology, and statistical inference overlap considerably. The present text generally focuses on research methods in clinical psychology. This focus will require excursions to issues related to the basis of knowing and interpretation, but clearly not into epistemological discussions. Similarly, we shall address selected statistical issues in which research design is inextricably bound. The excursions into other topics are all designed to serve the central goal, namely, to examine research methodology.

CHARACTERISTICS OF RESEARCH IN CLINICAL PSYCHOLOGY

Clinical psychology embraces standard features of scientific research such as defining the research idea, generating hypotheses, designing investigations, collecting and analyzing data, and so on. Yet in clinical psychology and related disciplines in which laboratory, clinical, and applied studies are conducted, the basic steps of research and methodological acumen of the investigator are challenged. The special demands for understanding research methods can be suggested by highlighting the substantive and methodological diversity of the field.

Substantive diversity refers to the content areas that clinical psychology encompasses. The content areas of the field are vast and would be difficult even to enumerate fully, much less describe. Consider for a moment just a few of the domains. Clinical psychology includes the study of diverse *populations* as illustrated by investigations of all age groups from infancy through the elderly; indeed, the field extends beyond these age limits by studying processes before birth (e.g., prenatal characteristics of mothers and families) and after death (e.g., the impact of death on relatives, treatment of bereavement). Also, a variety of special populations are studied such as those with special experiences (e.g., the homeless, prisoners of war), with psychological or psychiatric impairment (e.g., children, adolescents, or adults with depression, anxiety, posttraumatic stress disorder, autism, schizophrenia, to mention only a few), and with medical impairment and disease (e.g., cancer, Acquired Immune Deficiency Syndrome [AIDS], spinal cord injury, diabetes). People in contact with special populations (i.e., others who experience a condition directly) themselves are often studied (e.g., children of alcoholics, spouses of depressed patients, siblings of physically handicapped children).

Examples of a few of the populations in clinical research merely begins to convey the breadth of focus. Consider a few other research domains that might be mentioned. Research in clinical psychology is conducted in diverse *settings* (e.g., laboratory, clinics, hospitals, prisons, schools, industry) and in the absence of structured settings (e.g., homelessness). Clinical psychology research is also conducted in conjunction with *multiple disciplines* (e.g., medicine, psychiatry, neurology, pediatrics, criminology). In addition, central areas of research within the field have remarkable breadth in the topics they encompass. For example, rich and broad areas of research include the following: the study of personality characteristics; the assessment, diagnosis, treatment, and prevention of clinical dysfunction; and cross-cultural and ethnic variations in personality, adjustment, and maladjustment.

Understandably, diverse methods of study are required to meet alternative conditions in which clinical psychologists work and the special challenges in drawing valid scientific inferences from often complex situations. The methodological diversity of clinical research, as the substantive diversity, can be illustrated in many different ways. Considering the type of designs, research encompasses investigations where specific variables are experimentally manipulated (e.g., true experiments) and where subject characteristics are observed (e.g., correlational or passive-observational studies). Also, clinical research includes varied types of group designs as well as single-case experiments. In addition, the conditions of research vary widely including, at one extreme, brief, highly controlled laboratory studies with college students, and at the other extreme, long-term evaluations in clinical or applied settings (e.g., schools, hospitals, prisons) where manipulations and interventions may be less well controlled. We shall have the opportunity to detail diverse methodological practices and options. However, the point is merely to note that the field entails diverse areas of content and diverse methods of study.

The purpose of research is to draw scientifically based and sound inferences about the impact of a particular independent variable. This is accomplished by arranging the situation, through experimental control, close observation, and prediction and statistical evaluation, to draw valid inferences. Research in clinical psychology shares all of the usual obstacles in research to which experimental design is aimed. Yet there are special obstacles that the very subject matter often raises. The range of research topics means that an investigator can profit from understanding the issues underlying research methods. The reason is that the issues often need to be addressed in novel ways.

The purpose in highlighting the diversity and richness of clinical psychology is to underscore the importance of facility with the methods of research. Special demands or constraints are frequently placed on the clinical researcher. Ideal methodological practices (e.g., random assignment) are not always available. Also, restrictions (e.g., a control group might not be feasible, only small sample sizes are available) may limit the researcher's options. The task of the scientist is to draw valid inferences from the situation and to use methodology, design, and statistics toward that end. In clinical psychology and related areas of research, the options in methodology, design, and statistics must be greater than in more basic research areas to permit the investigator to select and identify creative solutions. Clinical research is not in any way soft science; indeed, the processes involved in clinical research reflect science at its best precisely because of the thinking and methodological ingenuity required to force nature to reveal its secrets. Deploying strategies to accomplish this requires an appreciation of the purposes of research in terms of the specific concerns that are to be addressed. We shall consider these concerns to provide the underpinnings of research strategies that follow.

THE "PSYCHOLOGY" OF RESEARCH METHODOLOGY

Methodology embraces the understanding of many principles and general strategies as well as several specific practices for conducting research. In detailing the research practices and goals toward which they are aimed, it is easy to depersonalize the research enterprise. At the outset, it is critical to underscore that research design, and science more generally, is basically a human enterprise. This does not mean that the methods and findings are subjective or that science is guided by whim. Yet researchers are "people" first. This obvious statement has broad implications for our subject matter. As people, we have ideas, beliefs, ambitions, individual histories and experiences, and so on. These natural human characteristics do not seep into science; they are central to it.

Consider, for example, the goal of research, namely, to draw clear inferences about the relations among variables. In subsequent chapters, we shall spend a great deal of time on ways to design investigations to maximize the clarity of the findings. Yet "clarity of the findings" is not a property of the results of a study. Rather, it has to do with the consensus among those who read the report of the study. Reaching a consensus extends beyond epistemology or that branch of philosophy that addresses how we come to know things. Of relevance as well is the substantive information from psychology (e.g., perception, learning, attitudes, beliefs, persuasion).

In most research, findings are not unequivocally clear. Research must accumulate for years to elaborate a phenomenon and to clarify the circumstances in which the effects are evident. In such circumstances, our individual *thresholds* for stating that the findings are established clearly assume an important role. At what point shall we believe that a particular finding is sound or true? The threshold varies as a function of the specific area of research, strength of our beliefs, prior training and experiences, and no doubt many other factors. A finding may more readily be embraced as "clear" or "valid" to the extent it is compatible with these factors.

Our thresholds for believing may vary for our own research versus the research of others. The language with which we refer to our own research and the research of others may belie our varied research thresholds for believability. For example, when *I* use weak measures in my studies and have an inadequate control group, I may regard and refer to the study as *somewhat weak, the best that could be done under the circumstances,* and *clearly better than prior work in the area.* When *you* conduct an experiment with similar characteristics, I may view this a bit more harshly. The study may *lack essential controls, be seriously flawed,* and *preclude conclusions about the phenomenon of interest.* We need not lament the different standards that individuals may apply to a given area of research, type of experiment, and so on. It is mentioned here to provide an important context for methodology and research design.

Methodology has to do in part with the persuasiveness of findings. We engage in specific strategies and practices to persuade ourselves individually as well as the scientific community at large. Often findings are so clear and repeated so often that consensus is great. Even here, clarity is a matter of degree and individual preference. For example, for years data on the dangers of cigarette smoking varied in their credibility to scientists and the public. At

first, individuals may have doubted the main finding (e.g., cigarettes are hazardous to one's health). As the evidence accumulated (and entered the mass
media), more people were persuaded and acknowledged this evidence as
"true." Some still are not persuaded; others are persuaded but retain their
original belief by stating that there are special circumstances in their case that
mitigates the dangers of smoking. Their belief is retained not by denying the
finding (a main effect) but by noting that the danger of cigarette smoking is
not applicable given their special circumstances (an interaction). The specific
hypothesis under which such people operate might well be accurate, namely,
that in their case some other variable may reduce the danger. That hypothesis
may be untrue, is unlikely to be well tested, and probably is inadvisable to
believe from the standpoint of physical health.

The example is mentioned here to convey crucial aspects about beliefs and
how they influence the clarity and impact of research findings. The task for
an individual study as well as for the field as a whole is to develop tests of
hypotheses that are convincing. "Convincing" in this context does not mean
that the results show a particular pattern, "prove" the hypotheses, or demonstrate that the investigator is "right." Rather, "convincing" relates to the
quality of the research design and those features that permit sound inferences
to be drawn. A well-designed study would provide a convincing test so that
the results, whatever their pattern, would be persuasive to the investigator as
well as to others in the scientific community.

The fact that research depends on beliefs and persuasion is not a weakness
of the enterprise. It is, however, important to accept this as a given and as a
critical point of departure. The task before us is to uncover the secrets of
nature. We adopt strategies of all sorts—theory construction, research methodology, and statistical evaluation—to aid in our task. Each strategy involves
decision points that may affect the clarity of the conclusions we draw. Reasonable people not only can disagree about the conclusions of individual studies
but do so routinely. Thus there are inherent limits to what we can expect from
an individual study not merely from the complexity of the subject matter but
because of the diversity of human characteristics upon which inferences and
interpretation depend. At the same time, there is much that we can do to
maximize the information from research and to accumulate knowledge in spite
of these limitations.

OVERVIEW OF THE BOOK

Research design can be viewed as a decision-making process. Decisions are
made at all stages of the process of an experiment ranging from deciding how
a particular idea should be tested in a concrete situation to how the data should
be evaluated and interpreted. It is not always possible to specify how each of

the decisions should be made in advance of considering a particular study. Each decision has its own implications and trade-offs in terms of the final product. Also, the decision may depend upon how the phenomenon examined in the experiment is conceptualized.

The present text describes and evaluates different methodological, design, and assessment options and the rationale for their use. The book focuses on many of the complexities of design by emphasizing the problems that arise in experimentation and techniques designed for their control. Advantages, limitations, and other considerations in using particular design practices are elaborated.

The purpose of research is to draw valid inferences about the relations among variables. Experimentation attempts to arrange the circumstances so as to minimize ambiguity in reaching these inferences. Many of the factors that can interfere with drawing clear conclusions from research can be readily identified. These factors are referred to as threats to validity and serve as the basis for why and how we conduct research. Alternative types of experimental validity and the factors that interfere with drawing conclusions serve as the bases for chapters 2 and 3.

The experiment begins with an idea that becomes translated into a specific question or statement. A particular subset of variables is selected for manipulation or scrutiny. Sources of research ideas, types of variables, alternative research questions, and the conditions under which these are investigated are described in chapter 4.

An initial decision in research is selecting among the many different design options. Alternative group and single-case designs provide different ways of evaluating a particular variable. Advantages and potential limitations of each design, problems that are likely to arise, and control techniques to improve the designs are presented. Group designs are detailed in chapter 5, and alternative control and comparison conditions upon which these designs rely are presented in chapter 6. Single-case research designs and their use in clinical work are discussed in chapter 7. The importance of the single case (e.g., case studies) is highlighted. Specific research design options are presented along with considerations that dictate their use. Also, efforts to adapt these designs to clinical work are discussed.

Independently of the design, a crucial aspect of the experiment is ensuring that the manipulation of the independent variable was effectively achieved. Checking on the experimental manipulation can greatly enhance the conclusions drawn from research. The procedures to assess the implementation of the experimental manipulation, the interpretation of the results of these techniques, and the problems that may arise are elaborated in chapter 8.

Selection of the dependent variable raises a number of conceptual and assessment issues. The requirements for "appropriate" and useful measures in a particular experiment are manifold. Different modalities of assessment may be selected and, within these, vast options are available for specific measurement techniques. Usually more than one assessment modality is incorporated into the design. The relative priority of different modalities and specific measures depends upon both the substantive and methodological considerations elaborated in chapter 9. Special topics in assessment, the focus of chapter 10, include reactivity of assessment, the methods and use of unobtrusive measures, and criteria to evaluate interventions such as psychotherapy. This chapter raises a number of issues especially pertinent to treatment research including client-, treatment-, and consumer-related measures of outcome, as well as the issues, problems, and procedures of follow-up assessment.

Many sources of artifacts and bias can interfere with drawing valid inferences. These may derive from the investigator who designs and analyzes the experiment, the experimenter who actually runs the subjects, demand characteristics of the experimental situation, the roles that subjects adopt as they participate in the study, and subject-selection biases prior to and during the experiment. Chapter 11 examines these influences, the manner in which they are likely to affect the results, and methods to minimize, assess, or eliminate their impact.

Evaluating the results of an experiment raises many options in clinical psychology. Chapter 12 focuses on alternative methods of data evaluation including statistical, nonstatistical, and clinical methods. Criteria, strengths, and weaknesses of alternative methods are discussed. Special topics related to data evaluation and interpretation are covered in chapter 13. Different types of effects produced by independent variables, negative results (no-difference findings), and replication of research are presented.

Conducting psychological experiments raises ethical issues that bear directly upon design considerations. The manner in which a hypothesis is examined may entail the use of deception, invasion of privacy, and violation of confidentiality. One reason the ethical issues are essential to consider is that they frequently specify the confines in which design options must be selected. Ethical issues in relation to the protection of subject rights, dilemmas of clinical research, guidelines for research, and responsibilities of the investigator in relation to the research enterprise and the scientific community are presented in chapter 14.

Finally, completion of an experiment is often followed by preparation of a written report that may be intended for publication. Communication of the results is not specifically part of the topic of methodology. However, the thought and decision-making processes underlying the design of a study must be conveyed in the written report. Chapter 15 discusses the written report and its preparation in relation to methodological issues presented in previous chapters. The special role that methodological issues and concerns play in the communication and publication of research is highlighted.

FOR FURTHER READING

Lakatos, I. (1978). *The methodology of scientific research programmes.* Cambridge, England: Cambridge University Press.

Laudan, L. (1984). *Science and values.* Berkeley: University of California Press.

Manicas, P.T., & Secord, P.F. (1983). Implications for psychology of the new philosophy of science. *American Psychologist, 38,* 399–413.

Serlin, R.C., & Lapsley, D.K. (1985). Rationality in psychological research: The good-enough principle. *American Psychologist,* 40, 73–83.

Chapter 2

DRAWING VALID INFERENCES I: INTERNAL AND EXTERNAL VALIDITY

The purposes of experimentation are to uncover relations between variables that otherwise could not be readily detected and to verify relationships that have been hypothesized. Without experimentation, potential relations between variables must be viewed in their full complexity as they appear in nature. Research design and statistical evaluation help simplify the situation in which the influence of many variables, often operating simultaneously, can be separated from the variable(s) of interest to the investigator. Without such simplification and isolation of variables, many if not an unlimited number of interpretations could explain a particular phenomenon. The interpretive chaos and ambiguity that may result without experimentation is evident in anecdotal case reports in which one attempts to infer the relation between such events as early childhood experience and later adjustment or treatment and therapeutic change. Yet so many alternative explanations can be offered to explain the present condition of interest, and selection among the alternatives is a judgment call. Uncontrolled case reports usually do not provide an adequate basis for drawing valid inferences.

The unique contribution of an experiment is that it helps rule out or make implausible different factors that might explain a particular phenomenon. An experiment does not necessarily rule out all possible explanations. The extent to which it is successful in ruling out alternative explanations is a matter of degree. From a methodological standpoint, the better the design of an experiment the more implausible it makes competing explanations of the results.

TYPES OF VALIDITY

The purpose of research is to reach well-founded (i.e., valid) conclusions about the effects of a given intervention and the conditions under which it operates. Different types of experimental validity address these purposes in different ways. Four types of experimental validity have been identified: internal, external, construct, and statistical conclusion validity (Cook & Campbell, 1979). Table 2.1 lists each type of validity and the general type of questions to which each is addressed. Research design and its constituent methods and procedures, as well as methods of data analysis, are used to address these questions. Each type of validity is pivotal. Together they convey the multiple considerations that investigators have before them when they design an experiment.

It is not difficult to argue in any given instance that one type is *the* most important. Indeed, we shall provide examples where the very nature of the investigator's interest dictates the priority of one over another. In designing an experiment, it is critical for investigators to identify their purposes and specific questions clearly and to emphasize validity issues within the design that these entail. The reason is that it is difficult to design an experiment to address each type of validity equally well. A weak experiment is one in which the type of inferences the investigators wish to draw are not addressed well within the investigation. The present chapter discusses internal and external validity. These are presented first because they are relatively straightforward and reflect the logic of experimentation rather well. Also, failures to consider internal and external validity often represent the most blatant flaws in research.

Table 2.1. Types of Experimental Validity and the Questions They Address

TYPE OF VALIDITY	QUESTIONS ADDRESSED
Internal Validity	To what extent can the intervention, rather than extraneous influences, be considered to account for the results, changes, or group differences?
External Validity	To what extent can the results be generalized or extended to people, settings, times, measures, and characteristics other than those in this particular experimental arrangement?
Construct Validity	Given that the intervention was responsible for change, what specific aspects of the intervention or arrangement was the causal agent, that is, what is the conceptual basis (construct) underlying the effect?
Statistical Conclusion Validity	To what extent is a relation shown, demonstrated, or evident, and how well can the investigation detect effects if they exist?

INTERNAL VALIDITY

The task for experimentation is to examine the influence of a particular intervention in such a way that extraneous factors will not interfere with the conclusions that the investigator wishes to draw. Experiments help to reduce the plausibility that alternative influences could explain the results. The better the design of the experiment, the better it rules out alternative explanations of the results. In the ideal case, only one explanation of the results of an experiment would be possible, namely, that the independent variable accounted for change.

An experiment cannot determine with complete certainty that the independent variable accounted for change. However, if the experiment is carefully designed, the likelihood that the independent variable accounts for the results is high. When the results can be attributed with little or no ambiguity to the effects of the independent variable, the experiment is said to be internally valid. *Internal validity* refers to the extent to which an experiment rules out alternative explanations of the results. Factors or influences other than the independent variable that could explain the results are called *threats to internal validity.*

Threats to Internal Validity

Several types of threats to internal validity have been identified (e.g., Cook & Campbell, 1979). It is important to discuss threats to internal validity because they convey the reasons that carefully designed experiments are needed. An experiment needs to be designed to make these threats implausible. To the extent that each threat is ruled out or made relatively implausible, the experiment is said to be internally valid.

History

This threat to internal validity refers to any *event* occurring in the experiment (other than the independent variable) or outside of the experiment that may account for the results. History refers to the effects of events common to all subjects in their everyday lives (e.g., at home, school, or work). The influence of such historical events might alter performance and be mistaken for an effect resulting from the intervention or treatment. In an experiment it is important to be able to distinguish the effect of specific events occurring in the life of the subjects from the effect of the experimental manipulation or intervention.

Although history usually refers to events outside of the experiment, it may include events that take place during the experiment as well. When subjects are run in a group, unplanned events may occur (e.g., power blackout, medical emergency of one of the subjects, fire drill). It may be conceivable that the event disrupted administration of the intervention and reduced or enhanced the influence that normally would have occurred. Insofar as such events provide plausible explanations for the results, they threaten the validity of the experiment.

Maturation

Changes over time may result not only from specific events but also from *processes* within the subjects. Maturation refers to processes changing over time and includes growing older, stronger, wiser, and more tired or bored. Maturation is only a problem if the design cannot separate the effects of maturational changes from the intervention.

History and maturation often, but not invariably, go together as threats to internal validity. Although in any given case, it may not be easy to determine whether historical events or maturational processes accounted for change, it may not be essential to make the distinction in pointing out flaws in a study. For example, the problem of history and maturation can be seen in a study designed to evaluate the effects of training courses on childbirth for expectant mothers (Klusman, 1975). The purpose was to examine whether two different training courses reduced self-reported anxiety. One of the courses trained expectant mothers to engage in special exercises that would facilitate delivery (Lamaze method); the other course merely provided information about labor, delivery, and child care (Red Cross course). In general, both groups of expectant mothers showed a reduction in anxiety and were not different from each other.

The findings would be very important if they provided clear information about treatment since another facet of this study demonstrated that the level of maternal anxiety is related to the amount of pain experienced during labor. Unfortunately, there is no clear basis for asserting that either training program was responsible for change. It is quite possible that *historical events* occurring over time in the life of expectant mothers (e.g., reading about children, labor, and delivery; chatting with other expectant or new mothers about their experiences) or *maturational processes* (e.g., becoming less concerned about the anxieties of delivery over time) could explain the results. Special training programs may not be necessary for reductions in anxiety over the course of pregnancy. To help rule out the possible influence of history and maturation, the investigator could have sampled mothers who did not undergo training (i.e., a no-treatment group). This latter group would have helped to separate treatment effects from naturally occurring events or processes extraneous to treatment.

Testing

This threat to internal validity refers to the effects that taking a test one time may have on subsequent performance on the test. In an experiment, pre- and postintervention tests might be given to evaluate how much an individual improves or deteriorates over time on a particular measure. Performance at the second testing may be influenced by practice or familiarity with the test because of the first testing. Changes at the second testing might not be due to an experimental manipulation or intervention but to the effects of repeated testing. For example, in the previously noted investigation on childbirth, two different training courses were associated with reductions in anxiety on the part of expectant mothers (Klusman, 1975). It is quite possible that reduction of anxiety from the first to last sessions had nothing to do with training. Merely repeating the test might have led to different responses. This is plausible since it has been known for some time that repeated testing on personality measures may be associated with improvements in apparent adjustment (e.g., Windle, 1954). A group that receives repeated testing without the intervention, such as a no-treatment control group, can help rule out testing as an explanation of changes evident in the intervention group.

Instrumentation

This refers to changes in the measuring instrument or measurement procedures over time. For example, in many clinical studies ratings of client improvement or observations of overt behaviors are made. The standards or scoring criteria that the therapists or clients use in rating or observing behaviors may change over time. Changes in the dependent variable over the course of treatment may result from changes in scoring criteria, rather than changes in actual behavior.

The problem of instrumentation, of course, does not usually arise when standardized paper-and-pencil tests are administered or when automated devices are used to score a response. The measuring devices, instruments, and scoring procedures are the same for each administration. Even so, it is conceivable that casual remarks by the experimenter at the time of the test administration might affect the subject's response and effectively alter the nature of the test and how the responses are obtained. For example, in a laboratory experiment on the reduction of arousal, stress, and anxiety, the experimenter might well say, "I'll bet you're really relieved now that the film (story, task) is over. Please complete this measure again." It is conceivable that the different instructions preceding the measure alters the assessment in systematic ways and leads to the report of less anxiety. The reduction may result from assessment changes rather than from the experimental manipulation.

Statistical Regression

As a threat to internal validity, regression refers to the tendency for extreme scores on any measure to revert (or regress) toward the mean of a distribution when the measurement device is readministered. If individuals are selected for an investigation because they are extreme on a given measure, one can predict on statistical grounds that at a second testing the scores will tend to revert toward the mean. That is, the scores will tend to be less extreme at the second testing.

For example, an investigator might want to study the effects of some form of therapy on socially withdrawn children. Many children might be given a test of social interaction or perhaps be observed by parents, teachers, or a therapist. For the study, an investigator might reasonably want only those children who are severely withdrawn (i.e., are extreme on their scores for withdrawal). These individuals would be treated and then reevaluated to see whether they had improved.

Regression effects would lead to the prediction that the extreme scores would on the average revert to the mean of all the tested children. Thus the children selected for the study would be very likely to improve and appear less withdrawn at the second testing. However, improvement might well have occurred anyway even if no treatment were provided. Regression is a threat to internal validity if the change due to the intervention cannot be distinguished from the effect of scores reverting toward the mean. (Regression is discussed in greater detail in chapter 5.)

Selection Biases

A selection bias refers to systematic differences in groups based upon the selection or assignment of subjects to experimental conditions. Obviously, the effects of an independent variable between groups can be unambiguously inferred only if there is some assurance that groups do not systematically differ before the variable was applied. Random assignment of subjects is the procedure commonly used to minimize the likelihood of selection biases.

The threat of selection to the internal validity of an experiment often arises in clinical, counseling, and educational research where intact groups are selected with patients from separate hospital wards, students from different classes, or samples from different schools. Groups are performed and cannot be rearranged for research purposes. Even when groups are not already formed, practical demands may interfere with randomly assigning subjects to groups.

For example, in a now classic study designed to evaluate processes and outcomes of client-centered therapy, clients were assigned either to a treatment or control group (Rogers & Dymond, 1954). The treatment group received client-centered therapy; the control group initially served as a waiting-list control group. Waiting-list clients received no treatment but were measured before and after this waiting period to provide comparison data for the treatment group. If clients were assigned randomly to these conditions, initial subject selection would not serve as a threat to internal validity. Yet subjects were assigned on the basis of whether it seemed that they could wait for treatment (i.e., serve in the waiting-list control group) without serious harm or discomfort. Thus clients assigned to treatment and control groups might differ in terms of severity of their psychological state and many other variables as well. Group composition changed even more once treatment began. Subjects assigned to the waiting-list group occasionally were reassigned to the treatment group if, during the waiting period, they became anxious or were advised by someone else (e.g., the student's college advisor) to receive treatment.

The general findings of the research were that therapy was superior to no treatment. There is some ambiguity about the findings because selection is a threat to internal validity. Subjects in treatment and waiting-list groups may have been very different to begin with or in their expected rate of improvement. Differences attributed to treatment effects may be confounded with subject characteristics, that is, selection.

Attrition or Experimental Mortality

The loss of subjects or attrition in an experiment may serve as a threat to internal validity. Loss of subjects does not refer to their veritable demise in most psychological experiments, although this too would present the same threat to validity. Attrition usually refers to subjects dropping out of the experiment over time. If there is a single group of subjects tested at different points in time, changes in overall group performance might be due to the gradual loss of subjects who scored in a particular direction, rather than to improvements in the scores as a function of some intervention. If the experiment is conducted over a long period or includes a follow-up period to assess the long-term effects of treatment, attrition is almost inevitable and may obscure the conclusions that can be drawn.

Attrition is a threat to internal validity if there is a differential loss of subjects between groups. Differential attrition is likely, for instance, in investigations in which experimental conditions are differentially attractive or effective. Subjects are more likely to remain available and cooperative during and after treatment if they are receiving a treatment that is interesting, has little or no cost or adverse side effects, seems plausible, and is effective than if they are receiving a condition that is less desirable on these and related dimensions.

For example, one study compared the effects of drug therapy (imipramine) with cognitive therapy for the treatment of depression (Rush, Beck, Kovacs, & Hollon, 1977). Cognitive therapy was found to be more effective. Interestingly, drug therapy led to significantly greater attrition during treatment than did cognitive therapy. The differential loss of subjects is an interesting and important outcome measure in its own right. Yet other comparisons pertaining to the differential efficacy of treatment on measures of depression might be the result of comparing groups of subjects that are no longer comparable in the way they were prior to treatment. Differences between groups might be due to the different treatments or to the different types of subjects remaining in each of the groups. Attrition has implications for each type of experimental validity. Hence we shall return to the topic again.

Combination of Selection and Other Threats

In designs where groups are not formed through random assignment, it is possible that procedures for selecting subjects will lead to combinations of threats to internal validity mentioned above. Specifically, selection of groups that are already formed prior to the experiment might lead to a combined confound of selection and some other threat to internal validity. The experience of one of the groups in the study (e.g., history, maturation) may differ systematically from that of the other group. The *differential influence* of this threat among groups is referred to as an interaction with selection (e.g., Selection × History, Selection × Maturation) and can produce group differences in the results that are mistakenly attributed to the intervention.

For example, one experiment was designed to compare the effects of behavioral-milieu therapy with routine ward care for the treatment of chronic psychiatric patients (Heap, Boblitt, Moore, & Hord, 1970). The behavioral-milieu therapy consisted of providing an incentive system on the ward for developing individualized self-care and social behaviors (behavioral part of the program). Patients were either assigned to the experimental ward or the control ward that received routine custodial care. Interestingly, the experimental group was moved to a special ward that was made available especially for the experiment. This ward included amenities such as drapes, bedspreads, rugs, clocks, and similar improvements not available in the control ward. Both the move and the addition of amenities to the ward constitute historical events within the experiment that were provided to experimental but not to control subjects. These events provided to only one of the groups constitutes a combined Selection × History threat to internal validity; the histories for the different groups varied.

Of course, it might seem academic to raise this example. After all, how much can a move to another ward with more livable household conditions alter the behavior of psychiatric patients? Actually, results from other studies have shown that merely moving to another ward, independently of whether a new treatment is given, can lead to durable therapeutic improvements in psychiatric patients (e.g., Gripp & Magaro, 1971; Higgs, 1970). In the Heap et al. (1970) example, the treatment program surpassed the effects of routine hospital care. It is difficult to attribute the difference to the special therapy program because other events covaried between the treatment and routine-care conditions.

Selection × History and Selection × Maturation interactions are likely to be the most frequent confounds involving selection, but other combinations are possible. For example, if the subjects in different groups are not tested at the same time, the results might be due to changes in the assessment procedures or criteria for scoring behavior over time (i.e., Selection × Instrumentation). As a general statement, if any single influence (e.g., history, testing) applies to only one of the groups or applies in different ways to the groups, the threat involves selection as an interaction.

Diffusion or Imitation of Treatment

It is possible that the intervention given to one group may be provided accidentally to all or some subjects in a control group as well. The administration of treatment to the control group may be inadvertent and, of course, opposite from what the investigator has planned. Nevertheless, the effects will be to diffuse what the investigator concludes about the efficacy of treatment. Rather than comparing treatment and no-treatment conditions or two or more distinct treatments, the investigator actually is comparing conditions that are more similar than intended. As a threat to internal validity, the effect of a diffusion of treatment will be to equalize performance of treatment and control groups in the study.

An example of a diffusion of treatment as a threat to internal validity was reported in an investigation that compared two treatments for psychiatric patients in a day (rather than residential) hospital program (Austin, Liberman, King, & DeRisi, 1976). One treatment was a behaviorally oriented program where patients received a wide range of techniques (e.g., incentive program, social skills training) to develop adaptive behaviors that would facilitate community adjustment. The other program, conducted at a different facility, had an eclectic-milieu therapy approach where group interaction, patient–staff planning meetings, and other forms of therapy were offered. The results, evaluated 3 and 6 months after treatment, showed a slight but nonsignificant superiority of the behavioral program in the extent to which patients improved on their individualized treatment goals.

At the end of the study, it was discovered that one of the therapists in charge of the eclectic-treatment condition used behavioral techniques extensively in her group, including some of the techniques that comprised the behavioral treatment group. This therapist had a close friend who was a behavioral psychologist and had taken workshops for further professional training in behavior therapy during the course of this project. Because the patients treated by this latter therapist really did not receive the eclectic-milieu treatment, their data were withdrawn so the results could be reanalyzed. The results then showed a significant difference between behavioral and eclectic-milieu treatments favoring the former.

The threat to internal validity is clear in this example only because the authors were able to detect that the treatment for subjects in one condition was inadvertently provided to some subjects in the other condition. Since the treatments were not as distinct as originally planned, the net effect was to diffuse the apparent treatment effect upon subsequent statistical analyses. A conclusion would be reached that treatments do not differ from each other in overall efficacy if such diffusion occurs and is not detected. In other studies, treatment conditions have not been fully conducted by all therapists or have been applied to individuals who were not intended to receive the intervention (e.g., Feldman, Caplinger, & Wodarski, 1983). Even when treatment differences remain, diffusion may occur when control subjects receive treatments intended to be restricted to the experimental group (e.g., Patterson, Chamberlain, & Reid, 1982). In such instances, there is a diffusion of the experimental effect that results in misleading conclusions about the impact of the intervention.

Special Treatment or Reactions of Controls

In an investigation where the intervention, treatment, or program is administered to the experimental group, the no-treatment control group may also be accorded special attention. This is likely to occur in applied settings such as schools, hospitals, and industry rather than in laboratory studies with college students. One group receives the special program that is viewed as generally desirable. The control group may receive some *compensatory treatment* to overcome the inequality.

Subjects in the no-treatment control group may not receive the specific intervention of interest, but they may receive other services such as more money, more monitoring of their well-being, or special privileges. The services provided to the control group are usually intended to redress the apparent inequality and to compensate for not providing the intervention. From the standpoint of internal validity, the no-treatment group may be receiving an "intervention" in its own right that obscures the effect of the program provided to the experimental group.

Even if no special compensation in attention or money is provided to no-treatment control subjects, the absence of treatment may lead to special performance. When subjects are aware that they are serving as a control group, they may react in ways that obscure the differences between treatment and no treatment. Control subjects may compete with the intervention subjects in some way. For example, teachers at control schools or managers in departments of a large business who learn they are not receiving the intervention may become especially motivated to do well and to show they can be just as effective as those who receive the special treatment program. On the other hand, rather than trying extra hard, control subjects may become demoralized because they are not receiving the special program. The control subjects may have experienced initial enthusiasm when the prospect of participating in the special intervention was announced. Their hopes may be dashed by the fate of random assignment. As a consequence, their performance deteriorates. By comparison, the performance of the intervention group looks better whether or not the intervention led to change.

Awareness of participating in an experiment can influence both intervention and control groups. From the standpoint of internal validity, a problem arises when this awareness differentially affects groups so that the effects of the intervention are obscured. At the end of the study differences between treatment and control subjects, or the absence of such differences, may be due to the atypical responses of the control group rather than to the effects of the intervention. The atypical responses could exaggerate or attenuate the apparent effects of treatment.

General Comments

Ideally, it would be instructive to select a single study that illustrated each of the threats to internal validity. Such a study would have failed to control for every possible threat and would not be able to attribute the results to the effects of the independent variable. A study committing so many sins would not be very realistic or represent most research efforts, which commit flaws only one or a few at a time. Thus detailing such an ill-conceived, sloppy, and uncontrolled study would have little purpose. (It would, however, finally give the author a place to report the design and results of his dissertation in detail.)

Most of the threats to internal validity can be readily seen in studies where only one group (or subject) receives treatment. In such cases, the changes over time cannot be unambiguously attributed to the intervention. In most treatment research the minimal experimental conditions include one group that receives a treatment with another group that does not. The purpose of using a no-treatment control group, of course, is to rule out as possibilities the threats listed previously. History, maturation, and so on could not account for group differences because both groups presumably would share the effects of these influences. Any group differences due to treatment are superimposed on changes occurring for these other reasons. One might hypothesize that groups differed systematically in history, maturation, regression, and so on. But this is the combined threat of Selection × History (or Selection × some other factor). However, if subjects were assigned randomly to groups, it may be difficult to explain how there were differences between groups on one of these dimensions. (Possible differences arising from random assignment are discussed in chapter 5.)

In the course of an experiment groups that are initially similar might become different for other reasons than the effects of the intervention. For example, it may well be that subjects in a no-treatment group of a therapy study drop out in higher numbers than those who are in treatment. Differential attrition across groups could account for group differences on the dependent measure. If one group loses more subjects than another group with scores that are better or worse than the rest of the sample in that group, subsequent group differences might be a function of who dropped out of the study rather than the independent variable. Similarly, participation in a control condition may generate reactions such as compensatory performance or demoralization. Treatment and control group differences emerge from reasons other than the intervention provided to the treatment group.

The threats to internal validity discussed previously are the major categories of alternative explanations of experimental results. Experiments must be designed with these potential threats in mind. Practically, it is useful to decide in advance whether the experiment, when completed, would be open to criticism to any of the threats, and if so, what could be done to rectify the situation. Of course, problems may arise during the experiment that later turn out to be threats (e.g., instrumentation or attrition). Even so, with many problems in mind prior to the study, specific precautions can be taken to optimize the clarity of the results.

If a threat to internal validity is not ruled out or made implausible in an experiment, it becomes an alternative explanation of the results. That is, whether the intervention or particular threat to validity operated to cause group differences cannot be decided and the conclusion about the intervention becomes tentative. The tentativeness is a function of how plausible the threat is in accounting for the results given the specific area of research. Some threats may be dismissed based upon findings from other research that a particular factor does not influence the results. The degree to which a rival interpretation can be dismissed may be a matter of debate and may require subsequent research to resolve.

EXTERNAL VALIDITY

The purpose of research is to establish general lawful relations that transcend a particular experimental arrangement. Internal validity addresses the initial question of whether an experiment has demonstrated an interpretable relation. External validity addresses the larger question. Specifically, *external validity* refers to the extent to which the results of an experiment can be generalized beyond the conditions of the experiment to other populations, settings, and conditions. External validity refers collectively to all of the dimensions of generality. Characteristics of the experiment that may limit the generality of the results are referred to as *threats to external validity*.

Threats to External Validity

Numerous threats to external validity can be delineated (Bracht & Glass, 1968; Cook & Campbell, 1979). Threats to external validity constitute questions that can be raised about the limits of the findings. Generally, the questions ask if any features within the experiment might delimit generality of the results.

It is useful to conceive of external validity as questions about the *boundary conditions* of a finding. Assume that a study has addressed the issues of internal validity and establishes a relation between an intervention and outcome. One is then likely to ask, "Yes, but does this apply to other groups of people (e.g., the elderly, nonhospitalized people, diverse ethnic or racial groups), to other settings (e.g., clinics, day-care centers), or to other geographical areas (e.g., rural, other countries)?" What are the boundaries or *limits* of the demonstrated relationship? Stated another way, one can discuss external validity in terms of *statistical interactions.* The relation between the intervention and behavior change applies to some people but not others or to some situations but not others; that is, the variable is said to *interact* with (or operates as a function of) these other conditions.

The factors that may limit the generality of an experiment usually are not known until subsequent research expands upon the conditions under which the relation was originally examined. The manner in which experimental instructions are given, the age, ethnicity, race, and sex of the subjects, whether experimenters are from the general population or are college students, the setting in which the experiment is conducted, and other factors may contribute to whether a given relation is obtained. The generality of experimental findings may be a function of virtually any characteristic of the experiment. Some characteristics, or threats to external validity, can be identified in advance of a particular study that might limit extension of the findings.

Sample Characteristics

The effect of an intervention is demonstrated with a particular sample in a given experiment. To what extent can the results be generalized to other persons who vary in age, race, ethnic background, education, or any other characteristic? It is possible that the subjects in a given study are in some way differentially responsive (or unresponsive) to the treatment. This threat frequently arises in psychological research in general as expressed in the pervasive concern about conducting research on university undergraduates. The concern is that findings obtained with college students will not necessarily extend to others whose age, education, motivation, and other characteristics would differ. The use of college student samples does not necessarily restrict generality of a finding. However, college students represent a very special sample in terms of subject and demographic characteristics, socioeconomic class, level of intelligence, experience, and other attributes. It may be plausible that some of these special characteristics relate to the independent variable of interest. Hence the findings may be limited to samples with these features.

In clinical research, the goal is often to evaluate a treatment for a particular patient population or clinical disorder. Demonstration that change occurs with college students who do not experience the problem or evince only mild levels of the problem may not be persuasive. The extent to which the findings would generalize to a group with very different subject and demographic characteristics (e.g., persons who are married, older, perhaps from lower socioeconomic status) and dysfunction (e.g., with a debilitating clinical disorder) can be cogently challenged.

Concerns over characteristics of the sample and the implications for generalizing the results can be well illustrated in medical research where the intervention (e.g., consumption of soft drinks or a particular food) is provided to subjects (e.g., *laboratory* rats) and is shown to cause cancer. No doubt *non-laboratory* rats would like to know whether these results would generalize to them and their everyday diets. Humans share this concern, namely, do the results generalize to people whose diets, activities, metabolism, longevity, and other factors differ? It is possible, if not likely, that critical features of the subjects (rats) made them differentially responsive to the intervention and restrict generality across species. Medical researchers, of course, are well aware of this threat and often select species where the mechanism or process of interest parallels the species to which generalization is sought.

Stimulus Characteristics

The usual concern in generality of results has to do with sample characteristics and whether the findings extend across different subjects. Equally relevant but less commonly discussed is the extent to which the results extend across the stimulus characteristics of the experiment (Brunswik, 1955). The stimulus characteristics refer to features of the study with which the intervention or condition may be associated. Characteristics of the setting, experimenters, interviewers, or other features of the stimuli to which subjects are exposed may restrict generality. The findings of the study may be restricted to a particular setting, situation, or feature of the experimental arrangement (Maher, 1978a).

The experimental setting in which treatment is conducted is one dimension that may restrict generality of the results. For example, the results of therapy studies conducted in university clinics may not extend to other outpatient clinics in the community because of the differences between the settings and the consequences of these differences for extending treatment. Clients and therapists as well as the investigator's ability to ensure that treatment is administered in a consistent fashion vary across settings.

As an example, the problem of extending treatments across settings was suggested in the expansion of a drug rehabilitation program for hard-core drug addicts (see Bernstein, Bohrnstedt, & Borgatta, 1975). The program sent addicts from the metropolitan area to a treatment center in a country setting where the addicts lived in a commune-type arrangement and participated in various self-help therapy programs. The program was expanded and instituted in the same metropolitan area rather than sending people to a rural setting. Apparently, the program was not as successful in the city as it had been in the country, perhaps because of the accessibility to drugs in the city. These results do not necessarily challenge the efficacy of the treatment program as originally demonstrated but suggest that the effects may depend upon characteristics of the setting (e.g., rural conditions).

The experimental setting is only one example of the stimuli conditions that may be relevant. The general concern is that some feature of the stimulus conditions within the investigation may restrict generality. Using one experimenter, several experimenters all of whom are college students, showing one videotaped vignette to convey the experimental condition, and other features may be assumed to be irrelevant by the investigator. However, the narrow range of stimuli may contribute to the findings and the results may not extend beyond these stimuli. The implications of including a narrow range of stimuli in an investigation extend beyond a threat to external validity. Hence we shall address and elaborate the issue again in the context of construct validity. At this point, it is important to note that the stimulus conditions of the experiment may very much relate to and hence limit generality of the results.

Contextual Characteristics

The context in which the intervention is presented may place restrictions on the generality of the results. The context refers to any of the conditions in which the intervention may be embedded. There is, of course, always some context in which the intervention is presented (e.g., time of the year in relation to other activities of the subjects). Yet several special arrangements may plausibly contribute to the relationship between the intervention and behavior and hence restrict generality of the findings.

Reactivity of experimental arrangements. As a threat to external validity, reactivity of an experimental arrangement refers to the influence of the subjects' awareness that they are participating in an investigation. The results of an experiment may be influenced by the fact that subjects know they are being studied or that the purpose is to examine a particular outcome. The external validity question is whether the results would be obtained if subjects were not aware that they were being studied.

In evaluating treatment in an outpatient clinic, the results may differ depending upon whether subjects know they are participating in an experiment. Participation in an experiment may elicit reactions such as trying to please the experimenter, avoiding responses that might lead the experimenter to evaluate the subject adversely, and so on. These influences presumably would not be present in an experiment where subjects were unaware of their participation.

Not all aspects of reactivity may be of interest to investigators wishing to explore the external validity of a given finding. For example, subjects' awareness that they are receiving treatment may not be important. Whether or not subjects are in an investigation, they invariably are aware that treatment is being administered. However, superimposed on this general awareness might be that they are being evaluated for scientific purposes. This latter aspect of reactivity might well alter the subjects' responses in some way. (The effects of awareness of participating in experiments and the resulting roles that subjects may adopt are discussed in chapter 11.)

Multiple-treatment interference. In some experimental designs, subjects are exposed to more than one experimental condition. Subjects might receive two or more different interventions or alternate between intervention and no-intervention conditions. Multiple-treatment interference refers to drawing conclusions about a given treatment when it is evaluated in the context of other treatments. The conclusion drawn about one treatment or intervention might be restricted by the administration of prior treatments.

The problem of multiple-treatment interference can be illustrated in a study designed to treat marital discord (Azrin, Naster, & Jones, 1973). Twelve married couples interested in marital counseling were seen for treatment. The purpose of the investigation was to examine a technique referred to as *reciprocity counseling,* which consists of a multifaceted program that helps spouses express mutual appreciation, provide feedback about areas of behavior that could be improved, and fulfill each other's fantasies to increase marital satisfaction, along with other procedures designed to enhance communication and sensitivity to the needs of the partner. Prior to receiving 4 weeks of reciprocity counseling, all couples received 3 weeks of *catharsis* counseling, where the couples met with a therapist and talked about their problems and feelings.

The results showed that reciprocity counseling was associated with marked improvements in marital satisfaction, whereas catharsis counseling did not improve satisfaction. Does reciprocity counseling work in improving marital satisfaction? From the study we can infer that this treatment, when preceded by the opportunity to discuss problems in a more traditional therapy format (catharsis), does produce change. The external validity of the reciprocity counseling may be restricted to those individuals who receive catharsis counseling. That is, the context or prior history of the catharsis treatment may be critical for reciprocity counseling to be effective. The results of the experiment may not be applicable to subjects who do not have a similar history or set of prior experiences within the experiment.

Novelty effects. As a threat to external validity, novelty effects refer to the possibility that the effects of an intervention may in part depend upon their innovativeness or novelty in the situation (Bracht & Glass, 1968). It is possible that the effects of the intervention depend upon the fact that it is administered under conditions where it is particularly salient, infrequent, or otherwise novel in some way.

Consider an example well outside of clinical psychology to illustrate the possible operation of novelty effects. Research has shown that automobile accidents, specifically rear-end collisions, are significantly reduced by having brake lights mounted near the car's rear window above the trunk (Nittany Motor Club, 1978). Apparently brake lights mounted near the rear window are more visible to motorists who travel immediately behind the car. Presumably, fewer rear-end collisions result because the motorist behind a car equipped with such lights can respond sooner to the need to slow down or stop than otherwise would be the case. Several years ago research compared the accident rates of taxicabs equipped or not equipped with rear-window mounted lights. The specially equipped cabs showed a 54% reduction in rear-end collisions.

When this research was completed, cars on the road did not have rear-mounted lights as they do now as a matter of course. The conclusions from this type of research prompted policymakers to require automobile manufacturers to install the specially equipped lights on all new cars. Over time, the proportion of newer cars on the road with such lights had increased. Now that most cars on the road have such lights, reductions in accidents may not be evident. It is possible that the effect of the lights in reducing the accidents stemmed in part from the fact that the positioning of lights near the rear window was novel to motorists who viewed them. Cars with such lights were conspicuous when they were relatively rare, that is, novel. Motorists may have paid closer attention to the lights only because they differed from what one ordinarily saw when driving. Placing the lights on all new cars as is now the case might eliminate the novelty of the intervention and perhaps the effects on reducing rear-end collisions.

The presence of novelty effects is difficult to evaluate. Thus a new treatment when first proposed may seem to be very effective. Changes in the effects of an intervention over time might be due to the novelty of the early applications in the context of other available interventions. However, alternative explanations are available. For example, in the case of therapy, early applications might prove to be more effective than later ones because over time interventions may be carried out less faithfully or diluted when combined with other procedures. Nevertheless, in planning and interpreting experiments it may be that treatments that are novel to the public and are "new and improved," very much like the soaps, cereals, automobiles, and shampoos we purchase, will be effective in part because of their novelty.

Assessment Characteristics

Several different facets of assessment within a study may affect generality of the results. These facets can refer to any condition of assessment that differs from those to which the investigator may wish to generalize and that may plausibly influence the results. Within clinical research, assessment conditions that may restrict generality readily come to mind.

Reactivity of assessment. For most measures used in psychological experiments, subjects or clients are aware that some facet of their functioning is assessed. The measures may include a variety of questionnaires or tests that subjects complete. If subjects are aware that their performance is being assessed, the measures are said to be *obtrusive.* Obtrusive measures are of concern in relation to external validity because awareness that performance is being assessed can alter performance from what it would otherwise be. If awareness of assessment leads people to respond differently from how they would usually respond, the measures are said to be *reactive.*

In clinical research, the fact that clients are aware of the assessment procedures raises an important question about the generality of the findings. If the results of a treatment study are evident on paper-and-pencil inventories or on interviews by a therapist in the clinical setting, one might question the generality of treatment effects. That is, to what extent do treatment effects demonstrated on reactive measures within the laboratory or clinic setting extend to measures that are not reactive and administered outside of the setting? Treated clients may show great reductions in anxiety on various questionnaires designed for this purpose. It is possible that the findings will be restricted to the characteristics that are measured in the confines of the experiment. Has anxiety decreased in the clients' actual experience in everyday life? An exceedingly important question is whether the changes carry over to actual experience of the clients in their ordinary everyday settings, a question of external validity of the results.

Test sensitization. In many experiments, particularly in therapy research, pretests are administered routinely. The purpose is to measure the client's standing on a particular variable before receiving the experimental manipulation or treatment. Administration of the pretest may in some way *sensitize* the subjects so that they are affected differently by the intervention, a phenomenon referred to as *pretest sensitization.* Individuals who are pretested might be more or less amenable or responsive to an intervention (e.g., treatment, persuasive message) than are individuals who are not exposed to a pretest merely because of the initial assessment.

Consider as an example that an investigator wishes to examine people's views toward violence. The hypothesis may be that viewing violent movies leads to an increase in aggressive thoughts and a positive evaluation of violence. The investigator may wish to evaluate views of people after they see a "war movie" at a movie theater. The investigator provides a questionnaire to persons in the theater lobby immediately before they enter the movie. Subjects complete the measure before entering the movie and then again when the movie is over. For present purposes we shall omit control conditions and other features that might be included in the experiment to focus our comments on sensitization. The investigator is interested in the impact of seeing a violent film on views toward violence. However, it is possible that administration of a test before the film, that is, the pretest, makes people view and react to the film somewhat differently than they usually do. Perhaps the questions heighten sensitivity to certain types of issues or to the entire topic of violence that may not have otherwise been raised. At posttest performance, how subjects respond is not merely a function of seeing the movie but also may be due in part to the initial pretest sensitization. Hence a possible threat to external validity is that the results may not generalize to subjects who have not received a pretest. Administering a pretest does not necessarily restrict generality of the results. It does, however, raise the question of whether nonpretested individuals, usually the population of interest, would respond to the intervention in the same way as the pretested population. (Pretest sensitization is discussed in chapters 5 and 10 where specific experimental designs and assessment problems are elaborated.)

Even when a pretest is not used, it is possible that assessment may influence the results. The posttest might sensitize subjects to the previous intervention that they have received and yield results that would not have been evident without the assessment. This effect, referred to as *posttest sensitization* (Bracht & Glass, 1968), is very similar to pretest sensitization where test administration may crystallize a particular reaction on the part of the subject. With posttest sensitization, assessment constitutes a necessary condition for treatment to show its effect. Essentially, treatment effects may be latent or incomplete and appear only when a reactive assessment device is administered. As a threat to external validity, posttest sensitization raises the question of whether the results would extend to measures that subjects could not associate with intervention or measures that were completely out of their awareness. The effect of posttest sensitization is slightly more difficult to assess than is pretest sensitization because it requires nonreactive assessment of treatment effects and a comparison of the results across measures varying in reactivity.

In passing, it is important to note that sensitization effects are not necessarily viewed as artifacts or threats to external validity. The effects suggest that a reactive forewarning may increase the impact of a subsequent intervention. A recent study demonstrating the importance of sensitization evaluated the impact of a television advertising campaign designed to reduce alcohol consumption among people who had been identified as drinkers (Barber, Bradshaw, & Walsh, 1989). Large-scale media campaigns designed to reduce substance abuse are not regarded as widely effective. The investigators evaluated whether sending a letter to people in advance of the campaign would sensitize community members to the television commercials that followed. The results indicated that people who were sent the letter alerting them to the upcoming campaign and who then received the advertising on television showed significant reductions in alcohol consumption and were significantly lower in consumption than those who received the advertising campaign without the letter or the letter without the advertising campaign. Thus in this study sensitization enhanced the impact of the intervention.

Time of measurement and treatment effects. The results of an experiment may depend on the point in time that assessment devices are administered. For example, an investigation may reveal that a particular type of psychotherapy surpassed no treatment or that one therapy was superior to another immediately after completion of treatment. An external validity question that can be raised is whether the same result would have been obtained had measurement been taken at another time, say, several months after treatment.

In psychotherapy outcome research, the effectiveness of treatment usually is evaluated immediately after the last therapy session (posttreatment assessment). It is possible that the conclusions at this point in time would not extend to a later period. For example, in one study, separate treatments were implemented at school to alter the behavior of maladjusted children (Kolvin et al., 1981). Two of the interventions (group therapy, behavior modification) yielded different effects depending on the point in time that assessment was completed. Immediately after treatment, relatively few improvements were evident. At follow-up, approximately 18 months later, improvements in these groups, relative to control subjects who had not received treatment, were marked. The effects evident at one point in time (posttreatment) were different from those at another point in time (follow-up). Other studies with adults and children can be identified to show that the conclusions reached about a particular treatment or the relative effectiveness of alternative treatments in a given study occasionally vary from posttreatment to follow-up assessment (see Kazdin, 1988).

General Comments

The previously discussed threats to external validity only begin to enumerate those conditions that might restrict the generality of a finding. All of the conditions of an experiment that are relevant to the generality of a finding cannot be specified in advance. In principle, any characteristic of the experimenters, subjects, or accoutrements of the investigation might later prove to be related to the results. If one of the threats applies, this means that some caution should be exercised in extending the results. The degree of caution is a function of several factors including the extent to which conditions introduced into the situation depart from those to which one would like to generalize and the plausibility that the specific condition of the experiment might influence generality. These are areas where reasonable people might well disagree.

One cannot simply discount the findings of a study as a very special case by merely noting that subjects were pretested or were aware that they were participating in an experiment, or by identifying another characteristic of the experiment. *Enumerating a list of threats that are possible in principle is insufficient to challenge the findings.* The onus is upon the investigator who conducts the study to clarify the conditions to which he or she wishes to generalize and to convey how the conditions of the experiment represent these. The onus upon those skeptical of how well this has been achieved is to describe explicitly how a particular threat to external validity would *operate and quite plausibly* restrict the findings.

Many conditions might be ruled out as threats to external validity on seemingly commonsense grounds (e.g., hair or eye color of the experimenter, season of the year, birth weight of subjects). In any given area, these seemingly remote factors might well be important. The task of the reviewer or the consumer of research (e.g., other professionals, laypersons) is to provide a plausible account of why the generality of the findings may be limited. Only further investigation can attest to whether the potential threats to external validity actually limit generality and truly make a theoretical or practical difference. Of course, there is no more persuasive demonstration than several studies in which similar findings are obtained with some consistency across various types of subjects (e.g., patients, college students), settings (e.g., university laboratory, clinic, community), and other domains (e.g., different researchers, countries).

The value of a finding is not always determined by the degree to which it can be generalized across other dimensions. Some findings are important precisely because their generality is very limited. For example, performance on a particular laboratory task or psychological test may distinguish schizophrenic patients from nonpatient samples functioning in the community. A question might be raised about the generality of this result and whether other populations might be separated from nonpatient samples as well. Yet there are important theoretical and clinical reasons for singling out schizophrenia. Hence it may be of interest not to demonstrate generality of the results to other diagnostic groups. If the test or task was shown in subsequent research to have wide generality across populations, the procedure might distinguish alcoholics, drug addicts, transvestites, and professors from individuals otherwise functioning normally. The value of the original finding is greatly attenuated. Rather than a specific criterion for distinguishing schizophrenia, the generality may be so great as to identify all sorts of dysfunction. Thus the extent to which external validity is important or desirable is a function of the specific research problem.

RELATION OF INTERNAL AND EXTERNAL VALIDITY

Internal and external validity convey critical features of the logic of experimentation. Internal validity is addressed by experimental arrangements that help rule out or make implausible factors that could explain the effects we wish to attribute to the intervention. Everyday life is replete with "demonstrations" that do not control basic threats to internal validity. For example, almost any intervention that one applies to oneself or a group can appear to "cure" the common cold. Consuming virtually any vitamin or potion from assorted animal parts or reading highly arousing material (e.g., on methodology and research design) in a few days will usually be associated with great improvements. Pre- and postassessments with one of the above interventions would, no doubt, reflect improvements. Did our intervention lead to improvement? Probably not.

We can muse at the example because we know that colds usually remit without the above interventions. The example is relevant because maturation (immunological and recuperative processes within the individual) is a threat to internal validity and can readily account for changes. For areas we do not understand as well and where the course and determinants are less clear, a host of threats can compete with the variable of interest in accounting for change. Experimentation and control of threats to internal validity become essential.

As a priority, the internal validity of an experiment is to be regarded as more important, or at least logically prior in importance, than external validity. One must first have an unambiguous finding before one can ask about its generality. Given the priority of internal validity, initial considerations of an experiment pertain to devising those conditions that will facilitate demonstrating the relation between the independent and dependent variables. A well-designed experiment maximizes the opportunity to draw valid inferences about the intervention.

By stressing internal validity, there is no intention to slight external validity. For research findings with applied implications, as is often the case in clinical psychology, counseling, and education, external validity is particularly important. A well-conducted study with a high degree of internal validity shows what *can* happen when the experiment is arranged in a particular way. Yet it is quite a different matter to show that the intervention has this effect and *does* operate this way outside of the experimental situation.

For example, as mentioned already, experiments on cancer may show that a particular soft drink or food additive may cause cancer in laboratory animals fed high doses of the item. Internally valid experiments of this sort are informative because they show what can happen. The findings may have important theoretical implications for how and why cancers develop. Yet a major question in addressing the immediate utility of the findings for applied purposes is whether cancers develop in this way outside of the laboratory. Do the findings extend from mice and rats to humans, to lower doses of the suspected ingredients, to diets that may include many other potentially neutralizing substances (e.g., water and assorted vitamins and minerals), and so on? These latter questions all pertain to the external validity of the findings.

Considerations pertaining to external validity often serve as the initial attraction of people who are beginning their psychological research careers.

Students early in their research careers often wish to study something "relevant," or at least more obviously relevant than the overworked experiments with college sophomores whose performance is evaluated under laboratory conditions. Thus research questions in such settings as a treatment clinic, psychiatric hospital, or the home may be very enticing because of their obvious relevance to applied questions that may motivate research. Unfortunately, research in applied situations where many questions of clinical interest arise often is difficult to complete because of practical limitations and obstacles. Moreover, such obstacles frequently lead to design problems that threaten the internal validity of the research. There are often trade-offs in addressing alternative types of validity, which we shall discuss in much further detail. The purpose at this point is to describe internal and external validity because the issues they raise provide the rationale for several methodological practices.

SUMMARY AND CONCLUSIONS

The purpose of research is to investigate specific relations between independent and dependent variables. The value of experiments derives from their capacity to simplify the situation in which variables may operate so that the influence of many variables can be separated from the variable of interest. Stated another way, an experiment helps rule out the influence of many alternative variables that might explain changes on the dependent measures.

The extent to which an experiment rules out as explanations those factors that otherwise might account for the results is referred to as *internal validity*. Factors or sources of influence other than the independent variables are referred to as *threats to internal validity* and include history, maturation, testing, instrumentation, statistical regression, selection biases, attrition, selection in combination with other threats (e.g., Selection × History), diffusion of treatment, and special treatment or reactions of controls.

Aside from evaluating the internal validity of an experiment, it is important to understand the extent to which the findings can be generalized to populations, settings, measurement devices, and experimenters other than those used in the original experiment. The generality of the results is referred to as the *external validity* of the experiment. Although the findings of an experiment could be limited to any particular condition or arrangement unique to the demonstration, a number of potential limitations on the generality of the results can be identified. These potential limitations are referred to as *threats to external validity* and include characteristics of the sample, the stimulus conditions of the experiment, the contextual conditions such as reactivity of the experimental arrangement, multiple-treatment interference, and novelty effects, and the conditions of assessment such as reactivity, test sensitization, and timing.

Internal and external validity address central aspects of the logic of experimentation and scientific research more generally. The purpose of research is to structure the situation in such a way that inferences can be drawn about the effects of the variable of interest (internal validity) and to establish relations that extend beyond the highly specific circumstances in which the variable was examined (external validity). There often is a natural tension between meeting these objectives. Occasionally, the investigator arranges the experiment in ways to increase the likelihood of ruling out threats to internal validity. In the process, somewhat artificial circumstances may be introduced (e.g., videotapes to present the intervention, scripts that are memorized or read to the subjects). This means that the external validity may be threatened. Yet considerations of the relation of internal and external validity are somewhat premature. There are other types of validity that need to be discussed to convey the full range of issues that researchers must consider in designing experiments. The next chapter turns to the notions of construct and statistical conclusion validity and then discusses the relation and priorities of all four kinds of validity.

FOR FURTHER READING

Cook, T.D., & Campbell, D.T. (Eds.). (1979). *Quasi-experimentation: Design and analysis issues for field settings.* Skokie, IL: Rand McNally.

Krathwohl, D.R. (1985). *Social and behavioral science research.* San Francisco: Jossey-Bass.

Mook, D.G. (1983). In defense of external invalidity. *American Psychologist, 38,* 379–387.

Reichardt, C.S., & Gollob, H.F. (1989). Ruling out threats to validity. *Evaluation Review, 13,* 3–17.

Chapter 3

DRAWING VALID INFERENCES II: CONSTRUCT AND STATISTICAL CONCLUSION VALIDITY

Internal and external validity are fundamental to research and nicely convey the underpinnings for many methodological practices. Two other types of validity, referred to as construct validity and statistical conclusion validity, must also be addressed to draw valid inferences. These types of validity are no less central to research design. Yet they are less familiar to researchers and consumers of research and reflect slightly more complex concepts and design considerations than do internal and external validity. This chapter considers construct and statistical conclusion validity and the interrelations and priorities of alternative types of validity. As in the previous chapter, the goal is to describe the nature of these types of validity and the threats they raise. Subsequent chapters will focus on alternative strategies to address these threats.

CONSTRUCT VALIDITY

Construct validity has to do with interpreting the basis of the causal relation demonstrated within an experiment. The meaning requires careful delineation of construct from internal validity. Internal validity, as you recall, focuses on whether some intervention is responsible for change or whether other factors (e.g., history, maturation, testing) are plausible accounts for the effect. Assume for a moment that these threats have been ruled out by randomly assigning subjects to treatment and control groups, by assessing both groups in the same way and at the same time, and so on. We can presume now that the group differences are not likely to have resulted from the threats to internal validity but rather to the intervention. It is at this point that the discussion of construct validity can begin. What is "the intervention" and why did it produce the effect? *Construct validity* addresses the presumed cause or the explanation of the causal relation. Is the explanation or interpretation of the investigator plausible? Is the reason for the relation between the intervention and behavior change due to the construct (explanation, interpretation) given by the investigator? Answers to these questions focus specifically on construct validity.

Construct validity is a more familiar term in the context of test development and validation (e.g., Wainer & Braun, 1988). For example, investigators may develop a psychological test that they believe measures anxiety. Several types of studies are completed to establish the construct validity or that it is anxiety that the scale measures rather than some other construct (e.g., intelligence, deviance, honesty, altruism). Thus in the use of test development, construct validity refers to the explanation of the measure or the dimension that it assesses. In a parallel way, construct validity of an experiment refers to the explanation of the outcome (see Cook & Campbell, 1979).

There are several features within the experiment that can interfere with the interpretation. These are often referred to as *confounds*. We say an experiment is confounded or that there is a confound to refer to the possibility that a specific factor varied (or covaried) with the intervention that could in whole or in part be responsible for the change. In an experiment, some component other than the one of interest to the investigator may be responsible for change. Those features associated with the intervention that interfere with drawing inferences about the basis for the difference between groups are referred to as *threats to construct validity*.

Threats to Construct Validity

Attention and Contact With the Clients

One type of threat to construct validity pertains to the delivery of the intervention and the impact on the client. The intervention or experimental manipulation may include components that the investigator may see as irrelevant but that may explain or partially explain the effects. Attention and contact accorded the client in the experimental group or differential attention across experimental and control groups may be the basis for the group differences. The intervention may have exerted its influence because of the attention provided rather than because of special characteristics unique to the intervention.

A familiar example from psychiatric research is the effect of placebos in the administration of medication. Suppose investigators provide a drug for depression to some patients and no drug to other patients. Assume further that groups were formed through random assignment and that the threats to internal validity were all superbly addressed. At the end of the study, patients who had received the drug are greatly improved and significantly differ in level of depression from those patients who did not receive the drug. The investigator may then discuss the effect of the drug and how this particular medication affects critical biological processes that control symptoms of depression. We accept the fact that the intervention was responsible for the outcome (internal validity). Yet "the intervention" consists of all those aspects associated with the administration of the medication in addition to the medication itself.

We know that taking any drug might decrease depression because of expectancies for improvement on the part of the patients and on those administering the drug. Indeed, such expectancies can exert marked therapeutic effects on a variety of psychological and medical dysfunctions (White, Tursky, & Schwartz, 1985). The intervention might have been effective because of such expectations and the change they generate. In the present example, these effects were not examined so the investigator cannot identify the explanation of the effect.

To examine the basis for the effects (construct validity), it would be essential to include a third group that received a placebo on the same schedule of administration. A *placebo* is a substance that has no active pharmacological properties that would be expected to produce change. A neutral substance is used that is known to be inactive in relation to the clinical problem. Administration of a placebo to another group would be extremely useful in this study to address construct validity. A placebo might be a pill, capsule, or tablet of the same size and shape, and perhaps share other characteristics of the active medication. Those who administer the drug (physicians or nurses) and those who receive the drug should be naive ("blind") to the conditions to which subjects are assigned. Thus expectations for improvement might be constant between drug and placebo groups. With a placebo-control group, attention and contact with the client and expectations on the part of experimenters or clients become less plausible constructs to explain the effects the investigator wishes to attribute to the medication.

In a somewhat parallel fashion, treatment and no-treatment are often compared in psychotherapy research. The treatment may, for example, focus on cognitive processes that the investigator believes to be critical to the clinical problem. Assessment completed after treatment may reveal that the treatment group is significantly better than the no-treatment group on various outcome measures. If the investigator explains the finding as support for the importance of altering cognitions or using this particular treatment, there is a construct validity problem. We must question whether there are plausible features associated with the intervention that ought to be ruled out.

In fact, treatment and no-treatment groups differ on several dimensions, including meeting with a therapist, generating patient expectations for improvement, working with someone on their "problems," and so on. Might these plausibly improve symptoms even if cognitions are not the focus of treatment? Some writers about psychotherapy answer affirmatively (e.g., Frank, 1982); in addition, evidence suggests that when control subjects are led to expect improvement, they often improve whether they received a veridical treatment or not (Bootzin, 1985). Hence, if the investigator wishes to explain the findings in terms of specific mechanisms within the treatment, some other factors might need to be controlled to show that these latter factors could not plausibly explain the findings. We shall discuss this further when control groups are examined (chapter 7).

In general, there is a threat to construct validity when attention, contact with the subjects, and their expectations might plausibly account for the findings and have not been controlled or evaluated in the design. A design that does not control for these factors is *not* necessarily flawed. The intention of the investigator, the control procedures, and the specificity of the conclusions the investigator wishes to draw determine the extent to which construct validity threats can be raised.

Single Operations and Narrow Stimulus Sampling

In any study, the investigator is usually interested in a phenomenon, variable, or intervention and its effects in some general way. For example, the investigator may believe that a particular intervention will reduce anxiety for patients who receive treatment. The investigator develops specific procedures to test the idea. In moving from the idea to the specific procedure, we know that decisions may raise concerns over external validity. Thus questions might emerge regarding whether the relation we demonstrate in our study will generalize to situations and variations of the intervention that depart from the ones we have selected. The way in which the idea is operationalized may affect construct validity as well, that is, our ability to decide whether the treatment of interest or some feature associated with the intervention is responsible for the results.

In many studies, the intervention is operationalized so that it is associated with and inseparable from features that are assumed to be irrelevant by the investigator. These irrelevancies cannot be ruled out as influences in explaining the basis of the intervention effect. For example, in a treatment study, two different treatment groups might be compared. The intention of the investigator, the control procedures, and the specificity of the conclusions the investigator wishes to draw determine the extent to which construct validity threats can be raised. Let us say we recruit therapists expert in Treatment A to administer one treatment and other therapists skilled in Treatment B to administer another treatment. Thus different therapists provide the different treatments. This is reasonable because we may wish to use experts who practice their special techniques (e.g., Sloane, Staples, Cristol, Yorkston, & Whipple, 1975). At the end of the study, assume that Therapy A is better than B in the outcome achieved with the patient sample. Because therapists were different for the two treatments, we cannot really separate the impact of therapists from treatment. We might *say* that Treatment A was better than Treatment B. Yet a colleague conversant in construct validity might state that therapists who administered A were generally better therapists than those who administered B and that this accounts for the results. The confound of treatment with therapists raises a significant ambiguity.

There is a more subtle variation that may emerge as a threat to construct validity. Say we are comparing two treatments and we use one therapist. This therapist provides both treatments and sees clients in each of the treatment conditions. At the end of the investigation, suppose that one treatment is clearly more effective than the other. The investigator may wish to discuss how one technique is superior and explain on conceptual grounds why this might be expected.

We accept the finding that one intervention was more effective than the other. In deference to construct validity we ask, "what is 'the intervention'?" In this example, the intervention was the therapist administering one treatment versus another treatment. That is, the comparison consisted of this therapist giving Treatment A versus this same therapist giving Treatment B. It is possible that the combination of this therapist with one of the treatments accounted for the pattern of the results. We cannot separate the influence of the therapist combined with the treatment in accounting for the results.

One might say that the therapist was "held constant" because he or she was used in both groups. But it is possible that this particular therapist was more credible, comfortable, competent, and effective with one of the techniques than with the other. Perhaps the therapist believed in the efficacy of one technique more than another, performed one technique with greater fidelity than the other, or aroused patients' expectancies for improvement more with one of the techniques. The differential effects of treatment could be due to the Therapist $\times$ Treatment interaction rather than to a main effect of treatment. The study yields somewhat ambiguous results because the effect of the therapist was not separable in the data analyses from the different treatment conditions.

Construct validity could be improved by sampling across a wider range of stimuli so that the effects of treatment can be evaluated in the design. Two or more therapists could be included, each of whom would administer both treatments. At the end of the study, the impact of therapists could be separated from the impact of treatment (in an analysis of variance). If the effectiveness of treatment varied between the therapists, this could be detected in the interaction (Treatment $\times$ Therapist) term.

Consider another example, a laboratory experiment designed to evaluate opinions held about mental illness. The purpose is to see if people evaluate the personality, intelligence, and likability of others differently if they believe they have been mentally ill. College students serve as subjects and are assigned randomly to one of two conditions. In the experimental condition, the students see a slide of a casually dressed 30-year-old man. They then listen to a tape that describes him as holding a factory job, living at home with his wife and two children, and so on. The description also includes a passage noting that the man has been mentally ill, experienced strange delusions, and was hospitalized 2 years ago. In the control condition, students see the same slide and hear the description except for those passages that talk about mental illness and hospitalization. At the end of the tape, subjects rate the personality, intelligence, and likability of the person in the slide. Alas, the hypothesis is supported, namely, subjects in the "mentally ill description" condition showed greater rejection of the person than did subjects who were in the control condition.

The investigator wishes to conclude that the content of the description that focused on mental illness is the basis for the differences between groups. After all, this is the only part of the content of the slide and tape description that distinguished experimental and control groups. Yet there is a construct validity issue here. The use of a single case in the slide (i.e., the 30-year-old man) is problematic. It is possible that rejection evident by subjects who received the mental illness description occurred because of special characteristics of this particular case presented on the slide. The difference could be due to the manipulation of the mental illness description or to the interaction of this description with characteristics of this case. These alternatives cannot be distinguished in the design. One would want slides of different persons varying in age, sex, and other characteristics of the case. In general, it is important to represent the stimuli in ways so that *potential irrelevancies* (e.g., the case, unique features of the task) can be separated from the intervention or variable of interest. Without separating the irrelevancies, the conclusions of the study are limited (Maher, 1978a).

The use of a narrow range of stimuli and the limitations that such use impose sound similar to external validity. Actually, sampling a narrow range of stimuli as a threat can apply to *both* external and construct validity. If the investigator wishes to *generalize* to other stimulus conditions (e.g., other therapists or types of cases in the above two examples), then the narrow range of stimulus conditions can be discussed as a threat to *external* validity. To generalize across stimulus conditions of the experiment requires sampling across the range of these conditions, if it is plausible that the conditions may influence the results (Brunswik, 1955). If the investigator wishes to describe why a change occurred, then the problem is one of *construct* validity, because the investigator cannot separate the construct of interest (e.g., treatment or types of description of treatment) from the conditions of its delivery (e.g., the therapist or case vignette).

Experimenter Expectancies

For purposes of discussion, we shall consider the *investigator* as the person who has responsibility for planning and designing the study and the *experimenter* as the person who is actively running the subjects and carrying out the procedures. This distinction is helpful despite the fact that the investigator and experimenter are occasionally the same person and that multiple individuals in a project may vary in the extent to which they share these roles. We focus here on the experimenter to emphasize the person in direct contact with the subjects.

In both laboratory and clinical research, it is quite possible that the expectancies, beliefs, and desires about the results on the part of the experimenter influences how the subjects perform.

The effects are sometimes referred to as *unintentional expectancy effects* to emphasize that the experimenter may not do anything on purpose to influence subjects' responses. Depending on the experimental situation and experimenter–subject contact, expectancies may lead to changes in tone of voice, posture, facial expressions, delivery of instructions, and adherence to the prescribed procedures and hence influence how subjects respond. Expectancy effects are a threat to construct validity if they provide a plausible rival interpretation of the effects otherwise attributed to the intervention.

Expectancy effects received considerable attention in the mid-1960s, primarily in the context of social psychological research (Rosenthal, 1966, 1976). However, it is not difficult to imagine their impact in clinical research. For example, in treatment research, the expectancy effects might be suspected in situations where the experimenter has a strong investment in the outcome and has contact with subjects in various treatment and control conditions. The history of the development of alternative forms of psychotherapy includes many instances in which experimenter expectancy effects provide a reasonable rival explanation of the results. As one illustration, psychoanalysis, psychoanalytically oriented psychotherapy, and rational-emotive therapy were compared for outpatient cases (Ellis, 1957). The investigator served as the therapist for all conditions. The results showed that rational-emotive therapy, the technique developed by the investigator, was superior to the two alternatives. Similarly, in a study contrasting insight-oriented therapy and systematic desensitization for phobic patients, one therapist was responsible for administering both conditions (Lazarus, 1961). Desensitization, the technique promoted by the author, was more effective.

In both examples, the treatment clearly known to be of central interest to the investigator led to greater therapeutic change. It is not at all fair to pose that the investigators were biased or that their expectancies, rather than or combined with treatment, were responsible for the results. There is, in each study, a problem of *narrow stimulus sampling* and an inability to separate treatment from Therapist × Treatment effects that threaten both external and construct validity. External validity is threatened because it might be plausible to question the generality of findings to other therapists less experienced or skilled or who did not prefer and promote the techniques that appeared to be effective. Construct validity is threatened because the effects of treatment could not be separated from the therapist effects and the plausibility that the therapist may be more effective with a technique he preferred—perhaps by rendering procedures of the comparison treatment less well or less consistently. Because of the investigators' positions, expectancy as a possible threat to construct validity cannot be easily dismissed. We would very much want to see the study replicated with more and different therapists and perhaps even assess therapist expectancies at the beginning of the study to see if these correlated with outcome.

The notion of experimenter expectancies, as a threat to validity, is not frequently invoked for at least two reasons. First, the construct as well as the ways through which it achieves its effects are unclear. Second and related, there are many more parsimonious interpretations that may serve as confounds before the notion of expectancies needs to be invoked. For example, differential adherence of the experimenter to the conditions, explicit and differential instructions to subjects, and changes in the measurement criteria (instrumentation) for subjects in different conditions might reflect more concretely why two conditions differ in their effects. Nevertheless, in a given situation, expectations on the part of the experimenter may plausibly serve as a source of ambiguity and threaten the construct validity of the experiment.

Cues of the Experimental Situation

Cues of the situation refer to those seemingly ancillary factors associated with the intervention that may contribute to the results. These cues have been referred to as the "demand characteristics of the experimental situation" (Orne, 1962). Demand characteristics may include sources of influence such as information conveyed to prospective subjects prior to their arrival to the experiment (e.g., rumors about the experiment, information provided during subject recruitment), instructions, procedures, and any other features of the experiment that may seem incidental to the overall manipulation.

The influence of cues in the experiment distinct from the independent variable was dramatically illustrated by Orne and Scheibe (1964) who examined the role of demand characteristics in a sensory deprivation experiment. Sensory deprivation consists of minimizing as many sources of sensory stimulation as possible for the subject. Isolating individuals from visual, auditory, tactile, and other stimulation for prolonged periods has been associated with distorted perception, visual hallucinations, inability to concentrate, and disorientation. These reactions usually are attributable to the physical effects of being deprived of sensory stimulation.

Orne and Scheibe suggested that cues from the experimental situation in which sensory deprivation experiments are conducted might contribute to the reactions. They completed an experiment where subjects were exposed to the accoutrements of the procedures of a sensory deprivation experiment but actually were not deprived of stimulation. Subjects received a physical exam, provided a short medical history, were assured that the procedures were safe, and were exposed to a tray of drugs and medical instruments conspicuously labeled "Emergency Tray." Subjects were told to report any unusual visual imagery, fantasy, or feelings, difficulties in concentration, disorientation, or similar problems. They were informed that they were to be placed in a room where they could work on an arithmetic task. If they wanted to escape, they could do so by pressing a red "Emergency Alarm." In short, subjects were given a variety of cues to convey that strange experiences were in store.

The subjects were placed in the room with food, water, and materials for the task. No attempt was made to deprive subjects of sensory stimulation. Subjects could move about, hear many different sounds, and work at a task. This arrangement departs from true sensory deprivation experiments where the subjects typically rest, have their eyes and ears covered, and cease movement as much as possible. A control group in the study did not receive the cues preparing them for unusual experiences and were told they could leave the room by merely knocking on the window. At the end of the "isolation" period, the experimental group showed greater deterioration on a number of measures including the report of symptoms characteristically revealed in sensory deprivation experiments. Because sensory deprivation was not administered, it appears that the cues usually associated with deprivation studies may contribute to or account for the results.

Demand characteristics can threaten the construct validity if it is plausible that extraneous cues associated with the intervention could explain the findings. The Orne and Scheibe (1964) demonstration conveyed the potential impact of such cues. Whether these demand characteristics exert such impact in diverse areas of research is not clear. Also, in many areas of clinical research, the independent variable may include cues that cannot be so easily separated from the portion of the manipulation that is considered to be crucial. For example, different variations of treatment or levels of an independent variable (e.g., high, medium, and low) may necessarily require different cues and hence be intertwined with different demand characteristics. The cues that may give subjects hints on how to perform may not be considered as extraneous but as part and parcel of the manipulation itself. In such cases, it may not be especially meaningful to note that demand characteristics accounted for the results.

On the other hand, when several conditions are different from control conditions (e.g., a no-treatment control group), one might weigh the plausibility of demand characteristics as an influence. It may be the case that there is an implicit demand conveyed to control subjects that they are not expected to improve from one test occasion to another. Presumably if cues were provided to convey this expectation, treatment and no-treatment differences might well be due to different demand characteristics across the assessment conditions. The means of evaluating demand characteristics are discussed further in chapter 11.

General Comments

The discussion has noted common threats to construct validity. However, construct validity threats are not easily enumerated in the general case. The reason is that the threats have to do with interpretation of the reason for the outcome in an experiment. Thus theoretical views and substantive knowledge about how the experimental manipulation works or the mechanisms responsible for change are also at issue, apart from the issue of experimental confounds. The questions of construct validity are twofold: "What is the intervention?" and "Why did this intervention lead to change?" The first question emphasizes the fact that the intervention may be embedded in or confounded by other conditions that influence and account for the outcome. The second question emphasizes the related issue of interpretation of what led the intervention to change performance. Here we do not speak of confound as much as better understanding of the mechanism, process, or theory to explain the change. The questions encompass construct validity because they affect interpretation of the basis for a given finding.

STATISTICAL CONCLUSION VALIDITY

Internal, external, and construct validity and their threats codify many of the concerns to which methodology is directed. The list of these concerns is long; what more can remain? Actually, a great deal. Assume we have designed our wonderful experiment to address the bulk of those threats already highlighted. Shall we find reliable differences between the groups? Even if the intervention and control conditions really would produce differences in their outcomes, whether we find such differences depends on multiple considerations. *Statistical conclusion validity* refers to those facets of the quantitative evaluation that influence the conclusions we reach about the experimental condition and its effect.

Statistical evaluation often is viewed and taught from two standpoints. The first of these pertains to understanding the tests themselves and their bases. This facet may emphasize what the tests accomplish and the formulae and derivations of the tests themselves. The second and complementary standpoint pertains to the computational aspects of statistical tests. Here statistical tests may be viewed as arithmetic tools with alternative methods of computation to help summarize the data and to reach conclusions.

There is another, more general facet, namely, the role of statistical evaluation in relation to research design and drawing valid inferences. Statistical conclusion validity reflects this level of concern with quantitative evaluation and is often the Achilles' heel of research. Because this type of validity is often neglected, failure to consider statistical issues often undermines the quality of an investigation. There are several features of the results and statistical evaluation that can obscure interpretation of the experiment. These are referred to as *threats to statistical conclusion validity.*

Overview of Essential Concepts

Statistical Tests and Decision Making

Before discussing the threats to validity, it is important to review a few of the essential concepts of statistical evaluation and to highlight the rationale for statistical evaluation. As the reader knows, in most psychological research, the conclusions in an experiment depend heavily on hypothesis testing and statistical evaluation. The null hypothesis specifies that there are "no differences" between groups (e.g., treatment vs. control group). Statistical tests are completed to evaluate whether the differences that are obtained are reliable or beyond what one is likely to find due to chance fluctuations. We can reject the null hypothesis of no difference if we find a statistically significant difference or accept this hypothesis if we do not. The rejection and acceptance of hypotheses are weighty topics, only part of which we can treat here.

The model of null hypothesis testing using statistical evaluation, the use of probability levels (alpha) as a basis for drawing inferences, and whether statistical tests are appropriate at all for data evaluation are a matter of debate (e.g., Lipsey, 1990). Many of these issues are addressed later. However, at this point, these issues are skirted in recognition of the fact that the bulk of research in psychology is based on drawing inferences from statistical evaluation. As such, there are common weaknesses of research that can be identified under the rubric of statistical conclusion of validity.

The decision-making process is based on selecting a probability level that specifies the degree of risk of reaching a "false" conclusion. If the statistical differences between groups passes this probability level, we state that the difference is reliable and represents an effect of the intervention. If the difference fails to pass the threshold, we say that the difference is not statistically significant and that in fact the groups are not truly different.

Figure 3.1 notes the outcomes of an investigation based on the conclusions we might draw from statistical evaluation. The four cells represent the combination of *our decision* (there is a reliable difference vs. there is no reliable difference) and *the state of affairs in the world* (there really is a difference, or there is no difference). Our goal in experimentation is to draw conclusions that reflect the true state of affairs in the world. That is, if there are differences between two or more conditions (i.e., if the intervention is truly effective), we wish to reflect that in our decision (Cell B in Figure 3.1). If there is no difference between the conditions in the world, we would like to conclude that as well (Cell C). Occasionally, there is a clear effect in our study, when in fact there really is no effect in the world (Cell A) or no effect in our study when in fact there is one in the world (Cell D). We specify our probability level (alpha) for concluding that the differences are significant. By doing so, we also fix the risk of concluding erroneously that there are differences when in fact there are none in the world and of concluding that there are no differences when in fact there are.

The cells in Figure 3.1 have established names that reflect critically important statistical concepts to refer to the decision-making process, outcomes of our experiment, and risk of reaching a false conclusion. Table 3.1 lists these and other concepts that we shall draw upon to elaborate the threats to statistical conclusion validity and later discussions of statistical evaluation more generally (chapters 12 and 13).

Effect Size

Among the concepts listed in Table 3.1, effect size is especially critical to highlight because it underlies several issues we shall consider. In general terms, effect size refers to a way of describing the magnitude of the difference between conditions or how much impact an intervention has had. Effect size refers to the magnitude of the difference between two (or more) conditions or groups. This magnitude is expressed in standard deviation units. Effect size *(ES)* is computed for a given measure in a study by evaluating the difference between means of the groups and dividing their difference by the standard deviation. Specifically,

$$ES = \frac{m_1 - m_2}{s}$$

where m_1 and m_2 are the sample means for two groups or conditions (e.g., treatment and control groups), and s equals the pooled standard deviation for these groups.

Consider a two-group study that evaluates treatment for patients who are experiencing anxiety. Patients are assigned to treatment or no-treatment con-

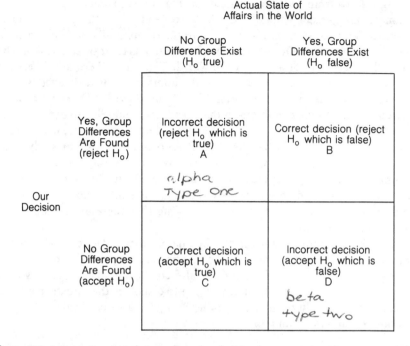

Actual State of
Affairs in the World

	No Group Differences Exist (H_0 true)	Yes, Group Differences Exist (H_0 false)
Yes, Group Differences Are Found (reject H_0)	Incorrect decision (reject H_0 which is true) A *alpha Type One*	Correct decision (reject H_0 which is false) B
No Group Differences Are Found (accept H_0)	Correct decision (accept H_0 which is true) C	Incorrect decision (accept H_0 which is false) D *beta type two*

Our Decision

Figure 3.1. A 2 × 2 matrix that conveys the decisions we reach based on our statistical evaluation of the results and in relation to the true state of affairs in the world. If H_0 (the null hypothesis) is true, this means there really are no group differences in the world. If H_0 is false, this means there really are group differences. The cells have other names as discussed in the text. In particular, it is worth noting here that Cell A is also known as alpha (α) or Type I error; Cell D is known as beta (β) or Type II error.

ditions. After the study, patients complete a measure of anxiety in which higher scores equal higher levels of anxiety. Suppose that treated subjects show a posttreatment mean of 10 on the scale, whereas control patients show a score of 16. We shall also suppose that the standard deviation is 8. Effect size equals .75 (derived from 10 minus 16 divided by 8). This means that in standard deviation units, the mean of the treatment group was .75 higher than the mean of the control subjects.

Effect size is a critical concept for statistical evaluation. Effect size is often assumed to reflect the magnitude of the difference as that difference exists in nature. Thus, if an investigator is exploring a truly effective technique or variable, this will produce a marked effect size and significant results. However, effect size is very much dependent on the design and methodology of the study. A poorly planned or executed study can produce small and nondetecta-

Table 3.1. Important Concepts in Relation to Statistical Conclusion Validity

CONCEPT	DEFINITION
alpha (α)	The probability of rejecting a hypothesis (the null hypothesis) when that hypothesis is true. This is also referred to as a Type I error (cell A).
beta (β)	The probability of accepting a hypothesis (the null hypothesis) when it is false. This is also referred to as a Type II error (cell D).
Power	The probability of rejecting the null hypothesis when it is false or the likelihood of finding differences between conditions when, in fact, the conditions are truly different. This probability is $1 - \beta$ (cell B).
Effect Size	A way of expressing the difference between alternative conditions (e.g., treatment vs. control) in terms of a common metric across measures and across studies. The method is based on obtaining the difference between the means of interest on a particular measure and dividing this by the common (pooled) standard deviation.
Standard Deviation	A measure of variation or variability about a mean. The standard deviation (also the square root of the variance) of a sample is given by the formula:

where X_i = an observation of Subject i,
$\bar{X}$ = mean of the sample,
N = sample size,
SS = sum of squared deviation,
df = degree of freedom.

ble effects. Effect size is basic to statistical conclusion validity because it is a common final pathway for entering methodological problems, sloppiness and error, and uncontrolled variation into the results.

We cannot control effect size in the sense of dictating how effective the variable is. Yet we can greatly influence effect size by reducing variability in the procedures of the study to minimize the error term (standard deviation) that is used in the effect size equation. Many efforts to control features of the experiment are designed to minimize "error" variance, that is, variability in the formula. The larger the variability (denominator), the smaller the effect size for a constant difference between means (numerator). Having described effect size, we can turn more specifically to threats to statistical conclusion validity.

Threats to Statistical Conclusion Validity

Low Statistical Power

Central to statistical evaluation is the notion of statistical power, which refers to the extent to which an investigation can detect differences between groups when differences exist within the population (see Table 3.1). *Power* is the probability of rejecting the null hypothesis (i.e., there are no differences) when that hypothesis is false. Stated differently, power is the likelihood of finding differences between treatments when, in fact, the treatments are truly different in their outcomes. Certainly, if there is a difference between groups, if the intervention or experimental manipulation is effective, we wish to detect this difference in our statistical tests.

The central threat to statistical validity in studies is relatively weak power or a low probability of detecting a difference if one truly exists. When power is weak, the likelihood is increased that the investigator will conclude there are no differences between groups. There might well be no differences in the world, and the intervention may in fact be no different in the effects it produces than a control condition. However, the study must be designed so as to detect a difference if there is one. Low power is a threat to statistical conclusion validity if the study provides a weak test of the hypotheses. The finding of "no differences" might be due to low power rather than to the absence of differences between groups. Power is not an exoteric concept of relevance only to researchers in the confines of their studies. Areas critical to everyday life are affected. For example, studies of alternative treatments for cancer occasionally have been unable to demonstrate differences due to weak statistical power (see Freiman, Chalmers, Smith, & Kuebler, 1978). More central to clinical psychology, the majority of comparisons of different psychotherapy techniques show no differences in treatment outcome. This could easily be due to the weak power of studies, given the relatively small samples and small effect sizes that characterize this research (Kazdin & Bass, 1989).

Statistical power of an experiment is a function of the criterion for statistical significance (alpha), the size of the sample *(N)*, and the differences that exist between groups (effect size). Although the most straightforward method of increasing power is to increase sample size, alpha and *ES* are under the control of the investigator in significant ways. The present discussion highlights the concepts to elaborate statistical conclusion validity. However, we shall address these matters in more detail later (chapter 12).

Variability in the Procedures

The notion of effect size is useful to discuss further threats to statistical conclusion validity. Consider as a hypothetical experiment, a comparison of two treatments, A and B, which are administered to different groups. Ordinarily, effect size is considered to be a function of the true differences in the effects of these treatments. That is, if Treatment A is more effective than Treatment B in the "real world," this will be evident in our experiment and be shown in our statistical evaluation.

Reconsider the formula for effect size. The denominator includes a measure of variability (standard deviation). Thus whatever the difference between Treatments A and B in our study, that difference will be in part a function of the variability in our experiment. This variability includes many influences, not all of which might even be specified here. Factors that influence variability include individual differences among the subjects, random fluctuations in performance on the measures, differences in experimenters or therapists in how they administer the intervention, and other sources. One source of variance has to do with how the interventions or experimental procedures are introduced and executed. Ideally, the procedures will be held relatively constant and implemented in a way that minimizes variation among subjects. This means that the procedures will be applied consistently, experimenters will be trained to administer the instructions and other procedures in a constant way, and so on.

Rigor in the execution of the procedures is not a methodological nicety for the sake of appearance. Consistency in execution of the procedures has direct bearing on statistical conclusion validity. A given difference between groups may or may not be regarded as reliable. Variation cannot be eliminated, especially in relation to those aspects of research involving human participants (e.g., as subjects, clients, experimenters, therapists) and in settings outside of the laboratory. However, in any experiment, extraneous variation can be minimized by attention to details of how the study is actually executed. If variability is minimized, the likelihood of detecting a true difference between the treatments or treatment and control conditions is increased. In terms of our effect size formula, the differences between groups will be divided by a measure of variability; this measure will be larger when there is uncontrolled variation than if this source of variation were minimized. The larger the variability, the lower the effect size that will be evident for a given difference between groups.

Sometimes one can tell from the way an experiment is designed that there will be relatively high levels of variability and consequently great difficulty in demonstrating differences between conditions. For example, several years ago, a now classic study compared behavior therapy and psychotherapy for the treatment of adults who came for treatment (Sloane et al., 1975). Clients were assigned to behavior therapy, psychotherapy, or a waiting-list control group. The way in which the two treatments were designed and implemented provided the opportunity for relatively large variability.

Specifically, treatment guidelines were provided to behavior therapists and psychotherapists; these were quite general and allowed remarkable latitude in what was actually done in the sessions. Each therapist was selected because of special expertise in the practice of one of the two approaches. Consequently, considerable freedom was given to therapists so they could treat the case as they wished within these broad guidelines. Essentially, each therapist (male) could and no doubt did provide his own brand of treatment. The individual characteristics of the therapists and what they actually did in treatment varied greatly within a given condition. In seeing this feature of the design, one might suspect on a priori grounds that there would be a great deal of within-group variability. Such variability could diminish the obtained effect size and the likelihood of obtaining statistical significance between conditions. The results in general showed few or no differences in the outcomes between behavior therapy and psychotherapy. It would be an oversimplification to state that this one aspect of the study, namely, high within-treatment variability, led to no differences. Indeed, there were other sources of variations that were rather broad as well, including heterogeneous subject characteristics (e.g., diverse clinical problems). Yet on the basis of the results, we are hard pressed to tell whether the paucity of differences is due to the equivalent effects of treatment in general or because of the manner in which the treatments were implemented in this study. This latter point might always be raised in a study where few or no differences are found. However, the design of this study heightens the concern because variability, usually controlled by specifying and administering treatment in a relatively standardized way, was given relatively free reign.

Subject Heterogeneity

Subjects in an investigation can vary along multiple dimensions and characteristics such as sex, age, background, race and ethnicity, marital status, and others. In the general case, the greater the heterogeneity or diversity of subject characteristics, the less likelihood there will be to detect a difference between alternative conditions. Critical to the statement is the assumption that subjects are heterogeneous on a characteristic that is related (correlated) with the effects of independent variable. For example, clients who were recruited for a psychotherapy study may vary widely (and "lengthly") in shoe size. Is this heterogeneity of great concern? Probably not. It is unlikely for most forms of psychotherapy that treatment effectiveness and performance on the outcome measures would be correlated with shoe size. On the other hand, clients may vary widely in their severity or duration of the clinical problem, employment, socioeconomic class, and the presence of other problems (e.g., substance abuse, depression, chronic medical disease) not of interest in the study. The impact of treatment and performance on the dependent measures might well be influenced by these factors. That these factors influence outcome is not inherently problematic nor undesirable. However, heterogeneity of the sample means that there will be greater variability in the subjects' reactions to the measures as well as to the intervention. This variability will be reflected in the denominator for evaluating effect size. The greater that variability (denominator), the less likely a given difference between means will be found to be statistically significant.

Consider our hypothetical example concerning Treatments A and B. Suppose we believe that these treatments might be effective for depressed individuals and test this in an experiment. We recruit all comers at some clinic and find that our subjects range in age from 15 to 60 years and include a broad range of socioeconomic classes, males and females, multiple ethnic groups, diverse IQ levels, and different types of depression (e.g., people who say they are sad, those who meet diagnostic criteria for major depression, those who are suicidal, those who have suffered the recent death of a close relative, and so on). After our recruitment, we are likely to praise ourselves for conducting a study with great external validity because of the representativeness of the subjects to the diverse patient samples and the "free world." Suppose further that Treatments A and B are different in their effectiveness for some of these depressed people but our study finds no differences. The absence of differences might have been due to the relatively great heterogeneity of the subjects. The variation would be reflected no doubt in performance on the measures with or without treatment and then in presumably quite different responses to treatment.

To show that one treatment is more effective than another would require massive differences between groups to overcome the large within-group variation. Perhaps equally likely would be different reactions of patients to the treatments. Some subgroups of depressed people (e.g., those who are merely sad) might well have profited from Treatments A and B, whereas those who are severely depressed may have responded to Treatment B. This differential responsiveness, if not evaluated separately as a variable in its own right in the design or data analysis, enters into the denominator as within-group variability and attenuates the likelihood of showing group differences.

This particular threat to statistical conclusion validity can be addressed in different ways. The first, of course, is to choose homogeneous samples. Homogeneity is a matter of degree. One might wish to limit the age range, type of clinical problem, educational level, and other variables within some reasonable boundaries. Ideally, the decision of what variables to consider and how narrow the confines is decided by theory or research on the effects of these and related variables on the measures of interest. If in doubt, one might select a relatively homogeneous set of subjects on diverse factors as a conservative way of addressing this threat.

A second alternative is to choose heterogeneous samples but to ensure that the impact or effect of the characteristics can be evaluated in the design. For example, subjects of different ages and type of depression can be included. In the design of the study and the data analysis, the effects of age (above vs. below the median) and type of depression (those diagnosed as clinically depressed vs. those experiencing bereavement) can be evaluated. When these factors are analyzed as separate effects in the analysis, they no longer become within-group or error variance and do not serve to increase the denominator in evaluating treatment differences. This point is elaborated further in the discussion of factorial designs (chapter 5).

Unreliability of the Measures

Reliability refers to the extent to which the measures assess the characteristics of interest in a consistent fashion. Reliability is, of course, a matter of degree and refers to the extent of the variability in responding. Performance on the measure may vary widely from item to item within the measure because items are not equally clear or consistent in what they measure, and performance may vary widely from occasion to occasion. To the extent that the measure is unreliable, a greater portion of the subject's score is due to unsystematic and random variation. This variation again means that in statistical evaluation, relatively large variability can be introduced. In studies with relatively unreliable measures, the obtained effect size is likely to be lower. Selection of assessment devices in designing a study is more than a quick shopping trip through the literature (see chapter 9). Selection of poorly designed measures where reliability and validity are in doubt is tantamount to flirtation with this particular threat to statistical conclusion validity.

Multiple Comparisons and Error Rates

Not all of the threats to statistical conclusion validity pertain to variability. Statistical evaluation of the results can be hindered by other problems that directly influence whether the investigator concludes that groups differed. In an investigation, several different measures are likely to be used to evaluate the impact of the intervention. For example, in a treatment study, the clients are likely to complete a few measures (e.g., depression, symptoms in diverse areas, social functioning); relatives of the clients or therapists may complete various measures as well. At the end of the investigation, Treatments A and B will be compared on each of the measures. The familiar *t* test may be used given that there are two groups and parametric data.

There are separate but interrelated problems that reflect a threat to statistical conclusion validity. The first has to do with the *number of statistical tests* that will be completed. The more tests that are performed, the more likely a chance difference will be found, even if there are no true differences between conditions. Thus the investigator may conclude mistakenly that there is a difference between groups and a true effect of the intervention (Type I error). The possibility of this occurring is evident in any experiment. The risk of such an error (Type I error) is specified by alpha or the probability level that is used as a criterion for statistical significance. Yet this risk and its probability level applies to an individual test. When there are multiple comparisons, alpha is greater than .05 depending on the number of tests. The risk across several statistical tests, sometimes referred to as *experiment-wise error rate,* is much greater.

The problem is not merely in the number of comparisons but also the fact that the comparisons are not really independent from each other. For example, all of the measures may reflect performance of the clients. In addition, for many measures the rater (e.g., who completed the measure) may be the same. Thus the measures are likely to be intercorrelated. The statistical evaluation ought to consider the fact that the measures are interrelated. Failure to do so may generate statistically significant differences among measures that are not truly independent.

In general, the number of comparisons in a study and the nonindependence of these comparisons, given the relations of the measures, can lead to misleading conclusions about group differences. At this point, it is important to mention these threats to statistical conclusion validity. Strategies to address statistical issues in the execution of research are detailed in chapter 12.

General Comments

The threats to statistical conclusion validity refer to the features of the study that affect the quantitative evaluation of the impact of the intervention. When the threats are made explicit, they may appear obvious. Yet they often serve as the tacit downfall of an experiment. Excellent ideas conducted in carefully controlled tests routinely have weak power, a topic we shall examine in more detail. Perhaps even more pervasive is the hidden variability that can emerge in all facets of experimentation that serves to obscure differences between conditions.

The notion of experimental control, when first introduced into the discussion of research, is usually raised in the context of control groups and threats to internal validity. However, a deeper understanding of the notion of control stems in part from its relation to statistical conclusion validity. The control and evaluation of variability in research, to the extent possible, are critical. The initial question of interest in designing a study is, "Are the groups or conditions different?" This question emphasizes the means on some measure or set of measures. The question beyond this usually guides statistical conclusion validity; namely, if there is a difference will this study be able to detect it? This latter question greatly influences several features of the design (e.g., selection, sample size) and procedures (e.g., implementation of the intervention, experimenter training). Many facets of research including recruitment of subjects, preparation and delivery of experimental instructions, and methods of scoring and checking data all become potential sources of uncontrolled variation and can introduce ambiguity into the results.

We have discussed variability and variation as if they were the enemy. There is some sense in which this might be true but great care is needed in making this point. The goal of our research is not to eliminate variability but rather to understand it. That means we wish to elaborate the full range of factors that influence personality and behavior including our interventions (e.g., a new treatment), those interventions of "nature" not under our experimental control (e.g., child-rearing practices, stress associated with bereavement, chronic disease, war), and individual differences (e.g., temperament, genetic predispositions, personality style). When any one or more of these serves as the basis of our investigations, we need to control other sources of variation. The reason is that the source of variation that is of interest in our study may be obscured by allowing free fluctuation of all other sources of variation. Experimental design and statistical evaluation serve to separate and evaluate these alternative sources of variation.

INTERRELATIONS AMONG VALIDITIES

In the present and previous chapters, we have covered internal, external, construct, and statistical conclusion validity. At the design stage, each type of validity needs to be considered along with its individual threats. Not all of the problems that can interfere with valid inferences can be predicted or controlled in advance (e.g., loss of subjects over time). However, most can be addressed in planning the experiment and its execution. Also, even those that cannot be resolved in advance are worth considering at the design stage. It is worth making explicit that addressing each threat to validity perfectly well is not possible. The reason is that addressing one type of validity often compromises another type of validity. It is useful to consider the occasionally inverse relations among alternative validities.

Threats to internal validity generally can be ruled out by allocating subjects randomly to conditions and controlling potential sources of bias (e.g., instrumentation, mortality) that might arise during the experiment. Yet in designing experiments, researchers usually are interested in more than ruling out threats to internal validity; they also are interested in providing the most sensitive test of the independent variable possible. Maximizing the likelihood of detecting the relation raises issues of statistical conclusion validity. The investigator wishes to minimize extraneous influences and sources of variation in how subjects respond in the experiment.

Increased precision is achieved by holding constant the potential sources of influence on subjects' behavior other than the independent variable. Conditions are held constant if they are identical or very close to that across subjects and experimental conditions. Of course, one cannot realistically expect to implement an experiment where all conditions are the same except for the independent variable. Just to cite an obvious problem, the subjects in the study vary because of their differences in genetic make-up, childhood experiences, physical capabilities, intelligence, age, ethnic background, and familiarity with experiments. Each of these factors and many others introduce variation into the experiment in terms of how subjects respond to the intervention.

The manner in which the independent variable is implemented may introduce extraneous variation into the experiment. Ideally, the conditions of administration among subjects within a given condition would not vary at all. Some features of the experimental manipulation might be held constant such as administering instructions or showing materials to the subjects by using audio- or videotapes. If an experimenter interacts with the subjects, this interaction may vary slightly across different subjects; if several experimenters are used in the study, even greater variation may be introduced. Other extraneous factors of the experiment such as the time of the day, weather, how the independent variable is implemented, and so on all may contribute to sources of variation. These factors can be *controlled* by having them vary unsystematically across groups. If there is no systematic bias with these sources of variation, the experiment is controlled. However, *holding* the factors *constant* may even be better from the standpoint of demonstrating the relation between the independent and dependent variable. By removing sources of variation, a more sensitive (powerful) test of the independent variable is provided.

At first glance, it may seem that experimenters should automatically maximize the sensitivity of all experimental tests by making the experiment as precise as possible in terms of minimizing extraneous sources of variation. However, experimental precision has its cost in the generality of the experimental results. *As a general rule, design features that make an experiment more sensitive as a test of the independent and dependent variables tend to limit the generality of the findings. Conversely, features of an experiment that enhance generality of the results tend to increase variability and to decrease the sensitivity of the experimental test.*

In clinical psychology, there often is concern about the relevance of research obtained in highly controlled situations for phenomena in applied situations. This question has arisen frequently in discussions of analogue research, in which a process of human interaction is purposely simplified for investigation (see Kazdin, 1978). For example, to evaluate the effects of psychotherapy, often college students are recruited as subjects and receive highly abbreviated treatments (e.g., four sessions) administered by students in training. The conditions of the experiment permit very careful control over the intervention and extraneous sources of variability (e.g., homogeneous subject sample). The control is admirable from the standpoint of design. The cost may be in the external validity of the results. Would the findings hold or apply in any way to patients seen in treatment, with more commonly used variations of the treatment, when administered by full-time and experienced therapists? Conditions of tightly controlled research may deviate so markedly from the ordinary situation that the plausibility of producing generalizable findings is commensurately decreased.

The problem for an investigator is that the more the conditions in the experiment resemble the natural situation, the fewer the factors that will be held constant in the experiment. And the fewer the factors that are held constant, the greater the potential variability in the study. Variation in an experiment in conditions other than the independent variable constitutes error variance or "noise" and can decrease the chances of obtaining a statistically significant finding.

It is not always the case that careful experimental control necessarily restricts the generality of a phenomenon in clinical research. Yet there seems to be a relation such that a gain in either experimental precision or generality may be associated with a sacrifice in the other. Once a finding has been established through well-controlled and internally valid studies, research emphasis can extend to external validity. External validity is evaluated by systematically broadening samples of subjects, the type of settings in which treatment is administered, variations of treatment that are attempted, the type of measures and constructs used to evaluate outcome, and so on.

SUMMARY AND CONCLUSIONS

Construct validity pertains to interpreting the basis for the causal relation that has been demonstrated in an investigation. The intervention or the variable of interest may be one of many factors that distinguishes intervention and control conditions or two or more intervention conditions. Factors that may interfere with or obscure valid inferences about the basis for the effect are *threats to construct validity*. Major threats include attention and contact with the clients, single operations and stimulus sampling, experimenter expectancies, and cues of the experimental situation.

Statistical conclusion validity refers to those aspects of the experiment that affect the quantitative evaluation of the study and can lead to misleading or false conclusions about the intervention. Several concepts basic to statistical evaluation were mentioned in passing because of their role in statistical conclusion validity. These included the probability of accepting and rejecting the null hypothesis, the probability of making such decisions when they are false, and the notion of effect size. Major factors that commonly serve as *threats to statistical conclusion validity* operate by influencing one or more of these concepts and include low statistical power, variability in the procedures of an investigation, subject heterogeneity, unreliability of the measures, and multiple statistical comparisons and their error rates.

The four types of validity, including internal, external, construct, and statistical conclusions validity, all need to be considered at the design stage of an investigation. It is not possible in any one experiment to address all threats well or equally well, nor is this necessarily a goal toward which one should strive. Rather, the goal is to address the primary questions of interest in as thorough a fashion as possible so that clear answers can be provided for those specific questions. At the end of that investigation, new questions may emerge or questions about other types of validity may increase in priority. The need for further information is not necessarily a flaw but rather the continued line of inquiry to which an important study invariably leads.

The obstacles in designing experiments not only emerge from the manifold types of validity and their threats, but also from the interrelations of alternative types of validity. Factors that address one type of validity might detract from or increase vulnerability to another type of validity. For example, factors that address statistical conclusion validity might involve controlling potential sources of variation in relation to the experimental setting, delivery of procedures, homogeneity of subjects, and so on. In the process of maximizing experiment control and making the most sensitive test of the independent variable, the range of conditions included in the experiment become increasingly restricted. Restricting the conditions such as the type of subjects or measures, the standardization of the independent variable, and so on may commensurately limit the range of conditions to which the final results can be generalized.

In this and the previous chapter we have discussed alternative types of validity and their threats. The purpose has been primarily to describe these threats and how they operate. In remaining chapters, we address several of these areas again and more concretely and discuss strategies that directly affect inferences drawn from research.

FOR FURTHER READING

Cowles, M., & Davis, C. (1982). On the origins of the .05 level of statistical significance. *American Psychologist, 37,* 553–558.

Lipsey, M.W. (1990). *Design sensitivity: Statistical power for experimental research.* Newbury Park, CA: Sage Publications.

Nunnally, J. (1960). The place of statistics in psychology. *Educational and Psychological Measurement, 20,* 641–650.

Wampold, B.E., Davis, B., & Good, R.H. (1990). Hypothesis validity of clinical research. *Journal of Consulting and Clinical Psychology, 58,* 360–367.

SELECTION OF THE RESEARCH PROBLEM AND DESIGN

Selection of the research problem refers to the focus of the investigation and the question that is to be addressed. The research focus may begin with an overall idea that serves as the impetus for investigation. Perhaps the general idea expresses the relation to be studied or specific hypotheses of what will happen when certain conditions are varied. However, the general idea must be reexpressed in concrete terms that specify the precise way in which the general concepts will be defined. The concrete terms refer to what will be done in the investigation and how performance will be measured. The present chapter discusses the initiation of research and specification of the idea. The chapter also previews many of the design options from which the investigator can select.

RESEARCH IDEAS AND OPERATIONS

Sources of Ideas

The research investigation begins with an idea. How the idea is derived may be more appropriately discussed in the context of creativity than methodology. Nevertheless, some comments might be made in passing about the source of research ideas because this is the beginning of the research design process. Presumably a scientist might be equipped with excellent research design skills and knowledge of how to execute the design. Yet in the absence of a specific research idea, he or she would be all dressed up with no place to go. Where one decides to go in research, that is, which question or problem will be addressed, may arise from many sources.

First, many ideas arise out of simple curiosity about a phenomenon. Curiosity is no explanation of why a particular course of research is pursued, but it helps convey that the motive for asking particular questions in the context of experimentation need not always germinate out of complex or highly sophisticated theoretical notions. This research may seek to describe how people are or perform in a particular situation and then expand to generate ideas about why this is the case.

Second, and related, theory is often devised to explain a phenomenon and then tested in research. In an effort to understand phenomena, investigators propose concepts to integrate different ideas and variables in an orderly fashion. The theory or model may explain different constructs and how they relate to each other and to other events. Research is completed to test predicted relations and other conditions that explain how the variables or processes operate. For example, theory might propose that there are certain styles of behavior (e.g., withdrawn, highly conforming) or beliefs (e.g., maladaptive cognitions) that account for a variety of phenomena. An investigation might be devised to place people in a situation to see if the expected type of performance is evident.

Third, a great deal of research in clinical psychology stems from the observations of clinical dysfunctions. Research attempts to describe and understand various types of problems (e.g., anxiety, depression), how they emerge, their course over time, and other characteristics. The correlates (e.g., in personality style, family background) and similarities and differences among alternative clinical problems encompass a wide range of investigations.

Fourth, research sometimes is stimulated by efforts to operationalize or measure various constructs. Developing assessment devices is central because measurement is a precondition for research. An investigator may be interested in studying empathy, risk taking, hopelessness, adjustment, and an indefinite number of other constructs. Research is begun to develop and validate a new measure.

Fifth, research is often stimulated by other studies. Research may evaluate the interpretation of a relation provided by the original investigator or test the generality of conditions across which the relation holds. A very large portion of the published research is directed at building upon, expanding, or reexplaining the results of other studies.

Finally, in clinical psychology, a prominent source of hypotheses has been the case study. A case study usually consists of the intensive evaluation of an individual over time. Close contact with an individual case provides unique information because of observation of many variables, their interactions over time, and views about the bases of personality and behavior. Cases can generate many hypotheses about all facets of functioning (e.g., impact of special events in childhood, why one relates to others in particular ways, and so on). The case study has played a special role in clinical psychology and in research and hence is treated further in a separate discussion (chapter 7).

The source of an idea for psychological experimentation is not restricted to the above options. The value of the source of the idea is determined by the empirical and conceptual yield the source provides in actual research. Ideas that are derived from everyday experience, common cultural wisdom, or stereotypic notions about behavior may be just as useful in generating hypotheses as are more complex psychological theories.

This brief discussion of the source of ideas does not address the quality of the idea. It is difficult to judge what a good research idea is because that judgment is based upon subjective evaluation, theoretical predilection, and ultimately its empirical yield. Despite the difficulty in judging the quality of ideas, professionals are called on to make these judgments all of the time; for example, judgment of the value or contribution of an idea occurs routinely in the process of reviewing research reports that are considered for possible journal publication or grant applications that seek funding for proposed research. Professionals are regularly called on to determine whether a completed or proposed study is "significant" in the sense that it addresses an important question, adds to existing knowledge, and focuses on an agreed-upon problem in an area of research.

An idea that may be viewed as a contribution to literature often involves focusing on a problem area or unresolved issue in the specific research area of interest to the investigator. To develop a study on a problem or unresolved aspect of a given literature requires detailed knowledge of that literature. Thus for developing research ideas in a given area, there is no substitute for knowing the area thoroughly. Reading incisive reviews and individual studies from the relevant literature is essential. The difficulty a novice researcher often suffers when under pressure for an idea (as in an honors or master's thesis) may stem from not knowing an area sufficiently well to identify central issues.

Although there is no substitute for expertise to generate a research idea that takes an important "next step," mastery of the literature can be delimiting as well. The literature in a given area reflects a set of agreed upon assumptions and methods, many of which are accepted on faith. Drawing upon areas outside of the content area to be researched frequently adds new dimensions that might not have been pursued otherwise. Thus the advantage of novice researchers often is, paradoxically, that their thinking is not confined by the standard topics and procedures for investigation.

Levels of Understanding and the Research Idea

The overall purpose of research in clinical psychology is to enhance understanding of human functioning broadly conceived. In any given study, the task is to add an increment of knowledge. At the planning stage, whether a particular study is likely to accomplish this goal is difficult to say. The idea and the way (methods) in which it is studied directly affect judgments about significance of the knowledge yield. In beginning work in a research area, it is important to have as a guide the current status of knowledge. This knowledge serves as a way of identifying the type of work that may contribute further and improve the level of understanding.

Level of understanding can be discussed in terms of what is known about a phenomenon, the manner in which it operates, the variables or factors of which it is a function, and the conditions under which it is or is not evident. Research begins at a rudimentary level, which may be largely descriptive. At this initial stage, the task may be to identify or describe relations between variables. For example, a study might show that two variables are correlated (e.g., personality style and medical illness), that is, they go together in some way. Showing that two or more variables are related, at a very basic descriptive level, is not automatically interesting or important. The reasons, either theoretical or practical, suggested by the investigator provide meaning to this relation. Occasionally the demonstrated relation may be of stark significance because the variables may not be expected to relate or because of some immediate and obvious implication. For example, demonstration that acquired immunodeficiency syndrome (AIDS) is related to intravenous drug use was important at the descriptive level. This connection between a disease and drug use is critical but by itself is only an initial step.

A higher level of understanding emerges when one can go beyond the relation of two or more variables to identify features about that relation. Knowing the direction of the relation (e.g., if one variable precedes another in time) or the mechanism of operation (e.g., how or why they are related) extend further our understanding. For example, in the AIDS example, it could be that drug use increases vulnerability to the AIDS virus. The substances that are abused conceivably could impair one's immune system and make one vulnerable to AIDS. However, the basis for the relation is known now to lie elsewhere. The mechanism relating these variables is sharing of needles for intravenous injection, which spreads the virus directly. This level of understanding is obviously greater than the mere connection of the two variables. Knowing the mechanism can be used to alter the spread of AIDS by decreasing the sharing of needles.

Research moves from description to explanation by elaborating the factors, mechanisms, directionality, and other factors that relate to variables. This movement reflects increased understanding. One can see the progression in clinical psychological research. For example, a well-established connection is evident between parent punishment practices and aggressiveness of the child. Parents of aggressive children often punish in inept ways by using harsh, frequent, and ineffective punishment (Patterson, 1986). This correlation (parent punishment practices and child behavior) is important at a descriptive level. A higher level of understanding has been achieved by showing that harsh punishment can lead to aggressive child behavior, that is, that there is a direction to this relation. This is not to say that all aggressive behavior is caused by inept parenting nor that child behavior does not influence parent child rearing. The findings show that one variable (parent punishment) is related to another (child deviance) and that variation in the former leads to variation in the latter. Further understanding emerges by identifying multiple influences that contribute to both parental punishment and child aggression, and how diverse factors emerge and conspire to produce their effects.

The search for direction of influence between two variables, the mechanisms or processes connecting the two variables, whether there is a causal connection, and the influence of other variables on the relation represent deeper levels of understanding of a phenomenon. In selecting the research focus or question, the investigator considers the current status of knowledge in regard to the variables of interest and develops a study to contribute to that knowledge base. When beginning research in an area, the investigator may consider the importance of selecting a problem that has not been studied before. The rationale may be that "these two variables have not been studied previously." However, in selecting the research problem, this criterion is not the direct one of interest. The relation of an infinite number of variables can be identified that have not previously been studied before (e.g., shoe size and schizophrenia; cognitive style and longevity of one's parents; diet as a graduate student and long-term professional success). The issue is the selection of an idea that can contribute to the knowledge base and that represents a relation of some interest in relation to understanding human functioning. Theory, explanation, and views of the implications of a possible connection between variables imbue the idea with meaning and potential significance.

Theory plays a critical role in the research process and deserves special comment. Theory, broadly defined, refers to a conceptualization of the phenomenon of interest. The conceptualization may encompass views about the nature, antecedents, causes, correlates, and consequences of a particular characteristic or aspect of functioning. Also, the theory may specify the relations of various constructs to each other. There are different levels of theory. In clinical psychology, theories of personality have been a central topic in which diverse facets of human functioning were explained. Psychoanalytic theory illustrates this well by posing a variety of constructs, mechanisms that are designed to explain intrapsychic processes and performance in everyday life, psychopathology, development, and so on. More circumscribed theoretical views characterize contemporary research in an effort to develop specific models or integrated sets of findings and relations among variables. The models may explain the relation between specific characteristics and a disorder (e.g., hopelessness and helplessness in relation to depression) and how these characteristics lead to other features of dysfunction.

In research, the investigator usually makes a prediction or has an expectation about the relation of the independent variable and dependent variable. The theoretical or conceptual connection between these variables is important because it suggests the basis of the relation and ideally implications for other domains of functioning beyond those examined in this particular demonstration. As a goal of understanding functioning, we wish not merely to accumulate facts or empirical findings, but to relate them to each other and to other phenomena in a cohesive way. For example, an investigator may demonstrate that there are sex differences regarding a particular personality characteristic or style of responding. However, by themselves sex differences are not necessarily inherently interesting. A theoretical understanding would explain how this difference develops, what implications the difference may have for understanding development, and so on. From the standpoint of research, theoretical explanations guide further studies after a particular finding. The presence or absence of a predicted difference has obvious implications for the prediction that guided the research, and these implications generate continued studies.

Defining the Research Idea

Operational Definitions

Whatever the original idea that provides the impetus for research, it must be described concretely so that it can be tested. It is not enough to have an abstract notion or question. For example, one might ask at a general level such questions as: "Do anxious people tend to withdraw from social situations?" or "Are college students put to sleep by the lectures of their instructors?" These and similar notions are adequate for initial leads for study but require considerable work before empirical research could be executed.

The concepts included in the abstract notion must be operationalized, that is, made into operational definitions. *Operational definitions* refer to defining a concept on the basis of the specific operations used in the experiment. For example, an operational definition of anxiety refers to the procedures or methods used to measure anxiety in the experiment. Anxiety might be defined as physiological responses to a galvanic skin response measure of skin resistance or to an individual's self-report of being upset, nervous, or irritable in several situations. Greater specificity may be required than noting the measure. For example, the above question, "Do anxious people tend to withdraw from social situations?", requires operational criteria for designating anxious and nonanxious individuals and for defining social withdrawal. "Anxious" may be operationalized by referring to persons who attain relatively high scores (e.g., at or above the 75th percentile) on a standardized measure of anxiety. Nonanxious or low-anxious persons might be defined as those who attain relatively low scores (e.g., at or below the 25th percentile) on the same scale. Specifying the measure and the cutoff criteria to define anxious and nonanxious groups would clearly satisfy the requirements of an operational definition. Similarly, for defining social withdrawal, the specific measure must be identified.

Although operational definitions are essential for experimentation, there are limitations that such definitions bear. To begin with, although the investigator may start with an abstract notion that is to be operationalized, the use of an operational definition may be incomplete or greatly simplify the concept of interest. For example, an operational definition of love might be based upon the expression of love on a self-report measure or overt physical expressions of affection. Although each of these measures is part of what people often mean by love, the measures, either separate or combined, are not the full definition that people usually have in mind when they talk about or experience love. From the standpoint of research, the purpose is to provide a working definition of the phenomenon. Yet the working definition may not be complete and all encompassing or even bear great resemblance to what people mean in everyday discourse.

A second limitation is that the operational definition may include features that are irrelevant or not central to the original concept. For example, anxiety might be operationalized by including persons who attend a clinic and complain of various symptoms. Yet this definition includes other components of interest than anxiety that can influence the conclusions of the study. Attending a clinic is determined by many factors other than experiencing a problem, including the availability of clinic facilities, concern over the expense, ethnic and/or cultural views about treatment and possible stigma, and encouragement by relatives and friends. There may be many other people in the community who are equally or more anxious than those who seek treatment. Thus there is always a possible concern that any single operation used to define a construct will be inadequate or incomplete or include components irrelevant to the original concept.

A third limitation of operational definitions pertains to the use of single measures to define a construct. There are limitations to all measurement devices due to special features of the device itself. Performance of the subject on a single measure is determined by more factors than the construct that is being measured. For example, although self-report of anxiety on a questionnaire is likely to be related to actual anxiety, the extent to which anxiety is reported is likely to be a function of such other factors as the purposes for which the test will be used (e.g., receiving free therapy vs. obtaining a job), how the subject feels on that day, how the questions are worded, the characteristics of the individual administering the test, and the subject's general likelihood of admitting socially undesirable characteristics. Simply stated, a single measure is not likely to be an adequate estimate of the construct of interest.

Investigators usually wish to describe general relations that go beyond single and narrowly circumscribed operations. For example, if possible, it is important to be able to make general statements about anxiety and its relation to other phenomena independently of the many different ways in which anxiety can be operationalized. Using a single measure to define a construct may impede drawing general relations among concepts.

The inadequacies of defining a concept with a single measure or operation (referred to as *single operationism*) had led to the use of multiple measures or operations *(multiple operationism)*. Although a concept may be imperfectly measured by individual operations, the commonalties among several measure may converge on the concept of interest. Thus self-report of anxiety, physiological responsiveness in anxiety-provoking situations, and overt behavioral performance together may help estimate a person's anxiety. Combined measures that attempt to explore a concept with different operations may allow an investigator to place more confidence in assessing the concept of interest.

Discrepancies Among Definitions

It is quite possible that different operational definitions lead to different conclusions about the phenomenon of interest. For example, an area of active research within clinical psychology is the nature of depression among children. There are many ways in which depression has been operationalized using different measures and different raters (child, parent, teacher, peers) to define depression of the child. Three commonly used ways consist of child or parent ratings on a standardized scale (e.g., Children's Depression Inventory) and psychiatric diagnosis (derived from separate interviews drawing upon parent and child information). A study was designed to evaluate three commonly used methods of defining depression and the differences they might yield (Kazdin, 1989a). From a sample of psychiatric inpatient children, child, parent, and diagnostic criteria were used as three independent methods of identifying depressed children. The results yielded little overlap in the cases who were defined as depressed. Thus children defined as depressed by one operational criterion were different from those defined as depressed by another criterion. In addition, the differences between depressed and nondepressed children on measures of cognitive processes, social behavior, and self-esteem varied as a function of the method of operationalizing depression. The point here is not to suggest that every different method of operationalizing a construct leads to a specific and unique result. However, differences are quite possible among alternative ways of operationalizing constructs, and these too need to be examined.

One might challenge the entire research enterprise if different ways of defining a construct lead to different findings. Yet different definitions do not invariably lead to differences. Also, we wish to understand discrepancies that might emerge. For example, one investigator may operationalize happiness based on the number of smiles and positive statements an individual makes in an interview; another investigator may operationalize the construct by having people complete a scale in which they report the degree to which they are happy. Differences or discrepancies in these methods of operationalizing the construct are not "problems." We wish to understand as part of the elaboration of human functioning what accounts for the fact that all people who smile frequently do not report themselves to be happy, and all people who say they are happy do not smile frequently.

Multiple Operations to Represent Constructs

As evident in the above discussion, the use of a single measure or operation to define constructs can be limited. Each method of operationalizing is fallible because it may depend on specific and unique characteristics of the measure. Most investigations in clinical psychology utilize a set of measures to operationalize different constructs. For example, an effective treatment might be expected to improve three domains of client functioning: client symptoms, work adjustment, and family interaction. Each domain of interest represents a construct. Each of these constructs would be represented by two or more measures. The reason is that individual measures are fallible and unlikely to capture the construct of interest. The investigator looks for consistency among measures of a given construct.

Recent advances in design and statistical analyses have expanded the methods of evaluating constructs and combining multiple measures. Within a given study, multiple (two or more) measures can be used to define a construct. The relations of the measures to each other and to the overall construct as well as to other measures or outcomes can be examined. The notion of *latent variable* has been used to reflect the idea of a construct represented by several measures. The specific measures are referred to as *observed variables* and represent the construct of interest. Correlational analyses can evaluate the associations among observed variables and the extent to which they represent a single latent variable of interest. Because that latent variable is defined by several different measures, it is not confounded by the measurement error of a single measure.

Consider an example of the methods of operationalizing latent variables. Newcomb and Bentler (1988) were interested in identifying critical paths toward deviance over the course of adolescence and young adulthood, with particular focus on the role of early drug use. They assessed youths over a period spanning 4 years to understand the factors that predict outcomes in young adulthood and to identify causal paths toward deviance. Several constructs or domains of functioning (latent variables) were assessed during adolescence, each represented by multiple measures. The domains included drug use, social conformity, criminal activity, deviant peer networks, and others.

Consider in more detail the construct, drug use, which was of primary interest. Three separate measures were used to operationalize this construct: frequency of alcohol use (beer, wine, liquor), cannabis use (marijuana and hashish), and hard drug use (tranquilizers, sedatives, barbiturates, heroin, cocaine, and several others). The three measures were assumed to reflect a general tendency toward drug use. Specific data analytic techniques (e.g., confirmatory factor analyses) demonstrated that the observed variables were highly related and reliably reflected the construct of interest.

In passing, it is worth noting that during adolescence, teen drug use was significantly related to lower social conformity, greater criminal activity, and having a deviant friendship network. Early drug use was related years later to reduction in academic pursuits (less involvement in college), job instability (unemployment, being fired), and increased psychoticism (e.g., disorganized thought processes). Although the latent variable, drug use, was associated with untoward long-term outcomes, the analyses permitted separate evaluation of different observed variables or operational definitions. As might be expected, among drug use measures in adolescence, hard drug use had particularly untoward outcomes in young adulthood.

General Comments

Research usually begins with an abstract notion or concept that reflects the construct of interest. For purposes of experimentation the concept is operationalized through one or more procedures or measures. The constructs that constitute both the independent and dependent variables are translated into specific procedures and measurement operations. The experiment demonstrates a relation between the independent and dependent variables, which are specified very concretely. After the experiment the investigator usually wishes to go beyond the specific operations and back to the more abstract level of concepts. Thus an experiment may demonstrate a particular relation under specific environmental conditions with concrete operational definitions of the independent and dependent variables; however, to go beyond the very specific demonstration requires assuming a broader relation. There are an infinite number of ways that a construct might be operationalized. In a given study it is valuable to utilize multiple measures of the construct of interest to evaluate the generality of findings among different concrete measures or operations and sources of measurement error.

VARIABLES TO INVESTIGATE

Types of Variables

Defining the research idea in operational terms is an important step in moving toward the investigation itself. Another way to consider the initial stage of the research process is in terms of the types of variables that are studied. The specific idea or hypothesis is expressed in such a manner that some independent variable can be altered and evaluated. The independent variable of a study refers to the conditions that are varied or manipulated to produce change or, more generally, to the differences among conditions that are expected to influence subject performance. Three types of independent variables that will be distinguished here include environmental or situational variables, instructional variables, and subject variables.

Environmental or Situational Variables

Many variables of interest consist of altering the environmental or situational conditions of an experiment. Manipulation of an environmental variable consists of varying what is done to, with, or by the subject. Environmental or situational variables may consist of providing a given condition or task to some subjects and not providing it to others (e.g., treatment vs. no treatment, medication vs. no medication). Alternatively, different amounts of a given variable may be manipulated (e.g., more treatment given to some subjects than to others). Finally, the environmental variable may consist of providing qualitatively different conditions to the subjects (e.g., one treatment vs. another treatment). The following questions illustrate the type of manipulations that would require varying an environmental or situational variable:

1. Does recording one's calorie consumption and weight after each meal alter eating habits? The environmental variable here would be the task of self-observation and might be invoked for some subjects but not for others.
2. Does a prenatal care program for pregnant women increase the birth weight and decrease birth complications of their newborns? Here the special intervention (e.g., home visits, counseling in diet, monthly physical exams) is an environmental variable.
3. Are specific forms of psychotherapy differentially effective with depressed clients? Here the type of treatment given is the environmental variable.

Instructional Variables

These variables refer to a specific type of environmental or situational manipulation. Instructional variables refer to variations in what the subjects are told or are led to believe through verbal or written statements about the experiment and their participation. In the simplest situation, when instructional variables are manipulated, other environmental variables are held constant. Instructional variables usually are aimed at altering the subject's perception or evaluation of a situation or condition. The following experimental questions consists of manipulations of instructional variables:

1. Does telling clients that they are participating in a "treatment project that should alter their behavior" enhance the effects of a veridical treatment technique relative to telling clients they are participating in an "experiment that is not expected to alter their behavior"? Here, the treatment procedure is constant across groups. However, different instructions are compared to examine the influence of client expectancies on treatment outcome.

2. Do therapists interpret psychological test results differently when they are told that the test responses were produced by disturbed patients rather than from people functioning adequately in everyday life? The sample test responses given to different therapists might be identical, but the instructions to the therapists about who completed them would vary.

3. Does telling subjects that their responses on psychological tests will be anonymous rather than identifiable influence their admission of socially undesirable behaviors? The task presented to the subject consists of a set of questions or items. Completion of the test is preceded by instructions that lead subjects to believe that their scores are anonymous or not.

Subject or Individual Difference Variables

These variables refer to attributes or characteristics of the individual subjects. The characteristics are not manipulated. Rather, they are varied in an experiment by selecting subjects with different characteristics, attributes, or traits. Subject variables may include such obvious characteristics as age, education, social class, sex differences, or standing on some personality measure. In clinical psychology, special samples are frequently studied such as depressed adults, physically or sexually abused children, families of patients with a diagnosis of schizophrenia, couples in conflict, individuals who are identified as intellectually gifted, individuals of various cultural or ethnic background, and others. In such studies, people with or without the characteristic of interest or people with varying degrees of that characteristic are compared.

The fact that the variables usually are called *subject variables* does not mean that only the attributes of individuals who usually serve as subjects are studied. Characteristics of therapists, interviewers, and experimenters also are subject variables and may be studied as such in experiments. Subject variable research may seek to elaborate differences and similarities among alternative groups. For example, depressed and nondepressed parents may be identified and then compared in the manner in which they interact with their newborn infants, children, or spouses. Also, subject variable research may evaluate the differential responsiveness or reactions of some people to other variables (e.g., psychotherapy, efforts to manipulate mood). The following questions illustrate the subject variable research approach:

1. Do clients with more formal education gain more from verbal psychotherapy than do clients with less education? Here education is the subject variable. Subjects may be categorized in the study as college versus no college degree or baccalaureate versus postbaccalaureate education.

2. Do people who have tested positive for AIDS have increased stress relative to those untested or who have tested negative? Here alternative groups are selected to evaluate the potential impact of diagnostic information.

3. Does birth order of the individual (position of birth among one's siblings) influence the professional accomplishments achieved in later life? Here adults who have, say, two siblings will be included. The adults might be placed into one of the three groups according to whether they were born first, second, or third in relation to their two siblings.

Investigation of Multiple Variables

The variables as described might imply that a given investigation is restricted to studying only one type of variable. Yet an investigation can examine multiple variables of a particular type or of different types of variables within a single study. Indeed, combining variables across categories in a given study is an excellent research strategy and may address a host of important questions. For example, for research in psychotherapy we do not merely wish to examine the effectiveness of alternative treatments. It is likely that the effects of a given treatment depend on a variety of other factors such as client characteristics (e.g., diagnosis, severity of problems) and therapist characteristics (e.g., competence, experience, warmth). To understand treatment as well as to identify optimally effective applications, multiple and different classes of variables must be studied together.

In general, a study that manipulates a single variable or single class of variables addresses a rudimentary question. This does not mean that the question is unimportant. The importance of the question cannot be evaluated in the abstract; it is determined by the relation of the study to the existing literature, theory, practice, and other considerations. However, the complexity of the question is increased by combining alternative variables and variables from separate classes (e.g., subject and environmental variables). The question addressed the impact of a given manipulation under alternative conditions and hence represents a deeper understanding of how the variables of interest operate.

RESEARCH DESIGN OPTIONS

The initial stages of research entail development of the research idea and operationalization and selection of the specific variables of interest, as already highlighted. There remain a variety of options for research related to how the idea is evaluated and the conditions in which study is conducted. The options have implications for diverse threats to validity and hence the conclusions that can be drawn. The different ways in which the study might be designed are detailed in subsequent chapters. As a way of an overview, it is useful to consider major design options in which the variables of interest may be evaluated.

Types of Research

Research in clinical psychology actively draws upon three major types of studies: true experiments, quasi-experiments, and passive-observational designs. *True experiments* consist of investigations in which the arrangement permits maximum control over the independent variable or manipulation of interest. The investigator is able to assign subjects to different conditions on a random basis, to include alternative conditions (e.g., treatment and control conditions) as required by the design, and to control possible sources of bias within the experiment. From the standpoint of demonstrating the impact of a particular variable of interest, true experiments permit the strongest basis for drawing inferences.

Occasionally the investigator cannot control all features that characterize true experiments. Some facet of the study such as the assignment of subjects to conditions or of conditions to settings cannot be randomized. *Quasi-experiments* refers to those designs in which the conditions of true experiments are approximated (Campbell & Stanley, 1963). For example, an investigator may be asked to evaluate a school-based intervention program designed to prevent drug abuse or teen pregnancy. The investigator wishes to use a nonintervention control group because the passage of time and course of development (e.g., history, maturation, testing, and other internal validity threats) can lead to change. However, for practical reasons a control condition is not permitted within the school that wishes the program. The investigator seeks other schools that will serve as nonintervention control groups and tested over time for comparison purposes. These other schools might be similar in some ways (e.g., in population, size, geography). Yet, we have already lost some features of true experiments. Assignment of children or schools to conditions is not random, and a host of factors (e.g., motivation for change among administrators) may differ greatly across conditions. Already the design is less ideal than one would like. Yet there are many design options and methods of drawing valid inferences.

True and quasi-experiments refer primarily to studies where an independent variable is manipulated in some way, as illustrated by providing treatment or an experimental condition to some people but not to others. In a great deal of clinical research, the interest is not in manipulating an independent variable. Rather, the focus is on studying a variable that "nature" has manipulated in some way. The investigator is interested in studying people who vary in the characteristic or experience of interest. For example, the investigator might wish to study differences between cigarette smokers and nonsmokers in relation to some personality traits or background characteristics; between marital partners who are physically violent with each other versus those who are not; between depressed versus nondepressed people; and between people who were former prisoners of war versus those who were not. Studies can provide critical insights about the nature of a problem, characteristic, or experience. However, the investigator has had no control over the event itself. Hence this type of research differs from true or quasi-experiments.

Passive-observational studies refer to research where the relations among variables are observed but not manipulated (Cook & Campbell, 1979). There is no universally accepted term for designs referred to as passive-observational designs. Historically, the designs have been referred to as correlational research to emphasize the fact that the studies explore the relations among phenomena as they exist, that is, without experimental manipulation. Correlational analyses (e.g., Pearson product-moment correlations) were the primary bases of analyses. The distinction between experimental and correlational research was drawn in classic papers about these separate traditions of research (see Cronbach, 1957, 1975). *Correlational research,* as a term, mixes a type of data analysis (correlation) with design (nonmanipulation of independent variables) and has been criticized for that reason (Cook & Campbell, 1979). Passive designs can be evaluated in many different ways beyond correlations; also, true and quasi-experiments can be evaluated with correlational techniques. Hence, there is virtue in avoiding mixing the data analysis with the design classification.

A passive-observational study emphasizes the fact that the experimenter does not intervene, manipulate, and control the intervention of interest. The most common use of this kind of study in clinical psychology is subject-selection research. The investigator varies the independent variable by selecting subjects with different characteristics (e.g., people who have experienced trauma vs. those who have not) or with varying degrees of that characteristic (e.g., people with high, medium, or low scores on a measure of risk taking, depression, or helplessness).

In another type of passive design, the investigator examines the relations (e.g., correlations) among different sets of measures (e.g., peer acceptance and aggression among children, level of stress experienced and views about health). A related example is when these relations are examined over time, as in prediction studies in which a group is followed (studied) longitudinally. One might, for example, wish to study those factors in childhood or adolescence that predict early marriage, large family size, adult criminality, and so on. The factors assessed in childhood or adolescence (e.g., absence of a parent, sexual abuse, presence of a gifted sibling) obviously are not manipulated by the investigator.

It is often the case that true experiments, as compared to passive-observational studies, are considered to be the only firm basis for drawing "causal" inferences in science, a clear demonstration that the independent variable led to the effects on the dependent variable. The strength of true experiments is without peer in demonstrating the impact of an independent variable, given the control afforded and the ways in which that control rules out a variety of explanations that might account for the results. Even so, true experiments are not flawless. A true experiment, however well controlled, does not provide the basis for certainty of the finding.

At the same time, passive-observational studies are not merely diluted experiments, invariably flawed, nor inherently incapable of yielding causal information. Advances in methodology and statistics (e.g., path analyses, causal modeling, structural equation modeling, cross-lagged panel correlations) have increased the strength of inferences that can be drawn from so called passive-observational studies. Interests of clinical research involve many questions about "nature's" interventions. Theory, methodology, and experimentation can be used to separate the impact of alternative variables when less than ideal experimental controls are available.

Design Strategies

Research in clinical psychology draws upon different types of designs. Group designs and single-case designs highlight the diversity of methods employed in clinical research. In *group designs*, several subjects are studied. In the usual experiment, groups are formed by the investigator who assigns subjects to conditions. The condition refers to the level of independent variable that is to be varied (e.g., treatment vs. no-treatment). Each group usually receives only one of the conditions. Occasionally, the general class of designs is referred to as between-group research because separate groups of subjects are used and each group receives only one of the conditions of interest. A between-group design includes at least as many groups as there are experimental conditions or treatments. In addition, depending on the precise question or hypothesis of interest, control groups add to the number of groups in the study.

The effects of different experimental and control conditions across groups are evaluated statistically by comparing groups on the dependent measures. Preliminary assignment of subjects to groups is usually determined randomly to produce groups equivalent on factors possibly related to the independent variable (intervention) or that might also account for group differences on the measures (dependent variables). If groups are equivalent on such factors *before* the experimental manipulation or treatment, any differences among groups *after* the manipulation are assumed to result from the effects of different experimental conditions. In clinical research, a wide range of group designs are used and the diversity of this general type of research alone raises a plethora of methodological issues.

In addition to group designs, the field also entails *single-case experimental designs.* These designs are characterized by investigation of a given individual, a few individuals, or one group over time. The underlying approach toward research for group and single-case designs is identical, namely, to implement conditions that permit valid inferences about the independent variable. However, in single-case research, this is accomplished somewhat differently. Typically, one or a few subjects are studied. The dependent measures of interest are assessed continuously over time (e.g., each day for several weeks). The manner in which the independent variable is implemented is examined in relation to the data pattern for the subject or group of subjects over time.

Single-case designs can be used to address diverse research topics and issues. The designs play a special role in the field because in clinical work, a central concern is the treatment of individual clients. Single-case designs can be used to experimentally evaluate the impact of a given intervention or alternative interventions. As with group designs, there are many different single-case designs, with their own requirements, advantages, and obstacles.

Conditions of Experimentation

The conditions under which the investigation is conducted to test the ideas of interest can vary widely. To convey the diversity, consider *laboratory versus applied research*. For example, laboratory research may consist of evaluation of the performance of college students who receive instructions designed to alter their mood, perform a task, or evaluate a video-tape of another person. In contrast, research in an applied setting may be at a clinic where patients are seen for treatment. The research may evaluate different types of treatment or evaluate different populations (e.g., people referred for one type of problem vs. another type of problem). In laboratory and clinic-based research, the differences encompass more than merely the settings. Characteristics of the subjects, the nature of the dependent variable, and the research problems that emerge can vary greatly as well.

The methodological differences between research in laboratory and applied settings have been elaborated in the context of psychotherapy and counseling research. There are obviously many questions about the effect of alternative forms of treatment and the factors that contribute to process and outcome. The complexities of psychotherapy often make research in the clinical setting impractical or prohibitive. Examining isolated variables or analyzing the impact of components of a treatment are often difficult, unfeasible, or ill-advised in clinical settings because of the diverse practical and ethical obstacles of research. Treatment research is often conducted under conditions *analogous* to those available in the clinic or other applied setting. Research that evaluates treatment under conditions that only resemble or approximate the clinical situation has been referred to as *analogue research*. An analogue study usually focuses on a carefully defined research question under well-controlled conditions. The purpose of the research is to illuminate a particular process or to study treatment that may be important in clinical applications.

Analogue research can refer to a wide range of studies. For example, one might conduct animal laboratory research to study the development or elimination of fears. Animal analogues are critical to clinical research and have served as the basis for establishing the underpinnings of alternative treatments for various clinical problems (e.g., anxiety). Also, analogue research has consisted of interpersonal interactions in laboratory studies where interviews or personal exchanges resemble in varying degrees the interactions of a therapist and patient in psychotherapy. The analogue conditions most widely discussed have been in relation to laboratory versus clinic study of alternative treatments. In this context, an analogue experiment has come to mean a study in which the conditions of the experiment depart from those conditions of clinical work (see Kazdin, 1978).

In a sense, virtually all experimental research with human subjects is analogue research insofar as it constructs a situation in which a particular phenomenon can be studied. Informing subjects that they are participating in research, evaluating controlled and time-limited interventions or experimental manipulations, using as outcome measures specific psychological assessment devices (e.g., questionnaires), and similar conditions make the situation analogous to one to which the investigator might wish to generalize. Thus the degree of similarity to the conditions of primary interest can vary widely. Clinical research methodology encompasses the different conditions and the problems and obstacles they raise.

Time Frame for Research

Research often varies in the time frame for investigation. The bulk of research is conducted in a concurrent time frame in which the independent variables of interest and the measures to evaluate this are administered and completed within a relatively brief period. An example would be a laboratory experiment in which subjects are exposed to an independent variable and complete the measures within one or two laboratory sessions. In contrast, the investigation may be conducted over an extended period of, say, several years. A frequent distinction is made between cross-sectional and longitudinal studies. *Cross-sectional studies* usually make comparisons between groups at a given point in time. *Longitudinal studies* make comparisons over an extended period, often involving several years. The results can be quite different even when similar questions are addressed.

For example, over the course of child development, research has indicated that many behaviors bothersome to children or parents (e.g., stuttering, anxiety, destroying objects, lying) are likely to occur and in fact may be quite common. The different problems wax and wane over the course of development, peak at different periods, and usually diminish to a very low rate among nonclinic samples. The pattern of behavior over the course of development can be assessed concurrently by evaluating children of different ages (e.g., Achenbach & Edelbrock, 1981). This would be a cross-sectional study and would show characteristic behaviors at different ages. This type of study *suggests* a developmental pattern, that is, how behaviors change in frequency over time. This is not the same as the yield from a longitudinal study in which one group of children (e.g., 2-year-olds) is followed and repeatedly assessed over several years (e.g., reassessed at age 4, 6, and 8 years; e.g., MacFarlane, Allen, & Honzik, 1954). The longitudinal study portrays how behaviors actually change in a given sample because the same children are studied over time.

One type of study is not inherently superior. Indeed, they have different types of problems. For example, a cross-sectional study may suggest that children show different characteristics at different ages. However, there is a possible *cohort* effect. This refers to the possibility that different age groups of subjects (cohorts) may have unique characteristics that are confounded with the variable of interest. In a cross-sectional study, different groups of children vary in their histories. Thus for example, 2-year-olds may not have the pattern of behavior of the 8-year-olds when they mature; possibly something about how the 2-year-olds are growing up (e.g., nutrition, different parenting styles with more or fewer parents in the home) influences their performance in ways not evident in the other group(s).

In a longitudinal study, history of the group is controlled because a group or more than one group is followed over time. Yet longitudinal studies have their own problems because over time it is often difficult to follow the subjects. Attrition or loss of subjects over time can diminish the strength of the conclusions because of selection biases if the sample is increasingly depleted.

Evidence from different time frames can be used to address different questions or even the same question differently. For example, the investigator may be interested in the correlates of viewing violence on television among children, a topic that has received considerable attention. Within a current time perspective, the investigator might compare children who view violent television versus those who watch as much television but who do not view violent programs. Children might be matched on diverse subject (e.g., age, sex, IQ) and demographic characteristics (e.g., socioeconomic status of parents, family constellation). Comparisons might then be made on some other measures such as personality characteristics of the child or parents or perhaps aggressive behavior of the child at home or at school. The purpose would be to elaborate the features associated with television viewing.

As an alternative, a more longitudinal focus might include following (assessing) children over time. Among the questions that might be asked is what are the correlates of early television viewing later in life. Both cross-sectional and longitudinal studies indicate that viewing violence on television is associated with aggressive behavior and that the relation is influenced by a variety of factors (e.g., sex of the child, success of children in school, social popularity; see Eron & Huesmann, 1984).

Many studies are neither cross-sectional nor longitudinal in the sense illustrated here. Rather, they vary in their time frame. For example, treatment studies usually evaluate the outcomes of therapy immediately after treatment is finished. Yet studies vary widely in whether they provide follow-up assessment and, if so, in how long they follow the cases. The time frame is important to consider because, as we shall elaborate later, conclusions often vary as a function of when assessment is conducted and the duration of follow-up.

SUMMARY AND CONCLUSIONS

The research idea that serves as a basis for experimentation may be derived from any of several sources, including curiosity about a particular phenomenon, the need to resolve an applied problem, resolution of issues raised by previous research, predictions derived from psychological theory, and others. Whatever the initial idea, ultimately it needs to be specified in operational terms. Specific experimental operations, procedures, and measures define the independent and dependent variables. When the experiment begins, it is not the overall concept that is manipulated but rather the specific operationally defined variable.

The variables that comprise clinical investigations usually include environmental, instructional, and subject variables. *Environmental variables* usually consist of manipulating what is offered, presented, or done to the client. *Instructional variables,* actually a subcategory of environmental variables, refer to what the client is told. *Subject variables* consist of attributes, traits, or characteristics of the subjects, experimenters, therapists, or others. Subject variables are examined by selecting subjects with specific characteristics rather than by manipulating specific conditions.

Developing the research idea and operationalizing and selecting the specific variables are initial stages of the study. A variety of design options emerge in relation to how the effect of the variables is actually examined. True experiments, quasi-experiments, and passive-observational studies were discussed to define major types of research. Alternative design strategies were noted by distinguishing group and single-case research. The conditions of experimentation can vary and include laboratory and applied or clinical settings. Analogue research was discussed to illustrate the issue of testing in the context of therapy research. Finally, the time frame of research was discussed as a condition that can vary among experiments. Cross-sectional and longitudinal research were noted to convey strategies that vary in the time frame.

Alternative design options along these and other dimensions warrant detailed discussion. Design and method options vary in the advantages and disadvantages they provide. In the next chapters, we shall elaborate alternative designs in clinical research and the issues they address and raise in relation to drawing valid inferences.

FOR FURTHER READING

Cattell, R.B. (1988). The principles of experimental design and analysis in relation to theory building. In J.R. Nesselroade & R.B. Cattell (Eds.), *Handbook of multivariate experimental psychology* (2nd ed.). New York: Plenum Press.

Serlin, R.C. (1987). Hypothesis testing, theory building, and the philosophy of science. *Journal of Counseling Psychology, 34,* 365–371.

Shakow, D. (1982). Perspectives on research in clinical psychology. In P.C. Kendall & J.N. Butcher (Eds.), *Handbook of research methods in clinical psychology.* New York: John Wiley & Sons.

Weiner, I.B. (1983). Theoretical foundations of clinical psychology. In M. Hersen, A.E. Kazdin, & A.S. Bellack (Eds.), *The clinical psychology handbook.* Elmsford, NY: Pergamon Press.

Wicker, A.W. (1985). Getting out of our conceptual ruts: Strategies for expanding conceptual frameworks. *American Psychologist, 40,* 1094–1103.

Chapter 5

ALTERNATIVE RESEARCH DESIGNS

Designing experiments to derive valid inferences can be accomplished in many different ways. By far the most common method within clinical psychology is to compare groups of subjects who are exposed to different experimental and control conditions. This general strategy can entail a variety of different arrangements depending on the groups included in the design, how assessment is planned, and when and to whom the intervention is presented. In the present chapter, we consider alternative group design strategies and their advantages and limitations.

SUBJECT ASSIGNMENT AND GROUP FORMATION

A fundamental issue in group designs is the assignment of subjects to groups. Group differences after the experimental manipulation is invoked become the basis for inferring a causal relationship between the experimental manipulation and performance on the dependent measures. Hence there must be some assurance that groups would not have differed without the experimental manipulation or interventions. The manner in which subjects are assigned to groups influences the confidence that one can place in the initial equivalence of groups and consequently the likelihood that subsequent group differences reflect the effects of the manipulation.

Random Selection

When investigators discuss randomization in experimentation, they usually are concerned with one of two concepts, namely, random selection of subjects from a population and random assignment of subjects to experimental conditions. In group designs, random assignment and related procedures to form groups are the central topics. Random selection is an independent issue that is not necessarily related to the particular design but warrants brief mention here.

Random selection of subjects is an issue that pertains to the generality (external validity) of experimental results among subjects. If we wish to generalize results from a sample of subjects in the experiment to a population of potential subjects, usually it is essential to select a representative sample of the population. For example, if we wish to draw conclusions about depressed patients in general, we would *not* want to restrict selection to patients in a particular hospital or clinic, in a particular city, state, or country but would want to sample from all available people. If subjects can be drawn from the entire population, it is more likely that the sample will represent that population. Generality of experimental results depends on the representativeness of the subjects in the experiment to those individuals who were not included, that is, the rest of the population. *Random selection* refers to drawing from the total population of interest in such a way that each member of the population has an equal probability of being drawn.

There is an obvious problem in meeting this requirement. Subjects in an experiment cannot be selected from a population unless that population is very narrowly defined. For example, for a population defined as "all introductory psychology students currently enrolled in a given term at this university," a random sample might be obtainable. However, a random sample of "introductory psychology students in general" could not be readily obtained. To sample this latter population would require being able to select from all individuals who have had introductory psychology already, including those no longer living, all those currently enrolled, and all who are yet to enroll (including unborn individuals) across all geographical settings. Sampling from all subjects in the population including those who are deceased or yet to be born, of course, is not possible. If generality of the experimental results to a population depends upon having randomly sampled from a population, conclusions would seem to be restricted to the narrowly confined groups of subjects.

Random selection from a population is often central to research. For example, epidemiological research identifies the distribution of various conditions (e.g., diseases, mental disorders) within a population. In such studies, special sampling procedures are used to ensure that the sample represents the current population of interest. Usually, different segments or subgroups of a population are identified to reflect demographic variables of interest such as social class, geography, and religion. Within such groups people are selected randomly so that the final sample reflects this distribution. In survey and opinion poll research as well, sampling from the population in this way is also critically important to ensure generality to that population, within some margin of error.

In clinical research, whether involving patient, college student, or community samples, random sampling from a population is not considered as essential nor is its absence viewed as an issue. A general operating assumption is that lawful relations derived from experiments with a given sample are likely to hold for other individuals who are similar. Results obtained with college students at one university would be expected in the usual case to hold for similar students at another university. Of course, many of the variables that would be assumed to be unimportant across samples, including geography, could very well lead to differences in experimental results.

Many variables across which one wishes to generalize may be irrelevant to the lawful relation discovered in the initial experiment. For example, assume we have developed an effective psychotherapy to treat agoraphobia (fear of open spaces) among young adults. It is parsimonious to assume initially that this treatment will be effective for males and females, young and old adults, and various ethnic and racial groups. Yet it is quite possible, and in a given case maybe even likely, that generality might not hold. As a general rule, the variables across which'the results of a given intervention can be extended must be determined empirically. Estimating the likelihood of the generality of findings depends upon the specific findings and the accumulation of knowledge about the factors that may influence a particular manipulation. After a phenomenon has been demonstrated, research can evaluate the findings across variations of conditions to assess directly the generality of the results.

The generality of experimental findings is not justified solely on the basis of random selection from a population of subjects. This is fortunate because truly random selection beyond a very narrowly defined population usually is not possible. The justification of generalizing results can come from direct experimental extensions or from inferences about the likelihood that basic processes demonstrated in research vary as a function of different subject or other variables.

Random Assignment

The central issue in group research is the assignment of subjects to groups. Once a sample of subjects has been specified, individual members can be assigned to groups in an unbiased fashion. *Random assignment* consists of allocating subjects to groups in such a way that the probability of each subject appearing in any of the groups is equal. This is usually accomplished by determining the group to which each subject is assigned by a table of random numbers.

The usual way to ensure that subjects are assigned randomly is to determine the groups to which subjects will be assigned prior to their arrival to the experiment. For example, if there are three groups in the experiment, a random numbers table can be consulted to draw numbers 1, 2, and 3 that correspond to each of the groups several times in random order. The numbers would be listed in the order in which they are drawn from the table (e.g., 1, 1, 3, 2, 3, 3, etc.). (Numbers other than 1, 2, or 3 in the table, of course, are ignored.) As the subjects arrive to the experiment, they are assigned to the groups in order according to the number that was drawn. So the first two subjects in our study would be assigned to Group 1, the third to Group 3, and so on in order. With such assignment, subjects are effectively assigned to groups randomly. No one can reasonably object to the assignment procedure as long as each subject is assigned to the group according to the predetermined schedule.

Drawing random numbers to determine group assignment does not guarantee that an equal number of subjects would be assigned to each group. In the above example, the number 3 may have been drawn from the table more times than the numbers 1 and 2, and thus more subjects would be assigned to this group than to the other groups. For power of statistical tests (statistical conclusion validity) and convenience in conducting several statistical analysis, it is better to have equal rather than unequal group sizes. This can be accomplished without violating random assignment by grouping subjects into *blocks*. Each block consists of the number of subjects that equals the number of groups in the experiment. If there are three groups, the first three subjects who appear in the experiment can be viewed as one block. One subject from this block of three would be assigned to each of the three groups. Importantly, the group to which any individual is assigned within a block is random. Assignment is accomplished by drawing numbers 1, 2, and 3 in any order as long as each block encompasses each number (1, 2, 3) only once. Assigning subjects based on numbers drawn in this way ensures that, as the experiment progresses and is completed, the number of subjects assigned to each group will be equal.

Random assignment obviously is important and seems too basic to warrant comment. However, the simplicity of random assignment as a procedure, that is, how it is accomplished, belies greater complexities. As we shall discuss later, random assignment does not necessarily ensure that groups are equivalent. In addition, for research in such settings as clinics, hospitals, and schools, random assignment is often unavoidably violated or simply not feasible. In cases where random assignment is violated, group differences might be due to subject characteristics rather than to the experimental manipulation.

For example, an investigator may assign subjects who serve in the early stages of the experiment to one group rather than to another. Perhaps, the investigator did not know whether there would be enough subjects for another control group that would be a desirable addition to the experiment. Each experimental group was run first with the available subjects. A control group might include available subjects who arrived after the other groups were completed. Even worse, control subjects may have been drawn from an entirely different sample. In such situations, where assignment was not random, unambiguous conclusions may be difficult to draw from the data. Group differences or even lack of differences could be due to subject assignment rather than to the intervention. In terms of experimental validity, selection becomes a threat to internal validity as a plausible explanation of the results.

Group Equivalence

Random assignment is important as a means of distributing characteristics of the sample among groups. There are several subject characteristics (e.g., age, sex, motivation for participation), circumstances of participation (e.g., order of appearance or entry into the study), and other factors that might, if uncontrolled, interfere with interpretation of group differences. In some studies, evaluating the impact of these variables may be the central purpose. In other studies, they might be regarded as "nuisance" variables that, if uncontrolled, will obscure interpretation. Random assignment is a way of ensuring that such "nuisance" variables will be distributed unsystematically across groups. An advantage of random assignment is that it does not require the investigator to be aware of all of the important variables that might be related to the outcome of the experiment. Over a sufficient number of subjects, the many different "nuisance" variables can be assumed to be distributed evenly among groups.

Random assignment sometimes is viewed as a dependable way of producing *equivalent groups*. Yet random assignment refers only to the *method* of allocating subjects to groups and in a given experiment has no necessary connection with a particular outcome. Randomly assigning subjects *can* produce groups that differ on all sorts of measures. Group differences are more likely when sample sizes are small and when there are extreme scores in the sample. For example, if there are 15 subjects to be allocated to three groups and the subjects vary widely in such dimensions as age, level of anxiety, and other subject variables, it is quite possible that groups may differ significantly on these variables even after random assignment.

It is important to underscore that random assignment does not necessarily produce equivalent groups. With random assignment, the likelihood that groups are equivalent increases as a function of the size of the sample. This means that with small samples, equivalence of the groups may not be assumed. This is especially relevant to clinical research, as for example in studies of psychotherapy, where sample sizes may be relatively small (e.g., 10–20 subjects per group; see Kazdin & Bass, 1989; Shapiro & Shapiro, 1983). Hsu (1989) has shown that when the total sample is relatively small (e.g., 24 subjects total in a two-group study), the likelihood that groups are *not* equivalent across a number of nuisance variables is relatively high. The net effect is that at the end of the study, the difference between groups due to the intervention may be obscured or misrepresented because of the nonequivalence of groups.

Investigators wish to establish that the groups are equivalent by comparing groups after their random assignment on such variables as age, sex, IQ, years of institutionalization, pretest performance on the measure of interest, and so on. The absence of differences (nonsignificant t tests or analyses of variance) may provide false comfort that the groups are equivalent. When the samples are relatively small, statistical tests are not adequate to reveal group differences on variables that might well influence the results. The reason is that the power (sensitivity) of such tests to detect differences is weak when sample sizes are small. Thus the situation in which random assignment is least likely to obtain equivalence (small samples) is also one in which such differences may be the most difficult to detect. With larger samples, the absence of differences between groups on alternative subject variables and pretreatment measures provides greater assurance of group equivalence. Even so, such results do not establish absolutely that the groups are equivalent. Groups still may differ on some variable, relevant or irrelevant to the experimental manipulation and performance on the dependent measures, that the investigator did not assess.

In general, random assignment remains vitally important as a concept and procedure. However, there is a belief that the procedure guarantees group equivalence in situations when this is not likely, that is, when the sample size is relatively small (Hsu, 1989; Tversky & Kahneman, 1971). Use of larger than usual sample sizes (e.g., > 40 subjects in each group) can increase the confidence in the equivalence of groups.

Matching

Often the investigator does not wish to leave to chance the equivalence of groups for a given characteristic of the sample. If a specific subject variable is known to relate to scores on the dependent measure, it is important to take this variable into account to ensure that groups do not differ prior to treatment. For example, it is possible that randomly assigning clients seeking treatment for anxiety could result in one of the treatment groups having subjects who were more anxious prior to treatment than those in one of the other groups. Group differences after treatment could be directly influenced by severity of anxiety of the groups before treatment began. It is undesirable to allow groups to differ prior to the intervention on a variable that is highly related to performance on the dependent measure. This is especially obvious if the difference is on the pretest measure of the treatment problem. Even with random assignment, groups might well differ in level of anxiety prior to treatment. Obviously, such initial differences can obscure any conclusions that will be drawn. The best way to ensure equivalence of groups on a particular dimension is to match subjects on the dimension and then to assign subjects randomly to groups. *Matching* refers to grouping subjects together on the basis of their similarity on a particular characteristic or set of characteristics. By matching, subjects at each level of the characteristic appear in each group and the groups will not differ on that characteristic prior to treatment.

Matching can be accomplished in different ways. Consider, for example, an experiment with two groups that is designed to investigate the effectiveness of treatments for depression. Prior to treatment, subjects complete a measure of depression. One way to match subjects is to look for pairs of subjects with *identical pretreatment scores.* When two subjects are found with the same scores, each is assigned to one of the two groups in an unbiased fashion (e.g., using a random numbers table or coin toss). This is continued with all pairs of subjects with identical scores. If enough pairs of subjects are available and are assigned to groups, pretreatment mean depression scores for the groups would be identical. Yet looking for sets of identical scores to match subjects is usually prohibitive because it means that most subjects who did not have a score identical with other subjects' score would not be used. Thus large numbers of subjects would need to be assessed to find enough subjects to fill the groups.

A more commonly used procedure is to *rank* all of the subjects, in this case from high to low depression scores. If there are three groups in the experiment, the first three subjects with the highest score form the first block. These three subjects are assigned randomly, so that one member of this block appears in *each* group. The next three subjects with the highest scores form the next block and are assigned randomly to each group, and so on until all subjects are used. This method of assignment utilizes all of the subjects by drawing them from the ranks in blocks of three (or whatever number of groups there are) and assigning them randomly to each of the groups. Matching, when followed by random assignment, can equalize groups on the characteristic of interest. The advantage of this procedure is that it does not leave to chance the equivalence of groups on the characteristic(s) of interest.

Implicit in the discussion is interest in the nature of the variables that are used for purposes of matching. Subjects are matched on these variables that are either known or assumed to be related to performance on the dependent measure. Pretest performance is likely to be correlated with posttest perform-ance because the same measures are used. Of course, it is not always possible to administer a pretreatment assessment device. However, other variables may be expected to relate to outcome (e.g., diagnosis, age, birth order, and self-concept) and serve as the basis of matching. Matching is not essential or inherently valuable in its own right. An investigator matches groups when he or she knows or suspects that the characteristic relates to performance on the dependent measures.

Mismatching

Matching used in conjunction with random assignment is widely used and very valuable as an experimental practice. The critical component of matching is random assignment. Subjects are matched first and then randomly assigned to groups. Occasionally, matching has been used in an attempt to equalize groups where random assignment is not possible. For example, psychiatric patients in two different hospital wards may serve as subjects in an experiment where different treatments are given to each ward. The investigator may be constrained by the preassignment of patients to their respective wards. The investigator might reasonably wish to evaluate treatment on patients who are equal in severity of impairment. Assume that the investigator assesses severity of patient dysfunction on a measure of psychoticism, perhaps obtained from nurses' ratings. Assume further, that the scores on the measures can vary from 1 to 100, with a higher score indicating greater severity of symptoms.

The patients in the two wards may differ in overall levels of psychoticism because slightly different (e.g., more severe, chronic patients) are referred to these wards. Yet there is likely to be some overlap of scores. The scores of patients from each of the two wards in this hypothetical example are illustrated in Figure 5.1. Each bar or column in the figure represents the range of scores for that ward. It is obvious from the figure that Ward 2 has a broader range of scores and patients in that ward generally have higher scores. However, the distribution of scores between Wards 1 and 2 overlap as reflected in those portions included between the two horizontal lines. The investigator may equalize severity by evaluating treatment with *only* those patients in one ward who have scores within this range and hence are similar to patients in the other ward. In some sense, the patients have been matched because those used in each ward have equal or approximately equal mean psychoticism scores. Unfortunately, this matching procedure is problematic.

Each patient's score is made up of a true level of psychoticism plus error associated with such factors as the unreliability of the assessment device and daily fluctuations in subject (patient) and rater (nurse) behavior, hospital routine, and other factors. The error in measurement is reflected in the fact that scores from one testing to another are imperfectly correlated. Scores that are extremely high on one day are likely to be slightly lower on the next. Conversely, scores that are extremely low one day are likely to be slightly higher on the next testing. As a general rule, the more extreme the score, the more likely it is to revert in the direction of the group mean on subsequent assessment. Not every high score will become lower and not every low score will become higher, but on the average the scores at each of these extremes will revert or *regress* toward the mean.

Regression toward the mean is a statistical phenomenon that is related to the correlation between initial test and retest scores. *The lower the correlation, the greater the amount of error in the measure, and the greater the regression toward the mean.* The problem with matching subjects who are in preassigned groups is that scores in each of the groups may regress toward a *different* mean. Even if subjects across groups are selected because their scores are equal, the groups may come from populations with different means and be at different

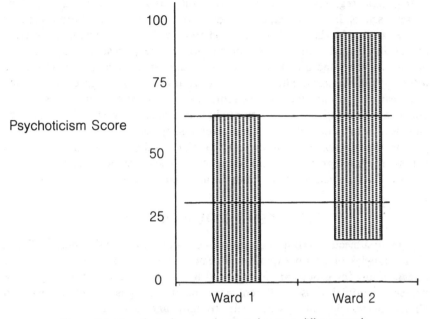

Figure 5.1. Hypothetical scores of patients from two different wards. The scores within the dashed lines represent the overlap of psychoticism scores between the two wards.

places in the distribution of scores in their respective groups. Hence subsequent testing might lead to group differences merely because the groups regress toward their respective means.

Regression can account for posttreatment differences even when treatment has no effect. In the present example, the patients selected for the experiment from the two different wards might be reassessed at some later point. One would expect merely on the basis of regression that certain changes would take place in scores on the psychoticism test. Patients in the experiment on Ward 1 would be expected to show a reduction in their scores on reassessment because patients selected from this group were above their group mean of psychoticism. In contrast, patients in the experiment from Ward 2 would be expected to show an increase in psychoticism because their scores tended to be below their group mean. In short, upon reassessment each of the samples will revert toward their group mean. If different treatments were given to the wards, the investigator might conclude that the treatment given to Ward 1 makes patients better (reduces psychoticism), whereas the treatment given to Ward 2 makes patients worse (increases psychoticism). Unfortunately, this change on reassessment may well have occurred independently of the interventions merely on the basis of regression.

In general, regression is of concern when subjects are selected because of their extreme scores. In such cases, depending on the test–retest correlation, subjects at the extreme levels are likely to revert toward the mean. The error in their scores that helped them have extreme scores on one occasion is less likely to operate in the same direction on the next assessment occasion. Thus upon retesting, their scores are likely to revert toward the mean. Regression toward the mean may occur whenever extreme cases are selected and the test–retest correlation is not high. Regression might lead scores to revert to the mean (i.e., change in a particular direction). However, if subjects are assigned randomly to groups, there is no reason to believe that there will be differential regression across groups. Regression would be expected to be the same for each group, so group differences can be attributed to the intervention rather than to regression.

SELECTED GROUP DESIGNS

Assigning subjects to groups in an unbiased fashion is one of the major defining characteristics of group experiments. Subject allocation, of course, merely refers to how the groups are formed and not to the experimental design. The present section discusses different experimental designs commonly used in clinical psychology along with their strengths and weaknesses.

To describe the designs, we shall employ the symbolic notation begun by Campbell and Stanley (1963). The symbols used to diagram the designs include the following notation: R stands for *random assignment* of subjects to conditions; O for *observation or assessment* of performance, and X for the *experimental manipulation or treatment*. The symbols are presented in temporal order so that, for example, $O_1 X O_2$ signifies that the first observation or pretest (O_1) was followed by an intervention (X), followed by the second observation or posttest (O_2).

Pretest–Posttest Control Group Design

The *pretest–posttest design* consists of a minimum of two groups. One group receives treatment and the other does not. The essential feature of the design is that subjects are tested before and after the intervention. Thus the effect of the intervention is reflected in the amount of change from pre- to postintervention assessment. In this design, subjects are assigned randomly to groups either prior to or after completion of the pretest. The design can be diagrammed as follows:

$$R \quad O_1 \quad X \quad O_2$$
$$R \quad O_3 \quad\quad O_4$$

(Again, the R denotes that subjects were randomly assigned; O an observation or assessment, and X the intervention.)

This design enjoys widespread use in clinical psychology. The administration of a pretest and posttest allows assessment of the amount of change as a function of the intervention. Although all experimentation is interested in change, assessment of the amount of change is particularly important in treatment research. Treatment research is devised to determine how much change was made and how many clients made a change of a particular magnitude. Also, severity of impairment prior to treatment may be an important source of information for predicting whether clients are likely to profit from certain kinds of treatment. For these reasons, a pretest is essential.

Considerations in Using the Design

The design has several strengths. To begin with, the design controls for the usual threats to internal validity. If intervening periods between pre- and posttreatment assessment are the same for each of the groups, threats such as history, maturation, repeated testing, and instrumentation are controlled. Moreover, random assignment from the same population reduces the plausibility that group differences have resulted from either selection bias or regression. Experimental mortality is not an inherent problem with the design, although as in any experiment differential loss of subjects could interfere with drawing a conclusion about the intervention.

The use of a pretest provides several advantages. First, the data obtained from the pretest allow the investigator to match subjects on different variables and to assign subjects randomly to groups. Matching permits the investigator to equalize groups on pretest performance. Second and relatedly, the pretest data permit evaluation of the effect of different levels of pretest performance. Within each group, different levels of performance (e.g., high and low) on the pretest can be used as a separate variable in the design. Thus, the investigator can examine whether the intervention varied in impact as a function of the initial standing on the pretested measure. Third, the use of a pretest affords statistical advantages for the data analysis. By using a pretest, within-group variability is reduced, and more powerful statistical tests of the intervention such as analyses of covariance or repeated measures analysis of variance are provided than if no pretest were used (see chapter 12).

Fourth, the pretest allows the researcher to make specific statements about change. For example, an investigator can assess how many clients improved, as determined by a certain percentage of change for each individual. Thus in clinical research where individual performance is very important, the pretest affords information beyond mere group differences at posttreatment. One can evaluate the individuals who did or did not change and generate hypotheses about the reasons. The pretest permits identification of people who changed.

Finally, by using a pretest, we can look at attrition in a more analytic fashion than would be the case without a pretest. If subjects are lost over the course of the study, a comparison can be made among groups by looking at pretest scores of those who dropped out. Of course, there are no formally accepted comparison procedures for evaluating whether subjects who are lost from each group differ on some dimension relevant to the results, particularly if only a few subjects drop out. However, we can compare the pretest scores of all groups by excluding the scores of those who completed a pretest but failed to complete a posttest. Such a comparison does not establish that subjects who dropped out from the groups were no different in some important attribute across groups or from the subjects who remained in the experiment. However, the pretest allows examination of the plausibility of these different alternatives.

There are some weaknesses to the pretest–posttest treatment control group design. The main restriction pertains to the influence of administering a pretest. A simple effect of testing, that is, repeatedly administering a test, is controlled in the basic design. What is not controlled is the possibility of an interaction of Testing × Treatment or a pretest sensitization effect. Possibly the intervention had its effect precisely because the pretest sensitized subjects to the intervention. This does not threaten the internal validity of the results. Rather, a pretest sensitization effect means that the results of the study can be generalized only to subjects who received a pretest.

Whether there is a pretest sensitization effect cannot be assessed in this design. The likelihood of sensitization depends upon several factors. If assessment and the intervention are not close together in time or are unrelated in the perceptions of the subject, sensitization probably is less likely. Therefore, a pretest administered immediately prior to an intervention in the context of the experiment is more likely to lead to sensitization than is assessment in a totally unrelated setting (e.g., in class or in a door-to-door survey of the subject at the subject's home) several weeks prior to treatment. Yet the more remote the pretest from the posttest in time and place, the less adequate it may be as a pretest. Intervening events and processes (e.g., history, maturation) between pretest and posttest obscure the effects that can otherwise be more readily attributed to the experimental manipulation. In general, the strengths of the design usually outweigh the threat that pretest sensitization will obscure the findings. The information about subject status prior to intervening, the use of this information to match cases and to evaluate change, and the statistical advantages are compelling.

Posttest-Only Control Group Design

The *posttest-only design* consists of a minimum of two groups and essentially is the same as the previous design except that no pretest is given. The effect of the intervention is assessed on a postintervention measure only. The design can be diagrammed as follows:

$$R \quad X \quad O_1$$
$$R \quad \quad O_2$$

The absence of the pretest makes this design less popular in clinical research. There are at least two reasons for this. First, in clinical research, it is often critical to know the level of functioning of persons prior to the intervention. For example, in studies designed to treat or prevent various disorders, it is important to establish that the clients were dysfunctional or at risk for dysfunction prior to the intervention. In cases where screening criteria are used to identify subjects, pretest assessment is critical to examine whether clients begin at the intended level of functioning. Second, the lack of a pretest raises the discomforting possibility that group differences after the intervention might be the result of differences between groups prior to the intervention. Of course, random assignment of subjects, particularly with large numbers of subjects, is likely to equalize groups. And there is no more likelihood that random assignment will produce different groups prior to treatment with this design than in the previous design. Admittedly, however, there is no assurance that groups are similar on specific measures prior to treatment, a luxury afforded by the previous design.

Considerations in Using the Design

The design controls for the usual threats to internal validity in much the same way as the previous design. The absence of a pretest means that the effect of the intervention could not result from initial sensitization. Hence the results could not be restricted in their generality to only those subjects who have received a pretest.

Often a pretest may not be desirable or feasible. For example, in brief laboratory experiments, the investigator may not wish to know the initial performance level or to expose subjects to the assessment task before they experience the experimental manipulation. Also, large numbers of subjects might be available and randomly assigned to different conditions in such experiments. With large numbers of subjects and random assignment to the groups, the likelihood of group equivalence is high. Assurances of equivalent performance on premeasures may be of less concern to the investigator.

Certainly another feature that must be considered is that a pretest is not always available in clinical research. In many cases the assessment effort is very costly, and a pretest might be prohibitive. For example, an extensive battery of psychological tests might serve as the outcome measures. The time required to administer and interpret an assessment battery may be several hours, which might make the pretest not worth the cost or effort. Indeed, from a practical standpoint, there may be no alternative but to omit the pretest. Ethical considerations also may argue for omission of the pretest, if for example, a pretest might be stressful to the subjects.

The weaknesses of the posttest-only control groups design derive from the disadvantages of not using a pretest. Thus the inability to ensure that groups are equivalent on the pretest, to match subjects on pretest performance prior to random assignment, or to study the relation between pretest standing and behavior change; the lack of pretest information to evaluate differential attrition across groups; and reduced statistical power are all consequences of foregoing a pretest. Apart from these disadvantages, demonstration of the equivalence of groups at pretest and of course prior to any intervention is often comforting both to the investigator and those who examine or review the work. As already noted, with small samples "no differences" on pretreatment performance may not mean that the groups are equivalent. However, invariably it is more assuring to have data in favor of equivalence than to omit a pretest altogether. In general, several of the advantages of a pretest may not interest the investigator. The statistical advantage of repeated observations that the pretest provides remains a decided advantage of the pretest–posttest design.

Solomon Four-Group Design

The main purpose of the *Solomon four-group design* is to evaluate the effect of pretesting on the effects obtained with a particular intervention (Solomon, 1949). In the pretest–posttest control group design, the possibility exists that pretest sensitization limits the external validity of the result. In the posttest-only design, pretest sensitization is eliminated because there is no pretest. In the Solomon four-group design the effect of pretesting is assessed directly. To accomplish this, a minimum of four groups is required.

The design can be readily understood by viewing it as a combination of the previous two designs. The four groups in the design are the two groups mentioned in the pretest–posttest control group design and the other two groups of the posttest-only control group design. The Solomon four-group design can be diagrammed as follows:

$$
\begin{array}{cccc}
R & O_1 & X & O_2 \\
R & O_3 & & O_4 \\
R & & X & O_5 \\
R & & & O_6
\end{array}
$$

Considerations in Using the Design.

The design controls for the usual threats to internal validity. The effects of testing per se can be evaluated by comparing two control groups that differ only in having received the pretest (i.e., comparison of O_4 and O_6). More important, the interaction of pretesting and the intervention can be assessed by comparing pretested and unpretested groups (i.e., comparison of O_2 and O_5). Actually, the data can be analyzed to evaluate the effects of testing and the Testing $\times$ Treatment interaction. To accomplish this, the posttreatment assessment data for each group are combined into a 2 $\times$ 2 factorial design and analyzed with a two-way analysis of variance. Only the following observations are used: O_2, O_4, O_5, and O_6. The factors in the analysis are testing (pretest vs. no pretest) and treatment (treatment vs. no treatment). Other methods of analyzing the data from the design are available (see Braver & Braver, 1988).

Another feature of the design is that it includes replication of treatment and control conditions. The effect of treatment (X) is replicated in several different places in the design. The effect of treatment can be attested to by one within-group comparison (O_2 vs. O_1) and several between-group comparisons (e.g., O_2 vs. O_4; O_5 vs. O_6; O_5 vs. O_3 or O_1). If a consistent pattern of results emerges from these comparisons, the strength of the demonstration is greatly increased over designs that allow a single comparison.

The restrictions in the use of this design do not pertain to methodological weaknesses. Indeed, the design has excellent properties that provide a more persuasive demonstration than other designs because of the replication of treatment effects and the assessment of the contribution of pretesting. If the results are obtained across different conditions of assessment, this increases confidence in the external validity of the effects.

The gain in elegance and power in drawing inferences from the Solomon four-group design certainly is compensated in costs. As noted earlier, the experiment can be conceptualized as two smaller experiments. Twice the effort and costs are involved in the number of subjects run, the amount of data collected, and so on. To justify the extra effort the investigator usually would want to be primarily interested in evaluating pretest sensitization.

The design may appear to be somewhat esoteric because sensitization effects rarely enter into theoretical accounts of clinical phenomena. However, sensitization occasionally has important implications beyond the design considerations. For example, in one study, a Solomon four-group design was used to evaluate the impact of a suicide awareness program for high-school students (Spirito, Overholser, Ashworth, Morgan, & Benedict-Drew, 1988). The intervention consisted of a school curriculum designed to increase knowledge about suicide and to prevent or decrease the likelihood of suicide. Some students received the curriculum; others did not. Within these groups, some were pretested on measures related to knowledge about and attitudes toward suicide and hopelessness. The curriculum increased positive attitudes and reduced hopelessness. The effects were more marked for those who received the pretest, which demonstrates a pretest sensitization effect.

The Solomon four-group design calls for randomly assigning subjects to conditions. In the Spirito, Overholser et al. (1988) study, students who were absent on the day of the pretest were assigned to the no-pretest condition; those who were in school were assigned to the pretest condition. Thus the effect of pretesting and the interaction with treatment effects is potentially confounded by selection bias, that is, the possibility that subjects who did not come to school are different. Replication is needed to demonstrate that pretesting rather than subject selection is clearly the basis for the finding.

Additional research efforts probably should be directed at studying the effects of pretesting. Because so much research uses the pretest–posttest control-group design, the influence of pretesting might be more extensive than normally is assumed. A few studies using the Solomon four-group design in well-researched areas might be very valuable. Demonstrations across dependent measures might establish that in clinical research with widely used measures or interventions pretest sensitization is restricted to a narrow set of conditions or may not occur at all. The pervasiveness of pretest sensitization effects is not that clear in clinical research.

Factorial Designs

The above designs consist primarily of evaluating the impact of a single independent variable. There may be several variations of the independent variable in the above designs. For example, the independent variable (e.g., treatment) may be given to one group but withheld from another group. Alternatively, different versions of treatment might be provided across several groups. Whatever the variations, the studies basically evaluate one independent variable.

Investigation of a single variable in an experiment has its limitations. The main limitation is that it often raises relatively simple questions about the variable of interest. The simplicity of the question should not demean its importance. In relatively new areas of research, the simple questions are the bedrock of subsequent experiments. However, more complex and refined questions can be raised. For example, a single-variable experiment might raise the question of which treatment works better for a particular clinical problem or whether experienced therapists exert more impact than do nonexperienced therapists. A more complex question might be raised by including more than one variable. For example, are certain treatments more effective with certain types of therapists or clients? The latter type of question is somewhat more specific and entails evaluation of the separate and combined effects of two or more variables.

Factorial designs allow the simultaneous investigation of two or more variables (factors) in a single experiment. Within each variable, two or more conditions are administered. In the simplest factorial design, two variables (e.g., therapist experience and type of treatment) would each consist of two different levels (e.g., experienced vs. inexperienced therapists and Treatment A vs. Treatment B). In this 2×2 design, there are four groups that represent each possible combination of the levels of the two factors, as shown in Figure 5.2.

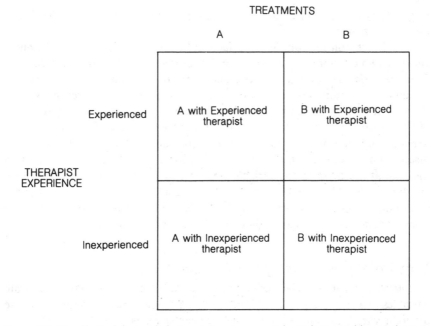

Figure 5.2. Hypothetical factorial design comparing two independent variables (or factors), therapist experience and type of treatment. Each factor has two different levels of conditions making this a 2 × 2 factorial design.

Of course, a factorial design is not a single design but rather a family of designs that vary in the number and types of variables and the number of levels within each variable. The variation of factorial designs also is influenced by whether or not a pretest is used. If a pretest is used, testing can become one of the variables or factors (time of assessment) with two (pretest vs. posttest) or more levels. The data can be analyzed to assess whether subjects changed with repeated assessment, independently of a particular intervention.

In single-variable experiments, one manipulation is of interest, and all other variables that might influence the results are controlled. In a factorial experiment, multiple variables are included to address questions about separate and combined effects of different variables. The variables that are included in the factorial design are not merely controlled; their effect is evaluated as distinct variables in the design. For example, a factorial design might evaluate the influence of characteristics of the subject (e.g., sex of the client), the therapist (e.g., degree of warmth during the therapy session), variations of treatment (e.g., Treatments A, B, or C), and conditions of therapy administration (e.g., number of sessions). These general classes of variables may be combined in a single study to ask pointed questions about the conditions under which variables exert their effects.

A major reason for completing a factorial experiment is that the combined effect of two or more variables may be of interest—that is, their interaction. The *interaction* refers to a synergistic effect resulting from the combination of variables. An interaction means that the effect of one of the variables (e.g., Treatment A or B) depends on the level of one of the other variables (e.g., sex of the patient). Essentially, an interaction denotes that the effect of a variable depends on some other condition under which it is administered. Earlier we discussed interactions in terms of external validity. In this light, the interaction means that the effect of one variable may or may not be generalized across all conditions. Rather, the impact of that variable occurs only under certain conditions or operates differently under those conditions (e.g., with men rather than women, with younger rather than older people, and so on).

Considerations in Using the Designs

The strength of a factorial design is that it can assess the effects of separate variables in a single experiment. The feature includes one of economy because different variables can be studied with fewer subjects and observations in a factorial design than in separate experiments for the single-variable study of each of the variables, one at a time.

In addition, the factorial design provides unique information about the combined effects of the independent variables. The importance of interactions cannot be overestimated in conducting research. Essentially, interactions provide the boundary conditions of independent variables and their effects. For example, in the context of treatment, a given intervention may not simply be effective or ineffective but rather may depend upon a host of qualifiers such as who administers treatment, what type of client problem, under what conditions of administration, for how long, and so on. These qualifiers refer to variables with which treatment is likely to interact. Finding that the effects of an independent variable does or does not interact with the levels of another variable is more than the evaluation of the generality of the experimental intervention. The implications may have important theoretical or practical value. In general, factorial designs can address more complex and sophisticated questions than do single-variable experiments (see also chapter 13).

The concerns about using the factorial designs are both practical and interpretive. On the practical side, one must remember that the number of groups in the investigation multiplies quickly as new factors or new levels of a given factor are added. For example, a design in its conceptual stages might simply begin as a 2 × 3 factorial design by looking at type of treatment (meditation training vs. biofeedback) and severity of anxiety (high, moderate, and low). This design already includes 6 (i.e., 2 × 3) groups. Yet it also might be interesting to study whether the treatment is administered in person by a live therapist or simply by prerecorded taped instructions. This third variable, manner of administering treatment, includes two levels, so the overall design now is a 2 × 2 × 3 and has 12 groups. Also, while we are at it, perhaps we could explore a fourth variable, instructions to the subjects. This variable might have two levels in which half of the subjects are told that the treatment was "discovered by a guru" and the other half that it was "discovered by a scientist engaged in basic laboratory research." We might expect meditation subjects who receive the "guru instructions" and biofeedback subjects who receive the "scientific researcher instructions" to do better than their counterparts. Now we have a 2 × 2 × 2 × 3 design, or 24 groups, a formidable doctoral dissertation to say the least. Instead of a study, we have a career.

As a general point, the number of groups in a study may quickly become prohibitive as factors and levels are increased. This means that the demand for subjects to complete each of the combinations of the variables will increase as well. In practice, there are constraints in the number of subjects that can be run in a given study and the number of factors (variables) that can be easily studied.

A related problem is interpreting the results of multiple factor experiments. Factorial designs are optimally informative when an investigator predicts an interactive relationship among two or more variables. Simple interactions involving two or three variables often are relatively straightforward to interpret. However, when multiple variables interact, the investigator may be at a loss to describe the complex relation in a coherent fashion, let alone offer an informed or theoretically plausible explanation. A factorial design is useful for evaluating the separate and combined effects of variables of interest when these variables are conceptually related and predicted to generate interactive effects. The inclusion of factors in the design is dictated by conceptual considerations of those variables and the interpretability of the predicted relations.

Quasi-Experimental Designs

The previous designs constitute basic between-group experimental designs and are *true experiments* because several facets of the study can be adequately controlled to eliminate threats to internal validity. The strength of the designs derives from the investigator's ability to control what treatment is administered to whom and at what point in time. Most important, subjects can be assigned randomly to conditions, thereby reducing the plausibility of potential threats to validity.

There are, however, many situations in which the investigator cannot exert such control over subjects and their assignment or the administration of treatment to particular groups. In clinical, counseling, and educational research investigators often are unable to shuffle clients or students to meet the demands of a true experiment but must work within administrative, bureaucratic, and occasionally even antiresearch constraints. As noted earlier, research designs where the investigator cannot exert control required of true experiments have been referred to as *quasi-experimental designs* (Campbell & Stanley, 1963).

Pretest–Posttest Design

There are many between-group quasi-experimental designs, the most common of which parallel the pretest–posttest and posttest-only experimental designs. For each of the quasi-experimental equivalents of these designs, the control group is not demonstrably equivalent to the experimental group, usually because subjects have been assigned to groups prior to the inception of the investigation. Because the groups are already formed, they may differ in advance of the intervention. This explains why the designs have been referred to as *nonequivalent control group* designs (Campbell & Stanley, 1963).

The most widely used version of a nonequivalent control group design is the one that resembles the pretest–posttest control group design. The design may be diagrammed as follows:

$$nonR \quad O_1 \quad X \quad O_2$$
$$nonR \quad O_3 \quad \quad O_4$$

In this version, nonrandomly assigned subjects (e.g., subjects who already may be in separate wards, separate clinics, or separate classrooms) are compared. One group receives the treatment and the other does not. The strength of the design depends directly upon the similarity of the experimental and control groups. The investigator must ask how the assignment of subjects to groups originally might have led to systematic differences in advance of the intervention. For example, two elementary schools might be used to evaluate an intervention, where the intervention is provided at one school but not at the other. Children in the schools may vary on such factors as socioeconomic status, IQ, or any number of other measures. It is possible that the initial differences on pretest measures or different characteristics of the groups, whether or not they are revealed on pretest measures, could explain the findings. The similarity of children across schools can be attested to partially on the basis of pretest scores as well as on various subject variables. Pretest equivalence on a measure does not mean that the groups are comparable in all dimensions relevant to the intervention, but it increases the confidence one might place in this assumption.

In the version of the design diagrammed previously, the results could not easily be attributed to history, maturation, testing, regression, mortality, and similar factors that might vary between groups. However, it is possible that these threats might differ between groups (i.e., Selection × History interaction or a Selection $\times$ Maturation interaction). These interactions mean that particular confounding events may affect one group but not the other, and hence might account for group differences. For example, one group might experience historical events (within the school) or differ in rate of maturation (improvements without treatment). These influences might account for group differences even if the subjects were equivalent on a pretest.

Differential regression toward the mean also might account for group differences if either group was selected because of its extreme scores on a measure related to posttest performance. Often differential regression might be caused by what the investigator does rather than occur as an inadvertent effect of an uncontrollable situation. As mentioned in the discussion of "mismatching," an investigator may try to equalize groups by selecting pairs of subjects (if there are two groups) who are similar. By matching in this fashion, and comparing only the subjects across groups who have matched partners, the investigator may make the groups numerically equivalent on pretest scores, age, diagnosis, years of institutionalization, or the like. However, differences in regression across groups might well result from this matching procedure.

As an illustration of a nonequivalent quasi-experimental design, Fisher et al. (1989) evaluated the effects of participating in group awareness training. Such training includes experiences that individuals sought to improve their daily life, personal effectiveness, decision-making skills, and interpersonal awareness. Adults ordinarily seek such training on their own and cannot easily be assigned to a control group. Thus, the authors began with a task of evaluating the impact of an intervention where treatment and control groups cannot easily be formed by random assignment of cases to groups.

The investigators devised a nonrandomly assigned control group to assist in reducing the plausibility of various threats to internal validity. The authors used a peer-nominated no-intervention group. Specifically, people who sought and participated in awareness training (intervention group) were asked to nominate other people not in their household who were the same sex, approximately the same age, from the same community, and whom they considered to be like themselves. These nominated individuals (control group) were recruited and asked to complete the assessment battery at different points in time, to coincide with the pre–post interval for subjects who received awareness training.

This control group clearly is not equivalent to a group comprised from random assignment of subjects to intervention and nonintervention groups. Was the group equivalent to the group that received awareness training? Data analyses revealed that at pretest, experimental and control subjects were no different in age, education, sex, income, and a variety of psychological measures of interest (e.g., social functioning, self-esteem). There was one initial preintervention difference on a measure of perceived control; training subjects attributed more internal control to themselves than did nonintervention subjects. However, across a very large number of variables and statistical tests the groups were not different prior to the intervention. There might well have been differences on some variables related to self-selection and interest in group awareness training in addition to the initial difference in perceived control on one of many measures. Yet the onus is on us as readers to pose a relevant difference that might plausibly influence the results. This nonequivalent group controls reasonably well for threats to internal validity (e.g., testing, history), even though our confidence would have been augmented with equivalent and randomly composed groups. In passing, the results indicated that group awareness training and control subjects were not different on virtually all of the measures at posttreatment and at 1-year follow-up.

Posttest-Only Design

A nonequivalent control group design need not use a pretest. The posttest-only quasi-experimental design can be diagrammed as follows:

$$\text{non}R \quad X \quad O_1$$
$$\text{non}R \qquad\ \ O_2$$

Of course the problems with this design, as with its true experimental counterpart, is that the equivalence of groups prior to the intervention cannot be assessed. In the posttest-only *experimental* design, discussed earlier, the absence of a pretest was not necessarily problematic, because random assignment increases the likelihood of group equivalence, particularly for large sample sizes. In a posttest-only *quasi-*experiment, the groups may be very different across several dimensions prior to treatment. Hence attributing group differences to the intervention may be especially weak. Aside from problems of probable group nonequivalence prior to treatment and the absence of a pretest to estimate group differences, this version of the nonequivalent control group design suffers from each of the possible threats to internal validity of the same design with a pretest. As with the experimental designs, the nonequivalent control group designs share the same relation to pretest sensitization effects and their control depending on whether a pretest is used. However, there is no need to discuss pretest sensitization because essentially the same points provided in the earlier discussion apply here. Also, by comparison with the other problems of quasi-experimental designs, pretest sensitization is of relatively less concern.

　　Although the posttest-only quasi-experiment is weak, occasionally this may be the most viable design available. For example, one study focused on the evaluation of an inpatient treatment program for chemically dependent adolescents (dependent primarily on alcohol, marijuana, speed, downers, and cocaine; Grenier, 1985). The intervention consisted of a multidisciplinary program in the hospital (e.g., individual, group, and family therapy; an Alcoholics Anonymous model stressing complete abstinence from alcohol, and other procedures). The investigator examined whether those who completed the program were any more improved than those who had not received the program. Random assignment was not possible. Consequently, the investigator completed an assessment of former patients and of persons on the waiting list. The abstinence rates of the groups were 65.6% of the youth who received the program and 14.3% for those who had yet to receive the program. The results are compatible with the view that the program improves outcome. Clearly, several questions remain unanswered. At the same time, this initial test provides critical information to suggest that the program may offer some benefit. Further work appears worthwhile including extension to a randomized trial as well as evaluation of components of the package. A quasi-experiment provides an excellent beginning, particularly when viewed against the alternative of little or no evaluation that characterizes most institutional programs.

Variations

Before completing the discussion on nonequivalent control group designs, it is important to mention variations of the above designs that also might be used. A variation of the nonequivalent control group design with a pretest might be diagrammed as follows:

$$\text{non}R \quad O_1 \quad X \quad O_2$$
$$\text{non}R \quad \quad O_3 \quad \quad O_4$$

(The version of the design without the pretest can be illustrated simply by omitting O_1 and O_3.) The diagram indicates that groups received the pre- and posttreatment assessments at different points in time. Obviously, such a design has more problems than designs in which measures are administered to groups at the same time. With this version, pretest equivalence of groups cannot really be determined because when one group is tested there is no basis to infer the standing of the other group on the same measures at that time. In addition, different historical events, maturation, and instrument decay across groups become increasingly plausible as rival hypotheses of the results as the time of assessment of different groups becomes disparate.

Occasionally, the experimental and treatment groups are assessed at different times, as diagrammed above, but staggering the conditions does not necessarily compete with the conclusions that can be drawn. Treatment and control conditions in institutional experiments often are staggered to keep patients in different conditions from interacting. For example, one quasi-experiment of this sort evaluated the effects of teaching problem-solving skills to male hospitalized alcoholic patients (Intagliata, 1978). Treated patients received 10 one-hour group therapy sessions, during which they were trained to recognize and define problems, to generate solutions, and to select alternatives. The purpose was to train people to handle real-life problems after discharge from the hospital.

The assignment of subjects was staggered; groups were not run or assessed at the same time. The first 32 admissions were assigned to the control group. The next 32 admissions were designated as the treatment group. This violation of random assignment was based on the author's interest in keeping control subjects (receiving routine ward treatment) from having direct contact with experimental subjects. Indeed, the experimental subjects did not begin their treatment until control subjects had been discharged. The results showed that training in problem solving enhanced these skills on paper-and-pencil measures and in helping individuals plan for their postdischarge community adjustment.

Given the design, it is possible to raise rival hypotheses such as the nonequivalence of groups or differential history, maturation, or instrumentation. However, these are not very plausible despite the quasi-experimental nature of the study, in part because pretest information showed that the groups did not differ in age, verbal IQ, marital status, and other variables and because the assignment to groups differed only by 3 or 4 weeks. Hence this quasi-experiment staggered assessment and evaluation of the different groups, but the plausibility of rival interpretations resulting from that were minimal.

The design might be conducted without a pretest. An experimental and control group might be assessed at different points without information attesting in advance to their equivalence on any measures. In such cases, of course, the problems of drawing unambiguous inferences about treatment are increased. In addition, the problems of history, maturation, and instrument decay are present and might readily account for group differences.

Despite the disadvantages of using control groups that are assessed at different points in time from the experimental group, the addition of the control group makes these designs better than using only one group that receives the intervention. If only one group were used with pre- and postintervention assessment—or, even worse, merely the postintervention assessment—not much more than an uncontrolled case study remains, and most threats to internal validity cannot be ruled out.

General Comments

Although the nonequivalent control group designs already mentioned constitute the most frequently used variations, all of the possible quasi-experimental designs cannot be enumerated. The general characteristics of these designs is that constraints inherent in the situation restrict the investigator from meeting the requirements of true experiments. This usually means that the investigator cannot assign subjects randomly to conditions and that many threats to internal validity will compete with the experimental manipulation in explaining the results.

The inability to meet the demands of true experiments does not invariably sentence the demonstration to ambiguity. Thus quasi-experimental designs are not inherently flawed. The issue that raises concern pertains to the plausibility that rival hypotheses could explain the findings. Plausibility might vary greatly in a given study. Examples provided previously were ones in which the way treatment was arranged made rival threats to internal validity not particularly strong contenders for explaining the results. This is not always the case.

For example, in one quasi-experiment using a pretest–posttest experimental design, different doses (12 vs. 18 sessions) of a cognitively based treatment were compared (Lochman, 1985). The goal of the intervention was to control classroom behavior of aggressive boys. The group that received 12 sessions was run approximately 1 year before the group that received 18 sessions. The latter treatment was found to be more effective. However, comparisons revealed that subjects in this latter treatment were younger to begin with and more well behaved. These latter differences might well account for or contribute to the different outcomes at posttreatment and hence rival the explanation accorded to the different amounts of treatment.

Often it is the case that constraints limit the investigator to quasi-experimental designs. In such cases, ingenuity is required to mobilize methodological weapons against ambiguity. The threats to internal validity may be handled by various control groups that can be used in the situation. These groups may help weaken one or more threats to internal validity and patch up an otherwise imperfect design. Indeed, groups added to designs to rule out various rival explanations of the results have been referred to as "patched-up" control groups (Campbell & Stanley, 1963) and are discussed in the next chapter.

MULTIPLE-TREATMENT DESIGNS

The defining characteristic of the multiple-treatment design is that each of the different treatments under investigation is presented to each subject. Although the evaluation of treatments is "within subjects," separate groups of subjects are usually present in the design. In most multiple-treatment designs in clinical research, separate groups are used so that the different treatments can be balanced across subjects, that is, so that treatments can be presented in different orders. Because separate groups are used in the multiple-treatment designs, points raised about random assignment and matching are relevant for constructing different groups for multiple-treatment designs.

There are different versions of multiple-treatment designs that depend upon the number of treatments and the manner in which they are presented. All of the designs might be called *counterbalanced designs* because they try to balance the order of treatment across subjects. However, it is worth distinguishing both the commonly used version of the multiple-treatment design as well as the general method for balancing treatments.

Crossover Design

A specific multiple-treatment design that is used in treatment research is referred to as the *crossover design*. The design receives its name because part way through the experiment, usually at the midpoint, all subjects "cross over" (i.e., are switched) to another experimental condition. The design is used with two different treatments. Two groups of subjects are constructed through random assignment. The groups differ only in the order in which they receive the two treatments. The design can be diagrammed as follows:

$$R \quad O_1 \quad X_1 \quad O_2 \quad X_2 \quad O_3$$
$$R \quad O_4 \quad X_2 \quad O_5 \quad X_1 \quad O_6$$

The diagram may appear complex because of the numbering of different interventions (X_1 and X_2) and the different observations (O_1 through O_6). However, the design is relatively straightforward. Essentially, each group is formed through random assignment *(R)*. A pretest may be provided to assess performance prior to any intervention. The pretest (designated in the diagram as O_1 and O_4) is not mandatory but is included because it is commonly used and provides the benefits of a pretest, discussed earlier. The crucial feature of the design is that the groups receive the interventions (X_1, X_2) in different order. Moreover, behavior is assessed after each intervention. Thus there is an assessment halfway through the study at the crossover point as well as after the second and final treatment is terminated.

As an example, Hackmann and McLean (1975) used a crossover design to compare two different treatments for eliminating obsessions in 10 patients with obsessional rituals and thoughts. Thought stopping and flooding were the two treatments. Thought stopping consisted of having the individual patient imagine situations that provoked an obsessional ritual or thought. As the patient signaled (by raising a finger) that the image or thought was clear, the therapist hit the desk with a ruler and shouted "stop!" The purpose of this treatment was gradually to interfere and thwart completion of the thought. Eventually control was transferred to the client who stated "stop" aloud and later "stop" subvocally to control his or her own thoughts. Flooding consisted of exposing patients to the feared situations that precipitated the anxiety that apparently led to obsessions. Patients were exposed to actual events (e.g., handling objects that the patient thought were contaminated) in the flooding condition.

The 10 patients were divided into two groups of 5. The first group received flooding first followed by thought stopping; the second group received the treatments in the opposite order. Each treatment was given for four sessions. Assessment of the obsessions was completed by ratings and inventories before treatment, after the first treatment, and again after the second. During each treatment there were within-group improvements from the previous assessment period. Both treatments were associated with change, and there were no differences between the treatments.

Multiple-Treatment Counterbalanced Designs

The crossover design as discussed here is a simple design, usually with two treatments, in which each client receives the different treatments but in a different order; that is, the treatments are counterbalanced. With an increase in the number of treatments, however, the counterbalancing procedures become more complex. In the design with only two treatments, counterbalancing ensures that both possible orders of treatment are given; that is, both treatments appear as the first and as the second treatment.

With additional treatments, the order in which the treatments are given is more difficult to balance. For example, consider the hypothetical experiment in which four treatments (A, B, C, and D) are to be compared. Each subject will receive each of the treatments. An important issue is deciding the order in which the subjects should receive treatment. One method is to determine the sequence of treatments randomly for each subject. Thus the sequence for each subject will vary depending upon "chance." This procedure would be adequate with a large number of subjects. However, it is possible, particularly with a small number of subjects, that the order of treatments will not be balanced. That is, one of the four treatments may appear at some point in the sequence (e.g., the first treatment) but not at the other points. More likely, the different treatments will not appear at each point in the sequence for an equal or approximately equal number of times. This inequality could interfere with the conclusions to be drawn about treatment effects.

For example, in one study, the effects of three forms of behavior therapy (systematic desensitization, implosion, and reinforced practice) were evaluated for reducing anxiety in 14 phobic patients in an outpatient psychiatric facility (Crowe, Marks, Agras, & Leitenberg, 1972). The patients included diverse phobias (e.g., fear of being alone, of social situations, of noises, and others). Each treatment was given to each patient for four sessions prior to shifting to another treatment until all three treatments were completed. The order of conditions was determined on a random basis for each patient. On behavioral measures, the reinforced practice procedure tended to be the most effective.

An important design consideration in evaluating these results is whether the treatments were distributed approximately equally across the different positions in the sequence (first, second, or third treatment). Purely random assignment alone could have ended in, say, a larger percentage of patients receiving the reinforcement condition at one particular point in the sequence (e.g., first). This is no minor matter because the study also found that the treatment given first tended to be the most effective independently of what it was. So the position in which treatment was administered in the sequence contributed to its effects. Without knowing when the treatments were presented in the random ordering of treatments to subjects, it is not possible to rule out an alternative explanation of the results in this study. The results might reflect a Treatment × Order interaction (showing the effects of a treatment because it appeared in one place in the sequence more than other treatments), rather than a simple treatment effect (showing that treatments differed independently of where they appeared in the sequence). It would have been desirable to select a set of sequences that would ensure that each treatment was presented an equal number of times in each position across subjects. (Actually, it would not be possible with 14 subjects to make this equal because 15 subjects would be needed; three groups of 5 subjects each that received a given treatment, first, second, and third, respectively.)

A useful procedure to ordering the treatments in a multiple-treatment design is to select a set of sequences in advance and to assign subjects randomly to the different orders. For example, suppose that there are four groups of subjects and each subject receives each of the four treatments. A few specified arrangements or sequences of treatments could be preselected in advance to which the subjects are randomly assigned. If there were four arrangements of the treatments, the design might be summarized as presented in Table 5.1.

The characteristic of this ordering is that each group has a different sequence that includes each of the four treatments (A, B, C, and D). Moreover, each

Table 5.1. Order of Four Treatments (A, B, C, D) in a Latin Square Design

		ORDER			
		1	2	3	4
	I	A	B	C	D
	II	B	A	D	C
Sequences					
	III	C	D	A	B
	IV	D	C	B	A

Each subject is assigned randomly to one of four groups (I, II, III, or IV), which constitutes a different sequence of the four treatments. Sequence refers to the set of treatments in a given order (i.e., the rows in the table); order refers to the position of a given treatment or whether it appears 1st, 2nd, 3rd, or 4th (i.e., the columns).

of the treatments is administered once in each of the available positions. The arrangement of treatments in such a way that each occurs once and only once in each position and in each group is referred to as a *Latin Square*. In a Latin Square, the number of groups (represented by rows in the table), orders or positions (represented by columns), and treatments (represented by A through D) are equal. The table represents only one way of ordering the treatments. Actually, for a given number of treatments, there are several Latin Squares. (For a discussion of procedures to select and to form Latin Squares for a given experiment and for a table of various squares, the interested reader is referred to other sources [Fisher & Yates, 1963; Kirk, 1968].) At the end of the investigation, analyses can compare different treatments and can assess whether there were any effects due to groups (rows), to order (columns), or treatment (As vs. Bs vs. Cs vs. Ds). (Although main effects of treatment, order, and groups can be extracted from Latin Square analyses, interactions among these effects present special problems that are beyond the scope of the present chapter [see Grant, 1948].)

One effect that is still left uncontrolled is the particular sequence in which the treatment appears. The sequence of treatments in the table (the rows) does not represent all possible sequences. Not every treatment is preceded and followed by every other treatment. For example, Treatment B never immediately follows Treatment D, nor does Treatment C follow Treatment A, and so on. Hence, it is not really possible with the above design to rule out the influence of different sequences as a contributor to the data for a given treatment. There may be an *interaction* between the effects of treatment and where treatment appears in the sequence. This interaction can be avoided as a source of confound by using all possible orders of treatment with separate groups of subjects. In a *completely balanced design,* each treatment occurs equally often in each order and each treatment precedes and follows all others. The problem with such a design is that the number of groups and subjects required may be prohibitive. The number of subjects for complete counterbalancing would be *k* factorial, where *k* equals the number of treatments in the experiment.

In general, the administration of multiple treatments to the same subject is relatively rare. When treatment studies use multiple-treatment designs, the most common version compares two treatments, as illustrated by the crossover design. Conducting additional treatments may require a relatively long period of continuous treatment so that each treatment has an opportunity to influence behavior. Moreover, the problem of reflecting change with multiple treatments, discussed below, makes testing for effects of several treatments a dubious venture. Consequently, several treatments are infrequently evaluated within subjects; when they are, the designs usually are not completely balanced to include all possible sequences of treatment.

Considerations in Using the Designs

The utility of multiple-treatment designs depends upon several factors, including the anticipated effects of juxtaposing different treatments, the type of independent and dependent variables, and the measurement of cumulative treatment effects with the same subjects.

Order and Sequence Effects

Perhaps the most important consideration in using a multiple-treatment design relates to the problem of ordering treatments. Actually there are different problems that can be distinguished. To begin with, if an experiment consisted of one group of subjects that received two different treatments (A and B) in a particular order, the results would be completely uninterpretable. For example, if Treatment B led to greater change than Treatment A, it would be impossible to determine whether B was more effective because of its unique therapeutic properties or because it was the second treatment provided to all subjects. Treatment B may have been more effective because a continuation of treatment, independently of what the treatment was, may have led to greater change. Thus the order in which the treatments appeared in this single group study might have been responsible for treatment differences and hence serves as a plausible alternative explanation of the results.

When the order of treatments might account for the results, this is referred to as an *order effect*. The effect merely refers to the fact that the point in time in which treatment occurred, rather than the specific treatment, might be responsible for the pattern of results. In most multiple-treatment designs, order effects are not confounded with treatments because of counterbalancing procedures, as illustrated in the discussion of crossover and Latin Square designs. Although order is not confounded with treatment where counterbalancing is used, it still may influence the pattern of results. Investigators occasionally report order effects in which early (or, less often, later) treatments are consistently more effective by virtue of when treatment is administered independently of what the treatment is (e.g., Crowe et al., 1972; Everaerd, Rijken, & Emmelkamp, 1973; Hackmann & McLean, 1975). Quite possibly the reason for this is related to ceiling and floor effects, discussed later, in that by the time the final treatment is provided in a series of treatments, the amount of change that can be reflected on the dependent measures is attenuated.

There is another way that the specific order of treatments may influence the results. Specifically, the transfer from one treatment to another is not the same for each treatment. Receiving Treatment A followed by Treatment B may not be the same as receiving Treatment B followed by Treatment A. The order in which these appear may partially dictate the effects of each treatment. When the arrangement of treatments contributes to their effects, this is referred to as *sequence effects*. The nature of the problem is conveyed by other terms that are sometimes used, such as *multiple-treatment interference* or *carryover effects*. The importance of the sequence in which different events appear in dictating their effects is obvious from examples of everyday experience. For example, the taste of a given food depends not only on the specific properties of the food but also on the taste and characteristics of the food or liquid that has immediately preceded it.

The effects of the sequence of different experimental interventions was nicely illustrated in an investigation designed to compare different amounts of isolation as a form of punishment (referred to as time-out) to reduce deviant behavior (e.g., aggressive acts, tantrums, self-destructive behavior) in institutionalized retarded residents (White, Nielson, & Johnson, 1972). Specifically, the purpose was to compare three different isolation periods. After deviant behavior, a resident was isolated in a special room for either 1, 15, or 30 minutes. The residents were divided into three groups, each group receiving the different time-out durations, each for a 2-week period. Other effects were controlled by providing each treatment in each of the positions (first, second, or third treatment given) in the fashion required by a Latin Square design.

Observations of disruptive behavior indicated that the longer durations (15 or 30 minutes) tended to suppress behavior to a greater extent than did the 1-minute duration. Yet the effects of the time-out duration partially depended on the order in which the duration appeared in the sequence. When the 1-minute duration of isolation was presented as the first treatment, it tended to be very effective and much more effective than when it appeared after one of the longer durations. Indeed, when a 1-minute duration followed other durations it tended to be no better than omitting punishment altogether.

As a general statement, multiple-treatment designs are quite susceptible to the influence of sequence effects. Whether these effects are viewed as nuisances depends on the purposes of the investigator. Sequence effects represent complex interactions (e.g., Treatment × Order of Appearance) and may be of interest in their own right. All events in one's life occur in the context of other events. Hence sequence effects embrace questions about the context in which events occur and the effects of prior experience on subsequent performance. Depending on one's purpose, the fact that sequence effects occur may be central. However, for treatment evaluation, sequence effects are rarely sought. The purpose is to produce therapeutic change and to determine which among alternative treatments effectively accomplishes this.

Restrictions With Various Independent and Dependent Variables

Considerations pertaining to the variables that are to be studied may dictate whether a multiple-treatment design is likely to be appropriate or useful for the experiment in question. Some variables of interest to the investigator are not easily studied in a multiple-treatment design. For example, the experimental instructions or subject expectancies may present particular problems, depending on the precise experimental manipulations. The problem is in providing to the subject separate interventions that may present conflicting information or procedures. For example, individual therapy and family therapy may be difficult to compare within a particular set of subjects. The respective treatment rationales may present conflicting information to the subjects about the appropriate focus of intervention (either on the individual or family). The second treatment might seem odd if it would contradict the theoretical basis and actual operations of the first treatment. Hearing the rationale and receiving one of these procedures first might influence the client's belief in the other one.

The problem of potentially conflicting information among the different treatments can sometimes be resolved. The solution may lie in the intricacy of the rationales that the experimenter provides so that the different treatments will not appear to conflict. Thus the creativity of the investigator argues against any absolute rules about which treatments can and cannot accompany another in a multiple-treatment design.

Discussing potentially conflicting interventions raises another side of the issue. It is possible to select interventions that are very similar. For example, the "different treatments" presented to the subjects may only vary in subtle characteristics. These "different" treatments may produce few detectable effects in a multiple-treatment design because clients do not distinguish the conditions. The first intervention may lead to a certain degree of change. The second intervention, or variation, may not be perceived as any different from the first one and hence may produce no differences within subjects; essentially, the second intervention is perceived as a continuation of the first. Although intervention differences would not be revealed by changes within subjects, a comparison between groups for the first treatment conditions administered might yield a difference.

Personality, demographic, physical, and other stable characteristics are not studied within subjects because they do not vary within the same subject for a given experiment. Obviously, subjects are not both male and female or a psychiatric patient and not a patient within the same experiment. Often, it is possible to provide experiences within the experiment that changes how a subject reacts to certain variables. A subject could be given a success or failure experience in an attempt to assess the impact of these experiences on dependent measures. Stable subject characteristics can be readily studied in factorial designs that combine group and multiple-treatment features. For example, a subject can be classified by one variable (e.g., sex, age, level of anxiety) and receive each of the different levels of another variable (e.g., Treatments A and B). This combined design can examine whether treatment effects differ according to subject characteristics.

Aside from restrictions on independent variables, there are restrictions on dependent measures that can be readily evaluated in a multiple-treatment design. Dependent measures involving such skills as cognitive or motor abilities may not readily reflect treatment effects within subjects. When one treatment alters a skill (e.g., bicycle riding or reading), the effects of other treatments are more difficult to evaluate than when transient changes in performance are made.

Ceiling and Floor Effects

A possible problem in evaluating different interventions within the same subjects is that ceiling or floor effects may limit the amount of change that can be shown. *Ceiling and floor effects* refer to the fact that change in the dependent measures may reach an upper or lower limit, respectively, and that further change cannot be demonstrated because of this limit. The amount of change produced by the first intervention may not allow additional change to occur.

Assume, for example, that two treatments are presented in a multiple-treatment design and evaluated on a hypothetical measure of adjustment that ranges in scores from 0 to 100. Here, a score of 0 equals "poor adjustment," which means the individual is constantly depressed, anxious, drunk, suicidal, and apathetic—and this is on the good days. Assume that 100 equals the paragon of adjustment or that the individual is perfectly adaptive, content, and self-actualizing even in the face of recent loss of family, possessions, job, fortune, and memory. In pretreatment assessment, subjects are screened and selected based on their poor adjustment on the scale; say, scores lower than 25. Then two treatments are provided, in counterbalanced order, to two groups of subjects. Suppose the initial treatment increases adjustment to a mean of 95. With this initial change, a second treatment cannot provide evidence of further improvements. For example, the data might show the pattern illustrated in Figure 5.3, in which it can be seen that the first treatment (A or B) led to marked increments in adjustment and administering the second treatment did not produce additional change. The conclusion would be that the treatments are equally effective and that one does not add to the other.

A different pattern might emerge if there were no ceiling on the measure. That is, if even higher scores were allowed and a greater amount of change could be shown, different conclusions might be reached. For example, if the adjustment scale allowed scores beyond 100 and additional degrees of adjustment, different results might have been obtained. The treatments might have been different at their first presentation. Treatment A might have led to a mean score of 95 but Treatment B to a score of 150. In that case, when the other (second) treatment was applied to each group, additional changes may have been detected, at least in going from A to B.

In general, the problem of ceiling or floor effects is not restricted to multiple-

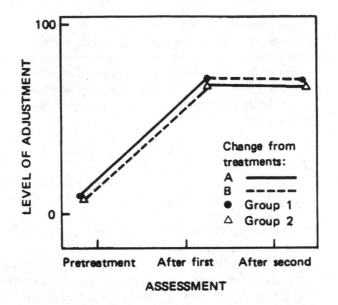

Figure 5.3. Hypothetical data for a crossover design in which each group of subjects receives the treatments, but in a counterbalanced order.

treatment comparisons. The absence of differences *between groups* on a measure may result from limits in the range of scores obtained on that measure. If scores for the different groups congregate at the upper and lower end of the scale, it is possible that differences would be evident if the scale permitted a greater spread of scores. For example, in one of our projects, we evaluated alternative treatments for antisocial children (Kazdin, Bass, Siegel, & Thomas, 1989). The treatments (variations of problem-solving skills training and relationship therapy) differed in outcome on a number of measures. As part of the study, parents and children rated the acceptability of treatment, that is, the extent to which they viewed treatment as appropriate, fair, and reasonable. Three treatments were rated quite positively and did not differ in level of acceptability. It is possible that the treatments were equally acceptable. However, the means for the groups were close to the upper limit of possible scores on the scale. Thus it remains possible that acceptability would differ if the scale range were not limited.

Although the problem of ceiling and floor effects can occur in any design, it is exacerbated by multiple-treatment designs because different treatments operate toward continued increases (or decreases) in scores. With repeated treatments, the limit of the scores may be approached with one or two treatments and not allow differentiation of later treatments. Thus one consideration in using a multiple-treatment design is whether the different measures provide a sufficient range of scores to allow continued increments in performance from a purely measurement standpoint.

In multiple-treatment designs, ceiling and floor effects are readily avoided when change is transient. For example, interventions based on administration of drugs or incentives for performance may produce effects only while the interventions are in effect. Assessment of behavior can be made while these interventions are in effect. After withdrawal of the intervention, perhaps with an intervening period so that drug or incentive effects are completely eliminated, the second intervention can be implemented. If the effects of an intervention are transient and only evident when the intervention is in effect, the improvements resulting from one treatment will not limit the scores that can be achieved by the second treatment.

The study of interventions with transient effects resolves the problem of ceiling and floor effects in the dependent measures. However, in areas of clinical or applied research as in psychotherapy, counseling, and educational interventions, the purpose is to produce a nontransient change. It is not reasonable to select interventions with transient effects for purposes of design if the goal is protracted change.

SUMMARY AND CONCLUSIONS

In most research in clinical, educational, and counseling psychology, the intervention of interest is evaluated by making comparisons between groups. Careful attention must be given to the assignment of subjects to groups. In experimental research, subjects are assigned in an unbiased fashion so that each subject has an equal probability of being assigned to the alternative conditions. Typically, *random assignment* is employed. As an adjunctive procedure, subjects may be matched on a given variable at the beginning of the experiment and randomly assigned in blocks to conditions. *Matching* followed by random assignment is an excellent way to ensure equivalence of groups on a measure that relates to the dependent variable. Occasionally, matching is used with intact or preexisting groups, with the goal of identifying subjects across groups who are equal on a measure prior to treatment. Although the intent of this matching procedure is well based, it may yield groups that regress to different group means. Independently of the intervention, groups may differ because of this regression effect. Because of the possible artifact in group differences, equalizing groups in this way was referred to as *mismatching.*

Several different designs were discussed including the *pretest–posttest control group design, posttest-only control group design, Solomon four-group design, factorial designs,* and *quasi-experimental designs.* The pretest–posttest control group was noted as particularly advantageous because of the strengths that the pretest provides for demarcating initial (preintervention) levels of functioning, evaluating change, and increasing power for statistical analyses. Factorial designs were also highlighted because they permit simultaneous study of the effects of two or more variables in a single experiment. In addition, these designs allow evaluation of *interactions* between variables, that is, whether the effects of one variable depend on different levels of another variable.

Multiple-treatment designs were also discussed. Although separate groups of subjects are included in these designs, their unique characteristic is the presentation of separate treatment or treatment and control conditions to the same subjects. In multiple-treatment designs, separate groups of subjects are used so that the different treatments can be *counterbalanced.* Counterbalancing is designed to ensure that the effects of the treatments can be separated from the order in which they appear.

In the simplest multiple-treatment design, referred to as the *crossover design,* two treatments are given to two groups of subjects but in different order. In more complex versions, several treatments may be delivered and either presented in a randomized or a prearranged order to randomly comprised groups of subjects. A *Latin Square* design refers to ways of arranging multiple treatments within subjects where the number of treatments is equal to the number of groups and where each treatment appears once in each position in the sequence in which treatments are arranged.

There are several considerations in using multiple-treatment designs. *Order and sequence effects* are controlled by ensuring that each treatment is administered at each point in the order of treatments (e.g., first, second, third, etc.). Sequence effects are more difficult to control unless each treatment precedes and follows all other treatments somewhere in the design. This latter balancing requirement is prohibitive with multiple treatments. The problem with leaving sequence effects uncontrolled is that the effects of one treatment may be influenced by previous treatments. That is, there may be a carryover effect from one treatment to the next.

Another consideration pertains to restrictions in the use of various independent and dependent variables in multiple-treatment designs. Independent variables such as subject characteristics or treatments that appear to present conflicting information or procedures to the subject may be impossible or extremely difficult to study within subjects. Dependent variables that reflect abilities or skills may be difficult to evaluate in multiple-treatment designs if multiple treatments are presented. Unlike most transient measures of performance, ability and skill levels may not readily reflect the cumulative effects of multiple treatments on many measurement devices.

Finally, studying multiple treatments may introduce problems of *ceiling and floor effects* that refer, respectively, to upper or lower limits on the response measure that will not allow subsequent interventions to reflect further change in performance. There must be some assurance that the dependent measure(s) do not restrict the range of performance allowed in view of the subjects' responses to early treatments.

FOR FURTHER READING

Campbell, D.T., & Stanley, J.C. (1963). Experimental and quasi-experimental designs for research. In N.L. Gage (Ed.), *Handbook of research on teaching.* Chicago, IL: Rand McNally. (Available as a separate booklet published in 1966.)

Cook, T.D., & Campbell, D.T. (1979). *Quasi-experimentation design and analysis issues for field settings.* Chicago, IL: Rand McNally.

Greenwald, A.G. (1976). Within-subjects designs: To use or not to use? *Psychological Bulletin, 83,* 314–320.

Kendall, P.C., & Butcher, J.N. (Eds.). (1982). *Handbook of research methods in clinical psychology.* New York: John Wiley & Sons.

Chapter 6

CONTROL AND COMPARISON GROUPS

The previous chapter conveyed the basic paradigms for several designs. A central feature was providing the experimental manipulation, condition, or intervention to at least one group. The effect of the conditions is evaluated by comparing alternative groups that receive various intervention or control conditions. In any of the designs, a number of experimental and control groups can be included. A single experimental group and a control group provide the minimal conditions of each design and hence are only illustrative.

In discussions of basic experimental design, we are often taught that an experiment requires a control group. The very name of one of the groups as a "control group" raises problems. Figure 6.1 conveys one problem with the concept of control group insofar as it suggests that the other group in the study is perhaps out of control. More seriously, the notion of *a* control group is misleading because it implies that the addition of a single group to a design may provide a general control for diverse biases, artifacts, and rival hypotheses that might plague the research. In fact, there are all sorts of groups that may be added or included in a design depending on the potential influences other than the intervention that may account for the results (threats to internal validity) and the specificity of the statements the investigator wishes to make about what led to change (threats to construct validity). The present chapter discusses control and comparison groups that are often used in clinical research, the design issues they are intended to address, and considerations that dictate their use.

Figure 6.1. Depiction of one meaning of control and "experimental" groups. Reprinted with permission from *The Spread of Terror* by Peter S. Mueller; copyright 1986, Bonus Books, Inc., 160 E. Illinois St., Chicago, IL.

ALTERNATIVE CONTROL GROUPS

Control groups are usually used to address threats to internal validity such as history, maturation, selection, testing, and others. Control of these and related threats is accomplished by ensuring that one group in the design shares these influences with the intervention group but does not receive the intervention or experimental manipulation. If the intervention and control groups are formed by random assignment and assessed at the same point(s) in time, internal validity threats are usually addressed. In clinical research, several control groups are often used.

No-Treatment Control Group

Rationale and Description

In evaluating a particular therapy or experimental intervention, a basic question can always be raised, namely, to what extent would people improve or change without treatment? The question can be answered by including a *no-treatment control group* in the experimental design. This group is so fundamental to intervention research that it was included in the basic descriptions and diagrams of the pretest–posttest control group and posttest-only control group designs discussed in the previous chapter. This is the group that is assessed but otherwise receives no intervention. By including a no-treatment group in the design, the effects of history and maturation as well as other threats to internal validity are directly controlled.

The performance of people in a no-treatment control group can change significantly over time, which underscores the importance of this group in providing a baseline level for purposes of comparison when evaluating intervention effects. For example, in psychotherapy research improvements often occur among clients who are in the no-treatment control condition. Historically, these improvements have been referred to as *spontaneous remission*. The term is not extremely informative because the reasons for the change (e.g., spontaneous) and the extent to which change has improved client functioning (e.g., remission) are arguable. Actually, spontaneous remission refers to changes made without receiving formal treatment in a given investigation. The term embraces history, maturation, and regression (reversion of extreme scores toward a less extreme mean on a given assessment device) but is usually not discussed as such in evaluations of therapy. In some cases, clear historical events are possible explanations. For example, people who do not receive treatment may seek alternative treatments. Even if another type of treatment is not formally sought, clients may improve as a function of more informal means of "treatment" such as talking with relatives, neighbors, members of the clergy, or general practice physicians. Improvements over time may also result from changes in the situations that exacerbated or precipitated the problem (e.g., adjustment after a death of a loved one) and other maturational influences that affect one's mood, outlook, and psychological status. Also, individuals who come for treatment may be at a particularly severe point in their problem. Hence one would expect that reassessment of the problem at some later point would show improvement for many individuals. It may not be true that "time heals all wounds," but ordinary processes occurring with the passage of time certainly are strong competitors for many therapeutic techniques.

In view of the multiple influences that may impinge on clients who are in a no-treatment group, it is difficult to specify whether changes over time are "spontaneous," whatever that means. From a methodological point of view, the important issue is to control for the amount of improvement that occurs as a function of these multiple, even if poorly specified and understood, influences. A no-treatment control group assesses the base rate of improvement for clients who did not receive the treatment under investigation.

Ideally, one would know in advance what the level of improvement is for clients with a particular problem so that treatment could be evaluated without using no-treatment control procedures. Yet even if improvement rates for various client disorders were well known, a no-treatment group would be needed in treatment research for other reasons. Changes in behavior may result from repeated assessment on the various dependent measures used to evaluate treatment. A no-treatment group is exposed to the same assessment procedures of the treatment group, thus making implausible the effects of testing and instrument decay as possible explanations of the results.

It is important to use as a no-treatment group clients who have been randomly assigned to this condition. Violation of random assignment reduces the confidence that can be placed in any between-group differences after treatment has been completed. For example, some individuals for one reason or another may choose not to participate in the program after pretreatment assessment or withdraw after a small number of treatment sessions. People who have withdrawn from treatment would of course not be appropriate to consider as part of or additions to the no-treatment control group. Although these clients might be considered to have received no treatment, they are self-selected for that status. Their subsequent performance on any measures might well reflect variables related to their early withdrawal rather than to the absence of treatment.

Special Considerations

There are obvious practical problems in utilizing a no-treatment control group. Difficulties are encountered in explaining to clients who apply that treatment is unavailable. Usually clients must be given a reason why treatment is unavailable; for example, they may be told that only some individuals who apply will be able to receive treatment and no guarantee can be made that they will be selected. Yet when people are told that they were not selected for treatment, they may seek treatment elsewhere. Even if they do not seek other treatments, they may resent not receiving treatment and fail to cooperate with subsequent attempts to administer assessment devices.

If a no-treatment group of clients is successfully formed, it is likely that there will be time constraints on the group. As a general rule, the longer that clients are required to serve as no-treatment control subjects, the more likely they will drop out of the study. Thus the use of a no-treatment group may be feasible only for a relatively short period, depending on such factors as severity of the client's problem and the availability of alternative treatments. The investigator may wish to know the effects of the intervention over an extended period (e.g., 1, 5, or 10 years of follow-up). However, continuation of a no-treatment control group usually is not feasible over an extended period. Few no-treatment subjects are likely to remain in the study over an extended period; those who do may be a select group whose data are difficult to interpret.

Aside from the practical problems, using a no-treatment control group presents obvious ethical problems. When clients seek treatment, it is difficult to justify withholding all attempts at intervention. Providing an experimental or exploratory treatment that is reasonable, even if unproven, is more ethically defensible than providing no treatment at all. When it comes to withholding treatment in a clinical situation, ivory tower pleas for experimental elegance, control groups, and the importance of scientific research may be unpersuasive to prospective clients. A partial solution to withholding treatment and meeting the requirements of a no-treatment control group is to use a waiting-list control group.

Waiting-List Control Group

Rationale and Description

The purpose of a no-treatment control group is to assess changes in clients who receive no formal treatment over the treatment period, that is, the pre- and posttreatment assessment interval. If this interval is not too long, it is possible to use a group that receives no treatment during this interval but does receive treatment immediately after this interval. As soon as the second (posttreatment) assessment battery is administered, these subjects receive treatment. Members of this group, referred to as a *waiting-list control group,* are told that their treatment will be delayed.

When clients originally apply for treatment, they can be asked whether they would participate even if treatment were delayed. Only those subjects who agree would be included in the study. These clients would be assigned randomly to either treatment or waiting-list control conditions. The control clients are promised treatment within a specified time period and in fact are called back and scheduled for treatment. Although it is tempting to assign those clients who indicate they could wait for treatment to the control group and those who could not wait to the treatment group, circumventing random assignment in this way is methodologically disastrous. Group differences or the absence of group differences could be the result of subject selection in combination with history, maturation, regression, and so on.

A few rudimentary features characterize a waiting-list control group. First, if a pretest is used, there must be no treatment between the first and second assessment period for the waiting-list control group. During this period, the group is functionally equivalent to a no-treatment control group. Second, the time period from the first to second assessment of the waiting-list control group must correspond to the time period of pre- and posttreatment assessment of the treatment group. This may be easily controlled if treatment consists of a particular interval (e.g., 2 months) and the pre-to-posttreatment assessment period is constant across treated subjects. Then, waiting-list control subjects can return for reassessment after that fixed interval has elapsed. If treatment duration varies, a waiting-list control subject can be scheduled for reassessment at the same time that a treated subject returns for posttreatment assessment. The waiting-list control and experimental subjects are paired in this way on the basis of having taken the pre- and posttreatment assessment devices over the same time interval (e.g., within 1 week), or perhaps even on the same days. This procedure, elaborated later in the discussion of Yoking, holds constant the assessment interval for waiting-list and treatment subjects. It is important to keep the time interval constant to control for history and maturation over the course of the assessment interval.

Waiting-list control clients complete pretest or posttest assessments and then receive treatment. An important practical question is how to have the waiting-list subjects return for reassessment immediately prior to providing them with treatment. Actually, this is not particularly difficult. Clients usually are required to complete the assessment again before receiving treatment. Essentially, reassessment is connected with the promise of scheduling treatment and serves as an immediate antecedent to the long-awaited intervention.

Special Considerations

There is an obvious limitation of the waiting-list control condition, particularly in comparison to a no-treatment group. Because subjects in the waiting-list group receive treatment soon after they have served their role as a temporary no-treatment group, the long-term impact of such processes as history, maturation, repeated testing, and other influences cannot be evaluated. Even if waiting-list subjects did not change very much in the time interval in which they waited for treatment, they may have improved or deteriorated greatly by the time of follow-up assessment even without treatment. One can follow the treatment group to see how they are doing 1 or 2 years later. Yet the waiting-list control group is no longer available for comparison; by this time this group will be another treatment group. Although this concern raises genuine interpretive problems, waiting-list control groups represent a reasonable compromise in treatment evaluation. The reason is that in principle and practice, protracted no-treatment control conditions are not feasible.

The use of a waiting-list control group has much to recommend it. From a practical standpoint, it usually is not as difficult to obtain waiting-list control subjects as it is to obtain no-treatment subjects. The difficulty partially depends on how long the control subjects are required to wait for treatment, the severity of the problem, their perceived need for treatment, and the availability of alternative resources. From the standpoint of experimental design, there is a decided advantage in the use of a waiting-list control group. This group allows careful evaluation of treatment effects at different points in the design. Because treatment eventually is provided to the waiting-list control subjects, its effects can be evaluated empirically. Essentially, a waiting-list control study using a pretest can be diagrammed as follows:

$$R \quad O_1 \quad X \quad O_2$$
$$R \quad O_3 \qquad\quad O_4 \quad X \quad O_5$$

The effects of treatment (X) is replicated in the design. Not only can the treatment be assessed by a between-group comparison (comparison of O_2 and

O_4) but by within-group comparisons as well (comparison of change from O_3 to O_4 with the change from O_4 to O_5). Of course, to accomplish this, waiting-list control group subjects must be reassessed after they finally receive treatment.

The waiting-list control group does not completely ameliorate the ethical problems of withholding treatment but may help a little. Now the issue is not withholding treatment from some of the clients. Rather, all clients receive treatment and differ only according to when they receive it. Ethical problems arise if clients request or require immediate treatment and delaying treatment may have serious consequences. Obviously, a waiting-list control group is not ethically defensible with acutely suicidal patients. Apart from such situations and as an alternative to the no-treatment control group, a waiting-list group offers a distinct advantage because clients eventually receive treatment.

No-Contact Control Group

Rationale and Description

The effects of participating in a study, even if only in the capacity of a no-treatment or waiting-list control subject, may have impact on the subjects as discussed previously as reactivity of the experimental arrangement. In the context of treatment research participating in a control group may exert some therapeutic change. Indeed, it has been known for some time that clients who receive the initial assessment battery on separate occasions prior to treatment show marked improvements (Frank, Nash, Stone, & Imber, 1963). Although regression alone might account for improvement upon repeated testing, the anticipation of relief from participating in a treatment project may be responsible as well. Thus, improvements could be due to error in measurement (regression) but also to veridical changes in the clients' views of their situation and dysfunction.

Occasionally it is possible to evaluate the impact of participation by using as a control group individuals who have no contact with the project. These individuals constitute a *no-contact control group.* The requirements for a no-contact group are difficult to meet because the subjects do not receive treatment and *do not realize that they are serving in this capacity.* To obtain such a group of subjects, pretest information usually is needed for a large pool of subjects who are part of a larger assessment project. Some of these subjects, determined randomly, are selected for the no-contact group. To obtain the initial pretest information requires that assessment devices be administered under some other guise (e.g., part of routine class activities in an undergraduate course). Also, obtaining subsequent test information must be conveyed as part of a routine activity so it is not associated with a treatment project.

It is worth illustrating this group briefly even though it is used relatively infrequently. As a classic example, Paul (1966) treated college students for speech anxiety and utilized several students who qualified for treatment as no-contact control subjects. Measures were administered under the guise of requirements for and a follow-up to ordinary college speech classes. No-treatment subjects, also a separate group in the study, received several assessment devices as part of the study, telephone contact and interviews, and other procedures related to the treatment project. A no-contact group received none of these and had no basis to infer that they were involved in a treatment study. Because the assessment before and after treatment was related to participation in the course, data were available without revealing use of the information as part of a treatment study. At the end, comparisons could be made assessing the effect of receiving contact with the program versus no contact. Among subjects who did not receive treatment, those who had no explicit contact with the study (no-contact control subjects) performed less well on various measures of anxiety and personality at the end of the study and at follow-up than those subjects who did. Thus serving as a no-treatment subject explicitly connected with the study was associated with some improvements that may not otherwise have been obtained.

Special Considerations

For research in clinic settings, a captive group of subjects analogous to college students is usually unavailable. In addition, administering measures under a guise other than treatment is likely to violate both the letter and spirit of current informed consent requirements for subjects who participate in research. Studies in institutional settings such as psychiatric hospitals, prisons, and schools might permit no-contact control groups. Assessment devices could be administered routinely on separate occasions and be used to provide data for comparisons with subsamples who serve in the study. However, use of data as part of research requires informing subjects and obtaining consent. Thus subjects may know they are serving in a study.

The main issue is not in whether a no-contact group could be formed but rather in the question that is being addressed. In most studies the investigator is not likely to be concerned with separating the effects of contact with the treatment or research project from no-contact; a no-treatment or waiting-list control group is likely to serve as the appropriate measure of improvement against which the effects of treatment can be evaluated. On the other hand, it might be important for conceptual reasons to evaluate whether serving in a project, even as a no-treatment subject, influences a particular set of measures or clinical problem.

An investigator may also wish to use no-contact procedures to avoid the influences associated with knowing that one is participating in an experiment. For example, in one program, over 500 7th graders from 10 different schools were included in a study to control classroom discipline (Matthews, 1986). Children within each school were assigned randomly to experimental or control conditions. Teachers in the experimental condition were trained to conduct relaxation exercises in their classes, which they did on a daily basis for approximately 7 months. The objective was to calm the children and to develop a means for coping with tension. Control children did not receive the special program. Neither teachers nor students were aware that they were participating in a study; the intervention was provided as part of the curriculum for some students in their homerooms. The dependent measure consisted of discipline infractions at the school (e.g., fighting, cutting class), information which was collected routinely and not associated specifically with this study. The results indicated that experimental youth, when compared with control students, showed significantly fewer discipline infractions. The fact that persons in experimental and control group(s) were uninformed about their participation minimizes the impact of potential threats to validity (e.g., special treatment or reactions of the control group, reactivity of the experimental arrangements, reactivity of assessment). In this study the no-contact feature applied to both intervention and control conditions. In general, no-contact procedures or control groups may be useful to address the impact of serving in a study or to eliminate the potential reactivity of such an arrangement. Counsel is required to ensure that subject rights are protected and that the study meets ethical requirements of informed consent (elaborated in chapter 14).

Nonspecific Treatment or "Attention-Placebo" Control Group

Rationale and Description

No-treatment and waiting-list control groups are employed primarily to address threats to internal validity. In the context of treatment research, a nonspecific treatment control group addresses these threats but focuses as well on threats to construct validity. In any treatment there are many seeming accoutrements that may contribute to or be solely responsible for therapeutic change. Such factors as attending treatment sessions, having personal contact with a therapist, hearing a logical rationale that describes the genesis of one's problem, and undergoing a procedure directed toward ameliorating the problem may exert influence on client performance and generate their own therapeutic effects. When a client participates in treatment, he or she is likely to believe in the procedures and have faith that some therapeutic change will result (Frank, 1973). Studies of medical treatments have shown that inert substances given under the guise of treatment *(placebos)* can alter a variety of disorders ranging in severity from the common cold to malignancy (Shapiro

& Morris, 1978). Placebo effects, by definition, result from factors other than active ingredients in the substance (e.g., sugar tablets) itself. Hence the belief of the patient in treatment and perhaps the belief in the physician who administers treatment and similar factors appear to be responsible for change.

Effects analogous to placebo reactions influence individuals who come to psychotherapy (see White et al., 1985). Indeed, the history of psychological treatments can be traced by drawing attention to procedures that produce change primarily through suggestion (Frank, 1973). From the standpoint of evaluating treatment, a specific control procedure may be used to exclude these nonspecific factors not necessarily peculiar to any particular treatment.

A simple comparison of treatment and no-treatment control groups does not establish what facet of "the intervention" led to change, that is, construct validity. To identify if the specific intervention or the unique properties of a treatment are important in producing change in the clients, a nonspecific treatment group can be included in the design. For example, a group may be included in which clients meet with a therapist, hear a rationale that explains how their problem may have developed, and discuss something about their lives in further sessions that are similar in number and duration to those in the treatment group. From the standpoint of the investigation, these subjects are considered to be receiving a psychological placebo, as it were. This is some procedure that might be credible to the clients and appear to be effective but is not based on theoretical or empirical findings about therapeutic change.

There are limits to what nonspecific control conditions provide. Consider as a hypothetical study in which a particular treatment technique (e.g., cognitive therapy) is compared to a nonspecific treatment group for depressed clients. Assume that subjects in the cognitive therapy receive a treatment that focuses on their beliefs, self-statements, and other cognitions that are considered to be responsible for their depression. Subjects in the nonspecific treatment control condition might meet with the therapist for the same number of sessions. Perhaps these subjects would talk about work or school in their present life. Therapists for this condition would be informed to avoid all discussion of depression, cognitive processes, psychological events and relations in the past, and other potentially emotionally laden or seemingly significant material. At the end of the study, suppose we find that cognitive therapy was significantly superior to the nonspecific treatment control condition on a variety of measures of depression and adjustment.

Have we established that treatment (cognitive therapy) works for the reason (construct) we propose, that is, dealing with critical cognitive processes? The comparison group and findings reduce the plausibility that coming to sessions, meeting with a mental health professional, and so on is the basis for change. Focusing on cognitive processes in treatment seems to add a significant increment in effectiveness over and above a nonspecific control condition. However, we might wish to see further studies to isolate the factors responsible for the effects of cognitive therapy. It is possible that talking about or focusing on depression, even if cognitive processes were ignored, would produce the same amount of change as the cognitive therapy condition. Tests with alternative control conditions may help cognitive therapy retain the explanatory edge over other constructs that might explain the finding. Further research and further comparison groups that address the critical part of the ingredients of cognitive therapy may be needed to explain why cognitive therapy works. The nonspecific treatment control group helps as a critical beginning by making implausible the effects of merely attending treatment.

Special Considerations

There are several issues that emerge in developing a nonspecific treatment control condition. To begin, the conceptual problems are not minor. Although the notion of a placebo illustrates the type of effect obtained in psychotherapy, the parallel of medical and psychological treatments is not entirely appropriate. A placebo in medicine is known in advance, because of its pharmacological properties (e.g., salt or sugar in a tablet), not to produce the desired effects. In psychological treatment, one usually does not know in advance that the properties of the nonspecific treatment group are inert. For example, merely chatting with a therapist, engaging in some activities that are related to one's problem, merely relaxing with a therapist all might be cast in theoretical language to make them seem plausible as genuine treatments. This is why in the therapy research business, one investigator's treatment group is another investigator's control group. For example, client-centered and relationship-based treatments have been used as veridical and primary treatments in some studies and as "attention-placebo" control conditions in others. It is difficult to devise an intervention that is at once credible to the clients and yet also is one that could not be construed by someone as a theoretically plausible treatment.

Another issue that emerges pertains to the credibility of the procedure. One ingredient in therapy is the client's beliefs that treatment will work. Presumably a plausible nonspecific treatment control group would have this ingredient as well so that client belief is not the construct that can explain the results. However, devising a credible control condition requires a rationale about why this "treatment" is likely to be effective and why procedures in or outside of the treatment sessions look like credible means toward therapeutic change. There is some evidence to suggest that highly credible control conditions are often as effective as treatment conditions (Kazdin & Wilcoxon, 1976). This has implications for conducting experiments (larger sample sizes are needed to detect small group differences) and for their interpretation (isolating the construct that accounts for change).

Ethical issues also emerge in providing nonspecific treatment conditions.

This issue is not merely one of providing a treatment that may not be well based on theory or empirical findings. As with other control conditions, if clients are in need of care, this type of group may not be defensible. There is a more subtle ethical issue. Participation in the present control condition might influence beliefs about therapy in general and have impact on clients' subsequent use of treatment. If clients learn that treatment is not very credible, does not help, or does not focus on their problems, this might remove a possible resource from them in their future. Conceivably, ordinary therapy might teach a given client such lessons; using a control condition without a veridical treatment merely increases the likelihood of such an effect.

Yoked Control Group

Rationale and Description

In many studies, select differences in procedures or events to which the subjects are exposed may arise during the investigation. Differences may develop as a function of executing the study or implementing a particular intervention. The problem with these differences is that they are not random but may vary systematically between groups. If the effect of the intervention is to be distinguished from these differences that inadvertently arise across groups, the latter influences must be controlled.

One procedure to rule out or assess factors that may arise as a function of implementing a particular intervention is called the *yoked control group*. The purpose of the yoked control group is to ensure that groups are equal with respect to potentially important but conceptually and procedurally irrelevant factors that might account for group differences (Church, 1964). Yoking may require a special control group of its own. More likely in clinical research, yoking can be incorporated into another control group. In this case, yoking refers to equalizing the groups on a particular variable that might systematically vary across conditions.

Yoking is used relatively infrequently, so it may be especially useful to consider an example in which it might be applied. Consider a hypothetical study designed to evaluate a specific therapy technique for the treatment of acrophobia (fear of heights). Three groups are used, including (a) the "new and improved" treatment, (b) a nonspecific treatment control group that meets with a therapist but engages in a task not likely to be therapeutic (e.g., discussing the development of fears among people they know), and (c) no treatment. Suppose that clients in the treatment group are allowed to attend as many sessions as needed to master a set of tasks designated as therapeutic. For example, clients might have to complete a standard set of anxiety-provoking tasks in therapy to help them overcome anxiety. The number of sessions that clients attend treatment could vary markedly given individual differences in the rate of completing the tasks. A nonspecific treatment control group might receive a bogus treatment in which group members merely come in and discuss fears of their friends and relatives. One might raise the question of how many sessions the control group subjects should receive. It would be important to design the study so that any differences in effects of treatment cannot be due to the different number of sessions that the various groups received. Yet the control subjects should not simply be given a fixed number of sessions because that would not guarantee equality of sessions across groups.

A solution is to yoke (match) subjects across groups by pairing subjects. The pairs might be formed arbitrarily unless matching was used to assign subjects to groups. A subject in the experimental group would receive a certain number of therapy sessions on the basis of his or her progress. Whatever that number turned out to be would be the number of sessions that would be given to the control subject to whom he or she was yoked. That is, the number of sessions for each control subject would be determined by the subject to whom he or she was paired or matched in the experimental group. Obviously, the yoking procedure requires running the experimental subject first so that the number of sessions or other variables on which yoking was made is known in advance and can be administered to the control subject. The behavior of the experimental subject determines what happens to the control subject. At the end of treatment, the number of treatment sessions will be identical across groups. Hence any group differences could not be attributable to the number of sessions to which clients were exposed.

The yoking might be extended to address the other group in the design, namely, the no-treatment control group. If pre- and posttreatment assessments are provided, how long should the interval between these assessments be for the group that does not receive any treatment? Subjects in the no-treatment group could also be yoked to people in the treatment group in terms of the number of weeks between pretreatment and posttreatment assessment. Thus at the end of the study, yoking would yield the following result. Both treatment and nonspecific control groups would have received the same number of sessions, and the time elapsed in weeks or days between pretreatment and posttreatment assessment would be the same for all treatment and control conditions. Stated in a more quantitative way, the means and standard deviations would not differ in relation to the number of sessions (for the two treatment groups) or the number of days or weeks between pre- and posttreatment for all groups. As evident from this example, the yoked control procedure may not necessarily constitute a "new" control group.

Special Considerations

Conceivably, an experimental and control group can be yoked on all sorts of variables that may differ between groups. Whether yoking is used as a control technique needs to be determined by considering on substantive grounds whether the variables that differ across these groups might plausibly account for the results. For example, in a given therapy study it might make sense to yoke on the number of treatment sessions, because the amount of contact with a therapist and treatment may contribute to the differences between a treatment and nonspecific treatment control group, particularly if therapy subjects receive many more sessions. Stated differently, it may be plausible that the number of sessions, rather than the content of the sessions, is viewed as a threat to construct validity. "The intervention" confounds content and amount of treatment and hence raises ambiguities about why the intervention was more effective. On the other hand, it may be unimportant to yoke subjects in such a way that the time of the day that therapy sessions are held or the attire of the therapists is perfectly matched across groups. The variables that serve as the basis of yoking are often based on considerations of construct validity, that is, what the investigator wishes to say about the treatment and what facets of treatment, if allowed to vary systematically, might plausibly account for the results. By yoking, the investigator controls those variables that potentially can confound the results.

Nonrandomly Assigned or "Patched-Up" Control Group

Rationale and Description

Many groups might be added to a between-group research design that utilizes subjects who were not part of the original subject pool and not randomly assigned to treatment. These groups are referred to as *patched-up control groups*. One use of nonrandomly assigned subjects is to help rule out specific threats to validity such as history, maturation, instrumentation, and so on. Such a group may be used when a no-treatment control group cannot be formed through random assignment. Although the purpose of this group is exactly that of the randomly assigned no-treatment group mentioned earlier, there may be special interpretive problems that arise because of the way in which the group is formed. The control groups in the nonequivalent control design discussed in the context of quasi-experiments constitute patched-up groups. These groups are useful in helping to rule out threats to internal validity, but they may be weak for comparative purposes depending on how they were formed.

As an example, Rogers and Dymond (1954) used a patched-up control group in their study that evaluated the effects of client-centered psychotherapy. Clients who applied for treatment at a university counseling center were assigned either to treatment (individual client-centered therapy) or waiting-list control conditions. Waiting-list control subjects waited for 60 days before they were reassessed and given treatment. This group, though similar to the treatment subjects in motivation for treatment and various personality factors, did not completely control for such threats to internal validity as history, maturation, and testing. The reason for this is that the interval between being assessed during the waiting period was shorter than the average interval that it took for therapy subjects to complete treatment. Technically, differences between these two groups might result from changes occurring over the different testing periods that elapsed, independently of treatment.

To help examine the plausibility of such threats to validity as history, maturation, and testing, the authors used a patched-up control. Specifically, volunteers were solicited for an experiment on personality. These subjects had not applied for treatment and hence were different from treatment and waiting-list subjects in that regard. Yet these patched-up control subjects were matched to subjects who applied for treatment in terms of sex, student–nonstudent status, approximate age, and socioeconomic status. One half of the patched-up control subjects were yoked to treatment subjects and the other half to control subjects in terms of the time that was allowed to elapse between testing periods. In other words, the patched-up group, although very different in subject composition, helped evaluate the effects of history, maturation, and testing on changes in the dependent measures. Moreover, this group assessed the influence of such threats over treatment and follow-up periods (6 to 12 months after treatment) by which time the waiting-list subjects had long since completed treatment. The patched-up control group was not comprised through random assignment among all subjects in the study and hence was not ideally comparable to the other groups. Yet the general failure of this group to show systematic improvements over the course of treatment helped to diminish the plausibility of various threats in accounting for the changes that occurred in the therapy group.

Special Considerations

Patched-up control groups can vary widely and have to be evaluated on their individual merit. Their purpose is to reduce the plausibility of alternative influences (internal validity or construct validity). Because the group is not comprised randomly, the data may not be as persuasive as parallel data resulting from a randomly comprised control or comparison group. Yet in any given case the absence of randomness may not be a fatal limitation. The question is whether some specific threat (e.g., Selection or History × Maturation) is as plausible as the interpretation the investigator wishes to place on the data. Although patched-up control groups are less than perfect control groups, they can serve to tip the balance of plausibility among alternative interpretations of the data.

Not all of the patched-up or nonrandomly assigned groups in clinical research address threats to internal validity. Groups might be added to provide useful information and to expand the conclusions that can be reached about the outcome. In treatment research, a valuable use of nonrandomly selected subjects is to compare the extent to which clients in the study are distinguished from their peers who have not been referred for treatment. By comparing individuals who have been identified as part of a treatment population with their peers who apparently are functioning with little or no problem, one can assess whether treatment has brought the clients within a normal range of behavior. The use of normative data to evaluate treatment is part of a larger area of evaluating the clinical importance of changes made in treatment (see chapter 12).

OTHER COMPARISON GROUPS

The notion of control groups is rudimentary. The familiar purpose of control groups is conveyed in a straightforward manner by discussing the no-treatment and waiting-list groups in which the threats to internal validity are controlled. A more in-depth understanding of research design might be pursued by discussing the broader concept of *comparison groups.*

Comparison groups refer to any group included in the design beyond the primary group or groups of interest. Comparison groups permit the investigator to draw various conclusions; alternative groups vary in the types of conclusions they permit. Control groups are merely one type of comparison group. Some control groups (e.g., no treatment, waiting list) primarily address the threats to internal validity; other types of control groups (e.g., nonspecific treatment) also address concerns of construct validity in the sense that they aid in interpreting the basis for the impact of the intervention. The investigator may wish to make any number of statements about the intervention and what accounted for the change. Because the range of possible conclusions varies widely with content area and investigator interest, all comparison groups of interest cannot be catalogued. Nevertheless, comparison groups often used in clinical research can be identified and illustrated.

Routine or Standard Treatment

In clinical research, assigning individuals to the usual control conditions may not be possible, feasible, or ethically defensible. The settings in which clients present themselves, the reasons for their referral, and the implicit contract that this entails may demand that the usual control conditions are unavailable. For example, in a clinic setting persons may seek treatment because of grief or are referred by the courts for physical, sexual, or spouse abuse. Obviously, no-treatment, waiting-list, and nonspecific-treatment control conditions, in most situations, would not be feasible.

In such circumstances, the investigator may wish to test whether a new treatment is effective. One alternative is to compare the new treatment with the standard one that is provided in the setting. The question of interest is whether the new treatment is effective with a particular clinical problem. The research question may be important to address with the sample of interest and in the setting, even though the full range of control group options are not available.

A reasonable compromise might be to compare the new treatment with the standard treatment that is usually provided. The advantage of this procedure is that all individuals will receive an active treatment. Thus demands for service and ethical obligations might well be met. At the same time, the new treatment can be provided and evaluated as a viable alternative. In such a study, the new treatment and standard treatment are compared. With random assignment of cases to groups and consistency in the assessment procedures, threats to internal validity can be ruled out as accounting for the results. Here a standard or routine treatment is used as a comparison to evaluate the intervention of interest.

The use of standard treatment as a comparison condition has obvious benefits. The "usual treatment" is ethically defensible in research, and hence its use attenuates concerns that arise in control conditions that withhold treatment. Also, all participants in a study receive treatment. Subjects in the standard treatment group presumably are subject to the nonspecific or generic factors that are provided in treatment. In addition, attrition that is jeopardized by no-treatment or less than credulous attention-placebo treatment conditions is less likely.

Standard and routine treatments or programs raise their own dilemmas. It is often difficult to know what these treatments actually entail at the clinic, hospital, or school, no matter what the descriptions and brochures actually say. The investigator ought to monitor and assess carefully what is carried out as part of routine treatment. If possible, it is better from the standpoint of the design for the investigator to administer the condition so that integrity of the procedure and assessment before, during, and after treatment can be closely monitored.

Other Active Treatments

The investigator may wish to compare the treatment of interest to another treatment. In a simple version of such a study, there is no "control" group in the usual sense. Assuming random assignment, the comparison group addresses the usual threats to internal validity (e.g., history, maturation). The comparison group in such studies may consist of active treatment conditions that are selected to permit specific substantive conclusions to be drawn.

For example, in one study, the investigators wished to see if combining two separate treatments led to greater therapeutic change than did the individual treatments presented separately (Horn, Ialongo, Popovich, & Peradotto, 1987). Specifically, hyperactive children were identified and assigned to one of three conditions: behavioral parent training, in which the parents were trained in social learning principles, self-control training, in which the children received problem-solving skills training to help them gain self-control, and both procedures combined. At posttreatment and 1-month follow-up, all three groups had improved. The combined groups did not produce greater change than did the other conditions. Thus the authors' question was addressed without the use of a control group.

Because cases were randomly assigned to groups and families completed the assessments at pre, post, and follow-up, the threats to internal validity were addressed. On the other hand, we do not know why change occurred. The absence of a no-treatment, waiting-list control group, or attention-placebo group makes interpretation of the reason for change somewhat difficult. This might be used as a basis to criticize the study. However, these questions extend beyond the investigators' purpose. The absence of a control group seems reasonable in the case of this study given the specific question and comparisons of interest. (A greater problem that we shall not elaborate here is one of statistical conclusion validity. The study included small sample sizes [6–7 cases per group], which provides a statistically weak test of the hypotheses [see chapter 12].)

Intact Groups in Subject-Selection Studies

Research in clinical psychology often involves passive-observational studies where subjects are selected because of special characteristics (e.g., patients with a particular diagnosis, the elderly, abused children). The purpose is to understand or describe unique features of the population along some dimensions of interest. As such, one or more comparison groups may be included. The investigator is concerned with attributing group differences to a particular construct. Thus the comparison groups are selected to be similar to the group of interest in subject, demographic, and other variables that may serve as competing explanations of the findings.

For example, the goal of one study was to identify whether mothers of children who were diagnosed with an anxiety disorder were likely to suffer from anxiety disorders themselves (Last, Hersen, Kazdin, Francis, & Grubb, 1987). The focus was important because of the paucity of research on the question of familial ties in anxiety disorders between parent and child. To that end, the primary group of interest was the mothers of children who received diagnoses of anxiety disorder. Mothers of these children were assessed to see if in the course of their lives or at the time of assessment they met psychiatric diagnostic criteria for an anxiety disorder, as assessed by persons unaware of the childrens' diagnoses. The results for this group by themselves would not be very informative because mothers of any child patient group might have a history of various disorders including anxiety.

A comparison group was added which consisted of youth who came to the same clinical facility and who met criteria for some other diagnosis than anxiety disorder. The comparison group included cases with diagnoses of attention deficit disorder (hyperactivity), conduct disorder, and oppositional disorder. The mothers of these children were assessed. The purpose of adding this comparison group was to see if mothers of anxious children were more likely to meet criteria for anxiety disorder than were "similar" mothers of nonanxious but clinically disturbed children. The comparison group permitted the authors to focus on whether any association between parent and child disorder is associated with child dysfunction or specifically with anxiety. Interestingly, 83% of the mothers of anxious youth had a history of anxiety disorders, whereas only 40% of the mothers of children without this diagnosis showed this history. The comparison group was obviously important because the rate of anxiety disorders in parents of children with other disorders was relatively high. From this study we know that mothers of anxiety disorder patients themselves are likely to have a history of anxiety disorder. The comparison group shows that the preponderance is not due merely to being a mother of a child with any diagnosis.

In studies evaluating the characteristics of intact groups, the usual goal is to identify the primary group of interest and then a comparison group that is similar on other variables that could possibly interfere with inferring the basis of group differences. Ideally, one would identify groups that differed only in the characteristic of interest but were identical on subject, demographic, and other variables irrelevant to the construct. Even so, it is possible in theory and practice that the groups differed in some characteristic not measured. This is one reason why research based on selection and comparison of intact groups is often regarded as more ambiguous in the conclusions that can be drawn in comparison to experiments in which some condition or intervention is manipulated experimentally. Nevertheless, critical questions in clinical psychology demand the study of intact groups. For example, we wish to know the following differences: between depressed and nondepressed patients; among parents who physically abuse, versus those who neglect their children, versus those who do neither; and between those children who are exposed to untoward family lives but who function well as adults versus those who suffer impairment. Evaluation of the characteristics of special groups or of those exposed to special environments are pivotal for theoretical understanding of human experience as well as for clinical work (e.g., diagnosis, treatment, and prevention). Designing such studies to obtain comparison groups to isolate the construct of interest (e.g., depression) is essential.

SELECTING CONTROL AND COMPARISON GROUPS

The previous discussion describes control and comparison groups that are likely to be of use in clinical research. It is tempting to provide rules or guidelines for selecting a particular group in certain kinds of situations but not in others. Yet the precise groups that should be used in clinical research depend on at least three considerations: the interests of the investigator, previous research findings, and practical and ethical constraints.

The interests of the investigator refer to the claims that he or she would like to make at the end of the experiment. The interests embrace internal and construct validity. The investigator wishes to rule out the usual threats and at the same time to say something about why the effect was obtained. Addressing internal validity is relatively straightforward; addressing construct validity is more intricate because it depends on the investigator's view of what is critical to the intervention and the specificity of the desired conclusions.

The same collection of groups would require different controls depending upon what the investigator wishes to conclude when the study is completed. For example, consider a study that compared client-centered and cognitive therapy. If the investigator were only interested in discussing which of two treatments is better for a particular disorder, this design without any of the familiar groups mentioned earlier would be adequate. On the other hand, another investigator may be interested in asking whether either one of these treatments exerts therapeutic effects beyond those that can be accounted for by nonspecific treatment effects. In this case, a control group that provided a nonspecific treatment "experience" would be critical. Thus if these client-centered and cognitive treatments were equally effective, one could compare these groups to a nonspecific treatment condition to determine whether the treatment effects were likely to be the result of attending treatment per se. The latter design, with its addition of a nonspecific treatment control group, is not necessarily superior to the previous one in which only the two treatment groups were included. The issue of superiority of one design over another is not measured by how many control groups there are but whether the question of interest to the investigator is adequately addressed. Both of the above experiments appear to address their respective questions adequately.

One could take a broader view of experimentation and note that the reader or consumer of research may wish to draw more inferences from an experiment than did the investigator, in which case an extra control group here and there might be useful. However, the main purpose of a given study should be to deploy resources to provide the best test of a limited question, rather than to try to control for or anticipate all of the questions that might be asked, even though they were not of direct interest.

There are no rules for deciding specifically what control groups to include, and investigators probably proceed in different ways to reach the final decisions. In my own research, it has been useful to ponder the anticipated patterns of results in order to decide some of the groups that might be included. Specifically, this procedure involves plotting possible variations of results (e.g., differences between or among groups) that might come from the study while the study is still in the design stage. Initially, the "ideal" or expected results with respect to a particular hypothesis and prediction, if they can be specified, might be diagrammed; then more likely data patterns are considered. As variations of possible results are considered, the following question can be asked: What alternative interpretations can account for this pattern of results? The answer to that question is likely to lead to changes in the experimental groups or addition of control groups to narrow the alternative interpretations that can be provided. Permutations of likely patterns or results and critical evaluation of rival interpretations of the findings are useful in generating additional comparison groups that are needed in a given study or bolstering the design by increasing the sample, to ensure a strong test of the major comparisons of interest.

Previous research also may dictate the essential control groups for a given investigation. For example, in the study of a particular treatment, it is not always necessary to use a no-treatment or waiting-list control group. If there are consistent data that the absence of treatment has no effect, at least on the dependent measures of interest, these groups might be omitted. Of course, to justify exclusion of a no-treatment group, one would want convincing data about the likely changes over time without treatment. Relying on data from studies completed by other investigators at different research facilities might not provide an adequate basis to exclude a no-treatment group unless there is consensus that the problem is immutable without treatment. For example, "depressed clients" in one investigator's research may vary markedly from the "same" sample at another facility because of the different measures used in screening and the different locales. On the other hand, within a research program, continued studies may reveal that no treatment leads to no change in the clients. In such a case, omitting a no-treatment group after several studies have been completed is somewhat more justifiable.

There is another way to view the elimination of particular groups such as no-treatment groups as a program of research progresses. As investigations build upon one another, the research questions become increasingly refined, and there may be no need for some of the control groups used early in the research. Again, it is difficult to be specific about when various groups can be abandoned; however, as noted earlier, experimental demonstrations vary in their persuasiveness to the scientific community depending on a host of factors. Hence, when in doubt it is probably advisable to include a control group to augment the persuasiveness of the experimental test.

As a final consideration, the selection of control groups is limited greatly by practical and ethical constraints. Practical issues such as procuring enough subjects with similar treatment problems, losing subjects assigned to control conditions for a protracted period, and related obstacles mentioned earlier may dictate the types of groups that can be used. Ethical constraints such as withholding treatment, delivering treatments that might not help or might even exacerbate the client's problem, deception about ineffective treatments, and similar issues also limit what can be done clinically. In the context of clinical samples, both practical and ethical issues may make it impossible to perform the comparisons that might be of greatest interest on theoretical grounds.

PROGRESSION OF CONTROL AND COMPARISON GROUPS

The use of alternative control and comparison groups isolated from an area of research is somewhat abstract. Also, the discussion does not convey the progression of research that can be measured in the level of sophistication of the questions that are asked and the complexity of the conditions to which an experimental group is compared. Psychotherapy research usefully illustrates the progression of research and the role of alternative control and comparison groups.

Evaluating Psychotherapy

A major task of psychotherapy research is to identify effective treatments, to understand the underlying bases of therapeutic change, and to elaborate those client, therapist, and other factors on which treatment effects depend (Gold-fried, Greenberg, & Marmar, 1990; Kiesler, 1971). At the general level, the tasks to which research is devoted have been cast as a question, namely, *"What* treatment, by *whom,* is most effective for *this* individual with *that* specific problem, under *which* set of circumstances?" (Paul, 1967, p. 111). This broad objective can be translated into several more specific strategies that can guide individual studies. Table 6.1 presents major strategies and the questions they are designed to address.

Treatment Package Strategy

Perhaps the most basic question is to ask whether a particular treatment or treatment package is effective for a particular clinical problem. This question is asked by the treatment package strategy that evaluates the effects of a particular treatment as that treatment is ordinarily used. The notion of a

Table 6.1. Alternative Treatment Evaluation Strategies to Develop and to Identify Effective Interventions

TREATMENT STRATEGY	QUESTION ASKED	BASIC REQUIREMENTS
Treatment Package	Does treatment produce therapeutic change?	Treatment vs. no treatment or waiting-list control
Dismantling Strategy	What components are necessary, sufficient, and facilitative of therapeutic change?	Two or more treatment groups that vary in the components of treatment that are provided
Constructive Strategy	What components or other treatments can be added to enhance therapeutic change?	Two or more treatment groups that vary in components
Parametric Strategy	What changes can be made in the specific treatment to increase its effectiveness?	Two or more treatment groups that differ in one or more facets of the treatment
Comparative Outcome Strategy	Which treatment is the more or most effective for a particular problem and population?	Two or more different treatments for a given clinical problem
Client and Therapist Variation Strategy	What patient, family, or therapist characteristics does treatment depend on for it to be effective?	Treatment as applied separately to different types of cases, therapists, and so on
Process Strategy	What processes occur in treatment that affect within-session performance and that may contribute to treatment outcome?	Treatment groups in which patient and therapist interactions are evaluated within the sessions

"package" emphasizes that treatment may be multifaceted and include several different components that could be delineated conceptually and operationally. The question addressed by this strategy is whether treatment produces therapeutic change. To rule out threats to internal validity, a no-treatment or waiting-list control condition is usually included in the design.

Strictly speaking, evaluation of a treatment package only requires two groups, namely, one which receives the intervention and the other which does not. Random assignment of cases to groups and testing each group before and after treatment controls the usual threats to internal validity. However, there has been considerable debate about the impact of nonspecific treatment factors and the effects they can exert on clinical dysfunction (e.g., Horvath, 1988). Consequently, treatment package research is likely to include a group that serves as a nonspecific treatment control condition that requires clients to come to the treatment and receive some "control" type of active experience.

As an example, Longo, Clum, and Yeager (1988) evaluated a multifaceted psychosocial treatment package for adults with recurrent genital herpes.

Herpes is a sexually transmitted viral disease with no known cure. Psychological treatment was considered to be appropriate because episodes of the disease are associated with and apparently fostered by stress and the experience of emotional distress. Individuals with recurrent herpes were assigned randomly to one of three groups. The psychosocial intervention package consisted of group meetings that provided training in stress management, relaxation, imagery, and planned exercises in these areas outside of the group treatment sessions. A second group was included in the design as a nonspecific treatment control condition. Individuals also attended group treatment sessions; instead of specific training experiences, persons in this group discussed interpersonal conflicts. This intervention was not considered by the investigators to be a procedure likely to effect change. A final group consisted of a waiting-list (no-treatment) control condition.

The results indicated that episodes of herpes were fewer, less severe, and of a shorter duration for cases who received the intervention package, relative to each of the other groups. A similar pattern favoring the intervention group was evident for measures of depression, stress, and emotional distress. These results suggest that the package produces greater change than did the passage of time and attending sessions that resemble treatment. Of course, the particular component(s) of the package that was responsible for change cannot be determined from the study. However, this is not a criticism, given the goal of evaluating the impact of the overall package. The study conveys the treatment package strategy well because of the specific comparisons included in the design and the conclusions they permit.

Dismantling Treatment Strategy

The dismantling treatment strategy consists of analyzing the components of a given treatment package. After a particular package has been shown to produce therapeutic change, research can begin to analyze the basis for change. To dismantle a treatment, individual components are eliminated or isolated from the treatment. Some clients may receive the entire treatment package, whereas other clients receive the package minus one or more components. Dismantling research can help identify the necessary and sufficient components of treatment.

As an illustration, Nezu and Perri (1989) evaluated social problem-solving therapy for the treatment of depressed adults. The problem-solving treatment included the following separate components: (a) a problem-solving orientation process that pertains to how individuals respond when presented with a problem or stressful situation, and (b) a set of skills or goal-directed tasks that enables people to solve a potential problem successfully. The investigators evaluated whether the full package of training was superior to an abbreviated version in which only the skills component was provided. Clients were assigned to one of two groups to receive either the full treatment or the skills component only. A waiting-list control group was included in the design. At posttreatment and at 6-month follow-up, clients who received the full package (orientation and skills training) were less depressed than were those who received the abbreviated treatment (skills training). The authors suggested that the orientation component provided a critical aspect of the treatment. The findings suggest that the package offers more than skills training alone. Of course, the effects of orientation process alone in relation to the overall package was not studied. For present purposes, it is important to note that the specific question about treatment led to a comparison group that itself was a veridical treatment.

Constructive Treatment Strategy

The constructive treatment strategy refers to developing a treatment package by adding components to enhance outcome. In this sense, the constructive treatment approach is the opposite of the dismantling strategy. A constructive treatment study begins with a treatment that may consist of one or a few ingredients or a larger package. To that are added various ingredients to determine whether the effects can be enhanced. The strategy asks the question, "What can be added to treatment to make it more effective?" A special feature of this strategy is the combination of individual treatments. Thus studies may combine conceptually quite different treatments such as verbal psychotherapy and pharmacotherapy.

An illustration of the constructive strategy was provided by Alden (1989) who evaluated treatments for adults with avoidant personality disorder, a syndrome that consists of long-standing patterns of social withdrawal, sensitivity to social criticism, and low self-esteem. The study examined the incremental value of two treatments. The first treatment was social skills training, which develops specific social interaction skills. The second treatment was graduated exposure designed to assist in the management of anxiety by developing the use of relaxation skills and practicing exposure to interpersonal situations in a gradual fashion. Clients were assigned to either a social skills group, a graduated exposure group, or a combination of the two. A no-treatment control group was also included.

After 10 weeks of treatment, clients in the treated groups showed greater improvement on a variety of measures of social anxiety and functioning. The three treatments were no different from each other at posttreatment or at a 3-month follow-up. These results suggest that the components are largely equivalent and do not enhance treatment when combined. The combined treatment did not improve on the effects of the constituent treatments. For present purposes, it is important to note that the study compared three active treatment conditions. Each represents a special variation of treatment to address the question of interest.

Parametric Treatment Strategy

The parametric treatment strategy refers to altering specific aspects of treatment to determine how to maximize therapeutic change. Dimensions or parameters are altered to find the optimal manner of administering the treatment. These dimensions are not new ingredients added to the treatment (e.g., as in the constructive strategy) but variations within the technique to maximize change. Increases in duration of treatment or variations in how material is presented are samples of the parametric strategy.

A basic parameter of treatment is duration. More treatment may not invariably lead to greater outcome (see Howard, Kopta, Krause, & Orlinsky, 1986). Yet in cases in which treatment is only mildly effective or where effects are evident but short-lived, duration or dose of treatment is a reasonable parameter to investigate. With this rationale in mind, Perri, Nezu, Patti, and McCann (1989) evaluated the effectiveness of behavior therapy in the treatment of obesity. Two versions of treatment were provided that varied in the number of weekly sessions (20 vs. 40). Both conditions included several components such as training in self-monitoring, stimulus control, self-reinforcement, cognitive modification, problem solving, and exercise, clearly a multifaceted package. At the end of 40 weeks, the group that had received the longer duration of treatment showed greater weight loss. The superiority of the former group was evident at a follow-up approximately 8 months later. The results indicate that duration of treatment was an important parameter that contributed to outcome. From the standpoint of control and comparison groups, the critical comparison was between two versions of treatment.

Comparative Treatment Strategy

The comparative treatment strategy contrasts two or more treatments and addresses the question of which treatment is better (best) for a particular clinical problem. Comparative studies attract wide attention not only because they address an important clinical issue but also because they often contrast conceptually competing interventions (e.g., Heimberg & Becker, 1984; Kazdin, 1986a).

As an illustration, Szapocznik et al. (1989) compared structural family therapy and psychodynamic therapy to treat Hispanic boys (6–12 years old) referred for a variety of different problems (e.g., conduct disorder, anxiety disorder, adjustment disorders). In the family therapy condition, families were seen. Treatment emphasized modifying maladaptive interactional patterns among family members. Psychodynamic therapy consisted of individual therapy with the child. Treatment focused on play, expression of feelings, transference interpretations, and insight. Diverse outcome measures were included to reflect changes unique to the individual treatments. In general, the results indicated that both groups attained equivalent reductions in behavioral and emotional problems at posttreatment. Both groups were better at posttreatment than was a nonspecific treatment control condition in which recreational activities were provided. Family therapy was superior to psychodynamic therapy on a measure of family functioning at a 1-year follow-up. However, there generally were no differences in child dysfunction at posttreatment and follow-up between treatment conditions. The use of a control group in this study was very helpful. If the two treatment groups were equally effective without this control, one could not separate whether the differences were due to nonspecific treatment influences such as attending sessions. The control group suggests that such minimal experiences did not lead to the types of changes associated with treatment.

Client and Therapist Variation Strategy

The previous strategies emphasize the technique as a major source of influence in treatment outcome. The effectiveness of treatments can vary widely as a function of characteristics of the patients and the therapists. The client and therapist variation strategy examines whether alternative attributes of the client or therapist contribute to treatment outcome. The strategy is implemented by selecting clients and/or therapists on the basis of specific characteristics. When clients or therapists are classified according to a particular selection variable, the question is whether treatment is more or less effective with certain kinds of participants. For example, questions regarding this strategy might ask if treatment is more effective with younger versus older clients, or with certain subtypes of problems (e.g., of depression) rather than with other subtypes.

An example of a client variation study was reported in the treatment of alcoholic patients (Kadden, Cooney, Getter, & Litt, 1989). The investigators evaluated two treatments: coping skills training and interactional group therapy. Three subject variables were investigated including sociopathy, overall psychopathology, and neuropsychological impairment, each of which has prognostic significance in relation to alcoholism. The authors reasoned that higher functioning patients (low on the three subject variables) would benefit from interactional experiences. Patients with greater impairment and relatively poorer prognosis would profit more from coping skills training that emphasized relapse prevention. In general, the findings indicated that patient characteristics interacted with type of treatment in outcome results, as reflected in days of drinking during the 6 months of treatment. Interaction-based treatment was more effective with higher functioning patients; coping skills was more effective for patients higher in sociopathy and psychopathology.

The type of research illustrated by this example is more sophisticated in the sense of the type of predictions that are made. Different types of variables (treatment, subject) are combined. Although the usual control conditions might be used, the question focuses on comparison groups that are composed of combinations of treatment and subject characteristics. Work of this ilk typically follows development of a technique to the point that it is known to be effective.

Process Research Strategy

The previously noted strategies emphasize outcome questions or the impact of variations of the intervention on clients at the end of or subsequent to treatment. The process research strategy addresses questions pertaining to the mechanisms of change of therapy by addressing manifold concerns of what transpires between the delivery of an intervention and the ultimate impact on the client. Topics may focus on the transactions between therapist and client and the impact of intervening events on the moment to moment or interim changes during treatment. Many issues address questions of process including the sequence, stages, and progression of client or therapist affect, behavior, and cognition over the course of treatment or within individual sessions.

As an illustration, Rounsaville et al. (1986) examined the relation of alternative therapy processes in predicting outcome for the treatment of depression. Patients (N = 35) received interpersonal psychotherapy for depression. Therapists (N = 11) who provided treatment were evaluated by their supervisors after observing tapes of several therapy sessions. Processes rated by the supervisors included therapist (exploration, warmth and friendliness, and negative attitude) and patient factors (participation, exploration, hostility, psychic distress), as measured by the Vanderbilt Psychotherapy Process Scale. Treatment outcome was assessed with measures of psychiatric symptoms, social functioning, and patient-evaluated change.

The results indicated that only one patient factor (hostility) was related to outcome on a measure of change completed by the patients. In contrast, therapist factors were much more strongly related to outcome. Therapist exploration was significantly and positively related to reductions in clinician evaluations of depression and patient-rated improvements. Therapist warmth and friendliness correlated significantly with improved social functioning and parent-rated improvements. These results convey the importance of specific therapist relationship characteristics in relation to treatment outcome.

In this study, none of the familiar control or comparison groups was used. The purpose was to correlate specific processes with specific outcomes within a particular technique. Here too this level of questioning is based on prior studies demonstrating that the treatment is effective when compared to alternative control conditions. After such demonstrations it becomes meaningful to ask about the factors that contribute to change.

General Comments

The strategies noted previously reflect questions frequently addressed in current treatment research. The questions posed by the strategies reflect a range of issues required to understand fully how a technique operates and can be applied to achieve optimal effects. The treatment package strategy is an initial approach followed by the various analytic strategies based on dismantling, constructive, and parametric research. The comparative strategy probably warrants attention after prior work has been conducted that not only indicates the efficacy of individual techniques but also shows how the techniques can be administered to increase their efficacy. Frequently, comparative studies are conducted early in the development of a treatment and possibly before the individual techniques have been well developed to warrant such a test. A high degree of operationalization is needed to investigate dismantling, constructive, and parametric questions. In each case, specific components or ingredients of therapy have to be sufficiently well specified to be withdrawn, added, or varied in an overall treatment package.

The progression requires a broad range of comparison groups that vary critical facets of treatment. The usual control conditions (no-treatment, attention–placebo control) may continue to play a role. However, the interest in evaluating change over time without treatment or factors common to treatment gives way to more pointed questions about specific facets of treatment that account for or contribute to change. Comparison groups are aimed to provide increasingly specific statements related to construct validity, that is, what aspects of the intervention account for the findings.

SUMMARY AND CONCLUSIONS

Control groups rule out or weaken rival hypotheses or alternative explanations of results. The control group appropriate for an experiment depends on precisely what the investigator is interested in concluding at the end of the investigation. Hence all, or even most, of the available control groups cannot be specified in an abstract discussion of methodology. Nevertheless, treatment research often includes several specific control procedures that address questions of widespread interest.

The *no-treatment control group* includes subjects who do not receive treatment. This group controls for such effects as history, maturation, testing, regression, and similar threats, at least if the group is formed through random assignment. The *waiting-list control group* is a variation of the no-treatment group. During the period that the experimental subjects receive treatment, waiting-list control subjects do not receive treatment. After treatment of the experimental subjects is complete, waiting-list control subjects are reassessed and then receive treatment. A *no-contact control group* may be included in the design to evaluate the effects of participating in or having "contact" with a treatment program. Individuals selected for this group usually do not know that they are participating in a treatment investigation. Hence their functioning must be assessed under the guise of some other purpose than a treatment investigation.

A *nonspecific treatment control group* consists of a group that engages in all of the accoutrements of treatment such as receiving a rationale about their problem, meeting with a therapist, attending treatment sessions, and engaging in procedures alleged to be therapeutic. Actually, the purpose is to provide the generic ingredients of the treatment to the nonspecific treatment control group and to address the question of whether the effects of veridical treatment were merely due to its nonspecific treatment components.

A *yoked control group* may be used to control for variations across groups that may arise over the course of the experiment. Implementing treatment procedures may involve factors inherent in but not relevant to the independent variables of interest to the investigator. Yoking refers to a procedure that equalizes the extraneous variables among groups so that the variable of interest is unconfounded. Yoking is conducted by matching or pairing subjects in the control groups (or one of the control groups) with subjects in an experimental group and using information obtained from the experimental subject to decide the conditions to which the control subject will be exposed.

Nonrandomly assigned or "patched-up" control procedures represent a category of groups that is characterized by selection of subjects. For example, in quasi-experiments, a nonrandomly assigned group might be used to control for various threats to internal validity such as history or maturation. The group, by virtue of its selection, imperfectly controls these threats but still strengthens the plausibility of the conclusions that can be drawn.

Apart from control groups, the investigator may wish to include a wide range of comparison groups. *Comparison groups,* under which control groups might be subsumed, refer to a broad range of conditions. They are usually included to address construct validity. Groups are selected to increase the specificity of the conclusions about the intervention or variable of interest. Frequently used comparison groups include routine or standard conditions provided to clients, alternative treatments, and various intact groups in subject selection studies to control for variables potentially confounded with the primary characteristic of interest.

The addition of control and comparison groups to experimental designs represents the manner in which group research rules out threats to internal and construct validity and in so doing adds precision to the conclusions that can be reached. The use of control and comparison groups and their relation to the progression of research were illustrated by a discussion of psychotherapy outcome research. Several different treatment evaluation strategies were discussed to convey alternative control and comparison groups and questions that do not require control conditions in the usual sense.

FOR FURTHER READING

Beck, J.G., Andrasik, F., & Arena, J.G. (1984). Group comparison designs. In A.S. Bellack & M. Hersen (Eds.), *Research methods in clinical psychology*. Elmsford, NY: Pergamon Press.

Boring, E.G. (1954). The nature and history of experimental control. *American Journal of Psychology, 68,* 573–589.

Kendall, P.C., & Norton-Ford, J.D. (1982). Therapy outcome research methods. In P.C. Kendall & J.N. Butcher (Eds.), *Handbook of research methods in clinical psychology*. New York: John Wiley & Sons.

O'Leary, K.D., & Borkovec, T.D. (1987). Conceptual, methodological, and ethical problems of placebo groups in psychotherapy research. *American Psychologist, 33,* 821–830.

Parloff, M.B. (1986). Placebo controls in psychotherapy research: A sine qua non or a placebo for research problems? *Journal of Consulting and Clinical Psychology, 54,* 79–87.

Chapter 7

THE CASE STUDY AND SINGLE-CASE RESEARCH DESIGNS

Group designs dominate research in clinical, counseling, and educational psychology, and indeed the field more generally. Hence alternative designs and comparison conditions are central topics. However, research design refers broadly to an approach toward evaluating phenomena and establishing valid inferences. The use of groups is not a necessary feature of this approach. Indeed evaluation and valid inferences can be readily accomplished with the individual subject or single case.

Single-case designs have been used in many areas of research, including psychology, psychiatry, education, rehabilitation, social work, counseling, and other disciplines. The designs have been referred to by different terms, such as *intrasubject-replication designs,* $N = 1$ *research,* and *intensive designs,* to mention a few. Although several alternative terms have been proposed to describe the designs, each is partially misleading. For example, *single-case* and "$N = 1$" designs imply that only one subject is included in an investigation. This is misleading and hides the fact that large numbers of subjects and entire communities and cities have been included in some "single-case" designs. The term *intrasubject* is a useful term because it implies that the methodology focuses on performance of the same person over time. Yet this term, too, is partially misleading because some of the designs depend on examining the effects of interventions across (i.e., between) subjects. *Intensive designs* has not grown out of the tradition of single-case research and is used infrequently. Also, the term *intensive* has the unfortunate connotation that the investigator is working intensively to study the subject, which probably is true but is beside the point. The term *single-case designs* has been adopted here to draw attention to the unique feature of the designs, that is, the capacity to conduct empirical research with individual subjects, and because this term enjoys the widest use.

The unique feature of single-case designs is the capacity to conduct experimental investigations with one subject. The designs can evaluate the effects of interventions with large groups and address many of the questions posed in between-group research. However, the special feature that distinguishes the methodology is the provision of some means of rigorously evaluating the effects of interventions with the individual case.

The present chapter discusses case studies and single-case experimental designs and their characteristics. The case study as a method of evaluating the individual has a long history in clinical work and serves as an important backdrop for experimental methods with the individual case. Single-case designs and the methods they share permit careful evaluation of individual cases in research and practice. The specific requirements and procedures of single-case experiments are presented to convey the logic of the designs and how they address threats to validity. Apart from describing and illustrating these single-case experimental designs, the chapter also identifies ways of adapting these designs in quasi-experiments for their use clinically.

THE CASE STUDY IN CLINICAL PSYCHOLOGY

Although research in psychology has relied extensively on the study of groups of subjects, major scientific advances have been made with the careful study of individual cases. Illustrations can be provided from virtually every branch of psychology where the individual subject has provided important information, as reflected in such diverse areas of psychology as memory, animal behavior, cognitive development in children, language, and psychopathology among others (Bolgar, 1965; Dukes, 1965). The case study has played a more central role in clinical psychology than in other areas of psychology. Indeed, clinical psychology has been defined as the application of psychological principles and techniques to the problems of the individual (Korchin, 1976; Watson, 1951). To understand the individual, the clinical psychologist may study a broad range of variables pertaining to the individual, his or her interpersonal relationships, and indeed the larger social matrix.

Traditionally, psychology has focused on experimentation with groups of individuals and has reached conclusions about important variables on the basis of group differences. Laws based on group analyses provide general statements that apply to many individuals on the *average*. That is, the laws based on group research tend to be made at the expense of the individuality of each of the members. In contrast, laws derived from the study of the individual are intended to characterize the performance of one person and the variables of which that performance is a function.

In clinical psychology, study of the individual person rather than groups of individuals was advocated by Allport (1961), a personality theorist. He recommended the intensive study of the individual (which he referred to as the *idiographic* approach) as a supplement to the study of groups (which he referred to as the *nomothetic* approach). Scientific psychology, as usually conceived, does not include a place for the uniqueness of the individual subject. Allport thought this needed to be corrected. Studying the uniqueness of the individual did not mean that general laws of behavior did not apply or served no function. Rather, Allport believed that general laws alone were incomplete. Other investigators in clinical (e.g., Chassan, 1967; Shapiro, 1966) and experimental research (e.g., Skinner, 1957) advocated the study of the individual in place of or in addition to the study of groups of subjects (see Kazdin & Tuma, 1982).

Although the distinction between studying individuals versus groups has been made in trying to delineate the domain of clinical psychology, the distinction requires extensive qualification. As a scientific discipline, contemporary clinical psychology consists primarily of group research. Perusal of texts or journals that publish research reveals that only a small fraction of research in the field focuses on the individual. Yet as a professional and applied field, contemporary clinical psychology devotes considerable attention to the individual. Psychological services continue to be provided for the individual client in diverse inpatient and outpatient settings. The practice of psychology often is characterized as the focus on the individual subject, usually in the form of case studies, where scientific rigor is sacrificed. In contrast, research in clinical psychology usually is characterized as rigorous experimentation in laboratory or applied settings, typically with groups of subjects.

Despite the commitment of clinical psychology to the study of the individual case in theory, traditionally there has been a bifurcation between the case study and empirical research. The bifurcation is based on methodological discrepancies of these two approaches for evaluating variables that contribute to behavior. The case study usually consists of uncontrolled observations of the individual client in situations where concrete and immediate concerns of that person must be given high priority. Experimentation usually consists of carefully controlled evaluations of groups of individuals in which the research question is accorded high priority. This bifurcation is unnecessary because methods of evaluation are available to study the individual case experimentally and to accord high priority to the clinical concerns of the individual.

Value of the Case Study

The lack of controlled conditions, carefully obtained objective measures of functioning, and scientific rigor have limited the case as a research tool. Yet the naturalistic and uncontrolled characteristics also have made the case a unique source of information that complements and contributes to experimental research.

The case study has served many useful purposes in clinical theory, research, and practice. First, the case study has served as a *source of ideas and hypotheses* about human performance and development. For example, case studies from quite different conceptual views such as psychoanalysis and behavior therapy (e.g., the case of Little Hans [Freud, 1933]; the case of Little Albert [Watson & Rayner, 1920]) were remarkably influential in suggesting how fears might develop and in advancing theories of human behavior that would support these views.

Second, case studies have frequently served as the *source for developing therapy techniques*. Here, too, remarkably influential cases within psychoanalysis and behavior therapy might be cited. In the 1880s, the treatment of a young woman (Anna O.) with several "hysterical" symptoms (Breuer & Freud, 1957) marked the inception of the "talking cure" and cathartic method in psychotherapy. Within behavior therapy, development of treatment for a fearful boy (Peter) followed by evaluation of a large number of different treatments to eliminate fears among children (Jones, 1924a, 1924b) exerted great influence in suggesting several different interventions that remain in some form or another in clinical practice.

Third, case studies permit the *study of rare phenomena*. Many problems seen in treatment may be rare. By definition, clients with such problems rarely present themselves in sufficient numbers at one time to be evaluated in controlled group research. The individual client with a unique problem or situation is studied intensively with the hope of uncovering material that may shed light on the development of the problem. For example, the study of multiple personality, in which an individual manifests two or more different patterns of personality, emotions, thoughts, and behaviors has been elaborated greatly by the case study. A prominent illustration is the well-publicized report of the "three faces of Eve" (Thigpen & Cleckley, 1954, 1957). The intensive study of Eve revealed quite different personalities, mannerisms, gait, psychological test performance, and other characteristics of general demeanor. The analysis at the level of the case provided unique information not accessible from large-scale group studies.

Fourth, the case is valuable in *providing a counterinstance* for notions that are considered to be universally applicable. For example, in the development of behavior therapy, case studies were often cited where overt symptomatic behaviors were successfully treated. In traditional forms of treatment such as psychoanalysis, treatment of overt symptoms were discouraged based on the notion that neglect of motivational and intrapsychic processes presumed to underlie dysfunction would be ill-advised if not ineffective. Repeated demonstrations that overt symptoms could be effectively treated without the emergence of substitute symptoms cast doubt on the original caveat (see Kazdin,

1982a). Although a case can cast doubt on a general proposition, it does not itself allow affirmative claims of a very general nature to be made. By showing a counterinstance, the case study does provide a qualifier about the generality of the statement. With repeated cases, each showing a similar pattern, the applicability of the original general proposition is increasingly threatened.

Finally, case studies have *persuasive and motivational value*. From a methodological standpoint, case studies provide a weak basis for drawing inferences. However, this point is often academic. Even though cases may not provide strong causal knowledge on methodological grounds, a case study often provides a dramatic and persuasive demonstration and makes concrete and poignant what might otherwise serve as an abstract principle. Seeing is believing even though philosophy and psychology teach that seeing is not invariably trustworthy as a way of knowing. Cases may be especially convincing because of the way anecdotal information is compiled to convey a particular point. The absence of objective measures or details that might be inconsistent often convey unqualified support for a particular belief.

Another reason that cases are often so dramatic is that they are usually selected systematically to illustrate a particular point. Presumably, cases selected randomly from all those available would not illustrate the dramatic type of change that typically is evident in the particular case provided by an author. This point can be readily illustrated by merely referring to advertisements for fad diets or exercise devices. Typically, such advertisements show "before and after" photographs of someone who has completed the recommended program. The case is used to illustrate the "miraculous" effects of the program and may show someone who has lost 50 pounds supposedly after being on the program for only 10 minutes! Even if the illustrated case were accurately presented, it is likely to be so highly selected as to not represent the reaction of most individuals to the program. Nevertheless, the selection of extreme cases does not merely illustrate a point; rather, it often compels us to believe in causal relations that reason and data would refute.

As noted earlier, case studies often have served as the basis for developing specific therapeutic techniques as well as hypotheses about the nature of clinical disorders. Successful applications of a treatment technique at the case level can be very persuasive to the therapist-investigator, but the persuasive appeal here is a mixed blessing. Often a case is so convincing that writers frequently fail to maintain scientific restraint before careful evaluation of the specific findings. On the other hand, rigorous endorsement of a position usually stimulates research by others who test and critically evaluate the claims based previously on only anecdotal information. Thus the very persuasiveness of a case study may lend it heuristic value. Because cases often provide dramatic and concrete examples, they often stimulate investigation of a phenomenon. Empirical research can put to the test the claims made previously on the basis of case studies alone.

Limitations of the Case Study

The case study has special value that stands on its own. Yet as a basis for establishing knowledge, it has limitations. First, an important limitation of the case is that *many alternative explanations usually are available* to account for the current status of the individual other than those provided by the clinician. Postdictive or retrospective accounts try to reconstruct early events and show how they invariably led to contemporary functioning. Although such accounts frequently are persuasive, they are scientifically questionable. Many events in the individual's past might have accounted for contemporary functioning other than those highlighted by the clinician or client. More important, there is no way to test a hypothesis with the usual case report to assess the causal events in the past. In many cases, one cannot even be assured that the events in the past believed to account for behavior actually occurred. Reports of a person are not necessarily reliable and cannot, without independent corroboration, be accepted uncritically.

Second, the heavy *reliance of cases on anecdotal information* provides for the possibility of quite biased presentation. Clinical judgment and interpretation play a major role in making sense out of the client's predicament. In the absence of objective measures, the conclusions cannot be accorded scientific status. Many inferences are based on reports of the clients; these reports are the "data" on which interpretations are made. The client's reconstructions of the past and remembered events, particularly those laden with emotion, are likely to be distorted and highly selective. The reports may have little bearing on what actually happened to the client in the past. Unless subjective accounts are independently corroborated, they could be completely unreliable. Many case reports give the appearance of literary descriptions of stories rather than scientific investigations, not merely because of the style of writing but also because of the type of information made available.

Third, a major concern about the information derived from a case study is the *generalizability to other individuals or situations.* Scientific research attempts to establish relations between independent and dependent variables. Although such relations may be demonstrated for an individual case, the assumed purpose of science is to develop general "laws" of behavior that hold without respect to the identity of any individual. It is possible that the individual case will reflect marked or unique characteristics and not provide widely generalizable findings. The absence of objective procedures to evaluate the case makes replication of the study often difficult. Hence, knowledge about several potentially similar cases is difficult to achieve.

Sometimes several cases may be studied as a basis for drawing general conclusions beyond the individual. Although each case is studied individually, the information may be aggregated in an attempt to reveal relations that have broad generality. For example, the development of psychiatric diagnosis, which is concerned with the identification and delineation of particular psychological disorders, was greatly advanced by Kraepelin (1855–1926), a German psychiatrist. He identified specific "disease" entities or psychological disorders by systematically collecting thousands of case studies on hospitalized psychiatric patients. He described the history of each patient, the onset of the disorder, and its outcome. From this extensive clinical material, he elaborated various types of "mental illness" and provided a general model for contemporary approaches to psychiatric diagnosis (Zilboorg & Henry, 1941).

When individual cases are aggregated, the resulting information may be more convincing than information obtained from a single case. Conclusions drawn from several individuals seem to rule out the possibility of idiosyncratic findings characteristic of one case. Yet the extent to which information from many combined cases can be informative depends on several factors, such as the manner in which the observations were made (e.g., anecdotal reports vs. standardized measures), the number of cases, the clarity of the relationship, and the possibility that the individuals studied were selected in a biased fashion. Generally the accumulation of cases provides a much better basis for inference than does an individual case, but it still falls short of the success in demonstrating relations that can be achieved in experimental research.

In clinical psychology and other mental health related disciplines, the accumulation of multiple cases is common among professionals involved in clinical practice. The absence of systematic observation and standardization of assessment has made difficult the codification and utilization of this experience as part of the knowledge base. Even so, aggregated experience among professionals involved in practice occasionally reveals consistencies in beliefs about factors that contribute to treatment and therapeutic change (Kazdin, Siegel, & Bass, 1990). Consensus based on experience does not substitute for demonstrated findings. However, the information provides important leads to be pursued in research.

The Case Study and Experimental Research

As traditionally conceived, the case study refers to investigating an individual or group of individuals in the absence of experimental controls. The lack of experimental control means that it is difficult to exclude many rival interpretations that could account for the client's behavior. Hence the case study can be distinguished from experimental research where causal relations are more readily identified because the variables that influence behavior are manipulated directly and, with the inclusion of appropriate control conditions, can be accorded a causal role in behavior change.

From a methodological standpoint, the case study provides several problems because sufficient experimental control techniques are lacking to determine what actually accounted for the client's behavior. For this reason the case study sometimes is viewed more basically as *uncontrolled evaluations* where the role of specific variables on performance cannot be isolated unambiguously. This broader meaning extends the definition of a case study beyond the study of individual subjects to evaluations where one or several individuals are studied in an uncontrolled way. Single-case designs permit one to draw valid inferences about factors that influence performance. The designs focus on individuals or groups of individuals who are studied over time. Both true and quasi-single-case experiments provide methods to improve upon the case study both for research and clinical ends.

SINGLE-CASE EXPERIMENTAL DESIGNS: GENERAL FEATURES

The underlying rationale of single-case experimental designs is similar to that of the more familiar group designs. All experiments compare the effects of different conditions (independent variables) on performance. In traditional group experimentation, the comparison is made between groups of subjects who are treated differently. Based on random assignment to conditions, some subjects are designated to receive a particular intervention and others are not. The effect of the intervention is evaluated by comparing the performance of the different groups. In single-case research, inferences are usually made about the effects of the intervention by comparing different conditions presented to the same subject over time. Experimentation with the single case has special requirements that must be met if inferences are to be drawn about the effects of the intervention. It is useful to highlight basic requirements before specific designs are considered.

Continuous Assessment

Perhaps the most fundamental design requirement of single-case experimentation is the reliance on repeated observations of performance over time. The client's performance is observed on several occasions, usually before the intervention is applied and continuously over the period while the intervention is in effect. Typically, observations are conducted on a daily basis or at least on multiple occasions each week.

Continuous assessment is a basic requirement because single-case designs examine the effects of interventions on performance over time. Continuous assessment allows the investigator to examine the pattern and stability of performance before treatment is initiated. The pretreatment information over an extended period provides a picture of what performance is like without the intervention. When the intervention eventually is implemented, the observations are continued and the investigator can examine whether behavior changes coincide with the intervention.

The role of continuous assessment in single-case research can be illustrated by examining a basic difference of group and single-case research. In both types of research, as already noted, the effects of a particular intervention on performance are examined. In the most basic case, the intervention is examined by comparing performance when the intervention is presented versus performance when it is withheld. In treatment research, this is the basic comparison of treatment versus no treatment, a question raised to evaluate whether a particular intervention improves performance. In between-group research, the question is addressed by giving the intervention to some people (treatment group) but not to others (no-treatment group). One or two observations (e.g., pre- and posttreatment assessment) are obtained for several different individuals. In single-case research, the effects of the intervention are examined by observing the influence of treatment and no treatment on the performance of the same people. Instead of one or two observations of several individuals, several observations are obtained for one or a few people. Continuous assessment provides several observations over time to allow the comparisons of interest within the individual subject.

Baseline Assessment

Each of the single-case experimental designs usually begins with observing behavior for several days before the intervention is implemented. This initial period of observation, referred to as the *baseline phase,* provides information about the level of behavior before the intervention begins. The baseline phase serves different functions. First, data collected during the baseline phase describe the existing level of performance. The *descriptive function* of baseline provides information about the extent of the client's problem. Second, the data serve as the basis for predicting the level of performance for the immediate future if the intervention is not provided. Even though the descriptive function of the baseline phase is important for indicating the extent of the client's problem, from the standpoint of single-case designs, the *predictive function* is central.

To evaluate the impact of an intervention in single-case research, it is important to have an idea of what performance would be like in the future without the intervention. Of course, a description of present performance does not necessarily provide a statement of what performance would be like in the future. Performance might change even without treatment. The only way to be certain of future performance without the intervention would be to continue baseline observations without implementing the intervention. However, the purpose is to implement and evaluate the intervention and to see if behavior improves in some way.

Baseline data are gathered to help predict performance in the immediate future before treatment is implemented. Baseline performance is observed for several days to provide a sufficient basis for making a prediction of future performance. The prediction is achieved by *projecting or extrapolating* into the future a continuation of baseline performance.

A hypothetical example can illustrate how observations during the baseline phase are used to predict future performance and how this prediction is pivotal to drawing inferences about the effects of the intervention. Figure 7.1 illustrates a hypothetical case in which observations were collected on a hypochondriacal patient's frequency of complaining. As evident in the figure, observations during the baseline (pretreatment) phase were obtained for 10 days. The hypothetical baseline data suggest a reasonably consistent pattern of complaints each day in the hospital.

The baseline level predicts the likely level of performance in the immediate future if conditions continue as they are. The projected (dashed) line suggests the approximate level of future performance. This projected level is essential for single-case experimentation because it serves as a criterion to evaluate whether the intervention leads to change. Presumably, if treatment is effective, performance will differ or depart from the projected level of baseline. For example, if a program is designed to reduce a hypochondriac's complaints, and is successful in doing so, the number of complaints should decrease well below the number projected by baseline. In any case, continuous assessment in the beginning of single-case experimental designs consists of observation of baseline or pretreatment performance. As the individual single-case designs are described later, the importance of initial baseline assessment will become especially clear.

Stability of Performance

Because baseline performance is used to predict how the client will behave in the future, it is important that the data are stable. A *stable rate* of performance

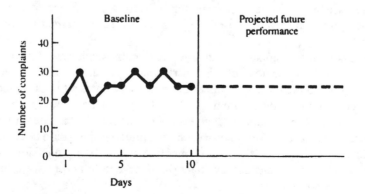

Figure 7.1. Hypothetical example of baseline observations of frequency of complaining. Baseline data (solid line) are used to predict the likely rate of performance in the future (dashed line).

is characterized by the absence of a trend (or slope) in the data and relatively little variability in performance. The notions of trend and variability raise separate issues, even though they both relate to stability.

Trend in the Data

A trend refers to the tendency for performance to decrease or increase systematically or consistently over time. One of three simple data patterns might be evident during baseline observations. First, baseline data may show no trend or slope. In this case, performance is best represented by a horizontal line indicating that it is not increasing or decreasing over time. As a hypothetical example, observations may be obtained on the disruptive and inappropriate classroom behaviors of a hyperactive child. The upper panel of Figure 7.2 shows baseline performance with no trend. The absence of trend in baseline provides a relatively clear basis for evaluating subsequent intervention effects. Improvements in performance are likely to be reflected in a trend that departs from the horizontal line of baseline performance.

If behavior does show a trend during baseline, behavior would be increasing or decreasing over time. The trend during baseline may or may not present problems for evaluating intervention effects, depending on the direction of the trend in relation to the desired change in behavior. Performance may be changing in the direction *opposite* from that which treatment is designed to achieve. For example, a hyperactive child may show an *increase* in disruptive and inappropriate behavior during baseline observations. The middle panel of Figure 7.2 shows how baseline data might appear; over the period of observations the client's behavior is becoming worse, that is, more disruptive. Because the intervention will attempt to alter behavior in the opposite direction, this initial trend is not likely to interfere with evaluating intervention effects.

In contrast, the baseline trend may be in the *same direction* that the intervention is likely to produce. Essentially, the baseline phase may show improvement in behavior. For example, the behavior of a hyperactive child may improve over the course of baseline as disruptive and inappropriate behavior decrease, as shown in the lower panel of Figure 7.2. Because the intervention will attempt to improve performance, it may be difficult to evaluate the effect of the subsequent intervention. The projected level of performance for baseline is toward improvement. A very strong intervention effect of treatment would be required to show clearly that treatment surpassed this projected level from baseline.

If baseline is showing an improvement, one might raise the question of why an intervention should be provided at all. Yet even when behavior is improving during baseline, it may not be improving quickly enough. For example, an autistic child may show a gradual decrease in head banging during baseline observations. The reduction may be so gradual that serious self-injury might

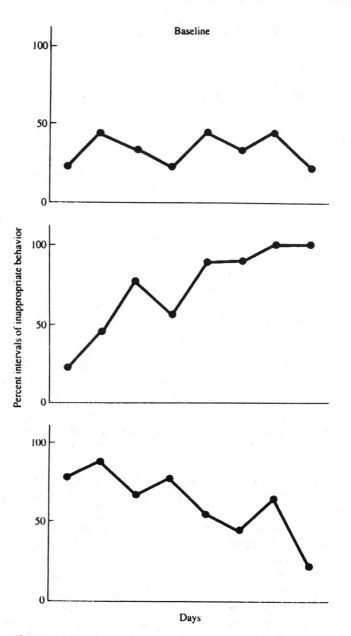

Figure 7.2. Hypothetical data for disruptive behavior of a hyperactive child. The upper panel shows a stable rate of performance with no systematic trend over time. The middle panel shows a systematic trend with behavior becoming worse over time. The lower panel shows a systematic trend with behavior becoming better over time. This latter pattern of data (lower panel) is the most likely one to interfere with evaluation of interventions, because the change is in the same direction of change anticipated with treatment.

be inflicted unless the behavior is treated quickly. Hence even though behavior is changing in the desired direction, additional changes may be needed.

Occasionally, a trend may exist in the data and still not interfere with evaluating treatments. Also, when trends do exist, several design options and data evaluation procedures can help clarify the effects of the intervention (see Kazdin, 1982b). For present purposes, it is important to convey that the one feature of a stable baseline is little or no trend, and that the absence of trend provides a clear basis for evaluating intervention effects. Presumably, when the intervention is implemented, a trend toward improvement in behavior will be evident. This is readily detected with an initial baseline that does not already show a trend toward improvement.

Variability in the Data

In addition to trend, stability of the data refers to the fluctuation or variability in the subject's performance over time. Excessive variability in the data during baseline or other phases can interfere with drawing conclusions about treatment. As a general rule, the greater the variability in the data, the more difficult it is to draw conclusions about the effects of the intervention.

Excessive variability is relative; whether the variability is excessive and interferes with drawing conclusions about the intervention depends on many factors, such as the initial level of behavior during the baseline phase and the magnitude of behavior change when the intervention is implemented. In the extreme case, baseline performance may fluctuate daily from extremely high to extremely low levels (e.g., 0% to 100%). Such a pattern of performance is illustrated in Figure 7.3 (upper panel), in which hypothetical baseline data are provided. With such extreme fluctuations in performance, it is difficult to predict any particular level of future performance.

Alternatively, baseline data may show relatively little variability. A typical example is represented in the hypothetical data in the lower panel of Figure 7.3. Performance fluctuates, but the extent of the fluctuation is small compared with the upper panel. With relatively slight fluctuations, the projected pattern of future performance is fairly clear and hence intervention effects will be less difficult to evaluate. Ideally, baseline data will show little variability. Occasionally relatively large variability may exist in the data. Several options are available to minimize the impact of such variability on drawing conclusions about intervention effects (see Kazdin, 1982b). However, the evaluation of intervention effects is greatly facilitated by relatively consistent performance during baseline.

ALTERNATIVE EXPERIMENTAL DESIGNS

Single-case designs vary in the ways that the effects of an intervention are demonstrated, the requirements for experimental evaluation, and the types of

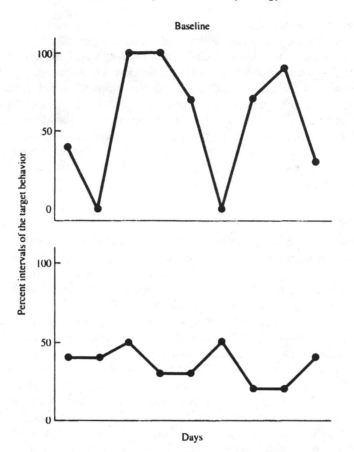

Figure 7.3. Baseline data showing relatively large variability (upper panel) and relatively small variability (lower panel). Intervention effects are more readily evaluated with little variability in the data.

questions that are addressed. The designs provide a range of options for careful evaluation of the individual case and hence contribute in an important way to the science and practice of clinical work. The major designs are presented and illustrated here. It is worth noting in advance that illustrations of the designs will be made with behavior modification applications. Although the designs are not restricted to a particular type of treatment, behavioral interventions have commonly been evaluated with these designs and provide a rich pool of examples.

Alternative research designs discussed to this point have used the Campbell and Stanley (1963) notation to convey the groups included in the design and when treatments and observations are provided. This notation tends to be very cumbersome in describing single-case designs. The reason for this is that observations (O) are conducted continuously with these designs. There usually is no discrete pretest or posttest, but there is continuous assessment before, during, and after treatment on a daily basis. The nature of scheduling interventions over time and across clients with single-case designs also would make the use of the X and O terminology unclear. Each design should be clear from the general description and from detailed examples provided in this chapter.

ABAB Design

The discussion to this point has highlighted the basic requirements of single-case designs. In particular, assessing performance continuously over time and obtaining stable rates of performance are pivotal to the logic of the designs. Precisely how these features are essential for demonstrating intervention effects can be conveyed by discussing *ABAB designs,* which are the most basic experimental designs in single-case research. ABAB designs consist of a family of experimental arrangements in which observations of performance are made over time for a given client (or group of clients). Over the course of the investigation, changes are made in the experimental conditions to which the client is exposed.

Description

The ABAB design examines the effects of an intervention by alternating the baseline condition (A phase), when no intervention is in effect, with the intervention condition (B phase). The A and B phases are repeated again to complete the four phases. The effects of the intervention are clear if performance improves during the first intervention phase, reverts to or approaches original baseline levels of performance when treatment is withdrawn, and improves when treatment is reinstated in the second intervention phase.

The design begins by observing behavior under baseline (no-treatment) conditions. When a stable rate of behavior is evident and is not accelerating or decelerating, treatment is implemented. Treatment may consist of a particular intervention conducted by a therapist, parent, spouse, or any other person and carried out in individual outpatient therapy sessions, at home, in an institution, and so on. Assume that the intervention is associated with some change in the observed behavior. When this change is stable, the intervention is temporarily withdrawn. The baseline condition or absence of treatment is reinstated. The return-to-baseline condition sometimes is referred to as a *reversal phase* because the behavior is expected to "reverse," that is, return to, or closely to, the level of the original baseline. After behavior reverts to baseline levels, the intervention is reinstated.

The design depends on continuous assessment of behavior, so within each phase several data points show the level of behavior. The logic of the design is based on comparing the level of behavior and the trends in the data across different phases. In each phase the data are used not only to describe current performance but also to predict what it would be like in the future if no changes were made in how the client is treated. When treatment is implemented, performance is expected to change. The change in performance moves the level of behavior from what it was at the baseline level and what it was predicted or extrapolated to be if baseline conditions were continued. Similarly, the new level of behavior during treatment predicts what behavior would be like if treatment were continued. When treatment is withdrawn, behavior should revert to baseline levels. If this pattern is obtained, the predicted level of treatment phase is violated. If the level of behavior changes as treatment is implemented or withdrawn, it suggests that treatment is responsible for the change. Other effects resulting from history or maturation would be expected to result in a continuation of the trend of a previous phase.

Illustration

The ABAB design and its use can be illustrated with a relatively simple treatment application to eliminate thumbsucking in a 9-year-old boy (Ross, 1975). The thumbsucking was associated with malocclusion of the front teeth, which could not be treated until sucking was eliminated. Thumbsucking was altered at home by the boy's mother. The parents recorded sucking at predetermined times during the day (while the boy watched television) and at night and early morning (while asleep). Treatment consisted of simply turning off the television set for 5 minutes if he was caught sucking his thumb during the day. His siblings also were told to help keep him from thumbsucking so that their TV time would not be lost also. This program was implemented and withdrawn in accord with requirements of the ABAB design.

The effects of the program are extremely clear (see Figure 7.4). When treatment was in effect, thumbsucking was almost eliminated. Sucking returned and approached baseline levels when treatment was withdrawn and again was virtually eliminated when treatment was reinstated. Interestingly, observations at night and in the early morning while the boy had been asleep showed a similar pattern even though the program was not introduced for nighttime thumbsucking. The daytime program was continued for 6 months beyond the 16th week as shown in the figure, with reportedly similar effects.

Considerations

The central requirement of the design is having stable levels of behavior. If behavior is decreasing or increasing while the baseline condition is in effect, this may interfere with drawing inferences about the relation between the intervention and behavior. Evaluating data in an ABAB design and drawing

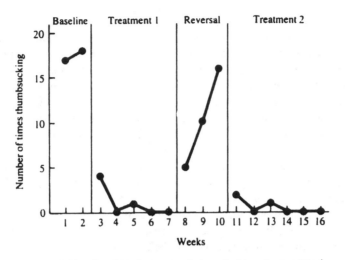

Figure 7.4. Thumbsucking frequency during television viewing (21 observations per week). Note: Adapted from Ross, J.A. (1975). Parents modify thumbsucking: A case study. *Journal of Behavior Therapy and Experimental Psychiatry, 6,* 248–249.

a conclusion about the causal role of treatment are difficult when treatment effects are consistent with the pattern of behavior already evident in the baseline phase. Hence most investigators recommend waiting until behavior is stable (i.e., no trend) and is relatively consistent over time, or shows a trend only in the direction opposite of the change anticipated with treatment. Statistical techniques have been developed to take into account baseline trends that might interfere with drawing conclusions about interventions (see Gottman, 1981; Kazdin, 1984a).

The ABAB design is not a single design but a family of designs in which treatment and nontreatment phases are alternated. The most commonly used version has been discussed here as a four-phase design that alternates a single treatment with baseline phases. However, designs are available that include more than one treatment and more than four phases. For example, suppose that the treatment (B_1) does not change behavior after the baseline phase. The clinician-investigator would not continue the phase but would try another treatment (B_2). This latter treatment would constitute a new phase and would probably be implemented later in the design. The design could be represented as an $AB_1B_2AB_2$ design. The variations of ABAB designs are too numerous to discuss here (see Barlow & Hersen, 1984; Kazdin, 1982b).

The ABAB design demonstrates a causal relation by showing that behavior reverts to or approaches the original baseline level after the intervention is withdrawn or altered (during the second A phase). This requirement introduces problems that restrict use of the design in clinical work. One problem is that withdrawing treatment does not always show a change in behavior. Indeed, it is the prime hope of therapists and patients alike that once treatment is terminated, its therapeutic effects will continue. Clinically, continued performance of the appropriate behavior is important; yet from the standpoint of an ABAB design, it could be disappointing. If behavior is not made to revert to baseline levels after showing an initial change, a causal relation cannot be drawn between the intervention and behavior. Some events other than treatment might account for change because behavior is not under the control of the administration or termination of treatment.

Even if behavior did revert to baseline levels when treatment was suspended temporarily, such a change would be clinically undesirable. Essentially, returning the client to baseline levels of performance amounts to making behavior worse. Of course, treatment can be withdrawn for only a brief period such as one or a few days. In most circumstances, the idea of making a client worse just when treatment may be having an effect is ethically unacceptable. There may be important exceptions if, for example, the required treatment has undesirable side effects and suspension of treatments tests whether the intervention is still needed. Aside from ethical problems, there are practical problems as well. It is often difficult to ensure that the client, therapist, or relatives responsible for conducting treatment will actually stop once some success has been achieved.

As a general rule, problems related to reversing behavior make the ABAB design and its variations undesirable in clinical situations. Yet the power of the design in demonstrating control of an intervention over behavior is very compelling. If behavior can, in effect, be "turned on and off" as a function of the intervention, this is a potent demonstration of a causal relation. Few threats to internal validity remain plausible in explaining the pattern of results. On the other hand, the investigator's desire for clear demonstrations of experimental control clearly conflicts with the clinician's (and client's) desire for protracted therapeutic change. Hence this design is not advocated strongly here in clinical work, where the roles of investigator and clinician should merge.

Multiple-Baseline Design

Description

The *multiple-baseline design* demonstrates the effect of an intervention by showing that behavior change accompanies introduction of the intervention at different points in time. Once the intervention is presented, it need not be withdrawn or altered to reverse behavior to or near baseline levels. Thus the clinical utility of the design is not limited by the problems of reverting behavior to pretreatment levels.

There are different versions of the multiple-baseline design. In each version, data are collected continuously and concurrently across two or more baselines. The intervention is applied to the different baselines at different points in time. The versions differ according to whether the baselines are *different responses* for a given individual, the same response of *different individuals,* or the same response for an individual across *different situations.*

For example, in the multiple-baseline design across responses, a single individual or group of individuals is observed. Data are collected on the performance of two or more behaviors, each of which eventually is to be altered. The behaviors are observed daily or at least on several occasions each week. After each of the baselines shows a stable pattern, the intervention is applied to only one of the responses. Baseline conditions remain in effect for the other responses. The initial response to which treatment is applied is expected to change while other responses remain at pretreatment levels. When the treated behavior stabilizes, the intervention is applied to the second response. Treatment continues for the first two responses while baseline continues for all other responses. Eventually, each response is exposed to treatment but at different points in time. A causal relation between the intervention and behavior is clearly demonstrated if each response changes only when the intervention is introduced and not before.

Illustration

As an example, an imagery-based flooding procedure was used to treat a 6½-year-old boy, named Joseph, who suffered a posttraumatic stress disorder (Saigh, 1986). This disorder is a reaction to a highly stressful event or experience and has a number of symptoms such as persistently reexperiencing the event (e.g., through thoughts, dreams), avoidance of stimuli associated with the trauma, numbing of responsiveness, outbursts of anger, difficulty in sleeping, and exaggerated startle responses. Joseph experienced the disorder after exposure to a bomb blast in a war zone where he lived. His reaction included trauma-related nightmares, recollections of the trauma, depression, and avoidance behavior.

To treat Joseph, five scenes were developed that evoked anxiety (e.g., one in which he saw injured people and debris, another where he approached specific shopping areas). To measure discomfort to the scenes, he rated his level of anxiety as each scene was described to him. During the sessions he was trained to relax, after which scenes were presented for extended periods (over 20 minutes). During this exposure period, he was asked to imagine the exact details of the scenes. The five scenes were incorporated into treatment in a multiple-baseline design, so that exposure to scenes occurred in sequence or at different points in time. In each of the sessions, discomfort was rated in response to all of the scenes.

The results, presented in Figure 7.5, showed that Joseph's discomfort consistently decreased after only 10 sessions (1 session of baseline assessment, 10 sessions of treatment). The reduction of anxiety for each scene was associated with implementation of the intervention. Assessment immediately after treatment and 6 months later indicated that he was no longer discomforted by the situations. The results from other measures also reflected change. Before and after treatment Joseph was assessed in the marketplace where the bomb blast had occurred. His performance had improved after treatment, which was reflected by his remaining in the area longer and thereby showing less avoidance. Other measures including assessment of anxiety, depression, and classroom performance at school indicated improvements after treatment as well. Thus the effects of treatment appeared to affect several important areas of functioning.

The multiple-baseline design can be extended across individuals. Baseline data can be collected for a behavior across different individuals (e.g., siblings

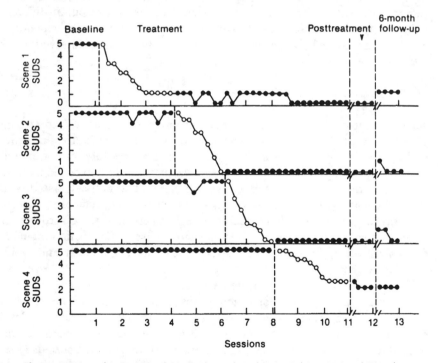

Figure 7.5. Joseph's Ratings of Discomfort referred to as Subject Units of Disturbance (SUDS) where .5 = *maximum discomfort* and 0 = *no discomfort*. Assessment was conducted to measure discomfort for each scene during the treatment sessions. Treatment (graphed as open circles) reflects the period in which imagery-based exposure (flooding) focused on the specific scene. Reprinted with permission from *Behaviour Research and Therapy, 24,* P.A. Saigh, In vitro flooding in the treatment of a 6-year-old-boy's posttraumatic stress disorder, 1986, Pergamon Press.

in a family, children in a classroom, patients on a ward), introducing the intervention at different points in time to each individual. Similarly, baseline data can be collected across different situations (e.g., in the ward, hospital grounds, and dining room) for a given individual, with the intervention at different points in time for each situation. In each version, the impact of the intervention is demonstrated if behavior changes when and only when the intervention is introduced.

Considerations

The multiple-baseline design demonstrates the effect of the intervention without a return-to-baseline conditions and a temporary loss of some of the gains achieved. Two major considerations that affect the clarity of the demonstration are the number and the independence of the baselines. The number of baselines adequate for a clear demonstration is difficult to specify. Although two baselines are a minimum, more baselines usually are desirable. The clarity of the demonstration across a given set of baselines is a function of such factors as the duration of baselines, the presence of trends or extensive variability of behavior during the baselines phase, the rapidity of behavior change after treatment is implemented, and the magnitude of behavior change. Depending on these factors, even a few baselines may provide a sufficiently convincing demonstration.

The number of baselines needed to demonstrate clear effects may depend on the problem of interdependence of the baselines. The design depends on showing that the behavior changes when and only when the treatment is implemented. Ideally, behaviors still exposed to the baseline condition do not change until the intervention is applied. If they do, it suggests that the intervention may not have been responsible for change. Rather, extraneous factors (e.g., history, testing) may have led to the change.

Occasionally, the effects produced by an intervention may be general rather than specific so that a change in one behavior is associated with changes in other behaviors. This interdependence of the baselines presents a potential problem for each version of the multiple-baseline design. When baselines consist of different behaviors in the same individual, change in one behavior may be associated with changes in other responses as well, even though these latter behaviors are not subjected to the treatment. The interdependence of baselines has been evident in other variations of the design (see Kazdin, 1982b). When baselines consist of a given behavior across separate individuals, change in the behavior of one individual may be associated with changes in other individuals as well. In addition, when baselines consist of a given behavior of one individual across separate situations, change in behavior in one of the situations may spread to other situations in which the intervention has yet to be introduced. Thus each version of the multiple-baseline design has the potential problem of interdependence of the baselines from which the data were gathered. Generalized effects across different baselines currently appear to be exceptions rather than the rule. When generalized effects are present, features from other single-case designs (e.g., a brief reversal phase) can be added in separate experimental phases to demonstrate a causal relation between treatment and behavior change.

Simultaneous-Treatment Design

Description

The *simultaneous-treatment* or *alternating-treatment design* allows comparison of different treatments within the individual subject (Barlow & Hayes, 1979; Kazdin & Hartmann, 1978). The design is unique in this sense. Although other single-case designs might be used to compare different treatments, they are not well suited for this purpose. For example, in the ABAB design, different treatments (B, C) could be provided in different phases (ABCABC). When this is done, however, the different treatments are obscured by multiple-treatment interference. One treatment may be more or less effective because of its specific treatment characteristics or because it preceded or followed the other treatment. The impact of a specific ordering of treatment can be ruled out if more than one individual is studied so that the treatments can be counterbalanced in separate ABAB designs. However, this is not equivalent to comparing different treatments with only one individual.

The simultaneous-treatment design provides different interventions in the same phase in such a way that a sequence or series of treatments are avoided. Thus treatments can be compared in situations where the investigator wishes to determine which among alternative treatments is most effective. As soon as the most effective intervention is identified, it can be implemented consistently to alter the behavior.

The design begins with baseline observations of a single response of a given subject. The behavior must be observed under different circumstances or at different times of the day so that there are at least two daily observation periods. After baseline is completed, two or more interventions are implemented to alter the response. The interventions are implemented concurrently but during the different observation periods. The interventions are varied daily so that they are *balanced* across the separate time periods and so that their effects can be separated from these time periods. The intervention phase is continued, varying the conditions of administration, until the response stabilizes under each of the separate interventions. If one of the interventions emerges as superior to the others, it can be implemented across each period in the final phase.

In the simplest version of the design, the separate treatments are balanced across different time periods only. In more complex versions, the interventions also are balanced across different individuals who administer treatment (e.g., parents at home or staff members in an institution) or other conditions (e.g., classrooms). If the different interventions are balanced across both time periods and treatment agents, at some point in the intervention phase the treatment agents need to administer each of the treatments at different points in time. However, this is not essential and often is difficult to arrange for practical reasons.

Illustration

A simultaneous-treatment design was used to evaluate different interventions designed to reduce the frequency of stereotyped repetitive movements among hospitalized mentally retarded children (Ollendick, Shapiro, & Barrett, 1981). Three children, ages 7 to 8 years old, exhibited stereotypic behaviors such as repetitive hand gestures and hair twirling. Observations of the children were made in a classroom setting while each child performed various visual–motor tasks (e.g., puzzles). Behavior was observed each day for three sessions, after which the intervention phase was implemented.

During the intervention phase, three conditions were compared, including two active interventions and a continuation of baseline conditions. One treatment procedure consisted of physically restraining the child's hands on the table for 30 seconds so he or she could not perform the repetitive behaviors. The second treatment consisted of physically guiding the child to engage in the appropriate use of the task materials. Instead of merely restraining the child, this procedure was designed to develop appropriate alternative behaviors the children could perform with their hands. The final condition during the intervention phase was a continuation of baseline. Physical restraint, positive practice, and continuation of baseline were implemented each day across the three different time periods.

Figure 7.6 illustrates the results for one child who engaged in hand-posturing gestures. As evident from the first intervention phase, both physical restraint and positive practice led to reductions in performance; positive practice was more effective. The extent of the reduction is especially clear in light of the continuation of baseline as a third condition during the intervention phase. When baseline (no-treatment) conditions were in effect during the intervention phase, performance remained at the approximate level of the original baseline phase. In the final phase, positive practice was applied to all of the time periods each day. Positive practice, which had proved to be the most effective condition in the previous phase, also led to dramatic reductions in performance when implemented across all time periods. Thus the strength of this intervention is especially clear from the design.

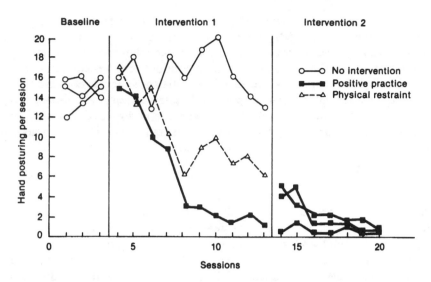

Figure 7.6. Stereotypic hand-posturing across experimental conditions. The three separate lines in each phase represent three separate time periods each session. Only in the initial intervention phase (Intervention 1) were the three separate conditions in effect. In the second intervention phase (Intervention 2) positive practice was in effect for all three periods. Source: Ollendick, T.H., Shapiro, E.S., & Barrett. R.P. [1981]. Reducing stereotypic behaviors: An analysis of treatment procedures using an alternating-treatments design. *Behavior Therapy, 12,* 570–577. Reprinted with permission.

Considerations

This design addresses the very practical question of which among alternative interventions is the most effective for a particular client. This question can be addressed without using a reversal or return-to-baseline phase to demonstrate the effects of treatment. If the different interventions have different effects on behavior, the pattern of results is not likely to be explained by extraneous events that coincided with the onset of the intervention phase. That is, history, maturation, repeated observation, and similar threats are not likely to be plausible rival interpretations of the results. The plausibility of the interventions accounting for change is bolstered by implementing the more or most effective intervention across all conditions of administration in the final phase of the experiment. When the most effective intervention is administered across all conditions of administration, performance should increase beyond the previous phase.

There are obstacles that may limit use of the design or particular variations of it. To begin with, it may be difficult to balance different interventions across both time periods and individuals who administer treatment. These latter conditions must be balanced in some way so that they are not confounded with treatment. Yet to balance interventions across these conditions may require a large number of treatment sessions, particularly if there are more than two interventions that are compared.

The design depends on showing changes for a given behavior across daily sessions or time periods. This means that behavior must shift rapidly as the intervention is changed at different points in time. Interventions that have carryover effects after they are terminated (e.g., drugs) would not be appropriate for this design. The interventions could not be kept distinct each day. Similarly, the behaviors studied with this design must be of the sort that can change readily within a given day. Behaviors that can vary from moment to moment or change rapidly (e.g., tantrums, anxiety, somatic complaints) are well suited to the design. Less transient response measures such as daily weight loss would not show the rapid change from shifts in interventions that were differentially effective in a single day. Thus some thought needs to be given to whether the interventions and behavior focused on can shift quickly enough to demonstrate the effects of interest.

A potential consideration in using the design is the client's ability to detect the differences between treatments. The treatments are not consistently associated with a given time period or therapeutic agent because these treatments are constantly varied across these conditions. If the treatments are very similar, the client may not be able to discriminate differences, especially if treatment is administered for only a few days or for a short time in any given day. Behavior may change across both treatments, but the treatment may not appear differentially effective because the client cannot detect which treatment is in effect at a given time.

A related concern is that the effects of administering each intervention in the same phase may differ from what they would be if the interventions were administered in separate phases. The effect of a given treatment is sometimes determined by other interventions administered in close temporal proximity, as discussed earlier under the notion of sequence effects. Similarly, in the simultaneous-treatment design there may be a unique form of multiple-treatment interference or sequence effects in which the effect of a given treatment is somehow determined by the other treatments to which it is compared.

The above cautions should not detract from the unique advantages of the simultaneous-treatment design. The design allows comparisons of different treatments with an individual client. In this sense, it provides an important addition to an investigator's armamentarium as a viable design option.

Changing-Criterion Design

Description

The *changing-criterion design* demonstrates the effect of an intervention by showing that behavior changes in increments to match a performance criterion. A causal relation between an intervention and behavior is demonstrated if behavior matches a constantly changing criterion for performance over the course of treatment (see Hartmann & Hall, 1976).

The design begins with a baseline phase after which the intervention is introduced. When the intervention is introduced, a specific level of performance is chosen as a criterion for the client. The daily criterion may be used as a basis for providing response consequences or an incentive of some sort. For example, a response may have to be performed at a certain level specified by the investigator. The criterion, of course, can be negotiated with the client. When the performance meets or surpasses the criterion level on a given day (e.g., certain number of cigarettes smoked, number of calories consumed), the response consequence (e.g., monetary reward) is provided. When performance consistently meets the criterion, say for a few days, the criterion is made more stringent (e.g., fewer cigarettes or calories consumed daily). Consequences are provided only for meeting the new criterion on a given day, and the criterion again is changed if the performance meets the criterion consistently. The criterion is repeatedly changed throughout the intervention phase until the terminal goal of the program is achieved. The effect of the intervention is demonstrated if behavior matches a criterion as the criterion is changed. If behavior changes with the criterion, it is likely that the intervention and criterion change rather than extraneous influences accounted for behavior change.

To demonstrate that performance matches the criterion, a particular criterion usually is invoked continuously for at least a few days. If performance attains the criterion and continues at that level for a few days, this suggests that the intervention accounts for change. By implementing a given criterion for at least a few days (or even longer), the behavior shows a step-like effect that is not likely to result from a general incremental change occurring as a function of extraneous events.

Illustration

In one study, a changing-criterion design was employed to evaluate a program for caffeine consumption in three adults (Foxx & Rubinoff, 1979). Caffeine consumed in large quantities has been associated with a variety of symptoms ranging in severity from general irritability and gastrointestinal disturbances to cardiovascular disorders and cancer. The intervention consisted of having participants, at the beginning of the program, deposit money ($20) that was returned in small portions if caffeine consumption fell below the criterion set for a given day. Participants signed a contract that specified how they would earn back or lose the money. Each person recorded daily caffeine consumption on the basis of a list of beverages that provided their caffeine equivalence (in milligrams).

The effects of the program for one subject, a female school teacher, are illustrated in Figure 7.7. During baseline, her daily average caffeine consumption was 1000 mg (equal to approximately eight cups of brewed coffee). When the intervention began, she was required to reduce her daily consumption by about 100 mg below baseline. When performance was consistently below the criterion (solid line), the criterion was reduced further by approximately 100 mg. This change in the criterion continued over separate subphases. In each subphase, money was earned back only if caffeine consumption fell at or below the criterion. The figure shows that performance consistently fell below the criterion. Assessment 10 months after the program had ended indicated that she maintained her low rate of caffeine consumption.

Considerations

The design depends on repeatedly changing the performance criterion and examining behavior relative to the new criterion. The design is especially well suited to those terminal responses that are arrived at gradually rather than responses acquired in one or a few trials. For most therapeutic problems, individuals usually must acquire the skills, overcome problematic situations, or gain comfort gradually so that this requirement may be met. If behavior

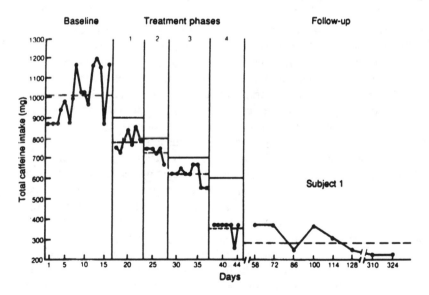

Figure 7.7. Subject's daily caffeine intake in milligrams during baseline, treatment, and follow-up. The criterion level for each treatment phase was 102 milligrams of caffeine less than that of the previous treatment phase. Solid horizontal lines indicate the criterion level for each phase. Broken horizontal lines indicate the mean for each condition. Source: Foxx, R.M., & Rubinoff, A. (1979). Behavioral treatment of caffeinism: Reducing excessive coffee drinking. *Journal of Applied Behavior Analysis, 12,* 335–344. Reprinted with permission.

change occurs in large steps and does not follow the criterion, the specific effect of the intervention in altering behavior will not be clear. Thus the design tends to be limited to demonstrating gradual rather than rapid changes because of the requirement of the changing criterion.

In general, the changing-criterion design is less powerful than other single-case designs because the effects of extraneous events could account for a general increase or decrease in behavior. The design depends on showing a unidirectional change in behavior (increase or decrease) over time. However, extraneous events rather than the intervention could result in unidirectional changes. The demonstration is unambiguous only if performance matches the criterion very closely and the criterion is changed several times. The design is strengthened by making bidirectional changes in the criterion during the intervention phase. Rather than simply making the criterion increasingly stringent, it can be made more stringent at some points and less stringent at others to weaken the plausibility that extraneous events account for the results. Of course, reversing behavior, even if only to a small degree and for a brief period, may be countertherapeutic.

General Comments

Single-case designs offer a distinct advantage for treatment research. To begin with, single-case methodology provides the means to investigate treatments empirically with individual clients. Traditionally, study of the individual client has been restricted to anecdotal reports about the course of change. Therapist impressions and uncontrolled implementation of treatment eliminate the possibility of drawing unchallenged causal inferences. In contrast, single-case designs allow careful evaluation of treatment by addressing threats to internal validity that serve as the basis for drawing causal inferences. Actually, several different questions can be addressed. The methodology permits evaluating the effects of an overall treatment package, withdrawing components of treatment over time to determine an essential treatment ingredient, adding components of treatment to enhance behavior change, and comparing different treatments.

Another advantage of single-case designs is that they permit investigation of problems that are not likely to be studied in between-group research. There are many clinical problems that are relatively rare so that it would be extraordinarily difficult to recruit subjects for a large-scale treatment evaluation project. Yet single-case designs allow careful investigation of an individual client. Thus information can be obtained from experimentation with a single case that otherwise might not be available.

For example, Barlow, Reynolds, and Agras (1973) reported the treatment of a 17-year-old male who desired to be a female. His behaviors and attitudes reflects his transsexual interest as evident in attraction to other males, a history of cross dressing, interest in traditionally feminine role behaviors such as knitting, crocheting, embroidering, sexual fantasies in which he imagined himself as a woman, effeminate mannerisms in sitting, standing, and walking, and so on. Extensive treatment based on modeling, rehearsal, and feedback was used to alter a variety of effeminate mannerisms, speaking patterns, social skills, sexual fantasies, and sexual arousal. The effects of training were demonstrated in a complex set of ABAB and multiple-baseline designs. This report is unique in experimentally demonstrating successful psychotherapeutic treatment of a transsexual. It is unlikely that this demonstration could have been accomplished with several transsexuals in a between-group design if for no other reason than the difficulty in recruiting such clients in sufficient numbers who would be interested in treatment other than direct physical change through surgery.

Although single-case designs provide an important contribution to treatment evaluation, they have distinct limitations. For example, single-case designs are weak in revealing subject characteristics that may interact with a specific treatment. Focusing on one subject or client, of course, does not allow systematically comparing treatments across multiple subjects who differ in various characteristics, at least within the same experiment. Examination of subject variables is more readily accomplished by group research, specifically factorial designs, where multiple subjects necessarily are required.

Related to the study of subject variables, the results of single-case investigations provide no hint of the generality of findings (external validity) to other subjects. Quite possibly, the effects of treatment demonstrated with the individual case will not generalize to other individuals. Within the single-case investigation, the investigator cannot determine how many clients would reveal the same pattern of change. However, it is important to note that the lack of generality of single-case findings is not a limitation of current research. Findings obtained in single-case experiments have had no less generality, and possibly greater generality, than findings from between-group research. Part of the reason for the generality of findings from single-case research is that treatment applications with the single case have sought extremely potent effects. Consequently, it has been argued that interventions with such effects for the single case are likely to generalize more broadly than are interventions that may meet the relatively weaker criterion of statistical significance (see Baer, 1977).

QUASI-EXPERIMENTS WITH THE SINGLE CASE

In our discussion of single cases, we have covered two methodological extremes. We began by mentioning uncontrolled case studies, which usually consist of narrative reports, undocumented interventions, subjectively filtered descriptions, and absence of experimental control. As a method of study, uncontrolled cases are wanting because they typically are subject to a vast range of validity threats. At the other extreme, we have discussed true single-case experimental designs. Such designs as the ABAB, multiple-baseline, and other designs provide arrangements that readily rule out threats to internal validity and permit causal conclusions about the effects of alternative interventions. Between the extremes of the uncontrolled case study and true single-case experiments are *quasi-experiments for the single case*. These consist of explicit efforts to incorporate several features of true experiments. In clinical work, occasionally the conditions of true single-case experiments cannot be met. Several alternatives exist to evaluate interventions and to meet clinical exigencies of the case.

Characteristics

The essential features of true single-case *experiments* are (a) controlling administration of the intervention (e.g., withdrawing and presenting alternative intervention and/or baseline conditions), (b) assessing performance continuously over time and under different conditions, and (c) looking for stable patterns to make and test predictions about performance. Consider these components in terms of their methodological role in drawing inferences. These features of the true experiments are weapons that directly combat threats to validity, particularly internal validity. Case studies can be arranged to deploy various combinations of these weapons to greatly increase the extent to which threats to validity are ruled out or made implausible (Kazdin, 1981). There are several characteristics we seek to add to the uncontrolled case to improve their yield.

Type of Data

Case studies may vary in the type of data or information that is used as a basis for claiming that change has been achieved. At one extreme, *anecdotal information* may be used, which includes reports by the client or therapist that therapeutic change has been achieved. At the other extreme, case studies can include *quantitative information,* such as scores from self-report inventories, ratings by other persons, and direct measures of overt behavior. Individual measures have their own problems (e.g., reactivity, response biases) but still provide a stronger basis for determining whether change has occurred than anecdotal accounts. If reliable quantitative information is available, at least the therapist has a better basis for claiming that change has been achieved. The data do not allow one to infer the basis for the change. Yet data serve as a prerequisite because they provide information that change has in fact occurred.

Assessment Occasions

Another dimension that can distinguish case studies is the *number and timing of the assessment occasions.* The occasions in which quantitative information is collected have extremely important implications for drawing inferences about the effects of the intervention. Major options consist of collecting information on a *one- or two-shot basis* (e.g., posttreatment only or pre- and posttreatment) or *continuously over time* (e.g., every day or a few times per week for an extended period). When information is collected on one or two occasions, there are special difficulties in explaining the basis of the changes. Threats to internal validity (e.g., testing, instrumentation, statistical regression) are especially difficult to rule out. With continuous assessment over time, these threats are much less plausible, especially if continuous assessment begins before treatment and continues over the course of treatment. Continuous assessment allows one to examine the pattern of the data and whether the pattern appears to have been altered at the point in which the intervention was introduced. If a case study includes continuous assessment on several occasions over time, some of the threats to internal validity related to assessment can be ruled out.

Past and Future Projections of Performance

The extent to which claims can be made about performance in the past and likely performance in the future can distinguish cases. Past and future projections refer to the course of a particular behavior or problem. For some behaviors or problems, an extended *history* may be evident indicating no change. If performance changes when treatment is applied, the likelihood that treatment caused the change is increased. Problems that have a short history or that tend to occur for brief periods or in episodes may have changed anyway without the treatment. Problems with an extended history of stable performance are likely to have continued unless some special event (e.g., treatment) altered its course. Thus the history of the problem may dictate the likelihood that extraneous events, other than treatment, could plausibly account for the change.

Projections of what performance would be like in the *future* might be obtained from knowledge of the nature of the problem. For example, the problem may be one that would not improve without intervention (e.g., terminal illness). Knowing the likely outcome increases the inferences that can be drawn about the impact of an intervention that alters this course. The patient's improvement attests to the efficacy of the treatment as the critical variable because change in the problem controverts the expected prediction.

Projections of future performance may derive from continuous assessment over time. If a particular problem is very stable, as indicated by continuous assessment before treatment, the likely prediction is that it will remain at that level in the future. If an intervention is applied and performance departs from the predicted level, this suggests that the intervention rather than other factors (e.g., history and maturation, repeated testing) may have been responsible for the change.

Type of Effect

Cases also differ in terms of the type of effects or changes that are evident as treatment is applied. The *immediacy and magnitude of change* contribute to the inferences drawn about the role of treatment. Usually, the more immediate the therapeutic change after the onset of treatment, the stronger a case can be made that the treatment was responsible for change. An immediate change with the onset of treatment may make it more plausible that the treatment, rather than other events (e.g., history and maturation), led to change. On the other hand, gradual changes or changes that begin well after treatment has been applied are more difficult to interpret because of the intervening experiences between the onset of treatment and therapeutic change.

Aside from the immediacy of change, the magnitude of the change is important as well. When marked changes in performance are achieved, this suggests that only a special event, probably the treatment, could be responsible. Of course, the magnitude and immediacy of change, when combined, increase the confidence one can place in according treatment a causal role. Rapid and dramatic changes provide a strong basis for attributing the effects to treatment. Gradual and relatively small changes might more easily be discounted as random fluctuations of performance, normal cycles of behavior, or developmental changes.

Number and Heterogeneity of Subjects

The *number of subjects* included in a case report can influence the confidence that can be placed in any inferences drawn about treatment. Demonstrations with several cases, rather than with one case, provide a stronger basis for inferring the effects of treatment. Essentially, each case can be viewed as a replication of the original effect that seemed to result from treatment. The more cases that improve with treatment, the more unlikely that any particular extraneous event was responsible for change. Extraneous events probably varied among the cases, and the common experience, namely, treatment, may be the most plausible reason for the therapeutic changes.

The *heterogeneity of the cases* or diversity of the types of people may also contribute to inferences about the cause of therapeutic change. If change is demonstrated among several clients who differ in subject and demographic variables (e.g., age, gender, race, social class, clinical problems), the inferences that can be made about treatment are stronger than if this diversity does not exist. With a heterogeneous set of clients, the likelihood that a particular threat to internal validity (e.g., history, maturation) could explain the results is reduced.

General Comments

The previously mentioned characteristics when applied to clinical cases can greatly increase the strength of inferences that can be drawn relative to uncontrolled case studies. Depending on how the different characteristics are addressed within a particular demonstration, it is quite possible that the inferences closely approximate those that could be obtained from a true single-case experiment. Not all of the dimensions are under the control of the clinician–investigator (e.g., immediacy and strength of treatment effects). On the other hand, critical features on which conclusions depend, such as collecting data and assessing performance on multiple occasions, can be controlled in the clinical situation and greatly enhance the demonstration.

Design Variations

Any given case study can be evaluated on each of the dimensions previously discussed. The extent to which valid inferences can be drawn and threats to internal validity eliminated or reduced are determined by where the case falls in relation to these characteristics. Of course, it would be impossible to present all the types of case studies that could be distinguished; an indefinite number could be generated, based on where the case lies on each characteristic. Yet it is important to look at a few types of quasi-experiments with the single-case based on the characteristics and to examine how adequately internal validity is addressed.

Table 7.1 illustrates a few types of uncontrolled case studies that differ on some of the characteristics mentioned previously. Also, the extent to which each type of case rules out the specific threats to internal validity is presented. For each type of case the collection of objective data was included because, as noted earlier, the absence of quantifiable data usually precludes drawing conclusions about whether change occurred.

Case Study Type 1: With Pre- and Postassessment

A case study in which a client is treated may utilize pre- and posttreatment assessment. The inferences that can be drawn from a case with such assessment are not necessarily strengthened by the assessment procedures alone. Whether specific threats to internal validity are ruled out depends on other characteristics noted previously. Table 7.1 illustrates a case with pre- and postassessment but without other characteristics that would help rule out threats to internal validity.

If changes occur in the case from pre- to posttreatment assessment, one cannot draw valid inferences about whether the treatment led to change. It is quite possible that events occurring in time (history), processes of change within the individual (maturation), repeated exposure to assessment (testing), changes in the scoring criteria (instrumentation), or reversion of the score to the mean (regression) rather than treatment led to change. The case included quantitative assessment, so that there is a firmer basis for claiming that changes were made than if only anecdotal reports were provided. Yet threats

Table 7.1. Selected Types of Hypothetical Cases and the Threats to Internal Validity They Address

TYPE OF CASE STUDY	TYPE I	TYPE II	TYPE III
Characteristics of case present (+) or absent (−)			
Quantitative data	+	+	+
Continuous assessment	−	+	+
Stability of problem	−	−	+
Immediate and marked effects	−	+	−
Multiple cases	−	−	+
Major Threats to Internal Validity Ruled Out (+)			
or Not Ruled Out (−)			
History	−	?	+
Maturation	−	?	+
Testing	−	+	+
Instrumentation	−	+	+
Statistical regression	−	+	+

Note. In the table, a "+" indicates that the threat to internal validity is probably controlled, a "−" indicates that the threat remains a problem, and a "?" indicates that the threat may remain uncontrolled.

In preparation of the table, selected threats were omitted because they arise primarily in the comparison of different groups in experiments. They are not usually a problem for a case study, which, of course, does not rely on group comparisons.

to internal validity were not ruled out, so the basis for change remains a matter of surmise.

Case Study Type 2: With Repeated Assessment and Marked Changes

If the case study includes assessment on several occasions before and after treatment and the changes associated with the intervention are relatively marked, the inferences that can be drawn about treatment are vastly improved. Table 7.1 illustrates the characteristics of such a case, along with the extent to which specific threats to internal validity are addressed.

The fact that continuous assessment is included is important in ruling out the specific threats to internal validity related to assessment. First, the changes that coincide with treatment are not likely to result from exposure to repeated testing or changes in the instrument. When continuous assessment is used, changes due to testing or instrumentation would have been evident before treatment began. Similarly, regression to the mean from one data point to another, a special problem with assessment conducted at only two points in time, is eliminated. Repeated observation over time shows a *pattern* in the data. Extreme scores may be a problem for any particular assessment occasion in relation to the immediately prior occasion. However, these changes cannot account for the pattern of performance for an extended period.

Aside from continuous assessment, this illustration includes relatively marked treatment effects, that is, changes that are relatively immediate and large. These types of changes produced in treatment help reduce the possibility that history and maturation explain the results. Maturation in particular may be relatively implausible because maturational changes are not likely to be abrupt and large. Nevertheless, a question mark ("?") was placed in the table because maturation cannot be ruled out completely. In this case example, information on the stability of the problem in the past and future was not included. Hence, it is not known whether the clinical problem might ordinarily change on its own and whether maturational influences are plausible. Some dysfunctions that are episodic (e.g., some forms of depression) in nature conceivably could show marked changes that have little to do with treatment. With immediate and large changes in behavior, history and maturation may be ruled out too, although these are likely to depend on other characteristics in the table that specifically were omitted from this case.

Case Study Type 3: With Multiple Cases, Continuous Assessment, and Stability Information

Several cases rather than only one may be studied where each includes continuous assessment. The cases may be treated one at a time and accumulated into a final summary statement of treatment effects or treated as a single group at the same time. In this illustration, assessment information is available on repeated occasions before and after treatment. Also, the stability of the problem is known in this example. Stability refers to the dimension of past–future projections and denotes that other research suggests that the problem does not usually change over time. When the problem is known to be highly stable or to follow a particular course without treatment, the investigator has an implicit prediction of the effects of no treatment. The results can be compared with this predicted level of performance.

As is evident in Table 7.1, several threats to internal validity are addressed by a case report meeting the specified characteristics. History and maturation are not likely to interfere with drawing conclusions about the causal role of treatment because several different cases are included. All cases are not likely to have a single historical event or maturational process in common that could account for the results. Knowledge about the stability of the problem in the future also helps to rule out the influence of history and maturation. If the problem is known to be stable over time, this means that ordinary historical events and maturational processes do not provide a strong enough influence in their own right. Because of the use of multiple subjects and the knowledge about the stability of the problem, history and maturation probably are implausible explanations of therapeutic change.

The threats to internal validity related to testing are handled largely by continuous assessment over time. Repeated testing, changes in the instrument, and reversion of scores toward the mean may influence performance from one occasion to another. Yet problems associated with testing are not likely to influence the pattern of data over a large number of occasions. Also, information about the stability of the problem helps to further make implausible changes due to testing. The fact that the problem is known to be stable means that it probably would not change merely as a function of repeated assessment.

In general, the case study of the type illustrated in this example provides a strong basis for drawing valid inferences about the impact of treatment. The manner in which the multiple-case report is designed does not constitute an experiment, as usually conceived, because each case represents an uncontrolled demonstration. However, characteristics of the type of case study can rule out specific threats to internal validity in a manner approaching that of true experiments.

Case Illustrations

The previous comments convey that a given pattern of information and data can contribute greatly to the extent to which case studies can make implausible threats to experimental validity. A few illustrations convey more concretely the continuum of confidence one might place in the notion that the intervention was responsible for change. Each illustration qualifies as a quasi-experiment because it captures features of true experiments and varies in the extent to which specific threats can be made implausible.

In the first illustration, treatment was applied to decrease the weight of an obese 55-year-old woman (180 lb., 5'5"; Martin & Sachs, 1973). The woman had been advised to lose weight, a recommendation of some urgency because she had recently had a heart attack. The woman was treated as an outpatient. The treatment consisted of developing a contract or agreement with the therapist based on adherence to a variety of rules and recommendations that would alter her eating habits. Several rules were developed pertaining to rewarding herself for resisting tempting foods, recording what she ate after meals and snacks, weighing herself frequently each day, chewing foods slowly, and following other guidelines. The patient had been weighed before treatment, and therapy began with weekly assessment for a 4½-week period.

The results of the program, which appear in Figure 7.8, indicate that the woman's initial weight of 180 was followed by a gradual decline in weight over the next few weeks before treatment was terminated. For present purposes, what can be said about the impact of treatment? Actually, statements about the effects of the treatment in accounting for the changes would be tentative at best. To begin with, the stability of her pretreatment weight is unclear. The first data point indicated that the woman was 180 lb. before treatment. Perhaps this weight would have declined over the next few weeks even without a special weight-reduction program. The absence of clear information regarding the stability of the woman's weight before treatment makes evaluation of her subsequent loss rather difficult. The weight loss is clear, but it would be difficult to argue strongly that the intervention rather than historical events, maturational processes, or repeated assessment could not have led to the same results.

The next illustration provides a slightly more persuasive demonstration that treatment may have led to the results. This case included a 28-year-old woman with a 15-year history of an itchy inflamed rash on her neck (Dobes, 1977). The rash included oozing lesions and scar tissue, which were exacerbated by her constant scratching. A program was designed to decrease scratching. Instances of scratching were recorded each day by the client on a wrist counter she wore. Before treatment, her initial rate of scratching was observed daily. After 6 days, the program was begun. The client was instructed to graph her scratching and to try to decrease her frequency of scratching each day by at least two or three instances. If she had obtained her weekly goal in reducing her scratching, she and her husband would go out to dinner. The results of the program appear in Figure 7.9, which shows her daily rate of scratching across baseline and intervention phases.

The results suggest that the intervention may have been responsible for the change. The inference is aided by continuous assessment over time before and during the intervention phase. The problem appeared at a fairly stable level before the intervention, which helps to suggest that it may not have changed

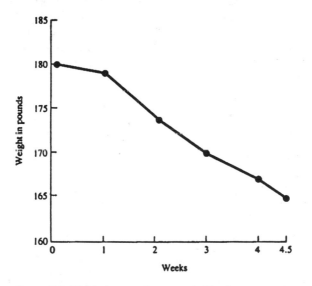

Figure 7.8. Weight in pounds per week. The line represents the connecting of the weights, respectively, on the days 0, 7, 14, 21, 28, and 31 of the weight-loss program. Reprinted with permission from *Journal of Behavior Therapy and Experimental Psychiatry, 4,* J.E. Martin and D.A. Sachs, The effects of a self-control weight loss program on an obese woman, 1973, Pergamon Press.

without the intervention. A few features of the demonstration may detract from the confidence one might place in according treatment a causal role. The gradual and slow decline of the behavior was intentionally programmed in the treatment, so the client reduced scratching when she had mastered the previous level. The gradual decline evident in the figure might also have resulted from other influences, such as increased attention from her husband (historical event) or boredom with continuing the assessment procedure (maturation). Also, the fact that the patient was responsible for collecting the observations raises concerns about whether accuracy of scoring changed (instrumentation) over time rather than the actual rate of scratching. Yet the data can be taken as presented without undue methodological skepticism. As such, the intervention appears to have led to change, but the quasi-experimental nature of the design and the pattern of results make it difficult to rule out threats to internal validity with great confidence.

In the next illustration, the effects of the intervention appeared even clearer than in the previous example. In this report, an extremely aggressive 4½-year-old boy served as the focus (Firestone, 1976). The boy had been expelled from nursery school in the previous year for his aggressive behavior and was on the verge of expulsion again. Several behaviors including physical aggression (kicking, striking, or pulling others and destroying property) were observed for approximately 2 hours each day in his nursery school class. After a few days of baseline, a time-out from reinforcement procedure was used to suppress aggressive acts. The procedure consisted of placing the child in a chair in a

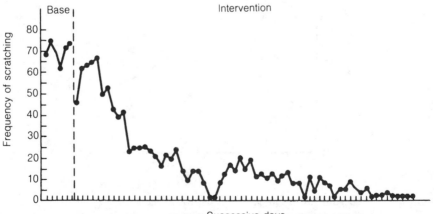

Figure 7.9. Frequency of scratching over the course of baseline and behavioral intervention phases. Reprinted with permission from *Journal of Behavior Therapy and Experimental Psychiatry, 8,* R. W. Dobes, Amelioration of psychosomatic dermatosis by reinforced inhibition of scratching, 1977, Pergamon Press.

corner of the classroom in which there were no toys or other rewarding activities. He was to remain in the chair until he was quiet for 2 minutes.

The effects of the procedure in suppressing aggressive acts are illustrated in Figure 7.10. The first few baseline days suggest a relatively consistent rate of aggressive acts. When the time-out procedure was implemented, behavior sharply declined, after which it remained at a very stable rate. Can the effects be attributed to the intervention? The few days of observation in baseline suggest a stable pattern, and the onset of the intervention was associated with rapid and marked effects. It is unlikely that history, maturation, or other threats could readily account for the results. Within the limits of quasi-experimental designs, the results are relatively clear.

Among the previous examples, the likelihood that the intervention accounted for change was increasingly plausible in light of characteristics of the report. In this final illustration, the effects of the intervention are extremely clear. The purpose of this report was to investigate a novel method of treating bed-wetting (enuresis) among children (Azrin, Hontos, & Besalel-Azrin,

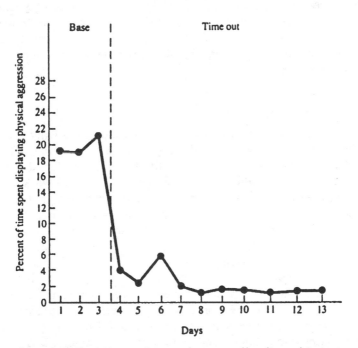

Figure 7.10. Physical aggression over the course of baseline and time out from reinforcement conditions. Reprinted with permission from *Journal of Behavior Therapy and Experimental Psychiatry, 7,* P. Firestone, The effects and side effects of timeout on an aggressive nursery school child, 1976, Pergamon Press.

1979). Forty-four children, ranging in age from 3 to 15 years, were included. Their families collected data on the number of nighttime bed-wetting accidents for 7 days before treatment. After baseline, the training procedure was implemented: The child was required to practice getting up from bed at night, remaking the bed after he or she wet it, and changing clothes. Other procedures were included as well, such as waking the child early at night in the beginning of training, developing increased bladder capacity by reinforcing increases in urine volume, and so on. The parents and children practiced some of the procedures in the training session, but the intervention was essentially carried out at home when the child wet his or her bed.

The effects of training are illustrated in Figure 7.11, which shows bed-wetting during the pretraining (baseline) and training periods. The demonstration is a quasi-experimental design, because several of the conditions discussed previously were included to help rule out threats to internal validity. The data suggest that the problem was relatively stable for the group as a whole during the baseline period. Also, the changes in performance at the onset of treatment were immediate and marked. Finally, several subjects were included who probably were not very homogeneous as a group (encompassing young children through teenagers). In light of these characteristics of the demonstration, it is not very plausible that the changes could be accounted for by history, maturation, repeated assessment, changes in the assessment procedures, or statistical regression.

General Comments

The use of features of single-case designs as aids in clinical situations addresses a broader point. Threats to internal validity in any given research and clinical situation warrant close scrutiny. Plausible threats when recognized in advance can be circumvented or addressed in many ways. In clinical work, adopting many of the features of true single-case experimental designs can greatly strengthen the conclusions that can be drawn. In any given case, the arrangement of approximations or quasi-experiments can reduce the plausibility of threats to validity in ways that are as clear as true experiments. The use of design features from single-case experiments are not mere methodological niceties. When integrated with clinical work, they can greatly improve upon evaluation of treatment progress and patient care. Such work no doubt entails complexities not addressed here such as developing measures to assess special characteristics and using standard measures in novel ways (e.g., continuous assessment of psychopathology and depression using standardized scales not designed to reflect changes over several brief periods). However imperfect quasi-experimental evaluations may prove to be, they offer distinct advantages over and above anecdotal cases with which they often compete.

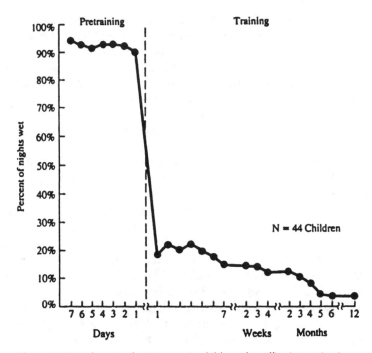

Figure 7.11. Bed-wetting by 44 enuretic children after office instruction in an operant learning method. Each data point designates the percentage of nights on which bed-wetting occurred. The data prior to the dotted line are for a 7-day period prior to training. The data are presented daily for the first week, weekly for the first month, and monthly for the first 6 months and for the 12th month. Source: Azrin, N.H., Hontos, P.T., & Besalel-Azrin, V. (1979). Elimination of enuresis without a conditioning apparatus: An extension by office instruction of the child and parents. *Behavior Therapy, 10,* 14–19. Reprinted with permission.

SUMMARY AND CONCLUSIONS

The study of the individual has played an important role in clinical psychology. Historically, *case studies* have led to important insights about the development of human personality, treatment, diagnosis of dysfunction, and other areas. As a method of study, uncontrolled and anecdotal case reports are limited. Results from a case study usually can be reinterpreted in so many ways that specific conclusions cannot be made without great ambiguity.

Single-case designs allow experimentation with the individual subject or client. The designs are *true experiments* in the sense that they address threats to experimental validity and demonstrate causal relations. The designs allow examination of several questions traditionally of interest in treatment evaluation: evaluating an overall treatment package, analyzing the components of treatment, building more effective treatments by adding components, and comparing different treatments. Several designs are available, including *ABAB, multiple-baseline, simultaneous-treatment,* and *changing-criterion designs,* each of which has its own variations depending precisely on how experimental control over performance is demonstrated. The designs vary in the questions that can be addressed, the way in which treatment effects are demonstrated, and the requirements for experimental evaluation. Also, the designs vary in their suitability in light of practical or clinical considerations. In clinical settings, the conditions for true single-case experiments cannot always be met. *Quasi-experiments* can be implemented that approximate true experiments in varying degrees.

Single-case designs have their limitations. Aside from limitations specific to each design, as a whole, the designs are not suited for evaluating subject characteristics by treatment interactions. Such interactions are more readily addressed in group factorial designs. Related to this, the designs do not allow immediate assessment of the generality of findings across subjects within a given experiment. Obviously, the investigator cannot assess how many of the subjects would show the same pattern of behavior if only one subject is included. These limitations do not impugn the value of the designs but rather only suggest limits in the questions for which they should be used.

FOR FURTHER READING

Barlow, D.H., & Hersen, M. (1984). *Single-case experimental designs: Strategies for studying behavior change* (2nd ed.). Elmsford, NY: Pergamon Press.
Bloom, M., & Fischer, J. (1982). *Evaluating practice: Guidelines for the accountable professional.* Englewood Cliffs, NJ: Prentice-Hall.
Johnston, J.M., & Pennypacker, H.S. (1980). *Strategies and tactics of human behavioral research.* Hillsdale, NJ: Lawrence Erlbaum Associates.
Kazdin, A.E. (1982). *Single-case research designs: Methods for clinical and applied settings.* New York: Oxford University Press.
Yin, R.K. (1984). *Case study research: Design and methods.* Beverly Hills, CA: Sage Publications.

Chapter 8

ASSESSING THE IMPACT OF THE EXPERIMENTAL MANIPULATION

Whatever the specific design of the research, the effects of some variable of interest is to be evaluated. For investigations in which some facet is varied by the investigator, the independent variable usually is manipulated by providing a particular condition to one group and omitting it from another group, providing varying degrees of a given condition to different groups, or presenting entirely distinct conditions to groups. However the independent variable is manipulated, the investigator seemingly needs only to provide these experimental conditions and then to assess whether subsequent performance of the subjects is altered. Actually, great care is required in manipulating the independent variable to ensure that the manipulation is likely to be a strong test of the hypothesis and that the variable or condition was manipulated as intended.

The strength of the test depends on quality control over the independent variable. Our goal as investigators is to convince ourselves as well as others that the hypothesis was well tested. Choosing the conditions or levels of a condition for the intervention or experimental manipulation of interest is essential to this end. Similarly, interpretation of the outcome of the experiment (construct validity) depends on assurances that the independent variable was implemented as intended. The focus on the independent variable and its manipulation or variation have a great deal to do with statistical conclusion validity as well. We not only wish to ensure that the independent variable is manipulated and varies between groups but also that there is consistency in how this is accomplished. Consistency of administration minimizes within-group variability and optimizes the sensitivity of the test.

The present chapter discusses the adequacy with which the independent variable is manipulated, the different ways in which the manipulation can be assessed, and the implications for interpreting the results of an experiment. The primary focus is on experimental research where the independent variable is controlled or manipulated by the investigator as in studies of variations in experimental conditions, instructions, tasks, or interventions presented to the subjects or clients. Much of clinical research involves subject-selection studies where groups are identified and compared. Hence analogous issues relevant to the adequacy of selection procedures are also discussed.

CHECKING ON THE EXPERIMENTAL MANIPULATION

The hypothesis of interest in the investigation is based on the assumption that the independent variable was effectively implemented. It is quite possible that the investigator will not manipulate the independent variable effectively enough to demonstrate the relation of interest or that those who implement the procedures (e.g., experimenters, therapists, parents, teachers) do not carry out the procedures as intended. It is extremely useful in clinical research to check whether the independent variable or intervention was implemented as intended.

Providing a check on the manipulation refers to independently assessing the independent variable and its effects on the subjects. The assessment is designed to determine whether the subject is exposed to conditions as intended. Assessment of the independent variable is distinguished both procedurally and conceptually from dependent variables included in the study. The check on the independent variable assesses whether the conditions of interest to the investigator were altered. This may mean merely that the stimulus was presented as intended or that the intervention was perceived by the subject. For example, in a psychotherapy study, a check on the independent variable would be achieved by ensuring that subjects actually received the treatment, that the number of sessions was provided as intended, that subjects in one group did not receive conditions appropriate for another group and so on. These are checks on the independent variable or interventions and are quite separate from the dependent measures (e.g., therapeutic change, symptom reduction, improved adjustment). Manipulation checks are critical in all studies where it is possible that the experimental condition is not faithfully rendered or presented.

In one sense, the best check on the effects of an independent variable is the dependent measure. The change in the independent variable is intended to alter the dependent measure, so the best test of the effects of the former is change in the latter. If the predicted results of an experiment are obtained, assessment of the independent variable to ensure that it has had the intended effect on the subject may not be essential. The predicted relation reduces ambiguity about the agent responsible for change. Presumably, the independent variable accounted for the results, barring obvious confounds. Even so, it is possible that the intervention produced the change by affecting a host of intervening processes in the individual and the construct of interest to the investigator was not the "crucial" one in the sense of being directly responsible for change. Also, it is possible that group differences at the end of the study support the prediction, albeit the independent variable was not manipulated well. Checking the extent to which the independent variable is effectively manipulated provides information that helps to rule out some of the different reasons that might account for the findings.

Types of Manipulations

The manner in which the success of the experimental manipulation can be assessed varies as a function of the type of manipulation. Manipulations vary in the types of variables (e.g., environmental, instructional, subject) and the precise conditions the investigator wishes to establish. Consider several different situations and the diverse manipulation checks that would be relevant.

Variations In Information

In many experiments, the manipulation refers to different information given to subjects across experimental conditions. The question to be answered for the check on the success of the manipulation is whether subjects received, attended to, and believed the information. Typically, subjects are provided with a questionnaire immediately after hearing the rationale or after exposure to the information to assess the success of the manipulation. For example, the independent variable might consist of varying the instructions about when personality change would occur. If different treatment rationales mentioned that a change would not occur for several weeks or that it would occur almost immediately, a postmanipulation questionnaire could assess approximately when subjects believed that personality changes would occur with the experimental manipulation. Presumably, if subjects respond to alternatives that reflect what they were told in their respective experimental conditions, the investigator could have more confidence that the independent variable was successfully manipulated.

When the manipulation relies on information, self-report questionnaires are frequently used to assess the success of the manipulation. A few questions might be all that are needed. These questions might be in true-false, multiple-choice, or open-ended (essay question) format. It is useful to include a true-false or multiple-choice format in most cases so that each question can be easily scored and answered. Open-ended questions might be used, such as "What is likely to happen in treatment?" or "Approximately when will behavior change?" These questions are useful because they do not divulge the purpose of the experiment or what the correct answers are as readily as true-false or multiple-choice questions. On the other hand, it is very difficult to score the subjects' responses to open-ended questions. Many subjects do not answer them, reply with only one or two words, or elaborate with extended discussions that miss the point of interest to the investigator.

In general, when the independent variable involves variation of information to the subject, the manipulation check is relatively straightforward. There usually is a check to ensure that the subjects received the appropriate information and that experimental groups are distinguishable on a measure that assesses that information. Self-report measures are commonly used because they are readily adaptable to the experiment by merely constructing examination-type questions.

Variations in Subject Behavior and Experience

Many manipulations consist of having subjects do something, engage in a particular task, actually carry out the instructions, or experience a particular emotion. The experimental question of interest is whether a certain task facilitates or hinders some outcome. Assessment of the success of the manipulation can take many forms, depending on what it is that subjects are supposed to do.

As an example, Dies and Greenberg (1976) were interested in assessing the importance of physical contact among participants in encounter groups on various personality measures. The manipulation consisted of having three different levels of physical contact in encounter groups that performed similar activities. One group made no physical contact during the sessions; another engaged in moderate physical contact; and a final group engaged in a high amount of physical contact (e.g., hand holding, embracing, sitting together with knees or shoulders touching). The groups engaged in similar encounter group exercises but were instructed to maintain differences in the amount of physical contact.

The investigators checked the manipulation to determine whether the groups really differed in the amount of contact. Several observers recorded the actual amount of physical contact they witnessed during the sessions. The conditions differed in the amount of physical contact and could be distinguished statistically. Incidentally, the results indicated that greater contact was associated with feelings of closeness, willingness to engage in risk-taking behaviors, and more positive attitudes toward oneself and others.

Not all tasks subjects are to perform are as readily observable as physical contact. Subjects may be asked to engage in various activities in their everyday lives (e.g., think specific thoughts, perform various activities in public or in private). When subjects are given different tasks to perform, usually direct observation or self-reports can assess whether they adhered to the task requirements. Unlike the assessment of the manipulation for independent variables based on information, the manipulation check for task variables assesses what subjects do rather than what they know. It is important to provide a check merely because providing different task instructions is very different from carrying out the task.

The manipulation consists of instructions, activities, or tasks that are designed to induce a particular state in the subject. Exposure to the experimental manipulation or task alone is insufficient as a manipulation check. The investigator wishes the subjects to experience something in a particular way and the experimental test depends on achieving this state. For example, the purpose of an experiment may be to induce high levels of euphoria or similar states in some of the subjects and moderate or low levels in other subjects. In these cases, it is useful to include items that allow individuals to check the extent to which they experience a particular emotion. For example, an item might have subjects rate on a 5-point scale how euphoric they feel (1 = *not at all euphoric*, 3 = *moderately euphoric*, 5 = *very euphoric*). The investigator could infer with some degree of confidence that the independent variable was successfully manipulated if groups differed in the extent of euphoria on their ratings according to the respective conditions to which they were assigned.

Variation of Intervention Conditions

Many interventions in clinical research consist of varying the conditions to which subjects are exposed. Actually, information or task manipulations could be categorized here. Yet the present category is much broader than varying information or tasks. Variation of therapist or experimenter behavior means that the manipulation is not what the subject knows or does to adhere to task requirements but what is done to the subject. Primary examples of this type of manipulation would be exposing subjects to different therapy, prevention, counseling, or remedial interventions. In this case, the success of the manipulation really is out of the hands of the client. Rather, the onus is on the therapist or trainer to carry out the manipulation as intended.

In the context of therapy, the type of check on the behavior of the therapist may be circumscribed or very broad, depending on the manipulation. For example, Abramowitz and Jackson (1974) were interested in comparing the effects of group therapy methods designed to improve personal adjustment and social relations in college students. The main purpose was to evaluate type of therapist comments in the group therapy sessions. Specifically, in one group, the therapist focused on "here-and-now" statements and kept the group discussing behavior, attitudes, and emotions occurring at the moment. In another group, the therapist focused on "there-and-then" statements and kept the group discussing the historical causes of their current behaviors, attitudes, and emotions. Another group included both "here-and-now" and "there-and-then" statements. An "attention-placebo" control group conversed but refrained from addressing clinically relevant material. In passing, it is worth noting that the focus of therapeutic discussion is no trivial question. Different therapy techniques have stressed the significance of discussing early childhood causes of behavior (e.g., psychoanalysis) or one's immediate experience (e.g., Gestalt therapy).

To check on the success of the manipulation, all treatment sessions were tape-recorded. Select sections of a few sessions were transcribed and examined by naive judges who tried to distinguish the conditions. In general, judges were able to separate the transcripts by the respective conditions. The ability of judges to distinguish groups strongly argues for the success in manipulating the temporal focus of the groups. Incidentally, the temporal focus did not make a difference in treatment outcome.

Variation in the behaviors of the experimenters or conditions to which subjects are exposed often can be readily checked and monitored. Some variables require more monitoring than others. When the different conditions depend on variations in the experimenter's behavior and potential difficulties may arise in prescribing or controlling these variations, manipulation checks may be especially useful. For example, if therapists are supposed to react in a friendly fashion for some clients and in an aloof fashion for other clients, manipulation checks are critically important. The ongoing nature of the therapist–client relationship may cause therapists to depart from the desired conditions of the experiment. On the other hand, when the manipulated variable consists of physical conditions to which subjects are exposed, such as decor of the therapist's office (e.g., Bloom, Weigel, & Trautt, 1977), the arrangement can be defined explicitly, implemented, and not checked for each subject.

Utility of Checking the Manipulation

Checking to see if the independent variable has been effectively manipulated is valuable in general. Data showing that the independent variable was manipulated as intended increase the confidence that can be placed on the basis for the results, that is, construct validity. Two situations are worth highlighting because manipulation checks provide particularly useful information, namely, where the experiment produced no significant differences between groups and where experimental conditions particularly need to be kept distinct.

No Differences Between Groups

If the predicted results of an experiment are not obtained and, in fact, no significant group differences are evident, assessment of the independent variable may prove to be remarkably helpful in interpreting the results. As an example, consider an experiment that provides treatment to two groups that differ only in what the subjects are told about treatment. One group is told that the treatment is an effective therapeutic procedure that is well established with a wide range of clinical problems; the other group is told that the procedure is experimental and is not yet known to work in improving adjustment. At the end of a treatment period, suppose there are no differences between groups on outcome measures. What can be said about the impact of the instructions on treatment outcome?

It is very important to ask whether the independent variable was manipulated adequately so that the different instructional sets were salient to the subjects. Certainly, we would want to know whether subjects heard, knew, or believed the instructions about treatment. If the subjects did not hear or attend to the crucial instructions, then the results of the study would be viewed differently than if the subjects fully heard and believed the instructions. If the subjects had not perceived the instructions, additional experimental research would be warranted to test the hypothesis under conditions in which the instructions were more salient.

On the other hand, if the subjects had perceived the instructions and the dependent measures reflected no group differences, this would suggest that the intervention was, in fact, manipulated and did not affect treatment outcome. In such a case, the investigator would be more justified in abandoning the original hypothesis. The results do not mean that all attempts to manipulate subjects' set or interpretations of treatment would produce no differences. However, the original hypothesis was at least tested. The adequacy of the test was partially demonstrated by showing that the subjects could distinguish the conditions to which they were assigned.

Keeping Conditions Distinct

Another way in which checking on the manipulation is useful is to ensure that the experimental conditions are, in fact, distinct. The investigator may intend to administer different conditions, instruct experimenters to do so, and provide guidelines and specific protocols of the procedures to ensure that this occurs. Yet the normal processes associated with the intervention may override some of the procedural distinctions envisioned by the experimenter.

One place where conditions may not remain distinct is in the evaluation of different therapy techniques. Part of the problem may be inherent in the subject matter and the way in which it is studied. In therapy investigations, the different techniques often are insufficiently specified, and thus the defining conditions and ingredients supposedly responsible for change are not distinguished across groups. Without sufficient specificity, nondistinct global procedures or loosely defined conditions, such as "supportive psychotherapy," "insight," or "behavior therapy," are implemented. Such treatments are likely to overlap with any other treatment that has some of the components of social interaction and interpersonal relationships (e.g., Sloane et al., 1975; Wallerstein, 1986). Overlap per se may not be detrimental so long as the areas that distinguish treatments are specified and corroborated by a manipulation check. Were the treatments implemented correctly and did they remain distinct along the supposedly crucial dimensions specified by their conceptual and procedural guidelines?

Therapy studies have reported difficulty in keeping techniques distinct even though systematic observations of these differences are not always reported. Therapists who administer different treatment conditions may include similar elements in both conditions despite efforts to keep treatments distinct. Also, clients assigned to specific treatments occasionally carry out procedures on their own that are included in other treatments. Comparisons of different treatments can be illuminated greatly by gathering information to ensure that the treatments are conducted correctly.

SPECIAL SITUATIONS IN CLINICAL RESEARCH

The above comments apply generally to experimental research in which conditions are manipulated across a wide range of topic areas. Clinical research often includes a variety of situations in which special issues emerge in ensuring the adequacy of the test of the independent variable.

Subject-Selection Studies

In much clinical research, the independent variable of interest is not manipulated directly. Rather, the investigator evaluates the construct(s) of interest by selecting persons who display the characteristic of interest. The "manipulation" is achieved by formation of groups. For example, the investigator may wish to compare depressed versus nondepressed persons; those who have experienced a trauma versus those who have not; couples who physically abuse each other versus those who do not; and so on. Subject-selection research is designed to illuminate crucial characteristics of the population of interest. These characteristics may shed light on the scope of dysfunction, possible theories of causes, ideas about interventions, and many other facets.

For example, much is known about the factors that place children at risk for becoming delinquents. These factors include early signs of misbehavior, academic dysfunction, marital discord and conflict in their homes, family history of antisocial behavior, and others. Being at risk means that youth have an increased likelihood of becoming delinquent. Many youth with these and other risk factors do not become delinquents. Subject-selection studies have evaluated those at-risk youth who do and those who do not become delinquent.

Interestingly, those who do *not* become delinquent seem to have other characteristics in their background such as a greater likelihood of being the first born among their siblings, higher self-esteem, more affection, and a supportive same-sex role model (Werner, 1987). Such findings are intriguing theoretically in helping us ponder the paths and methods of inhibiting paths toward delinquency.

Checking on the independent variable in subject-selection studies raises several issues for the investigator. Table 8.1 provides specific questions that are useful to address in order to establish that the independent variable or construct of interest serves as a basis for interpretation of the findings. The study begins by specifying the independent variable of interest (e.g., depression). Selection criteria are specified to identify groups and these are operationalized on specific measures (e.g., diagnostic instruments, depression scales). The specific measures and criteria are critical. Often the procedures are based on widely used psychological measures (e.g., standardized inventories and scales). In other cases, criteria or status designations external to the research program (e.g., prisoners, teen mothers, Alzheimer's patients) might be adopted as selection criteria.

Consider an example of the use of selection criteria and issues they raise for construct validity. One might wish to study parents who abuse their children physically and to see how they differ from parents who do not engage in abuse. In most major cities, social agencies have records of abusive parents and these might be used to obtain subjects. Parents with documented child abuse histories might serve as one of the groups in the study. As a comparison example, we might want parents of the same age, locale (city, neighborhood), family constellation (number of parents and children in the home), ethnic and racial composition, and so on. Of course, those in the nonabuse group would be people who are not on record as having abused their children or on record as suspected for abuse. Alas, we have our two groups. However, we also have a potential problem.

Table 8.1. Questions to Address in Subject-Selection Studies to Establish the Construct of Interest

---

1. What is the construct of interest?
2. What are the operational criteria to separate or delineate groups (e.g., the specific measures or selection criteria)?
3. To what extent is the assessment procedure (e.g., criterion, measure) known to reliably separate or select persons with and without the characteristic?
4. Are the groups with and without the characteristic of interest similar on subject and demographic variables (e.g., age, sex, race, socioeconomic status)?
5. Does the comparison group (without the characteristic) share all the characteristics but the one of interest? If not, how are these other characteristics to be evaluated, partialled out, or addressed in the data analyses?
6. Could the construct as described (e.g., depression) be interpreted to reflect a broader construct (e.g., having a disturbance, being a patient)?

People who are identified as abusive probably do abuse their children. Yet the identification process itself (i.e., report to social agencies) depends on many contingencies such as being reported by a neighbor, number of instances of abuse, conspicuousness of the abuse (e.g., if child and parents scream a lot), and severity of the abuse (e.g., if many emergency room visits occur). This raises two possible concerns that affect the validity of our study. The first is that parents in the abuse group may be an especially severe group or suffer from other characteristics that led to their identification by social agencies. This raises a problem of external validity if we are challenged that this does not represent all abused parents. That is not a major threat here because in fact many abusive parents are reported to social agencies, and we wish to learn about this group in its own right.

More subtle and damaging to the study is the potential threat to construct validity, namely, interpretation of the independent variable. It is possible that some number of abusive parents are included in the nonabuse group. Our selection criterion (being identified as abusive by a social agency) is far from perfect and many—probably most—abusive parents who might meet some legal definition of abuse are not on record. That means we are comparing a group of identified abusers with another group where abuse might also be present. Thus our group of abusers versus nonabusers may "really" consist of identified abusers versus other people who may or may not abuse their children. In all likelihood in this latter group most people are not abusive. However, there may well be abusive parents in the nonabuser group given the method of selecting subjects for the study. In the general case, it is important to maximize the assurances that subjects in a selection study are correctly classified according to the construct of interest. In our example, if abusers (or nonabusers) are in both groups, the differences on measures of interest would be diffused. It would be useful to add to the selection criteria further assessment in an attempt to establish that the two groups differ maximally on abuse status.

Apart from establishing the groups, questions in Table 8.1 alert us to establishing that the groups do not differ in ways other than the construct of interest, at least to the extent possible. It is always possible that some variable correlated with abusing one's children is the construct that separates the groups. Even though the investigator is interested in abuse, the groups could differ in other ways (e.g., age, sex composition, marital status, level of stress). Thus one needs as many assurances as available that the groups are different in abusive practices and not other characteristics that might equally explain the findings. Such control is not always possible because some characteristics often are associated and their separation is difficult.

Establishing the construct of interest in subject-selection studies is not always easy. In many cases the construct is not well established. The target group of interest is carefully identified. However, the group to which it is compared within the study greatly limits the conclusions that can be drawn. A common example of this is in subject-selection studies in which the investigator is interested in evaluating a special group (e.g., depressed patients, children with a specific disease, people exposed to a special experience) and where the investigator wishes to make specific statements about this group on a set of dependent measures. The difficulty often arises when that special group is compared to a "normal" (community sample) control group. This latter group includes people who are identified because they do not have the disorder, dysfunction, or special experience. The results invariably show that the special group is different from the "normal" group. Although the interpretation may focus on the special group, the "normal" comparison group is often insufficient to permit specific inferences to be drawn about the special group.

As an example, in one investigation, the authors proposed that antisocial youth would evince a particular type of personality organization according to object-relations theory (Matthys, Walterbos, Njio, & van Engeland, 1989). Children diagnosed as conduct disordered were compared with control children from an elementary school. The children wrote various descriptions about other children, adults, and themselves. These descriptions were scored to evaluate personality traits, organization of writing, affective statements, and other characteristics. The results indicated several differences in object–self relations between the conduct-disordered and control children.

The construct of interest from the independent variable side was conduct disorder and how children with this disorder respond on important measures of personality style. However, the comparison group of "normal" children raises interpretive ambiguity. Perhaps any patient group would show the demonstrated pattern. By design, the study does not speak specifically to conduct disorder. Several differences were evident between the conduct disorder and comparison group, including age and the proportion living in one-parent families, to mention a few characteristics. Also, conduct disordered youth were residents of an inpatient setting, whereas controls youth lived in their own homes. These latter group differences can be ignored for the moment to convey a more subtle point. The selection of a patient sample versus a community sample does not necessarily permit conclusions about the specific dysfunction of the patient sample. The primary conclusion one might draw is that patients and nonpatients differ. To draw more specific statements would require an additional group. A patient group without conduct disorder, if added to the design, would permit evaluation of whether unique object-relations and personality organization are specific to conduct disorder.

In general, subject-selection studies require special effort to isolate the construct of interest. Special attention is required in assessing the construct by making implausible other interpretations that might explain group differences. The selection of groups that vary in the construct of interest is only the beginning. Often, special data analyses and the inclusion of alternative control groups that vary on characteristics that might aid in interpretation are helpful in drawing conclusions about the specific construct of interest.

Treatment Integrity

Much of clinical research focuses on evaluating alternative interventions such as those provided in the context of treatment, prevention, counseling, and education. In the simplest case, one group receives the intervention and the other group does not (treatment vs. no treatment or a waiting-list control). Specification of the experimental manipulation pertains to clarification and evaluation of treatment delivery. Obviously, the implied hypothesis in that treatment when conducted appropriately, as intended, carefully, and so on, is likely to produce greater change than no treatment. Of primary interest is an evaluation of the extent to which treatment was conducted as intended, a concept referred to as *treatment integrity.*

Interpretation of intervention research depends on checking on the integrity of treatment. The importance can be conveyed by considering a study that evaluated alternative treatments for antisocial youth (ages 8 to 17 years) who attended a community activities setting where the interventions were conducted (Feldman et al., 1983). The study evaluated alternative treatments, experience of the therapist, and whether including peers without any dysfunction in the groups influenced treatment outcome. Consider only for a moment the impact of three treatments: (a) group social work (focus on groups processes, social organization, and norms within the group), (b) behavior modification (use of reinforcement contingencies in the group, focus on prosocial behavior), and (c) minimal treatment controls (spontaneous interactions of group members, no explicit application of a structured treatment plan). The treatments were provided to different groups of subjects.

The main objective was to evaluate changes in antisocial behavior of referred youths over the course of the intervention. Measures were obtained from parents, referral agents, the youths, and group leaders as well as direct observations of the groups. The intervention was conducted over a period of a year, in which the youths attended sessions and engaged in a broad range of activities and discussions (e.g., sports, arts and crafts, fund raising).

The results indicated few differences as a function of the specific treatment technique. Interestingly, checks on how treatment was carried out by direct observations of selected sessions revealed a breakdown in treatment integrity. Specifically, observations of treatment sessions indicated that only 25% of the leaders in the group social work condition and 65% of the leaders in the behavior modification condition correctly implemented procedures appropriate to their treatment. These percentages convey that a substantial portion of persons within a given treatment did not receive the appropriate condition. The minimal treatment condition that served as a control yielded interesting results as well. Approximately 44% of the leaders in this condition carried out systematic interventions, that is, treatment, even though none was supposed to do so. This alone would lead one to expect a diffusion of treatment effects, a bias operating to reduce any treatment differences. Based on the treatment integrity data, it is difficult to draw conclusions about the relative impact of alternative treatments. It is still possible that there would be significant outcome differences and substantially different conclusions about individual treatment conditions when the treatments are implemented as intended. It is to the original authors' credit to have assessed integrity, which greatly aids in interpretation of the findings.

The breakdown of treatment integrity is one of the greatest dangers in outcome research. In perhaps the most dramatic examples where integrity has been sacrificed, none of the intended treatment sessions was actually held with the clients (see Sechrest, White, & Brown, 1979). The difficulty is that in most intervention research, efforts to ensure or to assess the fidelity of treatment are omitted (Kazdin, Bass, Ayers, & Rodgers, 1990). Thus interpretation of the results often is obscured.

Interpretation of outcome assumes that the treatments were well tested and carried out as intended. Consider, hypothetically, a study in which two treatments are equally effective at posttreatment. The two treatments, if implemented as intended, may in fact be equally effective. A pattern of no difference might result from a failure to implement one or both of the treatments faithfully. Large variation in how individual treatments are carried out across patients within a given condition and failure to implement critical portions of treatments may also lead to no differences, such as between two or more treatment conditions. Even when two treatments differ, it is important to rule out the possibility that the differences are due to variations of integrity with which each was conducted. One treatment, perhaps because of its complexity or novelty, may be more subject to procedural degradation and appear less effective because it was less faithfully rendered. Thus integrity of treatment is relevant in any outcome study independent of the specific pattern of results.

There are several steps that can be performed to address treatment integrity. To begin with, the specific criteria, procedures, tasks, and therapist and patient characteristics that define the treatment can be specified as well as possible. Many investigators have described treatment in manual form, which includes written materials to guide the therapist in the procedures, techniques, topics, themes, therapeutic maneuvers, and activities (Lambert & Ogles, 1988; Luborsky & DeRubeis, 1984). Manuals also permit a basis to evaluate whether the sessions were carried out as intended.

Second, therapists can be trained carefully to carry out the techniques. Training is usually defined by the number of cases the therapist has seen or amount of time (years of experience) in using the techniques rather than proficiency in the constituent skills (see Kazdin, Kratochwill, & VandenBos,

1986). The training experience, however defined, obviously has important implications for how faithfully treatment is likely to be rendered.

Third, and related, when treatment has begun, it is valuable to provide continued case supervision. Listening to or viewing tapes of selected sessions, meeting regularly with therapists to provide feedback, and similar monitoring procedures may reduce therapist drift (departure) from the desired practices.

Whether treatment has been carried out as intended can only be evaluated definitively after the treatment has been completed. This evaluation requires measuring the implementation of treatment. Audio- or videotapes of selected treatment sessions from each condition can be examined. Codes for therapist and/or patient behaviors or other specific facets of the sessions can operationalize important features of treatment and help decide whether treatment was conducted as intended (e.g., DeRubeis, Hollon, Evans, & Bemis, 1982; Klosko, Barlow, Tassinari, & Cerny, 1990).

Treatment integrity is not an all-or-none matter. Hence it is useful to identify what a faithful rendition of each treatment is and what departures fall within an acceptable range. For some variables, decision rules may be arbitrary, but making them explicit facilitates interpretation of the results. For example, to consider a relatively simple characteristic, treatment may consist of 20 sessions of individual psychotherapy. The investigator may specify that treatment is administered adequately (i.e., is reasonably tested) only if a client receives 15 (75%) or more of the sessions. For other variables, particularly those within-session procedures that distinguish alternative treatments, specification of criteria that define an acceptable range may be more difficult. In some cases, the presence of select processes (e.g., discarding irrational beliefs, improving one's self-concept) might be sufficient; in other cases, a particular level of various processes (e.g., anxiety or arousal) might be required to denote that treatment has been adequately provided.

INTERPRETIVE PROBLEMS IN CHECKING THE MANIPULATION

Checking the effects of the manipulation can provide important information that not only aids in interpreting the findings of a particular investigation but also may provide important guidelines for further research. The increase in information obtained by checking on the manipulation and its effects is not without risk. The risk pertains to the possibility that there may be discrepancies between what is revealed by the check on the manipulation and the dependent measures of major interest. These discrepancies may introduce ambiguities into the experiment rather than eliminate them. To convey the interpretive problems that may arise, it is useful to distinguish various simple patterns of results possible in a hypothetical experiment.

Alternative Data Patterns

Consider a hypothetical experiment that checks whether the independent variable was in fact implemented as intended. After this manipulation check, subjects may complete the dependent measures. When the results are analyzed, it is possible to infer whether the intervention was implemented effectively from two sources of information, namely, the assessment of the independent variable manipulation check and the dependent measures. These two sources of information may agree (e.g., both suggest that the intervention had an effect) or disagree (e.g., where one shows that the intervention had an effect and the other does not). Actually, there are four possible combinations, which are illustrated as different cells in Figure 8.1. For each cell, a different interpretation can be made about the experiment and its effects.

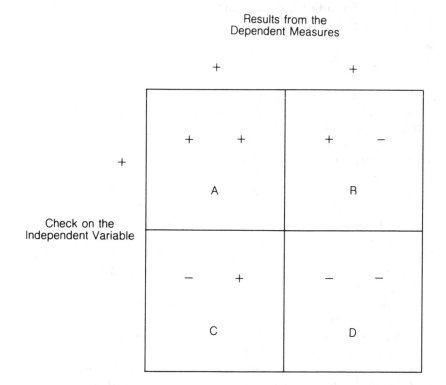

Figure 8.1. Possible agreement or disagreement between the manipulation check and dependent measures. A plus sign (+) signifies that the measure shows the effect of the manipulation or that experimental conditions differ on the dependent measures. A minus sign (−) signifies that the measure does not show the effect of the manipulation or that experimental conditions do not differ on the dependent measures.

Effects on the Manipulation Check and Dependent Measure (Cell A)

This first cell is the easiest to interpret. In this cell, the intervention had the intended effect on the measure that checked the manipulation. For example, subjects believed the instructions or performed the tasks as intended or the treatment was delivered to each subject as appropriate to his or her treatment condition. Moreover, the independent variable led to performance differences on the dependent measures. For present purposes, it is not important to consider whether the predicted relation was obtained but only that the independent variable was shown to have some effect on the dependent variable. In Cell A, the check on the manipulation is useful in showing that the procedures were executed properly but certainly is not essential to the demonstration. The positive results, particularly if they are in the predicted direction, attest to the effects of the independent variable. Because of the consistencies of the results for both the manipulation check and dependent measure, no special interpretive problems arise.

No Effect on the Manipulation Check and Dependent Measure (Cell D)

In this cell, there is no ambiguity in interpreting the results. However, the check on the manipulation greatly enhances interpretation of the investigation. In this cell, the check on the manipulation shows that the independent variable did not have the desired impact. The intervention was somehow missed by the subjects or was not sufficiently powerful to be perceived or noted by them. The lack of changes on the dependent measures should be expected. The investigator anticipated change in the dependent measures. Yet this change presupposed that the intervention was effectively manipulated. This pattern of results is instructive because it suggests that additional work is needed to perfect the experimental manipulation. The hypothesis of interest really was not tested. The manipulation check clarified the results by showing that the absence of the predicted effects of the independent variable might have resulted from providing a very weak manipulation.

It is quite possible that the pattern of Cell D only applies to some of the groups in an experiment; that is, select groups did not show the effect of the independent variable on either the manipulation check or dependent measures. Other groups may have reflected important changes. When the independent variable shows no effects on the manipulation check and dependent measures for some of the groups, this may be extremely useful. In these cases, the manipulation check may reveal that select groups are not different on the independent variable despite the conditions to which they are exposed and attest to the differential strength of the manipulation across conditions.

For example, Miller (1972) compared different versions of desensitization in treating college students with fears of harmless snakes. Among the conditions, some subjects received therapeutic instructions that said that treatment was designed to reduce fear. Another group received the same treatment but with no instructions, that is, the only information given them was that the purpose of the procedure could not be revealed. Yet another group received the treatment with instructions saying that the purpose was to study imagination. A check on the manipulation showed that subjects receiving therapeutic instructions were aware of the therapeutic goal of treatment. The majority of those who received misleading instructions (about imagination) were unaware of the therapeutic goal of treatment. Thus for these two groups, questionnaire data attest to the effects of the manipulation.

Interestingly, the majority of subjects who were given no information and told that the purpose of the study could not be revealed also believed in the therapeutic goals of treatment. This finding was important because in the analysis of fear reduction after treatment, the therapeutic-instruction group and the no-information group did not differ on outcome measures, although the misinformed (imagination) and therapeutic-instruction groups were different. The lack of difference in fear reduction between therapeutic-instructions and no-information groups might have been interpreted as the lack of importance of giving subjects an instructional set that they are receiving treatment. Yet the manipulation check revealed that subjects had a therapeutic set whether or not they received the instructions. Hence the lack of group differences is readily explained.

Effect on the Manipulation Check But No Effect on the Dependent Measure (Cell B)

In this cell, the manipulation check revealed that subjects were influenced by the intervention. On the other hand, the dependent variable did not reflect any effect. The conclusion that would seem to be warranted was that the intervention was well manipulated but that the original hypothesis was not supported. In fact, there may be no relation between the independent variable and the dependent measure, and perhaps this experiment accurately reflected this situation.

Failure to demonstrate an effect on the dependent measures despite the fact that the manipulation check reveals that the independent variable was successfully implemented does not prove the absence of a relation between the independent and dependent variables. It is possible that the manipulation was strong enough to alter responses on the measure of the manipulation but not strong enough to alter performance on the dependent measures. Some measures may be extremely sensitive to even weak interventions and others only to very strong interventions, a notion that is neither new nor speculative. Studies from several different areas could be brought to bear on the point. For

example, in social-psychological research, studies have shown that one's prejudice is more readily reflected on verbal self-report measures than on measures
of overt behavior (e.g., Kutner, Wilkins, & Yarrow, 1952; La Piere, 1934).
That is, when individuals are asked whether they will discriminate against or
not interact with others, they may readily express such negative intentions.
When these same individuals are placed in a situation in which they have to
exhibit an overt act to discriminate against others, they are much less likely
to show prejudicial behavior. Indeed, the strength of the prejudice might be
defined in part by the extent to which it is evident across different situations
and measures. Weak prejudice might be shown only across a few situations and
strong prejudice across diverse situations and measures.

In clinical psychology, one might view the strength of a given treatment in
much the same way. A therapeutic technique that is relatively ineffective may
only change the way an anxious individual talks about situations that arouse
anxiety. After treatment, the clients may say they are less bothered, as evident
on self-report inventories. Yet in the actual anxiety-provoking situation, physiological arousal and avoidance behaviors may or may not reflect improvements. As a general statement, more potent interventions would be expected
to effect broader and more consistent changes across dependent measures.

The pattern of results in Cell B may indicate that there is no relation between
the independent and dependent variable. On the one hand, it may indicate that
the potency of the manipulation was not sufficiently strong. If the investigator
has reason to believe that the manipulation could be strengthened, it might be
worth testing the original hypothesis again. On the other hand, there must
eventually be some point at which the investigator is willing to admit that his
or her hypothesis was well tested but not supported.

No Effect on the Manipulation Check But an Effect on the Dependent Measure (Cell C)

In this cell, the check on the manipulation reveals that the independent variable was not well manipulated, but the dependent measures do reflect the effect
of the intervention. In this situation, the experiment demonstrated the effects
of the independent variable, but ambiguity is introduced by checking the
manipulation. If this were to happen, the investigator would probably regret
having checked the effects of the manipulation at all.

The task of the investigator is to explain how the manipulation had an effect
on the dependent measures but not on the check of the manipulation. The
dependent measures, of course, are the more important measures and have
priority in terms of scientific importance over the measure that checked the
manipulation. Yet the haunting interpretation may be that the dependent
measures changed for reasons other than the manipulation of the independent
variable. There is no easy way to avoid the interpretation.

One reason that the dependent variable(s) may have reflected change when the available evidence suggests that the independent variable was not manipulated effectively pertains to the nature of statistical analysis. It is possible that the differences obtained on the dependent variable were the results of "chance." The results may have been one of the instances in which the subjects' responses between groups were different, even though there is no real relation between the independent and dependent variables in the population of subjects who might be exposed to the conditions of the experiment. In short, the null hypothesis of the original experiment, that is, that groups exposed to the different conditions do not differ, may have been rejected incorrectly and a Type I error was made. The probability of this error occurring, of course, is given by the level of significance used for the statistical tests (α).

An example in which the manipulation check yielded no group differences and the dependent measures did may help convey the dilemma in which the investigator is placed. Rosen (1974) was interested in evaluating the importance of client involvement in treatment as well as the instructional set that individuals had about treatment. The involvement manipulation, important for present purposes, consisted of telling individuals to get involved and work hard in treatment. Experimental subjects received desensitization involving relaxation and imagery. Subjects in the involved conditions were told to relax as deeply as possible and to imagine scenes as vividly and clearly as possible and, in general, to work hard. Subjects in the noninvolved conditions were not given these instructions. Several measures were used to check on the manipulation to see whether subjects who received instructions to work hard and to be involved in treatment differed from noninstructed subjects. One measure was how much tension subjects produced by squeezing a hand dynamometer, which was included as part of the procedures to tense muscles. Muscle tension was employed to help subjects distinguish tension from relaxation. Presumably, subjects who were trying harder would exert more tension. Other checks on the manipulation included self-ratings of vividness of imagery, muscle tension, and how hard subjects thought they worked. The only measure indicating that the involvement variable was effectively manipulated was self-ratings of muscle tension, and this was consistent over the course of treatment sessions. The other measures did not distinguish groups, which suggests that the manipulation was not effectively implemented. On the other hand, subjects showed significant changes on the dependent measures, which included overt behavior and self-report measures of fear. Thus the results are unclear because the independent variable did not appear to have been successfully manipulated yet still showed effects on the dependent measures.

The failure of the manipulation check to show group differences may reflect inadequacies with the measure itself. The most obvious question that arises is whether the measure assesses the construct reflected in the independent variable. Usually manipulation check assessment devices are based on *face validity*, that is, whether the items seem to reflect what the investigator's interests are. (Face validity is the psychologist's term to justify the basis for using specific items on a measure or a measure itself when in fact no good validation evidence has been obtained. Presumably, the reason this is called "face" validity is to emphasize how difficult it is for us to *face* our colleagues after having established the validity of an assessment device in such a shoddy fashion, especially when we know better.) It is quite possible for the manipulation check to reflect some other construct than the independent variable. It is of little consolation to raise this as a possibility after an investigation is completed. The manipulation check is part of the methodology for which the investigator can rightly be held responsible. Hence prior to the experiment, it is important for the investigator to have some assurance that the manipulation check will reflect actual differences across conditions. Reflecting change on the measure should be accomplished prior to the full experiment as a minimal validation criterion of the assessment device.

Other assessment problems with manipulation checks may explain why differences were not found across experimental conditions. For example, the items to assess the manipulation may have been too obscure or unclear. The subjects may have heard the information about the intervention but not have realized its relevance for the assessment device. Alternatively, the variability of the responses to the measure may have been great, leading to the absence of statistically significant group differences. Moreover, the information might not be recalled for the manipulation check (e.g., if fill-in items or essay questions were asked) but yet be easily recognized if questions were asked in another way (e.g., if multiple-choice questions were used). Whatever the reason, the failure of the manipulation check to agree with the changes in the dependent measure will interfere with interpretation of most results.

General Comments

Pointing out the ambiguities that can result from checking how successful the independent variable was manipulated could discourage use of such checking devices. This would be unfortunate because the investigator has much to gain from knowing how effectively the independent variable was manipulated. Such checks, as a supplement to information on the dependent measures, provide feedback about how well the hypothesis was tested. A failure to achieve statistically significant group differences on the dependent measures is instructive but does not convey specific details about the experimental manipulation. Changes in dependent measures reflect many events all working together, including whether the intervention was implemented effectively, whether the measures were appropriate for the intervention, whether procedural errors were sufficiently small to minimize variability, and so on. The absence of effects on dependent measures could be attributed to many factors, only one of which is the failure to implement the independent variable effectively. On the other hand, a manipulation check helps provide more specific information and hence can be very useful in interpreting a given study and guiding subsequent studies.

SPECIAL ISSUES AND CONSIDERATIONS

This chapter has advocated assessing how successfully the independent variable was manipulated. Introducing any additional components into an experiment is likely to have both potential gains and costs in terms of clarifying the results and hence must be weighed carefully. Checking on the manipulation is no exception, as illustrated by possible interpretive problems discussed previously. Different issues must be resolved to decide how and when to use manipulation checks.

Assessment Issues

One assessment issue relevant for deciding whether to check on the manipulation is the possible reactivity of assessment and the importance of reactivity for the particular experiment. By checking on the manipulation, an experimenter may arouse subjects' suspicions about the experiment and raise questions that ordinarily might not arise. It is quite possible that the manipulation may even sensitize subjects to the manipulation. The manipulation check, for example, in the form of a self-report questionnaire, may make salient events that previously happened to the subject.

Consider an extreme case. The experimental manipulation might consist of altering the content of a subject's conversation during a standard interview as a function of events that happen to the subject in the waiting room prior to the interview. *Confederates,* persons who work for the investigator, may pose as waiting subjects but, in fact, engage in prearranged discussions that might influence the subject. The prearranged discussions would vary across subjects depending on the exact experimental conditions. To check on this manipulation, the investigator could ask subjects at the beginning of the interview such questions as what they talked about in the waiting room, what their current mood is, and so on. The questions might suggest to the subjects that their previous interaction in the waiting room was part of the experiment. This, of course, would be stimulated further by an unsubtle question that asked the subject whether the individuals in the waiting room were part of the experiment.

As a general point, reactivity of the manipulation check per se might not be important, depending on how the investigator conceives the manipulation and the process through which it affects performance. For interventions involving subtle manipulations, the experimenter might not want to risk the possible influence of the manipulation check. Or, if the check is important, the investigator may wish to design unobtrusive measures that are less likely to arouse suspicions than are direct self-report measures (see chapter 10). For example, the experimenter might leave the subjects alone with another subject (actually a confederate) who asks, "Say, what is this experiment about anyway?" or "What did the experimenter say about what's going to happen?" Responses to a few such questions could be scored (e.g., from audiotapes, through a one-way mirror, or by the confederate) to address the question whether the subjects perceived the purpose of the study or to assess other specific aspects of the manipulation.

Alternatively, the investigator may administer the manipulation check after the dependent measures are assessed. Even if the manipulation check is reactive, this could not influence the results because the dependent measures have already been completed. The disadvantage with this alternative is that the longer the delay between the manipulation and assessment of the manipulation's impact, the greater the chances that the check will not discriminate groups. During the delay, subjects may forget precisely what they heard in the instructions or the original rationale. Also, it may be possible that the dependent measures, if completed first, could influence the results on the manipulation check.

To avoid reactivity of the manipulation check, the investigator might simply assess the manipulation and its effects in pilot work prior to the investigation. In this way, self-report questionnaires can be used without administering the dependent measures. In addition, the investigator will have a good basis for knowing in advance that the independent variable was effectively manipulated.

The decision whether to check on the effects of the manipulation also pertains to whether subject awareness of the independent variable is at all relevant. Effective manipulations do not necessarily operate through subjects' awareness. For some manipulations, it may be entirely irrelevant whether subjects know or could recognize what has happened to them in the experiment. For example, in cases where the manipulation involves administering different treatments to subjects, the check on the manipulation is likely to entail assessment of therapist behavior. Here, assessing subject involvement in the procedure per se is not of primary interest. Whether or not subjects perceive themselves as receiving supportive therapy as opposed to role-playing may not be important as long as the manipulation check shows that the defining conditions of these treatments were followed. As discussed earlier, the type of manipulation determines the manner and focus of the manipulation check. This means that in some cases subject perceptions are relevant and in others of ancillary importance.

The Influence of Nonmanipulated Variables

In addition to checking on the independent variable, many occasions arise in which it also may be important to determine whether there are extraneous variables that have changed over the course of the experiment. It is quite possible that the independent variable might change other features of subject behavior or of the situation that would serve as plausible rival hypotheses for the results.

If different treatments are to be compared, there might be several variables that could covary with treatment. For example, one might want to have subjects rate the warmth, congeniality, or competence of the therapist, the credibility of the treatment rationale, the confidence that the subjects have in treatment, whether treatment made them anxious, and so on. The number of dimensions that could be assessed in any one study is vast. There is no need and little value in merely including a large number of dimensions along with the check on manipulation. Rather, dimensions should be included only if they are of some direct interest and may in some way account for or elaborate the results. Stated another way, dimensions are assessed to help the construct validity of the study, which can mean either ruling out the influence of other factors or establishing the basis or mechanism that accounts for the construct itself.

In treatment evaluation, it is often difficult to decide in advance what nonmanipulated variables should be observed. The objective is to assess variables that might enhance interpretation of the results. The variables are determined by substantive findings of the content area itself. If certain variables covaried with the manipulation and could explain the results, it would be profitable to make some attempt to assess them.

Manipulation Effects and Analyses of Results

The discussion has presented the notion that an intervention is or is not effectively manipulated as determined by a check on the manipulation. The manipulation will usually not succeed or fail completely but will probably affect subjects within a given condition differently. A certain proportion of subjects may be affected by the intervention. This proportion could be defined by specific answers to particular questions. For example, subjects who answer all questions about the experimental manipulation correctly may be considered those for whom the condition was successfully implemented. Whatever the criteria, usually there will be some people for whom the experimental condition was effectively manipulated and others for whom it was not.

An important methodological and practical question is how to treat subjects who are differentially affected by the manipulation. This question pertains to the use of the subjects for the data analyses. On the one hand, it seems reasonable to include in the analyses only those subjects who were truly affected by the manipulation. After all, only those subjects provide a test of the hypothesis. On the other hand, merely using subjects who show the effects of the intervention on the manipulation check may lead to select groups of subjects that vary on several variables from the original groups that were formed through random assignment. Thus using only those subjects across different groups who reflect the effects of the intervention on the manipulation check might lead to systematic subject variable differences across groups. Mortality, in this case caused by the investigator excluding subjects from the analyses, can lead to subject-selection bias. Hence eliminating subjects who do not show the effect of manipulation usually is inappropriate.

As an illustration of this problem, large-scale intervention studies are often conducted in the schools to prevent maladjustment in children, substance abuse, teen pregnancy, and other threats to development. Interventions are implemented on a large scale, usually across several classrooms and schools. Treatment integrity is difficult to sustain and large differences are evident in the fidelity with which classroom teachers implement the interventions. Invariably, some teachers carry out the procedures extremely well, others less well, and still others not at all (e.g., Botvin, Baker, Filazzola, & Botvin, 1990; Hawkins & Lam, 1987). At the end of such a study, investigators often exclude classrooms (teachers and subjects) where the intervention was not carried out or not carried out well. Again, it seems reasonable to exclude teachers (and their classes) in the intervention group who did not conduct the intervention or who did not meet minimal criteria for delivery of the intervention. The investigator is interested in evaluating the effect of the intervention when implemented or implemented well relative to no intervention. Thus often the investigator selects those intervention classes where the program was well delivered. These teachers and classes are compared to nonintervention classes who, of course, did not receive the program.

The method of handling the intervention condition (all teachers and children in that large group) raises a significant problem. Selecting a subgroup of teachers who carried out the intervention adequately violates the original random composition of intervention and nonintervention groups or conditions in the study. Data analyses of the selected intervention group and nonintervention group now raise threats to internal validity (namely, Selection × History and Selection × Maturation, and other selection-related interactions). Group differences might simply be due to the special subset of teachers who were retained in the intervention group—these teachers are special. It is not the integrity of the intervention that is being evaluated as much as it is the specialness of the teachers who adhered to the procedures.

The most appropriate analysis of results is to include all subjects who were run in the various experimental conditions, ignoring the fact that only some of them may have shown the effect of the intervention on the manipulation check. There are different reasons for this. To begin with, an analysis that includes all subjects provides a more conservative test of the intervention effects. The original hypothesis of the study is the general one that administration of different conditions will lead to differences in performance. This is best evaluated by looking at subjects who received the different conditions. To look only at subjects who meet requirements on the manipulation check is to test a different hypothesis; namely, that individuals who are the most responsive to their respective conditions will show changes on the dependent measures.

Another reason for not discarding subjects in the analyses is that the manipulation may have accomplished the intended results without showing any effect on the manipulation check (see Cell C of Figure 8.1). It is important to stress that the dependent measures are the major measures of the effect of treatment. Hence data on the dependent measures should not be excluded on the sole basis that the manipulation check has not demonstrated an effect.

There might be some value in post hoc, unplanned, and exploratory analyses of the segments of data as a supplement to the major analysis of all of the data. These analyses could include only those subjects who showed the appropriate intervention effects on the manipulation check to see whether the scores on the dependent measures were suggestive of a more potent effect. It may not necessarily be the case that subjects who score in a particular way on the manipulation check do better or worse on the dependent measures with respect to the investigator's hypotheses. Presumably, another supplementary analysis might be completed by separating subjects who showed a predicted directional change in behavior (if pre- and posttest assessment data are available) and compare the scores of these individuals on the manipulation check. These analyses must be interpreted very cautiously and should only serve as a guide to the investigator for further work. The fact that the intervention did not produce effects in a number of subjects is not something merely to be expected and resolved by supplementary analyses. Rather, it is the investigator's responsibility to ensure in advance of the investigation that the intervention is manipulated in a potent fashion.

In some clinical studies, decisions are required to define in advance when the intervention can be said to have been applied. As noted earlier, in treatment studies, a prespecified regimen of say 20 sessions may be planned for the intervention group. We might agree in stating that those clients who completed all sessions would be considered to have received the intervention. Yet how should we handle clients who missed one or two sessions? How about five to ten sessions? For those who missed one or two sessions, does it make a difference which session(s) they missed? A decision needs to be made, ideally in advance of the study, to define what it means to receive a fair or reasonable rendition of treatment.

Apart from carefully defining the intervention, it is useful to note data evaluation issues here as well. Those clients who did not receive all of the sessions or meet some prespecified criterion might not be excluded entirely from any data analysis. The reasons are manifold. Perhaps those who completed treatment are a special group, self-selected through their persistence. Perhaps they have more (or less) severe clinical dysfunction than those who dropped out along the way. The deletion of cases for data analysis violates the random assignment to groups. A simple comparison of those who dropped out at specific points and those who completed treatment usually is insufficiently powerful (given the small and unequal samples) to identify reliable differences. For present purposes, it is important to be mindful of the differences within the experimental group in terms of the variations of the intervention subjects may have received. More than mindful, alternative data analyses are essential in an effort to uncover implications of these differences for the outcome measures (see Howard, Krause, & Orlinsky, 1986).

ESTABLISHING POTENT MANIPULATIONS

Establishing the efficacy of an experimental manipulation probably is best accomplished prior to an investigation, especially if an investigator is embarking in an area of research in which he or she has not had direct experience. Depending on the resources available and the cost of completing an investigation, a full-blown experiment usually is reserved as the place to test the relation between the independent and dependent variables rather than to work out basic dimensions required for effectively manipulating the intervention. Of course, over several experiments, the investigator may become increasingly adept at controlling the environmental arrangement and continually refining the intervention to produce more consistent and larger changes. However, this refers to refinement of the intervention over a series of studies. The initial study itself should be based on preliminary information that the manipulation can be implemented effectively.

Preliminary or pilot work to learn how to manipulate the independent variable successfully can be invaluable for the subsequent results of a research program. Pilot work usually consists of exploring the intended manipulations by running a set of subjects who may or may not receive all the conditions and measures that will be used in the subsequent experiment itself. In pilot work, the subjects can contribute directly to the investigator's conception and implementation of the manipulation. For example, the subject can receive the manipulation and complete the manipulation check. At this point, the subject can be fully informed about the purpose of the investigation and provide recommendations about aspects of the procedure that appeared to the subject to facilitate or detract from the investigator's overall objective. Detailed questions can be asked, and the ensuing discussion can reveal ways in which the manipulations can be bolstered.

Another reason for developing the manipulation in pilot work is that some of the problems of checking the manipulation can be eliminated. As discussed earlier, checking on the manipulation in an experiment may sensitize subjects to the manipulation and presumably influence performance on the dependent measures. Pilot work can check the success of the manipulation with, for example, self-report questionnaires. There is no need to obtain measures of performance on the dependent variable if preliminary work is to be used merely to establish that the experimental conditions are administered effectively. Once the manipulation has been shown to be effectively manipulated in pilot work, the investigator may wish to omit the manipulation check in the experiment to avoid the possibility of sensitization effects. Of course, a pilot demonstration does not guarantee that the experiment will achieve the same success in manipulating the independent variable, because subjects differ in each application. Yet, a pilot demonstration can greatly increase the confidence that one has about the adequacy of the experimental test.

To this point, the discussion presupposes a clear criterion for deciding when the manipulation has achieved sufficient potency. The main criterion is that the experimental manipulation produces change on the dependent measures. When such changes are demonstrated, the ambiguity about whether the intervention was effectively manipulated diminishes. Outside of potent changes on the dependent measures, it is unclear to this point what the investigator should aim for as he or she is developing the intervention. In most studies, the criterion to determine whether the independent variable was effectively manipulated is statistical significance. If experimental conditions reflect statistically significant differences (in the expected direction) on the manipulation check, the investigator usually infers that the intervention was effectively manipulated. Statistical significance may provide a weak criterion for determining whether the intervention was well manipulated.

Many studies that could be cited have provided clear evidence that the independent variable was not very effectively manipulated. It is unfair to be too critical of such studies because they did assess the effects of the manipulation and hence are exemplary at least in that regard. Nevertheless, the lack of effects on the manipulation check suggests that more preexperimental work might have been profitable.

For example, in the Rosen (1974) study mentioned earlier, some subjects were given a therapeutic set (that desensitization would reduce fear), whereas others were told that the investigation studied physiological reactions. On the manipulation check, approximately 72% of the subjects who received the therapeutic instructions thought that the study had a therapeutic purpose. This high percentage might suggest that the instructional set was effectively manipulated. However, approximately 61% of the group not given the therapeutic set also thought that treatment had a therapeutic purpose. These group differences are not large (and indeed not reliably different with statistical evaluation). In a finer analysis of the manipulation check, the author examined data for only those subjects who "firmly" held a belief in the therapeutic purpose of the experiment. This made the conditions appear more discrepant on the manipulation check, in that approximately 72% of the therapeutic instructions group and only 33% of the nontherapeutic instructions group showed a "firm belief" in the therapeutic purpose of the treatment. This difference approached a probability level of a $p < .10$ but still missed the usual criterion for statistical significance.

The issue here is not whether the groups could be distinguished with a test of statistical significance. The probability level of $p < .10$ is not the issue; even if the .05 level had been reached, the question could still be raised whether the manipulation had its desired effect on the subjects. The groups were not very different on the manipulation check. However defined, a relatively large proportion of subjects in each group were not well characterized by the instructional set provided in their respective conditions. Thus the instructions used to convey the sets could profit from considerably more preliminary work.

Pilot work can be very useful in advance of an investigation to develop distinct experimental conditions consistent with the desired manipulation. An investigation usually reflects a considerable amount of effort and resources, so it is important to ensure that the independent variable is successfully manipulated and the experimental conditions are as distinct as possible. If the manipulation is weakly implemented and doubt can be cast on the effectiveness with which the hypothesis is being tested, the interpretation of the final results may leave much to be desired.

SUMMARY AND CONCLUSIONS

The adequacy with which an independent variable is manipulated is a matter of degree. If the independent variable has its intended or predicted effects on the dependent measure, this is usually sufficient evidence that the intervention was adequately manipulated. It is desirable to have additional information to assess whether the independent variable was adequately manipulated. A check on the manipulation can be obtained by determining whether the subjects were affected by the particular changes in conditions or whether the procedures to which they were exposed were executed properly. This check, distinct from performance on the dependent variables, provides some assurance about the adequacy of the experimental test.

The manner in which this check is accomplished depends on the type of manipulation. When the manipulation consists of different kinds of information or instructions provided to the subjects, self-report questionnaires often are used to assess whether subjects noticed, heard, believed, or remembered the information presented. When the manipulation consists of varying the type of tasks subjects perform, self-report questionnaires or direct observation of subject performance may be used. When the manipulation consists of different treatment conditions to which the subjects are exposed, it may be checked by examining the behavior of the experimenters or therapists directly. Providing checks on the adequacy with which the independent variable was manipulated is particularly useful in situations where there are no differences between groups on the dependent measures, in clinical treatment where there is no therapeutic change or the amount of change is insufficient, and where there may be a problem in keeping experimental conditions distinct.

In clinical research, special types of studies raise critical issues in relation to the independent variable. Some studies are based on selecting samples with special characteristics, such as those exposed to particular experiences (trauma) or those who fulfill diagnostic criteria (e.g., depression). In such cases, the selection criteria need to be carefully specified and operationalized. More than that, careful attention must be accorded a wide range of other factors associated with the selection criteria that may serve as a competing construct in explaining the results. In treatment research, interpretation of the results depends on evidence that the intervention was, in fact, carried out as intended—that is, assessment of treatment integrity.

Occasionally, interpretive problems may arise if there are discrepancies between the information provided by a check on the manipulation and the dependent variables. Yet, as a general rule, assessing the adequacy with which the independent variable is manipulated can be extremely useful both for interpreting the results of a particular experiment and for proceeding to subsequent experiments. Interpretive problems that can arise in experiments can be attenuated in advance by conducting pilot work to explore different ways to manipulate the conditions of interest. Assessment of the experimental manipulation can ensure that the independent variable receives the most potent empirical test.

FOR FURTHER READING

Rezmovic, E.L. (1984). Assessing treatment implementation amid the slings and arrows of reality. *Evaluation Review, 8,* 187–204.

Schaffer, N.D. (1983). Methodological issues of measuring the skillfulness of therapeutic techniques. *Psychotherapy: Theory, Research and Practice, 20,* 486–493.

Vermilyea, B.B., Barlow, D.H., & O'Brien, G.T. (1984). The importance of assessing treatment integrity: An example in the anxiety disorders. *Journal of Behavioral Assessment, 6,* 1–11.

Yeaton, W.H., & Sechrest, L. (1981). Critical dimensions in the choice and maintenance of successful treatments: Strength, integrity, and effectiveness. *Journal of Consulting and Clinical Psychology, 49,* 156–167.

Chapter 9

ASSESSMENT METHODS AND STRATEGIES

Assessment is pivotal to all research. The results or outcomes of the independent variables of interest or intervention are to be reflected on some measure or outcome (dependent measure). What is assessed, how it is assessed, and interpretation of the assessment device are central to the study. Assessment plays a role beyond the measurement of outcomes or dependent variables. Assessment may be critical to the independent variable as in subject-selection studies where initial assessment is used to delineate groups such as people who are high versus low on a particular personality characteristic. In addition, assessment may be used to evaluate critical processes to check on the manipulation or to measure whether features within the individual (e.g., motives, cognitions) considered to moderate change in fact are altered by the independent variable.

The present chapter addresses fundamental issues pertaining to assessment. The primary focus is on assessment in the context of dependent measures or outcomes in clinical research. The chapter discusses selection of alternative measures, modalities of assessment, and issues and strategies to consider in assessment.

SELECTION OF DEPENDENT MEASURES

Selection of measures affects all studies because the impact of an independent variable is evaluated on some dependent variable. The implicit view in much research has been that the dependent variable can be selected almost as an afterthought. Good research ideas often are considered to be creative hypotheses about how independent variables should be manipulated. Indeed, the dependent variable infrequently is discussed in the notion of designing an experiment. The reason for this is based on the assumption that the effects of the independent variable probably will be broad and evident on any number of measures of the construct of general interest. Actually, results in many areas of clinical research may rely quite heavily on the dependent measures. Hence considerable thought needs to be given to how the effects of the independent variable will be demonstrated. No matter how important the independent variable may be from the standpoint of conceptual or applied considerations and no matter how much effort goes into manipulation, the end result may be totally uninformative if the dependent variable is not carefully considered.

Conclusions resulting from an investigation might be remarkably different depending on the measure that is used. Alternatively, the measures may differentially reflect the effects of the independent variable. For example, client and therapist ratings of overall client improvement may lead to different conclusions about the effects of psychotherapy. Indeed, only modest relations may exist among several different types of measures of adjustment and psychological status that the clients complete after treatment (Lambert, 1983). Thus the dependent variable is not merely a passive reflection of the effectiveness of the intervention but actually determines in part what will be found.

Criteria for Selecting Measures

Construct Validity

There are many requirements that should be met by the dependent measure. The initial criterion for selection of a measure is evidence that the measure assesses the construct of interest. In assessment, the term *construct validity* is used to refer generally to the extent to which the measure assesses the domain, trait, or characteristic of interest (Cronbach & Meehl, 1955). Construct validity has been used throughout this text to refer to a type of experimental validity that relates to the interpretation of the basis of the effect of the experimental manipulation. In the context of assessment, the interpretation of the measure is at issue, namely, to what extent does the construct underlying the measure serve as the basis for interpretation of the measure. Construct validity refers to the link between the concept behind the measure and the evidence or research in which that concept is supported. Construct validity does not reduce to a correlation between alternate measures or a measure and some other criterion. Rather, it refers more broadly to the evidence bearing on the measure and encompasses all types of validity.

In a given study, the investigator may be interested in measuring "adjustment," "emotional distress," or some other construct. There should be some initial assurance that the measure actually reflects the construct. Although this measurement requirement is obvious, evidence later in the chapter shows that prerequisites for ensuring that a particular construct is being assessed are not always met.

It is easy to be enticed by many available measures into the assumption that they assess a particular construct. Measures usually have names that reflect the *intention* of their creator. For example, it is typical that the titles of various inventories and questionnaires include the name of the construct of interest. Unfamiliar (and fictitious) examples readily convey the sorts of measures that are available, such as the Lipshitz Depression Inventory, The Step-On-Others Measure of Assertiveness, or the You-Bet-Your-Life Measure of Risk-Taking. The *names* of various measures often are far more a reflection of what the originator of the assessment method had in mind than of supporting evidence that a particular characteristic or construct in fact is assessed.

Similarly, many scales have been evaluated with factor analysis, a statistical procedure designed to identify sets of correlated items that cluster together. Names of the factors also suggest what is "really" measured. The connection between the name of the factor and the items is not always clear. Also, whether a scale, factor, or subscale with a given name is what the investigator means by the construct underlying the investigation is not axiomatic. Needless to say, there should be some evidence that the measure selected in fact assesses the construct of interest. If there is no evidence available, some means within the study should be taken to corroborate the method with a measure that is recognized as adequate to assess the construct.

Psychometric Characteristics

Psychometric characteristics refer here to reliability and validity evidence in behalf of a measure. Reliability and validity have diverse definitions. *Reliability* generally refers to consistency of the measure; *validity* refers to the content and whether the measure assesses the domain of interest. A more integrative definition weds the concepts. Reliability can be viewed as the relation between measures when they are maximally *similar* (e.g., alternative forms of the same measure, separate portions of a measure, or the identical measure administered at different points in time; Campbell & Fiske, 1959). Validity can be viewed as the relation between measures that are *dissimilar* (e.g., two different measures of the same construct).

Any single definition is hazardous because reliability and validity are broad concepts, each with several subtypes. Also, over the years the different types of reliability and validity and their meanings have varied (see Angoff, 1988). The net effect has been that at least in clinical psychology there have been inconsistencies in the terms and their definitions. Table 9.1 presents major types of reliability and validity that are commonly referred to and that are of clear relevance in evaluating measures for possible use in research.

The concepts of reliability and validity sensitize the investigator to a range of considerations. In any given situation, a specific type of reliability and validity may not be relevant. For example, high test–retest reliability over a period of a few months might be expected for a measure designed to assess a stable (e.g., trait) but not more transient (e.g., state) characteristic. Apart from characteristics of the construct, evaluation of the measure depends on its demonstrated psychometric characteristics. Measures known to reflect the construct of interest and to do so in a reliable and valid fashion bolster the confidence to which the investigator is entitled when interpreting the results of the study.

Sensitivity

Aside from reflecting the construct of interest, the dependent measure must be sensitive to the type and magnitude of change that the investigator is expecting. The sensitivity required to reflect change depends on the manner in which the independent variable is manipulated and, of course, precisely what the variable is. For example, if a study compared the effects of relaxation training versus no training to reduce anxiety among people visiting a dentist, a rather large difference (effect size) might be expected between these two conditions. But, if the comparison were between two treatments (e.g., brief vs. extended relaxation training), the differences might be more subtle. Whether an effect is obtained in either case might well be a function of the sensitivity of the dependent measure. Of course, a less sensitive measure would be needed to reflect change in the first comparison (relaxation vs. no relaxation) than in the case of the second comparison (very brief vs. more extended relaxation training).

Whether and how much a dependent measure is sensitive to change are difficult to specify in advance of a study. A few general desirable characteristics of the dependent measure can be identified. To begin with, the dependent measure should *permit a relatively large range of responses*. The measure must allow for the possibility that subjects can show a wide range of differences so that varying increments and decrements in performance can be detected. If subjects score at the extremes of the distribution at pretest, this, of course, will only allow the investigator to detect varying degrees of change in the opposite direction at postassessment. If it is necessary to be able to detect change in only one direction, as might be the case in studies designed to compare two treatments both known to be effective, then the measure need not allow for bidirectional changes. However, there should be some assurance in advance of the intervention that ceiling or floor effects will not be a limitation that could interfere with detecting differences among various experimental and control conditions.

An important guideline heavily relied on in research is whether a given dependent variable has reflected change in previous studies. Investigators

Table 9.1. Commonly Referred to Types of Reliability and Validity

TYPE	DEFINITION AND/OR CONCEPT
	RELIABILITY
Test–Retest Reliability	The stability of test scores over time; the correlation of scores from one administration of the test with scores on the same instrument after a particular time interval has elapsed.
Alternate-Form Reliability	The correlation between different forms of the same measure when the items of the two forms are considered to represent the same population of items.
Internal Consistency	The degree of consistency or homogeneity of the items within a scale. Different reliability measures are used toward this end such as split-half reliability, Kuder-Richardson 20 Formula, and coefficient alpha.
Interrater (or Interscorer) Reliability	The extent to which different assessors, raters, or observers agree on the scores they provide when assessing, coding, or classifying subjects' performance. Different measures are used to evaluate agreement such as percent agreement, Pearson product-moment correlations, and kappa.
	VALIDITY
Construct Validity	A broad concept that refers to the extent to which the measure reflects the construct (concept, domain) of interest. Other types of validity and other evidence that elaborates the correlates of the measure are relevant to construct validity. Construct validity focuses on the relation of a measure to other measures and domains of functioning of which the concept underlying the measure may be a part.
Content Validity	Evidence that the content of the items reflect the construct or domain of interest; the relation of the items to the concept underlying the measure.
Concurrent Validity	The correlation of a measure with performance on another measure or criterion at the same point in time.
Predictive Validity	The correlation of a measure at one point in time with performance on another measure or criterion at some point in the future.
Criterion Validity	Correlation of a measure with some other criterion. This can encompass concurrent or predictive validity. In addition, the notion is occasionally used in relation to a specific and often dichotomous criterion when performance on the measure is evaluated in relation to disorders (e.g., depressed vs. nondepressed patients) or status (e.g., prisoners vs. nonprisoners).

Table 9.1. *Continued*

TYPE	DEFINITION AND/OR CONCEPT
Face Validity	This refers to the extent to which a measure appears to assess the construct of interest; not regarded as a formal type of validation or part of the psychometric development or evaluation of a measure.
Convergent Validity	The extent to which two measures assess the similar or related constructs. The validity of a given measure is suggested if the measures correlate with other measures with which it is expected to correlate. The correlation between the measures is expected based on the overlap or relation of the constructs. A form of concurrent validity that takes on special meaning in relation to discriminant validity.
Discriminant Validity	The correlation between measures that are expected *not* to relate to each other or to assess dissimilar and unrelated constructs. The validity of a given measure is suggested if the measures show little or no correlation with measures with which they are not expected to correlate. The absence of correlation is expected based on the separate and conceptually distinct constructs.

Note: The types of reliability and validity presented here refer to commonly used terms in test construction and validation. The terms are used in various ways by authors. The purpose here is to highlight critical concepts for evaluating measures. For further discussion, the reader is referred elsewhere (Angoff, 1988; Kline, 1986).

examine published research in a particular area of study to see what measures have reflected change with what sorts of interventions. There is an advantage in looking to previous research in that it serves as a filter for many measures that probably would not reflect change for the type of intervention to be investigated. Measures that have reflected change in previous experiments in a sense have proven themselves to be sensitive to some manipulations. Another advantage is that by using previously reported measures, investigators can more readily compare their findings with those obtained in previous research. The use of similar measures across studies allows investigators to evaluate the magnitude of change in relation to prior work, whether groups were similar to begin with, whether the independent variable affected the dependent measure(s) in the same way, and so on. Of course, there may be disadvantages in using measures from previous investigations. Specifically, looking to other investigations for sources of dependent measures may lead to overreliance on a few measures, which can lead to stagnation in the development of new and perhaps more useful measures. Also, a given construct can be assessed in diverse ways. By assessing the construct in new and different ways, our understanding of the construct can be enhanced.

Overall, the sensitivity of a measure in an investigation should be assured in advance of manipulation of the independent variable, if possible. If a body of literature already shows the sensitivity of the measure to the intervention, then preliminary assessment work can be avoided. If such evidence is not available, preliminary work before the full investigation might evaluate whether different manipulations reflect change on the measure.

There is a major problem one is trying to avoid by determining whether the measure is sensitive prior to conducting the investigation. It is important to know whether the measure *could* reflect the predicted relation between independent and dependent variables. If no relation were demonstrated between the independent and dependent variables at the end of the investigation, it would be reassuring to know that the reason for this was not the insensitivity of the dependent measure. As a general rule, if there is no body of research showing that the measure can reflect change and assesses the appropriate construct, the investigator would wisely invest in pilot work. An alternative is to include the measure with several others on an exploratory basis and explicitly acknowledge in the investigation that one purpose is to explore the relation of a new measure with those already available in the literature.

Using Available or Devising Alternative Measures

Using Standardized Measures

In most cases, the investigator will use measures that are already available and whose psychometric characteristics are known to some degree. Many measures are available in an area of research, and there is usually tacit agreement that certain types of measures, modalities of assessment, and specific instruments are important or central. For example, in studying adult depression, it is very likely that an investigator will include a self-report measure (Beck Depression Inventory) and a clinician rating scale (Hamilton Rating Scale). These modalities and these specific instruments have enjoyed widespread use, a feature that does not necessarily mean that the measures are flawless or free from ambiguity (see Murray, 1989). These scales are considered to be the best researched within this area, and performance on the scales (e.g., scores) is quite meaningful among investigators. The frequent use of the measures has fostered continued use, and researchers embarking on a new study (e.g., evaluating treatment for depression) usually include one or both of these in the broader assessment battery.

Another reason for using standardized measures, of course, is because of the amount of work that may have gone into the measures by other researchers. That work facilitates interpretation of the measure. For example, to assess intellectual functioning or psychopathology among adults, one might rely on the Wechsler Adult Intelligence Scale—Revised (WAIS-R) and the revised Minnesota Multiphasic Personality Inventory (MMPI-2). Elaborate and extensive research on each of these measures facilitates their interpretation. Also, use of such well-studied measures lends credence that the study assessed the construct of interest.

Varying an Existing Measure

A standard measure of functioning, personality, behavior, or some other domain may be available to the investigator. Yet, some facet of the investigator's interest may make that measure not quite appropriate. The measure may have been developed, established, and very well validated in a context different from that of interest for the investigator's study. For example, one might wish to assess young children but the measure of interest has been developed, evaluated, or standardized with adolescents. Alternatively, the investigator may wish to assess a particular ethnic group whose language and culture differ from those samples with whom the measure was developed. The reason for selecting the measure is that the method or content seems highly suitable for the investigator's purposes. Yet the measure has not been used in this new way or validated in this context.

In such cases, the investigator may elect to use the measure. In so doing, it is essential to include within the study some independent means of validation. Independent means of validation refers to evidence that the measure "behaves" in a way that parallels the standard use of the measure. This might include calculating correlations of the measure in its new use with other measures in the study or using the measure to delineate subgroups and showing that the findings resemble those obtained in studies when the original measure has been used as intended. It may not be sufficient to show that the new use of the measure leads to predictable differences on the dependent measure. The complexity of the predicted relations and the plausibility of alternative interpretations of the measure are relevant to judge the new use of the measure. In the general case, it is advisable within the study, or as part of pilot work, to provide additional evidence that the construct of interest is still measured in the new use of the measure.

Use of existing measures in novel ways is often preferable to creating entirely new measures. The reason is that the available research on the existing measure is relevant for interpretation of the measure. Data on the original factor structure, correlations with other measures, and psychometric characteristics provide some information that may be relevant to the new application. If an entirely new measure were created instead, none of this background information would be available.

On the other hand, use of standardized measures in novel ways may be viewed and labeled by colleagues who review the research as "inappropriate" or beyond the intention of the founding fathers (and mothers) who devised the measure. This view is not extreme; there comes a point at which applicability of the measure to new samples, populations, and circumstances is strained. For many that point consists of any extensions beyond the specific purposes for which the measure has been developed and standardized. Reasonable people differ on this point; reasonable investigators provide data to ally the cogent concern that the novel use may not have validity data in its behalf.

Investigators often make slight variations in a standardized measure such as deleting a few items, rewording items, or adding new items. The purpose is to make the measure better suited to the new population or application. Whether or not one tinkers with the content or format, the requirements are similar. As a minimum, some evidence is needed within the study to show the measure continues to assess the construct of interest. To the extent that the measure is altered and that the new use departs from the one for which the measure was standardized, stronger and more extensive validity data are likely to be demanded by the research community.

As an illustration, in the work of our research group, we have been interested in measuring hopelessness in children. Hopelessness, or negative expectations toward the future, has been reliably assessed in adults with a scale devised for that purpose (e.g., Beck, Weissman, Lester, & Trexler, 1974). In developing the scale for children the items from the adult scale were rephrased and altered to simplify the content and to be more relevant to children's lives. Clearly such changes are not minor modifications of a scale, and hence it would not be reasonable to assume that the original validational evidence would apply. Two studies were conducted to evaluate alternative types of reliability and validity. Internal consistency data and analyses of items paralleled the results obtained with the adult scale. In addition, the construct of hopelessness in children generated results similar to those obtained with adults. For example, hopelessness was found to be related to suicide ideation and attempt and to be positively correlated with depression and negatively correlated with self-esteem (Kazdin, French, Unis, Esveldt-Dawson, & Sherick, 1983; Kazdin, Rodgers, & Colbus, 1986).

The initial findings on the Hopelessness Scale for Children were helpful but rather preliminary. One or two studies are limited for different reasons. In the case of our research, the children were within a restricted age range of 6 to 13 years and were all inpatients from a psychiatric hospital. Also, a limited range of constructs and other measures were examined as the basis for evaluating validity. The task in developing a measure is not necessarily to complete the infinite range of evaluations necessary. As an initial step, the investigator can provide preliminary evidence and place the measure and data analyses in the usual publication outlets, so that others can continue psychometric and construct validation research (e.g., Spirito, Williams, Stark, & Hart, 1988).

Developing New Measures

Sometimes the construct of interest is not measured by existing measures. The investigator may wish to develop a new measure to address the questions that guide the study. Under ideal circumstances, instrument development is a program of research in itself. The investigator can devote a research program and career to developing a new measure. In most cases, investigators are not interested in developing or evaluating a measure with that in mind. Rather, the goal is to address a set of substantive questions and a particular construct of interest is not operationalized in a way the investigator believes captures the construct adequately.

The investigator may develop a new measure and include this in the study of interest. In the process, there are obligations of the investigator to the research community. Specifically, some evidence is required either in pilot work reported in the write up of the study or as part of the study itself that attests in some way to the construct validity of the measure. The steps extend beyond face validity, that is, that the content of the items is reasonable or obvious. Alternative types of reliability and validity, as presented in Table 9.1, might be relevant. Particularly crucial would be evidence that supports the assertion that the measure assesses the construct of interest. One or more of the following types of information would be useful:

1. Differences between groups on the measure (e.g., older vs. younger, clinically referred vs. nonreferred cases) in ways that are consistent with the construct allegedly assessed (criterion validity);
2. The measure correlates in a predictable direction with other measures that are standardized, and the magnitudes of these correlations are consistent (e.g., low, moderate, high) with what would be predicted from the relation of the constructs encompassed by the new and standardized measures (concurrent, predictive, or concurrent validity);
3. The new measure is not highly correlated with standardized measure of some other, more established construct (e.g., $r \geq .80$), which might suggest that the new construct is fairly well encompassed by or redundant with the other (more established) construct (discriminant validity). (The level of correlation between two measures that might be viewed as reflecting their redundancy is somewhat arbitrary. A suggested criterion of $r \geq .80$ is provided here because the level of correlation is relatively high. Also the square of the correlation [r^2], which suggests the amount of shared variance, is 64% [i.e., $.80^2$]. Measures that share more than this amount of variance might be viewed with great care if one of the measures is proposed as a measure of a new construct.)
4. Over time, performance on the measure does or does not change depending on the nature of the construct (e.g., mood vs. character trait) (test–retest reliability).

With the use of a new measure, evidence on one or more types of validity is a minimum required to argue that the construct of interest is captured by the measure. As noted in the discussion of altering a standardized measure, it is usually insufficient to add the measure to the study and to show that it reflects changes that are predicted. Within the study, separate and *independent* types of evidence are needed about the measure apart from or in addition to how the measure reflects change as a dependent measure.

For example, an investigator may pose that after psychotherapy patients who receive Therapy A are better able to "smell the flowers of life" compared to those who received Therapy B. The Smell-the-Flowers Scale is developed with 50 true-false items (e.g., Item 1 = "Sunsets, which I never noticed before, are terrific"). Alas, the investigator shows that scale scores are higher (i.e., better) for Therapy A clients than for Therapy B clients. This type of evidence does not lobby particularly well for the validity of the scale. The minimal recommendations noted previously call for *independent* evidence within the study apart from the primary predictions. In the case of this study, it would be useful to show that the new scale does not correlate highly with symptom change on standardized outcome measures, attraction to one's therapist, socially desirable responding, and other reasonable constructs that are more readily measured by standardized instruments and that are more parsimonious. There are many other constructs that might account for client performance on the scale, other than the one that is posed. Efforts within the study are required to address this in at least a preliminary way. Without such efforts, the meaning of the performance on that measure remains at best quite tentative and more likely uninterpretable.

As an illustration, we have been interested in devising treatments for seriously disturbed children who engage in antisocial behavior (e.g., Kazdin, 1987). Although general scales are available to assess diverse symptom domains of children and relatively mild antisocial behaviors, we felt no scale truly captured the range of antisocial behaviors that characterized clinically referred youths. To that end, we devised a parent interview to assess severity and duration of a variety of antisocial behaviors (e.g., theft, fire setting, fighting) that paralleled many of the symptoms in current diagnostic criteria for Conduct Disorder (American Psychiatric Association, 1980, 1987). Evidence suggested that scores on the measure differentiated children with and without the diagnosis of Conduct Disorder, that performance on the scale correlated in the moderate to high range with other measures of disruptive and acting out behaviors, and that scores changed in response to treatment for antisocial behavior (Kazdin, 1989b; Kazdin & Esveldt-Dawson, 1986; Kazdin et al., 1989). All sorts of questions remain about the scale, content, and correlates. Developing a new scale, perhaps even more than revising an existing one, begins the path of validation completely anew.

General Comments

Using standardized measures, varying such measures to suit new situations, or developing new measures have as their final common pathway interpretation of the findings. The strength and specificity of the conclusions that the investigator can research is not based merely on statistical significance. With all of its vagaries, statistical significance and its determination are the "easy" parts of the research. The strength, specificity, and very likely the value or utility of the conclusions depend on interpretation of what was measured and the meaning of performance on the measures. If extensive evidence is available for the construct validity of the measure, which is often the case for standardized measures, the burden of interpretation is reduced. The burden is never eliminated even here because psychological measures by their very nature raise manifold issues about construct validity, external validity, potential bias, and so on. Intelligence tests, for example, tend to be the most well-studied psychological instruments. At the same time the tests are surrounded in controversy related to their interpretation and use (Hale, 1991). If extensive evidence is not available for the measure, if a standardized measure is altered in some way, either through application to novel circumstances or by item tinkering, or if a new measure is developed, validity data are essential to include within the study.

MODALITIES OF ASSESSMENT

The diverse measures available in clinical research and the range of characteristics they assess would be difficult to enumerate, let alone elaborate, here. Measures used in clinical psychology vary along a number of dimensions. Table 9.2 presents salient characteristics that vary among measures and that have implications for selecting measures. In a given study it is often valuable to select more than one measure of the construct of interest. Also, variation of the measures of that construct is important so that the methodological characteristics are not identical. In this way the investigator can be assured that the finding is not restricted to the construct as measured in a particular way. Characteristics in Table 9.2 help to identify different types of measures that may be selected.

The characteristic that may distinguish measures most sharply and not encompassed by Table 9.2 is the modality or type of measure. Although the different types of measures and the requirements for devising useful measures within each modality are beyond the scope of the present chapter, much can be gained by highlighting major modalities of assessment and the kinds of uses and problems they provide for clinical research.

Table 9.2. Alternative Dimensions and/or Characteristics of Psychological Measures

CHARACTERISTIC	DEFINITION AND/OR CONCEPT
Global—Specific	Measures vary in the extent to which they assess narrowly defined versus broad characteristics of functioning. Measures of overall feelings, stress, and quality of life are more toward the global side; measures of narrowly defined domains and experience are more specific.
Publicly Observable Information—Private Event	Measures may examine characteristics or actions that can be observed by others (e.g., cigarette smoking, social interaction) or assess private experience (e.g., headaches, thoughts, urges, and obsessions).
Stable—Transient Characteristics	Measures may assess trait-like characteristics or long-standing aspects of functioning or short-lived or episodic characteristics (e.g., mood immediately after being subjected to a frustrating experience in an experiment).
Direct—Indirect	Direct measures are those whose purpose can be seen by the client. Indirect measures are those that obscure from the client exactly what is being measured.
Breadth of Domains Sampled	Measures vary whether they assess a single characteristic (e.g., introversion, anxiety, risk-taking ability, or need for social approval), or reveal many different characteristics of personality or psychopathology (e.g., several personality traits or different types of symptoms within a single measure).
Format	Measures vary in the methods through which subjects can provide their replies such as true–false, multiple-choice, forced-choice, fill-in, and rating scale formats of self-report scales and inventories and extended narrative reports subsequently coded as in projective techniques.

Global Ratings by Others

Characteristics

Global ratings refer to efforts to quantify impressions of somewhat general characteristics. They are referred to as "global" because they reflect overall impressions or summary statements of the construct of interest. Typically, ratings are made by the therapist or by significant others who are in contact with the clients. A major justification for use of these ratings is that select individuals other than the client may be in a position by virtue of expertise (e.g., therapist, ward staff member of a psychiatric hospital) or familiarity with the client (e.g., spouse, parent) to provide a well-based appraisal.

The judgments may vary in complexity in terms of precisely what is rated. Very often global ratings are made in such areas as improvement in therapy, social adequacy, ability to handle stress, and similar general measures of overall adjustment. These ratings are usually made by having raters complete one or a few Likert-type items—that is, items rated on a multiple-point continuum where the degree of the rated dimension can be assessed. For example, two typical items might be:

To what extent has the client improved in therapy? (check one)

1	2	3	4	5	6	7
no improvement			moderate improvement		very large improvement	

How much do the client's symptoms interfere with everyday functioning?

1	2	3	4	5	6	7
not at all			moderately			very much

The above samples not only illustrate the format for global ratings but also the generality of the dimension frequently rated. Usually ratings ask for an appraisal of a multifaceted or complex area of functioning.

There are many features of global ratings that have made them popular. To begin with, ratings provide a very flexible assessment format for an investigator. Virtually any construct of interest to the investigator (e.g., symptomatology, overall functioning, ease in social situations) can be included. The flexibility also means that a general characteristic can be used to rate individuals who may differ greatly in their individual problems. By rating clients on a global dimension that encompasses diverse problems (e.g., degree of improvement, extent to which symptoms interfere with ordinary functioning), a similar measure can be used for people whose characteristics at a more molecular level vary greatly.

Another reason that global ratings have been popular is that they provide a summary evaluation of a client's status. The problems clients experience may include many facets. It is important to determine with specificity how these different facets have changed. It is often useful to have an overall statement that distills the effects of treatment into a relatively simple statement. Global ratings of client behavior often have been used for that purpose.

Global ratings also provide a convenient format for soliciting judgments of experts, peers, or other informants. Presumably, an expert in the nature of clinical dysfunction is uniquely skilled to evaluate the status of the client, the severity of the client's disorder, and the degree to which change, deterioration, or improvement has occurred. Similarly, individuals in the natural environment who interact with the client (e.g., peers, spouses, employers) also are in unique positions to evaluate performance. In this context, global ratings of client change often have been incorporated into treatment evaluation.

Potential Limitations

One of the major problems with global ratings is evaluating precisely what they measure. The phrasing of global ratings suggests what the item is designed to measure (e.g., symptoms). However, there is no assurance that this in fact is what is actually measured. Few or, more often, no concrete criteria are specified to the assessor who completes the ratings. The ratings by definition are rather general, and all sorts of variables may enter into the rater's criteria for evaluating the client.

Because the criteria are not well specified, it is possible that the global ratings may change over time independently of whether the client has changed, as reflected on some other, more specific measure. For example, therapists may view clients as improving over time simply because of changes in the criteria used in making their overall ratings of improvement. Thus a client's greater ease, candor, or warmth within the therapy session may influence a therapist's rating of client improvement at the end of therapy whether or not clinical change in the problem area (e.g., obsessions or compulsive rituals) has occurred. Changes in the measurement procedures or criteria over time were referred to earlier as *instrumentation,* a threat to the internal validity. Instrumentation can account for changes over time as a function of assessment rather than change in client behavior. Global ratings are especially subject to the instrumentation threat because the criteria that go into making ratings are general.

The absence of clear criteria in making ratings leads to yet another problem. An important feature of scientific research is that the results are cumulative. It is important to be able to examine a set of investigations to make conclusions about variables and their effects. Global ratings are often developed for a particular study and not subject to the usual validation steps. Consequently, little relation may exist between rating methods from one study to the next.

Another problem with global ratings, certainly related to the problem of what they measure, is their potential lack of sensitivity. Essentially, global ratings ask general questions for a given dimension, such as "How severe are the client's symptoms?" "How much improvement has there been?" and "How anxious is the client?". By posing general questions such as these, the measures lose some of the sensitivity that could be obtained from assessing very specific characteristics of the relevant dimensions of interest. For example, given the complexity of personality and behavior, it is very likely that therapy may change some aspects of behavior and not others. Anxiety, as a commonly treated disorder, is very complex and consists of many facets as reflected on self-report, behavioral, and physiological measures. Indeed, within each of these facets there are many additional components. Global ratings greatly oversimplify the nature of functioning and therapeutic change.

Self-Report Inventories, Questionnaires, and Scales

Characteristics

Certainly the most popular measures in clinical psychology are self-report inventories, questionnaires, and scales. These measures require clients to report on aspects of their own personality or behavior. Unlike global ratings, such measures typically include multiple items that are designed to sample specific aspects of a domain of functioning.

The widespread use of self-report measures can be traced to several factors. First, an obvious factor that makes self-report measures absolutely central is the fact that many states, feelings, and psychological problems are defined by what clients say or feel. Individuals may feel helpless, self-critical, generally unhappy, or have a low self-concept. Although there may be ways of looking for overt behavioral or physiological correlates of these states or ratings by various informants (e.g., peers, spouses), clients can report directly on them.

Second, self-report measures permit assessment of several domains of functioning that are not readily available with other assessment techniques. Obviously, the client is in a unique position to report on his or her own thoughts, feelings, wishes, and dreams, and overt acts. Also, the client can report on his or her states and behaviors across a wide range of different situations and hence can provide a comprehensive portrait of everyday performance.

Third, the ease of administration has made such measures especially useful for purposes of screening. Screening refers to the initial assessment phase where the investigator must select a small sample from a larger population. Often a simple assessment device (e.g., self-report scale) is used as a means to divide the sample. Individuals who meet particular criterion levels on the self-report measures or questionnaires can be selected and studied more intensively through other techniques. Indeed, the extensive use of self-report measures in military and educational settings has been precisely for this massive screening to identify individuals who should receive additional assessment (e.g., psychiatric diagnosis of potential recruits in the military or evaluation of learning-disabled children in education). Also in clinical, counseling, and community psychology, questionnaires and inventories completed by oneself or by others (e.g., parents, teachers) are commonly used as initial screening devices to select people for further evaluation or intervention.

There are many different types of self-report measures—so many that it is difficult to consider them as part of a single category. In fact, measures are available that constitute virtually all permutations of the characteristics noted in Table 9.2. For many self-report measures, extensive research exists. For example, one of the most widely investigated measures in clinical psychology is the Minnesota Multiphasic Personality Inventory (MMPI), an objective self-report test. The measure, recently revised (MMPI-2), includes multiple scales that measure personality and psychopathology (Butcher, Graham, Williams, & Ben-Porath, 1990). The measure has been used with diverse populations (e.g., psychiatric patients, prisoners) and for multiple purposes (e.g., screening of prospective employees, treatment planning, evaluation of therapy outcome). Apart from any single measure, a large range of measures are available; an overwhelming number of characteristics can be assessed including various traits, states, moods, feelings, impulses, strivings, and trepidations. Self-report measures can assess diverse aspects of a given characteristic or multiple characteristics merely by having the client respond to many different items. The number of measures available and the number of personality characteristics that can be assessed make self-report measures convenient and widely used.

Potential Limitations

Self-report measures used in treatment evaluation and personality research usually are not based on global ratings of a general state; instead, they include inventories designed to measure specific subject characteristics. There are two general categories of problems that characterize many self-report measures: (a) the biases on the part of the subject and (b) the lack of evidence that the measure assesses the characteristic of interest.

Self-report measures are a candidate for distortion on the part of the subjects. Distortion refers to the alteration of subjects' responses in some way in light of their own motives or self-interest. At the extreme, subjects can dissimulate to such a degree that the answers they report are simply untrue. Occasionally, inventories have special scales (e.g., Lie scales) to assess the extent to which the subject is not telling the truth, is being inconsistent, or endorsing response alternatives that are extremely unlikely.

Blatant dissimulation aside, subjects are likely to alter slightly the image of themselves that they present and to interpret very loosely the meaning of the items so that they appear to place themselves in the best possible light. The tendency to do this is referred to as *social desirability* and has been shown to be extremely pervasive on self-report measures. Inventories designed to measure specific psychiatric disorders and personality traits often correlate very highly with measures of social desirability (e.g., Edwards, 1957). Thus individuals who complete self-report items are likely to endorse the socially condoned behaviors rather than the socially inappropriate behaviors. The pervasiveness of social desirability as a response style has led investigators to posit a specific personality trait referred to as the *need for social approval* (Crowne & Marlowe, 1964). Individuals who are high in their need for social approval on a self-report measure behave in experimental situations in a way that maximizes approval from others. Thus the bias on self-report inventories goes beyond a specific set of measures.

In treatment evaluation, another source of bias that may operate on self-report measures pertains to the severity of self-reported symptoms or complaints. Before therapy, clients may exaggerate their complaints because these exaggerations may ensure that they receive treatment or increase the speed with which treatment is provided. After therapy, clients may respond to the same measures in a more socially desirable fashion in the sense that they provide the therapist and clinic with evidence of improvement, presumably the reward of providing treatment. The changes in self-report responses before and after therapy due to exaggeration and underplaying of problems has been referred to as the "hello-goodbye" effect (see Meltzoff & Kornreich, 1970). Of course, this effect is difficult to estimate because of the actual changes in treatment or because of influences such as statistical regression, that is, improvements that may result simply from having extreme scores at the initial assessment.

The range of biases that may operate on self-report measures and the voluminous literature devoted to these biases cannot begin to be sampled here. Suffice it to say that many biases are potential limitations to the information provided by self-report inventories. Depending on the assessment devices and response format (e.g., true–false or ratings), people have shown a tendency to acquiesce or agree with items regardless of their content, to check extreme values on rating scales, to give cautious or qualified answers, to be inconsistent across items, and so on.

The problems of distorting answers on self-report inventories (e.g., socially desirable responding) stem from the fact that the subjects are aware that they are being assessed and act differently than they ordinarily would respond without this awareness. Because subjects are aware of the assessment procedure, they can bring to bear their own motives and self-interest in responding. The extent to which distortion may occur is a function of many factors, including whether subjects can detect the purpose of the measure and whether their motives are consistent with those of the investigator. Presumably, the conditions for responding on self-report measures can be arranged in such a fashion as to minimize distortion, although how low the minimal level will be is open to question. Having clients complete tests under conditions of anonymity, ensuring confidentiality, providing incentives for candor, or conveying to the client that his or her best interests are served by honest self-evaluation are designed expressly for this purpose.

Projective Techniques

Characteristics

Projective techniques refer to a specific class of measures that attempt to reveal underlying intrapsychic characteristics, motives, processes, styles, themes, and sources of personality conflict. These characteristics are measured indirectly. Clients are provided with an ambiguous task where they are free to respond with minimal situational cues or constraints. The ambiguity of the cues and minimization of stimulus material allow the client to freely project onto the situation important processes within his or her own personality.

There are many projective techniques that differ according to the responses required of the subject, the type of stimuli presented, the manner in which content or style of responding is interpreted, the purposes of the test, and other factors. Among the most commonly used are the Rorschach and Thematic Apperception Test, which serve as a useful frame of reference. These tests present stimuli to the subject that consist of inkblot designs or ambiguous drawings, respectively. The subject is required to interpret what he or she sees. The stimuli are ambiguous so that they can be interpreted in an indefinite number of ways. The purpose of making the stimuli ambiguous is to examine the material or content the subject produces. Given the ambiguous stimuli, this material is considered to be a product of the individual's personality and reflect unconscious processes, underlying themes and motives, conflicts, and so on.

Responses to projective techniques are considered to be traceable to content themes and perceptual processes that unify and organize personality. Content domains such as how the individual handles sexual or aggressive impulses, relates to authority, or expresses need for achievement as well as stylistic or coping methods such as expressing affect and managing needs, are inferred. The many different interpretations provided by the subject usually are condensed to reflect a small number of themes or processes. Performance on projective tests has been viewed as a way to provide insights on the inner workings and organization of personality.

Potential Limitations

Projective techniques have received considerable attention in personality assessment. Their use and popularity have waxed and waned over the last 25 years due in part to their association with a particular theoretical approach toward the nature of personality (Klopfer & Taulbee, 1976). Several projective techniques have adhered to intrapsychic models, primarily psychoanalytic models, which explain human functioning in terms of underlying personality characteristics.

Research on projective techniques has enjoyed a resurgence of interest in personality assessment (Craik, 1986). Developments in psychoanalytic theory (e.g., object relations) and methods of scoring diverse scales have led to accelerated research on projective techniques (Erdberg, 1990; Striker & Healey, 1990). Nevertheless, use of the measures is generally restricted within clinical psychology. The measures are not routinely incorporated into studies related to such topics as the diagnosis, assessment, and treatment of clinical dysfunction, treatment process research, and studies of special populations.

To be sure, studies using projective techniques address diverse topics. However, when compared to other types of measures such as self-report inventories, projective techniques are less frequently employed. There are many reasons. First, many projective techniques traditionally have relied heavily on interpretations and inferences of the examining psychologist. These interpretations often have been shown to be inconsistent across examiners, which has lead researchers to question the basis for making judgments about personality. Second and related, projective techniques are associated with a particular theoretical orientation and level of analysis, namely, intrapsychic processes drawn to psychodynamic theories. Adherence to these views has waxed and waned as well. The development of more ecumenical and integrative views of human functioning and the impact of cognitive psychology have been associated with greater appreciation of internal workings of human personality. Third, scoring methods of many projective methods are somewhat cumbersome. Consequently, unless the investigator has specific interest in projective tests, the measures are not likely to be adopted casually to expand an assessment battery. Thus if the investigator would like to assess aggression, symptoms, or stress and wishes to choose multiple methods to operationalize the constructs, projective tests are not the usual choice. Investigators are more likely to select measures that are more convenient to administer and score.

Notwithstanding these considerations, projective techniques have occupied a very special place in clinical assessment. The full range of clinical topics including "normal" functioning of personality, characteristics of different diagnostic groups, personality and human performance, and other areas can be evaluated from the standpoint of intrapsychic processes and themes. Elaboration of the content areas of the field as well as development of alternative tests and scoring methods have made projective assessment an area of work in its own right.

Behavioral Measures

Characteristics

Assessment often relies on measures of overt behavior. Behavioral assessment requires an operational definition of the construct of interest in terms of overt behaviors that the client performs in everyday situations or in situations that are designed explicitly to reveal specific responses. Behavioral assessment attempts to assess directly the behavior of interest by looking at what the client actually does. Thus the resulting responses are considered to provide actual *samples* of the relevant behaviors.

The potential utility of direct assessment of overt behavior can be illustrated in the context of therapy. Many problems that arise in therapy consist of overt behavioral problems. Examples include such problems as enuresis, tics, stuttering, sexual dysfunction, inadequate social or dating skills, failure to approach situations because they evoke anxiety, and verbalizations of hallucinations and delusions. The fact that these problems include behavioral components does not in any way deny that other modalities of assessment are important or relevant. Yet as a modality of assessment, behavioral measures focus on what the individual actually does and operationalize problems in terms of ordinary types of performance.

An important feature of behavioral assessment is that measures can be constructed to suit the behaviors of individual clients. Such assessment procedures are constructed by carefully defining the behaviors that are to be observed and scoring these behaviors as the client functions in everyday situations. In many cases, behavioral assessment is conducted in the situations in which the client's behavior is to be altered. For example, investigations using behavioral assessment have been conducted in the home, classrooms, psychiatric hospitals, business settings, and the community (see Kazdin, 1989c).

Although behavioral assessment often has involved observing performance in the natural environment, this is not feasible in many situations. Many of the behaviors observed (e.g., sexual arousal) are not the sort that clients are interested in having monitored in the natural environment. Relatedly, the conditions in which some behaviors occur (e.g., at the office, while getting ready for school or work, at meals) may preclude direct assessment for practical reasons. Hence behavioral assessment often is conducted under contrived or simulated conditions. Special tasks or situations may be devised in which behaviors can be observed directly. For example, individuals may report anxiety in social situations. To assess this through overt performance, a number of role-play tasks may be devised in which people are asked to interact with others at the clinic. Subject performance may be videotaped and coded for specific characteristics (e.g., nonverbal and verbal behaviors) that might reflect anxiety or avoidance.

An advantage of overt behavioral assessment is that it can take into account the specificity of behavior across situations. Whether a given behavior occurs and the type of behavior that occurs are likely to be a function of specific environmental cues. Behavioral assessment attempts to assess behavior either in the situation directly or in situations designed to approximate those conditions closely. Sampling behavior under conditions of the natural environment or conditions resembling these should provide access to the behavior of interest or something very much like that behavior.

The importance of considering the situational and other stimulus conditions that may contribute to behavior is often taken advantage of directly in behavioral assessment. For example, assessment of child behavior in the home might be based on scoring the frequency of the child's compliance with parental requests and how often he or she engages in tantrums or other obstreperous behaviors. In addition to assessing the child's behavior, the assessment may focus on specific behaviors of the parents as well, such as their approval, disapproval, and commands in relation to the child (Patterson, 1982). These latter behaviors relate directly to and greatly influence the child's behavior. By assessing the parent's behavior in relation to that of the child's interrelations between various stimuli (behaviors of the parents) and responses (behaviors of the child) can be discerned.

Potential Limitations

One of the main considerations in evaluating behavioral measures is the extent to which the sample of overt behavior represents the construct of interest to the investigator. One of the strengths of behavioral assessment is that it examines the behavior of direct interest (e.g., cigarette smoking, social interaction, compulsive rituals). Because the behaviors of interest are observed directly, the measures seemingly are straightforward indexes of the problems. Even direct samples of behavior are not necessarily representative samples of what behaviors are like during periods when samples are not obtained. It is possible that the sampled behaviors or period of time when assessment is conducted do not accurately portray the client's performance at other times. If the periods of observation samples (e.g., 1 hour of observation per day) are to represent all of the potentially available observation periods (e.g., all waking hours), assessment methods need to ensure that there are no differences that occur across the available periods of assessment. This can be accomplished by randomly selecting periods throughout the day for behavioral assessment. Although this is not feasible for most behaviors because of practical considerations, it would seem to resolve the problem of obtaining a direct and representative sample of behavior.

As noted earlier, many behavioral measures are conducted under contrived situations. A contrived situation permits evocation of the behaviors so they can be readily assessed. Yet performance in contrived situations may be different from performance in ordinary situations. Subjects may be aware of the special assessment arrangement and respond differently as a result (see Kazdin, 1982c). In addition, contrived situations invariably remove or omit some of the stimulus conditions that may influence the extent to which behavior is performed. For example, drinking by alcoholics has been assessed in inpatient treatment settings where clients can sit and consume alcohol at a simulated bar (e.g., Sobell, Schaefer, & Mills, 1972). The simulated bar looks like an ordinary bar but is actually a special room in the hospital. Although the bar might seem to be a very close approximation of the situation in which much of the problem drinking outside of the laboratory would occur, it still is relatively distant from nonlaboratory situations. Indeed, reports suggest that alcoholics drink infrequently in treatment facilities when alcohol is made available (Skoloda, Alterman, Cornelison, & Gottheil, 1975). Apparently, many of the psychological cues of the natural environment (e.g., work demands, interactions with others), rather than the simple physical cues of the drinking situation, may precipitate drinking (Lawson, Wilson, Briddell, & Ives, 1976). If this is the case, simulated situations may be inherently limited. Obviously, individual problem areas and various simulated situations must be studied to assess whether they are related to performance in ordinary situations. Given the situational specificity of behavior, one might expect that departure of the situation from the natural setting might well lead to differences in behavior.

On balance, behavioral measures provide a unique focus that extends the method of evaluation beyond the more familiar and commonly used self-report scales and inventories. Also, for many facets of functioning studied in clinical psychology (e.g., agoraphobia, marital communication, child-rearing practices), overt behavior plays a major role. Evaluation of samples of behaviors can provide central information.

Psychophysiological Measures

Characteristics

Psychophysiological measures refer to assessment techniques designed to quantify biological events as they relate to psychological states. The number of available psychophysiological measures is vast and includes measures of different types of functions (e.g., arousal of the autonomic system) and systems (e.g., cardiovascular, gastrointestinal, neurological). In clinical research, psychophysiological measures have been used rather extensively to assess general states of arousal such as those associated with anxiety or more specific arousal states such as sexual arousal in response to particular stimuli.

A major area within psychology that has given great attention to psychophysiological response assessment is biofeedback. Biofeedback explicitly attempts to alter performance of psychophysiological functioning. A large number of different assessment procedures may be used to look at the effects of feedback on cardiovascular responses (e.g., heart rate, blood pressure), electromyographic responses (muscle tension), electroencephalographic responses (e.g., alpha activity, seizure-related neurological activity), skin temperature, gastrointestinal responses (e.g., activity of the colon, sphincter reflexes), and others. Biofeedback involves use of psychophysiological assessment devices and is unique in that sense.

Even outside of biofeedback, psychophysiological assessment procedures receive major use. These measures are considered to assess an important part of functioning that cannot be determined from other modalities. Depending on the target focus, physiological functioning may be viewed as a direct, or as the most direct, measure of the problem of interest. For example, in the area of sexual arousal, sexual stimuli can be presented in the actual situation, on slides, or on audiotape to determine whether they arouse the clients. Arousal to the stimuli can be assessed directly by looking at blood volume changes in the penis or lining of the vagina. Such assessment does not replace or obviate the need for a self-report assessment of arousal, but rather points to the possibility of direct assessment of the physiological side of arousal.

Psychophysiological measures have also figured prominently in the area of anxiety management and its treatments (Marks, 1987). Treatment studies have relied heavily on such measures as heart or pulse rate as measures of anxiety. Traditionally, physiological arousal has played a central role in conceptualizing emotional states such as anxiety. As a result, research has attempted to assess the level of physiological functioning as individuals experience specific emotional states. Obviously, when physiological measures can be uniquely associated with experienced states, such measures present important advances in psychological assessment. One reason for this is that physiological measures are less subject to some of the artifacts that seem to plague many other measures. For example, response patterns such as socially desirable responding, acquiescence, and so on do not seem relevant when monitoring such measures as heart rate, blood pressure, respiration rate, and so on. Also, voluntary alteration of responses to psychophysiological measures in light of demands of the experiment situation are likely to be less than the alteration likely on self-report or behavioral test measures. For these reasons, psychophysiological measures often have been regarded as direct measures to circumvent many sources of artifact and bias present in other modalities of assessment. Of course, psychophysiological measures have their own sources of artifact and bias, but these differ from those in traditional measures used in clinical psychology.

Potential Limitations

The view traditionally adhered to in psychophysiology is that many psychological states are based on or related to underlying physiological processes. That is, specific states can be identified with measures of physiological functioning. No doubt this general assumption has support depending on the measures used, the specific psychological states, and the intensity of that state. Yet, the assumption also tends to oversimplify the nature of psychophysiological measures. Research has demonstrated that response systems that can be measured physiologically are not isomorphic with psychological states.

For a set of measures within a given system (e.g., heart rate, blood pressure, and blood volume as measures of the cardiovascular system) and across systems (e.g., measures of cardiovascular functioning, respiration, skin resistance), responses to specific events may not be interrelated in a consistent fashion for different subjects (Lacey & Lacey, 1958). This state of affairs has led to much less emphasis on measuring general constructs such as anxiety or emotional states and more emphasis on viewing assessment alternatives as reflecting more specific psychophysiological functions. Specific research is needed to validate measures of physiological measurement to ensure that they are in fact related to the construct of interest.

There are considerations in using psychophysiological measures that are much more mundane than concerns about precisely what is being measured. For example, psychophysiological recording often requires rather expensive equipment, particularly if multiple response systems are monitored simultaneously. The expense is prohibitive for many research programs. Also, artifacts unique to particular assessment methods can influence responsiveness on measures. Movements of the subject, changes in respiration, electrical interference from adjacent equipment, and demands of the situation may enter into the responses of subjects who are connected to various devices. Whether the above potential sources of artifact occur is in part a function of the particular measures used and the nature of the recording system. For example, inadvertent or intentional changes in respiration on the part of the subject can affect heart rate data and can introduce artifacts. Such influences can be readily controlled or addressed by monitoring systems that might mediate changes in the response of interest or by ruling out the possibility of involvement in a specific system by removing its influence with a competing task or medication.

General Comments

The discussion of major modalities of assessment is not intended to be complete either in terms of the number of modalities available or the variations within each modality. Major options were reviewed that may be differentially relevant for an investigation, depending on the purpose and constructs of interest on the part of the investigator. Selection of a given modality of assessment might be dictated by theoretical predictions, the nature of the client's complaint, and interpretation of the therapist as to the primary modality of the problem. Practical decisions as well might dictate the methods of assessment finally selected.

Our discussion has focused on assessment modalities free from the content areas of clinical psychology. Often the measures are dictated by the content area and the interests they inherently reflect. For example, within clinical psychology a great deal of research focuses on neuropsychological assessment. The area considers the diagnosis and evaluation of functioning and damage to the brain as, for example, associated with injury, psychological dysfunction, medical illness, and aging. A variety of specific measures and tasks are routinely included to assess intellectual skills, sensation, memory, speech perception, tactile discrimination, and other domains (see Goldstein, 1990). Many measures are regarded as standard to address the range of questions that neurological assessment requires. For other areas of research in clinical psychology as well, one might identify measures and modalities in frequent use. The issue for our discussion was options for selecting dependent variables more generally.

In most studies it may be difficult to discern precisely why one modality of assessment was selected rather than another. Yet the description of the purpose of the research should directly state why a particular modality has been selected over another. Within that modality it is desirable to justify why a particular measure was selected. In most cases in which such a justification is not explicit, there may be extensive evidence attesting to the utility, reliability, and validity of the assessment technique. In other cases, many options might be available and the decision appears arbitrary. Specific hypotheses about the constructs that constitute the dependent measures may dictate not only the modality of assessment (e.g., psychophysiological measures) but also the particular measure within the modality (e.g., heart rate rather than skin conductance).

In the overview of assessment modalities, potential sources of limitations were discussed. Inadvertently, there may have been an implication that one type of measure was better than another. For a given research or clinical purpose, one modality may be more well suited than another because it reflects the construct and level of analysis of interest (e.g., projective techniques for unconscious processes; behavioral measures for samples of everyday interactions). However, one type of measure is not inherently superior to another. The investigator's purpose or concern over a particular source of bias or artifact may dictate which modality of assessment and measurement devices within a given modality will be appropriate.

The discussion of separate modalities of assessment also may have accidentally fostered the notion that the investigator should select only one modality for evaluating the results of an experiment. Actually, it is very useful to draw upon assessment devices from different modalities and to use multiple measures to reflect the dependent variable of interest. Although the importance of multiple measures is elaborated later, the utility of different measures should be clear from the review of select assessment modalities. Each modality includes different sources of bias and potential limitations. There is no single measure that overcomes all of the problems that arise in assessment. Indeed, the measures are complementary. Selecting several different measures, each with different sorts of problems, increases confidence that the response dimension of interest in fact is being assessed. Using separate measures can help distinguish those responses that may be due to methodological idiosyncrasies of a given assessment device from systematic changes in the construct or domain of interest.

MEASUREMENT STRATEGIES AND ISSUES

Use of Multiple Measures

The number of available measures in clinical psychology is unlimited. The advantage of such an availability, of course, is that it provides many options in evaluating diverse facets of performance. The disadvantage is that it makes selection difficult. The major question for any clinical investigation is, what measure should be used or is the most appropriate? If one were interested only in measuring such a familiar construct as "anxiety," the number of available measures for each type of modality would still be extraordinary (Bernstein, Borkovec, & Coles, 1986).

Guidelines for selecting measures were mentioned earlier. These general considerations help narrow the range of assessment devices likely to be useful. In addition, the utility of a measure is partially determined by the investigator's specific purposes. For example, if the independent variable is designed to affect the manner in which people talk about themselves, direct measures of overt speech or self-report inventories may be of primary importance. On the other hand, the independent variable might be expected to affect unconscious processes or how people perceive aspects of their environment. Projective techniques may be appropriate in such cases.

It is unlikely that the expected effects of an independent variable will pertain to only one modality of assessment or only one measure within a given modality. The independent variable may have many influences. Thus several different measurement devices might be used to examine the effects of the experimental manipulation more comprehensively. Actually, there are at least three reasons that favor the use of multiple dependent measures, including the multifaceted nature of clinical problems, the specificity of performance of subjects on various measures, and the need for multiple operationism in evaluating constructs of interest.

Multifaceted Nature of Clinical Problems

One reason for advocating use of several different dependent measures in an investigation pertains to the nature of the construct (e.g., personality characteristic, clinical problem). Most constructs of interest are multifaceted, that is, they have several different components. No single measure is likely to capture these different components adequately. Consider the construct of depression, which has received major attention in clinical research. Some components of depression are based on *self-report.* Individuals say that they feel sad and no longer are interested in activities that were previously pleasurable. In addition, there are *overt behavioral components* such as reduced social interaction, changes in eating (more or less eating), and reduced activity. Similarly, *psychophysiological components* include changes in sleep electroencephalogram activity. *Unconscious processes* may reflect sad affect and negatively valenced interpretations of alternative stimuli. These different facets of depression may overlap but they are not likely to be so highly related that one is redundant with another. Any evaluation of depression in, say, a test of alternative treatments would be incomplete if change were merely demonstrated in one modality. The exception to this would be if it were clear from the beginning that only one facet was defined as important and the sole focus of treatment. Ideally, treatment would alter each of the different components as they are relevant for a given client.

Clinical problems occasionally may not be multifaceted, or at least the assessment of various components that could be discerned are not crucial for treatment. Highly circumscribed problems such as enuresis, tics, isolated fears, and specific habit disorders may be assessed directly with measures of overt behavior. Although each of these behaviors may be part of a more complex set of problems, they often can be studied and treated specifically. In these latter cases a highly focused assessment of the problem may be perfectly suited to the purposes of the therapist and client. Multiple measures still might reflect broader changes in treatment than the measure of primary interest.

Specificity of Performance

The notion that performance and functioning may be multifaceted and consist of several different components addresses the response side of the assessment issue. There is another side of the coin that pertains to the situations or stimulus conditions. Specifically, performance may vary greatly as a function of changes in the conditions or situations. Multiple measures may be important to assess how an individual responds under different stimulus conditions.

Traditionally, personality has often been characterized as a set of traits. These traits reflect dispositions to respond in ways that are consistent over time and across situations. Trait views focus on determinants of performance within the individual. Broad dispositions (e.g., aggressiveness) might lead one to expect performance consistently over time and across diverse situations. However, performance often varies markedly across situations for a given individual. In other words, there is a specificity of performance so that individuals high in a particular trait may behave quite differently as the situation or stimulus conditions change.

An important example of the specificity of performance was provided by the "classic" studies of Hartshorne and May (1928; Hartshorne, May, & Shuttleworth, 1930), which examined the moral conduct of children in a variety of different settings. Children were given the opportunity to be dishonest about their performance and to steal in tasks at home, at school, in athletic contests, and so. One might expect to find rather high correlations among the measures of dishonesty, suggesting that individuals have general dispositions to be dishonest or honest and are consistent across diverse situations. In fact, there were small but consistently positive correlations across situations. The modest correlations suggest some consistencies in performance. Yet the correlations were lower than expected and raised the question about the existence of a trait of honesty. The major finding was that honesty varied considerably across situations. Thus how children performed tended to be situation-specific. The greater the differences among the situations, the lower the relation between cheating across these situations.

The research by Hartshorne and May illustrates the specificity of behavior across different situations and tasks. Even in the same situation, measures of performance considered to reflect the same general construct may not be highly related. For example, Sears (1963) examined the interrelations among different measures of dependency in preschool children. Different behaviors in a nursery school setting were observed, including seeking positive attention (e.g., approval), seeking negative attention (e.g., through disruptiveness), touching or holding another child or the teacher, seeking reassurance, and being near others. These behaviors showed few significant interrelations, that is, they were not very highly correlated. A child's performance in one category did not predict performance in another. The point of this study and others like it is that performance and alternative measures of a construct can be highly specific even in a given situation.

Recent personality research has indicated that understanding and predicting performance are greatly enhanced by knowing both the disposition or trait within an individual as well as the stimulus conditions and situational determinants in which the individual is placed (Magnusson, 1981). From the standpoint of assessment, this means that a person's performance and the conclusions to which that performance may lead are likely to vary across measures of a given construct. Thus the investigator should be prepared for the possibility that changes in dependent measures may be confined to peculiar aspects of a given problem or a particular aspect only in certain situations. Placing faith on demonstrating behavior change in any one situation or for any single facet of performance may be unwise. Measures designed to evaluate different facets of performance are more likely to reveal effects of an intervention.

Multiple Operationism

An individual's performance on a given measure is partially a function of the precise method in which assessment is conducted. The method of assessment may refer to the different modalities of assessment. Even among very similar methods of assessment, there seems to be a correlation between performance due to the format of assessment. For example, a subject may complete self-report devices in true–false, multiple-choice, or checklist formats, among others. Each of these measures may be designed to study a given construct such as self-esteem. The scores on any measure can be assumed to be a function, in part, of the individual's level of self-esteem. However, the way in which self-esteem is assessed alone will contribute to the individual's score and presumed level of the characteristic. There seems to be a specific portion of the score that is determined by the method of assessment.

The contribution of the method of assessment to the score for a given dependent measure can be seen by looking at some of the characteristics of measurement devices in general. The issue of the contribution of the assessment method per se was clarified by Campbell and Fiske (1959), who were concerned with the requirements for developing measurement devices. Specifically, Campbell and Fiske noted that any time investigators wish to develop a new measure of construct (e.g., altruism), they must show that the measure meets certain standards. These include evidence that the measure correlates with other measures of the same construct and that the measure does not correlate with measures of seemingly unrelated constructs. The notion of *convergent validity,* mentioned earlier, was used to denote that independent methods of assessing a given construct agree with each other, that is, correlate relatively highly. For example, if two measures that supposedly assess altruism correlate highly, this would be evidence of convergent validity. The fact that the measures *converge* suggests that they assess the same construct.

The notion of *discriminant validity* was introduced to denote that a newly proposed measure should be distinguished from measures of other constructs; that is, it should have little or no correlation (Campbell & Fiske, 1959). For example, if a newly proposed measure of altruism were found not to correlate highly with measures of other constructs such as intelligence, social desirability, anxiety, and so on, each of these demonstrations would be evidence of discriminant validity. Of course, if high correlations were found between the newly proposed measure and a more established measure of another construct, this would suggest that the measures really were assessing similar characteristics, no matter what the two assessment devices were called.

The way in which convergent and discriminant validity can be examined is to conduct a study designed to evaluate the interrelation among various measures. Whether one measure converges with other measures of the same construct, of course, can be assessed by administering two or more measures designed to assess the same construct and see whether they correlate highly. The way to see whether a measure diverges from others with which it should *not* correlate is achieved by including measures of constructs that are expected to be unrelated. Essentially, this means administering a number of measures to the same individuals. Some of the measures would be designed to assess the same construct or personality dimensions; some would assess different constructs or dimensions.

The correlations obtained to determine convergent and discriminant validity cannot be viewed uncritically. It is quite possible that correlations between two measures will be influenced not only by the construct that is being assessed but also by the format or method of assessment. For example, if two paper-and-pencil measures of altruism were administered, they might correlate rather highly. Is this evidence of convergent validity? Actually, it may be that the high correlation is due to the similarity in the method of assessment (two self-report scales) rather than the construct being assessed. In addition, it is possible that a high correlation will be obtained between measures because of a common source of bias or artifact. Subjects may respond in a socially desirable fashion across both measures, and this will be misinterpreted as convergent validity for the construct that the investigator originally had in mind.

To evaluate the contribution to the assessment method it is important to include with the assessment of multiple constructs or dimensions some measures that rely on different modalities or methods. Campbell and Fiske (1959) introduced the notion of the *multitrait-multimethod matrix*, which refers to the correlations obtained from administering several measures to the same subject. These measures include two or more traits or constructs each of which is measured by two or more methods. The purpose of the matrix is to evaluate convergent and discriminant validity and to see whether the correlation between measures is due to the similarities in the way the responses are assessed rather than in what constructs supposedly are measured.

The evaluation of different methods of assessing the same construct and of similar methods of assessing different constructs can lead to surprising results. For example, in studies of dysfunction among children, the strong role of method factors has been shown. Specifically, the correlation between different methods of assessing (self-report, other report) the same construct (e.g., depression) is often lower than is the correlation between measures of different constructs (depression, aggression) completed by the same method (e.g., self-report; Kazdin, Esveldt-Dawson, Unis, & Rancurello, 1983; Kazdin, French, & Unis, 1983). This suggests that the method of assessing constructs can greatly contribute to the result and to correlations between measures.

Assessment in experiments can profit from knowledge that both substantive and methodological characteristics of assessment devices contribute to a subject's score. If information is desired about a construct, it is important to use more than a single measure. Any single measure includes unique components of assessment that can be attributed to methodological factors. Evidence for a particular hypothesis obtained on more than one measure increases the confidence that the construct of interest has been assessed or the performance of the subject, independently of a particular method of assessment, has been altered.

Interrelations of Dependent Measures

Although the use of multiple measures is advocated as a general strategy for evaluating a construct, this strategy is not without problems. The main issue stemming from use of multiple measures is that the results for a given experimental manipulation may be consistent across measures. Some dependent measures may reflect changes or differences in the predicted direction and others may not. Indeed, some measures may even show changes or differences in the opposite direction. The discrepancies among measures means that the conclusions about the effect of the intervention depend on what measures are examined. This makes interpretation of the results more difficult and ambiguous than if the findings and conclusions were drawn on the basis of a single dependent measure. Thus for many investigators, discrepancies among dependent measures are a problem.

The failure of multiple measures to correspond is a "problem" only because of some traditional assumptions about the nature of personality and human behavior and the manner in which independent variables operate. Actually, there are many reasons to expect multiple measures not to agree. Four explanations of lack of correspondence among measures pertain to the contribution of method variance in assessing behavior, the multifaceted nature of behavior, the magnitude of a client's standing on the characteristic, and the course of changes across different facets of behavior.

Contribution of Method Variance

An overriding assumption of traditional assessment has been that there are different measures of a given construct and that these should correlate highly. The notions of convergent and discriminant validity, described earlier, embody this assumption. The notion of convergent validity fosters the view that measures of a given personality or behavioral characteristic have a common component that is highly correlated. The view encourages researchers to conceptualize constructs as unidimensional, that is, they are single and relatively simple constructs that measure roughly the "same thing" but in many different ways. Hence investigators should search for correlations among measures of a given trait.

The lack of correspondence among measures can be handled by the view that different measures of the same characteristic or trait should *not* necessarily go together or correlate highly in a given investigation. Specifically, if the methods of assessment differ (e.g., true–false vs. multiple-choice self-report measures, or self-report vs. behavioral measures), the lack of high correlations between the measures might be due to the contribution of method variance. With this explanation, method variance becomes the culprit that interferes with interpretation of experimental results. Indeed, method variance may account for the correlations or lack of correlations between measures.

The potential problem with this interpretation is that it implies that lack of correspondence between measures is merely a methodological artifact stemming from the assessment devices. Systematic error variance associated with the measurement devices is used to explain lack of correspondence between measures that seemingly would otherwise be related. However, we have come to learn that performance may well differ as a function of different stimulus, as well as situational and assessment conditions. The imperfect agreement among measures is not an artifact or limitation of the measure but an expected feature.

Multifaceted Nature of Personality and Behavior

The view that characteristics of personality or behavior are multifaceted has challenged the notions of convergent validation to some extent. As discussed earlier, if one views a given characteristic as multidimensional, the insistence on correspondence between dependent measures of that characteristic is reduced. Personality characteristics may have several different components that overlap but are not interchangeable, redundant, or isomorphic. For example, several measures are available to assess depression. However, depression is not a unidimensional characteristic or simply sadness. Manifold characteristics can be identified involving affect (e.g., sadness), cognition (e.g., beliefs that things are hopeless), and behavior (e.g., diminished activity). Within a given domain, several finer distinctions can be made. Thus within the cognitive domain of depression, measures are available to assess negative beliefs about oneself, hopelessness, helplessness, and others. Given the multidimensional nature of personality, behavior, and clinical dysfunction, as illustrated by depression, the lack of correspondence between measures might well be expected.

On a priori grounds, the different components of a given characteristic might be expected to diverge. For convenience and parsimony, psychologists have adhered to general construct labels such as anxiety, personality, and extraversion. Although proposing such constructs helps simplify findings across different areas of research or different measurement devices, it does not follow that all components of any one of these constructs occur together in a given individual (co-occur) or change together even if they are present (co-vary). There may be largely independent components that individuals refer to under a general construct label. Lack of correspondence among dependent measures related to a particular construct or target problem may not be a problem at all from the standpoint of interpreting research. Although some of the lack of correspondence could well be attributable to different methods of assessment, measuring different aspects of the problem could account for the low correlations as well.

Magnitude of the Characteristic

Another way to interpret the lack of correspondence among dependent measures relates to the magnitude of the characteristic, trait, disposition, or clinical problem. Different measures designed to assess the same characteristic of personality or behavior may covary as a function of the client's standing on the characteristic. For example, in the case of anxiety, clients may be measured on self-report, overt behavioral, and psychophysiological measures. The different measures may or may not correspond depending on the magnitude of the client's anxiety. Perhaps clients who are overwhelmed by anxiety would score at a very high level on each of the measures. At the other extreme might be individuals who show absolutely no anxiety and score the equivalent of zero or "none" on each measure. These extreme groups (very high vs. no anxiety) may show a consistent or a more consistent pattern across measures.

The very large intermediate group may show quite different patterns and variability across several measures. For example, individuals in this group with only slight or moderate anxiety might report anxiety on self-report measures. Such mild levels of reported anxiety may not be associated with any specific overt behaviors or autonomic arousal. Verbal reports may be more capable of reflecting gradations of reactions relative to measures of overt behavior or psychophysiological states. Thus some anxiety is evident on portions of the assessment battery.

There is some evidence that correspondence among different measures is related to the magnitude or intensity of arousal. For example, in one treatment study where clients were presented with a threatening stimulus, different psychophysiological measures (skin conductance and heart rate) did not correspond very highly (Marks, Marset, Boulougouris, & Huson, 1971). However, changes in these measures were correlated during exposure to the most threatening stimulus. This suggests that the greater the arousal, the more agreement there is likely to be between different measures. Whether this relation holds equally across measures within a given assessment modality or across measures of different modalities remains to be investigated.

Lack of correspondence among measures might be expected based on varying levels of intensity of the characteristic for which clients are selected. This is consistent with the notion of thresholds of responding (Campbell, 1963). Clients may have different thresholds for responding on the measurement devices. The threshold for endorsing a particular item or performing a task might vary for measurement devices within a modality (e.g., self-report inventories) or across modalities (e.g., self-report inventories, behavioral measures). Indeed, an investigator might even want to operationalize the notion of severity of a problem for research purposes on the basis of how many different measures in an assessment battery reflect extreme performance (as defined by some cutoff point).

Course of Behavior Change

The lack of correspondence between measures can be explained by considering the relations among components of personality and behavior over time. Quite possibly, different facets of behavior change at different rates or at different points in time. Hence, studies showing a lack of correspondence between measures from, say, pretreatment to posttreatment assessment, may only reflect the fact that different aspects of performance change at different rates.

Rachman and Hodgson (1974; Hodgson & Rachman, 1974) have introduced the notion that changes over time among multiple measures of a given client characteristic, state, or behavior might or might not go together. When changes across measures do correspond, this is referred to as *synchrony*. When changes do not go together, this is referred to as *desynchrony*. In the case of desynchrony, different measures of change might vary independently or even inversely. Rachman and Hodgson suggest that lack of correspondence between measures of change, or desynchrony, may occur because some aspects of personality or behavior change before others. The lack of correspondence may be a function of looking at the measures at one point only (e.g., immediately after treatment). The different facets of behavior may become synchronous as time progresses and separate response systems come into line with each other. Essentially, therapy may more readily alter some systems than others and alter some systems more rapidly than others. Indeed, analyses of behavioral and self-report measures among outcome studies have shown increases in the correspondence among measures over time (see Hodgson & Rachman, 1974). In general, the notions of synchrony and desynchrony allow for the correspondence or lack of correspondence among diverse measures and highlight the importance of evaluating the relations among measures over time.

SUMMARY AND CONCLUSIONS

Assessment is central to all research. Apart from the pivotal role in measuring the dependent variables, assessment may enter into other facets of the study such as delineation of groups in subject-selection studies, in evaluating the impact of the experimental manipulation, and in evaluating moderating factors posited to account for the relation between independent and dependent variables.

Selection of assessment devices for research can be based on several criteria including considerations related to construct validity, psychometric properties, and sensitivity of the measure to reflect change. Standard or currently available measures are usually used in a given study because properties of the measures are known including evidence that the construct of interest to the investigator is likely to account for performance on a given measure. Occasionally, investigators alter standardized measures to apply them to populations or in contexts in which the measures have not been used or intended. The measure may be used as is or modified slightly by rewording or omitting items. Investigators may develop an entirely new measure because a standard measure is not available or alteration of an existing measure would on prima facie grounds render this of limited value. If a measure is used in a novel way, altered in any way, or if a new measure is developed, it is essential to include validity data within the study or as pilot work to that study to support construct validity.

A vast number of measures are available. Several modalities were highlighted as a means of encompassing the broad range of measures used in clinical research. Commonly used measures fall within several modalities: global ratings; self-report inventories, questionnaires, and scales; projective techniques; behavioral measures; and psychophysiological measures. Within each modality an extraordinarily large number of specific measures exist. The modality of assessment and the specific measure within the modality should be carefully thought out and explicitly justified prior to the investigation.

In general, it is useful to rely on multiple measures rather than a single measure for several reasons. First, clinical problems tend to be multifaceted. There is no single measure that can be expected to address all of the components of a problem. Second, performance may vary as a function of the assessment modalities and devices used. Even within a given modality of assessment, individuals may respond quite differently as a function of exactly what measure is used (e.g., heart rate vs. skin conductance within psychophysiological assessment). Third, assessment devices do not perfectly reflect an individual's standing on a particular dimension. An individual's score on a measure is partially determined by the method of assessment. It is useful to demonstrate that changes in the construct of interest (e.g., anxiety) are not restricted to only one method of assessment. Essentially, demonstrations relying on multiple assessment techniques strengthen the confidence that can be placed in the relation between independent and dependent variables.

An important issue in using multiple measures pertains to the lack of correspondence among measures. Thus an investigation using multiple measures may demonstrate that the independent variable affects some measures in one way and has no effect or an opposite effect on others. Hence what might have been a clear conclusion with a single measure seems to be obfuscated by the use of several different measures. Actually, there are important reasons not to expect measures to agree in view of the contribution of method variance of different assessment devices, the multifaceted nature of personality and behavior, the client's standing on the characteristic of interest, and the course of change over time among different response modalities. Disagreement among multiple measures should not be construed as introducing ambiguity into the results, but rather should be regarded as a means of elaborating the specific effects of interventions. The relation between different measures itself is an important aspect of understanding human functioning and the way in which it is affected by independent variables.

FOR FURTHER READING

Conoley, J.C., & Kramer, J.J. (Eds.). (1989). *The tenth mental measurements yearbook.* Lincoln, NE: University of Nebraska Press.

Davis, R.V. (1987). Scale construction. *Journal of Counseling Psychology, 34,* 481–489.

Goldstein, G., & Hersen, M. (Eds.). (1990). *Handbook of psychological assessment* (2nd ed.). Elmsford, NY: Pergamon Press.

Kline, P. (1986). *A handbook of test construction: Introduction to psychometric design.* London: Methuen.

Wainer, H., & Braun, H.I. (Eds.). (1988). *Test validity.* Hillsdale, NJ: Lawrence Erlbaum Associates.

SPECIAL TOPICS IN ASSESSMENT

A variety of assessment issues emerge in clinical psychological research. These can vary considerably as a function of the content area (e.g., family studies, clinical neuropsychology). Nevertheless, a number of issues can be identified that raise methodological considerations with generality across areas. The present chapter considers assessment and methodological issues raised by alternative assessment situations and measures.

REACTIVITY OF ASSESSMENT

Measures most frequently used in research are presented to subjects who are well aware that their performance is being assessed. Such measures are said to be *obtrusive* to denote that subjects are aware of the assessment procedures. Obviously, subjects know that some facet of their personality or behavior is being assessed when they complete a self-report questionnaire or projective test, or they are placed into a somewhat contrived situation where their overt behavior is observed. Subjects are aware that their performance is being assessed, whether or not they know the specific purposes or foci of the measures.

Awareness raises the prospect that performance on the measure is altered or influenced by this awareness. If performance is altered by awareness of the measure, the assessment is said to be *reactive*. It is not necessarily the case that subjects' awareness (obtrusiveness) influences their performance (reactivity). Knowledge of the purposes of the measures, motivation of the subjects, and subject roles, among other influences, contribute to reactivity. Reactivity raises several methodological issues that can influence selection of assessment devices in a given study.

Problems of Reactive Assessment

Several interrelated problems are likely to result from a heavy reliance on reactive measures. These include the contribution of reactivity as a method factor in assessment, the external validity of the results, the motivation of the subjects to present a particular image, and the influence of the individual who administers the assessment device.

Reactivity as a Method Factor

Scores on separate assessment devices may be correlated because they measure the same construct (e.g., anxiety). Apart from measuring the same aspect of behavior, the methods of assessment (method factors) may be similar. The previous chapter discussed the possible contribution of method variance when two measures are similar in method of assessment (e.g., two self-report measures) or in format within a given modality of assessment (e.g., two true–false measures). The similarity in method factors may increase the correlation between the two measures.

Aside from similarity in the assessment device, reactivity is another method factor that may contribute to a subject's scores. Subjects may show a general set of responding such as placing themselves in a socially desirable light. To the extent that this response set influences each of the measures because they are both reactive, the correlation among different measures may be higher. The correlation between the measures might be lower if one measure were reactive and the other were not.

Essentially, reactivity may be viewed as a method factor that contributes to an individual's responses on an assessment device. In general, interpretation of psychological measures can be greatly enhanced by using multiple measures that vary in reactivity. If similar results are obtained across such measures, the investigator has greater assurance that conclusions are not restricted to some aspect of the assessment method. Thus when feasible, it is important to use measures that are nonreactive as well as those that are reactive and thereby broaden the conclusions that can be reached.

External Validity

The problem of reactivity of assessment can be elaborated further by discussing external validity more directly. Two different external validity issues can be raised. The first is whether the results of an experiment using obtrusive assessment differ from what they would be if assessment were unobtrusive. Because almost all psychological research relies on subjects who know that their performance is being assessed, this question is extremely important. The influence of obtrusive assessment on external validity is difficult to address directly because investigators usually cannot administer a given assessment device (e.g., questionnaire) under conditions where some subjects are aware of assessment and others are not. Obtrusive and unobtrusive assessment usually require entirely different methods (e.g., self-reports vs. observations reported by peers).

It is possible to see whether measures of the same construct that differ in potential reactivity reflect the same effect of the independent variable. For example, overt behavior could be sampled in a contrived situation in the laboratory and in the natural environment where a contrived situation is designed to appear as part of everyday experience. These would constitute obtrusive and unobtrusive assessment techniques, respectively. If performance is similar between the two measures and conclusions are similar, one can assume that the conclusions are not restricted to potentially reactive measures.

One difficulty in determining the relation between reactive and nonreactive assessment techniques is that lack of correlation is open to various interpretations. For example, one study evaluated social interaction skills of college students in a role-play situation (reactive assessment) and in a contrived laboratory situation where subjects were placed in a waiting room with a confederate (nonreactive assessment, Bellack, Hersen, & Lamparski, 1979). Videotapes made in each situation were used to obtain data on such behaviors as the amount of eye contact, verbalizations, smiles, duration of responding to the other person, instances of disclosing personal information, and questions asked. In general, few correlations across the different assessment methods were statistically significant. The results might be interpreted to imply that behavior varied across conditions as a function of reactivity. However, it is possible that the content of the situations and the types of social interaction required were so different, independent of reactivity, that responses would be varied under each condition even if both were assessed under reactive conditions. There is no guarantee that the lack of correspondence of responses was due to reactivity unless the specific tasks presented to the subject were the same or very similar.

Whether results of an experiment extend to unobtrusive measures is especially important in therapy research, in which the goal of treatment is to change ordinary behavior of the clients in everyday life, under conditions where they do not believe they are being specially monitored. Reactive assessment in a laboratory or clinic setting does not really provide the vital information needed about performance in everyday life, unless evidence is available that the laboratory or clinic-based measures in fact correlate with everyday experience assessed unobtrusively.

Another external validity issue worth noting in passing pertains to pretest sensitization that has been discussed earlier. Administering assessment devices prior to an intervention may sensitize subjects to the intervention, and the results therefore may not apply to individuals who do not receive a pretest. Whether a pretest limits generality of a particular finding is easily addressed either by studying the independent variable in separate investigations that include or omit the pretest or by using a Solomon four-group design, as elaborated earlier. The problem of reactive pretest as a threat to external validity could be avoided entirely if the pretest relied on an unobtrusive measure.

Motivation of the Subjects

One reason that reactivity is viewed as a potential problem pertains to how subject awareness might influence performance. If subjects are aware that their behavior is being assessed, they can often alter their responses accordingly to achieve their own purposes. In chapter 9, potential sources of bias and distortion were discussed in the context of self-report measures, where such biases as response styles have been studied extensively. Yet any obtrusive assessment method allows for the possibility that subjects will respond in a particular way to present a certain kind of image. For example, individuals may place themselves in a socially desirable light. This favorable impression can be accomplished on self-report measures by endorsing items that convey that the individual behaves in accordance with more widely accepted standards of behavior, whether or not the responses accurately reflect the individual's behavior. Yet questionnaires are not the only measures subject to these sorts of biases. Individuals performing on projective tests or on specific behavioral tasks can respond in a socially desirable fashion as well (Crowne & Marlowe, 1964).

The issue is not the modality of assessment per se but whether the assessment is reactive. Some methods of assessment (e.g., self-report questionnaires) may be more susceptible to distortion than others (e.g., psychophysiological measures). Yet the reactivity of each of the different methods alone allows for some distortion. The individual may respond in a way other than he or she would if the measures were unobtrusive.

Influence of the Assessor

The responses of subjects in an experiment can be influenced by various characteristics of the individuals who administer the assessment devices (assessors). For example, results obtained from psychological inventories or from interviews may be influenced by such variables as age, sex, race, social class, and even religion of the assessor or interviewer (e.g., Masling, 1960; Rosenthal, 1969). The personal or demographic attributes of an assessor usually are not of interest in clinical investigations, where an assortment of assessment devices are administered; nevertheless, these attributes can influence the response pattern on the dependent measures.

Investigators often console themselves by the fact that a given experiment may hold potential sources of artifact constant. Thus if a single assessor administers the assessment devices across all subjects, assessor characteristics could not differentially influence the data. Yet, in principle, statistical interactions may result from complex relations between the independent variable and characteristics of the assessor. The influence of the assessor may operate differentially across experimental conditions or types of subjects in the experiment. Using two or more assessors may help evaluate the influence of the assessor, but it does not eliminate the possible contribution of the assessor on subject performance.

The assessor may be a source of influence primarily because the subject is aware that assessment is conducted and is exposed to someone in the role of an assessor. Assessor characteristics could not as readily exert their direct influence if assessment did not expose the subject to someone in the position of an assessor. That is, this source of bias can be reduced or eliminated through unobtrusive assessment.

Attempted Solutions

The problems mentioned previously provide only a sample of major limitations of results obtained in experiments with reactive assessment. A host of other influences, extending beyond assessment, are related to the reactivity of the experimental situation itself. (Influences such as demand characteristics and subject roles that characterize reactive experimental arrangements are detailed in the next chapter.) Whether reactivity pertains to assessment or to the experimental arrangement, it raises the possibility that subjects perform in a particular way unrepresentative of their performance under unobtrusive conditions.

Several solutions have been proposed to minimize, or even to eliminate entirely, the influence of subject awareness on performance. These solutions vary as a function of the specific method of assessment. With self-report questionnaires and rating scales, the instructions given to the subjects often are designed to increase their candor and to decrease the influence of reactivity. One tactic is to tell the subjects that their answers to the test items are anonymous and that their individual performance cannot be identified. Of course, in most investigations these claims are accurate, although the subjects may not believe them. Subjects are more likely to respond candidly and less likely to place themselves in a socially desirable light if they believe they cannot be identified.

Another strategy to minimize the influence of subject awareness on performance is to add "filler" items on a given measure. The filler items are provided to alter the appearance of the focus or to make the measure appear less provocative or intrusive. In the process, the true purpose of the measure, that is, the construct of interest, is obscured. For example, a self-report measure of various psychiatric symptoms, criminal activity, or sexual practices might be infused with items about interests, hobbies, and more neutral subject characteristics. The subjects are aware of the assessment procedures but the filler items may obscure or diffuse the singular focus that would heighten reactive responding. The filler items may soften the impact of the measure and the reactions that might otherwise be prompted.

Another solution is to vary what subjects are told about the task and how it should be performed. For example, the purpose of the test may be hidden, or subjects may be told that their test responses have no real bearing on their future and will not be used for or against them. Alternatively, subjects may be told to respond to the self-report items very quickly. The purpose of "speed instructions" is to have subjects give little attention to what actually is measured and hence not deliberate about the content or purpose of the items. These instructional ploys may or may not be plausible, depending on the circumstances of testing and the exact facets of personality or behavior that are assessed.

The use of computers in psychological assessment may have implications for reducing the reactivity of assessment. Computers can serve several roles in psychological assessment (see Butcher, 1985). One of these is to permit subjects to answer questions directly by responding to items presented on a monitor or screen. The questions are presented and answers are recorded automatically without a human examiner. Computerized assessment, when compared to the measure administered by an examiner, often yields more information about sensitive topics such as alcohol consumption and sexual problems (see Erdman, Klein, & Greist, 1985). In addition, respondents often report favorable attitudes toward computerized test administration. In any case, it is possible computerized administration of tests will decrease subjects' reactive responding to assessment.

Assessment occasionally consists of direct observation of overt behavior over an extended period. With such measures, different solutions have been sought to decrease the influence of reactivity. For example, when overt behavior of children is observed directly, in a naturalistic situation such as the home or at school, subjects may be exposed to the observer on several occasions prior to the actual assessment. Observers may assess the behavior of the children for a week or two merely to have the children become accustomed to the observation procedures. It is assumed that after a period of time, obtrusive assessment will become less reactive over time and exert little or no influence. The children would be expected to habituate to the presence of the observers and eventually respond in the way they normally would if observers were not present.

When reactive procedures are used because of the unavailability of alternative assessment devices, one of the strategies that might be adopted is to encourage subjects to respond as honestly as possible. Although this may be naive when subjects have a particular interest in their performance in light of some goal (e.g., job procurement, discharge from a hospital), the overall approach may be sound. In many cases, such as evaluation of progress in therapy, it is usually in the best interests of the client to respond as candidly and accurately as possible. In such cases, this message may be worth elaborating to the respondents to obtain samples of performance during assessment that are as representative of daily performance as the measures allow.

Nevertheless, whether performance under obtrusive and unobtrusive assessment conditions is similar requires empirical evaluation. Even under ideal conditions of administration, the fact that subjects are aware that their behavior is to be assessed might limit generality of the results. Possibly the results of an experiment have little bearing on behavior outside of the reactive assessment procedures.

Artifact Versus Treatment

To this point, reactive assessment has been discussed as a potential source of artifact that may influence the type of data obtained. In the context of methodology and research design, the possibility that an individual's behavior changes because he or she is aware that assessment is being conducted presents a problem. On the other hand, in clinical psychology, the fact that measures may be reactive is sometimes relied on as an important part of treatment. If assessment influences how an individual responds, can assessment procedures be used to change behaviors of clinical relevance?

One way to assess behavior reactively is to have individuals observe their own behavior, a procedure referred to as self-monitoring or self-observation (Bornstein, Hamilton, & Bornstein, 1986). Self-monitoring merely consists of having the individual observe some behavior that he or she wishes to change such as cigarette smoking, eating, interacting with others, nail biting, and others. Research has shown that observing one's own behavior can decrease or increase a variety of behaviors, depending on whether the behaviors are negatively or positively valued, respectively. The therapeutic effects of self-monitoring are inconsistent. When behavior is altered, the effects of self-monitoring often are transient. Although this means that self-monitoring is not likely to be consistently effective as a *treatment* technique, it suggests that reactive observation may contribute to the responses that are obtained in research, at least in the short run.

UNOBTRUSIVE (NONREACTIVE) MEASURES

The obtrusiveness of measures used in virtually all clinical research does not in any way make the results necessarily inaccurate or unreliable. The only limitation might be that the responses of the subjects under conditions when they are aware of assessment may not resemble responses under conditions when they are unaware of assessment. The conclusions that can be drawn in a given study can be greatly bolstered by showing that the results are similar across obtrusive and unobtrusive measures.

Measurement Techniques

Although the importance of unobtrusive measures may be readily apparent, incorporating such measures into research may seem extremely difficult. Non-reactive assessment requires measuring performance without arousing any suspicions that assessment is being conducted. It is useful to mention the major types of unobtrusive measures and illustrate their relevance for clinical and social psychological research (see Webb, Campbell, Schwartz, Sechrest, & Grove, 1981). The major techniques of unobtrusive measurement are listed in Table 10.1. The techniques include simple observation, observation in contrived situation, archival records, and physical traces. Within the social sciences, numerous examples are available that illustrate how these methods have been used.

Table 10.1. Major Methods of Unobtrusive Measurement

TYPE OF MEASURE	DEFINITION	EXAMPLES
Simple Observation	Observing behavior in a naturalistic situation where the assessor does not intervene or intrude. The assessor is passive and does nothing to alter the normal behavior or to convey that behavior is being observed.	Observing nonverbal gestures or body distance as a study of social behavior; recording the clothing individuals wear to reflect mood states.
Observations in Contrived Situations	Simple observation of behavior in naturalistic situations in which the experimenter or assessor intervenes or does something to prompt certain kinds of performance. The assessor plays an active role without violating the reactivity of the situation.	Using confederates who seem to be in need of assistance to test for altruism; testing for honesty in a situation that allows for cheating.
Archival Records	Records kept for reasons other than psychological research such as institutional, demographic, social, or personal records.	Records of birth, marriage; institutional data such as discharge records or patient history; documents.
Physical Traces	Physical evidence, changes, or remnants in the environment that may stem from accumulation or wear resulting from performance.	Wear on pages to discover magazine or book passages read; deposits of trash to study littering; graffiti to study sexual themes.

Simple Observation

Observing behavior as it occurs in naturalistic settings consists of an especially relevant assessment method for clinical and social psychological research. The goal of such research is to understand personality, behavior, and human interaction and is only approximated by the usual psychological devices such as questionnaires and laboratory tasks. Simple observations in naturalistic settings sample behavior unaffected or less affected by the situational constraints of the laboratory and methodological characteristics of the more commonly used assessment procedures.

An interesting example of simple observation derived from the study of people touching each other. One function of touching other individuals (e.g., having a hand on another person's back, putting an arm around someone's shoulder, holding someone's arm while talking to him or her) is to convey status or power (Henley, 1977). Higher status or more powerful individuals may be more likely to touch others than to be touched by others. If touching is a sign of power, then status variables such as socioeconomic standing, age, race, and gender all might be related to touching. Higher status individuals (e.g., those of higher socioeconomic status, older individuals, and males) all would be expected to touch others more than be touched.

Individuals were observed in public regarding whether they touched another person and whether the touch was reciprocated. The individuals were classified according to the status variables of interest. Touching was defined as intentional contact with the hand and was observed unobtrusively. In general, the results supported the predictions. Individuals who were male, older, and rated as higher in socioeconomic status more frequently touched others (females, younger individuals, persons of lower socioeconomic status, respectively) than were touched by them. (Too few observations were available to examine race.) By itself the findings do not establish that touching necessarily assesses status or power. Yet the observational data have supplemented questionnaire research that has related touching others to dominance, status, and being placed in a position of power (see Henley, 1977). Thus direct observation adds credence to other assessment methods for evaluating social behavior.

Simple observation is very useful because of the almost unlimited situations in everyday life that are open to scrutiny and direct tests of hypotheses. Of course, the method has potential problems. One problem that may arise that would defeat the value of unobtrusive observation in naturalistic situations is detecting the presence of the observer qua observer. As an unobtrusive measure, the observer must not influence the situation. Usually this amounts to disguising the role of the observer, if an observer actually is required in the situation. If performance can be sampled without observers, perhaps by hidden cameras, even less opportunity might be present to alter the nonreactivity of the situation.

Another problem with simple observation is ensuring that the behaviors of interest occur with sufficient frequency to be useful for research purposes (e.g., differentiation of groups, data analyses). Merely watching subjects in the situations of interest does not guarantee that the responses will occur. The response of interest may be so infrequent as to make assessment prohibitively expensive, inefficient, or of little use.

A final problem with simple observation pertains to the standardization of the assessment situation. The environmental conditions in which the response occurs may change markedly over time. Extraneous factors (e.g., presence of other individuals) may influence behavior and introduce response variability in the measure. The net effect of this variability might be to obscure the effects of the independent variable. Simple and naturalistic observation can be influenced by uncontrolled factors that make it difficult to assess performance in a relatively uniform fashion.

Observation in Contrived Situations

Observations in contrived situations resolve some of the problems of simple observation. Contrived situations maximize the likelihood that the response of interest will occur. Hence the problem of infrequent responses or conditions that do not precipitate the response is resolved. Also, arranging the naturalistic situation allows for standardizing extraneous factors, and hence the data are less subject to uncontrolled influences. The important requirement of observations in contrived situations, of course, is to control the situation while maintaining the unobtrusive conditions of assessment. This may be accomplished by utilizing an observer, experimenter, or confederate working with the observer, to help stage the conditions that are designed to evoke certain kinds of behaviors.

A prime example of contrived situations for the purposes of assessment are television programs *(Candid Camera, Totally Hidden Video)* that place people into situations varying in degrees of frustration. The situations are well planned so that as each new unwitting subject enters into the situation (e.g., a cafeteria), the stimulus conditions presented to him or her are held relatively constant (e.g., someone sitting next to the subject wearing a feathered hat that keeps hitting the subject in the face while he or she is eating at the counter). The subject's behavior is recorded on film, which serves as the basis for the television program. The reactions of the subjects when they are informed that they are really being filmed for the show often reveal success in hiding the contrived nature of the situation.

One potential problem in contrived situations is ensuring that the measure remains unobtrusive. Although most people do not suspect that their behaviors are being monitored in everyday situations, they should not be underestimated about occasionally seeing through a ruse. The fact that conditions are contrived and relatively natural does not ensure that subjects will not see through them.

Archival Records

Records of all sorts provide a wealth of information about people and have been sampled in psychology to test many hypotheses. The unique feature of records is that they usually can be examined without fear that the experimenter's hypothesis or actions of the observers may influence the raw data themselves.

A classic study in clinical psychology that used archival records was completed by Barthel and Holmes (1968), who examined whether schizophrenic patients had a history of social isolation prior to their hospitalization. One characteristic of schizophrenic patients is social withdrawal and isolation. Barthel and Holmes examined this relation by looking at the history of hospitalized patients. The archival record used to examine social isolation was high school yearbooks. The number of social activities in which each patient participated was counted from the yearbooks from each patient's senior year. Social activities included participation in clubs, organizations, special interest groups, student government, and others. The activities of hospitalized schizophrenics, hospitalized "neurotics," and control subjects (individuals presumed to be with little or no psychological impairment) were tallied. The control subjects were individuals in the yearbooks who were pictured next to the schizophrenic or neurotic subject. (*Neurotic* and *neuroses* are terms that were previously used to denote disorders that were distinguishable from *psychotic* and *psychoses*. Neuroses refer to less severe disorders where there is less impairment in perceptions, beliefs, behavior, and other domains. Schizophrenia is an example of psychosis; phobias are an example of what would have been referred to as a neurotic disorder. In contemporary diagnosis, neuroses is not usually used. More specific terms are applied for individual disorders [e.g., phobias] and broader classes in which they are grouped [e.g., mood disorders, anxiety disorders].)

Schizophrenic patients were found to engage in significantly fewer activities than did "normal" control subjects. Neurotic patients fell between schizophrenic and normal subjects and did not differ from either group significantly in the number of social activities. The results tend to support the notion that schizophrenic patients are socially isolated prior to hospitalization. The results add considerably to existing information by looking at archival records as another way of measuring isolation.

Archival records have their own sources of measurement problems. One problem is the possible changes in criteria for recording certain kinds of information. For example, records of crime rate may vary over time as a function of changes in the definition of crime or sociological variables that may alter the incidence of reporting certain crimes (e.g., rape). The changes in the criteria for recording information (an example of instrumentation) may lead to interpretive problems.

A related problem is the selectivity in the information that becomes archival. For example, historical records of births are likely to omit many individuals. Before more extensive methods of recording births and population statistics came into use, many births were likely to have gone unrecorded. Those births unlikely to be recorded may have varied as a function of socioeconomic status, age, and marital status of the mother, geographical location, and race. Thus there may be a selective deposit of the information that becomes archival for subsequent research.

Physical Traces

Physical traces consist of selective wear (erosion) or the deposit (accretion) of materials. Either the wear or deposit of materials may be considered to reflect specific forms of behavior. An interesting trace measure was used by Barthel and Crowne (1962) who studied the phenomenon known as *perceptual defense*. Perceptual defense consists of recognizing and reporting taboo words—that is, words that are socially censured as a part of ordinary conversation or viewed as vulgar (e.g., "whore," "penis," "bitch"). College students were exposed to the words by a tachistoscope for very brief periods that made the words difficult to discern. The subjects were instructed to write the words when they could recognize them. The investigators used erasures and obliterations of the answer as a measure of avoidance in acknowledging and reporting these words. They hypothesized that individuals high in the need of approval from others, as measured by a questionnaire, would inhibit their report of such words. Subjects who were high in their need for social approval erased more of their answers and thus avoided reporting the taboo words than did those low in social approval. The use of erasures is a creative physical trace measure because it is one that subjects are not likely to expect as an important dimension of the investigation.

An excellent example of a physical trace measure has been used to evaluate the long-term impact of lead exposure in children. Lead is a heavy metal to which individuals can be exposed through multiple sources, including water, air (e.g., from leaded automobile fuel exhaust), paint, and others. Studies completed by Needleman and his colleagues (Needleman & Bellinger, 1984; Needleman, Schell, Bellinger, Leviton, & Alldred, 1990) have shown that relatively low doses of lead exposure in children are associated with hyperactivity, distractibility, lower IQ, and overall reduced school functioning in children. Follow-up assessment of children with relatively high levels of lead

11 years later have shown that intellectual, motor skills, and academic performances are significantly lower than in those with less lead exposure.

A critical measure of this research program has been based on a physical trace of lead exposure. Lead tends to collect in the bones and teeth. One cannot easily remove bone samples of children to make the necessary assessments. However, Needleman collected baby teeth that were normally extruded. Teeth were collected from thousands of children to evaluate lead exposure. From this measure, high and low lead exposure groups could be formed and compared in their academic and classroom performance over a period of several years.

One area in applied intervention research that has relied on physical trace measures is littering. Several investigations have evaluated the effects of various incentive systems and instructional manipulations on individuals who attend zoos, athletic stadiums, movie theaters, and national parks, or who live in university settings or urban areas (see Geller, Winett, Everett, 1982). In these programs, small monetary incentives or tickets for raffles have increased the deposit of trash in appropriate containers or have encouraged the pickup of littered trash. Litter is weighed or counted to provide a physical trace measure of the success of the interventions.

A potential problem with physical trace measures is that changes over time may occur as a function of the ability of certain traces to be left. For example, research on wall inscriptions (graffiti) in public bathrooms has shown differences in the frequency of inscriptions by males and females and cross-cultural differences in erotic themes (see Webb et al., 1981). If one wished to study graffiti over time, as a physical trace, this might be difficult. Many institutions have "seen the writing on the wall" and have tried to use surface materials that are less readily inscribed or cover marks before they accumulate. Thus the material on which traces are made may change over time.

The selective deposit of physical traces is another potential problem. Physical trace measures may be subject to some of the same limitations of archival data. It is possible for the traces to be selective and not represent the behavior of all the subjects of interest. Also, physical traces may be influenced by a number of variables that determine what marks are left to evaluate and hence what data will be seen. For example, fingerprints are the example par excellence of a physical trace measure. However, they are not always available as signs of someone's presence at the scene of a crime. Individuals not interested in leaving such traces are well aware of the necessary procedures to ensure that their presence and fingerprints go unrecorded.

A final problem with physical traces is that they may become reactive. Once the trace becomes known as a measure of interest, potential subjects may become aware of this and respond accordingly. For example, social scientists and news reporters occasionally have a keen interest in the trash of celebrities and politicians as a means of measuring their private affairs (e.g., correspondence) and potential vices (e.g., weekly consumption of alcohol). Publicity about these practices probably has limited the types of items that are publicly discarded for trash pick up. Secretive, cautious, and perhaps wise celebrities alike may use other means of disposal (e.g., paper shredder, trash compactor).

General Comments

Unobtrusive measures provide a rich source of information. The value of these measures is to supplement more commonly used techniques and thereby to add strength to the external validity of research findings. Extending the external validity of findings is important in any research endeavor. Yet this is particularly important in clinical psychology, where the goal of research often is to address issues and phenomena outside of the laboratory. For example, unobtrusive measures of therapy outcome (e.g., hospital visits, days of work missed) would provide tremendously important information about treatment efficacy and would uniquely supplement the data obtained from the more frequently relied upon self-report questionnaires and inventories.

Unobtrusive measures are not necessarily better than other types of measures. Whether one method is more useful than another is a function of the purposes for which the measure is employed and characteristics of the measure insofar as they help achieve these purposes. Because each assessment method is incomplete and methodologically imperfect on its own, it is desirable to use as wide a range of measures as is available for a particular construct of interest.

If findings are obtained across diverse measures with different methodological features (e.g., obtrusive and unobtrusive measures), this suggests the robustness of the relation between the independent and the dependent variables. In addition, unobtrusive measures often are based on data drawn from everyday life (e.g., archival records, physical traces). In areas of research with applied implications, such as clinical, counseling, and educational psychology, use of such measures can help integration and utilization of the findings. Measures of relevance in everyday life can convey the applied implications of the lawful relation for daily functioning and facilitate the adoption of findings in society.

Unobtrusive measures have their own problems. Apart from the issues mentioned already, each of the measures must be interpreted with some caution. Unlike more commonly used measures, unobtrusive measures usually undergo little validation research, so there are few assurances that they measure what the investigator wishes to measure. In addition, whether the unobtrusive measure will be sufficiently sensitive to reflect the relation of interest is difficult to determine in advance. In general, there is less collective experience with a given unobtrusive measure than with standardized measures such as questionnaires and inventories. The diverse types of reliability and validity are not readily known for most unobtrusive measures.

Unobtrusive measures need to be corroborated with other measures in the usual way that assessment devices are validated. This can be done both by empirical research that examines the relation among different measures and by theoretical formulations that place a particular measure into a context that makes testable predictions. Increasingly greater confidence can be placed in the measure as additional predictions are corroborated. This logic, of course, applies to any psychological measure, whether or not it is unobtrusive.

Unobtrusive measures can raise very special ethical issues. Research obligations to subjects require that they provide informed consent regarding assessment and intervention facets of the experiment. Unobtrusively observing performance in everyday life and using information to which subjects have not consented violate the letter and spirit of consent (see chapter 14). On the other hand, unobtrusive measures may vary widely in the ethical issues they raise. For example, archival measures and physical traces may not raise concern because they address past performance and could not threaten or jeopardize in any way the identity of the subjects. The very nature of unobtrusive assessment means that the investigator must be sensitive to possible ethical concerns in the use of specific strategies.

EVALUATING INTERVENTIONS

A major area of assessment in clinical psychology pertains to the evaluation of interventions. Interventions refer here to efforts to alter performance of individuals or groups to improve functioning. Treatment, prevention, educational, and enrichment programs encompass a variety of interventions across the life-span. Evaluating interventions raises unique issues depending on the clients, goals, and procedures. Psychotherapy outcome is used here to illustrate several points about assessment strategies.

Overall Assessment Strategy

Several points about assessment of dependent variables in general apply to intervention research. Prominent among these is the use of multiple measures. The multifaceted nature of human functioning, the broad impact of clinical problems in the context of a treatment focus, the limitations of any singular modality and source of information, and the different perspectives and contexts relevant for treatment evaluation dictate the use of several measures for reasons outlined in the previous chapter. In clinical, counseling, and educational work, the cost of interventions in time and money is often quite high. The treatment program may require years to complete; follow-up evaluation may span one to several additional years (e.g., Kolvin et al., 1981; Seitz, Rosenbaum, & Apfel, 1985). Repetition of the experiment (replication) is not very feasible. Hence one wishes to maximize the information obtained from the initial and possibly only test of the specific hypothesis.

Evaluation of client functioning is obviously important as part of intervention research. However, the applied nature of such research raises other types of measures and criteria. Several of these are highlighted here to encourage the development and use of measures other than client change and symptomatic or social functioning.

Criteria for Evaluating Therapy

Typically, the criteria for evaluating treatment include methods selected from global ratings, self-report inventories, projective techniques, overt behavior, and psychophysiological measures. Occasionally, unobtrusive measures supplement these methods. Although traditional assessment criteria are important in evaluating client change, the manner in which they have been used has been restricted. Much more information about the impact of treatment and client change can be culled from the data than is ordinarily obtained. The present discussion addresses a broad range of criteria for evaluating treatment and includes the extent of client change, the efficiency and the cost of treatment, and consumer evaluation of treatment.

Client-Related Criteria

In treatment research, one limitation is how traditional assessment devices are used. Independently of the specific assessment device, conclusions about treatment or the relative effectiveness of different treatments are drawn on the basis of comparing average (mean) scores of clients among various treatment or control conditions. Statistical analyses serve as the basis for concluding that groups differ. From group differences, conclusions have been reached that one treatment is more or less effective than another or, in the case of no differences, equally effective. Group differences in mean performance on some measure provide an important, but extremely limited, criterion for evaluating treatment. Other criteria that reflect improvement are important measures of change as well.

Importance of the Change

For clinical research, a major criterion for evaluating treatment should be whether the change is clinically significant, that is, whether the improvement enhances the client's everyday functioning. Recent research has begun to address clinical significance as a criterion for evaluating treatment. Clients may be identified as evincing problems worthy of treatment by virtue of their departure from socially acceptable levels of performance (e.g., conduct-disordered children, socially withdrawn adults).

Even if the change in functioning for a treatment group is statistically significant (from pre- to posttreatment), the change may make little difference in the clients' lives. Assessing the clinical significance of change can be examined by defining a level or range of functioning that is adaptive or that constitutes a normative range. The importance of the change is evaluated in light of these latter criteria. (Chapter 12 elaborates the evaluation of clinical significance and application of these criteria.)

In general the magnitude of therapeutic change warrants attention in treatment evaluation. The importance of therapeutic change may be even more useful in evaluating a given technique or the relative strength of different techniques than the usual statistical comparison of mean differences. In chapter 6 the notion of normative data was introduced in the discussion of "patched-up" control groups. Treatment studies can profit from adding such a group to determine whether change on a particular assessment device (e.g., overt behavior) has placed the client appreciably closer to normative levels of functioning as shown by peers whose behaviors have not been brought to treatment.

Proportion of clients who improve. A problem with a statistical evaluation of group differences is that it averages the amount of change across all clients within a given treatment group. Conceivably, one treatment might make some clients worse but still produce a better overall average change than another treatment. One therapy technique may be recommended over another based on the proportion of clients who are likely to improve. Selecting a treatment that produces improvements in the largest proportion of clients maximizes the probability that a given client will be favorably affected by treatment. In contrast, selecting a treatment that produces the greatest average change may not improve the highest proportion of clients.

For example, in one study, cognitive-behavior therapy and medication (Alprazolam) were compared for the treatment of panic disorder among adults (age 18–65 years; Klosko et al., 1990). At the end of treatment, the therapy and medication groups generally were not different from each other on mean (average) amount of change. Yet the proportion of clients who reported zero panic attacks in a 2-week period after treatment provided a clear pattern. The percentage of clients who completed the study and who were free from panic attacks was 87% for cognitive-behavior therapy and 50% for medication. Both treatments produced better results than attention-placebo and waiting-list control subjects (36% and 33% free from attacks, respectively). In terms of the proportion of clients favorably affected by treatment, the therapy procedure was apparently more effective than medication.

The proportion of clients who improve may not in itself be an important criterion in cases in which the actual amount of improvement is very small and of little clinical significance. The magnitude of behavior change needs to be considered in conjunction with the proportion of clients who improve. The primary interest is to evaluate which among alternative treatments produces the greatest proportion of clients who have achieved a clinically significant change.

Breadth of changes. The efficacy of treatment may be appropriately judged on the basis of how well it alters the problem for which the client sought treatment. Another criterion that might differentiate treatments is the breadth of changes that are produced. Both case reports and experimental research have shown that treatment effects often extend beyond the target focus of therapy. For example, treatments of phobias, obsessive–compulsive disorders, and moderate to severe personality disorders have been associated with decreases in anxiety in areas beyond the treatment focus and in depression, and improvements in work, social, and sexual adjustment (e.g., Hodgson, Rachman, & Marks, 1972; Sloane et al., 1975; Wilson, 1989).

Included in the breadth of changes are the side effects of treatments. Two treatments may be equally effective in altering the target problem but differ in important side effects. For example, in one study drug treatment (Ritalin) was shown to be as effective as an incentive program in reducing hyperactivity in children in a classroom situation (Ayllon, Layman, & Kandel, 1975). Yet the untoward side effects of the drug (in suppressing desired behaviors not focused on in treatment) made the incentive program the treatment of choice. A comparison of the different treatments without additional data on the side effects would have led to the misleading conclusion that the treatments were equally beneficial.

Generally, the breadth and nature of side effects are important criteria for evaluating a given treatment and for comparing the utility of different treatments (see Dewan & Koss, 1989). Beneficial and deleterious side effects of treatment have been sufficiently documented to warrant their systematic evaluation. Side effects may include whether clients complete treatment. Independently of their efficacy, various inpatient and outpatient treatments have been shown to differ in attrition or loss of subjects (e.g., Davis, 1973; Rush et al., 1977). Such data may provide supplementary information to the usual assessment criteria for evaluating a given treatment.

Durability of improvements. An obviously important criterion for evaluating treatment is the durability of therapeutic change. In clinical research there is a paucity of follow-up data, so the long-term effects of many treatments are a matter of surmise. Follow-up data are important in part because they may alter the conclusions about the effects of different treatments. Even if two techniques are equally effective immediately after treatment, the course of change during follow-up may differ considerably. Several studies of alternative forms of individual psychotherapy, behavior therapy, and cognitive therapy have shown that the relative effectiveness of two or more treatments varies at posttreatment and follow-up several months or a year later (e.g., Heinicke & Ramsey-Klee, 1986; Jacobson, 1984; Kingsley & Wilson, 1977).

Sometimes treatment techniques may differ in efficacy immediately after treatment but not differ at follow-up. For example, Staudt and Zubin (1957) found that somatotherapies such as psychosurgery, insulin, electroconvulsive shock, and other treatments were superior to custodial care in treating hospitalized schizophrenics. However, after 2 to 3 years of follow-up, these treatments were no more effective than custodial care. Because of the importance of follow-up, several methods for follow-up assessment that can be incorporated into research are discussed later in this chapter.

Impact of treatment on significant others. The primary focus of treatment obviously is the individual who seeks treatment. Yet treatment may have consequences for others involved with the client in some way (Brody & Farber, 1989). In many instances, an important criterion for evaluation is the impact on others involved in the lives of individuals in treatment.

On conceptual grounds, some dysfunctions draw on a broader focus than a given individual. For example, family-based therapies usually consider the people referred for treatment as the "identified patient." The problem or dysfunction is considered to reflect a process or pattern in the family. Thus changes beyond a single person referred for treatment are central. Apart from a particular conceptual approach, there are cases where the problems are likely on prima facie grounds to have impact on others who share a close relationship with the client. Some areas identified for treatment (e.g., sexual dysfunction) might well be expected to have impact on significant others. Yet other areas that may seem less interpersonal can have broad impact on others. For example, individuals who experience posttraumatic stress disorder, panic attacks, agoraphobia, and depression may have life-styles to accommodate their dysfunction. These life-styles can affect the interpersonal functioning of spouses and offspring.

Depending on the treatment focus, evaluation of the impact of the intervention of nontreated significant others can be an important criterion. For example, in the treatment of antisocial children, parent management training is a viable intervention. Apart from changes in the child referred for treatment, occasionally the impact of treatment on others is assessed. Treatment has been shown to improve behavior of the siblings of the child identified for treatment and to decrease maternal psychopathology, particularly depression (see Kazdin, 1985). These changes are important because siblings are at risk for antisocial behavior, and mothers of antisocial youth often evince depression. Consequently, the extended impact of the treatment to other family members is quite relevant in evaluating the intervention. More generally, the impact of treatment on the client may be a primary focus. However, the broader impact may be relevant as well.

Efficiency and Cost-Related Criteria

The above criteria refer to treatment efficacy and the ways in which efficacy can be assessed. The client-related criteria actually involve the methods of psychological assessment addressed in chapter 9. However, these methods are not the only ones relevant to treatment evaluation. Other criteria exist related to the efficiency and cost of treatment. Assessment of these criteria extend beyond the usual evaluation methods but can greatly supplement measures of efficacy.

Duration of treatment. The length of time required for a particular treatment to achieve a given level of effectiveness is an important criterion for evaluating treatment. A technique that reaches a specified level of improvement in a shorter period of time is preferable in general. Hence showing that two or more treatments do not differ on client-related criteria does not attest to all of the relevant differences among treatments. Two treatments for a given clinical problem may vary in the speed with which they achieve a given level of therapeutic change.

There appears to be a dose-response relation in psychotherapy (Howard, Kopta, Krause, & Orlinsky, 1986). Approximately 50% of adult patients show marked improvement after about 8 treatment sessions; 75% show such improvement after 26 sessions. Even if a shorter term therapy (e.g., 10 sessions) were slightly less effective than a longer term therapy (e.g., 30 sessions), the shorter term therapy might be preferred by clients, therapists, and agents acting in behalf of insurance companies. The duration of different treatments provides very useful and relatively easily obtainable information relevant to evaluation of alternative interventions.

Administration of treatment. Treatments vary in the method and efficiency of administration. A familiar distinction in administering treatment is between individual and group therapy. If individual and group treatments were equally effective, group treatment might be preferred because of its efficiency in terms of number of clients per therapist and treatment session. Yet there is more to efficiency in administration than individual versus group treatment.

Some techniques can be widely disseminated because they can be implemented by clients themselves or because they might be able to be presented through mass media (e.g., television). For example, many self-help manuals are designed to treat diverse problems including overeating, cigarette smoking, sexual dysfunction, anxiety, inadequate social skills, conduct problems, and so on (Glasgow & Rosen, 1984). Often extravagant claims are made about the effectiveness of "do-it-yourself" treatments where empirical evidence is absent. However, some treatments have evidence in their behalf. For example, self-administered desensitization has been shown to be as effective as therapist-directed desensitization in treating phobias (Rosen, Glasgow, & Barrera, 1976). Even if it were slightly less effective, the self-administered treatment may be preferred because it is more easily disseminated to the public on a larger scale than individual outpatient treatment. Completely self-directed treatment represents an extreme in which clients, often unrealistically, are expected to obtain materials and to provide adequate and effective treatment. This is a worthy goal when feasible. Yet, many psychological problems (e.g., depression, substance abuse) are likely to influence the feasibility of providing self-help, even if effective self-help strategies are available. Perhaps the use of self-help materials along with some guidance could be provided. Such treatments might be widely disseminable for diverse problems and clients.

There are no simple measures to assess the ease of disseminating a treatment. Several variables may determine disseminability such as the cost of professional training, complexity of the procedures, and need for ancillary equipment or apparatus. Some of these latter criteria should be assessed carefully when contemplating the widespread use of a particular treatment.

Costs of professional expertise. An important criterion for evaluating treatment pertains to the cost of professional training. Treatments that require relatively little therapist training or can be conducted without therapists may be preferred to those that require professionals to have extensive training. Treatments that do not require highly skilled professionals can be disseminated more easily to the public and thus may be preferable. Many treatment and rehabilitation programs have enlisted the aid of parents, teachers, hospital attendants, or college students to administer programs for inpatient and outpatient treatment. Another use of nonprofessionals consists of self-help groups such as Alcoholics Anonymous (AA), Take Off Pounds Sensibly (TOPS), or Synanon (for ex-addicts).

Client costs. A multifaceted criterion for evaluating treatments is the cost of treatment to the clients. The most obvious cost is monetary expenditure, which no doubt is related to other criteria such as the amount of professional training required to administer treatment and the disseminability of treatment. Yet there are psychological costs as well, such as the amount of stress associated with different treatments. For example, treatment techniques such as flooding or implosion, which involve exposure of the clients to highly stress-provoking situations, may be less attractive than other, less stressful interventions. The psychological and physical costs of completing treatment might be relevant to assess in evaluating therapy, particularly with those techniques that are likely to be aversive to clients. The psychological costs of treatment may be too great to entice participants independently of the data pertaining to treatment efficacy.

Cost and outcome analyses. Increasing attention is given in program and treatment evaluation to costs of treatment as they relate to outcome. The overall question both in large-scale social interventions as well as individual treatments is whether the costs are justified given the returns. Many different types of analyses are available. One of these is *cost–benefit analysis,* which attempts to compare the monetary costs of an intervention with the benefits that are obtained. The benefits must be measured in monetary terms also. This requirement makes cost–benefit analysis difficult to apply to many psychological interventions where the beneficial effects might extend well beyond monetary gains (Yates, 1985). For example, providing programs to help parents rear their children may have monetary benefits (e.g., preventing some children from entering treatment or from being adjudicated). Another gain may be to increase harmony in the homes of many families, an effect that cannot be so readily evaluated in monetary terms. Of course, many returns of treatment can be examined in terms of social benefits such as those derived from the fact that clients return to work, miss fewer days of work, have fewer car accidents, stay out of hospitals or prison, and from other measures that can be translated into monetary terms. Other criteria including changes on psychological measures are important to consider from the standpoint of treatment costs.

Cost-effectiveness analysis does not require placing a monetary value on the benefits and can be more readily used for evaluating treatment. Cost-effectiveness analysis examines the costs of treatment relative to a particular outcome. The value for therapy evaluation is that it permits comparison of different treatment techniques if the treatment benefits are designed to be the same (e.g., reduction of drinking, increase in family harmony). Such information would be very useful and address important questions independently of narrow debates about statistical differences that distinguish treatments.

As yet there are no agreed-upon methods for calculating cost-effectiveness in psychotherapy. In the area of psychological treatment, the measure of effectiveness would be disputed across different techniques. Indeed, estimating both cost and effectiveness is reasonably complex because of the decisions that have to be made about costs, information about changing costs, and the evaluation of both narrow and broad effects that might be achieved in the long and short run. In light of the complexities of estimating costs and effectiveness, it is obvious there is no simple or single formula to be applied for treatment evaluation. However, investigations could examine and report some of the costs of different treatments to provide relevant data.

Consumer-Related Criteria

Efficacy and cost considerations are not the only factors that can be used to measure the value of treatment. The acceptability of treatment to consumers (i.e., potential clients) raises all sorts of issues that warrant attention in clinical research.

Acceptability of treatment. Alternative treatments for a given problem may not be equally acceptable to prospective clients. Efficiency and cost considerations may contribute to the acceptability of a treatment, but there are other factors as well. Procedures may be more or less objectionable in their own right independent of their efficacy. Indeed, many procedures that are readily accept-able to clients often have few or no demonstrated effects. For example, com-monly advertised procedures to control diet or cigarette smoking are highly sought by clients despite the lack of demonstrated efficacy. In addition to efficacy, it is important to evaluate how acceptable or palatable treatments are to clients. Those treatments that are acceptable are more likely to be sought and adhered to once clients have entered into treatment. The wider audience that such highly acceptable treatments attract will make techniques more disseminable.

Techniques might be selected by clients not only for their likely effects but also because of the manner in which these effects are obtained. Thus stress-inducing techniques (e.g., aversion therapy, flooding) may not be as acceptable as viable alternatives (e.g., incentive systems, desensitization). Different treat-ments also may vary in their objectives. These objectives may be more or less acceptable to clients. For example, some treatments for alcoholism aim for complete abstinence, whereas others aim for controlled (social) drinking. These different goals may make treatments differentially preferred by prospec-tive clients. In making treatment decisions, it would be useful to have clients evaluate the procedures in their own right in terms of acceptability (e.g., Kazdin, 1984b, 1986b; Kazdin, French, & Sherick, 1981). Such information can greatly supplement data on effectiveness.

General Comments

Evaluation of therapy techniques should extend beyond traditional measures of change on a narrowly defined set of outcome criteria. Psychological mea-sures of different modalities are essential and need not be replaced. However, by themselves, they do not address the range of important outcome questions that might be raised both from substantive and decision-making perspectives. The value of various treatments and whether they should be used either for the individual client or for large-scale application depend on much more than the average amount of change produced among clients. Multiple criteria are required to address the diverse interests that various parties have in treatment and its effects. Interests vary among those who receive (e.g., clients), deliver (e.g., therapists), evaluate (e.g., researchers), and financially support (e.g., health insurance) treatment. Hence the criteria used for evaluation necessarily depend on many different considerations (Krause & Howard, 1976).

FOLLOW-UP ASSESSMENT

Assessment immediately after treatment is referred to as *posttreatment* assess-ment; any point beyond that ranging from weeks to years typically is referred to as *follow-up* assessment. Follow-up raises important issues for psychotherapy outcome research such as whether gains are maintained and whether conclusions can be reached at all given patient attrition. Conclusions about the efficacy of a treatment or relative effectiveness of alternative treatments may vary greatly depending on when assessments are conducted. For example, in the Kolvin et al. (1981) study, two of the interventions (group therapy and behavior modification) provided to maladjusted children showed different effects depending on the point in time that assessment was completed. Immediately after treatment, relatively few improvements were evident in the areas of neuroticism, antisocial behavior, and total symptom scores. These areas improved markedly over the course of follow-up approximately 18 months after treatment. The authors discussed a "sleeper effect," that is, improvements that are not evident immediately after treatment but emerged and/or increased over time.

Several other studies involving child and adult samples point to the significance of the timing of outcome assessments (see Kazdin, 1988; Wright, Moelis, & Pollack, 1976). Conclusions about the effectiveness of a given treatment relative to a control condition or another treatment differed at posttreatment and follow-up. Thus the treatment that appeared more or most effective at posttreatment did not retain this status at follow-up.

Not all studies find that the pattern of results and conclusions about a given treatment relative to another treatment or control condition vary from posttreatment to follow-up assessment. Indeed, a review of treatment studies has suggested that as a rule the pattern between treatments evident at posttreatment remains evident at follow-up (Nicholson & Berman, 1983). However, the number of clear exceptions suggests that the conclusions about a given treatment in any particular study might well depend on when the assessment is conducted. The possibility of quite intricate relations between timing of assessment and outcome results exist when one considers that changes on different types of measures (e.g., self- or parent-report, psychophysiology) and measures of different constructs (e.g., specific symptoms, adjustment) may also vary with the point in time that assessments are administered.

The possible dependence of conclusions on the timing of follow-up assessment has different implications. To begin with, it is important to determine whether therapeutic changes are maintained and whether they surpass the gains that may be associated with the passage of time without that particular treatment. More than that, it is important to identify the function, curve, or course of change on the outcome measures associated with different techniques. If a few assessment points were obtained during follow-up, the function might be extrapolated so that whether and how change continues can be inferred.

Decisions regarding the timing of follow-up assessment may be influenced by several considerations. First, the nature of the treatments may be a critical consideration. Some treatments may be expected to produce a more rapid rate of change, whereas others, possibly equally or more effective in the long run, may be initially slower in their rate of therapeutic change. The occasional finding that treatment effects are delayed (e.g., Heinicke & Ramsey-Klee, 1986; Kolvin et al., 1981) and that changes at follow-up are often greater than those immediately after treatment (e.g., Wright et al., 1976) underscore the possibility that a given treatment may vary in outcomes at different assessment points.

Second, characteristics of the symptoms or dysfunction may influence the decision regarding when to conduct follow-up assessment. For example, for treatment of overeating and substance use or abuse (alcohol consumption, drug abuse, cigarette smoking), relapse is relatively high. Dramatic changes at posttreatment are noteworthy. However, follow-up assessment is usually regarded as essential given the usual modest and short-lived effects that are demonstrated. Characteristics of the clinical problems such as whether they are chronic or episodic and transient or of high or low frequency may dictate the timing of following assessment. For example, for very low-frequency behaviors that are occasionally treated (e.g., fire setting), long follow-up periods may be needed to allow for the accumulation of the behaviors over time to even occur. A brief follow-up of, say, 6 months, is unlikely to be sensitive to differences among groups.

Third, age or developmental stage of the sample may influence timing of follow-up. If special milestones or transitions (e.g., entry into adolescence) follow treatment, follow-up assessment may be planned to avoid or consider the impact of any changes. Also, the normal rate of change in various behaviors may dictate the evaluation period. If marked changes are expected over a follow-up interval as a function of maturation, a briefer follow-up interval may be selected.

Attrition

An unspoken ideal in treatment research literature is to report long-term follow-up data that evaluate clients years after treatment. Generally, most studies do not report follow-up; among those that do, the follow-up interval usually is a matter of months rather than years (e.g., Kazdin, Bass, Ayers, & Rodgers, 1990; Shapiro & Shapiro, 1983). There are many methodological problems involved in obtaining and interpreting follow-up data. These problems seem to be greater as the interval between posttreatment and follow-up assessment increases.

Certainly the main problem is attrition. Usually, the longer the follow-up period, the greater the loss of subjects. Obviously, over time it is increasingly difficult to locate or to induce subjects to respond. Subjects change addresses, change their names (usually through marriage), enter institutions, die, and do other things that show that the original treatment investigation in which they participated is not the highest priority in their lives. Even if subjects can be located, they do not always wish to comply with requests for follow-up data. This, of course, may depend on their view of the treatment and the actual requirements of follow-up. The methods of obtaining follow-up information, as discussed later, differ greatly in the extent to which they may inconvenience subjects.

Loss of subjects is a problem because the follow-up data may not represent the "true" level of performance if the overall sample of subjects were reassessed. The remaining subjects at follow-up may represent a highly select sample and vary from other subjects within the same treatment group in ways that are directly related to the treatment outcome. For example, subjects who are located 1 year after treatment, compared to those not located at follow-up, may vary in subject and demographic variables, mobility (moving from city to city), severity of the target problem or related problems, and other factors. There can never be certainty that those located represent the group that could not be located. Hence it is difficult to interpret the follow-up data when attrition takes a significant toll.

Loss of subjects may lead to even greater ambiguity if there is a differential loss among groups in a study comparing several different treatments. Treatments may be responsible for differential loss of subjects. Some treatments may be more acceptable than others or lead to more positive changes at posttreatment or follow-up. Subjects may vary in their cooperativeness with attempts to obtain follow-up data as a function of their impressions and benefits of treatment. Hence, there may be a differential responsiveness to solicitations for follow-up data among groups. If two treatments differ significantly in their loss of subjects at follow-up, the resulting follow-up data may be difficult to interpret. The fact that different numbers of subjects responded may signify something important about the different treatment. However, the psychological status of the treated clients across groups cannot be meaningfully compared.

Methods of Follow-up Assessment

Decisions about the kind of follow-up data that are appropriate for the clients' problems, therapy techniques, and resources of the experimenter need to be made in advance. Thus it is useful to outline available options and factors that might contribute to their selection.

Questionnaires and Inventories

Questionnaires and inventories are useful for collecting follow-up information. The advantage is that these measures can be mailed to the subjects and can encompass diverse dimensions of assessment. Also, the assessment devices may have independent information attesting to various forms of reliability and validity so that the stability and correlates of questionnaire responses can be inferred. Also, questionnaires and inventories can provide reports from the clients themselves as well as reports from significant others (e.g., spouses, parents). Hence the options for different perspectives and performance in different contexts are great.

One problem with self-report questionnaires and inventories is that clients may assume a "set" during follow-up that differs from what it may have been during treatment. Self-report questionnaires and inventories in general may have problems pertaining to the response sets and styles. However, long after treatment subjects may view the assessment procedures as a way to reward the experimenter for his or her interest or for satisfaction with the program. Of course, dissatisfaction on the part of the subjects also might dictate whether they respond, and if so, the impression they provide regarding their functioning.

Interviews

Interviews might be used for follow-up assessment and consist of a standardized series of questions presented to individuals on the phone or in the laboratory-clinic setting to which the subject returns. If the follow-up interviews are conducted in the laboratory or clinic situation itself, the clients can be seen and evaluated by trained assessors or can be observed directly for their behavior in the interview situation. Of course, any advantages of having clients come in for an interview are likely to be offset by a greater loss of subjects. Asking subjects to come in makes follow-up more difficult and costly for the subjects. Subjects are likely to be more willing to chat on the phone for a few minutes at their convenience.

The problems of self-report inventories, mentioned earlier, extend to interview data. The "set" of the subject or motives in answering the questions may change from treatment to follow-up assessment. The advantage of the interview, especially if conducted in the clinic setting, is that some facets of performance during the interview might be assessed unobtrusively. For example, videotaped samples of the interview might be used to rate signs of anxiety during the interview and supplement the information obtained from the verbal report. Alternatively, the interview might be tape-recorded. Additional data might be culled from the reports such as anxiety during speech, responses to specific questions, and so on.

Overt Behavior

Many different ways of sampling overt behavior have been used for follow-up assessment. One method is to observe what the client does directly in the natural environment. For example, observations might be conducted in the home to observe interactions among spouses or children. Clients themselves can observe their own behavior as long as some means are taken to ensure consistency in scoring behavior. Parents, spouses, roommates, or others might be able to check behavior unobtrusively to attest to the veracity of the report or the margin of error in assessment.

Overt behavior may be assessed in contrived situations either as part of everyday experience or in the laboratory setting. Contrived situations may be used in the laboratory situation. Clients may be instructed to report to the laboratory where they are placed through a situation that requires performance of the behaviors developed in therapy. For example, parents may interact with their children after being given a task to see whether they are managing their child more effectively; outpatients treated for anxiety may complete a series of tasks in a potentially anxiety-provoking situation; and delinquents might role-play responses as they practice interacting with peers who place pressure on them to commit antisocial acts.

In many ways, it is ideal to observe behavior of the clients in their natural environment to see whether the changes in treatment have transferred and are maintained in everyday life. If the clients or experimenter cannot accomplish this, individuals in contact with the client may be able to provide select information. One of the problems is the lack of standardization of the situations in which clients are observed. Clients cannot all be observed at home or at work because the differences in their individual situations might make the responses difficult to combine or compare. Assessment may require contacting subjects in the different groups or within a given group under relatively homogeneous conditions. Depending on the focus of treatment, the variation in living situations may not interfere with observing the relevant behavior. For example, eating, smoking, exercising, and other responses might be converted to some unit across all subjects in their everyday situations (e.g., calories, cigarettes smoked, minutes or miles jogged or calories expended, respectively) and be used for follow-up assessment. On the other hand, other problems (e.g., pervasive anxiety, anxiety at work, urges to write books) may present greater obstacles for standardizing measures.

Other problems may restrict the use of overt behavioral measure in the natural environment. Many behaviors may occur at a low rate in some clients but are clinically important when they occur. For example, panic attacks, obsessive–compulsive rituals, and instances of child abuse may be difficult to detect in observations over a brief period in which observers can be used for such assessment. Also, many problems treated in therapy occur at times when observers are unlikely to be available. For example, deviant sexual acts, sleepwalking, and feelings of loneliness may not coincide with periods in which observers are sent to the client's home.

Archival Records

Records of overt behavior may be extremely useful in evaluating follow-up. For example, the effects of intervention programs with psychiatric patients, prisoners, and the unemployed have been measured by hospital readmission rates, contact with the police, and unemployment records (e.g., Paul & Lentz, 1977). Records such as these are not always available. In many cases where useful information is available, it is infrequently used. For example, days absent from work might be used as a relevant follow-up measure for treatment of outpatient alcoholics; divorce and remarriage records for marital discord; and emergency room visits as a measure of child or spouse abuse.

The advantage of such records is that they usually are nonreactive since it is not expected by clients that they might ever be used to evaluate the constructs of interest. Another advantage is that they usually reflect measures considered to be socially relevant to the social benefits of treatment. The measures provide dramatic illustrations of the social impact of treatment or the effects of treatment on the client's life.

Of course, there are disadvantages as well regarding archival measures. The measures may be influenced by variables other than treatment. For example, readmission of psychiatric patients may reflect much more than the psychiatric status of the patient. Reentering the hospital may reflect such considerations as change in family ties, loss of job, or season of the year. In addition, record keeping among public agencies frequently provides crude information from the standpoint of evaluating treatment. Contact with the police, for example, does not provide a very complete indication of how well the client is doing 1 or 2 years after rehabilitation. It is one thing not to be on record with the police, but quite another to be functioning well on a job, earning a living, and displaying other positive or prosocial behaviors. Nevertheless, archival records provide information that supplements other measures and, depending on the target problem, may serve as very relevant outcome measures.

Sources of Information

The methods of assessment provide options for obtaining follow-up information. With some of the methods, decisions have to be made about the source of the information. The source refers to who provides the information.

The Client

Obviously, the client is in a unique position to provide information about the benefits of treatment. The client can be assessed by virtually all of the different methods mentioned above. Even overt behavior in the natural environment can be readily assessed by the client himself or herself. For many clinical dysfunctions, clients are the primary or occasionally the sole source of information, especially when private events and subjective states (e.g., headaches, obsessive thoughts, feelings of despair, urges) are evaluated. Concomitant behaviors might well be assessed by observers, but self-report is viewed as the most direct assessment of such states. Even outside of the context of private events, the perspective of the client is usually central. Consequently, most follow-up assessment uses the clients themselves as the source of information.

Informants

People in contact with the client such as peers, a spouse, roommates, teachers, employers, friends, colleagues, and others can be contacted to provide information. The information may be in the form of questionnaires, inventories, or overt behaviors. The precise format depends on the method of interest and the relationship of the informant to the client.

Excellent research has been completed on the use of informants to evaluate the effects of inpatient and outpatient treatment of psychiatric patients (e.g., Ellsworth, 1975; Ellsworth, Foster, Childers, Arthur, & Kroeker, 1968; Penk, Charles, & Van Hoose, 1978). Patients admitted for treatment were asked to identify a relative or close friend who could be contacted by mail for information about the patient's home and community adjustment before and after treatment. The relatives received a questionnaire that asked them to rate a number of concrete behaviors rather than more global evaluations (e.g., ratings of the patient's "depression") related to various dimensions of psychopathology. The informant ratings were very useful in their own right and for corroborating other sources of information (e.g., hospital staff ratings).

There are obvious practical problems in soliciting and using informants. It is important to ensure that the informants have access to the problem focused on in treatment. This is readily accomplished if parents are reporting on the problem behaviors of young children in the home. In contrast, if employers, spouses, or friends are reporting on alcoholic consumption, smoking, or compulsive rituals, the behaviors may not be apparent to the informant selected. In general, there must be assurances across subjects that the informants have access to the relevant information.

Experimenters

Obviously, the most reliable way to obtain follow-up information is somehow to use an experimenter or assessor. Assessors can be used to measure overt behavior either at the research setting or at home. On the other hand, practical constraints alone usually prohibit sending someone to measure behavior to each individual client. Telephone follow-up assessment is a compromise that uses the assessor to evaluate behavior of the client directly in a contrived phone situation. Sending an assessor to the client or using a contrived situation introduces reactivity into the situation. Thus the results obtained might be a partial function of changing the natural situation, a disadvantage that the use of informants may not incur.

General Comments

The discussion of different methods and sources of follow-up information does not exhaust the available alternatives. Yet even with the methods presented, multiple options exist from which researchers may select. Of course, as with assessment of behavior change in a treatment study, the ideal follow-up strategy would be one that involves multiple response formats. However, in advocating the use of multiple measures at follow-up we may fail to appreciate the practical difficulties in accomplishing follow-up assessment. The paucity of follow-up data in general, and beyond a few months after treatment, in particular, leads one to recommend follow-up assessment by at least one of the methods.

Methods of Contacting Clients

Face-to-Face Assessment

Questionnaires, inventories, and interviews are the most commonly used methods of obtaining follow-up information. A critical decision is how to obtain the information. One option is to ask clients at follow-up to return to the setting where the study was completed and to complete various measures. Face-to-face or "live" follow-up assessment is desirable because the assessment conditions are similar, if not identical, to those in which prior assessments (pre, posttreatment) were conducted. Thus conditions of assessment are held constant. Also, face-to-face assessment permits the use of a broad range of measurement strategies (e.g., self-report, direct observation, psychophysiological measures). More extensive assessment (i.e., more constructs, more measures) is available because once clients are in the setting, a large block of time may be available. Although more assessment is not invariably better assessment, the options provided by face-to-face contact are noteworthy.

A disadvantage of live assessment is the likelihood of attrition or loss of subjects. Returning to the setting is costly in client time and effort. Monetary incentives for participation may minimize loss of subjects. Even so, returning to the clinic or laboratory is likely to be inconvenient for many persons. One option is to visit the clients in their homes and to complete the assessments there. For many projects, home visits are expensive because of the cost of assessors, travel, and missed visits when clients are not home for a scheduled visit. Aside from the fact that face-to-face assessment is not always convenient, it is not feasible in situations where multiple informants (e.g., clients, employers, teachers) are asked to evaluate client functioning.

Mailing the Measures

A second option is to mail the measures to the clients or to those who are to complete the follow-up assessment. Individuals are asked to complete the measures and to return them, perhaps in a self-addressed, stamped envelope. This assessment option has the advantage that one can usually reach a large number of participants and diverse informants. Also, completing measures at home (for the clients or relatives) is more convenient than coming to the clinic or research setting. Hence a higher rate of compliance (lower attrition) may be more likely.

Mailing measures has its own liabilities. To begin with, the investigator is restricted in the range of measures that can be used, namely, to those self- or other-report measures that can be completed with little verbal instructions. The breadth of available measures varying in degrees of readability and clarity makes this disadvantage surmountable.

Another issue is that measures are likely to be completed under diverse "testing conditions." Some subjects will complete the measures after work, while watching TV, while sipping beer, while listening and nodding half-attentively to a roommate or spouse, and so on. The uncontrolled and diverse testing conditions raise the likelihood of introducing additional variability in the measure. If expected differences (effect sizes) between groups is small, if sample sizes are small, or if power is weak, the addition of a small amount of variability can present large problems.

A related consideration has to do with the quality of the data. Assessment by mail can lead to missing data among those subjects who complete and return the measures. Individual items invariably are omitted, completed inaccurately, or are otherwise undecipherable. These problems are less likely in face-to-face assessment because an examiner can query at the moment or remind the person to answer a given item or measure.

Telephone Assessment

Another option is to contact clients or significant others by telephone. The individual is called and the measure is presented item by item over the phone. The caller can be experimentally naive (blind) to the conditions in which the subject participated. The caller can complete the measure as the call progresses by transcribing the verbal answers to the questionnaire or inventory. For later checking, the call can be tape-recorded, pending client permission.

As an example, one measure used to evaluate children with behavior problems is referred to as the Parent Daily Report (Chamberlain & Reid, 1987). The measure consists of a list of deviant or otherwise bothersome behaviors that children can perform at home. Assessment consists of calling the parent for several (e.g., 6–10) days. Each day, the parent is queried about each behavior on the list. The parent's task is to report whether the behavior has occurred in the previous 24 hours. The specific time period and well-defined nature of the behaviors are designed to provide information that reflects child performance rather than overall impressions of deviance.

The convenience of telephone follow-up assessment is obvious. Clients can respond to items without the effort of either visiting the clinic or taking the additional time to read and complete measures on their own. From the standpoint of the investigator, more subjects are likely to comply with telephone assessment than the other options. Also, less missing or incomplete data among cases who do complete the assessment is likely because the caller can ensure the integrity of the measure. Given the ease of administration, it is encouraging to note that evidence suggests that telephone contact can yield results that are equivalent to face-to-face interviewing in the assessment of clinical dysfunction (Wells, Burnam, Leake, & Robins, 1988).

General Comments

Alternative methods of contacting persons at follow-up vary in their advantages and disadvantages. Convenience, cost in experimenter time, geographical area (e.g., all cases are on campus vs. in a large metropolitan area) across which subjects are dispersed, anticipated attrition, and funds available to pay participants are all major elements that influence the investigator's decision on the method to use. What is not clear is whether the different methods provide equivalent data, that is, the same types of responses. Investigators often select the method based on the nature of the measures that are required. For example, family interaction and marital communication can be assessed by self-report. However, many investigators wish to sample these through direct observation.

In some studies, all three methods might be used to assess clients. For example, those who have not agreed to live assessment might receive the packet in the mail; those who do not return the measures might be called. The use of diverse methods is a case where maximizing the number of subjects who will be obtained is a reasonable compromise against holding all assessment conditions constant. It would be important to document and, to the extent possible, avoid in the procedures a situation where cases in one group (e.g., the control group) are more likely to have completed their assessments under one condition (e.g., telephone) than cases in another group (e.g., treatment group).

SUMMARY AND CONCLUSIONS

Subjects are usually aware that some facet of their performance is being assessed (obtrusiveness of assessment). The methodological issue with obtrusive measures is that performance may be altered in some way as a result of that awareness (reactivity of assessment). The possibility exists that the results may be restricted to circumstances in which subjects know their performance is being assessed and that the measures have contributed to the pattern of performance that is obtained.

To ensure that conclusions are not restricted to reactive conditions of assessment, unobtrusive or nonreactive measures can be used. Because subjects are unaware that behavior is assessed, the resulting data can be considered free from reactive influences and be used to corroborate or extend more commonly used assessment methods. *Unobtrusive measures* may be conducted in different ways including *simple observation,* observation in *contrived situations, archival records,* and *physical traces.* Each of these has been used creatively in clinical research to extend greatly the conclusions that can be drawn.

The *criteria for assessing therapy outcome* have been restricted. Many dimensions seemingly important for evaluating client change and treatment have been ignored as outcome criteria. Several criteria relevant for evaluating therapy beyond those commonly used in treatment include the following: the clinical importance of behavior change, the proportion of clients who achieve clinically important change, the breadth of change, the durability of change, the impact of treatment on significant others, the duration of treatment, the ease of administering treatment, the professional and client costs of treatment, cost and outcome analyses, and the acceptability of treatment to the clients. These criteria greatly extend the research questions that can be asked of treatment.

The durability of treatment is generally accepted in clinical research as an important treatment criterion. However, follow-up data are infrequently collected to evaluate long-term treatment effects. Many methods of follow-up assessment can be used such as self-report questionnaires and inventories, interviews, samples of overt behavior, and archival records of performance. Alternative sources of information for follow-up assessment include the clients, informants, and experimenters; alternative methods of contacting clients include face-to-face assessment, sending the measures through the mail, or calling subjects. The assessment options are so rich that follow-up assessment can be readily incorporated into treatment in some form.

FOR FURTHER READING

Kazdin, A.E., & Wilson, G.T. (1978). Criteria for evaluating psychotherapy. *Archives of General Psychiatry, 35,* 407–416.

Lambert, M.J., Christensen, E.R., & DeJulio, S.S. (Eds.). (1983). *The assessment of psychotherapy outcome.* New York: John Wiley & Sons.

Strupp, H.H., & Hadley, S.W. (1977). A tripartite model of mental health and therapeutic outcomes. *American Psychologist, 32,* 187–196.

Webb, E.J., Campbell, D.T., Schwartz, R.D., Sechrest, L., & Grove, J.B. (1981). *Nonreactive measures in the social sciences* (2nd ed.). Boston: Houghton Mifflin.

Chapter 11

SOURCES OF
ARTIFACT AND BIAS

Artifacts and biases in experimental research refer to extraneous influences that may threaten the validity of an experiment. Each type of experimental validity can be affected by extraneous influences. However, artifacts and biases generally raise concerns with the interpretation of the experiment and outcomes that might be incorrectly attributed to the intervention. Thus interpretative issues are central to construct validity.

There is no predetermined set of artifacts that can be enumerated. What constitutes an extraneous influence in an experiment refers to all those variables that the experimenter is not interested in examining. The factors that can give rise to conclusions in an experiment are virtually unlimited. Which ones are artifacts and biases depend on the focus of the investigation. For example, one investigator may wish to study the effects of therapist beliefs on treatment efficacy and view beliefs as the independent variable. Another experimenter may be interested in the efficacy of different treatments and regard therapist beliefs as a potential source of artifact. Thus a given source of influence may be viewed at times as an artifact and at other times as an independent variable.

McGuire (1969) suggested that influences commonly identified as artifacts evolve through three stages. The first stage is *ignorance*. During this stage, investigators are unaware that an extraneous variable is operative in an experiment and may account for the results. When such a source of artifact is posed, it may be denied. The second stage is *coping*. In this stage the existence and possible importance of the artifact are recognized. Investigators increasingly recognize the potential influence of the artifact in their experiments and implement control procedures to assess, minimize, or eliminate its impact. The third and final stage is *exploiting* the source of artifact in its own right; rather than trying to minimize or eliminate the effect, research attempts to examine the source of influence as an independent variable. The influence is maximized in experiments, and variations are examined to establish the way in which the variable operates. At this stage substantive knowledge accrues, and the variable is more widely understood as a source of influence.

The present chapter examines several sources of influence often regarded as artifacts in psychological research. Conceptualization of many of these influences has evolved and they are recognized as important independent variables in their own right. From a methodological standpoint, however, it is important to consider methods of coping with these influences in research and hence to look at different influences as potential contaminants of experimental results. Several types of influence are discussed that may interfere with drawing conclusions about a given independent variable. These include biases stemming from those who conduct research, demand characteristics, subject roles, and subject selection.

INVESTIGATOR AND EXPERIMENTER SOURCES OF BIAS

Several sources of artifact and bias may enter into research as a function of who designs the investigation (referred to as the *investigator*) and who actually executes it (referred to as the *experimenter,* Barber, 1976). Distinguishing an investigator and experimenter may oversimplify the different roles because the same person may serve as investigator and experimenter. Alternatively, there may be multiple investigators and experimenters, or, in automated and mechanized experiments, no real experimenter in the usual sense. However, the different roles or functions of an investigator and experimenter help delineate a number of problems that may contribute to the results of an experiment.

Rationales, Scripts, and Procedures

Nature of the Problem

Potential sources of bias in an experiment include the instructions and experimental materials or procedures to which subjects are exposed. The source of bias varies depending on precisely what the experimenter and subject are supposed to do. A major source of bias may result from imprecision in the script or protocol that the experimenter should follow in the experiment. The script refers to the specific activities, tasks, and instructions that the experimenter should administer. Depending on the investigation, this may entail delivering a rationale, providing a brief interview, answering questions, assisting the subject, and performing a task or implementing the experimental manipulation. The experimenter's script must be well specified by the investigator. Failure to specify in detail the rationale, script, and activities of the experimenter has been referred to as the *loose protocol effect* (Barber, 1976).

Several problems may result from failing to specify how the experimenter should behave. First, the lack of specificity of the procedures means that the investigator does not know what actually was done with the subjects and hence cannot convey the procedures to other investigators. The study cannot be repeated either by the original investigator or by others because of the lack of important details.

A second problem resulting from not specifying the script is inconsistency among different experimenters when two or more of them are used to run the experiment. The procedures may vary systematically from experimenter to experimenter in terms of what is said to the subject, the general atmosphere that is provided, and other features. This variation in experimenter behavior is more likely when details of implementing the procedures are not well specified. For example, in one study interviewers obtained different sorts of data when the procedures they conducted were not well structured and when they had latitude in devising the questions for the subjects (Feldman, Hyman, & Hart, 1951). On the other hand, very similar data were obtained when the procedures were structured and the questions were specified in advance. Interactions that can be or by design are somewhat unstructured or free-flowing (e.g., interviews, psychotherapy sessions), unlike many laboratory arrangements, might maximize the influence of the experimenter (interviewer, therapist) because of the nature of the interaction.

Inconsistencies among experimenters may readily obscure the effects of an independent variable. When the experimenters perform differently, this introduces "noise" into the data. Within-group variability (error variance) is increased, which can reduce the obtained effect size and power of an experiment and threatens the statistical conclusion validity. The effect of the independent variable may need to be extremely potent to overcome this variability. For this reason alone, it is advisable to standardize the performance of the experimenters so that they perform alike and so that each experimenter performs consistently over time.

Standardizing the rationales, procedures, and experimenter's script is a matter of degree. In clinical research it may not be possible or desirable to codify all statements and types of comments made by the experimenter. For example, a therapist may adhere to procedures that are well spelled out. Yet the very process of therapy will call for statements on the part of the therapist that cannot be completely specified in advance. In the context of therapy, specifying the procedures requires delineating those aspects of treatment considered to be important for change. Additional comments that may arise as distressed clients report events in their lives may be necessary at some point over the course of treatment. In many areas of research other than therapy, the interactions between an experimenter and subject can be completely specified, and the experimenter may not have to deviate from a carefully detailed script except for an occasional and unpredicted question from the subject.

Even if the investigator specified the procedures in careful detail, another problem that can arise is the failure of experimenters to adhere to these procedures. There is no guarantee that the experimenter will carry them out as specified. The experimenter may alter the procedures to suit his or her own personality or neglect specific aspects that appear irrelevant, awkward, or redundant. Over time, experimenters may become increasingly divergent in how they run subjects, and hence they may deviate from the original procedures. The task of the investigator therefore is not only to specify the experimenter's script in detail but to ensure that the script is executed as specified.

Recommendations

Several procedures can help ensure that the experiment is conducted in a consistent fashion. To begin with, the procedures should be explicit and standardized for the experimenters. For laboratory research, and in varying degrees in applied research, many aspects of the procedures can be automated or taped in advance. Tape recordings of instructions and videotapes of visual material to be presented to the subject ensure standardization.

When these options are unavailable or seem undesirable by virtue of the goals of the intervention, the statements to be made by the experimenters may be spelled out verbatim. Detailed specification of the rationale or instructions guarantees a certain amount of consistency. Experimenters may vary some of the words used and introduce their own statements but these do not necessarily compete with the overall consistency of the script.

One source of variation among experimenters is how they respond to sensitive questions on the part of the subject (e.g., "Am I just a guinea pig?", "Is this the control group?"). Depending on the experiment, it may be useful to try to anticipate the range of questions that may arise and to provide guidelines or particular statements for answering them. Of course, variations in handling an occasional question may reflect inconsistencies among experimenters but are not likely to be as serious as basic differences in how subjects are routinely run.

Another recommendation is to train experimenters together. During training, experimenters can practice conducting the experiment on each other or the investigator as subjects to see how the procedures are to be performed. By having individuals practice and receive feedback together, relatively homogeneous behavior during the actual experiment is more readily assured. Homogeneity in performance can be sustained by continuing training sessions periodically with all experimenters as a group while the experiment is actually being run. One procedure to examine and sustain consistency of performance among experimenters is to include "subjects" in the study who are working for the investigator. These subjects, referred to as confederates, enter the study as if they were completing the experiment. However, their task is to discuss with the investigator what was done, how it was done, and so on after they participate in the experiment.

In my own work, occasionally I have utilized as confederates people who know the procedures well because of their prior work as experimenters. Perhaps the most useful facet of the procedure is to tell experimenters at the beginning of the project that individuals will be coming through the experiment as subjects. These confederates are unannounced, of course, and interspersed with other subjects. Probably, the most interesting aspect of this procedure is that it may increase vigilance in the experimenters. For example, experimenters in our own work have always speculated on who was working as a confederate and seemingly are especially careful in adhering to the experimental script.

Another procedure to evaluate the consistency in performance among experimenters is to interview the subjects after the experiment. Subjects can be interviewed by someone not involved with the experimental manipulation to reduce the bias conveyed to subjects to respond in a particular way during the interview. An interview may compound the problem because it constitutes another experimental arrangement. Assurances may be needed that this interview is conducted consistently. An alternative is a questionnaire administered to the subject after the experiment that asks questions about the experimenter's behavior and the manner in which the procedures were executed. A problem with a questionnaire is that the answers are based on the subjects' perceptions. As such they may not reflect accurately what the experimenter did. Also, questionnaire responses based on an individual subject's perceptions may not be sensitive enough to reveal inconsistencies in how subjects were treated by different experimenters. On the other hand, if subjects' responses differ systematically among different experimenters, this may provide important clues about the procedures.

If there is some reason why the experimenter's behavior needs to be very closely monitored, video or audiotape recordings can be made of all experimenter–subject interactions. This might be completed as part of the experiment as in the case of studying process variables in psychotherapy research. Yet even if the interaction is not of interest, occasional and perhaps even unobtrusive recordings of an experimental session may be desirable.

Experimenters should be encouraged to report sessions in which they have deviated from the script. Experimenters should not be expected to perform consistently beyond a certain point and to be entirely free from error. For example, subjects may be run in a condition other than the one to which they were assigned, receive a portion of some other condition, or through some unusual event receive a diffuse or interrupted version of their condition. Ideally, the investigator establishes a climate where high standards of performance are expected yet errors are readily acknowledged and reported to serve the goals of the research, namely, to provide a meticulous test of the hypotheses. Encouraging experimenters to report instances where they inadvertently deviated from the script or were forced to deviate by virtue of the subject's behavior will help the investigator monitor the sorts of inconsistencies that transpire. Gross deviations from the procedures may require excluding subjects from data analysis.

Although it is important to specify the script of the experimenters, this requirement must be placed in context. A considerable amount of research, usually laboratory based, includes straightforward procedures on the part of the experimenter where deviation from the script may not be very serious. Experimenters frequently provide simple instructions, play tape recordings, show slides, administer questionnaires, explain the tasks and benefits of treatment, and so on. Presumably, loose protocols are less likely than in more complex social interaction or intervention studies involving more intricate manipulations.

In some studies, however, it may be important not to standardize heavily what experimenters do. For example, the research questions may be based on providing general guidelines that convey how the conditions are to be distinct. Experimenters may be allowed to act within these boundaries. This approach occasionally is taken in therapy outcome research. Experimenters are instructed to follow guidelines characteristic of one technique and to avoid the guidelines that characterize the other treatment technique (e.g., Sloane et al., 1975). Of course, unless the general guidelines are well specified and can be expressed as a set of operations in the experiment, the investigator may still have no firm idea of what experimenters actually are doing.

Experimenter Expectancy Effects

Nature of the Problem

One source of potential bias in experimental research that received considerable attention in the mid-1960s is experimenter expectancy effects. These effects refer to the influence of the experimenter's belief and desires about the results on how the subject performs. The effects are considered to be unintentional because the experimenter may not do anything on purpose to influence subjects' responses. Rather, through tone of voice, posture, facial expressions, and other cues, the experimenter may influence how the subject responds.

Initial research in this area was completed by Rosenthal (1966, 1976), who found that leading experimenters to expect certain results in fact influenced how the subjects actually performed. This research included a series of investigations that showed expectancy effects with human and infrahuman subjects. The research on unintentional expectancy effects has been critically reviewed by challenging the statistical analyses and treatment of data in many of the studies. Nevertheless, some evidence has shown that experimenters' expectancies influence what the subjects do (see Barber, 1976). In addition, characteristics of experimenters and how they behave (e.g., those who act more professional, competent, and relaxed) systematically relate to the magnitude of the expectancy effects (Rosenthal, 1976).

In treatment research, the problem of expectancy effects might be particularly acute in situations where the experimenter may have a strong investment in the outcome and is completely responsible for running subjects in the various treatment and control conditions. For example, in an investigation mentioned earlier, psychoanalysis, psychoanalytically oriented psychotherapy, and rational-emotive therapy were compared for the treatment of neurotic outpatients (Ellis, 1957). The investigator served as the therapist for all conditions. The results showed that rational-emotive therapy, the technique developed by the investigator, was superior to the two alternatives.

It is quite plausible in this study that expectancies might have exerted influence on the results. The investigator's interest and enthusiasm for the particular treatment that he had created might have inadvertently conveyed cues not available in the other treatments. The plausibility of expectancies operating is increased further because the investigator was responsible for rating client improvements across each of the conditions. Thus in the administration or evaluation of treatments, expectancies may have accounted for the results.

Expectancies can threaten the construct validity of the experiment. Features of the experimenter considered to be irrelevant to the experimental manipulation (e.g., expectancies, enthusiasm, suggestions for improvement) may vary systematically with the conditions. Expectancies alone or in combination with the manipulation may be responsible for the pattern of results. Whether expectancies of the experimenter represent a plausible account of the results is difficult to say in the general case.

Recommendations

Current evidence suggests that the experimenter's expectancies can influence results, although the pervasiveness of this influence among different areas of research is not known. There is debate about the manner in which experimenter expectancies exert their influence. It is important to know the different ways in which experimenter expectancies operate because this will suggest the type of control procedures needed. For example, expectancies operating through loose protocols or systematic errors in calculating data would lead the investigator to control some features, whereas expectancies operating through subtle verbal or nonverbal cues would lead the investigator to control entirely different procedures.

Currently the most conservative practice would be to keep experimenters naive or "blind" with respect to the purpose of the experiment and to evaluate the extent to which this is accomplished. (The term *blind* is used to denote procedures in which the investigator, experimenter, and others [e.g., staff, assessors] are kept naive with respect to the hypotheses and alternative experimental or control conditions of the study. The term continues to be used in research. Because of confusion of the term with the loss of vision and the potential pejorative reference to that condition, terms other than blind [e.g., experimentally naive, masked conditions] are often preferred. The term has a well-established meaning, continues to have wide usage in research, and consequently is retained here.)

In medical research, keeping experimenters blind usually refers to not informing experimenters about which conditions or treatments subjects receive. For example, different drugs might be administered in coded capsule form. Although experimenters may be involved in the administration of the capsules, they are not informed about who receives the active drug (or which active drug) and who receives a placebo; moreover, they have no way of telling from the capsules themselves.

In psychological research, keeping the experimenters naive usually refers to withholding the hypotheses of the experiment. The experimenters who administer the different treatments cannot always be kept blind in the sense of not knowing who receives treatment or who receives one variation of treatment rather than another. Thus even though experimenters are not told about the hypotheses, they are likely to guess what the study is about and to make plausible estimates about those conditions that are likely to effect greater change. In treatment research, for example, therapists are likely to develop hypotheses about what treatments should produce more change than others and what treatments actually are control procedures for the investigation. The hypotheses that are developed may be quite similar across experimenters because of some of the obvious differences among treatments. Of course, whether the investigators' hypotheses are accurately guessed may depend on the complexity of the hypotheses (e.g., whether complex interactions among variables are predicted), the similarities among different conditions, and whether the individual experimenter has access to all the relevant information delineating treatments.

Even if experimenters are naive to begin with, the effects of the interventions may well develop expectancies and hypotheses that are fairly accurate. In drug research, for example, not telling experimenters what drug conditions are administered does not always really keep them blind. As the therapeutic effects or side effects of drugs become apparent, active drugs and placebos can often be identified. For example, in three studies comparing different drugs with a placebo for the treatment of hyperactive children, "blind" psychiatrists correctly identified between 96% and 100% of the patients receiving active drugs and between 80% and 90% of the patients receiving placebos (Weiss, Minde, Douglas, Werry, & Sykes, 1971). Thus the psychiatrists were hardy making random guesses about the conditions to which children were assigned.

In psychology experiments, it may be difficult to keep experimenters naive. For some experimental arrangements, it is possible that crucial aspects of the interventions might be administered by tape recorder or by experimenters who differ from those who are in charge of assessing the subject's performance. In this way, the experimenters who administer the conditions may not be naive but those who obtain the data from the subject are.

Obviously, it is especially important to keep those individuals in charge of data collection blind. Whether this is successfully accomplished can be determined empirically. A relatively simple procedure has been proposed to assess whether experimenters or observers (e.g., assessors in contact with the subject) are blind (Beatty, 1972). Specifically, observers are asked to guess which of the specific treatments subjects have received. If the observers guess among the available alternatives, the investigator can compare the frequency of correct identifications obtained with those expected by chance. If observers correctly identify a larger proportion than expected by chance, this suggests that they were not naive. If the observer can distinguish conditions, the bias and expectancies during assessment might well have influenced the results.

The above method of estimating whether experimenters can identify the conditions to which subjects are exposed does not solve the problem of keeping experimenters naive. However, it provides information that can greatly enhance the interpretation of the findings. At present, researchers routinely say that the experimenters are blind merely because they were not explicitly told what the hypotheses are. Whether experimenters are blind can be evaluated empirically. This may mean assessing the expectancies about the outcome of different conditions, or correctly identifying the conditions to which subjects are exposed, depending on the role of the experimenter. In either case, information about the actual expectations of the experimenters would be very useful.

Experimenter Characteristics

Nature of the Problem

Several different characteristics of the experimenters may influence subject behavior. Subject and demographic variables of the experimenters may interact with the independent variable or characteristic of the subjects to produce the results. Characteristics of the experimenter, such as age, gender, race, ethnic identity, level of anxiety, friendliness, and prestige, have been found to affect responses given by the subjects on self-report and projective tests, measures of intelligence, and various laboratory tasks (Barber, 1976; Johnson, 1976; Masling, 1960).

Under most circumstances the influence of experimenter characteristics may only restrict the external validity of the findings. Conceivably, the relation between the independent and dependent variables may hold up only with experimenters who have specific characteristics. In most experiments this is not likely to be a problem. Two or more experimenters may be used and run subjects across all conditions. The results can be analyzed to determine whether experimenters affected subjects differently. If no differences are obtained, this suggests that the results are not restricted to a particular characteristic of the experimenter. Of course, it is possible that all experimenters share a characteristic (e.g., all are college students) that contributes to the results. This possibility becomes less likely as the number of experimenters and the heterogeneity of experimenters increase and as the amount of interaction between the experimenter and subject in the experiment decreases.

Characteristics of the experimenter could threaten the construct validity of the results. This is possible where one experimenter administers one experimental condition and another experimenter administers another condition. When experimenters are perfectly confounded with conditions, the characteristics of the experiments rather than the independent variable may account for the pattern of results. The confounding of experimenters with conditions occasionally arises (e.g., Sloane et al., 1975) and raises the prospect that experimenter characteristics accounted for or contributed to group differences.

The characteristics of experimenters as a source of influence are not well studied in psychology in general. In clinical psychology, an important exception is research in psychotherapy where characteristics of persons who administer the interventions (therapists) are often studied (Beutler, Crago, & Arizmendi, 1986). A variety of therapist characteristics can play an important role in treatment outcome such as level of empathic understanding, amount of experience, degree of openness, and directiveness, to mention a few. Thus in the case of treatment delivery, therapist characteristics can make an important difference.

Recommendations

The range of experimenter attributes that may influence the results and the pervasiveness of this influence across experimental paradigms and areas of research are not known. Many tests of experimenter characteristics have been reported in interview, testing, or therapy situations in which the amount of interaction between subjects and experimenter is relatively great and where the subject may be placed in a situation where he or she might be evaluated. The literature would not seem to justify the potentially great experimental effort of routinely sampling a broad range of experimenter characteristics in an investigation. Experimenter characteristics are not easily balanced across conditions or groups in an experiment because so many different characteristics (e.g., sex, ethnicity, race, age) might easily be identified.

It would be useful if investigators more carefully specified the characteristics of experimenters in their reports of research. This would at least allow other investigators to examine their characteristics in subsequent research and to evaluate whether the characteristics are important for a particular area of inquiry. Also, many investigators could analyze for experimenter characteristics (e.g., therapist sex, experience) that might provide additional information about the generality of the results. If particular characteristics cannot be examined, data at least can and should be analyzed for differences among experimenters.

Data Recording, Analysis, and Fabrication

Nature of the Problems

Several different kinds of problems pertain to the data obtained in an experiment. These include making errors in recording or computing the data, analyzing select portions of the data, and fabricating or "fudging" the data. Errors in recording or calculating the data include inaccurately perceiving what the subject has done, arithmetic mistakes, errors in transposing data from one format to another (e.g., questionnaires to data sheets or computer files), and similar sources of distortion. These errors are not necessarily intentional or systematic.

Evaluation of recording and arithmetic errors across several studies has yielded a rate of approximately 1%. This refers to the percentage of data points incorrectly recorded or scored. Several studies have found that errors tend to be in the direction of the investigator's or experimenter's hypotheses (see Barber, 1976; Rosenthal, 1984). For example, in one study, experimenters made errors in adding scores of their subjects and most of these errors (75%) were in the direction of the expected findings (Lazlo & Rosenthal, 1971). Not all studies show that the errors are systematically in the direction of the investigator's hypotheses or that the errors would alter the conclusions (Rusch, Walker, & Greenwood, 1975). However, the directionality of the errors is not the point. Errors in scoring or calculating data obviously are important because they may lead the investigator to make unwarranted conclusions. Systematic errors in the data may alter the affirmative conclusions; unsystematic or random errors in the data may negate or obscure group differences because the errors add variability to the data.

The heavy reliance on computers might seem to aid in reducing computational errors. To be sure, there are obvious advantages in the use of computers in checking data and computing or transforming scores based on operations that previously would be completed by calculator or by hand. However, computers do not necessarily reduce data errors. Coding subjects incorrectly in reference to the experimental condition they received or to their sex, age, and other characteristics can be made easily by one or two numbers of entries in a data base. The fact that computers alone play a critical role in data entry, scoring of measures, and so on does not reduce the importance of checking the data. Hopefully, the benefit of computers is that they facilitate verification of the data because of the relative ease of entering the data independently on separate occasions and checking to ensure the numbers are correct.

It is likely that many investigators check their data, particularly data that depart from the expected findings. In fact, if data are not routinely checked, investigators are likely to assume that data supporting a hypothesis are accurate and are more likely to check data that are discrepant with a hypothesis. The biases resulting from selective checking are obvious and are likely to apply to published studies that have yielded data consistent with their predictions.

Biases in the data analyses may refer to a host of problems. Many of these problems stem from biased selection on the part of the investigator of those data that should be analyzed or reported. An investigator may select data from the experiment that appear most promising and subject them to extensive analyses. Alternatively, all of the data may be analyzed but only select portions are reported. The implication of these selective uses of the data is that the predicted results were achieved. The conclusions will be misleading because they fail to include all of the data and all of the analyses that were completed.

The problem may be relatively common when many different dependent measures are used and only a small number are reported. The reader of the published account of the investigation may not know that a particular percentage of the analyses would be expected to be statistically significant on the basis of "chance." Without knowing how many analyses are expected to be significant, the results might be attributed to nonchance differences. The percentage of statistically significant differences expected on the basis of chance often is much higher than the frequently cited 5% [for analyses conducted at the .05 level of confidence]. The percentage of chance differences may increase depending on the nature of the tests, independence of the sets of data included in the tests, and other factors, all of which are discussed in chapter 12.

A related issue pertains to the specific statistical tests and the implications their selection may have for the conclusions. Often the investigator has many choices of different methods of analyzing the data. The different analyses may lead to different conclusions. The different analyses do not refer to choosing between alternative statistical tests (e.g., analysis of variance or multiple regression), although the point applies here as well. Within a given type of analysis, changes in seemingly minor decisions can generate a different set of significant results and lead to different conclusions. The problem is exacerbated by the use of a fixed threshold calling effects statistically significant (i.e., $p. < .05$). As such, seemingly minor decisions such as adoption or alteration of default criteria in statistical software programs or the treatment of missing data within the analysis can alter the findings regarded as statistically significant. In using factor analysis to identify the internal structure of the scale, selecting among alternative multiple comparison tests to compare means, entering and deleting variables into discriminant functions to predict group status, using multivariate versus univariate analyses of variance, and conducting cluster analyses to identify typologies, to mention a few cases, require several decisions by the investigator. A bias can occur if the results are analyzed in several different ways and then selectively reported based on the pattern of statistically significant findings.

The selective reporting of data and data analyses has a broader manifestation. Many experiments are completed and yield findings that are not statistically significant. The results of such experiments usually are not reported but merely allocated to a file drawer. The *file drawer problem* (Rosenthal, 1979), as this is sometimes called, refers to the possibility that the published studies represent a biased sample of all studies that have been completed for a given hypothesis. Those that are published may be the ones that obtained statistical significance (i.e., the 5% at the $p < .05$ level). There may be many more studies, the other 95%, that did not attain significance. Methods can be used to estimate how many studies with no-difference findings would be needed to place reasonable doubt on a finding that has attained significance (see Rosenthal, 1984). Thus the bias can be addressed. For present purposes the broader point is critical, to wit, findings must be viewed in a broader context of other findings and other studies that attempt to replicate the research.

Certainly, the most misleading type of bias in data analysis is reporting fraudulent data. If the investigators have sole access to the data, systematic fudging on a large scale may be difficult to detect. Instances of making up the data instead of running the investigation or changing aspects of the results are difficult to detect. Many dramatic instances across diverse areas of scientific research have been documented (see Barber, 1976; Mahoney, 1976). Also, recent attention has focused on instances in which investigators report results that were not actually run or report results quite different from those actually obtained (e.g., National Academy of Sciences, 1989; US Congress, 1990). Efforts to monitor research and to underscore the responsibilities of the researcher to the broader scientific community are responses to such instances. We shall discuss this issue further in the context of ethical issues that guide research (chapter 14).

Some attention has been given to faking data on the part of the experimenter who actually runs the subjects. Research suggests that when experimenters have to run particularly difficult subjects or the experimental conditions cannot be easily administered, they may make up part or all of the data. For example, in one investigation, students were required to serve as experimenters in a project designed to verbally condition individuals in normal conversation (Azrin, Holz, Ulrich, & Goldiamond, 1961). Students were required to positively reinforce opinion statements of individuals in ordinary conversation outside of the laboratory by agreeing with such statements. The experiment could not be completed because subjects terminated conversations when an experimenter agreed with them. Yet students reported successfully obtaining the data. Several admitted to a confederate that they could not obtain the data unless they deviated from the procedures they were supposed to carry out. Others reported simply fabricating the data.

Recommendations

The recommendations for handling various biases that may enter into the data vary greatly depending on the precise source of error. Misrecording and miscalculating the data are relatively easily controlled, although they may be difficult and costly to eliminate entirely in very large data bases. Obviously, individuals who record the data should be kept uninformed of the experimental conditions so that the possibility of directional (biased) errors in favor of the hypotheses is removed. Scoring and entry of the data can include a variety of steps that may vary as a function of the nature of the data, such as whether the dependent measures (e.g., questionnaires) are scored by hand or by computer, whether data are entered directly from scored forms or are first entered onto data sheets, and so on.

The scoring of data and transposition to data sheets or computer should be checked at each stage. The very beginning step is ensuring that the subject has completed all the measures (e.g., all items, all assessments) and that the marks or subject responses can be unambiguously scored. Interim steps vary but are determined by places where error could reasonably enter the process. Checking of the data is a process that one can integrate into the routine activities of the research team, given that errors can be expected and need to be found and corrected. Eventually, the data are usually entered on computer files for analyses. Here editing of the data can be completed to check accuracy for the number of subjects in each condition, on each assessment occasion, and for each measure, whether the range of scores for a given measure represents a legitimate (i.e., possible) score, whether there are outliers, and so on.

Compulsive checking may be time-consuming, but it involves a relatively small cost considering the amount of time that goes into the planning and implementation of the experiment. If all of the data cannot be checked, certainly a generous proportion from all conditions should be randomly checked to provide an idea of whether errors occurred and what their influences on the results might be.

It is more difficult to address the problems of selectively reporting data or data analyses. Presumably, instructing investigators about the need to plan analyses in advance, conveying their responsibilities in the reporting of data and their analyses, and noting the consequences of selectively reporting data may help. Yet the problems here extend beyond the individual investigator. Publication practices continue to emphasize investigations that find statistically significant differences. The message is clearly conveyed to most investigators to find significance rather than to report whatever results come from their experiments. When significance is obtained for some dependent variables but not others, journal editors occasionally require authors to delete parts of their results that did not obtain significance. Also, the pressure for journal space may delete details and qualifications about the results such as different patterns across different analyses. The intent is to save journal space, but the effect is that the conclusions the readers may draw from the published report are greatly altered.

The problem of fudging is also difficult to control directly. The threat of expulsion from the scientific community and the strong demands for accurate reporting in science are likely to hold data fabrication in check (Barber, 1976; Snow, 1961). Cases of fudging may be difficult to detect if data are kept secret. Conveying the purposes and goals of research, modeling responsible practices in the training of reseachers, requiring investigators to make raw data available, and encouraging investigators to replicate each other's work are possible solutions. Probably one of the best checks is to replicate work that has been reported. This not only addresses the veridical nature of the findings but serves many other functions in the accumulation of scientific knowledge (see chapter 13).

DEMAND CHARACTERISTICS

Impact of the Cues of the Experiment

Demand characteristics, discussed in the context of construct validity, refer to cues in the experimental situation that may influence how subjects respond. Their significance derives from the possibility that these cues, rather than or in conjunction with the experimental manipulation, account for the pattern of results. The range of cues that may contribute to subject behavior is difficult to specify. Any facet of experimental behavior, the setting, experimental materials, and context of the research that are irrelevant conceptually to the variables of interest that might foster certain types of performance could contribute to demand characteristics.

Of course all experiments include multiple characteristics that are unique to the study. These cues do not necessarily contribute to demand characteristics. Those cues that are plausibly related to the pattern of results (e.g., differences between groups) and are confounded with the groups can be considered as demand characteristics. Demand characteristics may be a plausible rival interpretation of results attributed to a particular independent variable. For example, in the Orne and Scheibe (1964) study described earlier, the extraneous cues of sensory deprivation research were shown to lead to effects resembling those attributed to diminished sensory input. The nature of the research area allowed for a rather clear separation of the extraneous cues and the independent variable.

In many areas of research, the independent variable may include cues that cannot be so easily separated from the portion of the variable that is considered crucial. Whether demand characteristics are germane may partially be a function of the conceptualization of the independent variable. Different variations of treatment or levels of an independent variable may necessarily require different cues and hence be intertwined with different demand characteristics. The cues that may give subjects hints on how to perform may not be conceived of as extraneous but as part and parcel of the manipulation itself. In such cases, it is not particularly meaningful to say that demand characteristics accounted for the results.

For example, in psychotherapy research the intervention usually carries with it a strong expectation for the desired change on the part of the subject. Many of the cues associated with treatment may lead subjects to expect change. These cues are not always alterable. Of course, subjects can be given an instructional set that attempts to negate the implicit expectancy. For example, subjects might be told not to expect change at all or not until a particular time elapses. Yet other cues of treatment (e.g., individual treatment sessions, focus on a problem) may make it impossible to eliminate demand from treatment.

Evaluation of Demand Characteristics

In an investigation, there may be special cues associated with the experimental condition or cues may vary greatly between different conditions. Special equipment or arrangements (e.g., unusual activities) that vary across conditions would be examples. If it is plausible or perhaps conceivable that differences in these cues could affect the dependent measures in systematic ways, the role of demand characteristics may be worth evaluating.

Three procedures have been suggested to evaluate the influence of demand characteristics (Orne, 1969). These techniques assess whether the cues of the experimental situation alone would lead to performance in the direction associated with the independent variable. If the cues of the situation do not lead subjects to perform in any way that they would when exposed to the experimental manipulation, this suggests that demand characteristics do not account for the results.

Postexperimental Inquiry

One method of estimating whether demand characteristics account for the results is to assess whether subjects are aware of the purpose of the experiment and the performance that is expected of them. This is referred to as a *postexperimental inquiry* and is accomplished by asking the subjects after the experiment what their perceptions are about the purpose of the experiment, what the experimenter expected from them, and how subjects were supposed to respond. Presumably, if subjects are aware of the purpose of the experiment and the performance expected of them, they can more readily comply with the demands of performance. Hence their responses may be more a function of their information about the experiment than of the manipulation itself.

The postexperimental inquiry of subjects may convey useful information but has unique restrictions. The inquiry may generate its own set of demands to subjects who will not tell all they know or feign their motivation for responding. Also, subjects may not have perceived the demand characteristics but still have responded to them in the experiment. The cues of the experiment that dictate performance may be subtle and depend on behaviors of the experimenter or seemingly irrelevant procedures. The subject may not necessarily integrate all of these and be able to verbalize their net effect. Even if the subjects respond in a way that indicates awareness of the purpose of the experiment, it is possible that the inquiry itself, rather than the experiment, stimulated this awareness. The questions may stimulate insights that were not present while they were responding to the manipulation.

The overall limitation of the postexperimental inquiry is that it does not prevent or anticipate the operation of demand characteristics. Measuring the influence of bias is useful but inferior to identifying bias and preventing or minimizing its influence in advance of the study. Other strategies for evaluating demand characteristics are more appropriately suited to these latter goals.

Preinquiry

Another technique for evaluating the demand characteristics of an experiment is the *preinquiry*. This technique is referred to as a preinquiry or nonexperiment because subjects are not actually run through the procedures in the usual way (Orne, 1969). Rather, subjects are asked to imagine themselves in the situation to which subjects would be exposed. These subjects may see the equipment that will be used, hear the rationale or instructions that will be provided, and receive all of the information that will be presented to the subject short of actually going through the procedures. Essentially, the procedures are explained but not administered. After exposing the subject to the explanations of the procedures and the materials to be used in an experiment, the subjects are asked to complete the assessment devices as if they actually had been exposed to the intervention. The task is to respond as subjects would who experienced the procedures.

The preinquiry assesses the extent to which the cues of the experimental setting and the specific experimental condition can generate certain kinds of responses. Differences among experimental conditions suggest the direction in which demand influences may operate. Preinquiry research can inform the investigator in advance of conducting further investigations whether demand characteristics operate in the direction of expected results derived from actually running the subjects.

Preinquiry data also may be useful when compared with data from actually conducting the investigation and running subjects through the procedures. If the preinquiry data and experimental data are dissimilar, this suggests that the cues of the experimental situation alone are not likely to explain the findings obtained from actually being exposed to treatment. If the preinquiry data and experimental data are similar, this makes the influence of demand characteristics a potential explanation of the results and something to be considered or controlled for in subsequent research. The fact that preinquiry and experimental data are similar does not mean that demand characteristics were responsible for change in the subjects. The independent variable may produce veridical changes similar to those associated with demand characteristics alone. Thus preinquiry information is especially useful when it provides data that are discrepant from data derived from actually completing the investigation.

Simulators

Another method for examining demand characteristics is to use *simulators.* Subjects who serve as simulators are asked to act *as if* they received the experimental condition or intervention even though they actually do not. These simulators are then run through the assessment procedures of the investigation by an experimenter who is "blind" as to who is a simulator and who is a real subject (i.e., a subject run through the procedures). Simulators are instructed to guess what real subjects might do who are exposed to the intervention and then to deceive a "blind" experimenter. If simulators can act as real subjects on the assessment devices, this means that demand characteristics could account for the results. As noted with the preinquiry data, correspondence in the data does not mean that demand characteristics are responsible for the results. If the data do not correspond, it suggests that simulators apparently were unable to derive the demand characteristics of the actual conditions or to act consistently with these characteristics in the expected direction.

General Comments

If data from postinquiry, preinquiry, or simulators and from real subjects who completed the experiment are similar, the data are *consistent* with a demand-characteristics interpretation. The consistency does not mean that demand characteristics account for the results. Both demand characteristics and the actual effects of the independent variable may operate in the same direction. The consistency raises issues for construct validity and interpretation of the basis for the findings. If the data from evaluation of demand characteristics and real subjects do not correspond, this suggests that the cues of the situation do not lead to the same kinds of effects as actually running the subjects. Yet even here there is some ambiguity. Being exposed to an explanation of treatment (as in preinquiry or simulator techniques) is not the same as actually undergoing treatment and could generate different demand characteristics. Thus differences between these subjects do not completely rule out demand characteristics.

Efforts to evaluate the role of demand characteristics are to be actively encouraged if demand is a plausible and conceptually interesting or important threat to construct validity. If demand characteristics generate results different from those generated by subjects who completed the experimental conditions, interpretation of the findings can be clarified. If demand characteristics can threaten construct validity, it is useful to design experiments so that merely exposing subjects to the cues (irrelevancies) of the experiment is not plausible as an explanation of the results. This can be accomplished by controlling or holding fairly constant all of the cues or designing experiments so the predicted results are counterintuitive, that is, they go in a direction opposite from what experimental demands would suggest.

SUBJECT ROLES

Demand characteristics draw attention to the cues of the experiment that may influence subject behavior. Subjects are assumed to respond to these cues in such a way as to give the experimenter what he or she wants in the way of results. Yet exposure of subjects to a particular set of cues does not invariably result in certain responses. The discussion of demand characteristics glosses over the fact that subjects may interpret cues differently and respond as a function of their own perceptions and purposes rather than the purposes of the investigator.

Alternative Roles

Subjects may adopt different ways of responding to the experimental cues of the experiment. These different ways of responding are referred to generally as *subject roles* and reflect how the subject intends to respond to the task or problem of the experiment. Several different roles have been distinguished in the social psychological literature including the good, negativistic, faithful, and apprehensive subject roles (see Greenberg & Folger, 1988; Weber & Cook, 1972).

The *good subject role* refers to the attempt of subjects to provide responses in the experiment that will corroborate the investigator's hypotheses. This role may reflect a subject's concern that his or her responses provide information that is useful to science. To adopt this role, the subject must identify the hypotheses and then act in a fashion that would be consistent with these hypotheses.

The *negativistic subject role* refers to the attempt to refute or inform the investigator's hypotheses. The negativistic subject is assumed to provide evidence for some alternative, perhaps opposing, hypothesis or to provide information that will be of no use. This role may result from the subject's concern over being controlled, predictable, or in a position where he or she is somehow forced to respond.

The *faithful subject role* refers to the attempt of subjects to follow carefully the experimental instructions and to avoid acting on the basis of any suspicions that they might have about the actual purpose of the investigation. This role may be performed passively if subjects apathetically follow the instructions of the experiment or actively if subjects are highly motivated to help science and take special care in not letting their suspicions or preconceptions enter into their responses.

The final role is the *apprehensive subject role,* which is adopted when subjects are concerned that their performance will be used to evaluate their abilities, personal characteristics (e.g., adjustment), or opportunities (e.g., employment). Subjects often are motivated to present themselves favorably to psychologists, who presumably are regarded as experts in evaluating psychological adjustment and other characteristics (Rosenberg, 1969). When subjects respond in a socially desirable fashion and hence place themselves in a desirable light, such responding may reflect the apprehensive subject role.

The adoption and impact of different subject roles have been difficult to evaluate in part because the different roles can lead to similar predictions in how subjects will behave. Also, subjects often need information (e.g., knowledge of the experimenter's hypothesis) to enact a particular role. Studies rarely provide evidence that this condition is met (see Greenberg & Folger, 1988). Among the roles most likely to be relevant in clinical psychology is the apprehensive subject role. Subjects frequently attempt to place themselves in a desirable light. Adoption of the apprehensive role might be expected given the stereotypes and suspicions that subjects have about research. Research may foster the apprehensive role if subjects assume the focus is designed to assess psychological adjustment and psychopathology. Indeed, telling subjects that the experiment is related to clinical psychology and determining responses that are "normal" elevates the apprehensiveness of the subject and further evokes apprehensive role behavior (Rosenberg, 1969).

Subject roles can threaten the validity of an experiment in different ways. If roles are likely to vary systematically with conditions, the construct validity of the study may be threatened. If a particular condition fosters diverse roles, variability of performance among the subjects may be increased and threaten statistical conclusion validity. External validity might be threatened if the results only apply to subjects who adopt a particular role. The influence of subject roles may restrict the generality of experimental findings in some research areas more than others. For example, areas such as persuasion and attitude change may be especially vulnerable to subject roles as a threat to external validity (Weber & Cook, 1972). Subject roles apparent in these experimental situations may differ from the set of the subject in everyday life. The subject in an experiment may be exposed to persuasive appeals and statements that could easily be avoided or terminated early in everyday life. In general, the influence of subject roles on the external validity of experimental results is not well studied.

Minimizing the Influence of Subject Roles

Several different procedures might be implemented to minimize the influence of subject roles in an experiment. Perhaps the greatest attention should be paid to the apprehensive subject role because evidence suggests this is the most pervasive role that subjects select. If subjects are apprehensive that their behavior is to be evaluated, attempts might be made to reduce these concerns. Precisely how this is accomplished might be a function of the particular goals of the experiment. As a general guideline, the procedures may assure the subjects that their performance will not be used to infer psychological adjustment or mental health. It may be useful to convey that their responses will be valuable and important no matter what they are. Essentially, subjects can be assured that there are no right or wrong answers or that some responses are not more appropriate than others. In practice, this may be difficult to convey to subjects if the questions included in the measures (e.g., about the presence of deviant behaviors) arouse apprehensiveness about being evaluated.

Any inducements for performance normally included as part of the experiment, such as money or course credits, might be given prior to the subject performance. Subjects otherwise might believe that the rewards for participating in some way depend on how well they do or the impression they convey. Despite disclaimers at the beginning of an experimental session, subjects occasionally associate the rewards for participating in the session with how well they perform.

Apprehensiveness may be minimized by conveying to subjects that their responses are anonymous and confidential. Presumably, subjects who believe that their responses cannot be identified are less motivated to convey a specific image. In addition, feedback from the experimenter about how well subjects are doing should be minimized. The feedback, unless part of the independent variable, conveys the responses that are highly valued and provides guidelines on how subjects are to perform if they wish to appear in a favorable light.

Subject roles might be minimized by ensuring that the subjects do not perceive the hypotheses of the experiment. Research has shown that when subjects know what the hypotheses are (e.g., by speaking to a confederate or receiving the hypotheses as part of the procedures), their responses may be altered (see Weber & Cook, 1972). Subjects are less readily able to respond in a manner consistent with the role they may have adopted if they are unaware of the specific hypotheses.

Ideally, an experiment should be designed so that the hypotheses are difficult to discern. The less obvious the hypotheses, the less likely it is that subjects will be able to respond in a biased fashion to support or refute the hypotheses. At one extreme, the hypotheses may involve complex interactions among different variables in a factorial design; at the other, a single treatment group may be compared to a waiting-list control group. Subjects in these different types of experiments are likely to vary in their accuracy in guessing the expected results from the conditions to which they are assigned.

One alternative to minimizing the influence of subject roles is to assess these roles as part of the experiment. A postexperimental inquiry, as discussed earlier, might reveal whether subjects were aware of the hypotheses, whether they wished to cooperate, whether they were concerned about being evaluated, and so on. Postexperimental inquiries must be interpreted cautiously because they may generate their own subject roles, and thus the motives operative during the experiment itself may be obscured.

Subjects might always be said to have some role or specific reaction to the experiment. An exception would be when they do not realize they are participating as in the evaluation of archival records. In studies when subjects are aware of their participation, the experimenter may wish to foster a set that encourages candid and honest responding. The task is to convey to subjects that their participation and responses, rather than the direction of the results, are critical. This response set may be conveyed explicitly by the experimenter to the subjects. The set may be equally important to convey from investigator to experimenter, namely, that accurate information rather than support for a specific hypothesis is critical.

SUBJECT-SELECTION BIASES

Subject-selection biases refers to influences attributable to types of subjects who participate in experiments. Different selection biases may operate at different points in the experiment beginning with the type of person who is recruited for participation and ending with those who finally complete the experiment. Two major sources of selection biases are the use of alternative samples and the loss of subjects during an experiment.

Alternative Samples

Nature of the Problem

A pervasive concern about psychological research is the restricted range of subject populations that are sampled. A frequent criticism of psychological research is that experiments on humans rely very heavily on college students, particularly students enrolled in psychology courses. Typically, students are enticed into participation in an experiment by receiving credit toward an undergraduate psychology course, monetary incentives, or by being solicited as volunteers by experimenters who circulate among psychology classes. An issue of concern is whether the findings obtained with college students will generalize to other samples of subjects. As mentioned in the discussion of external validity, the issue may be significant in areas of clinical research. For example, psychotherapy research has occasionally used student samples whose subject and demographic characteristics and types and severity of dysfunction depart from those of persons who are referred for treatment. The generality of findings of such samples to people who are referred for treatment might plausibly be challenged.

Apart from college students, occasionally there is concern about the using of *samples of convenience.* This refers to the selection and use of subjects merely because they are available. Obviously, a sample of subjects must be available to be included in a study. However, occasionally subjects are included without a clear rationale of why they were selected. Sometimes subjects are selected because they are present in a convenient situation (e.g., waiting room, hospital ward) or are available for a quite different purpose (e.g., participation in another experiment that requires a special population). An investigator may use an available sample to test a particular idea or to evaluate a measure he or she has just developed. The use of a highly specialized population that is selected merely because it is convenient raises concern. The specialized population and the factors that make them particularly convenient may have implications for generalizing the results.

A more pervasive way of delineating subjects that could lead to selection biases has to do with volunteer status. In most psychological research, subjects are volunteers in some sense. Informed consent procedures require subjects to agree to participate voluntarily, rather than to participate under duress of any kind. One can define volunteer status in a more restricted sense. From a large group of available subjects (e.g., college students, samples of convenience, community members), participants may be solicited through newspapers, notes posted on kiosks on college campuses, and public radio or television announcements. Some individuals agree to serve (volunteers) and participate in the study; others do not (nonvolunteers). The subjects determine whether they will participate. The possibility that those who volunteer to participate may differ in important ways from those who do not can restrict the generality of experimental findings.

Obviously, an important question is whether volunteer subjects differ in any important ways from nonvolunteer subjects. Considerable research has been conducted comparing individuals who volunteer to participate with those nonvolunteers whose responses can also be assessed within the experiment (e.g., through routine administration of test batteries, or by pursuing contact with nonvolunteers to induce their participation). Several variables have been related to volunteering for experiments. Major variables and their relation to volunteering are listed in Table 11.1. The literature is equivocal in many areas and, no doubt, the impact of volunteer status may vary greatly among areas of research and type of experiment. For most purposes, it is important to note that sufficient evidence is available indicating that individuals who volunteer for psychological experiments differ on a number of dimensions from nonvolunteers. Thus findings obtained with volunteer subjects may be limited in their generality across certain subject characteristics.

Recommendations

Perhaps the most obvious recommendation that might be made is to increase the range of people from among whom volunteers are sought. Certainly, as behavioral scientists, psychologists should be able to devise techniques to encourage individuals to volunteer when solicitations are made. More intense efforts at recruiting presumably would bring into experiments individuals who would not usually volunteer. Also, better understanding of the determinants of subject participation may be helpful. Many variables known to influence the rate of volunteering have been identified such as aversiveness of the task, the magnitude of incentives for participation, apparent importance of the subject's participation to the experimenter, and others. Structuring the situation so that the research actively fosters greater participation and serves a need or interest of the subjects is likely to increase the rate of volunteering.

The differences between volunteers and nonvolunteers do not necessarily restrict the generality of the results obtained with volunteer subjects. It is likely that some findings are not influenced by whether subjects were volunteers and

Table 11.1. Relation Between Subject, Demographic, and Personality Variables and Volunteering for Experiments

VARIABLE[a]	VOLUNTEERS, RELATIVE TO NONVOLUNTEERS, TEND TO . . .
1. Education	. . . be better educated
2. Socioeconomic Status	. . . have higher occupational status
3. Intelligence	. . . be higher in intelligence
4. Need for Approval	. . . be higher in the need for social approval
5. Sociability	. . . be more social
6. Arousal Seeking	. . . seek out more sources of stimulation
7. Conventionality	. . . be less conventional in their behavior
8. Sex	. . . be female
9. Authoritarianism	. . . be less authoritarian
10. Religious Affiliation	. . . be Jewish more likely than Protestant and Protestant more likely than Catholic
11. Conformity	. . . be less conforming
12. Town of Origin	. . . be from a smaller town
13. Religiosity	. . . be more interested in religion
14. Altruism	. . . be more altruistic
15. Self-Disclosure	. . . be more self-disclosing by providing information about their beliefs, aspirations, and preferences
16. Adjustment	. . . be more maladjusted when volunteering for unusual situations
17. Age	. . . be younger

[a]The variables are ordered according to the confidence that has been placed in the relation indicated based on current evidence (Rosenthal & Rosnow, 1975). The material presented here serves as a guideline; volunteer status and its correlates can vary as a function of the type of task and experiment.

other findings are influenced in varying degrees. In cases where findings are influenced by the volunteer status of the subjects, the research conclusions may merely vary in terms of the magnitude of performance on the dependent variables. For other findings, the volunteers may behave in a diametrically opposed fashion to nonvolunteer subjects. Experiments are required to assess the extent to which external validity is jeopardized across independent and dependent variables and experimental arrangements and tasks.

There are situations in clinical work in which volunteer status can be readily studied. For example, in treatment and institutional programs, occasionally within the same program some people vary in the "volunteeriness" of their participation (e.g., self-referred for treatment, court referred). The difficulty in evaluating volunteer status is that it often covaries with other characteristics (e.g., such as clinical problems, demographic variables). In laboratory research, volunteers might be examined and compared with people who initially did not volunteer. Further attempts to recruit these latter subjects would provide an opportunity to evaluate the impact of volunteer status on the measures of interest.

In general, the plausibility and relevance of volunteer status in contributing to the results must be considered for the individual research area. The concern emerges in those circumstances where the investigator draws sweeping conclusions about the effect of a manipulation without acknowledging that how subjects were recruited might well contribute to generality of the findings. In advance of information about the generality of findings with volunteer subjects, it is essential to specify how subjects are recruited and any factors that may operate to select some subjects over others. In treatment research, selection factors often refer to screening requirements used to select clients who are reasonably homogeneous (e.g., with respect to psychiatric diagnosis). In experimental research, variables related to subject selection such as year or major in college, circumstances of solicitation, and others might warrant specification because they may relate to who volunteers to participate and who does not. If recruitment and subject-selection practices relate to the results, the failure of findings to be replicated among separate studies may be accounted for by these variables.

Attrition

Nature of the Problem

Whether subjects volunteer for research constitutes a potential selection bias that operates prior to the experiment. Yet there is a continuation of the selection process during the experiment. If assessment of subject behavior is important after the experiment, as in the case of follow-up assessment, the selection process goes on even further.

The loss of subjects during the course of an investigation can affect virtually all facets of experimental validity by altering random composition of the groups and group equivalence (internal validity), limiting the generality of findings to those subjects who are persistent (external validity), by raising the prospect that the intervention combined with special subject characteristics account for conclusions the investigator would like to attribute to the intervention (external and construct validity), and by reducing sample size and power (statistical conclusion validity).

In laboratory research with one or two sessions to complete the experiment, loss of subjects is not likely to be a major problem. In clinical research in the context of treatment, prevention, and longitudinal studies, loss of subjects is common. In psychotherapy research attrition has been the subject of considerable study and hence offers examples of some of the major problems.

First and most obvious, subjects who drop out of an investigation are likely to differ from those who remain in the study. Dropouts may differ on a range of variables (e.g., type, severity, or chronicity of dysfunction, family history, past treatment experiences) that could interact with the intervention. Conclusions about the effect of treatment may be restricted to a highly select group, depending on the proportion of subjects lost.

Second, it is possible that people drop out from separate groups within the study and that characteristics of these individuals vary among the separate groups. That is, the people who drop out from one condition may differ systematically from those who drop out from another condition. For example, if 5 subjects drop out of a psychotherapy condition and 5 other subjects in the study drop out of a medication condition, it is not necessarily the case that these people are "the same." There may be systematic differences in the conditions leading to attrition in ways that affect different types of people. Perhaps, those psychotherapy subjects who did not wish to chat about their past and never considered their therapists to be like a father (transference) tired of psychotherapy and left; those medication subjects who were discomforted by a dry mouth and heart palpitations (side effects) may have quit their treatment. The subjects remaining in each of the groups and included in statistical comparisons may be different kinds of subjects in terms of subject, demographic, and personality characteristics; this cannot be easily tested given the small sample sizes and absence of available information on a vast range of possible differences in these characteristics. Usually, the number of attrition cases is too small to compare groups in a statistically sensitive way. Indeed, investigators may show no statistically significant differences between dropouts from two or more groups. This could provide illusory comfort that attrition did not lead to any selection biases that would favor one group.

Third, the number of subjects who drop out may vary significantly between or among groups. For example, in a classic study of cognitive therapy, this form of treatment was shown to be superior in reducing depression in adults when compared to medication (imipramine; Rush et al., 1977). Interestingly, medication led to a significantly larger number of cases leaving treatment before posttreatment assessment. Differential attrition across groups itself is an interesting outcome and may say something important about treatment conditions. Treatments that generate relatively high attrition rates may be relatively aversive, place special demands on the clients, have untoward side effects, or perhaps simply not work. In the case of this study, differential attrition between the two treatment groups clearly raises questions for all comparisons at posttreatment. Were the two treatments differentially effective on measures of depression or were group differences due to differential selection? The question is not easily resolved.

Finally, it is possible that so many cases drop out that valid conclusions about treatment cannot be made. For example, in one large-scale investigation noted earlier, youths (N = 450) received one of three treatment or control conditions designed to reduce antisocial behavior (Feldman et al., 1983). The design evaluated several factors (therapist experience, type of treatment, type of group) in a factorial design (2 × 3 × 3, or 18 groups). A 1-year follow-up was conducted. Almost 90% of the cases (396 of 450) who completed treatment were lost 1 year later. The small sample (n = 54) divided among the set of experimental conditions precluded evaluation of the effects of treatment. The loss of a large number of studies in intervention research is not at all rare. Upwards of 50% of cases who begin treatment may drop out (e.g., Pekarik & Stephenson, 1988; Vaile-Val, Rosenthal, Curtiss, & Marohn, 1984). In such cases, selection biases are readily plausible. Also, the large number of lost cases has dire consequences for sample sizes and hence statistical conclusion validity. Studies of treatment in clinical research usually begin with samples that are relatively small (see Kazdin & Bass, 1989; Rossi, 1990). Attrition further weakens the sensitivity of statistical tests.

The problem of subjects dropping out or terminating their participation may be exacerbated greatly by investigators. Investigators may use subjects who drop out in such a way as to obfuscate further the conclusions that might be drawn by reassigning subjects to conditions in the investigation on the basis of whether they have dropped out. For example, in one study the goal was to improve studying and grades of college students (Beneke & Harris, 1972). A behavioral program was administered either individually or in groups and involved incentives and training in study skills. Because it generally is useful to know what changes occur without treatment, the authors wanted to have a no-treatment group. Subjects were not assigned to this control group in the usual fashion.

At the beginning of treatment, a substantial percentage of subjects (15 of 53, or 28%) dropped out of the program after the initial meeting. The authors decided to use these subjects as a no-treatment control group since they did not receive treatment. As might be expected, treatment subjects improved in their course grades in the semesters after training significantly more than did no-treatment subject. (There were no differences between the individual and group methods of providing treatment.) Ordinarily, differences among treatment groups and a no-treatment control group would be readily interpretable. However, the use of subjects who dropped out of the program as the control group obfuscates any conclusions about treatment. It is not clear whether treated subjects would have improved to a greater extent than did control subjects who had been assigned randomly to a no-treatment condition at the inception of the study.

In general, attrition can create many different problems for an investigator. The conclusions that can be drawn tend to be restricted even further if those subjects who are lost are reassigned to some conditions within the experiment. The assumption that lost subjects are no different from those who continue along important subject variables can be easily challenged (see Flick, 1988; Gould, Shaffer, & Kaplan, 1985). Threats to internal validity become plausible as rival hypotheses in explaining group differences or the absence of differences.

Recommendations

There are several options available to address the problem of attrition. Special orientation (pretreatment) interviews, various mailings during the course of treatment, reminders and methods of scheduling appointments, and monetary incentives have been effective (see Baekeland & Lundwall, 1975; Flick, 1988). For example, a frequently used technique to decrease attrition in treatment research is to request that clients provide a deposit that will be refunded after treatment. Clients are told that the deposit will be refunded if they attend all or a specified percentage of sessions. Requesting and holding a deposit has been found to reduce attrition, and larger deposits (e.g., $20.00) have been more effective in this regard than smaller ones (e.g., $5.00; Hagen, Foreyt, & Durham, 1976). The use of a deposit has its own problems. For one thing, it may actually be or be viewed by clients, investigators, or research evaluation committees as a form of coercion. On the other hand, it may be reasonable to ask clients at the beginning of treatment to make a commitment to participate. If services are rendered as part of the study, a deposit from clients may be acceptable to all parties.

Another strategy for minimizing attrition is to identify variables correlated with attrition and utilize the information to decide who participates in subsequent research. For example, in a study of antisocial children seen for outpatient treatment, a few variables (number of child symptoms of antisocial behavior, level of stress of the mother, and family socioeconomic disadvantage) reliably predicted who remained in and who dropped out of treatment (Kazdin, 1990). From this type of information, one might identify cutoff scores or a profile of families at risk for attrition and use this as the basis for selecting clients for research. Such a strategy raises other compromises. With more stringent selection, a larger number of subjects will need to be recruited and screened. Also, there may be greater restrictions on the generality of the results with more exclusions.

An additional and perhaps wiser strategy is to devise specific procedures to combat attrition and to evaluate the efficacy of such procedures. For example, in one study intervention techniques were developed for families of adolescent drug users to increase participation in treatment (Szapocznik et al., 1988). Special pretreatment and early treatment contacts designed to foster alliances with the family increased entry into treatment and reduced attrition.

Attrition is likely to occur in studies that extend beyond more than one or a few sessions. In studies of several months or years, researchers understand at the outset that attrition will occur. Several statistical approaches to attrition have been developed and provide useful strategies to complement active efforts to minimize attrition. Statistical approaches utilize existing data (e.g., the last available data point) from cases who drop out and utilize other data in the study to estimate what the lost data might reflect. These methods allow researchers to identify the likely bias that attrition introduces into the data and the conclusions that would be warranted if the lost subjects had improved, remained the same, or became worse (see Flick, 1988; Howard, Krause, & Orlinsky, 1986; Little & Rubin, 1987).

SUMMARY AND CONCLUSIONS

Sources of artifact and bias in an experiment are a function of what the investigator is interested in studying. Extraneous factors that may account for the results may be viewed as artifacts and threaten each type of experimental validity. Major sources of artifact include biases stemming from those who conduct research, demand characteristics, subject roles, and subject selection.

Artifacts and biases may derive from the investigator (who designs the experiment) as well as the experimenter (who actually runs the subjects). The results may be influenced by the investigator's failure to specify the rationales, scripts, and procedures of the experiment, by the experimenter's failure to implement these consistently, by the experimenter's expectancies and characteristics, and by errors resulting from recording, analyzing, and even fabricating the data.

Another source of artifact consists of *demand characteristics,* which are defined as characteristics of the experimental situation that may influence the subjects' performance. Demand characteristics include all extraneous cues that convey to subjects how they should perform in the experiment. Techniques for assessing the potential influence of demand characteristics include the *postexperimental inquiry,* the *preinquiry,* and the use of *simulators.*

Demand characteristics draw attention to the cues of the experiment that influence subject behavior. Subjects are assumed to respond to these cues in a uniform fashion. However, subjects may react differently to cues of the situation. Four different styles of responding to the experiment have been identified and referred to as *subject roles.* They include the good, negativistic, faithful, and apprehensive subject roles. Evidence suggests that subjects are most likely to be concerned with evaluation of their performance in an experiment and hence adopt the apprehensive subject role. Adoption of subject roles can be minimized by attempting to reduce subject concern about being evaluated, dissociating any inducements for participation in the experiment with the results or responses that the subject produces, informing subjects that their responses are confidential and anonymous, and keeping subjects "blind" about the specific hypotheses.

Subject-selection biases encompass different types of considerations. The use or overuse of specific populations (e.g., college students), samples selected merely because they are available (samples of convenience), and persons who are asked to volunteer often raise general concerns of generality of the results (external validity). Selection biases arouse greater concerns when groups may differ in composition. Attrition or premature termination from the investigation raises special problems. Differential attrition in terms of number of types of cases may lead to bias in groups that can threaten each type of experimental validity.

FOR FURTHER READING

Greenberg, J., & Folger, R. (1988). *Controversial issues in social research methods.* New York: Springer-Verlag.

Kruglanski, A.W. (1975). The human subject in the psychology experiment: Fact and artifact. In L. Berkowitz (Ed.), *Advances in experimental social psychology* (Vol. 8). Orlando, FL: Academic Press.

Rosenthal, R., & Rosnow, R.L. (1969). *Artifact in behavioral research.* New York: Academic Press.

Rosenthal, R., & Rosnow, R.L. (1975). *The volunteer subject.* New York: John Wiley & Sons.

Chapter 12

ALTERNATIVE METHODS OF DATA EVALUATION

Evaluating and interpreting results of an experiment raise all sorts of methodological issues. Already discussed was the notion of statistical conclusion validity and selected factors in the design and quantitative evaluation that can impede drawing valid inferences. Statistical evaluation encompasses broad issues such as the utility or value of statistical tests and more focused concerns such as which tests, among alternatives, are appropriate.

In psychological research, data from an investigation typically are evaluated by statistical methods. Journals in clinical psychology and other areas of the field consistently illustrate the application of statistical analysis as the method of data evaluation. But statistical analyses, however important, have some limitations as a general method of evaluation that need to be put in perspective. Moreover, in clinical psychology, other methods of evaluating data are especially important. The present chapter considers methods of data evaluation, including statistical, nonstatistical, and clinical methods.

STATISTICAL EVALUATION

The general characteristics of statistical evaluation are sufficiently clear to most individuals that they need not be elaborated. Essentially, in most research, statistical evaluation examines whether groups receiving different conditions can be distinguished statistically on the dependent measure(s). Statistical evaluation consists of applying a test to assess whether the difference obtained on the dependent measure in likely to have occurred by "chance." Typically, a level of confidence (such as .05 or .01) is selected as the criterion for determining whether the results are statistically significant. The difference between groups on the dependent measure is evaluated with a statistical test that yields a probability value. A statistically significant difference indicates that the probability level is equal to or below the level of confidence selected, for example, $p < .05$. That is, the probability is .05 or some other value lower than that (e.g., .03). This means that if the experiment were completed 100 times, a difference of the magnitude found in the experiment would be likely to occur only five times on a purely chance basis. If the probability obtained in the study is lower than .05, most researchers would concede that group differences probably were *not* the result of chance but reflected a genuine relation between the independent and dependent variables.

To state that a relation in an experiment is statistically significant does not mean that there is necessarily a genuine relation between the variables studied. Even a statistically significant difference could be the result of a chance event. Chance is the one rival hypothesis that can never be completely ruled out. There may be no relation between the variables in reality but a statistically significant difference in the experiment because of sampling of subjects and other factors. Nevertheless, by tradition, researchers have agreed that when the probability yielded by a statistical test is as low as .05 or .01, that is a sufficiently conservative level of confidence to permit one to conclude that there probably is a relation between the independent and dependent variables.

Essentially, statistical evaluation provides a criterion to separate probably veridical from possibly chance effects. Although subjectivity and bias can enter into the process of statistical evaluation, for example, in terms of the tests that are applied and the criteria for statistical significance, the goal of statistics is to provide a *relatively* bias-free and consistent method of interpreting results. The prevalent use of statistics does not imply that agreement on their value is universal. Diverse facets of statistical evaluation have been challenged including the arbitrary criterion that a particular confidence level such as $p < .05$ represents the all-or-none decision making reached based on that criterion, the absence of information regarding the strength or practical value of the relation whether or not statistical significance is attained, and the likelihood that the null hypothesis upon which tests are based is never really true (Chow, 1988; Kupfersmid, 1988; Meehl, 1978).

Debates are extremely valuable because they draw attention to the limits of central features of the scientific enterprise and foster diversity of evaluative methods and techniques. Also, criticism of prevalent methods of statistical evaluation has helped spawn alternative means of evaluation other than null hypothesis testing. However, hypothesis testing and statistical evaluation to detect relations among variables dominate current research. Although the reliance on statistical evaluation is often lamented, the methods provide fairly consistent criteria for determining whether an effect is to be considered as veridical. This advantage is critically important.

Consider the fundamental value of a consistent criterion. Consider, for example, the development of a "new" therapy technique in clinical work. It is likely that a proponent of the new therapy will allege that therapeutic effects are produced and that the effects are superior to those produced by other treatments. In more experimentally based terms, the new treatment is proposed to be one that will produce greater change than no-treatment or other control conditions. Claims for effective treatment, for example, for facilitating dieting or reducing cigarette smoking, as advocated in trade books and magazine articles are rarely based on experimental methods and statistical criteria. Testimonials by proponents of the technique or those who have participated in the program serve as the basis for evaluation. It would be valuable in these cases to apply experimental methods and to evaluate the results statistically.

Statistics provide a tool to help separate veridical effects from those that might have occurred by chance. Endorsement of statistical evaluation does not mean that statistics provide "the answer," "real truth," and so on. Statistical evaluation is subject to all sorts of abuses, ambiguities, and misinterpretation. Alternative methods of analyzing the same data can lead to different conclusions, even with seemingly minor variations in decision points and default criteria in the analyses. Yet an advantage is that these ambiguities can be made explicit, studied, and understood. The explicitness of statistical procedures helps us raise questions and understand the limits of the conclusions.

Statistical evaluation is strongly emphasized in psychology; indeed, statistical significance often is regarded as the definitive test of whether the variables under investigation are important or worth pursuing. Yet statistical significance is a function of many different features of an experiment, only *one* of which is whether there is a relation between the independent and dependent variables. Several critical issues related to a statistical evaluation influence the conclusions that are drawn.

Significance Level (alpha)

The unswerving tradition to use alpha of $p < .05$ and $.01$ for decision making is well known. Because alpha is critical to decision making in an experiment, it cannot be neglected here. Two facets of alpha warrant special attention.

Sample Size

An initial issue pertains to the relation between sample size and statistical significance. The number of subjects in groups that are studied greatly affect whether group differences on the dependent measures at the end of the experiment are statistically significant. It can be assumed that groups will not have identical means on the outcome measures simply because of normal fluctuations and individual differences when several subjects are used. Even if the observed difference is not statistically significant, the investigator can be assured that the same magnitude of difference between groups might be significant or much closer to the level of significance if two or three times as many subjects were used.

Statistical significance is in part a function of sample size. That is, the larger the sample size, the smaller the group differences needed for statistical significance at a given level of confidence. Stated another way, a given difference between two groups will gradually approach statistical significance as the size of the samples within each group is increased. Indeed, if a large number of subjects is included, statistical significance is virtually assured. For example, investigations using hundreds or even thousands of subjects, often available when large-scale testing results are studied as in the military, have reported that statistical significance is virtually guaranteed no matter what the independent variable is to categorize the data into different groups (Bakan, 1966; Nunnally, 1960). (The importance of the sample size in relation to statistical significance is particularly evident with correlations. For example, with a sample of 40,000 subjects, a correlation of only $r = .01$ is significant at the .05 level.)

Varying Alpha

Obviously, a decision of whether a difference is veridical may vary as a function of whether alpha is set at .10, .05, or some other value. Although tradition is rather fixed, there are separate circumstances in which we may wish to reconsider the alpha level we select.

The first set of circumstances might be referred to as *rational flexibility.* Under these circumstances, the investigator may decide to relax the alpha level (reduce the probability of Type I error) based on substantive or design issues that are decided in advance of data collection. Several circumstances may lead to such a decision. For some of these, the investigator may anticipate specific constraints that will attenuate the likely effect size.

First, the criterion for selecting groups in a subject-selection study might be known to be imperfect or somewhat tenuous. Thus some individuals in one group (e.g., low scores on a measure or members of the community presumed not to experience psychiatric symptoms) might through imperfect classification belong in the other group (e.g., high scores on a measure or clinic-referred people with psychiatric symptoms). Comparison of groups will be obscured by variability and imperfect classification. Second and related, the measures in the area of research may not be very well established. The unreliability of the measure may introduce variability into the situation that will affect the sensitivity of the experimental test.

Third, the specific comparison of interest may be expected to generate a very small difference between groups. If we expect small differences, the usual advice would be to increase sample size so that power will be high for this small effect. When college student samples can be run and a large subject pool is available, that alternative is quite useful. In clinical settings, large samples of the populations of interest are often unavailable or are relatively uncommon (e.g., children with a particular chronic disease, two cohabiting adults of the same gender raising children, 5- to 10-year-old children exposed to both physical and sexual abuse). Obtaining large numbers of cases, sampling across a wide geographical area, or continuing the study over a protracted period to accumulate cases may not be feasible. Altering alpha might be reasonable as a way of evaluating predicted differences between groups.

Fourth, we might alter our criterion for alpha based as well on consideration of the consequences of our decisions. Consequences here may refer to cost, patient treatment (benefit, suffering), policy issues (e.g., ease of dissemination, providing the greatest care to the greatest number of people), and other decision areas where the weight of accepting or rejecting the null hypothesis has greatly different implications and value. For example, if we are studying whether a particular procedure has side effects, we might want to alter alpha to, say, $p < .20$. In such a study, we may wish to err (Type I, II) on the side of stating that the side effects exist if there is any reasonable suggestion in the data that they might.

In a given experiment, alpha is one of many decision points. The fact that the level is deeply ingrained in tradition does not exonerate the investigator to consider thoughtful departures based on circumstances of the particular experiment. There are circumstances in advance of seeing the results when the investigator may plan on using different levels of alpha within an experiment.

Suppose we are studying three conditions in a psychotherapy study: (a) Treatment A, (b) Treatment A with an added ingredient to enhance outcome, and (c) no-treatment control. We sample 75 people who meet various criteria (e.g., diagnosis, age, physical health). We then assign subjects randomly to conditions with the restriction that an equal number will appear in each group. What shall we use for our alpha level?

We could use an alpha of .05 and let the matter rest. Alternatively, we might in advance of the study consider the comparisons of interest and their likely effect sizes. The difference between treatments versus no treatment is likely to be large. The usual alpha level ($p < .05$) to detect a difference might well be reasonable here. In contrast, the differences between Treatment A with and without a special ingredient is likely to be smaller. A sample of 75 subjects with 25 cases per group in our hypothetical study is larger than the samples of most studies in psychotherapy research (Kazdin & Bass, 1989). With a clinic sample and constraints of time, perhaps it may not be reasonable to increase the sample size. Yet the sample size is not very large for detecting group differences between two viable treatments. Small effect sizes may be too difficult to detect. It might be reasonable to use a more lenient alpha level (e.g., $p < .20$) for comparisons of the two treatments.

The adjustment of alpha is referred to here as rational flexibility to emphasize the critical thought required in advance of the study. Evidence in many data sets may reveal that several findings would be significant if alpha had been set at $p < .10$ or if one-tailed rather than two-tailed tests were used. The adoption of a more relaxed alpha may be convenient to support a hypothesis. The danger of *convenient flexibility* is to be avoided in which the alpha level is altered in light of peeking at the results. Investigators could not be faulted for the temptation because few believe that a finding has been supported at $p < .05$ but is unsupported at a p level above that (e.g., $p < .06$). The issue for statistical evaluation has been the selection of some generally agreed-upon criterion. Whatever that is, there would always be instances that just miss and in which the investigator, but not many others of the scientific community, would say that the effect is close enough to be regarded as reliable.

In general, in a given instance it may be useful to reconsider the alpha level in advance or for some of the tests or comparisons in an experiment. If on a priori grounds special conditions within the design can be expected to attenuate sensitivity of an effect, a more lenient alpha may be justified. Both theoretical and applied concerns might lead to reconsidering alpha. Altering the alpha level might be guided by evaluating the nature of the consequences of different decisions, that is, concluding that there is or is not a reliable difference between conditions.

Power Revisited

Power, or the extent to which an investigation can detect a difference when one exists, was discussed earlier. It is important to revisit the issue because weak power is the Achilles heel of psychological research. Moreover, repeated lamentations about the problem of power in clinical psychology and other areas as well, over the course of more than 3 decades has had little impact on research (Rossi, 1990; Sedlmeier & Gigerenzer, 1989). Although our discussion can hardly be expected to exert further influence, it is clearly worth the effort here.

Power or weak power relates to substantive conclusions drawn about research. The implications can be major. For example, noted before was the finding in psychotherapy outcome research that treatments infrequently differ from each other in individual outcome studies. In a treatment study, comparison of a treatment with no treatment usually leads to significant effects in the published studies. The difference between treatment and no treatment is likely to be relatively large, as reflected in a reasonably large effect size (e.g., .70 to .80). As a general rule, the larger the effect size, the less powerful (sensitive) must the tests be to detect a difference. Small sample sizes (e.g., 10–30 cases per group) are often quite sufficient to detect differences when effect sizes are large.

In contrast, comparison of two treatments is likely to produce a much smaller difference or effect size. Much larger samples may be needed to detect such differences. A conclusion that treatments are no different, that is, support of the null hypothesis, is often interpreted to indicate that treatments are equally effective. It is quite likely that power was relatively weak for this comparison. For much of psychotherapy research, weak power is a rival threat to interpretation of the absence of differences between two or more conditions (see Kazdin & Bass, 1989).

Selecting the Size of the Sample

Deciding the size of the sample is critical to power. Sample size is often decided on the basis of prior research in an area or time constraints, given the flow and availability of subjects for the period in which the investigator wishes to complete the study. These criteria are understandable but can be ill informed. Through some minor and even casual calculations, one might decide the requisite sample size to ensure adequate power.

Four different concepts of statistical inference have been discussed at varying points, including the criterion for statistical significance (alpha), power, effect size, and sample size. These concepts are interrelated in the sense that when three of these are known, the remaining one can be determined. Their interrelations are critical in that they permit one to consider all sorts of options in an experiment such as what power is (given a specific level of alpha, effect size, and fixed N), what effect size is needed (if alpha, power, and sample size are predetermined), and so on.

The most frequent use is likely to be to decide *how many subjects to include* in a study. Thus to identify our sample size, we need to make decisions to fix the other three parameters, alpha, power, and effect size. At this point, let us adopt an alpha of .05 to adhere slavishly to tradition. As for level of power, we also might follow convention and accept a power of .80. The level of power that is "adequate" is not justified or derived mathematically. As with the level of confidence (alpha), the decision is based on convention about the margin of protection one should have against falsely accepting the null hypothesis (beta). Cohen (1965) recommended adoption of the convention that $\beta = .20$ and hence power $(1 - \text{beta}) = .80$ when $\alpha = .05$. This translates to the likelihood of 4 in 5 in detecting an effect when a difference exists in the population. Although power $\geq .80$ is used as a criterion here, higher levels (.90, .95) are often encouraged as the acceptable criterion (e.g., Freiman et al., 1978; Friedman, Furberg, & DeMets, 1985).

In any case, assume for now that we adopt power of .80. Now we must estimate effect size. How can we possibly do this because the effect size formula requires us to know the difference between groups of interest to us and the standard deviation $(ES = [m_1 - m_2]/s)$?

There are separate answers and alternatives. First, in many areas of research, effect size has been studied. The secondary analysis procedure referred to as *meta-analysis* has been used extensively for evaluating many areas of research. Meta-analyses provide estimates of effect sizes for research in a given area. The effect size is used as a common metric to combine studies using different dependent variables. We can consult such analyses to identify likely effect sizes for the study we propose to undertake.

For example, if we are about to conduct a psychotherapy study comparing treatment versus no treatment, we can estimate effect size from many of the meta-analyses of psychotherapy (e.g., see Brown, 1987). Effect size for such comparisons tend to be about .70. We can adopt this effect size as an estimate and be finished with the information we need to select our needed sample size. Alternatively, if we are comparing two or more treatments to each other, we know that effect sizes are likely to be smaller (e.g., in the range of .40 to .60). The point is that effect size estimates can be obtained from published research including individual studies or more conveniently from meta-analyses. Effect sizes vary across measures so there is no one effect size. These subtleties are of lesser importance at this point. One is advised to err on the side of conservative estimates of effect size by choosing a lower bound estimate with the idea that one's own investigation may not generate effects that are as potent.

A second way to estimate effect size is on rationale grounds. The investigator may believe that there is no precedent for the type of work he or she is to conduct given the intervention or measures. Hence the literature may be seen as little help in guiding the investigator on how to proceed, a claim often made by readers of the literature. That is fine as well. The investigator may estimate whether the effect size is likely to be small, medium, or large. Cohen (1988) provided us with admittedly arbitrary but quite useful guidelines in this regard by noting small, medium, and large effect sizes to reflect approximately .2, .5, and .8, respectively. It is helpful again to select a conservative estimate. If the investigator is new to an area of research (e.g., first or second study), it is likely that the strength of the experimental manipulation and many sources of variability may be unfamiliar and difficult to control. In such cases, the investigator may be slightly overoptimistic regarding the effect sizes that are expected and may underestimate the sources of variability that attenuate group differences.

In any case, assume that by one of the above methods we consider the likely effect size to be about .40. We have alpha = .05, power = .80, and effect size estimated at .40. At this point, we can enter tables of various books provided to us (e.g., Cohen, 1988; Kraemer & Thiemann, 1987). Entering the tables requires that we have selected three values (in our case alpha, power, and effect size) to decide the remaining value (sample size). The tables tell us the size of the groups (n) we need (e.g., 40 Ss/group) to detect an effect size estimated at .40 (see Cohen, 1988). We might learn that to detect such an effect size, we need a much larger N than we can obtain. This is excellent to identify before the study. We can then decide to vary alpha (e.g., $p < .10$) or reduce power slightly (e.g., power = .75) or select alternative conditions in which effect size is likely to be larger than .40. These are informed deliberations; they are praised when completed prior to an investigation but often chastised (hopefully by the investigators themselves but invariably by reviewers and journal editors) after an investigation. The use of power tables helps one to experiment intelligently with possible options regarding alpha, power, effect size, and N.

One further point about sample size and power is worth noting. Power pertains to the statistical comparisons the investigator will make including subanalyses that may divide groups into various subgroups. For example, the investigator may have $N = 100$ subjects in two groups. The main comparison of interest may contrast Group 1 ($n = 50$) with Group 2 ($n = 50$). The investigator may plan several analyses that further divide the sample, for example, by sex (males vs. females), age (younger vs. older), intelligence (median IQ split), or some other variable. Such comparisons divide the groups into smaller units (or subgroups). Instead of group $ns = 50$, the subgroups are much smaller. Power is commensurately reduced as the comparisons entail subgroups with smaller group ns. The lesson is simple: Ensure adequate power for the comparisons of primary interest.

Variability in the Data

Power is a function of alpha, N, and effect size. However, there is more to power than the formula for its computation. Noted already was the notion that excessive variability within an experiment can threaten statistical conclusion validity. Variability is inherent in the nature of subject performance in any investigation. However, the investigator can inadvertently increase variability in ways that will reduce the obtained effect size. Obviously, if the mean difference between groups equals a constant (e.g., 8) on some outcome measure, effect size will increase or decrease depending on the size of the standard deviation by which that difference is divided. Thus the more heterogeneous the subjects (e.g., in age, background, sex, socioeconomic class, and other variables), the more variable the effects of the independent variable are likely to be. The heterogeneity of the subjects is reflected in a larger within-group variability. This variability, referred to as error variance, is directly related to effect size and statistical significance. For a given difference between groups on the dependent measure, the larger the error variance, the less likely will the results be statistically significant. Thus statistical significance is influenced by the diversity of subjects who are employed in the investigation.

Other sources of variability are pivotal for the investigator to consider. The assessment instruments play an important role in the variability of the results. Measures vary in their reliability in assessing the construct of interest. To the extent that the measures assess true scores of the subjects on the construct, error variance in the study will be reduced. In developing and designing an experiment, the quality of the measures, as reflected in various psychometric characteristics, is quite important.

Error variance is also a function of variation in the experimental procedures. If experimenters administer conditions in an experiment slightly differently from each other, or if a single experimenter administers conditions differently over time, error variability will increase. Hence the magnitude of group differences will need to be greater to achieve a given level of statistical significance. If the procedures are unvarying across subjects, this eliminates a source of error variance. Understandably, many investigators attempt to run experiments using automated equipment where human experimenters are not needed at all or use such aids as audio- or videotape equipment. As a rule, mechanization of the procedures ensures greater consistency over the course of the experiment than using humans to administer the same conditions. In clinical settings, there are obvious limits in the options for mechanization.

Statistical Tests to Augment Power

The discussion of efforts to minimize error variability in an investigation as a means toward increasing power points to additional alternatives. The design and statistical evaluation of the study can greatly affect power. Noted previously were designs that used pretests. From a design standpoint, advantages of using pretests were manifold and included issues related to the information they provide (e.g., about magnitude of change, number of people who change, and so on). The statistical advantages of using a pretest are the most universal basis for using such designs.

Alternative statistical analyses can be used in which the pretest plays a prominent role. The power of the pretest is that with alternative analyses, the error term in evaluating effect size is reduced. With repeated assessment of the subjects (pre- and posttest), the within-group (subject) variance can be taken into account to reduce the error term. Consider the impact on the effect size formula.

We have noted previously that the formula for effect size $(ES) = (m_1 - m_2)/s$. When there is a pretest measure or another measure that has been assessed and is related to performance at posttreatment (e.g., covariate), the effect size error term is altered. The formula is represented by $ES = (m_1 - m_2)/s\sqrt{1 - r^2}$ where r equals the correlation between the pretest (or other variable) and posttest. As the correlation between the pre- and posttest increases, the error term and hence power of the analysis increases. Several statistical analyses can be used that take advantage of the use of a pretest. Prominent among these are analyses of covariance, repeated measures analyses of variance, and gain scores (see Lipsey, 1990).

Another statistical test issue related to power is the controversial matter of one- versus two-tailed tests. In significance testing, alpha is used to decide whether a difference between groups is reliable. Consider a two-group study and a *t* test to evaluate group differences. The null hypothesis is that the groups do not differ, that is, $ES = O$. A two-tailed test evaluates the obtained difference in light of departures from O in either direction, that is, whether one group is better or worse than another. The alpha of .05 refers to both "tails" or ends of the normal distribution that are used as the critical region for rejection.

In much research, the investigator may have a view about the direction of the differences. He or she may not wish to test if the effect size is different from zero but rather whether the treatment is better than the control condition or whether Treatment A is better than Treatment B. The hypothesis to reject is not bidirectional but unidirectional. As such, the investigator may wish to use a one-tailed test. A lower *t* value is required for the rejection of the null hypothesis if a one-tailed directional test is provided.

Most hypotheses in research are directional in the sense that investigators have an idea and interest in differences in a particular direction. For this reason, some authors have suggested that most significance testing should be based on one-tailed tests (e.g., Mohr, 1990). However, there is resistance to this to which the reader should be alerted. There is often an implicit assumption that investigators who use one-tailed tests may have done so because the results would not be statistically significant otherwise. It is unclear whether the use of one-tailed tests was decided in advance of seeing the results. The implicit assumption does not give the benefit of doubt to the investigator. At the same time, relatively few studies in clinical psychology and related areas use one-tailed tests. One rarely sees such tests or sees them in situations where the results would be significant whether the tests were completed as one- or two-tailed tests.

In general, investigators are encouraged to be conservative in their analyses of the data and in drawing conclusions about relations that are reliable or statistically significant. The discussion of multiple comparisons (later in the chapter) conveys this tradition rather well. Yet directional hypotheses and use of one-tailed tests warrant consideration. Critical to their use is clarification of the basis of the prediction so that consumers of research can identify whether the tests are reasonable. Also, because one-tailed tests are occasionally viewed suspiciously, the investigator might wish to note in passing those tests that would or would not have been significant with two-tailed tests. Comments on both type of tests within a study do not reflect concerns of the statistician who might lobby for a rational evaluation of using one or the other form of tests (but not both). Yet comments about the conclusions drawn from statistical tests raise broader issues. Among these is the importance of informing colleagues about the dependence of conclusions on assumptions and methods of analyses.

Statistical Significance and Magnitude of Effect

Statistical evaluation of the data usually consists of testing to see if differences between groups are statistically significant. In addition to the presence of group differences, it would be useful to know how strong the effect was or how strong the relation was between our independent variable and performance on the dependent measures. The strength refers to the magnitude of the contribution of the independent variable to performance on the dependent variable. Magnitude or strength of the relation can be expressed in different terms such as the amount of variance accounted for by the independent variable or the correlation between the independent and dependent variable.

In clinical research, the notion of the strength of the relation is obviously important. For example, if we wish to compare parents who abuse their children with parents who do not, we do not merely wish to demonstrate statistically significant differences on several measures (e.g., parent psychopathology, family functioning). In addition, we wish to know the strength of association and magnitude of the relation between parent status and other variables. If all of the variables we study differentiate abusive from nonabusive parents, we would like to know the strength of these connections and the relative contribution of each.

Magnitude of effect or strength of the relation can be expressed in many different terms including omega^2 (ω^2), eta (η), epsilon^2 (ϵ^2), and correlation squared (r^2; e.g., Haase, Ellis, & Ladany, 1989; Rosenthal, 1984). One measure of strength of association we have already discussed is effect size which illustrates nicely the informational yield provided beyond statistical significance. As mentioned already, in the simple case of two groups, effect size represents the magnitude of the differences between groups in terms of standard deviation units $(ES) = (m_1 - m_2)/s$. It is important to note that magnitude of effect, and in our illustration effect size, is *not* the same as noting that a finding is or is not statistically significant. However, there is a relation between measures of statistical significance and measures of magnitude of effect. The relation varies as a function of the specific statistical test and measure of strength of effect. In the case of effect size, this relation is worth highlighting in passing.

Consider for a moment that we have completed a study and obtained an effect size of .70. This magnitude of effect is one that is about the level of effect size demonstrated when psychotherapy is compared with no treatment. An effect size of this magnitude indicates a fairly strong relation and would be considered as a moderate to large effect size. Would an effect size of this magnitude also be reflected in statistically significant group differences? The answer depends on the sample size.

Consider two studies both with an effect size of .70. In one case, we have a two-group study with 10 cases in each group ($N = 20$). In another study, suppose we have two groups with 30 cases in each group ($N = 60$). We complete each study and are ready to analyze the data. In each study, we have two groups, so we decide to evaluate group differences using a t test. The test formula can be expressed in many ways. The relation between statistical significance and effect size for our two-group study can be seen in the formula:

$$t = ES \times \frac{1}{\sqrt{1/n_1 + 1/n_2}}$$

where $ES = (m_1 - m_2)/s$.

When $ES = .70$, and there are 10 cases in each of the two groups, the formula above yields a $t = 1.57$ with degrees of freedom (df) of 18 $(n_1 + n_2 - 2)$. If we consult a table for the Student's t distribution, we note that a t of 2.10 is required for $p = .05$ when $df = 18$. Our t does not meet the $p < .05$ level, and we conclude that there is no difference between Group 1 and Group 2.

When $ES = .70$ and there are 30 cases in each of the two groups, the above formula yields a $t = 2.71$, with a df of 58. If we consult Student's t distribution, we note that it is higher than the t of 2.00 we required for this df at $p < .05$. Thus we conclude that Groups 1 and 2 are different. Two points are worth noting from this example. The first is that strength of effect is different from statistical significance. The second point underscores sample size again as a critical determinant in relation to statistical significance.

Considerations

Experiments that use statistical tests could increase their informational yield by also including measures of strength relations between variables. The difficulty is deciding among many contenders how to best measure strength of the relation. Among the available options, no single measure has been adopted. Effect size has been discussed in the present chapter and as well in other contexts to illustrate points in relation to power. Effect size, the methods of its computation, and virtues of alternative methods are topics of discussion and debate as well (e.g., Haase et al., 1989; Murray & Dosser, 1987; O'Grady, 1982; Rosenthal, 1984). Considerations regarding alternative measures cannot be covered here (see Further Readings). However, the main point to emphasize is the importance of including measures of strength of the relation such as effect size or one of the many correlational measures.

Multiple Comparisons

In an experiment, the investigator is likely to include multiple groups and to compare some or all of them with each other. For example, the study may include four groups, say, three treatment and one control group. The investigator may conduct an overall test (analysis of variance) to see if there are differences. If the results are statistically significant, several individual comparisons may be made to identify which groups differ from each other. Alternatively, the investigator may forego the overall test and proceed to the individual comparisons. In each case, several two-group (pair-wise) comparisons are completed as each treatment is compared to each other treatment and to the control group. Alpha might be set at $p < .05$ to protect against the risk of a Type I error. This alpha refers to the risk for a given comparison, sometimes referred to as a *per comparison error rate.* Yet, there are multiple comparisons. With multiple tests, the overall error rate or risk of a Type I error can be much higher. This increase is sometimes referred to informally as *probability pyramiding* to note the accumulation of the actual probability of a Type I error increases with the number of tests. How much higher the p level increases depends on the number of different comparisons. In fact, with a number of comparisons, each held at the per comparison rate of .05, the probability of concluding that some significant effect has been obtained can be very high.

In our hypothetical example with four groups, the investigator may make all possible comparisons of the groups (six total pair-wise comparisons). The alpha selected must account for the number of pair-wise comparisons. Although the pair-wise error rate is .05, the risk of a Type I error for the experiment is higher because of the number of tests. This overall rate is referred to as the *experiment-wise error rate.* We must control for the probability of a Type I error for all of the comparisons or for the experiment-wise error rate.

There are alternative multiple comparison tests that are available to address the problem of experiment-wise error rate and to control the increased Type I risk (see Hochberg & Tamhane, 1987). Many of the more familiar multiple-comparison tests are known by the name of the individuals primarily responsible for their development (e.g., various tests by Tukey, Duncan, Scheffé). A relatively simple alternative is referred to as the Bonferroni procedure and consists of a way to adjust alpha in light of the number of comparisons that are made. Consider the most common variation of the procedure.

In a set of comparisons, the upper boundary of the probability of rejecting the null hypothesis is the number of comparisons (k) times alpha $(\alpha$; e.g., $p = .05)$. Obviously, if there are 10 comparisons to be made then the overall error rate is $k\alpha$ or .50. As a protection against a Type I error, $p = .50$ would clearly be unacceptable. To control the overall error rate, alpha can be adjusted for the number of comparisons.

The Bonferonni adjustment is based on dividing alpha $(p = .05)$ by the number of comparisons. In our four-group study, there are six possible pair-wise comparisons. If we set alpha at .05, we know our risk is actually much higher given the number of comparisons. To make an adjustment, we divide alpha by the number of comparisons. In our example, we divide .05/6, which yields $p = .0083$. For each of the individual pair-wise comparisons we complete (Treatment 1 vs. Treatment 2, Treatment 1 vs. control group, etc.), we use $p < .0083$ as the criterion for significance. If we use this criterion, then our overall experiment-wise error rate is controlled at $p < .05$.

The adjustment of alpha as noted previously arises when several pair-wise comparisons are made on a given measure. A similar concern, that is, elevated alpha, emerges when there are multiple outcome measures and several tests comparing the same groups are made across each measure. For example, if two groups of patients (anxious vs. nonanxious patients) are compared on several different measures, the chance of finding a significant difference, when there is none in the population, is higher than $p < .05$ for a given comparison. Here, too, the Bonferroni adjustment can be used for the number of comparisons where k still refers to the number of comparisons or tests. As before, for each test, the adjusted level is used to decide whether the effects are statistically significant.

Considerations

There is general agreement that multiple comparisons require some adjustment. Failure to consider the multiplicity of the comparisons has direct implications for statistical conclusion validity, in this case, often concluding that there are significant differences when, by the usual criteria for alpha, there is none. Beyond these general points, and at the point investigators need to make data analytic decisions, agreement diminishes. For example, which multiple comparison tests are appropriate and whether a given test is too conservative or stringent are two areas where reasonable statisticians can disagree.

Use of an adjustment such as the Bonferroni procedure is fairly common. Although the adjusted alpha is reasonable, the consequence can be sobering in a given study. In practice, the number of significant effects is likely to decrease when an adjusted level is used. Stated differently, as the alpha for individual pair-wise comparisons becomes more stringent, power decreases, and the probability of a Type II error increases.

Investigators are reluctant to adjust for the large number of tests that are often completed. There are alternatives for the investigator who believes central findings are supported by the statistical comparisons but sees them disappear when alpha is adjusted to control the experiment-wise error rate. First, the investigator can present the results for both adjusted and nonadjusted alpha levels. The results can note the tests that remain significant under both circumstances and those that are significant only when the overall rate is uncontrolled. Second, the investigator can select an experiment-wise alpha that is slightly more lenient than $p < .05$ such as $p < .10$ prior to making the adjustment. The Bonferroni adjustment will divide this alpha by the number of comparisons. The per comparison alpha is still below .05 depending on the number of comparisons. Adopting an experiment-wise rate of .10 is usually less of a concern to other researchers than adopting this rate for individual comparisons (per comparison rate). Finally, the investigator may not be interested in all possible comparisons, but rather in only a preplanned subset that relates specifically to one or two primary hypotheses. Adjusting alpha for this smaller number of comparisons means that the per comparison rate (of alpha) is not as stringent.

The alternatives do not exhaust the range of possibilities. For example, among the options is the use of less conservative variations of the Bonferroni adjustment (Simes, 1986) or a variety of other procedures to control Type I error (Hochberg & Tamhane, 1987). The central point is not to argue for any one solution but rather to underscore the importance of addressing the issue in the data analyses. Any data analytic issue that can be anticipated also requires consideration at the design stage before the study is completed. Identifying the major comparisons of interest in the study, the statistical tests that will be used, the number of tests, and so on may have implications for sample size and power. All such matters directly affect the conclusions to which the investigator is entitled and hence are critical.

Multiple Outcomes: Multivariate and Univariate Analyses

In most clinical research, multiple measures are used to evaluate the impact of an intervention. For example, in a therapy outcome study, several measures may be obtained to assess the different perspectives (e.g., clients, relatives, therapists), domains of functioning (e.g., depression, self-esteem, adjustment at home and at work), and different assessment formats (e.g., direct observations, questionnaires). As noted in the previous discussion, the data analyses may include a number of individual tests. Each group can be compared to each other group in the design on each of the outcome measures. Although the per comparison rate might be .05, we already noted that the actual likelihood of a chance finding multiplies quickly as the number of comparisons increases. The number of comparisons can increase when there are many groups compared to each other and/or a few groups that are compared when there are multiple measures. The Bonferroni adjustment is an alternative to address the issue of Type I error when such comparisons are made.

When there are multiple outcome measures, another issue emerges, namely, the interrelations of the measures. Performance on several outcome measures may be conceptually related, because they reflect a domain the investigator views as a unit, or empirically related, because the measures correlate significantly with each other. If we have, say, 10 dependent measures, we could analyze these separately with t or F tests. We could avoid the problem of an inflated Type I error with the adjustment noted previously. Yet, the other issue pertains to the fact that the measures may be interrelated.

Univariate tests, that is, separate tests for each measure, do not take into account the possible redundancy of the measures and their relation to each other. It is possible, for example, that two outcome measures show significant effects due to treatment. The high correlation of these measures may account for that difference. It is possible as well that none of the measures would show a difference but when viewed as a conceptual whole in fact show an effect.

When there are multiple outcome measures, we can consider the data to be *multivariate*. It may be desirable to conduct multivariate analyses (e.g., such as multivariate analyses of variance). Multivariate analyses include several measures in a single data analysis, whereas univariate analyses examine one measure at a time. We do not use multivariate analyses merely because we have several dependent measures. Rather, the primary basis is when the investigator is interested in understanding the relations among the dependent measures. The multivariate analyses consider these relations by providing a linear combination of the measures, and evaluate if that combination yields a statistically significant effect. If an overall multivariate analysis indicates a significant effect, this suggests that some combination of variables has shown the effect of the intervention or independent variable of interest.

After this finding with the overall effect of the multivariate analysis, one might then conduct univariate tests (individual F tests on each measure) to identify the specific differences on each of the dependent variables. As before, the alpha would need to be adjusted to avoid an elevated Type I error. Univariate tests may or may not show significant effects following an overall multivariate analysis. The multivariate analysis takes into account the relation of the measures to each other and evaluates the combination of measures. The univariate analyses ignore this facet of the structure of the data and may not lead to similar conclusions.

Considerations

In many experiments, multivariate analyses are used when there are several measures and then univariate analyses are completed if the overall multivariate analysis is statistically significant. Whether multivariate analyses are appropriate is based on several considerations. The mere presence of several measures is not sufficient to proceed to conduct multivariate analyses. It may be quite appropriate to analyze the multiple outcome measures with multivariate analyses or with several univariate tests (see Haase & Ellis, 1987; Huberty & Morris, 1989).

Multivariate analyses are particularly appropriate if the investigator views the measures as conceptually interrelated and is interested in various groupings of the measures separate from or in addition to the individual measures themselves. For example, there may be several measures of patient adjustment and family functioning. Within the study, the investigator may group all of the measures of patient adjustment and conduct a multivariate analysis to identify a combination for this overall conceptual domain and do the same for the measures of family functioning. Separate analyses may also be conducted for the individual scales within each conceptual domain if they are of interest as well.

Multivariate analyses evaluate the composite variables based on their inter-relations. This is a unique feature and is not addressed by performing several separate univariate tests. Separate univariate tests might be appropriate under a variety of conditions if the investigator does not view the measures as conceptually related, if the measures in fact are uncorrelated, or if the primary or exclusive interest is in the individual measures themselves rather than how they combine or relate to each other. Whether one should use multivariate tests when this option is available is based on several considerations beyond the scope of the present chapter (see For Further Reading).

Investigators occasionally use the multivariate analysis as an overall test. Once significant, they proceed with several univariate tests. Usually, these latter tests are conducted with a per comparison alpha of .05, and hence the overall risk of Type I error is greatly increased. The multivariate test was assumed to control for a Type I error at the level of alpha ($p < .05$). Yet the individual univariate tests, if conducted, still are required to consider the number of tests and the experiment-wise error rate.

General Comments

Statistical evaluation is not merely fundamental but is the mainstay of contem-porary research. Application of statistical tests is not that straightforward. The complexities and options as well as their implications for experimental validity lobby for careful consideration of the methods of statistical evaluation at the design stage. Alpha, power, and error rates, to mention a few considerations, are critical to address as the study is being planned. These are not esoteric issues nor merely quantitative issues. Rather, they will squarely affect the conclusions the investigator wishes to draw and the strength and quality of the design that tests the investigator's hypotheses or predictions.

NONSTATISTICAL EVALUATION

In areas of clinical research where single-case designs are used, typically data are evaluated without relying on statistics. Given the training of most students and professionals in psychology, nonstatistical evaluation seemingly represents an inappropriate form of analysis. The primary reason for rejection of non-statistical evaluation is the concern that by not using statistical techniques, subjective judgment may enter into deciding which findings are significant or veridical and which are not. The concern is reasonable because however arbi-trary statistical evaluation or decision making seems, the criteria appear quite explicit (e.g., for Type I and II errors, power).

The reader familiar with statistical tests, particularly with direct experience from his or her own research, would pause to note that judgments are often involved in statistical evaluation with the statistical tests themselves. Use of diverse tests (e.g., factor analyses, regression, cluster analyses, time-series analyses, path analyses) include a number of decision points about various solutions, parameter estimates, levels to continue or include variables in the analysis or model, and so on. These decisions are rarely made explicit in the data analyses. In many instances "default" criteria in the data analytic programs do not convey that a critical choice has been made. Descriptions of the material in statistical manuals that describe how to run the program are not intended to present the many rational and subjective criteria that can enter into the decisions.

Nonstatistical evaluation usually refers to examining the data and determining whether the intervention had an effect by *visual inspection.* Visual inspection is commonly used in single-case research where continuous data are available for one or several subjects. With single-case designs, the investigator has the advantage of seeing the data for a single subject for consecutive periods without the intervention, followed by similar data with the intervention in effect. If the intervention abruptly changes the pattern of data, an inference about the effect of the intervention is clearer than simply looking at pre- and postintervention differences across two observations. Assessment of the individual's performance on several occasions makes examination of the data through visual inspection less arbitrary than the method might appear at first glance. The use of visual inspection as a method of determining whether the effects of the intervention were reliable or not is very much related to the logic of the designs (as described in chapter 7).

Criteria for Visual Inspection

Evaluation of data nonstatistically has the same goal as statistical analysis, namely, to identify if the effects are consistent, reliable, and unlikely to have resulted from chance fluctuations between conditions. Although visual inspection is based on subjective judgment, this is not tantamount to noting that decisions are by fiat or vary with each person making the judgment. In many uses of single-case designs where visual inspection is invoked, the applied or clinical goals are to achieve marked intervention effects (Baer, 1977). In cases where intervention effects are very strong, one need not carefully scrutinize or enumerate the criteria that underlie the judgment that the effects are veridical.

Several situations arise in applied research in which intervention effects are likely to be so dramatic that visual inspection is easily invoked. For example, whenever the behavior of interest is not present in the client's behavior during the baseline phase (e.g., social interaction, exercise, reading) and increases during the intervention phase, a judgment about the effects of the intervention is easily made. If the behavior never occurs during baseline, there is unparalleled stability in the data. Both the mean and standard deviation equal zero. Even a minor increase in the target behavior during the intervention phase would be easily detected. Similarly, when the behavior of interest occurs frequently during the baseline phase (e.g., reports of hallucinations, aggressive acts, cigarette smoking) and stops completely during the intervention phase, the magnitude of change usually permits clear judgments based on visual inspection. In cases in which behavior is at the opposite extremes of the assessment range before and during treatment, the ease of invoking visual inspection can be readily understood. Of course, in most situations, the data do not show a change from one extreme of the assessment scale to the other, and the guidelines for making judgments by visual inspection need to be considered more deliberately.

Visual inspection depends on many characteristics of the data, but especially those that pertain to the magnitude of the changes across phases and the rate of these changes. The two characteristics related to magnitude are changes in *mean* and *level*. The two characteristics related to rate are changes in *trend* and *latency* of the change. It is important to examine each of these characteristics separately, even though they act in concert.

Changes in means across phases refer to shifts in the *average rate* of performance. Consistent changes in means across phases can serve as a basis for deciding whether the data pattern meets the requirements of the design. A hypothetical example showing changes in means across phases is illustrated in an ABAB design in Figure 12.1. As evident in the figure, performance on the average (horizontal dashed line in each phase) changed in response to the different baseline and intervention phases. Visual inspection of this pattern suggests that the intervention led to consistent changes.

Changes in level are a little less familiar but very important in allowing a

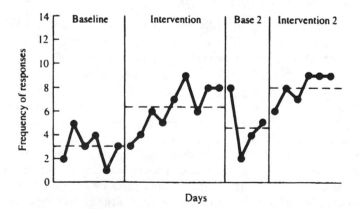

Figure 12.1. Hypothetical example of performance in an ABAB design with means in each phase represented with dashed lines.

decision through visual inspection as to whether the intervention produced reliable effects. Changes in level refer to the shift or discontinuity of performance from the end of one phase to the beginning of the next phase. A change in level is independent of the change in mean. When one asks about what happened immediately after the intervention was implemented or withdrawn, the implicit concern is over the level of performance. Figure 12.2 shows change in level across phases in ABAB design. The figure shows that whenever the phase was altered, behavior assumed a new rate, that is, it shifted up or down rather quickly. It so happens that a change in level in this latter example was also accompanied by a change in mean across the phases. Yet, level and mean changes do not necessarily go together. It is possible that a rapid change in level occurs but that the mean remains the same across phase or that the mean changes but no abrupt shift in level has occurred.

Changes in trend are of obvious importance in applying visual inspection. Trend or slope refers to the tendency for the data to show systematic increases or decreases over time. The alteration of phases within the design may show that the direction of behavior changes as the intervention is applied or withdrawn. Figure 12.3 illustrates a hypothetical example in which trends have changed over the course of the phase in an ABAB design. The initial baseline trend is reversed by the intervention, reinstated when the intervention is withdrawn, and again reversed in the final phase. A change in trend would still be an important criterion even if there were no trend in baseline. A change from no trend (horizontal line) during baseline to a trend (increase or decrease in behavior) during the intervention phase would also constitute a change in trend.

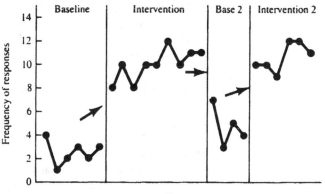

Figure 12.2. Hypothetical example of performance in an ABAB design. The arrows point to the changes in level or discontinuities associated with a change from one phase to another.

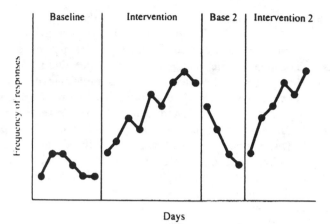

Figure 12.3. Hypothetical example of performance in an ABAB design with changes in trend across phases. Baseline shows a relatively stable or possibly decreasing trend. When the intervention is introduced, an accelerating trend is evident. This trend is reversed when the intervention is withdrawn (Base 2) and is reinstated when the intervention is reintroduced.

Finally, the *latency of the change* that occurs when phases are altered is an important characteristic of the data for invoking visual inspection. Latency refers to the period between the onset or termination of one condition (e.g., intervention, return to baseline) and changes in performance. The more closely in time that the change occurs after the experimental conditions have been altered, the clearer the intervention effect. A hypothetical example is provided in Figure 12.4, showing only the first two phases of separate ABAB designs. In the top panel, implementation of the intervention after baseline was associated with a rapid change in performance. The change would also be evident from changes in mean and trend. In the bottom panel, the intervention did not immediately lead to change. The time between the onset of the intervention and behavior change was longer than in the top panel, and it is slightly less clear that the intervention may have led to the change.

As a general rule, the shorter the period between the onset of the intervention and behavior change, the easier it is to infer that the intervention led to change. The rationale is that as the time between the intervention and behavior increases, the more likely that intervening influences may have accounted for behavior change. Of course, the importance of the latency of the change after the onset of the intervention depends on the type of intervention and behavior studied. For example, one would not expect rapid changes in applying diet and exercise to treat obesity. Weight reduction usually reflects gradual changes after treatment begins. Similarly, some medications do not produce rapid effects. Change depends on the buildup of therapeutic doses.

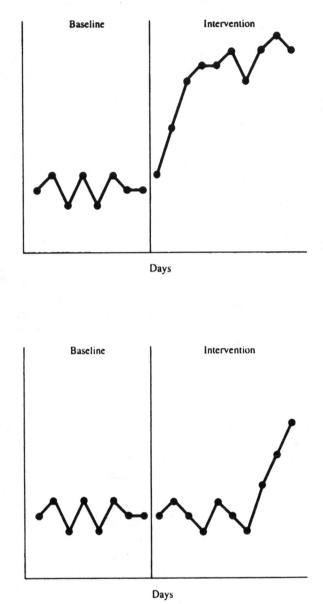

Figure 12.4. Hypothetical examples of first AB phases as part of larger ABAB designs. The upper panel shows that when the intervention was introduced, behavior changed rapidly. The lower panel shows that when the intervention was introduced, behavior change was delayed. The changes in both upper and lower panels are reasonably clear. Yet as a general rule, as the latency between the onset of the intervention and behavior change increases, questions are more likely to arise about whether the intervention or extraneous factors accounted for change.

Changes in means, levels, and trends, as well as variations in the latency of change across phases frequently accompany each other. Yet they are separate characteristics of the data and can occur alone or in combination. Visual inspection is conducted by judging the extent to which changes in these characteristics are evident across phases and whether the changes are consistent with the requirements of the particular design. When changes in mean, level, trend, and latency of change go together, visual inspection is relatively more easy to invoke. In such cases, the data across phases may not overlap. *Nonoverlapping data* refer to the pattern in which the values of the data points during the baseline phase do not approach any of the values of the data points attained during the intervention phase.

It is important to note that invoking the criteria for visual inspection requires judgments about the pattern of data in the entire design and not merely changes across one or two phases. Unambiguous effects require that the criteria mentioned above be met throughout the design. To the extent that the criteria are not consistently met, conclusions about the reliability of intervention effects become tentative. For example, changes in an ABAB design may show nonoverlapping data points for the first AB phases but no clear differences across the second AB phases. The absence of a consistent pattern of data that meets the criteria mentioned above limits the conclusions that can be drawn.

Problems and Considerations

Visual inspection has been quite useful in identifying reliable intervention effects both in experimental and clinical research. When intervention effects are potent, the need for statistical analysis is obviated. Intervention effects can be extremely clear from graphic displays of the data in which persons can judge for themselves whether the criteria have been met.

The use of visual inspection as the primary basis for evaluating data in single-case designs has raised major concerns. Perhaps the major issue pertains to the lack of concrete decision rules for determining whether a particular demonstration shows or fails to show a reliable effect. The process of visual inspection would seem to permit, if not actively encourage, subjectivity and inconsistency in the evaluation of intervention effects. Studies of how individuals invoke the criteria for visual inspection have shown that judges, even when experts in the field, often disagree about particular data patterns and whether the effects were reliable (e.g., DeProspero & Cohen, 1979; Gottman & Glass, 1978). The disagreement among judges using visual inspection has been used as an argument to favor statistical analysis of the data as a supplement to or replacement of visual inspection. The attractive feature of statistical analysis is that once the statistic is decided, the result that is achieved is usually consistent across investigators. And the final result (statistical significance) is not altered by the judgment of the investigator.

Another criticism levied against visual inspection is that it regards as significant only those effects that are very marked. Many interventions might prove to be consistent in the effects they produce but are relatively weak. Such effects might not be detected by visual inspection and would be overlooked. Overlooking weak but reliable effects can have unfortunate consequences. First, weak but reliable effects may have theoretical significance in relation to understanding personality, dysfunction, or treatment. Second, the possibility exists that interventions when first developed may have weak effects. It would be unfortunate if these interventions were prematurely discarded before they could be developed further. Interventions with reliable but weak effects might eventually achieve potent effects if investigators developed them further. On the other hand, the stringent criteria may encourage investigators to develop interventions to the point that they do produce marked changes before making claims about their demonstrated efficacy.

A final problem with visual inspection is that it requires a particular pattern of data in baseline and subsequent phases so that the results can be interpreted. Visual inspection criteria are more readily invoked when data show little or no trend or trend in directions opposite from the trend expected in the following phase and slight variability. Of course, trends and variability in the data do not always meet the idealized data requirements. In such cases visual inspection may be difficult to invoke. Other criteria, such as statistical analyses may be of use in these situations.

Visual inspection does not reflect an inferior method of data evaluation. The method differs from those associated with hypothesis testing and statistical evaluation and is subject to different types of objections. It is also important to recognize that visual inspection might be superior in many situations where statistical evaluation is insensitive. There are many situations where visual inspection would lead investigators to infer that the intervention produced a reliable effect but statistical evaluation might not yield a statistically significant effect. For example, the effects of a program designed to increase social interaction of a withdrawn child appeared to be reasonably clear (see Figure 12.5). The program was evaluated in an ABAB design that included the following phases: baseline, praise for social interaction of the child with her peers, praise for solitary play, and praise again for social interaction. Social interaction changed in the predicted fashion across all phases, showing an effect that probably would be endorsed as reliable or significant by most advocates of visual inspection. Interestingly, reanalysis of these data, using time-series analysis (Gottman, 1973), revealed that the results were not statistically significant. (Time-series analysis involves t tests across phases that assess whether changes in the level of behavior or in the trend are statistically significant. The test is a t test between adjacent phases. Additional details about time-series analysis have been presented in other sources [see Kazdin, 1982b].) If one had to put to a vote which method, statistical or visual, reflects whether there is an intervention effect, the "eyes" would have it. In the example of Figure 12.5, it is very likely that too few data points were available to provide a sensitive statistical evaluation. In any case, the pattern of data suggests that statistical significance is not infallible as a criterion for deciding the reliability of treatment effects.

General Comments

Nonstatistical data evaluation methods are generally unfamiliar to researchers. Objections to these methods also are strong because the methods, by their very nature, appear not merely to permit subjectivity but to embrace it directly. Yet visual inspection can be reliably invoked and has generated a body of research with outcomes that are at least as reliable and replicable as those obtained through statistical evaluation. Whether the criteria are adopted or not in a given study, the criteria of visual inspection are worth noting. Changes in mean, level, slope, and latency of change sensitize us to critical properties of the data. In the evaluation of continuous data and in clinical and research situations where performance is scrutinized over time, these properties can greatly influence decision making, treatment planning, and evaluation.

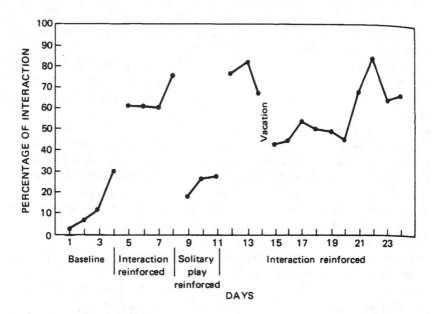

Figure 12.5. Percentage of time a withdrawn boy spent in social interaction before treatment began, during periods when social behavior toward peers was positively reinforced, and during periods when teachers gave attention for solitary play. Source: Harris, F.R., Wolf, M.M. & Baer, D.M. (1964). Effects of adult social reinforcement on child behavior. *Young Children, 20,* 8–17. Copyright 1964 by the National Association for the Education of Young Children, Washington, D.C. Reprinted with permission.

CLINICAL SIGNIFICANCE OF THERAPEUTIC CHANGE

One problem with statistical evaluation, especially in clinically relevant research, is that it detracts from the question of the applied importance of the outcome or effect. This issue is central to intervention research or efforts to change performance or functioning for some applied end. Intervention research is no small part of the field when one considers the diverse populations (e.g., school students, medical and psychiatric patients, the elderly) and settings (e.g., schools, clinics, the home, hospitals, industry, the community) in which psychologists work. Also, both treatment and prevention for a broad range of psychological and physical problems reflect areas where outcomes are quite relevant.

By searching for statistically significant effects, it is easy to lose sight that one goal is to produce clinically important changes. Visual inspection draws attention to the importance of achieving marked changes. Yet marked changes evident graphically by sharp changes in means, level, and slope do not necessarily signal that improvements are meaningful or important in the experience of the client.

In clinical psychology and other research areas with applied concerns, the difference between statistical and clinical (or applied) significance is frequently raised. Statistical significance refers to the probability-based criterion mentioned earlier for judging whether an effect is reliable. *Clinical significance* refers to the practical value or importance of the effect of an intervention, that is, whether it makes any "real" difference to the clients or to others. Investigators frequently lament the notion that a statistically significant difference does not necessarily reveal an important difference. Calls to supplement statistical significance with measures of the strength of relations (e.g., effect sizes) have emerged in part from the concern of evaluating the importance of the finding. Yet strength of the relation between the independent and dependent variables does not necessarily reflect on the experience of the individual client.

Recently, clinical research has attempted to assess the extent to which changes in behavior are important for the client. Evaluation of the clinical or applied importance of the change usually is used as a supplement to statistical or nonstatistical methods of determining whether group differences or changes over time are reliable. Once reliable changes are evident, further efforts are made to quantify whether treatment has moved the client appreciably closer to adequate functioning, that is, whether the change is important.

For some areas of treatment, one may be able to tell readily whether the change moves the client close to adaptive functioning. For example, treatment that eliminates the self-injurious behavior (such as headbanging of an autistic child) would be regarded as producing a clinically significant change. All self-destructive acts would be regarded as maladaptive and their elimination as an important change. However, reducing self-injurious behavior from, say, 500 to 200 instances per day might not be regarded as clinically important. Without a further reduction or complete elimination, the client may still self-inflict serious damage. The magnitude of the change might meet criteria for statistical significance or reflect a reliable difference by criteria for visual inspection. Yet its clinical value could be challenged. Virtual if not complete elimination of self-injurious behavior would be required to effect a clinically important change. Of course, in many cases, the presence or absence of a behavior at the end of treatment is not necessarily the criterion for deciding whether an important change was achieved.

Several other methods of evaluating the clinical significance of treatment effects have been elaborated. In each method, the focus is on identifying the importance of the change or level of functioning at the end of treatment. Three general strategies can be delineated including comparison with other groups, subjective evaluation, and social impact (see Jacobson, 1988; Kazdin, 1977; Wolf, 1978).

Comparison Methods

Normative Samples

Comparison methods, as the name suggests, involve direct comparison of clients with others. Prior to treatment, presumably the patient sample would depart considerably from their well-functioning peers in the area identified for treatment (e.g., anxiety, depression, social withdrawal, aggression, tics). One measure of the extent to which treatment produced clinically important changes would be the demonstration that at the end of treatment the patient sample was indistinguishable from or well within the range of a normative, well-functioning sample on the measures of interest.

Evaluating the extent to which individuals perform at or within the normative range is the most commonly used method of evaluating clinical significance. To invoke this criterion, a comparison is made between treated patients and peers who are functioning well or without significant problems in everyday life. A typical example was a treatment study designed to evaluate alternative interventions for aggressive and antisocial children ages 7 to 13 years (Kazdin, Esveldt-Dawson, French, & Unis, 1987). The effectiveness of three conditions was examined including problem-solving skills training (PSST), relationship therapy, and minimal treatment contact. Children were hospitalized in a short-term inpatient setting where treatment was begun and then continued on an outpatient basis. PSST consisted of a cognitive–behavioral treatment administered individually to children for 20 sessions. In the sessions children were trained to apply problem-solving skills to interpersonal interactions in which the children had engaged in aggressive and antisocial behavior. Individual relationship therapy consisted of 20 sessions in which the play and the thera-peutic relationship were used to develop self-acceptance to encourage expression of feelings. Minimal contact children met individually in sessions with a therapist and played games or engaged in other activities; this condition provided contact but no specific treatment regimen to alter antisocial behavior. The results showed statistically significant improvements on antisocial behavior and other symptom areas for youths who received PSST, as reflected on parent and teacher checklists immediately after treatment and up to 1 year later. PSST youths were more improved than relationship therapy and minimal contact youths. The effects were statistically significant but were they clinically important?

To answer the question, comparisons were made among treated youths and the normative data obtained for children of the same age and gender. Data are presented here for a parent-completed measure of deviant behavior (Child Behavior Checklist [CBCL]; Achenbach & Edelbrock, 1983). On this measure, the total score reflects an index of overall symptoms of dysfunction or psychopathology. Extensive data have been obtained on the scale that facilitate evaluation of the performance of clinic and nonreferred samples (Achenbach & Edelbrock, 1983). In this work, the 90th percentile on the total behavior problem scale of the CBCL has been found to discriminate clinic and non-referred samples; this percentile was adopted as the *upper limit for defining a normative range*. At the end of treatment, children who had been referred for aggressive and antisocial behavior were considered to show clinically important changes if they fell below this upper limit of the normative range.

The results in Figure 12.6 (upper panel) show the level of performance of each group in relation to the upper limit of the normative range. Both at posttreatment and follow-up, the means for all groups were well above (i.e., outside of) the upper limit of the normative range. Thus treatment did not bring the mean level of the group within the normative level. The data for individual children in the PSST group, the most effective condition, also reflected limited clinical impact. At posttreatment and 1-year follow-up assessments approximately 18% and 23%, respectively, of youths who received the PSST fell within the normal range for total behavior problems. Thus the vast majority of children did not improve to the extent that their behavior fell within the normative range.

Similar data were obtained for a measure completed by the children's teachers (School Behavior Checklist [SBCL], Miller, 1977). This measure also included an overall or total deviance score that was evaluated similarly. As shown in Figure 12.6 (lower panel), the data were slightly more encouraging. At posttreatment, the mean level of performance of the PSST group fell within the normal range. Yet by the 1-year follow-up, deviant behavior had increased and exceeded the upper limit of this range. The data for the individual children in the PSST group also convey the clinical impact of this intervention. At

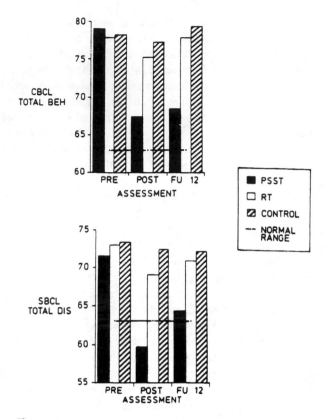

Figure 12.6. Mean scores (*T* scores) for the Problem Solving Skills Training (PSST), Relationship Therapy (RT), and Contact Control groups for the Total Behavior Problem Scale of the CBCL (upper panel) and the Total Disability Scale of the SBCL (lower panel). The horizontal line in each graph represents the *upper* limit of the nonclinical (normal) range of children of the same sex and age. Scores *below* this line fall within the normal range. Source: Kazdin, A.E., Esveldt-Dawson, L., French, N.H., & Unis, A.S. (1987). Problem-solving skills training and relationship therapy in the treatment of antisocial child behavior. *Journal of Consulting and Clinical Psychology, 55,* 76–85. Copyright © 1987 by the American Psychological Association. Reprinted by permission.

posttreatment and 1-year follow-up assessments, respectively, approximately 67% and 39% of the youths who received PSST fell within the normal range on the SBCL.

There are many other studies that might be cited that use the normative range (see Kazdin, 1977; Kendall & Grove, 1988). In each case, the study depends on identifying nondeviant peers who can serve as a basis for comparison. The performance of these peers is assessed to identify normative functioning. The mean and some range or interval about that mean are used to provide a window of functioning that is considered to represent people in the normal range. This is completed for each of the measures of interest in a study or for a smaller number of measures that are considered by the investigator to be particularly important.

Dysfunctional Samples

Another comparison that has been devised is a comparison of clients after treatment with a dysfunctional sample that has not been treated. The notion is that at posttreatment clients who have made a clinically significant change will depart markedly from the original sample of dysfunctional cases. Departure of 2 standard deviations from the mean of the dysfunctional sample is one criterion proposed to delineate that magnitude of change as to be clinically significant (Jacobson & Revenstorf, 1988). Thus at posttreatment, individuals whose scores depart at least 2 standard deviations from the mean of the dysfunctional group (untreated cases with demonstrated dysfunction) would be regarded as an important change.

At first blush, this criterion seems similar to the one used for ordinary statistical significance, namely, a comparison of two groups with the same problem; one group is treated, the other is not. However, the criterion for clinical significance is invoked in relation to the performance of individual clients. Clinically significant change is evaluated in relation to whether a given client departs from the mean by 2 standard deviations and the percentage of individuals who do so within a given experimental condition. To be considered as clinically significant, the changes of course must reflect a departure from the deviant sample in the direction of a decrease of symptoms or increase in prosocial functioning.

A criterion of 2 standard deviations has been suggested for separate reasons. First, if the individual is 2 standard deviations away from the mean of the original group, this suggests that he or she is not represented by that mean; indeed, 2 standard deviations above the mean reflects the 98th percentile. Second and related, 2 standard deviations approximates the criterion used for statistical significance when groups are compared (e.g., 1.96 standard deviations for a two-tailed t test that compares groups for the $p < .05$ level of significance).

As an illustration, a recent study compared two variations of problem solving to treat depression (Nezu & Perri, 1989), as highlighted previously. In evaluating the clinical significance of change, the investigators examined the proportion of cases in each group whose score on measures of depression fell 2 or more standard deviations below (i.e., less depressed) the mean of the untreated sample. For example, on one measure (the Beck Depression Inventory), 85.7% of the cases who received the full problem-solving condition achieved this level of change. In contrast, 50% of the cases who received the abbreviated problem-solving condition achieved this level of change. The comparisons add important information about the impact of treatment.

Problems and Considerations

These methods compare clients to a normative group and/or a deviant group. Identifying a normative group, the more commonly used method, raises critical questions. The initial question is who should serve as the normative group? For example, to whom should mentally retarded, chronic psychiatric patients, or prisoners be compared in evaluating intervention programs. Developing normative levels of performance might be an unrealistic ideal in treatment, if that level is based on individuals normally functioning in the community. Also, what variables would define a normative population? It is unclear how to match subjects included in the normative group along the diverse variables. The normative group might well be defined differently.

For example, in one program, social behaviors such as eye contact and verbalizations were developed in three hospitalized psychiatric patients whose social and verbal behaviors were deficient (Stahl, Thomson, Leitenberg, & Hasazi, 1974). Consider the results for one of the patients whose verbal behavior was altered after training. The patient's verbalizations increased to a level very close to (within 9% of) that of other hospitalized psychiatric patients of similar education who were not considered verbally deficient. Yet the increase in verbalizations was very discrepant (about 30% away) from the level of intelligent, normally functioning individuals. Thus the clinical impact of treatment would be viewed differently depending on the standard used for comparison.

Even if a normative group can be identified, exactly what range of their behaviors would be defined as within the normative level? Among individuals whose behaviors are not identified as problematic there will be a range of acceptable behaviors. It is relatively simple to identify deviant behavior that departs markedly from the behavior of "normal" peers. But, as behavior becomes slightly less deviant, it is difficult to identify the point at which behavior falls within the normative range. Is the normative range within some measure of variability of the average (mean) behavior of the normal peers, say plus or minus one standard deviation? A subjective judgment is required to assess the point at which the individual has entered into the normal range of performance.

Another issue has to do with the criterion for normative functioning. For many behaviors and measures of interest, bringing individuals into the normative range is a questionable goal. Consider, for example, reading skills of elementary school children. A clinically significant change might well be to move children with reading dysfunction so that they fall within the normal range. Yet, perhaps the normal range itself should not be viewed as an unquestioned goal. The reading of most children might be accelerated from current normative levels. Thus normative levels themselves need to be reconsidered.

Finally, it is quite possible that performance falls within the normative range or departs markedly from a deviant group but does not reflect how the individual is functioning in everyday life. Paper-and-pencil measures, questionnaires, interviews, and other frequently used measures may not reflect adaptive functioning for a given individual. Even for measures with high levels of established validity, performance of a given individual does not mean that he or she is happy, doing well, or adjusting in different spheres of life.

Subjective Evaluation

The subjective evaluation method refers to determining the importance of behavior change in the client by assessing the opinions of individuals who are likely to have contact with the client or who are in a position of expertise. The question addressed by this method of evaluation is whether behavior changes have led to differences in how the client is viewed by others. The views of others are relevant because people in everyday life often have a critical role in identifying, defining, and responding to people they may regard as dysfunctional or deviant. Subjective evaluations permit assessment of the extent to which the effects of an intervention, whether or not statistically significant on primary outcome measures, can be readily noticed by others.

As an example of the role of subjective evaluation as a measure of clinical significance, consider the case of Steven, a college student who wished treatment to eliminate two muscle tics (uncontrolled movements; Wright & Miltenberger, 1987). The tics involved head movements and excessive eyebrow raising. Individual treatment sessions were conducted in which he was trained to monitor and identify when the tics occurred and in general to be more aware of their occurrence. In addition, he self-monitored tics throughout the day. Assessment sessions were conducted in which Steven read at the clinic or college library and observers recorded the tics. The impact of self-monitoring and awareness training procedures was evaluated in a multiple-baseline design in which each tic was focused on in sequence. The demonstration showed that each tic declined in frequency when treatment was applied.

A central question is whether the reduction is very important or makes a difference either to Steven or to others. At the end of treatment Steven's responses to a questionnaire indicated that he no longer was distressed by the tics and that he felt they were no longer very noticeable to others. In addition, four observers rated randomly selected tapes without knowing which tapes came from before or after treatment. These were videotapes of assessment periods in which direct observations were made of Steven's tics. Observers rated the tics from the posttreatment tapes as not at all distracting, normal to very normal in appearance, and small to very small in magnitude. In contrast, they had rated tics on the pretreatment tapes as much more severe on these dimensions. Observers were then informed which were the posttreatment tapes and asked to report how satisfied they would be if they had achieved the same results as Steven had. All observers reported they would have been satisfied with the treatment results. The evaluations from Steven and independent observers help attest to the importance of the changes that were achieved and provide information that cannot readily be discerned from the reductions graphed from direct observations.

Subjective evaluation of treatment effects have been used to assess whether improvements in writing skills of children are reflected in ratings of creativity or interest value of the compositions; whether individuals who are trained in public speaking skills are evaluated more positively by the audience; and whether people in contact with deviant children see their behaviors differently after treatment (see Kazdin, 1977). The opinions of others in contact with the client are important as a criterion in their own right because they often serve as a basis for seeking treatment in the first place and also reflect the evaluations the client will encounter after leaving treatment.

In light of the very heavy reliance on global ratings in therapy research in general, a special caution is needed in mentioning and implicitly advocating such ratings here. In intervention research, subjective evaluations would be extremely limited and of unclear value as the sole or primary outcome measure for most clinical dysfunctions. However, as supplementary data, subjective ratings can reflect important information regarding how the problem is viewed.

Problems and Considerations

There are problems with the subjective evaluation method as well. The greatest potential concern is the problem of relying on the opinions of others for determining whether treatment effects were important. Subjective evaluations and the global ratings on which they depend appear to be more readily susceptible to biases on the part of raters than are overt behavioral measures (Kent, O'Leary, Diament, & Dietz, 1974). Thus one must treat subjective evaluations cautiously; it is possible that subjective evaluations will reflect change when other measures of change do not.

In addition, the fact that people associated with a client claim to notice a qualitative difference in behavior as a function of the client's treatment does not mean that the extent of the client's change is clinically significant. Persons in contact with the client may perceive a small change and report this in their ratings. But this says nothing about whether treatment has accomplished enough to alleviate the problem for which treatment was sought or to bring the client within normative levels of behaving.

Social Impact Measures

Another type of measure that helps to evaluate the clinical or applied importance of treatment outcomes is to see if measures of social impact are altered.
Social impact measures refer to outcomes assessed in everyday life and of
importance to society at large. These measures often are gross indexes of
change. For example, measures for programs designed to improve academic
functioning, to decrease aggressive behavior, and to prevent coronary illness
might include grades in school, arrest record, and mortality rate, respectively.

Consider as an illustration a program designed to aid economically disadvantaged families (Lally, Mangione, & Honig, 1988). Low socioeconomic
status mothers in the last trimester of pregnancy were recruited. The intervention consisted of contact with paraprofessionals who provided diverse services
related to mother and child care (e.g., nutrition, child development, parent–
child interactions, assistance with community services, and other features).
Home visits were provided weekly to assist families with such issues as child
rearing, family relations, employment, and community functioning. Day-care
was also provided to children for approximately 5 years. Intervention families
were compared to a nonrandomly comprised control group selected in the
same way as the intervention group and matched on several subject and
demographic variables. Follow-up evaluation was completed 10 years after the
program had ended at which point the children were between 13 and 16 years
of age. Among the many changes, several reflected social impact measures.
Intervention youth, compared to control subjects, showed fewer instances of
probation, less severity of recorded offenses, lower degrees of chronicity, and
lower costs (e.g., court costs, probation, placement, detention and related
costs). The effectiveness of the program on such measures is important. Such
measures are often regarded by consumers of treatment (i.e., those who request
and pay for treatment) as the "bottom line." A measure of the social impact
of treatment, or measures significant to consumers of treatment, often are
considered to reflect whether the change is one that affects functioning in
everyday life.

Social impact measures have often been used in clinical and applied studies.
For example, early parent- and family-based programs for children have
shown long-term benefits in subsequent attendance in high school, reliance on
welfare, and levels of mental retardation—outcomes with clear social impact
(Schweinhart & Weikart, 1988). In a very different area of research, psychosocial interventions that improve safety practices in business and industry, the
benefits are often reflected in the number of injuries and accidents (Fox,
Hopkins, & Anger, 1987). Similarly, efforts to alter habits of drivers have not
only reduced speeding, the primary intervention focus, but also are reflected
in reductions in accidents (Van Houten, Malenfant, & Rolider, 1985). In these
studies, injuries and accidents reflect measures of obvious social importance.

In raising the notion of social impact, one cannot avoid cost as a measure.

Interventions in clinical and applied settings often vary widely in their costs (e.g., outpatient vs. inpatient treatment, brief vs. long-term psychotherapy). Costs are obviously of keen interest to society for diverse parties (parents, clients, policy makers). Although cost is a measure that reflects social impact, it is not elaborated here for separate reasons. To begin with cost is not usually a measure of a psychological construct of interest and on which hypotheses about human functioning are directly tested, at least within clinical psychology. In this sense, other impact measures such as grades, delinquency, and so on are slightly different. In addition, cost and derivative measures (e.g., cost–benefit) are not straightforward and require special training beyond psychology.

Problems and Considerations

Measures of social impact have a number of liabilities that prompt interpretive caution. Measures (e.g., grades, crime rates, fatalities) are often relatively insensitive as measures of intervention effects. They are gross measures and subject to a variety of influences other than those associated with the intervention and investigation. Stated more precisely, error in the measures can be relatively high. Random error may come from variations in how consistently the measures are recorded, as in the case of many archival records (e.g., attendance in school, records in city hall). We take for granted that most psychological measures have a standardized method of administration. Social impact measures are more likely to be recorded and scored somewhat haphazardly over time, which introduces noise (error variability) into the results. Also, systematic error may be introduced by systematic changes in how the measure is scored (instrumentation) over time. Changes in policy, procedures, persons responsible for recording, formula for scoring, budget cuts, and so on all may operate in a systematic way to influence the measure. Both random and systematic error can introduce variability into the measure and make the measure insensitive as an outcome measure.

Also, social impact measures, because they may not be recorded consistently, can omit a great deal of behavior. For example, any program designed to reduce delinquent behavior might measure the extent to which a child or adolescent has contact with the police or the courts, or has an arrest record. Yet police often do not count all contacts with a youth and even if they do, most delinquent acts are not detected officially (Empey, 1982). Consequently, it is difficult to expect such measures to reflect change.

Social impact measures are often seized on by nonresearchers as reflecting the "bottom line" to evaluate the value and effectiveness of a program. Thus if the intervention has not shown social impact, this is often considered in the media or by nonresearchers as evidence that the intervention makes no difference, is not important, and perhaps has failed. In a given case, it is quite possible that this accusation is accurate. Yet, social impact measures need to be thoughtfully evaluated and interpreted. The absence of change on such a measure, given the very nature of many of these measures, may not be an adequate, reasonable, or interpretable index of the program's effect. The danger of social impact measures comes from their two most salient characteristics, namely, their high believability and credibility coupled with their often poor psychometric properties (e.g., alternative types of reliability and validity). Notwithstanding these caveats, social impact data can be quite useful to see if the improvements identified on specific psychological measures are reflected directly on measures of primary interest to consumers of treatment and to society at large. When such measures show a change, they convey important evidence that the impact of the intervention was socially important.

General Comments

The use of normative data, global evaluations of client behavior, and social impact measures represents an important step towards quantifying the extent to which outcomes produced with treatment really have made a difference in the clients' everyday lives. Because the methods address somewhat different questions about the importance of change, they should be used together whenever possible. Methods of evaluating clinical significance have been adopted relatively recently. As yet there is no standard or uniformly adopted procedure or measurement strategy in widespread use. Also, several critical issues that affect use and interpretation of alternative methods remain to be resolved (see Jacobson, 1988). These issues do not detract from the significant step such measures represent in examining the outcomes of intervention programs.

In many areas of interest in clinical psychology, standards are available for comparison purposes that are readily available. For example, in health psychology there are relatively well-accepted standards for normative and healthy levels of weight, hypertension, levels of cholesterol, and others. Interventions with extreme populations can be evaluated in relation to the extent to which they return individuals to a "normative" range. For many psychological tests, extensive normative data also exist. Examples would include standardized intelligence tests (e.g., Weschsler Intelligence Scales) and measures of personality and psychopathology (e.g., MMPI-2). From such measures, means and standard deviations can be used to identify ranges of performance associated with adaptive levels of functioning. Normative ranges on standardized psychological measures as well as indexes of optimal health are prone to change over time as a function of new knowledge and data. Thus standards and criteria for evaluating functioning are not immutable. Nevertheless, the levels provide useful targets toward which interventions can aim.

The message for evaluation is not to endorse one specific measure to reflect clinical or applied significance of an intervention. Any individual measure will possess its own problems. Rather, the issue is to incorporate some measures of clinical significance within intervention research. The measures expand on statistical and nonstatistical methods noted previously and increase the yield from intervention research. They also address a critical issue including the extent to which an intervention has genuine impact on client functioning. This latter issue, critical for clinical psychology, is often lost when statistical comparisons alone are made between alternative treatment and control conditions.

In many ways the comparison and subjective evaluation methods embody features of statistical and nonstatistical evaluation, which were mentioned earlier. As with nonstatistical evaluation, the comparison and subjective evaluation methods are concerned with assessing marked changes in behavior, those that clearly bring the clients within more appropriate levels of responding. As with statistical evaluation, these methods enable one to test in a quantifiable way whether treatment produced change. Comparison and subjective evaluation methods require statistical evaluation in the sense that comparisons need to be made along quantifiable dimensions to assess whether the extent of change brings clients to a level so that they are not different (statistically) from their peers or so that others rate them as improved in terms of a statistically significant improvement. Normative and judgmental criteria need to be more readily incorporated into treatment evaluation.

SUMMARY AND CONCLUSIONS

The chapter discussed three methods of data evaluation, namely statistical evaluation, nonstatistical evaluation, and clinical significance of change. Data evaluation usually consists of applying statistical analyses to the raw data. Statistical tests yield probability levels that are used to judge whether the findings are statistically significant. Issues critical to statistical evaluation and statistical conclusion validity were discussed, including significance levels, power, sample size, significance and magnitude of effects, multiple comparison tests, and multivariate data.

The rationale and arguments favoring statistical methods of data evaluation are deeply ingrained in graduate students and professionals conducting psychological research. Yet there are other methods of data evaluation that have been used in clinical research. Nonstatistical evaluation or visual inspection of the data has been used in single-case research. One reason for using visual inspection is to help investigators seek and report only those findings that are so strong as to be evident by merely looking at the data. Single-case designs help draw inferences through visual inspection because continuous data are available for the subject(s). Nonstatistical criteria for judging whether independent variables have produced reliable effects include changes in mean, level, and slope and in the latency of changes across phases. Judgments are required to invoke these criteria in situations that are not always clear.

Another method of evaluation is to assess the clinical or applied importance of therapeutic change. If the effects of an intervention are statistically significant, this really does not address whether the changes in the subjects are important for their everyday functioning. Comparison methods, subjective evaluation, and social impact measures have been used to assess the clinical importance of behavior change. The *comparison methods* usually demonstrate clinically significant change by showing that performance of the clients after treatment falls within the range of a normative comparison sample and/or departs markedly from the level of functioning that characterizes the sample who continue to evince the problem for which treatment was applied. The *subjective evaluation method* consists of having individuals in contact with the client to provide qualitative evaluations of performance. The *social impact method* consists of evaluating interventions on measures of direct interest to consumers and society at large. These three methods address in different ways the importance and magnitude of behavior change for the client's functioning and provide criteria not available in other forms of data evaluation.

FOR FURTHER READING

Cohen, J. (1990). Things I have learned (so far). *American Psychologist, 45,* 1304–1312.

Folger, R. (1989). Significance tests and the duplicity of binary decisions. *Psychological Bulletin, 106,* 155–160.

Gelso, C.J. (Ed.). (1987). Special issue: Quantitative foundations of counseling psychology research. *Journal of Counseling Psychology, 34* (Whole Issue No. 4).

Jacobson, N.S. (Ed.). (1988). Special issue: Defining clinically significant change. *Behavioral Assessment, 10* (Whole Issue No. 2).

Kazdin, A.E. (1982). *Single-case research designs: Methods for clinical and applied settings.* New York: Oxford University Press. (Appendix A and B on methods of visual inspection and statistical analyses for single-case designs.)

Mohr, L.B. (1990). *Understanding significance testing.* Newbury Park, CA: Sage Publications.

Rossi, J.S. (1990). Statistical power of psychological research: What have we gained in 20 years? *Journal of Consulting and Clinical Psychology, 58,* 646–656.

Stevens, J. (1986). *Applied multivariate statistics for the social sciences.* Hillsdale, NJ: Lawrence Erlbaum Associates.

Chapter 13

SELECTED TOPICS IN THE INTERPRETATION OF DATA

Interpretation of the findings in an investigation obviously depends on the methods of data evaluation, as discussed in the previous chapter. The different methods of evaluation alert us to different facets of the data. In the process, the range of outcomes (e.g., clinical and statistical significance) and our understanding of the impact and nature of interventions are increased. Notwithstanding the contribution of diverse methods, the fact remains that research in the sciences in general and within the many specialty areas of psychology relies almost exclusively on statistical evaluation in determining if an effect is reliable and veridical. The differences between groups or the absence of such differences are used to make claims about the impact of interventions or independent variables of interest. Within this framework, several issues can be identified regarding the interpretation of research findings. In the present chapter, we consider topics related to interpretation of findings that affect individual investigations as well as the accumulation of studies. The topics include data patterns and types of experimental effects, negative findings, and replication.

DATA PATTERN AND TYPE OF EFFECTS

The type of effects that a given investigation yields refers to the impact of the experimental conditions. The presence or absence of alternative effects and their interpretation can be illustrated by considering factorial designs and their yield. As discussed in the chapter on alternative research designs, in a factorial design two or more independent variables are studied simultaneously. In the simplest version, two variables (or factors) are studied, each of which has two different levels or conditions. This version of the factorial design would be referred to as a 2×2 design. (If one of the variables had three levels, it would be a 2×3 design.)

There are different reasons for singling out factorial designs for discussion. First, factorial designs are extremely common in the literature; the efficiency of factorial designs and the types of questions they uniquely address make them popular. Second, the designs permit evaluation of intervention effects of varying complexity. Specifically, with a factorial design one can look at the effects of a single independent variable alone or in combination with other independent variables. The effect of independent variables is referred to as a *main effect;* the effects of variables in combination with others are referred to as *interactions.* Third, factorial designs draw attention to broader issues regarding data interpretation. The effect of a given variable may depend on other variables. This might be evident in a given experiment when a statistically significant interaction is obtained. However, an experiment may show no effect of the independent variable. The result may be due to a hidden interaction because some other condition of which the investigator is unaware may not be at the level to permit the independent variable to show an effect.

Main Effects and Interactions

Statistical evaluation of the results of a factorial experiment may yield significant main effects, interactions, or both. The main effect is equivalent to an overall effect of an independent variable. For example, an investigation might consist of a 2 × 2 design in which Sex of Subject (males vs. females) and Type of Instructions (instructions to subjects leading them to expect therapeutic improvement vs. no instructions) are combined. The effects of these variables might be evaluated on changes in treatment for a particular clinical problem. The study would consist of four groups (2 × 2), representing all combinations of the different levels of each of the variables. Figure 13.1 illustrates how the study might be diagrammed with the four groups.

Statistical analyses (two-way analysis of variance) of the outcome measure might reveal no, one, or two main effects. Consider the hypothetical results where a main effect of Sex of Subject is statistically significant. This would mean that male and female subjects showed different amounts of therapeutic change. The statistical difference that accounts for the main effect is the mean level of performance across all male and all female subjects in the experiment ignoring the specific instructions that they received. If a main effect of Type of Instructions were obtained, it would mean that what subjects were told made a difference in their performance independently of their sex. The final possibility for the design is an interaction. The interaction refers to the pattern of results where the effect of one variable depends on the specific conditions of the other variables. In an experiment, an interaction may be statistically significant whether or not there are any significant main effects.

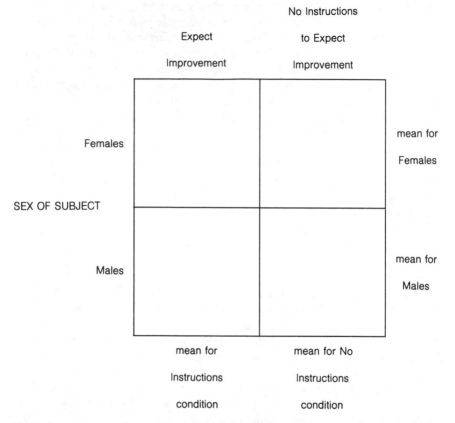

Figure 13.1. A 2 × 2 factorial design evaluating the separate (main effects) and combined (interaction) influences on a dependent measure.

Many different patterns of data might be evident when an interaction is statistically significant. In the above example, Sex of Subject and Type of Instructions might interact. In general the interaction would mean that the impact of instructions depended on the sex of the subject. Yet the precise effect and specific statement that would characterize this interaction depend on the nature of the data. Figure 13.2 shows some of the different patterns of the interactions that could result from the above hypothetical study. The interaction (top portion of the figure suggests) that male subjects were not affected by the instruction conditions. In contrast, female subjects showed greater treatment effects in the instruction condition than in the no-instruction condition. The middle portion of the figure shows a different type of interaction.

Male subjects responded differently across the two instruction conditions, whereas female subjects did not. In the bottom portion of the figure, a more complex interaction is illustrated. Here it can be seen that male and female subjects were affected by instructions but in the opposite fashion. Male subjects showed greater therapeutic change when they received instructions; female subjects showed greater change when they did not.

The purpose in highlighting the notions of main effects and interactions here is to raise more general issues about evaluating results. Thus a simple example and variations of results of the factorial design were selected. (Interactions are complex subjects in their own right and are treated extensively elsewhere [see For Further Readings, this chapter].)

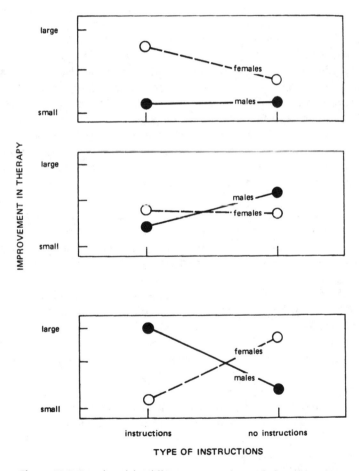

Figure 13.2. Samples of the different patterns that might be reflected in a statistically significant interaction.

In designing an experiment, the minimal prediction involved in a factorial design would be a significant main effect for one or both of the independent variables. Simply stated, this means that the investigator predicts that conditions for the variables or factors will differ statistically. A factorial design is efficient because it allows the experimenter to study more than one main effect, that is, more than one variable in a single experiment, and for that reason alone, it is a highly valued design.

If at all possible, it is especially useful to predict and search for interactions among variables. Predictions about the interactions of independent variables often reflect greater understanding of how the independent variables operate than do predictions about main effects. Interactions refer to the specific conditions under which effects of a given independent variable are obtained and are much more specific than global statements about main effects. In the above example, it might be useful to find that instructions leading subjects to expect therapeutic improvement leads to greater therapeutic change than not providing instructions (main effect of Type of Instructions). Yet a more sophisticated understanding of instructions would be evident if the precise conditions under which these instructional effects were obtained were known. Research examining variables in combination with instructions might show that the effects of instructions vary as a function of sex, therapists, and other factors. As these interactions are enumerated in research, the boundary conditions for the effects of instructions are drawn and a more complete understanding is available than from the demonstration of a straightforward main effect.

Aside from the understanding afforded by identifying interactions, these effects often are the most intriguing. Consider an example of an experiment that looked at factors that contribute to how clients view their therapists (Bloom et al., 1977). In this study the main task of the subject was to rate how qualified, dynamic, and generally believable the therapist was. The investigators proposed that people have stereotypes about therapists based on many different characteristics of the therapy situation. One of these characteristics may be the decor of the therapist's office. So they varied office decor, which was one factor in the design with two different levels: namely, a "traditional professional office" and a "humanistic office."

The traditional professional office was a room with a therapist's chair behind a desk, a file cabinet, and various books. Diplomas were on the wall to help convey the traditional office decor. In the humanistic professional office, using the same room, the desk was placed in a corner so it did not separate the therapist's and client's chairs. Indeed, these chairs were placed relatively close together. In lieu of diplomas, posters were displayed around the room with slogans, such as "Love makes the world go round." Throw pillows and a beanbag chair were also in the room. In short, office decor was varied to create different atmospheres. The authors considered the possibility that the decor might lead to different reactions depending on the sex of the subject and the sex of the therapist. Thus the design then included three factors each with two levels: Sex of Subject (male, female), Sex of Therapist (male, female), and Office Decor (traditional, humanistic).

The subjects came to the room individually and read a description of the therapist who supposedly occupied the office. The descriptions were the same for all subjects and for each decor but varied in whether the therapist was said to be a male or female. Subjects never actually met the therapist but filled out a questionnaire about the kind of therapist that was likely to occupy the office.

The major results yielded an interaction of Sex of Therapist $\times$ Office Decor. Female therapists were rated as more credible when seen to occupy a traditional professional office than a humanistic office. The opposite was found for male therapists, who were seen as more credible in the humanistic than in the traditional office. One explanation offered for this interesting finding pertains to the stereotypic reactions that individuals might have toward therapists. The investigators suggested that traditional offices might trigger reactions about the occupant being well trained, scientific, and authoritarian. Traditionally, these characteristics might also be stereotypically applied more frequently to males than to females. In contrast, a humanistic office might convey cues that the occupant is sensitive, warm, and caring. These latter characteristics may be more stereotypic of females.

Credibility was the greatest in situations where office cues and gender cues were complementary. Complementary characteristics might convey to subjects the best of both worlds, namely that the person they are seeing is professional and well trained, but also warm and sensitive. Of course, the precise explanation of the findings remains to be tested further. The interaction demonstrates an intriguing result that only could be evaluated by combining separate factors in a single experiment.

General Comments

Although the search for interactions was advocated here, certainly this point can be debated. Whether one looks for main effects or interactions in his or her research depends largely upon the state of knowledge in a given area of research, the purpose of the research, and one's view of the world. In a relatively new or unexplored area of research, investigators usually attempt to discover those variables that have any effect at all (main effects). Only later, after initial work, do the interactions take on more significance as the qualifying conditions are unraveled. Yet interactions may be important for theoretical as well as applied purposes by elaborating how a particular variable operates.

Research would be much simpler if variables operating in the world were restricted to main effects. Results of experiments could be accepted or rejected more easily if a given variable were always shown to have either an effect or no effect. Because variables often do interact with each other, it is difficult to interpret the results of a single experiment. If a variable has no effect, it is always possible that it would have an effect if some other condition of the experiment were altered. That is, the variable may produce no effect for certain subjects, experimenters, or other specific conditions but later produce great effects when any of these other conditions is altered. Often in research, we question the external validity (generality) of the findings obtained in a study. Equally, we can question the generality of the findings when an effect is *not* obtained, that is, whether the variable would have no impact if tested under other conditions.

In one sense, variables studied by psychologists always can be considered to interact with other variables rather than to operate as individual main effects. That a variable produces a main effect in an experiment does *not* mean that the effect is not qualified by other conditions. The conditions of the experiment that are held constant may reflect a narrow set of circumstances under which the variable produces a statistically significant effect. The effect might not be produced as these conditions change. To make the point, one can mention variables in which most investigators are not very interested: for example, repetition of most psychological experiments with a different species, with infants rather than adults (or vice versa), with individuals who have learning deficits, and so on might show few statistically significant findings. Few, if any, results obtained by psychologists would be replicated across all possible variations in conditions that could be studied. That is, there are implicit interactions among the conditions studied.

The point here is to show that so-called main effects are likely to be greatly qualified by other variables and really be part of interactions. Investigators may not study the other variables in light of their own interests or the theoretical questions underlying the experiment. Yet, from the standpoint of conceptualizing experiments and the results that may be obtained, it is important to recognize that main effects and interactions are more readily distinguished as concepts in a given experiment rather than ways in which independent variables may operate more generally. It is likely that all variables interact with some other variables in some way. Some of these interactions are of interest to psychologists in a given area; others are not. Also, some interactions are more likely to be detected in experiments than are others.

NEGATIVE RESULTS OR NO-DIFFERENCE FINDINGS

In most investigations, the impact of variables of interest are evaluated by statistical criteria. The presence of an effect is decided if the null hypothesis (H_o) is rejected. Despite the limitations of statistical criteria, they are used frequently to evaluate whether a study has merit and, for example, warrants publication in a journal. Yet as researchers know all too well, many investigations do not yield statistically significant findings or any other evidence that the independent variable influenced the subjects. The frequently discussed notion of *negative results* is used to refer to such an experimental outcome.

The term *negative results* has come to mean that there were no statistically significant differences between groups that received different treatments or that the result did not come out the way the investigator had hoped or anticipated. Usually the term is restricted to the finding that groups did not differ, which leads to acceptance of the null hypothesis. The null hypothesis states that the experimental conditions will not differ, that is, that the independent variable will have no effect. Typically, rejection of this hypothesis is regarded as a "positive" or favorable result, whereas failure to reject this hypothesis is regarded as a "negative" result. Advances in research usually are conceived as a result of rejecting the null hypothesis.

The search for group differences, often so that the results of a study will be publishable, may encourage sacrifice of methodological criteria, the possibility of inadvertent bias, or outright dissimulation (Barber, 1976). Group differences might occur at the expense of methodological rigor. Poor methodology and sources of experimental bias are more likely to be overlooked when a predicted or plausible finding of significant differences is obtained. The implicit view is that group differences demonstrate that, whatever failings of the experiment, they were not sufficient to cancel the effects of the independent variable. In contrast, negative results often imply that the independent variable was weak or that the dependent variable was a poor test of the treatment.

Actually, the value of a study can be assessed as a function of its conceptualization and methodological adequacy, rather than whether differences are found. The conceptualization and design of an investigation bear no necessary relation to the outcome of an experiment. Many sloppy, ill-conceived, and horrendously uncontrolled studies can lead to systematic group differences. Indeed, the directional operation of experimenter biases, as detailed earlier, may contribute directly to group differences. In contrast, meticulously conducted experiments with proper controls may well show no effect. As investigators, we wish to proceed with the best or strongest available design and greatest methodological care so that the results, whatever their pattern, will be interpretable.

It may be that methodological adequacy rather than statistical significance should be adopted as a more important criterion for evaluating the contribution of an investigation (Greenwald, 1975; Kupfersmid, 1988; Lykken, 1968). The difficulty in judging the value of any study is that neither the importance of a finding nor methodological adequacy is invariably agreed upon by those who do the judging. Statistical criteria may have been overly relied on because they present relatively simple bases for evaluating research.

Ambiguity of Negative Results

The absence of group differences in an experiment is usually not met with enthusiasm by the investigator nor by reviewers and journal editors who may be evaluating the manuscript for possible publication. This reaction derives from the ambiguity usually associated with negative results. The ambiguity can be clarified by keeping in mind that negative results are tantamount to accepting the null hypothesis. The reason for or basis of "no difference" findings usually cannot be identified in the experiment. The most straightforward reason for accepting the null hypothesis is that there is in fact no relation between the independent and dependent variables. There are, however, many other explanations for a "no-difference" finding.

Assume for a moment that there is a relation between the independent and dependent variable. A large number of factors might preclude showing these differences. Consider a simple investigation with an experimental and control group. Any factor within the experiment that operates to keep the means near each other can lead to no difference. To begin with, the intervention may not have been manipulated adequately. As noted in chapter 8, whether the independent variable was successfully manipulated often can be assessed. The failure to demonstrate that the manipulation was delivered appropriately to the experimental group would serve as a plausible explanation of the absence of group differences. For example, in one treatment study of antisocial youth mentioned earlier (Feldman et al., 1983), alternative treatments (behavior modification, traditional group social work, activity control) did not differ in their impact. The investigation demonstrated that treatment was not implemented faithfully and that treatment was inadvertently applied to the control group. The absence of group differences is understandable. In many studies, implementation is not assessed in a way that would even permit this type of evaluation.

The absence of group differences may also result from the particular levels of the independent variable selected for the study. Group differences might have resulted if other levels of the same variable had been studied. For example, the relations between different levels of an independent variable and group differences in outcome can be illustrated by the relation between the amount of treatment and therapeutic change. In general, the adult psychotherapy literature has tended to show a duration or dose effect of psychotherapy (Howard, Kopta, Krause, & Orlinsky, 1986). Across a large number of patients and studies, more sessions were associated with greater patient improvements. However, the relation is not linear. As shown in Figure 13.3, 50% of the patients are markedly improved by Session 8 (solid line) and 75% markedly improved by Session 26.

Assume we did not know of this relation and conducted a study to evaluate treatment duration. We may compare a group that receives 20 sessions with another group that receives 30 sessions. The difference between these groups, in terms of percentage of patients improved (see Figure 13.3), may be too small to produce a statistically significant difference. On the other hand, if the levels of the independent variable were more discrepant and at different stages of treatment (e.g., 10 vs. 30 sessions), group differences might be more likely. The example is provided to illustrate the potential problem of not selecting sufficiently discrepant levels of the independent variable to reflect change or inadvertently selecting levels from a range where the discrepancy may not be as relevant to outcome.

Alternatively, the nature of the relations between different levels of an independent variable and behavior change may lead to no differences even when grossly discrepant levels are compared. The relations between levels of the independent variable and outcome may be curvilinear rather than linear. For example, a hypothetical relation between anxiety level and behavior

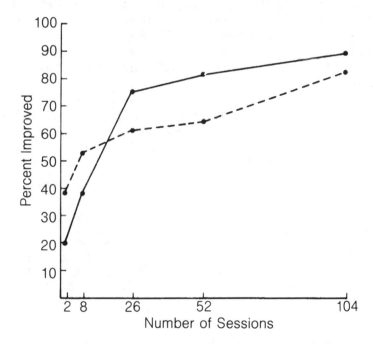

Figure 13.3. The relation between the number of sessions of psychotherapy for adult patients and the percentage of patients improved. The solid line reflects ratings at the end of treatment completed by researchers based on chart review. The broken line reflects patient self-report ratings during the course of treatment. Source: Howard, K.I., Kopta, S.M., Krause, M.S., & Orlinsky, D.E. (1986). The dose–effect relationship in psychotherapy. *American Psychologist, 41,* 159–164. Copyright © 1986 by the American Psychological Association. Reprinted by permission.

change for a particular treatment may be as illustrated in Figure 13.4. Subjects who are high and low in anxiety on a particular measure may not respond differently to treatment; that is, they may show equal change. A conclusion that there is no relation between anxiety level and outcome would not be accurate because a comparison of low and moderately anxious subjects or moderately and highly anxious subjects would have shown a relation.

Any factor in the experiment that operates to increase within-subject variability also may increase the likelihood of finding no differences. As we discussed in relation to statistical conclusion validity, the magnitude of an effect can be measured in terms of effect size or the difference between group means divided by the standard deviation. A given difference is lower in the effect size that is generated as the standard deviation (denominator) increases. The sensitivity of the experiment in detecting a difference can be reduced by allowing uncontrolled sources of variation or "noise" into the experiment. Allowing such factors as the adequacy of training of different experimenters and methods of delivering instructions to vary can increase the variance within-treatment groups and reduce the likelihood of finding group differences. Indeed, negative results have on occasion been implicitly used to infer that the investigator may be incompetent for not controlling the situation well enough to obtain group differences (Greenwald, 1975).

Inconsistencies across or within experimental conditions can override a relation between independent and dependent variables that otherwise would be detected. Also, if a finding is very well established and has been replicated under a variety of conditions, a failure of replication may well reflect upon the skills of the investigator. For example, if an experimenter finds that food-

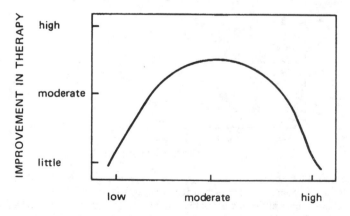

Figure 13.4. Hypothetical relation between degree of anxiety (on a personality inventory or behavioral test) and the amount of therapeutic change.

deprived laboratory animals do not learn to respond to a lever to obtain food under rather standard conditions, questions are likely to be raised about how the food was delivered or some other aspect of the experimenter's procedures. Developing responses in such circumstances is so common that failure to replicate might reflect on the competence of the experimenter rather than on the robustness of the original finding.

Several areas of an experiment that do not necessarily reflect procedural sloppiness are related to the sensitivity of the experimental test and the likelihood that group differences will be found. The assessment device(s) may show sufficiently variable performance that only the most robust relations would emerge as statistically significant. In addition, even when variability is small, the devices selected may not be the most appropriate for detecting a relation of interest. Assessment devices are often selected because of what they are called rather than what they have been shown to measure empirically, or because they are readily available, inexpensive, and expedient.

Several statistical considerations directly influence the sensitivity of the experiment. For example, sample size is related directly to whether the differences between groups on the dependent measure will be statistically significant. Whether group sizes are equal, whether the assumptions of the analyses are met, and similar factors dictate the sensitivity of the experimental test. As already detailed, the power of statistical tests raises the question, "What chance did the investigator have of detecting a difference between groups in the study if a difference exists in the population?" Evaluation of research in clinical psychology has shown that most investigations have very little chance of demonstrating treatment differences when such differences exist in the population (Rossi, 1990). As a rule, experiments are too weak to detect differences unless the actual effect of the intervention is relatively large. Because most treatment effects are not likely to be very large, experimenters can expect to have negative results simply because of the lack of power of their statistical tests.

When Negative Results Are Interpretable

The absence of group differences is routinely dismissed as ambiguous and is often given much less attention than it should receive. There are several situations in which negative results are very informative and interpretable. Negative results in the context of a program of research can be very informative. A program of research refers to a series of studies conducted by an investigator or group of investigators. The studies usually bear great similarity to each other along such dimensions as the independent variables, subjects, and assessment devices. In a program of research, presumably several of the studies would have produced some group differences (otherwise it would be difficult to explain why the work was continued). The demonstration of group differences in some of the studies means that the experimental procedures are sensitive to at least some interventions. Thus one can usually rule out the problem that the experiments are conducted poorly or that the methodology is too insensitive to detect group differences. In any given instance, these explanations may be true of one of the experiments. Yet, if the program of research has established itself in terms of demonstrating group differences, research showing no differences for a related variable can be viewed with greater confidence than would be the case in an isolated study.

A second situation in which negative results are informative is when these results are replicated (repeated) across several different investigators. A problem in the psychological literature, and perhaps in other areas as well, is that once a relation is reported, it is extremely difficult to qualify or refute with subsequent research. If negative results accumulate across several studies, however, they strongly suggest that the original study either resulted from very special circumstances or possibly through various artifacts. Examples are provided later in the discussion of replication.

A final circumstance in which negative results may be informative is when the conditions under which these results are obtained were predicted as well as explicated. An excellent research strategy is to predict the conditions under which the independent variable produces and fails to produce differences across groups. The way in which this is easily achieved is through a factorial design that permits assessment of an interaction. An interaction between the different factors indicates that the effect of one variable depends on the level of another variable. An interaction may be reflected in the finding that there are no differences between groups for some levels of the variables but statistically significant differences between groups for a different level of the variables; that is, negative results occur in only some of the experimental conditions. If such results were predicted, their occurrence would be quite informative.

Another type of interaction, although not usually referred to as such, is an interaction of independent and dependent variables. The absence of group differences might be predicted or obtained on some measures but not on others. It might be useful to show that the effects of different variables, or indeed whether an effect was obtained at all, depended on the specific measures that were used. Here negative results are predicted but only across some of the measures included in the experiment.

When Negative Results Are Important

Noting that negative results are interpretable suggests that a no-difference finding is salvageable. Actually, finding no difference under a variety of circumstances may be very important (Yeaton & Sechrest, 1986). Many questions of interest in clinical and applied research are important in relation to demonstrating no difference. Does consumption of a particular fruit laced with pesticide increase risk for cancer? Is a less painful, expensive, or invasive treatment as effective as the usual treatment alternative? Do children who spend time in day-care differ in psychological dysfunction from those who spend that time at home with a parent? No difference between the appropriate comparison groups in well-conducted studies for these questions would be quite informative and socially important.

As an example of a valuable no-difference finding, consider the treatment of breast cancer. Research has shown that for many women a radical mastectomy (complete removal of the breast) is no more effective in terms of long-term mortality than a lumpectomy (a more circumscribed operation in which the tumor and a small amount of surrounding tissue is removed; Fisher et al., 1985). This no-difference finding in terms of outcome is critically important because the two treatments are very different in their cost, risk, psychological impact, and other measures.

No-difference findings may also be of importance because of the potential questions they raise. For example, programs that are extremely costly and mandated for treatment for special populations may be shown to have little or no impact in the outcomes they produce (e.g., Weisz, Walter, Weiss, Fernandez, & Mikow, 1990). Such findings may stimulate innovative intervention and evaluation efforts.

In the general case, negative results may be important based on substantive *and* methodological considerations. The substantive considerations refer to the significance of the experimental or clinical questions that guide the investigation. As in the above example, the question may be one in which no differences between two groups, conditions, or interventions are actively sought. The methodological considerations refer to the care with which the study is planned, implemented, and evaluated. In particular, given documented weaknesses of research, the power of the study to have demonstrated differences if they exist is pivotal. Power analyses, of the type discussed earlier, can be completed before and after a study is conducted to provide the investigator and reader with a statement of the sensitivity of the test in light of expected or obtained effect sizes. No-difference findings in a well-conceived and controlled study with adequate power (e.g., $\leq .80$) ought to be taken as seriously as any other finding.

REPLICATION

Evaluation of the results of an experiment, whether or not a significant difference is demonstrated, entails more than scrutiny of that experiment alone. The reliability of a finding across studies greatly enhances evaluation of any particular investigation. Replication is a pivotal topic that relates to evaluation of findings and accumulation of knowledge.

Types of Replication

Replication refers to repetition of an experiment. Different types of replication can be distinguished, namely, direct or exact replication and systematic or approximate replication (see Carlsmith, Ellsworth, & Aronson, 1976; Lykken, 1968; Sidman, 1960). *Direct replication* refers to an attempt to repeat an experiment exactly as it was conducted originally. Ideally, the conditions and procedures across the replication and original experiment are identical. *Systematic replication* refers to repetition of the experiment by purposely allowing various features to vary. The conditions and procedures of the replication are deliberately designed only to approximate those of the original experiment. Actually, direct and systematic replication are not qualitatively different. An exact replication is not possible because repetition of the experiment involves new subjects tested at a different point in time and by different experimenters, all of which conceivably could lead to different results. Thus all replications necessarily allow some factors to vary; the issue is the extent to which the replication study departs from the original investigation.

A replication that is "direct" would follow the original procedures as closely as possible. This is the easiest to do for the researcher who conducted the original investigation, given that many of the procedures are not sufficiently described in written reports and articles of an investigation. Journals routinely limit the space available in which authors may present their studies. Consequently, authors are restricted to communicating only the most rudimentary information. Although the procedures of an investigation often seem clear when reading the concise report, this clarity quickly evaporates when one tries to replicate the study in an actual experimental situation. The investigator usually makes many decisions about what should be done about matters not specified in the original report. Thus most research attempting to replicate directly is actually a systematic replication, but one which resembles the original investigation very closely. Ideally, an individual interested in a close replication of the original experiment would use as many of the original experimental materials in the repetition as possible. These materials might include therapist manuals, assessment devices, protocols related to all experimental behavior, and so on, all of which may be available directly from the original investigator.

A replication that is "systematic" would vary the experiment deliberately along one or more dimensions. For example, a systematic replication might assess whether the relation between the independent and dependent variable holds when subjects are older or younger than those in the original experiment, when subject (patient) diagnoses differ, when the instructions on the experimental task are given orally or by tape recorder rather than in written form, when the therapists are inexperienced rather than experienced, and so on. Of course, a systematic replication tends to vary only one or a few of the dimensions along which the study might differ from the original experiment. There is a good reason to limit the number of variations introduced into the systematic replication. If the results of a replication differ from the original experiment, it is desirable to have a limited number of differences between these experiments so the possible reason for the discrepancy of results might be more easily identified. If there are multiple differences between the original and replication experiments, discrepancies in results might be due to a host of factors not easily discerned without extensive further experimentation.

Importance of Replication

The importance of replication in scientific research cannot be overemphasized. Unfortunately, the importance is not commensurate with the number of replications that seem to be attempted or at least reported. The sweeping statement about the dearth of replication studies has important exceptions. For example, research within experimental psychology frequently includes replications. Within a single article, several studies may be reported in which a demonstrated relation is repeated and elaborated in further investigations of the same type (e.g., see issues of the *Journal of Experimental Psychology: Learning, Memory, and Cognition*). In many cases, the nature of the study (e.g., laboratory study of memory using college students who attend a single session) facilitates repetition. In contrast, in clinical, counseling, and educational psychology, as well as other areas, recruiting and running subjects may be more protracted. However, the concern here is not with practical impediments to replication but a broader ethos in which replication and its critical role in science are uniformly appreciated.

It is often stated that there are few professional rewards for replication attempts, particularly direct replication attempts. Direct replications may be met with indifference because the outcome may be considered as either uninformative or ambiguous. If the results of the original study are successfully replicated, the replication project may be given little attention because it does not add new information to the literature. If the replication study does not yield the same results, the onus is implicitly on the second investigator to explain and demonstrate why there was a difference across the investigations.

The major reason that replications are not usually viewed with great excitement is that, by definition, they are partly *repetitions* of experiments that already have been done. Repetition of the experiment at first blush seems undramatic and certainly lacking in originality. Indeed, at cocktail parties with psychologists, one would not want to boast about the fact that his or her research is devoted to replication of work done by other experimenters! Yet replication experiments should not be viewed as mere repetitions of previous work. Rather, replications can be better conceptualized either as tests of robustness and generality of the original finding or more careful evaluations of the original hypotheses. This is not merely a terminological change but rather, I believe, a more accurate and useful characterization of the status of replications.

Replication studies are direct tests of robustness and the generality of the original experimental findings. They ask whether the relation holds across changes in the conditions of the experiment. If the results of a replication do not support the original research, they do not necessarily impugn the original finding. Rather, they may suggest that the relation only holds for a narrow set of conditions or relates to a specific circumscribed set of factors, perhaps some even unspecified in the original report. The original finding may be veridical and not the result of experimental biases or artifacts, but still insufficiently robust to have wide generality.

Replications as tests of generality are particularly important in clinical psychology where research and application are often intertwined. Tests of generality partially address the applied value of many findings and have implications for decisions about treatment. Researchers and clinicians alike wish to know how widely the results of a given treatment can be applied or, indeed, whether the results can be applied at all beyond a very narrow set of experimental conditions. Direct and systematic replications add to knowledge in different ways. Replications that closely approximate the conditions of the original experiment increase one's confidence that the original finding is reliable and not likely to result from a particular artifact. Replications that deviate from the original conditions suggest that the findings hold across a wider range of conditions. Essentially, the greater the divergence of the replication from the conditions of the original experiment, the greater the generality of the relation that was demonstrated.

Several replication attempts may reveal findings that show the original relation to be evident across a wide range of laboratory and even field conditions. On the other hand, several unsuccessful replication attempts may reveal findings that show the original relation not to be present anywhere. Unless the original finding is of unusual theoretical significance, it then may be viewed as trivial in the sense that it is narrowly restricted to a very specific set of circumstances. Alternatively, the original finding may have resulted from uncontrolled factors or biases not evident in the original report.

Aside from tests of generality, replications often provide much more careful evaluations of the hypothesis studied in the original experiment. Typically, these evaluations have implications for the interpretation (construct validity) of the original experiment. The very basis for conducting a replication may be that there is an alternative explanation of the results that the original investigator did not rule out. A replication may repeat the original experiment with additional control conditions and provide a methodological and theoretical advance.

Obviously, replication attempts do not invariably produce the same results as the original experiment. There are many dramatic examples where one study reported particularly interesting or influential findings and several unsuccessful replications followed. An interesting example is illustrated in a study completed several years ago (Valins & Ray, 1967) that was designed to assess the importance of people's cognitions about their own behavior. In this study, subjects who feared harmless snakes received false feedback about their physiological arousal. The feedback, consisting of noises that subjects were told was their heart rate, was supposed to lead them to believe that they were not aroused in the presence of snake stimuli (slides showing various kinds of snakes). The false heart rate information indicated no arousal (no rapid beating) during exposure to the slides. The results suggested that subjects who thought the noises were their heart rates and that they had not become aroused performed better on a subsequent measure of avoidance behavior than did subjects who were told that the feedback noise was random sounds. The authors interpreted the results as showing that one's own beliefs that fearful stimuli do not increase arousal will lead individuals to behave less fearfully.

Several subsequent studies attempting to replicate the findings found no group differences on avoidance measures after the false feedback (e.g., Gaupp, Stern, Galbraith, 1972; Sushinsky & Bootzin, 1970). These latter studies included control groups to rule out the influence of alternative processes in the false feedback group and any actual changes in physiological arousal. The consistent pattern in these latter studies suggests that the original results were due to uncontrolled factors in the experimental situation or depended on unspecified dimensions not clear from the report. (Another possibility is that the original results were a "chance" occurrence and that the null hypothesis [no group differences] was rejected falsely.)

Another example of a failure to replicate was evident in a single-case experiment. In a study completed several years ago, self-instruction training was used to alter the behavior of three children in a Head Start program who were highly disruptive in class (Bornstein & Quevillon, 1976). Training was conducted for 2 hours outside of the classroom, where the children and a trainer worked on tasks to develop problem-solving skills. The skills were intended to alter their on-task behavior in the classroom. The children were instructed to administer instructions to themselves—first aloud, then in a whisper, and finally without sound (covertly). Self-instruction training was administered and evaluated in a multiple-baseline design across children. The results indicated marked increases in on-task behavior in the classroom for each of the children. Moreover, the markedly improved classroom performance was maintained several weeks after treatment.

Several investigators have since tried to repeat this demonstration with little or no success (e.g., Bryant & Budd, 1982; Friedling & O'Leary, 1979). One of the replication efforts tried to follow very closely those procedures implemented in the original study using children in a Head Start program who were disruptive in class (Billings & Wasik, 1985). The results revealed that classroom performance was not improved by the procedures and the original effects were not replicated. Clearly, the original findings raise questions. Some of the ambiguities have prompted different types of studies to understand when and how self-instruction training can alter child behavior.

The failures to replicate the original findings in the examples lend emphasis to the importance of routine replication studies. The nature of publication practices undoubtedly fosters biases about the information disseminated in the literature. A given investigator or journal may report only "positive effects" (i.e., group differences) and systematically exclude all similar studies that find no differences. The statistical likelihood of obtaining significant group differences among the many attempted experiments alone would be expected to inflate the number of unreplicable positive effects in the literature. It is not clear how many published findings are unlikely to be replicated because they represent chance group differences brought to public light because of publication biases. The paucity of replication research may obscure the number of findings that can be confidently embraced as robust.

From the standpoint of a prospective investigator, replication work is important to consider as a research strategy, particularly at the inception of one's work in an area, when it is important to ensure that the phenomenon can be reproduced. After a phenomenon has been reproduced, it can be analyzed and elaborated in subsequent research. Although replication research is advocated here as an important focus, it would be naive to neglect the point noted earlier that simple replication may conflict with professional rewards. The rewards are for "original experimentation" or for something that has not been done before. (In many areas, any well-controlled research would meet this latter criterion.) An excellent strategy is to include in one's investigation a partial replication of previous research; for example, an experimenter could include conditions that closely resemble those in a previous experiment. In addition, conditions can be included that conceptually extend the experiment and the experimental conditions. Essentially, this strategy includes an attempt to combine direct and systematic replication strategies in a single experiment. The results of such research, assuming that the study meets methodological desiderata at least equal to the original experiment, not only allows one to comment on the reliability of the phenomenon but its generality all within the same experiment. Also, the researcher may be able to predict an interaction indicating the conditions across which the original findings may hold.

SUMMARY AND CONCLUSIONS

Three areas were discused related to interpretation of research findings. Data patterns and types of experimental effects were discussed in relation to factorial designs. Within factorial designs, the impact of a given variable can be studied alone (main effect) or in combination with other variables (interactions). The designs alert us to the fact that the impact of a given variable must be viewed in relation to other variables that may influence its impact. Factorial designs permit the combination of several variables that can reveal different effects of one variable as a function of the other. This concept (interaction) has important implications for the types of research we conduct, but also for interpretation of research and the presence or absence of effects more generally. The presence or absence of a finding or relation may well be due to or restricted by other conditions.

Another topic critical to interpretation of data is the notion of *negative results,* a concept which has come to mean that no statistically significant differences were found in the experiment. The concept has received attention because the importance of a given study and its publishability often have been associated directly with whether statistically significant results are obtained. Unfortunately, such an emphasis has detracted considerably from methodological considerations, that is, whether the conclusions can be accepted independently of statistical evaluation based on the quality of the design. Hence methodologically weak studies with statistically significant results often are published, and methodologically sound studies or studies at least as sound as those published often go unpublished.

Related to the topic of "negative" results is the notion of replication. *Replication* refers here to repetition of a previously conducted study. Replications can vary in similarity to the original experiment. *Direct replications* attempt to copy as exactly as possible the original experiment, whereas *systematic replications* deliberately attempt to vary the conditions of the original experiment. Replication research may lead to "negative" results, which can bring into question the basis for the results of the original experiment or the generality of the original findings.

Replication research is exceedingly important because it is the most reliable test of whether the finding is veridical. The logic of statistical analyses suggests that occasionally statistical significance will be achieved even when there are no group differences in the population, that is, findings significant by "chance" alone. Because these are likely to be published due to the bias for "positive" findings, there could well be a great many findings that would not stand up under any replication conditions. Thus to distinguish those findings in the field that have a sound basis requires replication research. Replications need not merely repeat previous experiments but can include previous experiments as a part of a new investigation.

FOR FURTHER READING

Cronbach, L.J. (1982). *Designing evaluations of educational and social programs.* San Francisco: Jossey-Bass.

Fagley, N.S. (1985). Applied statistical power analysis and the interpretation of nonsignificant results by research consumers. *Journal of Counseling Psychology, 32,* 391–396.

Jaccard, J., Turrisi, R., & Wan, C.K. (1990). *Interaction effects in multiple regression.* Newbury Park: Sage Publications.

Jules, G., & Mohr, L.B. (1989). Analysis of no-difference findings in evaluation research. *Evaluation Review, 13,* 628–655.

Rosnow, R.L., & Rosenthal, R. (1989). Definition and interpretation of interaction effects. *Psychological Bulletin, 105,* 143–146.

Wimsatt, W.C. (1981). Robustness, reliability, and multiple determination in science. In M.B. Brewer & B.E. Collins (Eds.), *Scientific inquiry and the social sciences: A volume in honor of Donald T. Campbell.* San Francisco: Jossey-Bass.

ETHICAL ISSUES AND GUIDELINES FOR RESEARCH

Psychological experimentation raises a number of ethical issues and dilemmas. First, experiments require manipulation of variables, which often may subject participants to experiences that are undesirable or even potentially harmful, such as stress, failure, and frustration. Whether participants in research should be subjected to such experiences is in part an ethical decision.

Second, implementing many experimental manipulations may require withholding information from the subject. The experimental question may address how subjects respond without being forewarned about exactly what will happen or the overall purpose. Withholding information from the subject also raises important ethical issues.

Third, experimentation requires assessment or observation of the subject. Many dependent measures of interest pertain to areas that subjects may consider private such as views about themselves, beliefs about important social or political issues, and signs of adjustment or maladjustment. Even if the observations themselves do not threaten the privacy of the individual subject, public disclosure of the information might be damaging. Hence issues pertaining to invasion of privacy and violation of confidentiality are raised by assessment of personality and behavior.

Fourth, the methodological requirements of psychological experiments also raise ethical issues that are particularly acute in intervention research. For example, assigning clients randomly to one of several treatment or control conditions entails an ethical decision favoring experimental design, rather than the seeming appropriateness of one condition over another for the client's problem. Also, whether treatment should be withheld also reflects an ethical decision made by an investigator.

Aside from substantive and methodological issues, the relationship between the investigator or experimenter and the subject raises ethical concerns. The difference in the power and status of experimenter and subject allows for potential abuses of the rights of the individual subject (Kelman, 1972). Research subjects, particularly in clinical research, often are disadvantaged or dependent by virtue of their age, physical and mental condition, captive status, educational level, or political and economic position. For example, by virtue of their status, children and adolescents, the aged, college students, psychiatric patients, prisoners, and military recruits have relatively much less power than the investigator. Such a power differential increases the vulnerability of these individuals to abuse. The subjects may be more readily induced into research and have, or at least feel they have, relatively little freedom to refuse or discontinue participation.

The status of the experimenter is sustained by several factors. The investigator structures the situation in which the subject participates. He or she is seen as an expert and as justified in determining the conditions for performance. The legitimacy, prestige, and importance of scientific research all place subjects in an inferior position. Although subjects can withdraw from the research, that may not be viewed as a realistic option given the status differential. Subjects may see themselves as lacking both the capacity and right to question the investigator and what is being done. Subjects are at a disadvantage in terms of the information about the experiment at their disposal, the risks that are taken, and the limited means for counteracting objectionable aspects of the treatment.

Investigators have become increasingly sensitive to many of the issues and desired practices required for experimental research. These practices ensure that the rights of the individual subject are protected and are given the highest priority in research. The present chapter raises a number of ethical issues as well as highlights contemporary guidelines for ethical research practices and professional obligations in the conduct and reporting of research. The focus of this chapter is on those issues primarily in the context of research with human subjects. Ethical and practical issues pertaining to infrahuman species are in no way less significant. However, the vast majority of research in clinical and counseling psychology and related areas is with human subjects.

CRITICAL ISSUES IN RESEARCH

Although many ethical issues can be identified, a few seem particularly salient: using deception in experiments, informing subjects about the deception after the experiment is completed, invading the subject's privacy, and obtaining informed consent.

Deception

Deception may take many different forms and often refers to quite different operations. At one extreme, deception can involve the entire misrepresentation of the nature of an experiment. At the other extreme, deception can also entail being ambiguous about the experiment or not specifying all or many important details. The extent to which these various active (e.g., misrepresentation) or passive (e.g., failure to mention specific details) forms of deception are objectionable in part depends on the situations in which they are used and the effects they are likely to have on the subjects. Misleading the subject may not be very objectionable in many experimental arrangements. For example, when subjects perform a memory task involving lists of words or syllables, they may be told initially that the purpose is to measure the way in which individuals memorize words. In fact, the purpose may be to assess the accuracy of recall as a function of the way in which the words are presented. In this situation, there seems to be little potential harm to the subjects or their evaluations of themselves. Alternatively, subjects may be placed under psychological stress or led to raise important questions about themselves. For example, subjects may be told they have latent adjustment or sexual problems.

The ethical dilemma lies in deciding whether deception is justified in a given experiment and whether its possible risks to the subject outweigh its potential benefits in the knowledge the study is designed to yield. Both the risks to the subject and potential benefits usually are a matter of surmise, so the decision is not at all straightforward. The dilemma is particularly difficult because the risks to the individual subject are weighed against the benefits to society. In most psychological experiments, the benefits of the research are not likely to accrue to the subject directly. Weighing potential benefits to society against potential risks to the individual subject is difficult, to say the least. The safest way to proceed is to minimize or eliminate risk to the subject by not using active forms of deception.

The potential harm that deception may cause for the individual subject certainly is a major ethical objection to its use. Moreover, aside from its harmful consequences for the subject, the act of deception has been objected to because it violates a value of honesty between individuals, in this case the investigator and subject. Investigators engage in behaviors as part of deception that would not be condoned outside the experimental setting because these behaviors violate the basic rights of individuals. Thus deception fosters a type of behavior that is objected to on its own grounds independently of its other consequences. Alternatively, it may not be the deceptive acts in which investigators may engage as much as the context in which these behaviors occur. Many forms of deception occur in everyday life and individuals occasionally object to these as well (e.g., surprise parties). The problem with forms of deception and surprises in an experiment is that the professional context of an experiment leads people to expect full disclosure, candor, and respect for individual rights.

Actually, deception in research rarely involves efforts to mislead subjects. The central issue for research is the extent to which subjects should be aware of the purpose and procedures of the experiment. Ideally, investigators would fully disclose all available information about what will take place. Complete disclosure would entail conveying to subjects the nature of all of the procedures, even those to which the subjects in any particular condition will not be exposed, and revealing the investigator's view and expectations about what the results might yield.

In most psychological experiments with human subjects, full disclosure of available information may not be realistic. If the subject knows about the purpose, hypotheses, and procedures, this information could influence or alter the results. To begin with, full knowledge about the experiment could raise all of the problems associated with demand characteristics and subject roles, as discussed in chapter 11. These influences are much more likely to occur when subjects are aware of the purpose of the experiment. More generally, the conclusions reached in an experiment may differ drastically when subjects are completely aware of the facets of the experiment from when they are unaware.

Resnick and Schwartz (1973) demonstrated the effects of disclosing the purpose and hypotheses of one type of experiment. College students participated in a verbal conditioning experiment in which their selection of pronouns in a sentence-construction task was reinforced by the experimenter by saying "good" or "okay." Some subjects (informed group) were told that the purpose was to increase their use of "I" and "we" pronouns in order to determine whether telling subjects the purpose of the experiment affected the results. These subjects were told the true purpose (i.e., to evaluate the effects of full disclosure). Other subjects (uninformed group) were told that the experiment was designed to study verbal communication. They were not informed of the experiment's real purpose. Subjects in both groups constructed sentences and received approval when "I" or "we" pronouns were used in the sentences.

As expected, the uninformed subjects showed an increase in the use of the target pronouns that were reinforced over their base rates in a practice (non-reinforced) period. This finding has been shown many times in the verbal conditioning literature. In contrast, the informed subjects showed a decrease in the use of target pronouns relative to their initial practice rates. Thus the results demonstrate that disclosing information about the purposes of the experiment altered the findings.

The results suggest that informing subjects about the purposes and expected results of an experiment might dictate the specific relation that is obtained between the independent and dependent variable. Of course, one might view the results in another way, namely, that not telling subjects about the experiment dictates a specific relation as well and one that is not more or less "real" or informative than results obtained under other circumstances. Yet, a major goal of psychology is to study affect, cognition, and behavior and to extrapolate findings to those circumstances in which individuals normally function. Thus investigators wish to understand how subjects respond to events when not forewarned about their anticipated effects and the purpose of exposure to these events. Although investigators would, in principle, like to avoid deception, it may be necessary in some form to understand certain behavioral processes.

In general, guidelines for informing subjects are dictated by law and by ethical principles that govern research and informed consent. Such guidelines do not require elaborating all of the views, hypotheses, expectations, and related possibilities to the subjects. Thus some information invariably is withheld. Of special concern in relation to deception are active efforts to mislead subjects. Such efforts are quite rare in clinical, counseling, and educational research. Research proposals that include efforts to mislead subjects must establish that deception is essential to achieve the research goals and that special procedures to protect subjects are provided to reduce any lingering effects of the experience.

First, the scientific investigation must merit the type of deception that is used. The investigator who designs the experiment may argue persuasively that deception is justified given the importance of the information that is to be revealed by the experiment. Yet an investigator may not be the best judge because of his or her investment in the research. Hence review committees involving individuals from different fields of inquiry ordinarily examine whether the proposed procedures are justifiable. The committees, formally developed in most universities and institutions where research is conducted, follow guidelines for evaluating research and for protecting subjects. (Guidelines for psychological research are discussed later in the chapter.)

Second, if there is any deception in the planned experiment, there must be assurances that alternative methods of investigation that would produce similar information are unavailable. This too is difficult to assess because whether similar methods would produce the information proposed in an experiment that uses deception is usually an empirical matter. Researchers genuinely disagree about the extent to which deception is essential.

Third, the aversiveness of the deception itself bears strongly on the justification of the study. The aversiveness refers to the procedures and degree of deception and the potential for and magnitude of harmful effects. Deceptions vary markedly in degree, although ethical discussions usually focus on cases where subjects are grossly misled about their own abilities or personal characteristics.

Research begins with the view that individual rights are to be protected. Investigators are to disclose to the extent possible details of the design, purposes, risks, benefits, and costs (e.g., monetary or other). The purpose is to permit the subject to make an informed decision regarding participation. If deception is to be used, either by withholding critical information or misrepresenting the study, the onus is on the investigator to show cause at the research proposal stage that this is essential for the necessary benefits of the research. Unless the case can be made to review committees that evaluate such proposals, the work may not be permitted.

In many cases, if deception seems necessary, the investigator's creativity and methodological and statistical skills can provide a path that avoids deception. It is useful to begin with the premise that there may be no need to deceive subjects. Alternative experimental procedures may address whether deception is necessary. For example, the investigator may present to different groups varying degrees of information and see if this affects the findings. Alternatively, perhaps the methods used to evaluate demand characteristics such as the preinquiry or use of simulators can be explored to evaluate if subjects would be likely to perform differently under different conditions of disclosure. The absence of differences between groups studied in this way are consistent with the view that deception may not be critical to the research findings and methods of study in the area of work. These alternatives are not perfect in providing unambiguous answers that might be obtained with deception. These options begin to develop the empirical basis for deciding if disclosure of information would in some way tarnish the empirical relations of interest to the investigator.

Debriefing

If there is any deception in the experiment or if crucial information is withheld, the experimenter should describe the true nature of the experiment to the subject after the subject is run. Providing a description of the experiment and its purposes is referred to as *debriefing*. The purpose of debriefing is to counteract or minimize any negative effects that the experiment may have had. By debriefing, the experimenter hopes the subjects will not leave the experiment with any greater anxiety, discomfort, or lowered self-esteem than when they arrived. Apart from overcoming possible deleterious effects of deception, debriefing is often considered to convey educative objectives such as communicating the potential value of research and acknowledging the subjects' contribution to research (Kidder & Judd, 1986). These features focus on conveying the benefits of subject participation in research and are of value in their own right.

Debriefing is usually discussed in the context of overcoming the deleterious effects of deception. The manner in which debriefing is conducted and the information conveyed to the subject vary enormously among experiments. Typically, subjects meet with the experimenter immediately after completing the experimental tasks. The experimenter may inform the subject about what the experiment was "really" about and explain the reasons that the stated purpose did not convey this. The importance of debriefing varies with the type of experiment and the nature of the deception. As part of the experiment, subjects may have been told that they have tendencies toward mental illness or an early grave. In such situations subjects obviously ought to be told that the information was not accurate and that they are "normal." Presumably such information will be a great relief to the subjects. On the other hand, subjects may be distressed that they were exposed to such a deception or that they were gullible enough to believe it.

Debriefing has been assumed to be a procedure that resolves the potentially harmful effects of deception. Yet debriefing has its own problems and may not achieve its intended purposes. To begin with, subjects may believe that the debriefing session is merely a continuation of the experiment and the deception by the experimenter. Suspiciousness on the part of the subject has a reasonable basis. Although quite rare, historical examples can be cited in which subjects were told that the experiment was over and were then "debriefed," when in truth the debriefing itself involved deception and the subject continued unwittingly to serve in the experiment (e.g., Festinger & Carlsmith, 1959).

Even if subjects are not suspicious about debriefing, questions can be raised about whether the effects of the manipulation can be nullified with a postexperimental explanation. The effectiveness of debriefing is likely to depend on several considerations, including the characteristics of the subject, the nature of the deception, and the time interval between deception and debriefing. Yet the available evidence suggests that debriefing subjects by providing full information about the deception does not necessarily erase the false impressions (e.g., about subject skills) established during the experiment (Ross, Lepper, & Hubbard, 1975; Walster, Berscheid, Abrahams, & Aronson, 1967). The fact that the effects of deception may linger even after debriefing provides us with further caveats. If deception is to be considered, it must be quite clearly justified to assure the risks to individual rights and integrity.

Debriefing requires considerable thought in research, particularly where subjects are deliberately misguided about the experiment. Debriefing must convey to the subject what the experiment was about, what the purpose was, and how reactions of the subject were typical. It may be necessary to individualize debriefing to meet questions of the individual subjects. The timing of debriefing may be important as well. Sometimes experimenters wait until all subjects are run in the experiment and contact subjects with a printed handout or class announcement. The reasons for this are that information provided early in the experiment might filter down to other subjects before they are run. Yet, delayed debriefing may not be as effective as immediate debriefing. If subjects are potentially harmed by the deception, the experimenter's obligation is to debrief as soon and as effectively as possible.

An investigator using deception should *demonstrate* that the debriefing procedures effectively eliminate incorrect beliefs induced in the experiment. Whether subjects are debriefed should refer more to the outcome of providing certain kinds of information rather than simply to the experience to which subjects are exposed. The effectiveness of a particular debriefing technique could be demonstrated in the experiment itself or as part of pilot work prior to the investigation.

Invasion of Privacy

Invasion of privacy represents a broad concept that encompasses practices extending well beyond research. Generally, invasion of privacy refers to seeking information of a personal nature that intrudes upon what individuals view as private. Information may be sought on such topics as religious preferences, sexual beliefs and behaviors, income, and political views. Individuals vary considerably regarding the areas they regard as sensitive and private. For example, one survey reported that married women provided detailed answers to questions about the use of contraceptive devices, a topic that might be viewed as very sensitive (Clark, 1967). The respondents were very cooperative in providing answers until they were asked to reveal their family's income, at which point they refused to answer. This question apparently invaded what subjects thought was private information, presumably because it was not part of the topic they had agreed to discuss. Surveys assess attitudes on all sorts of personal topics. Beyond surveys, other sources solicit information from individuals including credit bureaus, investigative and sales agencies, and potential employers.

In psychology, one of the major topics pertaining to invasion of privacy is the use of personality tests. Test results can reflect directly on an individual's psychological status, adjustment, and beliefs and uncover personal characteristics that the subject might regard as private. Moreover, the information obtained through psychological testing might be potentially damaging if made public. The threat of personality testing to the invasion of privacy has been a topic of considerable concern. Indeed, in the United States congressional hearings have addressed the use of psychological tests for selecting employees in the government (see *American Psychologist,* 1965). Personality inventories, particularly those studied in the area of psychopathology, had been used routinely to screen potential government employees. Many of the questions asked of prospective employees seemed to be of a personal nature and not clearly related to the tasks for which individuals were being selected.

In psychological research, the major issues regarding invasion of privacy pertain to how the information from subjects is obtained and used. Ordinarily, information provided in experiments must be provided willingly. Obviously, there are many kinds of research where consent of the individual is neither possible (e.g., in cases of severe psychiatric or neurological impairment) nor especially crucial (e.g., in the case of studying archival records for groups of unidentifiable subjects).

Two conditions designed to protect the subject's right to privacy in research are anonymity and confidentiality. Subjects who agree to provide information must be assured that their responses are anonymous. Anonymity can be assured at the point of obtaining the data as, for example, when subjects are instructed not to identify themselves on an answer sheet. Alternatively, anonymity can be assured after the information is obtained and the names are disconnected from the measures. Typically, data are coded so that subjects' names cannot be associated with a particular set of data. Only the investigator may have the information revealing the identity of a subject. In most research, confidentiality is maintained by obtaining the data under conditions of anonymity or converting the data through coding or data reduction procedures to a format where the individual's identity cannot be discerned. Research with clinic populations or in special settings may require specific safeguards regarding the protection of confidentiality. The reason is that many persons may have special interest in the information obtained as part of the research (e.g., employers, relatives, school administrators) and that the nature of the information (e.g., measures of adjustment, psychopathology) may be potentially damaging if misinterpreted or misused.

Invasion of privacy extends beyond the process of obtaining information. Once the information is obtained, subjects must be assured that their performance is confidential. Confidentiality means that the information will not be disclosed to a third party without the awareness and consent of the subject. Conceivably, situations might arise where confidentiality is violated as, for example, when the information might conceal some clear and imminent danger to an individual or society (APA, 1982). For example, clinical psychologists are involved with research on the evaluation, treatment, and prevention of AIDS. Confidentiality about who is participating in the research and about test results for infection are obviously important. The information, if inadvertently made available, can serve to stigmatize research participants and subject them to discrimination in several areas of everyday life (e.g., employment, housing).

Invasion of privacy enters into many different areas in clinical research. For example, privacy is an important issue in writing the results of research investigations and treatment applications. Clinical research reports often are prepared for publication where an individual case is involved. In these instances, efforts to maintain confidentiality require the investigator to disguise the ancillary information about the client in such a way that his or her identity could not be recognized. Typically, pseudonyms are used when a case is described in published form. Yet for many case reports a change in the name may not protect the subject's confidentiality. The details of the case or treatment may be unique and reveal the identity of the individual. If there is any risk that preparation of a research report could reveal the identity of a subject, the subject must be informed of this in advance and provide appropriate consent.

Another area in clinical research where invasion of privacy is possible is in the use of informants for data collection. Occasionally, treatment research with a client or group of clients may solicit the aid of friends, spouses, neighbors, teachers, or employers. The purpose is to ask these individuals to provide data about the client. The information is used to evaluate the effects of treatment or the severity of the client's problem, although the client may not be aware of this assessment. Seeking information about the client may violate his or her right to privacy and confidentiality. The client may not want his or her problem widely advertised, and any attempts at unobtrusive assessment may violate this wish. For example, asking employers to assess whether the client's alcohol consumption interferes with work performance may apprise the employer of a problem of which he or she was unaware.

Invasion of privacy is often discussed at the level of individual subjects or comparable small units (e.g., a given married or cohabiting couple, privacy of one's home). However, much larger units are relevant and of deep concern in clinical research. Privacy of communities and cultural and ethnic groups emerge as well. For example, a clinically relevant study was designed to survey alcohol use in an Inupiat community in Barrow, Alaska (Foulks, 1987; Manson, 1989). Impetus of the study was to examine cases of alcohol abuse and to evaluate community detention programs for acute alcohol detoxification. A representative sample of people ($N = 88$) over the age of 15 was drawn from the community and interviewed regarding their attitudes, values, and behavior in relation to alcohol use. Other measures of functioning were assessed as well including church membership and social and work behavior. The results indicated that 41% of the population considered themselves to be excessive drinkers; over 50% said that alcohol use caused problems with their spouse and family; 62% said they regularly got into fights when drinking. These and similar types of descriptive statements suggested that alcohol use was a problem in this community.

Reports of the findings were viewed by the community as highly objectionable and invasive. The community's view was that alcohol use and associated problems resulted from a new way of life imposed on them rather than on implied deficits, biological or otherwise, or problems inherent to the people. The report was criticized as denigrating, culturally imperialistic, and insensitive to the values of American Indian and Alaskan native culture (Foulks, 1989). Great simplification of the findings by the news media (e.g., a byline stating, "Alcohol Plagues Eskimos" in *The New York Times,* January 22, 1980) and emphasis of alcoholism and violence in various articles exacerbated the problem.

The consequences of this study might be used to illustrate many issues, only one of which is invasion of privacy (e.g., relations with the members of the population of interest at the design and reporting stages, dissemination of research findings, and contact with the media, to mention a few). In relation to invasion of privacy, individual community members could not be identified by the report. Nevertheless, community members, whether or not they participated as subjects, viewed their privacy as violated and objected that they were misrepresented (see Manson, 1989). Such examples convey that investigations do not merely describe relations and report findings of abstract scientific interest. The methods of obtaining information, the reporting of that information, and the way information is and could be used are part of the ethical considerations of research.

Informed Consent

Conditions and Elements

A pivotal ethical issue in research is informed consent. This issue is central because it encompasses many other topics including deception and invasion of privacy. An ethical imperative is that investigators obtain informed consent from the subjects for them to be able to participate in research. Of course as is usually the case with imperatives, there are occasional exceptions (e.g., archival research when subjects are no longer living and cannot consent). Also, implementing the imperative raises special obstacles. In principle, consent can never be completely informed. All possible consequences of the experimental procedures, measures, and participation cannot be known and hence cannot be presented to inform the subject. Even basic features of the procedures may be known imperfectly because the nature of research is to include elements where knowledge is the desired outcome. Thus information of interest to both investigator and subject is not completely available.

Stating the logical status and limits of presenting information is important as a backdrop for the tasks of the investigator. Information cannot be complete. Yet the responsibility of the investigator is to provide available information and reasonable statements of repercussions so that the subject can make a rational decision. Informed consent consists of three major elements: competence, knowledge, and volition (see Lidz et al., 1984). *Competence* refers to the individual's ability to make a well-reasoned decision and to give consent meaningfully. *Knowledge* refers to understanding the nature of the experiment, the alternatives available, and the potential risks and benefits. *Volition* refers to the basis of agreeing to participate. Subjects must provide their consent free from constraint or duress. To ensure that subjects' participation is and remains voluntary, they may revoke their consent at any time.

In the usual psychological experiment, where college students are studied, competence is not an issue. Subjects are considered capable of making rational decisions on the basis of the information provided. Also, the procedures (e.g., listening to tapes of innocuous interactions, reading passages and remembering details) raise little or no concern over physical or psychological consequences to the subject.

Knowledge about the experiment is essential. To provide adequate knowledge for informed consent, investigators must provide and describe all facets, risks, and sources of discomfort that might influence a subject's decision to participate willingly. All the conceivable risks need not be described; only those that might plausibly result from the procedure should be included. All of the information must be presented to the subject in an easily understandable fashion. In addition, subjects should be allowed to raise questions to clarify all of the issues that might be ambiguous.

Volition means that the subject agrees to participate without coercion. Participation in the experiment cannot be required to fulfill a class assignment, according to current requirements for consent. For subjects to provide consent, they must have a choice pertaining to their involvement in the investigation. The choice cannot be one in which participation in the experiment is substituted for some aversive or coercive alternative (e.g., completing two extra term papers), although in any given case, this may be difficult to discern. Whether the subject can "freely" choose to participate is sometimes evident from the consequences for not agreeing to participate or from withdrawing once consent has been provided. The absence of any penalty partially defines the extent to which the subject's consent was voluntary.

The differences in power and status in the experimental setting between the investigator or experimenter and subjects can militate against voluntary consent. Subjects may not feel they can choose freely to participate or to withdraw because of their position in relation to the investigator. Because the research situation is structured by the investigator, the subject depends almost completely on the information provided to make choices about participation or continuation in the investigation. Thus consent at any point in the research may not be completely informed because the subject may not have access to important information.

Operationally, informed consent is obtained in research when subjects sign a consent form. The form usually includes several ingredients, such as a description of the purpose of the study and the procedures to be followed and a statement of potential risks to the subjects as well as any benefits for the subject or for society. Moreover, statements are usually included in the form indicating that the client was permitted to ask questions of the experimenter and actually received answers to his or her satisfaction, that he or she does give permission to participate, that the information included will remain confidential, and that he or she is free to withdraw from the experiment at any time without penalty. The subject signs the form indicating that each of the above conditions have been met and that he or she agrees to participate.

Competence to provide consent is a central issue of concern that is heightened with populations who may be incapable or less than fully capable of providing consent (e.g., fetuses, young children, people with intellectual impairment, comatose patients, and institutionalized populations such as psychiatric patients and prisoners). Determining whether individuals are competent to provide consent presents many problems in its own right (Roth, Meisel, & Lidz, 1977). For individuals regarded as incompetent, parents or guardians may give permission, but in medical research a parent or guardian may *not* consent to participation of an incompetent person in a treatment that promises no direct therapeutic benefit. Competent guardians may not sign away the rights of their incompetent wards.

Even when consent can be sought and obtained from the people themselves, it is often unclear whether consent is adequate or meaningful. For example, Palmer and Wohl (1972) studied informed consent among voluntarily admitted psychiatric patients. Within 10 days after admission, 60% of the patients were unable to recall signing the admission form consenting to hospitalization. Some 33% of the patients did not recall or could not recall accurately the content of the form. Some of the patients even denied having signed it.

Similarly, an evaluation of biomedical research in the Veterans Administration hospital system revealed that approximately 28% of patients interviewed were not aware that they were participating in a research investigation (Committee on Biomedical Research in the Veterans Administration, 1977). This is particularly surprising given that all of the patients had received carefully implemented informed consent procedures and had signed the appropriate forms. Moreover, at least 20% of the individual patients had very little or no idea of what the research was about. These investigations raise questions about the competence of the patients or the adequacy of the procedures to secure informed consent.

Providing knowledge about the treatment often is a problem in clinical research. The risks and potential benefits of treatment are not always well known, particularly for populations that have been refractory to conventional treatments. Last-resort or experimental techniques may be improvised. Hence the necessary information for making a knowledgeable decision is unavailable. For example, in one very extreme case, psychosurgery was recommended to control aggressive behavior in a psychiatric patient. The patient consented to the procedure. In a landmark decision, the court ruled that consent could not be "informed" because of the nature of the treatment and the lack of available information about its benefits and risks *(Kaimowitz v. Michigan Department of Mental Health).*

Whether institutionalized populations can truly volunteer for treatment or research is also an issue. Individuals may agree to participate because they feel compelled to do so. They may anticipate long-term gains from staff and administration whose opinions may be important for status or commodities within the institution or for release from the institution. The lure of release and the involuntarily confined status of many populations for whom treatment is provided may make voluntary consent impossible.

In research and treatment, informed consent has become the central issue for ensuring the protection of the individual subject. This does not mean that all facets of an experiment are routinely described to the subject prior to participation. However, it does mean that, prior to research, procedures that might affect the subject's willingness to participate are described, and subjects are informed of their right to information about the experiment. Moreover, subjects are assured that they may terminate their participation at any time if they so desire.

Consent Forms

In advance of a study, a consent form is provided to convey information about the study that the subject needs to know to make an informed decision. Usually, institutional review boards and committees (e.g., at colleges, universities, hospitals, prisons) are charged with evaluating the research proposal, consent procedures, and consent form. Members who review the proposal are drawn from diverse disciplines. The research proposal is evaluated to examine the research design, specific procedures, the conditions to which the subject will be exposed, and risks and benefits. Evaluation of the research design deserves comment. The general plan of the research must be made clear to permit committee members to determine if the questions underlying the investigation are reasonable and can be answered by the study. If the questions cannot be answered by the study, then the subjects should not be placed at any risk or inconvenience.

Most psychological experiments do not involve risk situations and are designated as "minimal" risk. The subjects (e.g., college students), experimental tasks (e.g., memorizing lists of words, completing personality measures), and risks (e.g., mild boredom if that task continues too long) do not exceed the risks of normal living. Review of such studies is relatively straightforward because concerns about subject rights are not raised by the research paradigm. In some cases, review of the study or even informed consent procedures are omitted because the experiment is considered to be in a class of procedures that is innocuous. In clinical work, several features often extend the situation well beyond "minimal risk" by virtue of the population (e.g., patient samples), focus of assessment or intervention (e.g., suicidal intent, depression), special ethical dilemmas (e.g., random assignment, delaying treatment), as discussed further below. Understandably, the review of proposals and consent procedures of such studies are more stringent. In many universities, separate review committees are available for different types of research. For example, psychological experiments with minimal risk are often reviewed by a social sciences review committee. In contrast, research with clinical populations are likely to be reviewed by a biomedical committee.

Critical to the consent procedure is the consent form that the subjects sign to indicate their willingness to participate. The overall purpose of the form is to convey information, to do so clearly and simply, and to ensure that subjects are aware of what they will be participating in. Although specific details of the forms vary as a function of the type of research and level of risk, several components are common. Table 14.1 lists and highlights these components, each of which might be represented by a brief paragraph or two within the consent form.

Letter and Spirit

Concretely, the investigator is required to describe the procedures to the subject and to obtain signed consent. The signed consent form satisfies the research requirements and hence follows the "letter" of the rules that govern research and the investigator's responsibilities. In addition, there is a "spirit" of informed consent, which refers more nebulously to the overall intent of the procedures and the goal to ensure that clients genuinely understand what they are signing, what the study entails, and the risks, costs, and benefits. In most research (e.g., laboratory studies with college students) presentation of the consent information followed by the subject's signing of the form is sufficient for the letter and spirit of the consent procedures.

Research that is any way service related (e.g., treatment) or that involves personally or physically invasive procedures (e.g., obtaining private information that could be solicited by the courts, medical tests with remote, albeit real risks) or people who are or may not be competent to represent themselves fully (e.g., children, disadvantaged individuals) raises special obstacles. Clients may be less likely to understand options, choices, opportunities to change their minds about participation, risks, and so on. In such cases, satisfying the letter of the informed consent requirements may not approach the spirit or intent of these requirements.

Interestingly, there are no formal research requirements that subjects actually understand what is presented to them. Thus presentation of information and signing of consent forms might be accomplished without genuinely informed consent. For this reason the spirit as well as the letter of consent are important. The spirit of consent emphasizes the investigator's responsibility to maximize the clients' understanding of the investigation. Of course, all information is not known and hence cannot be presented. The spirit of consent refers to the researcher's "best effort" to convey the purpose, procedures, and risks of participation and generally to meet the consent conditions.

Presentation of the content by repeating significant facets of the study,

Table 14.1. Components of Informed Consent Forms

SECTION OF THE FORM	PURPOSE AND CONTENTS
Overview	Presentation of the goals of the study, why this is conducted, who is responsible for the study and its execution.
Description of Procedures	Clarification of the experimental conditions, assessment procedures, requirements of the subjects.
Risks and Inconveniences	Statement of any physical and psychological risks and an estimate of their likelihood. Inconveniences and demands to be placed on the subjects (e.g., how many sessions, requests to do any thing, contact at home).
Benefits	A statement of what the subjects can reasonably hope to gain from participation, including psychological, physical, and monetary benefits.
Costs and Economic Considerations	Charges to the subjects (e.g., in treatment) and payment (e.g., for participation or completing various forms).
Confidentiality	Assurances that the information is confidential and will only be seen by people who need to do so for the purposes of research (e.g., scoring and data analyses), procedures to assure confidentiality (e.g., removal of names from forms, storage of data). Also, caveats are included here if it is possible that sensitive information (e.g., psychiatric information, criminal activity) can be subpoenaed.
Alternative Treatments	In an intervention study, alternatives available to the client before or during participation are outlined.
Voluntary Participation	A statement that the subject is willing to participate and can say no now or later without penalty of any kind.
Questions and Further Information	A statement that the subject is encouraged to ask questions at any time and can contact an individual (or individuals) (listed by name and phone number) who is available for such contacts.
Signature Lines	A place for the subject as well as the experimenter to sign.

paraphrasing the consent form, asking questions of the subject at critical points to assess understanding, and similar strategies may be helpful. The time allowed to explain the procedures and to obtain consent may need to be extended to foster the atmosphere required to inform the client. Obviously, protracted consent procedures, clinically oversensitive presentations, and ad nauseam requests for feedback on the part of the experimenter ("But do you really understand that you could have nightmares from meeting with such an ugly therapist? O.K., tell me what a nightmare is.") are likely to be inappropriate as a general strategy. This is why the spirit of consent is so important. The rules or letter of consent procedures specify the minimal conditions to be satisfied in discharging responsibilities to the subject. Beyond that, judgment, experience, and common sense are needed to ensure the goals of consent and to balance research interests and subject rights.

Different types of presentation can be identified, including the following: perfunctory presentation of the consent form ("Here [consent form is handed to the subject], as soon as you sign this, we can begin"), lengthy deliberations of individual phrases and concepts (e.g., "You are probably wondering what "random" assignment really is and why we do this . . . Did you ever hear of R.A. Fisher—I didn't either. . . ."), and possibly overly empathic and mushy understanding ("O.K., how do you feel about all of what I have said so far? I'll bet this is a little threatening"). The sample and circumstances of the experiment obviously dictate the letter and spirit of consent and how these are to be achieved. The variability of each of these can be great in clinical research because of the wide range of circumstances in which researchers enter.

INTERVENTION RESEARCH ISSUES

Each of the above issues pertains to research generally. In studies of alternative interventions such as psychotherapy, counseling, and education, additional ethical issues arise or nuances emerge that warrant consideration.

Informing Clients About Treatment

An important issue is the information that is provided to the client about treatment. Outside of the rationale and procedures themselves, the investigator is required to convey the current status of the treatment, assuming that the client is able to understand the information. Whether treatment has been shown to be effective or not in previous applications would seem to be important as routine information. Many treatments are experimental and the subject normally can be provided with a statement to that effect.

Therapy research raises an interesting dilemma because honesty about the basis of treatment might well dispel some of the therapeutic effects that ordinarily would result. In the process of mentioning the current status of treatment, the investigator might well attenuate the "placebo" effects that ordinarily might occur. Suspicions about treatment efficacy might be raised by full disclosure. In some treatment studies, the independent variable is the expectancy for success conveyed to the subjects. Hence a treatment is claimed to be very effective or ineffective depending on the condition to which the subject is assigned. Disclosure of the current status of the technique would compete with this manipulation.

Information about treatment in an experiment may extend to the treatments in which the subject will not participate. Conceivably, subjects could be told that there are different treatments, only one of which they will receive. Subjects might want to know whether some treatments are more effective than others and whether they have been assigned to a control group. In addition, subjects may show a clear preference for an alternative treatment and react adversely to one to which they are assigned. As alternative treatments become known, skepticism about a particular treatment may arise and therapeutic improvement may be affected.

At the beginning of treatment, subjects might be told that there are alternative treatments offered, assuming that this is in fact the case. There may be no need to convey precisely what the alternative treatments are at this point. Although subjects are rarely pleased to learn that their assignment to treatment was random, the importance of randomness in assessing the impact of different treatments might be stressed.

Withholding Treatment

Therapy studies often withhold treatment by assigning subjects to no-treatment or waiting-list control conditions. Although these conditions are essential to answer specific research questions (as discussed in chapter 6), their use raises obvious ethical questions. Assigning a client to one of these conditions withholds treatment from which a person may benefit. At the very least, treatment for the client is delayed. If the client's condition does not deteriorate, the delay has increased the duration of misery that may have precipitated seeking treatment. At the worst, the client's condition may deteriorate during the period that treatment is withheld.

An investigator is obligated to consider seriously whether a group that delays or completely withholds treatment is necessary for the questions addressed in the research. Because of the ethical problems, it may be more appropriate to reserve questions comparing treatment with no treatment to situations where subjects are willing to wait and are unlikely to suffer deleterious consequences. Obviously, volunteer clients solicited from the community may be more appropriate for a study in which a waiting-list group is required than clients who seek treatment at a crisis intervention center. Where clients have severe problems and warrant or demand immediate intervention, questions comparing treatment with no treatment are more difficult to justify and to implement.

In some cases, assigning subjects to a waiting-list control group will not really delay treatment. Waiting lists are common at many clinics. A delay before entering treatment may average a few or several months before clients are seen. All subjects who are to serve in the study and who agree to participate can be moved up on the list. Those who are randomly assigned to treatment are treated immediately; those who are assigned to wait, can be assessed and then wait out the usual delay period of the clinic before receiving treatment.

Ethical issues are not eliminated by rearranging waiting-list status. Moving some clients up on the list may delay the treatment of others who are not in the study. Some of the problems of delaying treatment can be alleviated by informing clients at intake of the possibility that they will not be assigned to treatment for a particular (specified) interval. The investigation would only use subjects who agree with this stipulation and then randomly assign them to the various treatment and control conditions.

Using Treatments of Questionable Efficacy

In outcome research, some treatments in a given study might be expected to be less effective than others. This expectation may derive from theoretical predictions, previous research, or from the nature of the design. For example, in a simple 2×2 factorial design, an investigator may study the effects of such variables as therapist experience (experienced vs. inexperienced therapists) and duration of treatment (1 session vs. 10 sessions). Subjects in one of the groups resulting from this design will be exposed to inexperienced therapists for one treatment session, a condition likely to be less effective than the others. The use of treatments that have a low probability of being effective raises an ethical issue for the investigator.

In passing, it is interesting to note that in research, the investigator may be expected to convey to the subject what is known about treatment or to qualify the expectations about treatment effectiveness. In contrast, in clinical practice the therapist is not required to clarify the status of the technique or knowledge base. The vast majority of psychotherapy techniques—over 400 for the treatment of adults—have not been subject to empirical evaluation and do not have data attesting to their efficacy. One might argue that those without evidence on their behalf are "experimental" whether they are examined or used in research or clinical practice.

The questionable efficacy of an intervention condition is much clearer in using groups that are designed to control for "nonspecific" treatment factors such as attending treatment sessions, meeting with a therapist, and believing that treatment may produce change. These groups are designed with the expressed idea that there are few if any components that will actively help the client. The group provides a base against which another treatment can be evaluated. A control group of this sort may be relatively difficult to justify in clinical settings because it is deliberately designed to be of minimal help to the clients.

Providing a treatment designed to be weak or a control condition designed to be ineffective raises obvious ethical problems. First, the client's dysfunction may not improve or may even become worse without an effective treatment. Purposely to withhold a treatment expected to be relatively effective renders these possibilities more salient. Second, clients may lose credulity in the process of psychological treatment in general. Clients expect to receive an effective treatment and to improve. If treatment is not reasonable in their judgment and does not produce change, clients may be generally discouraged from seeking help in the future.

In general, the control conditions or treatments that may "fill out" the design warrant ethical evaluation by the investigator and review boards. This of course applies to any special control condition in which the likelihood of improvement is unexpected or minimal. Other contextual issues such as who the clients are (e.g., patients seeking treatment, community volunteers) and provisions after the study is completed (e.g., free treatment and care) may affect evaluation of the issues.

General Comments

The ethical issues raised in intervention research depend on the precise research question and the control groups that form the basis of the design. Use of no-treatment or waiting-list control groups is essential in research that asks the basic question, "Does this treatment work?" The question normally requires assessing the extent of change without treatment. Similarly, use of a nonspecific treatment control group may be important in research that asks the question "Why does this treatment work?" Such research may require a group to look at the influence of "nonspecific treatment factors" alone.

The research questions that require ethically sensitive control conditions are fundamental to progress in understanding treatment. The questions themselves cannot be abandoned. However, the conditions under which these questions are examined can be varied to attenuate partially the objections that normally arise. For example, questions requiring control conditions that withhold treatment or provide nonspecific treatment control groups need not be conducted in settings where clients are in need of treatment and have sought a treatment to ameliorate an immediately felt problem. On the other hand, where volunteer subjects are solicited and can be informed about the experimental nature of all treatment procedures, a wider range of experimental conditions is more readily justified. In short, where the setting has service delivery as the higher priority, the use of groups that withhold treatment or present "nonspecific" treatments that are expected to produce minimal change is generally unacceptable. Where research, rather than service delivery, has the higher priority and clients can be informed of the implications of this priority, the use of such groups may be more readily justified.

Some of the ethical issues of treatment can be ameliorated by providing all subjects with the more (or most) effective treatment in the project after they have completed the treatment to which they were assigned. After treatment, clients who served as a no-treatment control group also should receive the benefits of treatment. Indeed, this is exactly what the waiting-list control group receives. In studies with several different treatments or a nonspecific control condition, clients who are not completely satisfied with their progress eventually might be given the most effective treatment. Thus clients may benefit from the project in which they served by receiving the better (or best) treatment. From an experimental standpoint, this strategy is useful in further examining the extent of change in clients who continue in the superior treatment. Essentially, there is a partial replication of treatment effects in the design. From an ethical standpoint, providing all subjects with the most effective intervention may attenuate objections against assigning subjects to treatments varying in anticipated effectiveness.

ETHICAL GUIDELINES FOR RESEARCH PRACTICES

Many ethical problems that arise in research seem to be inherent in the research process itself. The use of human subjects often requires weighing alternatives that balance the individual rights of the subject against the search for scientific knowledge. Decisions about potential harm, deception, invasion of privacy, withholding of potential beneficial treatment practices, and similar issues have helped stimulate guidelines for research both at the professional and federal levels.

The American Psychological Association (1973, 1982, 1990a) has provided a set of principles designed to guide psychological research with human subjects. The guidelines are formulated in such a way as to emphasize the investigator's responsibilities toward individuals who participate in research. The principles are listed in Table 14.2.

As guidelines, the principles are necessarily ambiguous about concrete experimental practices. For example, the principles do not say that deception can or cannot be used. Indeed, the thrust of the principles is to point out the obligations of the investigator and to raise those areas of concern where caution and deliberation are required. The guidelines point to the considerations included in making decisions about whether a given research project should be undertaken. Although it may be difficult to make decisions in any given case, the overriding concern must be given to the protection of the subject. Indeed, the guidelines specify that as the pros and cons of the research are weighed, priority must be given to the research participant's welfare. Whether a given investigation adequately protects the rights of subjects usually is decided on the basis of an evaluation of the research by one's colleagues. As mentioned previously, universities and many other institutions where research is conducted rely upon review committees to evaluate the extent to which a proposed investigation provides safeguards for subjects and is consistent with the type of guidelines listed in Table 14.2.

Table 14.2. Ethical Principles in the Conduct of Research With Human Participants

The decision to undertake research rests upon a considered judgment by the individual psychologist about how best to contribute to psychological science and human welfare. Having made the decision to conduct research, the psychologist considers alternative directions in which research energies and resources might be invested. On the basis of this consideration, the psychologist carries out the investigation with respect and concern for the dignity and welfare of the people who participate and with cognizance of federal and state regulations and professional standards governing the conduct of research with human participants.

A. In planning a study, the investigator has the responsibility to make a careful evaluation of its ethical acceptability. To the extent that the weighing of scientific and human values suggests a compromise of any principle, the investigator incurs a correspondingly serious obligation to seek ethical advice and to observe stringent safeguards to protect the rights of human participants.

B. Considering whether a participant in a planned study will be a "subject at risk" or a "subject at minimal risk," according to recognized standards, is of primary ethical concern to the investigator.

C. The investigator always retains the responsibility for ensuring ethical practice in research. The investigator is also responsible for the ethical treatment of research participants by collaborators, assistants, students, and employees, all of whom, however, incur similar obligations.

D. Except in minimal-risk research, the investigator establishes a clear and fair agreement with research participants, prior to their participation, that clarifies the obligations and responsibilities of each. The investigator has the obligation to honor all promises and commitments included in that agreement. The investigator informs the participants of all aspects of the research that might reasonably be expected to influence willingness to participate and explains all other aspects of the research about which the participants inquire. Failure to make full disclosure prior to obtaining informed consent requires additional safeguards to protect the welfare and dignity of the research participants. Research with children or with participants who have impairments that would limit understanding and/or communication requires special safeguarding procedures.

E. Methodological requirements of a study may make the use of concealment or deception necessary. Before conducting such a study, the investigator has a special responsibility to (1) determine whether the use of such techniques is justified by the study's prospective scientific, educational, or applied value; (2) determine whether alternative procedures are available that do not use concealment or deception; and (3) ensure that the participants are provided with sufficient explanation as soon as possible.

F. The investigator respects the individual's freedom to decline to participate in or to withdraw from the research at any time. The obligation to protect this freedom requires careful thought and consideration when the investigator is in a position of authority or influence over the participant. Such positions of authority include, but are not limited to, situations in which research participation is required as part of employment or in which the participant is a student, client, or employee of the investigator.

G. The investigator protects the participant from physical and mental discomfort, harm, and danger that may arise from research procedures. If risks of such consequences exist, the investigator informs the participant of that fact. Research procedures likely to cause serious or lasting harm to a participant are not used unless the failure to use these procedures might expose the participant to risk of greater harm or unless the research has great potential benefit and fully informed and voluntary consent is obtained from each participant. The participant should be informed of procedures for contacting the investigator within a reasonable time period following participation should stress, potential harm, or related questions or concerns arise.

Table 14.2. *Continued*

H. After the data are collected, the investigator provides the participant with information about the nature of the study and attempts to remove any misconceptions that may have arisen. Where scientific or humane values justify delaying or withholding this information, the investigator incurs a special responsibility to monitor the research and to ensure that there are no damaging consequences for the participant.

I. Where research procedures result in undesirable consequences for the individual participant, the investigator has the responsibility to detect and remove or correct these consequences, including long-term effects.

J. Information obtained about a research participant during the course of an investigation is confidential unless otherwise agreed upon in advance. When the possibility exists that others may obtain access to such information, this possibility, together with the plans for protecting confidentiality, is explained to the participant as part of the procedure for obtaining informed consent.

Note. For a discussion of principles and guidelines, the original source should be consulted. See *Ethical principles in the conduct of research with human participants*, American Psychological Association, Committee for the Protection of Human Participants, 1982. Copyright © 1982 by the American Psychological Association. Reprinted by permission.

The review process has been mandated by federal regulations for medical and psychological research. For example, in 1966, the Surgeon General of the Public Health Service required institutions that received federal monies for research to establish review committees to consider subjects' rights and to ensure that informed consent was procured for the proposed research. This policy was extended to cover all research in the behavioral and social sciences. The Public Health Service guidelines for research have been revised and elaborated periodically (USDHHS, 1983). Current federal regulations are designed to evaluate whether any risks to the subjects are outweighed by the potential benefits to them or by the likely benefits to society in light of the information obtained.

In 1974, Congress mandated a special commission to draft ethical guidelines for research with human subjects. The National Commission for the Protection of Human Subjects in Biomedical and Behavioral Research was established to examine research and applications in areas where human rights have been or are likely to be violated. The Commission studied and made recommendations for practices in research with fetuses, prisoners, individuals considered for psychosurgery, and children. These guidelines do not apply to the bulk of research in clinical psychology but are important to mention insofar as they reveal Congress' strong interest in ethical issues raised by research with human subjects.

To examine the risks and benefits and protection of the subject's welfare, research proposals in a university setting are reviewed by a committee that critically examines the procedures and possible risks to the subjects. The committee is referred to as an Institutional Review Board (or IRB) in the federal codes to protect subjects (USDHHS, 1983). The committee evaluates whether subjects are provided with the opportunity to give informed consent, and they are made aware of their ability to withdraw consent and terminate participation at any time. Subjects must sign an informed consent form that explains the procedures and purpose in clear and easily understandable language and describes any risks and benefits. Risks are defined broadly to include the possibility of injury—physical, psychological, or social—as a consequence of participation in the experiment. Subjects must also be told that they are free to withhold information (e.g., of a personal nature) and to withdraw from the investigation at any time without penalty. Subjects must also be guaranteed that all information they provide will be anonymous and confidential and told how these conditions will be achieved.

The bulk of clinical psychological investigations includes procedures that may be without risk to the subject and hence do not provide special problems for review committees to evaluate. Procedures that receive scrutiny are those projects involving a failure to disclose fully the purpose of the study, those that are deceptive, those that contain the possibility of deleteriously affecting the subject's psychological or physical status, or those with special populations where competence to consent is in question (e.g., children). The committee must weigh the merits of the scientific investigation and the advance in knowledge it may provide against possible potential discomfort to the subject.

Ethical responsibility for research cannot be placed solely on the formal review procedures that are used to evaluate research. Ethical guidelines for research encourage investigators to seek advice of others and diverse perspectives to assess whether procedures that extend beyond minimal risk (e.g., covert observations, invasion of sensitive topics) are warranted. When weighing scientific merit and the likely benefits of the knowledge against subject rights, the investigator is advised to seek input from colleagues over and above formal review procedures (APA, 1982). In other words, the ultimate responsibility for the ethical integrity of the research falls to the investigator.

ETHICAL ISSUES AND SCIENTIFIC INTEGRITY

Ethics in research usually are discussed in relation to the subject and subject rights as, for example, illustrated in the issues raised by informed consent. Professional organizations have guidelines for ethical behavior of their members. The guidelines are intended to outline standards of integrity that pertain to diverse contexts beyond those associated with research and investigator and/or experimenter and subject interactions (see APA, 1990a). Although the full range of ethical standards are not entirely relevant to methodology and research design (e.g., contacts with clients in therapy), several research-related issues deserve comment. A set of ethical issues might be identified that is essential for maintaining the integrity of science. These issues encompass the obligations and responsibilities of the investigator in relation to one's colleagues, the profession, and scientific disciplines more generally.

Fraud in Science

Scientists are not immune to error, deception, and fraud in their work. Historical accounts of science provide a long line of examples in which scientists have made major errors in recording or interpreting their work, in directly trying to deceive others about their findings, and in making up or altering their data (see Broad & Wade, 1982; Kohn, 1988). The issues were mentioned briefly in the discussion of sources of artifact and bias in research. In the context of threats to validity, altering and making up data obviously bias research findings and their interpretation; in the context of ethical issues, they raise broader issues of great significance.

The distinction between error and fraud in research is major. Errors refer to honest mistakes that may occur in some facet of the study or its presentation. The processes entailed by collecting data, scoring measures, transcribing and entering data, and publishing raise multiple opportunities for error and for errors by many different persons. To err is human; to err frequently is careless. The investigator has responsibilities in relation to research errors. In general, the responsibility is to minimize error by devising procedures to check, monitor, and detect errors and then to rectify them to the extent possible. When errors are detected (e.g., as in published reports), investigators are encouraged to acknowledge them. Often journal publications include isolated notes where corrections can be written in the same outlet in which the original paper appeared.

Fraud in science refers to explicit efforts to deceive and misrepresent. Of all issues, fraud is the most flagrant because it undermines the foundations of the entire enterprise of scientific research (National Academy of Sciences, 1989). Although fraud is not new in science, recent attention has focused on deliberate efforts of researchers to mislead colleagues and the public (U.S. Congress, 1990). Dramatic instances have come to light where critical procedures, treatments, or potential breakthroughs could not be replicated or were known by one's colleagues to reflect explicit attempts to misrepresent the actual findings. Evaluations of scientific research have suggested that instances of fraud are likely to be quite rare (National Academy of Sciences, 1989). The rarity does not mean that the status quo is acceptable. The impact and implications of any instance of fraud can be tremendous for the specific area of work (e.g., suggesting a new principle or treatment procedure) as well as for the enterprise in general (e.g., threaten the credibility of science and scientists).

No single or simple cause of fraud is likely to be identifiable. Several influences can conspire to produce fraud including pressures of investigators to publish for recognition and career advancement, to produce critical breakthroughs, and to obtain funding for promising avenues of research, to mention a few. Protections to counter fraud include training in the central values of science, emphasis on the importance of the integrity of the investigator in advancing science generally, repeated opportunities in which an individual's work is subjected to review and evaluation by one's colleagues (e.g., as part of review processes in advance of the study, when the report is submitted for publication), public access to data records, and efforts to replicate research. In addition, there are severe sanctions within the profession as well as legal consequences for scientific fraud (e.g., in the use of public funds) and these can be professionally and personally devastating. Notwithstanding the multiple factors to protect against fraud, the key remains the ethical commitment and responsibility of the individual investigator to the discipline by conducting studies, reporting data, and preparing reports in as honest and objective a fashion as possible and to train those working under one's charge (e.g., students) in these standards and practices as well.

Allocation of Credit

Another issue related to obligations of the investigator pertain to allocation of credit. Several separate issues are encompassed including failure to acknowledge one's sources and reference to other material and the division of credit among collaborators in research and published projects of that research. Perhaps the most obvious and flagrant issue is that of plagiarism or the direct use and copying of someone else's material without providing credit or acknowledgement. The misconduct that plagiarism represents is generally brought to the attention of students early in their education. Special problems and opportunities emerge in science in the circulation of unpublished materials (e.g., manuscripts that are reviewed, convention presentations circulated in writing). A virtue of science is the public nature of the enterprise. Colleagues are encouraged to exchange ideas, to seek and to provide feedback, and to interact with colleagues to advance research ideas and objectives. The process generally works quite well without repeated claims of plagiarism or theft of ideas.

A more delicate and perhaps less concrete issue pertains to the credit accorded to those involved in research. Projects are usually collaborative. They involve multiple investigators and a team of people who have responsibility of varying types and in varying degrees for completion of the study. The different components of research and responsibilities from idea to the final published report are numerous. Allocation of credit emerges in such contexts as how to list and whom to list as authors on research articles and the relation between junior and senior scientists or faculty and students and how the different roles and contributions affect authorship. There are no obvious rules that can handle the range of circumstances in which issues of credit emerge. Investigators are encouraged to discuss these matters explicitly at the inception of research not merely to address issues of authorship but to decide credit and responsibility in relation to all facets of the study.

Sharing of Materials and Data

A central feature of science is the ability to replicate the work of others. Indeed, replication is the primary guarantee of reliability of research findings. Replication is usually discussed in the context of repeating the procedures of a prior investigation. The obligations of an investigator are to provide colleagues with the materials to permit them to conduct replication work. This might entail providing further descriptions of procedures and specific measures or responding to various questions that facilitate replication of the study.

Often critical features of a study have required years to develop (e.g., treatment manuals) or have important financial implications (e.g., software, a new psychological test) that make investigators reluctant or occasionally unwilling to share specific materials. However, the obligation to share materials begins when the individual enters the role of scientific investigator and places his or her work in the scientific domain (e.g., presentation of a paper, publication of a scientific article). At that point, the investigator has entered an implied contract with the rest of the scientific community in which he or she will aid in continuation and evaluation of the research. As part of that contract, the scientific community is obligated to provide credit where this is due in relation to the original investigator and to restrict use of the materials to those related to the research project.

The procedure generally appears to work well based on the exchange of a great deal of information informally among scientists. The information exchange is often prompted by a published report that helps to establish communication among scientists who begin a dialogue and exchange of materials. There are some formal protections to aid in making research information available. Funding agencies, both federal and private, often include significant material in the project proposal and final report (e.g., measures, detailed descriptions of procedures, raw data). This information is available by request or as a matter of public record for further scrutiny and use.

One of the most frequently discussed issues pertains to the sharing of data. This, too, is related to replication. Can one obtain the same or similar findings when analyzing the original data that were published? A colleague may believe that the original data were not analyzed correctly or in the most appropriate fashion, or would lead to quite different conclusions if analyzed differently. Data are viewed as part of the public domain, to be shared with others if requested.

There is often reluctance of investigators to share data. One reason is that a given study may be drawn from a larger data base. Several other projects may be planned and the investigator may be unwilling to circulate the data until the projects have been completed, analyzed, and reported. Here, too, once an article has been published in a scientific journal, it is difficult to justify withholding the specific data set on which that article was based. That data set, even if not the entire data base, might well be considered to be part of the information available to the scientific community.

Increasingly in research, data bases and raw data are made publicly available to other researchers to permit further analyses. Apart from placing data within the public domain, there are other virtues of this strategy. A given data set can represent a rich resource. The interests and creativity of a given investigative team that obtained and analyzed the data may not exhaust the knowledge available within that set. Other investigators with novel hypotheses, reconceptualizations of the issues, and different training or orientations may extract new knowledge. There may be ethical constraints here given that some review committees restrict use of data for the specific purposes outlined in the original proposal and by the investigator who provided that proposal. The purpose is to protect subjects whose consent does not extend to its use beyond the original project.

Guiding Principles and Responsibilities

The issues highlighted here are weighty to say the least and reflect areas where ambiguity often remains. Obviously, in the case of fraud, the ethical and professional standards and sanctions are clear. Guidelines for allocation of credit, sharing of data, and related matters are actively discussed and concrete rules cannot easily be provided.

Guiding principles have been provided by the American Psychological Association to address these matters and to convey explicitly the ethical obligations of the investigator. Samples of selected principles to cover these obligations are presented in Table 14.3. The guidelines convey important facets of research obligations. In some ways they can be seen to fall beyond the scope of methodology and research design. However, they are pivotal to the use and interpretation of research and the accumulation of findings.

It is clear from the implications of research, that science and scientists occupy a central role in society. In clinical psychology in particular, research may have critical implications that bring researchers into areas of social concern (e.g., day-care, criminal behavior, child rearing, treatment regimens, custody disputes). Quite apart from the specific line of work and social implications that work may bear, the integrity of each researcher is critical. The guidelines convey that the integrity of the enterprise and obligations of the researcher to maintain these are essential.

Table 14.3. Ethical Guidelines for Researchers

Fraudulent Research
   1. Psychologists do not engage in fraudulent research or distort, fabricate, misrepresent, or bias their results. They never suppress disconfirming data, and they acknowledge the existence of alternative hypotheses and explanations of their findings.

Allocation of Credit
   1. Psychologists take credit only for work they have actually done, including publication credit.
   2. Publication credit accurately reflects the relative contribution of the individuals involved, regardless of professional status. A student generally is listed as the principal author of any multiply authored articles based primarily on the student's thesis or dissertation. Minor contributions to publications are acknowledged in footnotes or in an introductory statement.
   3. Plagiarism in either written or oral form is unethical. Acknowledgement through specific citations is made for unpublished as well as published material that has directly influenced the research or writing.

Sharing of Data
   1. After research results are in the public domain, psychologists do not withhold the data on which their conclusions are based from other competent professionals, assuming the confidentiality of the participants can be protected.

Other
   1. Psychologists provide a discussion of the limitations of their studies, especially where their work touches on social policy or might be construed to the detriment of persons in groups of specific age, disability, ethnicity, gender, national origin, race, religion, sexual orientation, social class, or other vulnerable groups.
   2. Psychologists attempt to prevent distortion or misuse of psychological findings by their employing institution or agency.

Note. These guidelines constitute expectations regarding a broader set of principles outlined elsewhere, which should be consulted. Source: American Psychological Association, 1990, June. Ethical principles revised: Comments are sought on proposed revision, *APA Monitor, 21*(6), pp. 28–32. Copyright © 1990 by the American Psychological Association. Reprinted by permission.

General Comments

Ethical issues of the researcher in relation to the scientific community are significant. In addressing these, it is important not to lose sight of some givens of science. To begin with, scientists are human. Thus the full panoply of human characteristics, motives, and foibles are likely to be evident. This does not mean that the negative virtues are pervasive; it does mean that we should not be shocked to hear instances when less than desirable samples of humanness are evident, as when researchers argue ad hominem about their theoretical differences, when beliefs are held tenaciously in the face of seemingly persuasive counterevidence, when differential standards are applied to interpretation of some kinds of work rather than others, and so on. As humans, we are by our very nature limited. We are motivated viewers; we bring subjectivity to our experience and its interpretation. Not only is it true that, "seeing is believing," but more critically to our goals, "believing is seeing." Fraud, interests in primary credit, possessiveness of ideas, procedures, and data, as discussed previously occur and hence always warrant attention.

That scientists are human does not excuse lapses that compete with the very purposes of science. Indeed, that humanness has invented science. Another given is the very method of seeking knowledge. Science consists, among other things, of methods, procedures, practices, and values aimed at increasing objectivity of our work. Strategies of research, methods, and evaluation procedures have been devised to reduce the role of subjectivity and to increase replicability. Some of the methods used to decrease subjectivity introduce their own sources of error and artifact. For example, statistics are used to provide a criterion to determine if there is a reliable effect; yet chance could in any given case explain group differences. Also, measures are used to permit evaluation of constructs and to provide more objective means of assessment than impressions and personal opinions of the investigator; reactivity of assessment and low validity of the measures are potential limits assessment often introduces. However, these sources of error can be placed within the scientific arena, investigated, and evaluated.

SUMMARY AND CONCLUSIONS

Psychological research raises many ethical issues that are intertwined with methodology. Experimental questions and design options, such as those considered throughout the text, do not always make explicit the need to protect the rights and welfare of the subject. Salient issues pertaining to the rights of subjects include deception and debriefing, invasion of privacy, and informed consent. *Deception* is a major concern when subjects are misguided about the purpose of the experiment and the misinformation may deleteriously affect their beliefs about themselves or others. Deception is infrequently used or permitted in clinical research. If deception is used, subjects must be informed about the true purposes after they complete the experiment. Providing such information, referred to as *debriefing,* is designed to erase the effects of deception. However, the effects of deception are not invariably erased. Leaving aside the effects of debriefing, many investigators object to deception in its own right because of the relationship it fosters between experimenter and subject.

Invasion of privacy is often protected by ensuring that the responses subjects provide are completely anonymous. Subjects who agree to provide information also must be assured that the information will be confidential. Confidentiality requires that the information will not be disclosed to others without the awareness of the subject. In most research situations, anonymity and confidentiality are assured by removing the identity of subjects when the data are evaluated and conveying information publicly (in research reports) only on the basis of group performance. In clinical work, however, threats to invasion of privacy may derive from reports of individual cases where the individual's identity might be revealed. Also reports from research may affect large segments of society (e.g., ethnic and/or racial groups) even when the individual identity of the subjects is not at issue.

Informed consent is a central issue that encompasses many ethical concerns and means of protecting subjects in experimentation. Informed consent requires that the subject willingly agrees to participate in an experiment and be fully aware of the procedures, risks, and benefits when making the choice to participate. Procuring and interpreting informed consent is not entirely straightforward because the subject must be competent to provide consent, know the relevant information to make a meaningful choice, and consent completely voluntarily. Whether these criteria are met in any given case often is a matter of debate.

Treatment research raises a number of special ethical issues. These include informing the client completely about treatment, withholding treatment, and using treatments of questionable efficacy. Withholding treatment or using control procedures that may not be therapeutic are ethically objectionable and difficult to justify in situations where clients are in need of immediate care. Questions requiring these control procedures may be conducted in situations where clients are not in immediate jeopardy and agree to the conditions of participation. Some of the ethical issues raised in treatment research can be addressed by providing all clients with the most effective treatment, if they have not achieved marked improvements after participation in a less effective condition.

The many ethical issues raised in research have prompted guidelines designed to protect the rights of individual subjects. The guidelines apprise investigators of their obligations and the priority of ensuring protection of the subject at all times. The guidelines do not necessarily rule out practices that might be objectionable (e.g., deception). The onus is on the investigator to show that there are likely benefits of the research and that these require a departure from full disclosure of the purposes and procedures.

Not all ethical issues and obligations pertain to the relation of the investigator to research subjects. The investigator has obligations to the profession, scientific community, and public more generally. These obligations pertain to the conduct of research. Three issues were discussed to convey concerns in relation to fraud in science, allocation of credit, and sharing of materials and data. Ethical guidelines also are provided to convey these responsibilities as well.

FOR FURTHER READING

American Psychological Association, Committee for the Protection of Human Participants in Research. (1982). *Ethical principles in the conduct of research with human participants.* Washington, DC: Author.

Annas, G.J., Glantz, L.H., & Katz, B.F. (1977). *Informed consent to human experimentation: The subject's dilemma.* Cambridge, MA: Ballinger.

Greenberg, J., & Folger, R. (1988). *Controversial issues in social research methods.* New York: Springer-Verlag.

Handlesman, M.M., & Galvin, M.D. (1988). Facilitating informed consent for outpatient psychotherapy: A suggested written format. *Professional Psychology: Research and Practice, 19,* 223–225.

Miers, M.L. (1985). Current NIH perspectives on misconduct in science. *American Psychologist, 40,* 831–835.

National Academy of Sciences, Committee on the Conduct of Science. (1989). *On being a scientist.* Washington, DC: National Academy Press.

Schuler, H. (Ed.). (1982). *Ethical problems in psychological research.* New York: Academic Press.

Chapter 15

PUBLICATION AND COMMUNICATION OF RESEARCH FINDINGS

CHAPTER OUTLINE

After an investigation or set of investigations is completed, the results are often published so that they can be disseminated to the scientific community and become part of the accumulated knowledge base. Publication and communication of results of research findings involve a process with many decision points and steps. For examples, decisions are required regarding *whether* to publish the paper, *what* to publish (e.g., when a large data base may need to be subdivided in some way), *where* to publish (e.g., journal article, chapter, book), and *when* to publish (e.g., in an ongoing longitudinal study when interim segments of the data may be of interest). Also, authorship, responsibilities for completion and preparation of the paper, obligations to the scientific community in executing and reporting research, and making information and data available raise central issues. The many components of publication and communication are of keen interest because publications address both professional (e.g., development of the field) and personal (e.g., career advancement) issues and because these issues span diverse scientific disciplines. The breadth of interest means that authors from many disciplines have written on the topic and the literature is rich in substance.

The issues associated with publication and communication are weighty and the topic of several treatises that discuss useful strategies, frustrations, guidelines for authors, and technical preparation of manuscripts (e.g., Agnew & Pyke, 1987; Garfield, 1984; Maher, 1978b; Meinart, 1986; Sindermann, 1982). The purpose of the present chapter is to address a narrow facet of publication and communication and hence not to supplant other sources. Specifically, the purpose is to discuss publication and communication of results in light of design and methodological issues raised in previous chapters. The task of the author is to translate methodological, design, and evaluation decisions raised in previous chapters into a rational and readable manuscript.

In previous chapters, methodology has been discussed from the standpoint of specific strategies in planning, designing, and implementing research. At a broader level, methodology can be conceived as an approach toward thinking and problem solving. The approach considers specific types of obstacles to knowledge. These obstacles are codified in various ways under such rubrics as threats to validity, biases, and artifacts. The skill of the investigator in addressing these obstacles is often reflected in the quality of the design. In clinical settings, the skill of the investigator may be especially important because the characteristics of the sample, settings, and clinical issues may place methodological constraints. The quality of a given investigation is invariably a matter of degree and is evaluated both in relation to the criteria for experimental validity and to the constraints placed on the research setting. In relation to manuscript preparation, the task is to convey the rationale for method and design decisions. The thrust of the present chapter is to emphasize those facets of the manuscript and publication that pertain to methodology and research design. As such, the content is not intended to be a complete guide to manuscript preparation in general.

PUBLICATION PROCESS: AN OVERVIEW

Within psychology and other scientific disciplines, professional journals serve as the primary publication outlet for research. This chapter focuses on preparing papers for journal publication, even though the remarks may apply to other formats (e.g., conference presentations, chapters and books in which research is described). The publication process is usually conceived as beginning with preparation of a manuscript for journal submission. The process might be traced to a much earlier point. Indeed, decisions made at the design stage, including the focus of the study, the type of question, the strength of the planned design, and events throughout the investigation all may govern or restrict the eventual publication choices.

In discussing the publication process, we shall begin with the assumption of a completed study that contributes to the area of investigation in some substantive way and adds important knowledge. Inherent in this assumption is that the study is sufficiently well designed to generate experimentally valid conclusions. This assumption does not invariably mean that a study will end in a published report of the findings. Not all studies that are begun are completed; of those completed, not all are prepared for publication; of those prepared for publication, not all are submitted to journals for review and evaluation; of those that are, not all are accepted and published.

We begin here with an assumption that the study is completed and the author or authors wish to publish the results in a journal within or related to clinical psychology. After completion of the study, the author(s) prepare a written version of the paper in a highly specific format. This format in psychology is specified by the American Psychological Association (APA, 1983) but used and illustrated in many journals beyond the discipline of psychology. The manuscript consists of several sections, discussed later, that convey the rationale for the study, procedures, analyses, and the knowledge yield.

Once the manuscript is prepared, it is submitted to a journal the author has selected as a desirable and suitable publication outlet. Selection of the journal is often based on any of several criteria, including the journal that is viewed as most relevant to the topic, the breadth and number of readers or subscribers, the discipline and audience one wishes to address (e.g., psychology, psychiatry, medicine, social work, health, education), the prestige value of the journal in an implicit hierarchy of journals in the field, the likelihood of acceptance, and others. Several hundred journal outlets are available in the behavioral and social sciences. Journals in psychology within the English language have been described for purposes of aiding authors in the selection of appropriate outlets for their manuscripts (APA, 1990b). The information includes editorial policy, content areas, and guidelines for manuscript preparation for each of the journals.

Once the manuscript is submitted, the journal editor usually sends the paper to two or more reviewers. The reviewers are usually selected because of their knowledge and special expertise in the area of the study or because of familiarity with selected features of the study (e.g., novel methods of data analyses). Some reviewers are consulting editors who review often for the journal and presumably have a perspective of the type and quality of papers the journal typically publishes; other reviewers are ad hoc reviewers and are selected less regularly than consulting editors. Both consulting editors and ad hoc reviewers are often experts and active researchers in the specific area of the study and can evaluate the contribution well.

Reviewers are asked to evaluate the substance and methods of the study. They evaluate specific details including those features related to threats to internal, external, construct, and statistical conclusion validity, although the threats are not usually referred to by name in the reviewers' comments. The reviewers are instructed to evaluate the paper critically and to offer opinions about its merit.

Once the paper is reviewed, the editor evaluates the manuscript and the comments of the reviewers. There are major individual differences in journals and editors in this step. In some cases, the editor may provide an extensive review of the paper; in other cases he or she may not review the paper at all but defer to the comments and recommendations of the reviewers. The editor writes the author and notes the editorial decision. Usually, one of three decisions is reached: (a) the manuscript is *accepted* pending a number of revisions that address points of concern in the reviewers' comments; (b) the manuscript is *rejected* and will not be considered further by the journal; or (c) the manuscript is *rejected but the author is invited to resubmit* an extensively revised version of the paper for reconsideration.

The *accept* decision usually means that the overall study provides important information and was well done. Typically, reviewers and the editor have identified several points for further clarification and analysis. The author is asked to revise the paper to address these points. The revised paper would be accepted for publication. Occasionally, several revisions may be needed as the author and editor work toward achieving the final manuscript.

The *reject* decision means that the reviewers and/or editor considered the paper to include flaws in conception, design, or execution, or that the research problem, focus, and question did not address a very important issue. For the journals with high rejection rates, papers are usually not rejected because they are flagrantly flawed in design. Rather, the importance of the study, the suitability of the methods for the questions, and specific methodological and design decisions conspire to serve as the basis for the decision. In many of these cases, preparation of the manuscript in ways that emphasize the rationale for methodological practices selected by the investigator might readily lead to different reactions on the part of reviewers.

The *reject-resubmit* decision may be used if several issues emerged that raise questions about the research and the design. In a sense, the study may be viewed as basically sound and important but many significant questions preclude evaluation. The author may be invited to prepare an extensive revision that includes further procedural details, additional data analyses, clarification of many decision points pivotal to the findings and conclusions, and in general major changes. The revised manuscript may be entered into the review process anew to reach an accept or reject decision.

No individual study can address all concerns (or threats to validity). Consequently, the task of the reviewer is to assess what has been done and to judge whether the knowledge yield warrants publication in the journal. Concretely, reviewers examine such general issues as whether:

- the question(s) is important for the field,
- the design and methodology are appropriate to the question,
- the results are suitably analyzed,
- the interpretations follow from the design and findings, and
- the knowledge yield contributes in an incremental way to the field.

In noting these general areas, one cannot help but be struck by the judgments reviewers are asked to make. The judgments require a subjective as well as intellectual evaluation of the study. Science is an enterprise of people and hence cannot be divorced from subjectivity and judgment. In noting subjectivity in the manuscript review and evaluation process, there is a false implication of arbitrariness and fiat. Perhaps manuscript quality, as beauty, is in the eye of the beholder. However, this is not tantamount to noting that everyone sees manuscripts or beauty differently.

In addition to individual judgment, the decision to accept or reject is influenced by contextual factors. Individual journals can vary widely in their base rates of acceptance and the types of studies they are likely to accept. A given article might be reviewed quite differently as a function of the journal and in the recommendations for its publication, not to mention reviewers.

Although beyond our purpose, the review process deserves passing comment. The entire process of manuscript submission, review, and publication has been heavily lamented, debated, and criticized. The imperfections and biases of peer review, the lack of agreement between reviewers of a given paper, the influence of variables (e.g., prestige value of the author's institution, number of citations of one's prior work within the manuscript) on decisions of reviewers, and the control that reviewers and editors exert over authors have been and continue to be vigorously discussed (e.g., Bailar & Patterson, 1985; Bradley, 1981, 1982). Of special concern is the review process and the ways authors are treated. Understanding the review process can be aided by underscoring the one salient characteristic that authors, reviewers, and editors share: to wit, they are all human. This means that they (we) vary widely in skills, expertise, sensitivities, motives, and abilities to communicate. Consequently, the content, quality, and other features of manuscripts, comments of reviewers, and editorial decision letters vary in multivariate ways. As a new investigator begins to enter into the journal publication process, he or she quickly develops a set of stories about irrational features of the process, unreasonable judgments against one's own study, and so on.

If the reader has submitted a journal article but does not yet have a horror story to share about the review process, here is a guideline for developing such a story. Submit one paper for publication and have it rejected. Usually only one manuscript is required to reach this stage. When reviewers and the editor provide comments for the basis of the rejection, sift through the comments meticulously. Choose the most trivial point mentioned by any one of the parties. Usually, typographical errors, inappropriate format for citing a reference or two, or margin spacing [e.g., right justification] can be identified. Such comments are likely to be embedded in broader criticisms about the significance of the study and its methodology. These latter criticisms are to be ignored to develop this horror story. Once the trivial point has been identified, proceed to tell others [friends, colleagues] that the study was rejected because of that point. The story is good for approximately 5 years. After that point, authors often have different views about the original study. If they reread the original reviews, the salience and cogency of the original concerns increase.

METHODOLOGICALLY INFORMED
MANUSCRIPT PREPARATION

Overview

In psychology, one's initial introduction to manuscript preparation often occurs at the undergraduate level in a course devoted to experimental psychology or selected topics (learning, motivation) in which experimental design is also taught. The goal at this early stage of development is to encourage descriptive and objective scientific writing. Understandably, a particular view is fostered to distinguish the style of scientific writing from other forms in which opinion, subjectivity, and description are appropriately intertwined (e.g., a literary style where the full range of experience, emotions, and views are encouraged). The style of science writing is to be descriptive and to convey what was actually done so that the methods and procedures can be replicated. Concrete, specific, operational, tangible, objective, precise, and impersonal are some of the characteristics that capture the introduction to writing of scientific papers.

The above characteristics are not listed here to be cast aside as unimportant. The effort to describe research in concrete and specific ways is critical. Yet, the task of the author goes well beyond description. The general task of the author is to convey to the reader (reviewers) that the study contributes to knowledge in an important way and that the many decisions the author has made to address experimental validity are reasonable in pursuit of the questions the study is designed to address. Knowledge of methodology and research design is extremely helpful in making the case.

Sections of the Manuscript

It is useful to consider portions of manuscripts that are prepared for journal publication. The purpose here is to emphasize issues that relate primarily to methodology and research design that infuse the major sections of the manuscript. Obviously, there is more to manuscript preparation, submission, and publication than attention to methodology and design. There is no substitute for innovative and creative ideas and for brilliant and highly informed investigators. Most of us publish products of our research without the benefit of extremes of these other advantages. In all cases of publishing research in scientific journals, however, manuscript preparation and publication can be greatly aided by major attention to methodology and design.

The material that follows discusses the purposes of individual sections of the manuscript, with emphasis on the intended content. The major sections of a manuscript can also be conceived from the standpoint of answering critical questions. Table 15.1 presents questions that warrant consideration in each section of the manuscript. Studies can vary widely in clinical psychology and each question is not necessarily appropriate to each study. Hence the goals of the sections and the authors' obligation are discussed more generally.

Title

The selection of the title of a paper is worth mentioning. Usually one attempts to address the key variables, focus, and population with an economy of words. If the study focuses on diagnosis, assessment, treatment, or prevention, one of these words or variations might well be included. Similarly, if a specific disorder (e.g., depression), personality characteristic (e.g., repression-sensitization), treatment technique (e.g., structural family therapy), or sample (e.g., infants, elderly) is critical, the pertinent terms are likely to be integrated into the title.

Occasionally, one has a hint toward methodology in the title. Key terms are included, perhaps in the form of subtitles, to alert us to methodological points. Terms like "a pilot study" or "preliminary report" may mean many different things such as the fact that this is an initial or interim report of a larger research program. These words could also be gently preparing readers for some methodological surprises that threaten experimental validity and not to expect much from the design. In some cases, terms are added to the study such as, "A Controlled Investigation," which moves our expectation in the other direction, namely, that the present study is somehow well conducted and controlled, and perhaps by implication stands in contrast to other studies in the field (or the author's repertoire).

Abstract

The purpose of the Abstract is of course to provide a relatively brief statement of purpose, methods, findings, and conclusions of the study. Questions noted in Table 15.1 direct the writer to the content of this section. Critical methodological descriptors pertain to the subjects and their characteristics, experimental and control groups or conditions, design, and major findings. Often space is quite limited; indeed a word limit (e.g., 100 or 150 word maximum) may be placed on the abstract by the journals. The abstract is critically important because of the circulation in international data bases in which it is reprinted. Consequently, the limited word space that journals invariably invoke on their abstracts must be used judiciously. Vacuous statements ("Implications of the results were discussed") are better omitted and replaced with further details about the findings and conclusions.

Introduction

The Introduction is designed to convey the overall rationale and objectives for the study that follows. The task of the author is to convey in a crisp and concise fashion why this particular study is needed and the current questions, void,

Table 15.1. Major Questions to Guide Journal Article Preparation

---

ABSTRACT

What are the main purposes of the study?
Who was studied (sample, sample size, special characteristics)?
How were subjects selected and assigned to conditions?
To what conditions were subjects exposed?
What type of design was used?
What are the main findings and conclusions?

INTRODUCTION

What is the background for the study (briefly)?
What in current theory, research, or clinical work makes this study useful, important, or of interest?
What is different or special about the study in focus, methods, or design to address a need in the area?
Is the rationale clear regarding the constructs to be assessed?
What specifically are the purposes, predictions, or hypotheses?

METHOD

Subjects

Who are the subjects and how many are there in this study?
Why was this sample selected in light of the research goals?
How was this sample obtained, recruited, and selected?
What are the subject and demographic characteristics of the sample (e.g., sex, age, ethnicity, race, socioeconomic status)?
What, if any, inclusion and exclusion criteria were invoked, that is, what were the selection rules to obtain participants?
How many of those subjects eligible or recruited actually were selected and participated in the study?
Was informed consent solicited? How and from whom, if special populations were used?

Design

How were subjects assigned to groups or conditions?
How many groups were included in the design?
How are the groups similar and different in how they are treated in the study?
Why are these groups critical to address the questions of interest?

Procedures

Where was the study conducted (setting)?
What measures, materials, equipment, or apparatus were used in the study?
What is the chronological sequence of events to which subjects were exposed?
What intervals elapsed between different aspects of the study (assessment, treatment, follow-up)?
If assessments involve novel measures created for this study, what data can be brought to bear regarding pertinent types of reliability and validity?
What variation in administration of conditions emerged over the course of the study in ways that may introduce variation within and between conditions?
What procedural checks were completed to avert potential sources of bias in implementation of the manipulation and assessment of dependent measures?
What checks were made to ensure that the conditions were carried out as intended?

Table 15.1. *Continued*

METHOD

What other information does the reader need to know to understand how subjects were treated and what conditions were provided?

RESULTS

What are the primary measures and data on which the predictions depend?
What analyses are to be used and how specifically do these address the original hypotheses and purposes?
Are the assumptions of the data analyses met?
If multiple tests are used, what means are provided to control error rates?
Prior to the experimental conditions, were groups similar on variables that might otherwise explain the results (e.g., diagnosis, age)?
Are data missing due to incomplete measures (not filled out completely by the subjects) or due to loss of subjects? If so, how are these handled in the data analyses?
Are there ancillary analyses that might further inform the primary analyses or exploratory analyses that might stimulate further work?

DISCUSSION

What are the major findings of the study?
How do these findings add to research and support, refute, or inform current theory?
What alternative interpretations can be placed on the data?
What limitations or qualifiers must be placed on the study given methodological and design issues?
What research follows from the study to move the field forward?

---

or deficiency the study is designed to address. The section should not review the literature in a study-by-study fashion but rather convey issues and evaluative comments that set the stage for the study that is to follow.

It may be relevant to consider threats to validity of prior work if they serve as the impetus of the present study. These threats may entail criticism of prior work if conclusions have been reached prematurely. Alternatively, the study may build along new dimensions to extend the theory, hypotheses, and constructs to a broader range of domains of performance, samples, settings, and so on. The rationale for the specific study must be clearly established.

There may be essential material about a problem area that serves as contextual information. For example, in studies of diagnosis, treatment, assessment, or prevention of dysfunction, the Introduction invariably includes a paragraph to orient the reader about the seriousness, prevalence or incidence, economic and social costs of the disorder. Opening material provides basic information about a problem area that is not likely to be widely known. However, the material must be limited so that the bulk of the Introduction can be devoted to the more focused rationale for this particular study. Space for the Introduction may be limited (e.g., 2–4 manuscript pages) by tradition or actual constraints of the journal. A reasonable use of this space is in brief paragraphs or implicit sections that describe the nature of the problem, current status of the literature, the extension that this study is designed to provide, and how the methods to be used are warranted.

In the Introduction, the author is making a case for the study. Commonly made statements that may not be well received by reviewers are that the study: "is important," "is the first time" that something has been done, or that "the phenomenon has never been studied before." Each of these statements, when explicit, can be unfortunate *if* it holds the primary weight for the basis of the study. The statements, in isolation and without the underlying rationale, do not serve as strong bases for a study. The author need not and perhaps even should not state that the study is important. This is a conclusion to which the reader should be led through the writer's scholarship. The author's task is to develop the case based on a firm grasp of the issues and literature. Stating that a study is important may not only circumvent this process, but may also suggest that the author has not made the case or perhaps could not make the case that the study is important. The author is asking the reader to take his or her word for the importance of the area. Few reviewers or readers are likely to do so.

It is also not very useful to state or at least to emphasize that this study represents a first and that the variables have not heretofore been studied. The study might be the first to examine the relation of shoe size, empathic skills in therapy, and sex-role orientation (androgyny) among experienced gestalt therapists. The issue is whether the study represents a theoretically, empirically, or clinically important or interesting focus. The range of variables that could be selected and combined to produce a first is infinite. The Introduction must establish that the variables are of some interest well beyond this criterion. To the extent that the author conveys a grasp of the issues in the area and can identify the lacunae that the study is designed to fill can greatly increase the chances of acceptance for journal publication.

Method

This section of the paper encompasses several points related to who was studied, why, how, and so on. The section not only describes critical procedures, but also provides the rationale for methodological decisions. Initially, the subjects, clients, or research participants are described. From a method and design standpoint, information beyond basic descriptors can be helpful. Why was this sample included and how is this appropriate to the substantive area and question of interest? In some cases, the sample is obviously relevant because the subjects have the characteristic or disorder of interest (e.g., parents accused of child abuse) or is in a setting of interest (e.g., nursing home residents). In other cases, samples are included merely because they are available (college students, a clinic population recruited for some other purpose than this study). Such samples of convenience often serve as a count against the investigator. The rationale for the sample should be provided. If a sample is included that is potentially objectionable, the rationale may require full elaboration to convey why the sample was included and how features of the sample may or may not be relevant to the conclusions the author wishes to draw. More generally, subject selection, recruitment, screening, and other features warrant comment. The issue for the investigator is whether features of the subject-selection process could restrict (external validity) the conclusions in some unique fashion or worse, in some way represent a poor test given the purpose of the study.

The design is likely to include two or more groups that are treated in a particular fashion. From the standpoint of methodology and design, the precise purpose of each group and the procedures to which they are exposed should be clarified. Control groups should not merely be labeled as such with the idea that the name is informative. The author should convey precisely what the group(s) is designed to control, in terms of threats to validity. It is possible that some control procedures are not feasible under the circumstances of the study. Why and how the threats will be addressed should be clarified.

Reviewers often criticize a study because certain control conditions were not included. After the paper is rejected by the journal, authors retort in an understandably frustrated way that the control procedure was not feasible, that the threats were not plausible anyway, and so on. Generally, the responsibility here lies with the author. The author is advised to identify the critical threats in the area and to convey how these are controlled in the design. Plausible threats that are uncontrolled deserve explicit comment to arrest the reasonable concerns of the reviewers. Similarly, other features of the design that are not obvious or that address threats to validity of special concern in the design or to the content area may deserve comment.

Several measures are usually included in the study. Why the constructs were selected for study should be clarified in the Introduction. The specific measures and why they were selected to operationalize the constructs should be presented in the Method section. Information about the psychometric characteristics of the measures is often highlighted. This information relates directly to the credibility of the results. Do the measures assess constructs of interest and do so reliably? Are predictions and findings limited, qualified, or impeded by characteristics of the measures? Apart from individual assessment devices, the rationale for including or omitting areas that might be regarded as crucial (e.g., multiple measures, informants, settings) deserves comment. The principle here is similar to other sections, namely, the rationale for the author's decisions need to be explicit.

Results

The results are occasionally assumed by authors to be the most straightforward portion of the manuscript. This is easily arguable. The vast majority of studies in clinical psychology utilize *t* tests, analyses of variance, or regression analyses. There is an ever increasing range of statistical alternatives for evaluating a data set, regrettably few of which are regularly covered in graduate training programs (see Aiken, West, Sechrest, & Reno, 1990).

From the standpoint of methodology and design, it is important to convey why specific analyses were selected and how a particular test or comparison addresses the hypothesis or purpose presented earlier in the paper. It is often the case that analyses are reported in a rote fashion in which, for example, the main effects are presented and then interactions for each measure. The author presents the analyses in very much the same way as the computer printout that provided multiple runs of the data. Similarly, if several dependent measures are available, a particular set of analyses is automatically run (e.g., omnibus tests of multivariate analyses of variance followed by univariate analyses of variance for individual measures). The tests may not relate to the hypotheses, predictions, or expectations outlined at the beginning of the paper (Wampold, Davis, & Good, 1990). Knowledge of statistics is critical for selecting the analysis to address the hypotheses of interest and conditions met by the data. In presentation of the Results, it is important to convey why specific tests were selected and how these serve the specific goals of the study.

It is often useful to begin the Results by presenting basic descriptors of the data (e.g., such as means, standard deviations for each group or condition) so the reader has access to the numbers themselves. The main body of the Results is to test the hypotheses or to evaluate the predictions. Organization of the Results (subheadings) or brief statements of hypotheses before the analyses are often helpful to prompt the *author* to clarify how the statistical test relates to the substantive questions.

It is often the case that several additional or ancillary analyses are presented to elaborate the primary hypotheses. For example, one might be able to reduce the plausibility that certain biases accounted for group differences. Ancillary data analyses may be more exploratory and diffuse than tests of primary hypotheses in the minds of the authors and readers. Manifold variables can be selected for these analyses (e.g., sex, race, height differences) that are not necessarily interesting or important. The rationale for selection of this set of subanalyses in relation to the focus of the study is critical.

The author may wish to present data and data analyses that were unexpected, were not of initial interest, and were not the focus of the study. The rationale for this excursion and the limitations of interpretation are worth noting. From the standpoint of the reviewer and reader, the results should make clear what the main hypotheses were, how the analyses provide tests of them, and what conclusions can be reached as a result.

Noted earlier (chapter 12) were alternative methods of data evaluation (statistical, nonstatistical, clinical). It is useful to go beyond statistical significance when possible to look at magnitude of effects (e.g., effect size, correlational terms) and the applied importance of change. Such analyses can expand on the range of outcomes and deepen our understanding of the data.

Discussion

The Discussion consists of the conclusions and interpretations of the study and hence is the final resting place of all methodological issues and concerns. Typically, the Discussion includes an overview of the major findings, integration or relation of these to theory and prior research, limitations and ambiguities and their implications for interpretation, and future directions. The extent that this can be accomplished in a brief space (e.g., 2–5 manuscript pages) is to the author's advantage.

Description and interpretation of the findings invariably raise a potential tension between what the author wishes to say about the findings and their meaning versus what can be said in light of how the study was designed and evaluated. Authors and reviewers usually do not make an inventory of each threat to validity and how the study falls on each one. However, such an inventory would quickly pinpoint ambiguities that influence the Discussion section, that is, interpretation of the results.

The author's interpretation of the results extends beyond consideration of threats to validity, although these remain salient. Occasionally in the Discussion, the author conveys for the first time or most clearly what he or she wishes to say about the phenomenon of interest and what the present study was designed to accomplish. The interpretation by the author and how it follows from the study can be evaluated more clearly. The task of evaluating the methodology becomes clearer at this point. Specifically, as a reader or reviewer of the study, one can examine the interplay of the Introduction to the study, the Methods and Results, and the Discussion as to whether these broad sections "fit."

For example, the author might draw conclusions that are not quite appropriate given the method and findings. The Discussion conveys flaws, problems, or questionable methodological decisions within the design that were not previously evident. They are flaws *only* in relation to the Introduction and Discussion. That is, the reader of the paper can now state that if these are the types of statements the author wishes to make, the present study is not well suited. The slight mismatch of interpretative statements in the Discussion and the methodology is a common, albeit tacit basis for not considering a study as well conceived and executed. A slightly different study may be required to support the specific statements the author makes in the Discussion; alternatively, the Discussion might be more circumscribed in the statements that are made.

It is usually to the author's credit to examine potential sources of ambiguity because he or she is in an excellent position by familiarity with procedures and expertise to understand the area. The sources of ambiguity and plausible threats warrant mention. In this regard, data from the present study, findings from other studies, logic, and common sense are appropriate to make threats less plausible than they might otherwise seem. Of course, critically important threats to the area should have been addressed in the design itself. The plausibility of alternative treatments and the adequacy with which each was handled is an area where readers may disagree.

It is advantageous for readers to have the benefit of the author's candid evaluation of the study and its limitations. The comments permit readers to understand further the rationale for various methodological decisions within the design and hence to evaluate the overall study and its merit. At the same time, occasionally stark flaws in the study preclude interpreting the results. Authors may acknowledge critical flaws (e.g., absence of a needed control group, too few subjects due to attrition to evaluate a central hypothesis). In research (as in psychotherapy), insight into one's problems has its own merit, but it is no substitute for a "cure" or elimination of those problems. Saying that, "the author realizes that a control group was omitted" or "that the single outcome measure does, of course, need to be supplemented with further data" cannot be expected to redress the problems of the study. Also, calling a weak study "Preliminary" may not help either. At some point, the flaw is sufficient to preclude publication whether or not it is acknowledged by the author. At other points, acknowledging potential limitations conveys critical understanding of the issues and directs the field to future work. This latter use of acknowledgment augments the contribution of the study and the likelihood of favorable evaluation by readers.

General Comments

Preparation of the manuscript was discussed in light of methodological and design issues rather than from all the facets that may be important to include or address. General points can be culled from the effort to highlight each section. Briefly, the rationale for decisions within the design must be explicit. The rationales often address features that are likely to be of concern to reviewers and to encompass decisions related to experimental validity. Relatedly, it is useful for the author to consider threats to validity and to prepare the manuscript with these in mind. The author does not need to mention the threats explicitly but, rather, is required to anticipate the concerns that are likely to emerge.

Although the task of the author is to describe the research, the demands extend beyond clear description. Thought processes underlying methodological and design decisions will greatly influence the extent to which the research effort is appreciated and viewed as enhancing knowledge. The author is not advised to write a persuasive appeal about how important the study is and how this or that way was the best way to study the phenomenon. Yet it is useful to convey that decisions were thoughtful and that they represent reasonable choices among available alternatives to reach experimentally valid conclusions.

FINAL COMMENTS

Publication and communication of results of research represents a complex process involving many issues beyond methodology and research design. Diverse abilities are taxed, beginning with the author's skills in identifying and selecting critical substantive questions and culminating with skills in communicating the results. Methodology and design play major roles throughout the processes of planning, conducting, and communicating research results. In preparing the manuscript, the author invariably wishes to make a statement (conclusion). The strength of that conclusion is based on the extent to which the study addresses issues highlighted in prior chapters. It is important for the author to convey the focus and goals of the study clearly and concisely. The design decisions and the rationale for these decisions, when presented clearly, greatly augment the manuscript.

FOR FURTHER READING

Agnew, N.M., & Pyke, S.W. (1987). *The science game* (4th ed.). Englewood Cliffs, NJ: Prentice-Hall.

American Psychological Association. (1983). *Publication manual of the American Psychological Association* (3rd ed.). Washington, DC: Author.

American Psychological Association. (1990). *Journals in psychology: A resource listing for authors* (3rd ed.). Washington, DC: Author.

Maher, B.A. (1978). A reader's, writer's, and reviewer's guide to assessing research reports in clinical psychology. *Journal of Consulting and Clinical Psychology, 46,* 835–838.

Sindermann, C.J. (1982). *Winning the games scientists play.* New York: Plenum Press.

GLOSSARY

ABAB Design—A single-case experimental design in which the performance of a subject or group of subjects is evaluated over time across baseline (A) and intervention (B) conditions. A relation is demonstrated between the intervention and performance if performance changes in each phase in which intervention is presented and reverts to baseline or near baseline levels when it is withdrawn. Also called Reversal design.

Alpha (α)—The probability of rejecting a hypotheses (the null hypothesis) when that hypothesis is true. This is also referred to as a Type I error.

Alternate-Form Reliability—The correlation between different forms of the same measure when the items of the two forms are considered to represent the same population of items.

Analogue Research—Research that evaluates a particular condition or intervention under conditions that only resemble or approximate the situation to which one wishes to generalize.

Archival Records—Institutional, cultural, or other records that may be used as unobtrusive measures of performance.

Artifact—An extraneous influence in an experiment that may threaten validity, usually construct validity.

"Attention-Placebo" Control Group—A group in treatment research that is exposed to common factors associated with treatment such as attending treatment sessions, having contact with a therapist, hearing a logical rationale that describes the genesis of one's problem, and so on.

Attrition—Loss of subjects in an experiment. The loss of subjects can threaten all facets of experimental validity.

Baseline Assessment—Initial observations used in single-case designs that are obtained for multiple occasions (e.g., several days) prior to the intervention.

Baseline Phase—The initial phase of most single-case experimental designs in which performance is observed on some measure for several occasions (e.g., days) prior to implementing the experimental condition or intervention.

Behavioral Measures—Assessment that focuses on overt performance in laboratory or everyday settings. The performance attempts to sample directly the behavior of interest.

Beta (β)—The probability of accepting a hypothesis (the null hypothesis) when it is false. This is also referred to as a Type II error.

Blind—A term used to denote a procedure in which the experimenter and others associated with the investigation (e.g., staff, assessors) are kept naive with respect to the hypotheses and experimental conditions. Because of the confusion of the term with loss of vision and the pejorative reference to that condition, terms other than "blind" (e.g., experimentally naive, masked conditions) are often used.

Carryover Effect—In multiple-treatment designs, the impact of one treatment may linger or have impact on a subsequent treatment. This is equivalent to multiple-treatment interference.

Case Study—An intensive, and usually anecdotal, evaluation and report of an individual subject. Contrast with Single-Case Experimental Designs.

431

Ceiling Effect—This refers to a limit in the range of scores of a measure. The limit of the score may not differentiate among alternative groups that receive different conditions or may not permit demonstration of further movement or changes as a function of subsequent conditions in a multiple-treatment design. Ceiling or floor effect is sometimes used as a term depending on whether the upper or lower limit of the scale provides the restriction.

Changing-Criterion Design—A single-case experimental design that demonstrates the effect of an intervention by showing that performance changes in increments to match a performance criterion.

Clinical Significance—The extent to which the effect of an intervention makes an "important" difference to the clients or has practical or applied value.

Comparison Methods—Methods of comparing clients with others such as a normative sample as a means of evaluating the clinical significance of the changes achieved with an intervention.

Concurrent Validity—The correlation of a measure with performance on another measure or criterion at the same point in time.

Confederate—A person who works as an accomplice in the investigation, although he or she appears to be another subject or part of the natural arrangement of the setting (e.g., someone in a waiting room).

Confound—A factor, other variable, or influence that covaries with the experimental condition or intervention.

Construct Validity—In the context of experimental design, this refers to a type of experimental validity that pertains to the interpretation or basis of the effect that was demonstrated in an experiment. In the context of psychological assessment, the term refers to the extent to which a measure has been shown to assess the construct (e.g., intelligence) of interest.

Content Validity—Evidence that the content of the items of a measure reflect the construct or domain of interest. The relation of the items to the concept underlying the measure.

Continuous Assessment—A feature of single-case experimentation in which observations of performance are obtained repeatedly (e.g., daily) over time.

Convergent Validity—The correlation between measures that are expected to be related. The extent to which two measures assess the similar or related constructs. The validity of a given measure is supported if the measure correlates with other measures with which it is expected to correlate. Contrast with Discriminant Validity.

Counterbalanced—A method of arranging conditions or tasks presented to the subjects so that a given condition or task is not confounded by the order in which it appears.

Criterion Validity—Correlation of a measure with some other criterion. This can encompass concurrent or predictive validity. In addition, the notion is occasionally used in relation to a specific and often dichotomous criterion when performance on the measure is evaluated in relation to selected groups (e.g., depressed vs. nondepressed patients).

Crossover Design—A design in which two interventions are presented to each subject at different points in time. Halfway through the investigation, each subject is shifted to the other intervention or condition. The intervention is evaluated by comparing subject performance under the separate conditions.

Cross-Sectional Study—Research that seeks to understand the course of change or differences over time. Different subjects or groups at different ages or stages are selected and evaluated at a single point in time. Contrast with Longitudinal Study.

Debriefing—Providing a description of the experiment and its purposes to the subject after the investigation when deception was used or information was withheld about the investigation. The purpose is to counteract or minimize any negative effects that the experiment may have had.

Deception—Presentation of misleading information or not disclosing fully procedures and details of the investigation.

Demand Characteristics—Cues of the situation that are associated with the experimental manipulation or intervention that may seem incidental but may contribute to or even account for the results.

Dependent Variable—The measure designed to reflect the impact of the independent variable, experimental manipulation, or intervention.

Diffusion or Imitation of Treatment—The inadvertent administration of treatment to a control group that diffuses or obscures the impact of the intervention. More generally, any unintended procedure that may reduce the extent to which experimental and control conditions are distinct.

Discriminant Validity—The correlation between measures that are expected *not* to relate to each other. The validity of a given measure is supported if the measure shows little or no correlation with measures that, on a priori grounds, should measure different or unrelated constructs. Contrast with Convergent Validity.

Effect Size—A way of expressing the difference between alternative conditions (e.g., treatment vs. control) in terms of a common metric across measures and studies. The method is based on computing the difference between the means of interest on a particular measure and dividing this by the standard deviation (e.g., pooled standard deviation of the conditions).

Environmental Variables—Variables that consist of the environmental or situational conditions that are manipulated within an experiment. Alternative conditions (e.g., treatments) or tasks provided to subjects are classified here as environmental variables. Contrast with Subject Variables.

Experimenter Expectancies—Hypotheses, beliefs, and views on the part of the experimenter that may influence how the subjects perform. Expectancy effects are a threat to construct validity if they provide a plausible rival interpretation of the effects otherwise attributed to the intervention.

Experimenter—The person who conducts the experiment, runs subjects, or administers the conditions of research. See also Investigator.

Experiment-Wise Error Rate—The probability of a Type I error for all of the comparisons in the experiment given the number of tests. Contrast with Per Comparison Error Rate.

External Validity—The extent to which the results can be generalized or extended to people, settings, times, measures, and characteristics other than those in this particular experimental arrangement.

Face Validity—The extent to which a measure appears to assess the construct of interest. This is not regarded as a formal type of validation or part of the psychometric development or evaluation of a measure.

Factorial Designs—Group designs in which two or more variables are studied concurrently. For each variable, two or more levels are studied. The designs include the combinations of the variables (e.g., 2×2 design that would encompass four groups) so that main effects of the separate variables as well as their combined effect (interactions) can be evaluated.

File-Drawer Problem—The possibility that the published studies represent a biased sample of all studies that have been completed for a given hypothesis. The published studies may reflect those that obtained statistical significance (i.e., the 5% at the

$p < .05$ level). There may be many more studies (the other 95% somewhere in a file drawer) that did not attain significance and were not published (Rosenthal, 1979).

Follow-up Assessment—Evaluation of performance after posttreatment assessment.

Global Ratings—A type of measure that quantifies impressions of somewhat general characteristics. Such measures are referred to as "global" because they reflect over-all impressions or summary statements of the construct of interest.

History—A threat to internal validity that consists of any *event* occurring in the experiment (other than the independent variable) or outside of the experiment that may account for the results.

Independent Variable—The construct, experimental manipulation, intervention, or factor whose impact will be evaluated in the investigation.

Informants—People in contact with the client, such as a spouse, peers, roommates, teachers, employers, friends, colleagues, and others who might be asked to complete assessment or to provide information.

Informed Consent—Agreeing to participate in research with full knowledge about the nature of treatment, the risks, benefits, expected outcomes, and alternatives. Three elements are required for truly informed consent, namely, competence, knowledge, and volition.

Instructional Variables—A specific type of environmental or situational manipulation in which the investigator varies what the subjects are told or are led to believe through verbal or written statements in the experiment.

Instrumentation—A threat to internal validity that refers to changes in the measuring instrument or measurement procedures over time.

Interaction—The combined effect of two or more variables as demonstrated in a factorial design. Interactions signify that the effect of one variable (e.g., sex of the subject) depends on the level of another variable (e.g., age).

Internal Consistency—The degree of consistency or homogeneity of the items within a scale. Different reliability measures are used (e.g., split-half reliability, Kuder-Richardson 20 Formula, coefficient alpha).

Internal Validity—The extent to which the experimental manipulation or intervention, rather than extraneous influences, can be considered to account for the results, changes, or group differences.

Interrater (or Interscorer) Reliability—The extent to which different assessors, raters, or observers agree on the scores they provide when assessing, coding, or classifying subjects' performance.

Invasion of Privacy—Seeking information of a personal nature that intrudes upon what individuals or a group may view as private.

Investigator—The person who is responsible for designing and planning the experiment.

Latin Square—The arrangement of experimental conditions in a multiple-treatment design in which each of the conditions (task, treatments) occurs once in each ordinal position. Separate groups are used in the design, each of which receives a different sequence of the conditions.

Longitudinal Study—Research that seeks to understand the course of change or differences over time by following (assessing) a group or groups over time, often involving several years. Contrast with Cross-Sectional Study.

Loose Protocol Effect—A term to refer to the failure of the investigator to specify critical details of the procedures that guide the experimenter's behavior, including the rationale, script, or activities of the investigation (Barber, 1976).

Main Effect—The main effect is equivalent to an overall effect of an independent variable. In a factorial design, main effects are the separate and independent effects of the variables in the design and are distinguished from interactions. See Interaction.

Magnitude of Effect—A measure of the strength of the experimental effect or the magnitude of the contribution of the independent variable to performance on the dependent variable.

Matching—Grouping subjects together on the basis of their similarity on a particular characteristic or set of characteristics that is known or presumed to be related to the independent or dependent variables.

Maturation—Processes within the individual reflecting changes over time that may serve as a threat to internal validity.

Meta-Analysis—A quantitative method of evaluating a body of research in which effect size is used as the common metric. Studies are combined so that inferences can be drawn across studies and as a function of several of their characteristics (e.g., types of interventions).

Methodology—Refers to the diverse principles, procedures, and practices that govern research.

Mismatching—A procedure in which an effort is made to equalize groups that may be drawn from different samples. The danger is that the sample might be equal on a pretest measure of interest but regress toward different means upon retesting. Changes due to statistical regression might be misinterpreted as an effect due to the experimental manipulation.

Multiple-Baseline Design—A single-case experimental design strategy in which the intervention is introduced across different behaviors, individuals, or situations at different points in time. A causal relation between the intervention and performance on the dependent measures is demonstrated if each behavior (individual or situation) changes when and only when the program is introduced.

Multiple Comparisons—The number of comparisons or statistical tests in an experiment.

Multiple Operationism—Defining a construct by several measures or in several ways. Typically, researchers are interested in a general construct (e.g., depression, anxiety) and seek relations among variables that are evident beyond any single operation or measure to define the construct.

Multiple-Treatment Designs—Designs in which two or more different conditions or treatments are presented to each subject. In most multiple-treatment designs in clinical research, separate groups are used so that the different treatments can be presented in different orders.

Multiple-Treatment Interference—A potential threat to external validity when subjects are exposed to more than one condition or treatment within an experiment. The impact of a treatment or intervention may depend on the prior conditions to which subjects were exposed.

Multitrait-Multimethod Matrix—The set of correlations obtained from administering several measures to the same subject. These measures include two or more constructs (traits or characteristics), each of which is measured by two or more methods (e.g., self-report, direct observation). The primary purpose of the matrix is to evaluate convergent and discriminant validity.

Negative Results—A term commonly used to refer to a pattern of experimental results in which the differences or findings are not statistically significant.

No-Contact Control Group—A group that does not receive the experimental condition or intervention; subjects do not know they are participating in the research.

Nonequivalent Control Group—A group, often used in quasi-experiments, which is selected to control for selected threats to internal validity. The group is referred to as nonequivalent because it is not formed through random assignment in the investigation.

Nonmanipulated Variables—Variables that are studied through selection of subjects or observation of characteristics imposed by nature. See Subject-Selection Study.

Nonspecific Treatment Control Group—See "Attention-Placebo" Control Group.

Nonstatistical Evaluation—A method of data evaluation based on visual inspection criteria. Characteristics of the data (e.g., changes in means, trends, and level, as well as the latency of change) are used to infer reliability of the impact of the experimental manipulation.

Normative Range—A range of performance among a nonreferred, community sample that is used as a point of reference for evaluating the clinical significance of change in intervention studies.

No-Treatment Control Group—A group that does not receive the experimental condition or intervention.

Novelty Effects—A potential threat to external validity when the effects of an intervention may depend in part on their innovativeness or novelty in the situation.

Null Hypothesis (H_o)—The hypothesis that specifies that there is no difference between conditions or groups in the experiment on the dependent measures of interest.

Obtrusive Measures—Any measure or measurement condition in which subjects are aware that some facet of their performance is assessed. See Reactivity.

Operational Definition—Defining a concept by the specific operations or measures that are to be used in an experiment. The specific way in which the construct will be defined for inclusion in the investigation.

Order Effects—In multiple-treatment designs, the impact of a treatment may depend on whether it appears first (or in some other place) in the treatments that are presented to the subjects. If the position of the treatments influences the results, this is referred to as an order effect. Compare with Sequence Effects.

Passive-Observational Study—A type of research design in which the relations among variables are observed but not manipulated. Typically, the focus is on characteristics of different subjects or the relations among nonmanipulated variables. See also Subject-Selection Study.

Patched-up Control Group—A group that is not randomly composed from the pool of subjects in the study. The group is added to the design to help rule out specific rival hypotheses and decrease the plausibility of specific threats to internal validity.

Per Comparison Error Rate—The probability of a Type I error for a specific comparison or statistical test of differences when several comparisons are made. Contrast with Experiment-Wise Error Rate.

Physical Traces—Unobtrusive measures that consist of selective wear (erosion) or the deposit (accretion) of materials.

Placebo—A substance that has no active pharmacological properties that would be expected to produce change.

Postexperimental Inquiry—A method of evaluating whether demand characteristics may account for the results by asking the subjects after the experiment about their perceptions of the purpose of the experiment, what the experimenter expected from them, and how they were supposed to respond.

Posttest-Only Control Group Design—An experimental design (with a minimum of two groups) in which no pretest is given. The effect of the experimental condition across groups is assessed on a postintervention measure only.

Power—The probability of rejecting the null hypothesis (that there are no differences) when in fact that hypothesis is false. Alternatively, detecting a difference between groups when in fact a difference truly exists.

Predictive Validity—The correlation of a measure at one point in time with performance on another measure or criterion at some point in the future.

Preinquiry—A method of evaluating whether demand characteristics may account for the results by conveying information to the subjects about the experiment without actually running them through the conditions. Subjects are also asked to complete the dependent measures to see if their performance yields the expected results.

Pretest–Posttest Control Group Design—An experimental design with a minimum of two groups. Usually, one group receives the experimental condition and the other does not. The essential feature of the design is that subjects are tested before and after the intervention.

Pretest Sensitization—Administration of the pretest may alter the influence of the experimental condition that follows.

Probability Pyramiding—The error rate or risk of a Type I error rate that comes from conducting multiple comparisons (e.g., *t* tests) in an experiment.

Projective Techniques—A class of measures that assess facets of personality based on the presentation of ambiguous tasks or materials. Subjects respond with minimal situational cues or constraints.

Psychometric Characteristics—A general term that encompasses diverse types of reliability and validity evidence in behalf of a measure.

Psychophysiological Measures—Assessment techniques designed to quantify biological events as they relate to psychological states.

Quasi-Experimental Design—A type of design in which the conditions of true experiments are only approximated. Restrictions are placed on some facet of the design such as the assignment of cases randomly to conditions that affects the strength of the inferences that can be drawn.

Random Assignment—Allocating or assigning subjects to groups in such a way that the probability of each subject appearing in any of the groups is equal. This is usually accomplished by determining the group to which each subject is assigned by a table of random numbers.

Random Selection—Drawing subjects from a population in such a way that each member of the population has an equal probability of being drawn.

Reactivity—Performance that is altered as a function of subject awareness (e.g., of the measurement procedures, of participation in an experiment).

Regression Effect—See Statistical Regression.

Replication—Repetition of an experiment or repetition of the findings of an experiment.

Research Design—The plan or arrangement that is used to examine the question of interest; the manner in which conditions are planned so as to permit valid inferences.

Reversal Phase—A phase or period in single-case designs in which the baseline (nonintervention) condition is reintroduced to see if performance returns to or approximates the level of the original baseline.

Samples of Convenience—Subjects included in an investigation that appear to be selected merely because they are available whether or not they provide a suitable or optimal test of the hypotheses or conditions of interest.

Sample Size—The number of cases included that might refer to the overall number of subjects in the study (N) or the number of subjects within a group (n).

Sequence Effects—In multiple-treatment designs, several treatments may be presented to the subject. A series of treatments is provided (e.g., Treatment A, B, then C for some subjects and B, C, then A for other subjects, and so on for other combinations).

If the different sequences yield different outcomes, this is referred to as sequence effects. Compare with Order Effects.

Self-Report Inventories—Questionnaires and scales in which the subjects report on aspects of their own views, personality, or behaviors.

Significance Level—See Alpha.

Simulators—A method of estimating whether demand characteristics may operate by asking subjects to act *as if* they received the treatment or intervention even though they actually do not. These simulators are then run through the assessment procedures of the investigation by an experimenter who is "blind" as to who is a simulator and who is a real subject.

Simultaneous-Treatment Design—A single-case experimental design in which two or more interventions are implemented concurrently in the same treatment phase. The interventions are balanced or varied across different conditions such as the time period of the day in which the interventions are implemented. The design is useful for comparing the relative effectiveness of two or more interventions.

Single-Case Experimental Designs—Research designs in which the effects of an intervention can be evaluated with the single case, that is, one subject.

Single Operationism—Defining a construct by a single measure or one operation. Contrast with Multiple Operationism.

Social Impact Measures—Measures in outcome research that are important in everyday life or to society at large.

Solomon Four-Group Design—An experimental design that is used to evaluate the effect of pretesting. The design can be considered as a combination of the pretest-posttest control group design and a posttest-only design in which pretest (provided vs. not provided) and the experimental intervention (treatment vs. no treatment) are combined.

Stable Rate—Performance obtained from continuous observations over time, as in single-case designs, in which there is little or no trend (slope) or variability in the data.

Statistical Conclusion Validity—The extent to which a relation between independent and dependent variables can be shown based on quantitative and statistical considerations of the investigation.

Statistical Evaluation—Applying statistical tests to assess whether the obtained results are reliable or the differences in performance are likely to have occurred by "chance."

Statistical Power—See Power.

Statistical Regression—The tendency of extreme scores on any measure to revert (or regress) toward the mean of a distribution when the measurement device is readministered. Regression is a function of the amount of error in the measure and the test–retest correlation.

Subject Roles—Alternative ways of responding that subjects may adopt in response to the cues of the experiment.

Subject Variables—Those variables that are based on features within the individual or circumstances to which they were exposed. These variables are usually not manipulated experimentally.

Subjective Evaluation—A method of evaluating the clinical significance of an intervention outcome by assessing the opinions of clients themselves, individuals who are likely to have contact with the client, or people in a position of expertise. The question addressed by this method of evaluation is whether changes in treatment have led to differences in how the client perceives the changes with treatment or is viewed by others.

Subject-Selection Biases—Factors that operate in the selection of subjects or selective loss or retention of subjects over the course of the study that can affect experimental validity. Primary examples would be selection, recruitment, or screening procedures that might restrict the generality (external validity) of the findings and loss of subjects that might alter group composition and lead to differences that would be mistaken for an intervention effect (internal validity).

Subject-Selection Study—A type of passive-observational study in which the investigator varies the independent variable by selecting subjects with different characteristics (e.g., persons who have experienced trauma vs. those who have not) or with varying degrees of that characteristic (e.g., people with high, medium, or low scores on a measure of risk taking, depression, or helplessness). Groups are formed based on selection criteria.

Testing—A threat to internal validity that consists of the effects of taking a test on repeated occasions. Performance may change as a function of repeated exposure to the measure rather than to the independent variable or experimental condition.

Test-Retest Reliability—The stability of test scores over time; the correlation of scores from one administration of the test with scores on the same instrument after a particular time interval has elapsed.

Test Sensitization—Alteration of subject performance due to administration of a test before (pretest) or after (posttest) the experimental condition or intervention. The test may influence (e.g., augment) the effect of the experimental condition. A potential threat to external validity if the effect of the experimental condition may not generalize to different testing conditions.

Threats to Construct Validity—Those features associated with the experimental condition or intervention that interfere with drawing inferences about the basis for the difference between groups.

Threats to External Validity—Characteristics of the experiment that may limit the generality of the results.

Threats to Internal Validity—Factors or influences other than the independent variable that could explain the results.

Threats to Statistical Conclusion Validity—Considerations within the investigation that undermine the quantitative evaluation of the data.

Treatment Integrity—The fidelity with which treatment is rendered in an investigation.

True Experiment—A type of research in which the arrangement permits maximum control over the independent variables or conditions of interest. The investigator is able to assign subjects to different conditions on a random basis, to include alternative conditions (e.g., treatment and control conditions) as required by the design, and to control possible sources of bias within the experiment, that permit the comparison of interest.

Unobtrusive Measures—Those measures that are outside of the awareness of the subject.

Visual Inspection—A method of data evaluation commonly used in single-case research based on examining the pattern of change (means, level, trend, and latency of change) over phases.

Waiting-List Control Group—A group that is designed to control for threats to internal validity. The experimental condition or intervention is not provided during the period that experimental subjects receive the intervention. After this period, subjects in this control group receive the intervention.

Yoked-Control Group—A group or control condition designed to ensure that groups are equal with respect to potentially important but conceptually and procedurally irrelevant factors that might account for group differences. Yoking refers to equalizing the groups on a particular variable that might systematically vary across conditions.

REFERENCES

Abramowitz, S.I., & Jackson, C. (1974). Comparative effectiveness of there-and-then versus here-and-now therapist interpretations in group psychotherapy. *Journal of Counseling Psychology, 21,* 288–293.

Achenbach, T.M., & Edelbrock, C.S. (1981). Behavioral problems and competencies reported by parents of normal and disturbed children aged four through sixteen. *Monographs of the Society for Research in Child Development, 46,* Serial No. 188.

Achenbach, T.M., & Edelbrock, C.S. (1983). *Manual for the Child Behavior Checklist and Revised Child Behavior Profile.* Burlington, VT: University Associates in Psychiatry.

Agnew, N.M., & Pyke, S.W. (1987). *The science game* (4th ed.). Englewood Cliffs, NJ: Prentice-Hall.

Aiken, L.S., West, S.G., Sechrest, L., & Reno, R.R. (1990). Graduate training in statistics, methodology, and measurement in psychology: A survey of PhD programs in North America. *American Psychologist, 45,* 721–734.

Alden, L. (1989). Short-term structured treatment for avoidant personality disorder. *Journal of Consulting and Clinical Psychology, 57,* 756–764.

Allport, G.W. (1961). *Pattern and growth in personality.* New York: Holt, Rinehart & Winston.

American Psychiatric Association. (1980). *Diagnostic and statistical manual of mental disorders* (3rd ed.). Washington, DC: Author.

American Psychiatric Association. (1987). *Diagnostic and statistical manual of mental disorders.* (3rd ed., Rev.). Washington, DC: Author.

American Psychological Association, Committee for the Protection of Human Participants in Research. (1973). *Ethical principles in the conduct of research with human participants.* Washington, DC: Author.

American Psychological Association, Committee for the Protection of Human Participants in Research. (1982). *Ethical principles in the conduct of research with human participants.* Washington, DC: Author.

American Psychological Association, (1983). *Publication manual of the American Psychological Association* (3rd ed.). Washington, DC: Author.

American Psychological Association (1990a, June). Ethical principles revised: Comments are sought on proposed revision. *APA Monitor,* pp. 28–32.

American Psychological Association (1990b). *Journals in psychology: A resource listing for authors* (3rd ed). Washington, DC: Author.

American Psychologist. (1965). *20* (11). [Entire Issue].

Angoff, W.H. (1988). Validity: An evolving concept. In H. Wainer & H.I. Braun (Eds.), *Test validity.* Hillsdale, NJ: Lawrence Erlbaum Associates.

Annas, G.J., Glantz, L.H., & Katz, B.F. (1977). *Informed consent to human experimentation: The subject's dilemma.* Cambridge, MA: Ballinger.

Austin, N.K., Liberman, R.P., King, L.W., & DeRisi, W.J. (1976). A comparative evaluation of two day hospitals: Goal attainment scaling of behavior therapy vs. milieu therapy. *Journal of Nervous and Mental Disease, 163,* 253–262.

Ayllon, T., Layman, D., & Kandel, H.J. (1975). A behavioral–educational alternative to drug control of hyperactive children. *Journal of Applied Behavior Analysis, 8,* 137–146.

Azrin, N.H., Holz, W., Ulrich, R., & Goldiamond, I. (1961). The control of the content of conversation through reinforcement. *Journal of the Experimental Analysis of Behavior, 4,* 25–30.

Azrin, N.H., Hontos, P.T., & Besalel-Azrin, V. (1979). Elimination of enuresis without a conditioning apparatus: An extension by office instruction of the child and parents. *Behavior Therapy, 10,* 14–19.

Azrin, N.H., Naster, B.J., & Jones, R. (1973). Reciprocity counseling: A rapid learning-based procedure for marital counseling. *Behaviour Research and Therapy, 11,* 365–382.

Baekeland, F., & Lundwall, L. (1975). Dropping out of treatment: A critical review. *Psychological Bulletin, 82,* 738–783.

Baer, D.M. (1977). Perhaps it would be better not to know everything. *Journal of Applied Behavior Analysis, 10,* 167–172.

Bailar, J.C., III, & Patterson, K. (1985). Journal of peer review: The need for a research agenda. *The New England Journal of Medicine, 312,* 654–657.

Bakan, D. (1966). The test of significance in psychological research. *Psychological Bulletin, 66,* 423–437.

Barber, J.G., Bradshaw, R., & Walsh, C. (1989). Reducing alcohol consumption through television advertising. *Journal of Consulting and Clinical Psychology, 57,* 613–618.

Barber, T.X. (1976). *Pitfalls in human research: Ten pivotal points.* Elmsford, NY: Pergamon Press.

Barlow, D.H., & Hayes, S.C. (1979). Alternative treatments design: One strategy for comparing the effects of two treatments in a single subject. *Journal of Applied Behavior Analysis, 12,* 199–210.

Barlow, D.H., & Hersen, M. (1984). *Single-case experimental designs: Strategies for studying behavior change* (2nd ed.). Elmsford, NY: Pergamon Press.

Barlow, D.H., Reynolds, J., & Agras, W.S. (1973). Gender identity change in a transsexual. *Archives of General Psychiatry, 29,* 569–576.

Barthel, C.E., & Crowne, D.P. (1962). The need for approval, task categorization, and perceptual defense. *Journal of Consulting Psychology, 26,* 547–555.

Barthel, C.N., & Holmes, D.S. (1968). High school yearbooks: A nonreactive measure of social isolation in graduates who later became schizophrenic. *Journal of Abnormal Psychology, 73,* 313–316.

Beatty, W.W. (1972). How blind is blind? A simple procedure for estimating observer naivete. *Psychological Bulletin, 78,* 70–71.

Beck, A.T., Weissman, A., Lester, D., & Trexler, L. (1974). The measurement of pessimism: The Hopelessness Scale. *Journal of Consulting and Clinical Psychology, 42,* 861–865.

Beck, J.G., Andrasik, F., & Arena, J.G. (1984). Group comparison designs. In A.S. Bellack & M. Hersen (Eds.), *Research methods in clinical psychology.* Elmsford, NY: Pergamon Press.

Bellack, A.S., Hersen, M., & Lamparski, D. (1979). Role-play tests for assessing social skills: Are they valid? Are they useful? *Journal of Consulting and Clinical Psychology, 47,* 335–342.

Beneke, W.N., & Harris, M.B. (1972). Teaching self-control of study behavior. *Behaviour Research and Therapy, 10,* 35–41.

Bernstein, D.A., Borkovec, T.D., & Coles, M.G.H. (1986). Assessment of anxiety. In A.R. Ciminero, K.S. Calhoun, & H.E. Adams (Eds.), *Handbook of behavioral assessment* (2nd ed.). New York: John Wiley & Sons.

Bernstein, I.N., Bohrnstedt, G.W., & Borgatta, E.F. (1975). External validity and evaluation research: A codification of problems. *Sociological Methods and Research, 4,* 101–128.

Beutler, L.E., Crago, M., & Arizmendi, T.G. (1986). Therapist variables in psychotherapy process and outcome. In S.L. Garfield & A.E. Bergin (Eds.), *Handbook of psychotherapy and behavior change* (3rd ed.). New York: John Wiley & Sons.

Billings, D.C., & Wasik, B.H. (1985). Self-instructional training with preschoolers: An attempt to replicate. *Journal of Applied Behavior Analysis, 18,* 61–67.

Bloom, L.J., Weigel, R.G., & Trautt, G.M. (1977). "Therapeugenic" factors in psychotherapy: Effects of office decor and subject–therapist pairing on the perception of credibility. *Journal of Consulting and Clinical Psychology, 45,* 867–873.

Bloom, M., & Fischer, J. (1982). *Evaluating practice: Guidelines for the accountable professional.* Englewood Cliffs, NJ: Prentice-Hall.

Bolgar, H. (1965). The case study method. In B.B. Wolman (Ed.), *Handbook of clinical psychology.* New York: McGraw-Hill.

Bootzin, R.R. (1985). The role of expectancy in behavior change. In L. White, B. Tursky, G.E. Schwartz (Eds.), *Placebo: Theory, research, and mechanisms.* New York: Guilford Press.

Boring, E.G. (1954). The nature and history of experimental control. *American Journal of Psychology, 60,* 573–589.

Bornstein, P.H., Hamilton, S.B., & Bornstein, M.T. (1986). Self-monitoring procedures. In A.R. Ciminero, K.S. Calhoun, & H.E. Adams (Eds.), *Handbook of behavioral assessment* (2nd ed.). New York: John Wiley & Sons.

Bornstein, P.H., & Quevillon, R.P. (1976). The effects of a self-instructional package on overactive preschool boys. *Journal of Applied Behavior Analysis, 9,* 179–188.

Botvin, G.J., Baker, E., Filazzola, A.D., & Botvin, E.M. (1990). A cognitive–behavioral approach to substance abuse prevention: One-year follow-up. *Addictive Behaviors, 15,* 47–63.

Bracht, G.H., & Glass, G.V. (1968). The external validity of experiments. *American Educational Research Journal, 5,* 437–474.

Bradley, J.V. (1981). Pernicious publication practices. *Bulletin of the Psychonomic Society, 18,* 31–34.

Bradley, J.V. (1982). Editorial overkill. *Bulletin of the Psychonomic Society, 19,* 271–274.

Braver, M.C.W., & Braver, S.L. (1988). Statistical treatment of the Solomon Four-Group Design: A meta-analytic approach. *Psychological Bulletin, 104,* 150–154.

Breuer, J., & Freud, S. (1957). *Studies in hysteria.* New York: Basic Books.

Broad, W., & Wade, N. (1982). *Betrayers of truth.* New York: Simon & Schuster.

Brody, E.M., & Farber, B.A. (1989). Effects of psychotherapy on significant others. *Professional Psychology: Research and Practice, 20,* 116–122.

Brown, J. (1987). A review of meta-analyses conducted on psychotherapy outcome research. *Clinical Psychology Review, 7,* 1–23.

Brunswik, E. (1955). Representative design and probabilistic theory in a functional psychology. *Psychological Review, 62,* 193–217.

Bryant, L.E., & Budd, K.S. (1982). Self-instructional training to increase independent work performance in preschoolers. *Journal of Applied Behavior Analysis, 15,* 259–271.

Butcher, J.N. (Ed.). (1985). Perspectives on computerized psychological assessment. [Special series]:. *Journal of Consulting and Clinical Psychology, 53,* 745–838.

Butcher, J.N., Graham, J.R., Williams, C.L., & Ben-Porath, Y.S. (1990). *Development and use of the MMPI-2 content scales.* Minneapolis, MN: University of Minnesota Press.

Campbell, D.T. (1963). Social attitudes and other acquired behavioral dispositions. In S. Koch (Ed.), *Psychology: A study of science.* New York: McGraw-Hill.

Campbell, D.T., & Fiske, D. (1959). Convergent and discriminant validation by the multitrait-multimethod matrix. *Psychological Bulletin, 56,* 81–105.

Campbell, D.T., & Stanley, J.C. (1963). Experimental and quasi-experimental designs for research and teaching. In N.L. Gage (Ed.), *Handbook of research on teaching.* Chicago: Rand McNally.

Carlsmith, J.M., Ellsworth, P.C., & Aronson, E. (1976). *Methods of research in social psychology.* Reading, MA: Addison-Wesley.

Cattell, R.B. (1988). The principles of experimental design and analysis in relation to theory building. In J.R. Nesselroade & R.B. Cattell (Eds.), *Handbook of multivariate experimental psychology* (2nd ed.). New York: Plenum Press.

Chamberlain, P., & Reid, J.B. (1987). Parent observation and report of child symptoms. *Behavioral Assessment, 9,* 97–109.

Chassan, J.B. (1967). *Research design in clinical psychology and psychiatry.* New York: Appleton-Century-Crofts.

Chow, SL. (1988). Significance test or effect size? *Psychological Bulletin, 103,* 105–110.

Church, R.M. (1964). Systematic effect of random error in the yoked control design. *Psychological Bulletin, 62,* 122–131.

Clark, K.E. (1967, April). *Invasion of privacy in the investigation of human behavior.* Paper presented at the meeting of the Eastern Psychological Association, Boston, MA.

Cohen, J. (1965). Some statistical issues in psychological research. In B.B. Wolman (Ed.), *Handbook of clinical psychology.* New York: McGraw-Hill.

Cohen, J. (1988). *Statistical power analysis in the behavioral sciences* (2nd ed.). Hillsdale, NJ: Lawrence Erlbaum & Associates.

Cohen, J. (1990). Things I have learned (so far). *American Psychologist, 45,* 1304–1312.

Committee on Biomedical Research in the Veterans Administration. (1977). *Biomedical research in the Veterans Administration.* Washington, DC: National Academy of Sciences.

Conoley, J.C., & Kramer, J.J. (Eds.). (1989). *The tenth mental measurements yearbook.* Lincoln, NE: University of Nebraska Press.

Cook, T.D., & Campbell, D.T. (Eds.). (1979). *Quasi-experimentation: Design and analysis issues for field settings.* Chicago: Rand McNally.

Cowles, M., & Davis, C. (1982). On the origins of the .05 level of statistical significance. *American Psychologist, 37,* 553–558.

Craik, K.H. (1986). Personality research methods: An historical perspective. *Journal of Personality, 54,* 18–51.

Cronbach, L.J. (1957). The two disciplines of scientific psychology. *American Psychologist, 12,* 671–684.

Cronbach, L.J. (1975). Beyond the two disciplines of scientific psychology. *American Psychologist, 30,* 116–127.

Cronbach, L.J. (1982). *Designing evaluations of educational and social programs.* San Francisco: Jossey-Bass.

Cronbach, L.J., & Meehl, P.E. (1955). Construct validity in psychological tests. *Psychological Bulletin, 52,* 281–302.

Crowe, M.J., Marks, I.M., Agras, W.S., & Leitenberg, H. (1972). Time-limited desensitization, implosion and shaping for phobic patients: A crossover study. *Behaviour Research and Therapy, 10,* 319–328.

Crowne, D.P., & Marlowe, D. (1964). *The approval motive: Studies in evaluative dependence.* New York: John Wiley & Sons.

Davis, R.V. (1987). Scale construction. *Journal of Counseling Psychology, 34,* 481–489.

Davis, W.E. (1973). The irregular discharge as an unobtrusive measure of discontent among young psychiatric patients. *Journal of Abnormal Psychology, 81,* 17–21.

DeProspero, A., & Cohen, S. (1979). Inconsistent visual analysis of intrasubject data. *Journal of Applied Behavior Analysis, 12,* 573–579.

DeRubeis, R.J., Hollon, S.E., Evans, M.D., & Bemis, K.M. (1982). Can psychotherapies for depression be discriminated? A systematic investigation of cognitive therapy and interpersonal therapy. *Journal of Consulting and Clinical Psychology, 50,* 744–756.

Dewan, M.J., & Koss, M. (1989). The clinical impact of the side effects of psychotropic drugs. In S. Fisher & R.P. Greenberg (Eds.), *The limits of biological treatments for psychological distress.* Hillsdale, NJ: Lawrence Erlbaum & Associates.

Dies, R.R., & Greenberg, B. (1976). Effects of physical contact in an encounter group context. *Journal of Consulting and Clinical Psychology, 44,* 400–405.

Dobes, R.W. (1977). Amelioration of psychosomatic dermatosis by reinforced inhibition of scratching. *Journal of Behavior Therapy and Experimental Psychiatry, 8,* 185–187.

Dukes, W.F. (1965). N = 1. *Psychological Bulletin, 64,* 74–79.

Edwards, A.L. (1957). *The social desirability variable in personality assessment and research.* New York: Dryden Press.

Ellis, A. (1957). Outcome of employing three techniques of psychotherapy. *Journal of Clinical Psychology, 13,* 344–350.

Ellsworth, R.B. (1975). Consumer feedback in measuring the effectiveness of mental-health programs. In M. Guttentag & E.L. Struening (Eds.), *Handbook of evaluation research* (Vol. 2). Beverly Hills, CA: Sage Publications.

Ellsworth, R.B., Foster, L., Childers, B., Arthur, G., & Kroeker, D. (1968). Hospital and community adjustment as perceived by psychiatric patients, their families, and staff. *Journal of Consulting and Clinical Psychology, 32* (5, Pt. 2).

Empey, L.T. (1982). *American delinquency: Its meaning and construction.* Homewood, IL: Dorsey Press.

Erdberg, P. (1990). Rorschach assessment. In G. Goldstein & M. Hersen (Eds.), *Handbook of psychological assessment* (2nd ed.). Elmsford, NY: Pergamon Press.

Erdman, H.P., Klein, M.H., & Greist, J.H. (1985). Direct patient computer interviewing. *Journal of Consulting and Clinical Psychology, 53,* 760–773.

Eron, L.D., & Huesmann, L.R. (1984). Television violence and aggressive behavior. In B.B. Lahey & A.E. Kazdin (Eds.), *Advances in clinical child psychology* (Vol. 7). New York: Plenum Press.

Everaerd, W.T.A.M., Rijken, H.M., & Emmelkamp, P.M.G. (1973). A comparison of "flooding" and "successive approximation" in the treatment of agoraphobia. *Behaviour Research and Therapy, 11,* 105–117.

Fagley, N.S. (1985). Applied statistical power analysis and the interpretation of nonsignificant results by research consumers. *Journal of Counseling Psychology, 32,* 391–396.

Feldman, J.J., Hyman, H., & Hart, C.W. (1951). A field study of interviewer effects on the quality of survey data. *Public Opinion Quarterly, 15,* 734–761.

Feldman, R.A., Caplinger, T.E., & Wodarski, J.S. (1983). *The St. Louis conundrum: The effective treatment of antisocial youths.* Englewood Cliffs, NJ: Prentice-Hall.

Festinger, L., & Carlsmith, J.M. (1959). Cognitive consequences of forced compliance. *Journal of Abnormal and Social Psychology, 58,* 203–210.

Firestone, P. (1976). The effects and side effects of timeout on an aggressive nursery school child. *Journal of Behavior Therapy and Experimental Psychiatry, 7,* 79–81.

Fisher, B., Bauer, M., Margolese, R., Poisson, R., Pilch, Y., Redmond, C., Fisher, E., Wolmark, N., Deutsch, M., Montague, E., Saffer, E., Wickerham, I., Lerner, H., Glass, A., Shibata, H., Deckers, P., Ketcham, R., Dishi, R., & Russell, I. (1985). Five-year results of a randomized clinical trial comparing total mastectomy and segmental mastectomy with or without radiation in the treatment of breast cancer. *New England Journal of Medicine, 312,* 665–673.

Fisher, J.D., Silver, R.C., Chinsky, J.M., Goff, B., Klar, Y., & Zagieboylo, C. (1989). Psychological effects of participation in a large group awareness training. *Journal of Consulting and Clinical Psychology, 57,* 747–755.

Fisher, R.A., & Yates, F. (1963). *Statistical tables for biological, agricultural and medical research.* Edinburgh: Oliver & Boyd.

Flick, S.N. (1988). Managing attrition in clinical research. *Clinical Psychology Review, 8,* 499–515.

Folger, R. (1989). Significance tests and the duplicity of binary decisions. *Psychological Bulletin, 106,* 155–160.

Foulks, E.F. (1987). Social stratification and alcohol use in North Alaska. *Journal of Community Psychology, 15,* 349–356.

Foulks, E.F. (1989). Misalliances in the Barrow Alcohol Study. *American Indian and Native Alaska Mental Health Research, 2*(3), 7–17.

Fox, D.K., Hopkins, B.L., & Anger, W.K. (1987). The long-term effects of a token economy on safety performance in open-pit mining. *Journal of Applied Behavior Analysis, 20,* 215–224.

Foxx, R.M., & Rubinoff, A. (1979). Behavioral treatment of caffeinism: Reducing excessive coffee drinking. *Journal of Applied Behavior Analysis, 12,* 335–344.

Frank, J.D. (1973). *Persuasion and healing: A comparative study of psychotherapy* (2nd ed.). Baltimore: Johns Hopkins University Press.

Frank, J.D. (1982). Therapeutic components shared by all psychotherapies. In J.H. Harvey & M.M. Parks (Eds.), *Psychotherapy research and behavior change* (Vol. 1). Washington, DC: American Psychological Association.

Frank, J.D., Nash, E.H., Stone, A.R., & Imber, S.D. (1963). Immediate and long-term symptomatic course of psychiatric outpatients. *American Journal of Psychiatry, 120,* 429–439.

Freiman, J.A., Chalmers, T.C., Smith, H., & Kuebler, R.R. (1978). The importance of beta, the Type II error, and sample size in the design and interpretation of the randomized control trial. *New England Journal of Medicine, 299,* 690–694.

Freud, S. (1933). Analysis of a phobia in a five-year-old boy. In *Collected papers* (Vol. 3). London: Hogarth Press.

Friedling, C., & O'Leary, S. (1979). Effects of self-instructional training on second- and third-grade hyperactive children: A failure to replicate. *Journal of Applied Behavior Analysis, 12,* 211–219.

Friedman, L.M., Furberg, C.D., & DeMets, D.L. (1985). *Fundamentals of clinical trials* (2nd ed.). Littleton, MA: PSG Publishing.

Galton, F. (1872). Statistical inquiries into the efficacy of prayer. *Fornightly Review, 12,* 125–135.

Garfield, S.L. (1984). The evaluation of research: An editorial perspective. In A.S. Bellack & M. Hersen (Eds.), *Research methods in clinical psychology.* Elmsford, NY: Pergamon Press.

Garfield, S.L, & Bergin, A.E. (Eds.). (1986). *Handbook of psychotherapy and behavior change: An empirical analysis* (3rd ed.). New York: John Wiley & Sons.

Gaupp, L.A., Stern, R.M., & Galbraith, G.G. (1972). False heart-rate feedback and reciprocal inhibition by aversion relief in the treatment of snake avoidance behavior. *Behavior Therapy, 3,* 7–20.

Geller, E.S., Winett, R.A., & Everett, P.B. (1982). *Preserving the environment: New strategies for behavior change.* Elmsford, NY: Pergamon Press.

Gelso, C.J. (Ed.). (1987). Quantitative foundations of counseling psychology research [Special issue]:. *Journal of Counseling Psychology, 34* (Whole No. 4).

Glasgow, R.E., & Rosen, G.M. (1984). Self-help behavior therapy manuals: Recent developments and clinical usage. In C.M. Franks (Ed.), *New developments in behavior therapy: From research to clinical application.* New York: Haworth Press.

Goldfried, M.R., Greenberg, L.S., & Marmar, C. (1990). Individual psychotherapy: Process and outcome. *Annual Review of Psychology, 41,* 659–688.

Goldstein, G. (1990). Comprehensive neuropsychological assessment batteries. In G. Goldstein & M. Hersen (Eds.), *Handbook of psychological assessment* (2nd ed.). Elmsford, NY: Pergamon Press.

Goldstein, G., & Hersen, M. (Eds.) (1990). *Handbook of psychological assessment* (2nd ed.). Elmsford, NY: Pergamon Press.

Gottman, J.M. (1973). N-of-one and N-of-two research in psychotherapy. *Psychological Bulletin, 80,* 93–105.

Gottman, J.M. (1981). *Time-series analysis: A comprehensive introduction for social scientists.* Cambridge, England: Cambridge University Press.

Gottman, J.M., & Glass, G.V. (1978). Analysis of interrupted time-series experiments. In T.R. Kratochwill (Ed.), *Single-subject research: Strategies for evaluating change.* New York: Academic Press.

Gould, M.S., Shaffer, D., & Kaplan, D. (1985). The characteristics of dropouts from a child psychiatry clinic. *Journal of the American Academy of Child Psychiatry, 24,* 316–328.

Grant, D.A. (1948). The Latin square principle in the design and analysis of psychological experiments. *Psychological Bulletin, 45,* 427–442.

Greenberg, J., & Folger, R. (1988). *Controversial issues in social research methods.* New York: Springer-Verlag.

Greenwald, A.G. (1975). Consequences of prejudice against the null hypothesis. *Psychological Bulletin, 82,* 1–20.

Greenwald, A.G. (1976). Within-subjects designs: To use or not to use? *Psychological Bulletin, 83,* 314–320.

Grenier, C. (1985). Treatment effectiveness in an adolescent chemical dependency treatment program: A quasi-experimental design. *International Journal of the Addictions, 20,* 381–391.

Gripp, R.F., & Magaro, P.A. (1971). A token economy program evaluation with untreated control ward comparisons. *Behaviour Research and Therapy, 9,* 137–149.

Haase, R.F., & Ellis, M.V. (1987). Multivariate analysis of variance. *Journal of Counseling Psychology, 34,* 404–413.

Haase, R.F., Ellis, M.V., & Ladany, N. (1989). Multiple criteria for evaluating the magnitude of experimental effects. *Journal of Counseling Psychology, 4,* 511–516.

Hackmann, A., & McLean, C. (1975). A comparison of flooding and thought stopping in the treatment of obsessional neurosis. *Behaviour Research and Therapy, 13,* 263–269.

Hagen, R.L., Foreyt, J.P., & Durham, T.W. (1976). The dropout problem: Reducing attrition in obesity research. *Behavior Therapy, 7,* 463–471.

Hale, R. (1991). Intellectual assessment. In M. Hersen, A.E. Kazdin, & A.S. Bellack (Eds.), *The clinical psychology handbook* (2nd ed.). Elmsford, NY: Pergamon Press.

Handelsman, M.M., & Galvin, M.D. (1988). Facilitating informed consent for outpatient psychotherapy: A suggested written format. *Professional Psychology: Research and Practice, 19,* 223–225.

Harris, F.R., Wolf, M.M., & Baer, D.M. (1964). Effects of adult social reinforcement on child behavior. *Young Children, 20,* 8–17.

Hartmann, D.P., & Hall, R.V. (1976). The changing criterion design. *Journal of Applied Behavior Analysis, 9,* 527–532.

Hartshorne, H., & May, M.S. (1928). *Studies in nature of the character. I: Studies in deceit.* New York: Macmillan.

Hartshorne, H., May, M.A., & Shuttleworth, F.K. (1930). *Studies in the nature of character. III: Studies in the organization of character.* New York: Macmillan.

Hawkins, J.D., & Lam, T. (1987). Teacher practices, social development, and delinquency. In J.D. Burchard & S.N. Burchard (Eds.), *Prevention of delinquent behavior.* Newbury Park, CA: Sage Publications.

Heap, R.F., Boblitt, W.E., Moore, C.H., & Hord, J.E. (1970). Behavior-milieu therapy with chronic neuropsychiatric patients. *Journal of Abnormal Psychology, 76,* 349–354.

Heimberg, R.G., & Becker, R.E. (1984). Comparative outcome research. In M. Hersen, L. Michelson, & A.S. Bellack (Eds.), *Issues in psychotherapy research.* New York: Plenum Press.

Heinicke, C.M., & Ramsey-Klee, D.M. (1986). Outcome of child psychotherapy as a function of frequency of session. *Journal of the American Academy of Child Psychiatry, 25,* 247–253.

Henley, N.M. (1977). *Body politics: Power, sex, and nonverbal communication.* Englewood Cliffs, NJ: Prentice-Hall.

Higgs, W.J. (1970). Effects of gross environmental change upon behavior of schizophrenics: A cautionary note. *Journal of Abnormal Psychology, 76,* 421–422.

Hochberg, Y., & Tamhane, A.C. (1987). *Multiple comparison procedures.* New York: John Wiley & Sons.

Hodgson, R., & Rachman, S.H. (1974). Desynchrony in measures of fear. *Behaviour Research and Therapy, 12,* 319–326.

Hodgson, R., Rachman, S., & Marks, I.M. (1972). The treatment of chronic obsessive-compulsive neurosis: Follow-up and further findings. *Behaviour Research and Therapy, 10,* 181–189.

Horn, W.F., Ialongo, N., Popovich, S., & Peradotto, D. (1987). Behavioral parent training and cognitive–behavioral self-control therapy with ADD-H children: Comparative and combined effects. *Journal of Clinical Child Psychology, 16,* 57–68.

Horvath, P. (1988). Placebos and common factors in two decades of psychotherapy research. *Psychological Bulletin, 104,* 214–225.

Howard, K.I., Kopta, S.M., Krause, M.S., & Orlinsky, D.E. (1986). The dose-effect relationship in psychotherapy. *American Psychologist, 41,* 159–164.

Howard, K.I., Krause, M.S., & Orlinsky, D.E. (1986). The attrition dilemma: Toward a new strategy for psychotherapy research. *Journal of Consulting and Clinical Psychology, 54,* 106–110.

Hsu, L.M. (1989). Random sampling, randomization, and equivalence of contrasted groups in psychotherapy outcome research. *Journal of Consulting and Clinical Psychology, 57,* 131–137.

Huberty, C.J., & Morris, J.D. (1989). Multivariate analysis versus multiple univariate analyses. *Psychological Bulletin, 105,* 302–308.

Intagliata, J.C. (1978). Increasing the interpersonal problem-solving skills of an alcoholic population. *Journal of Consulting and Clinical Psychology, 46,* 489–498.

Jaccard, J., Turrisi, R., & Wan, C.K. (1990). *Interaction effects in multiple regression.* Newbury Park, CA: Sage.

Jacobson, N.S. (1984). A component analysis of behavioral marital therapy: The relative effectiveness of behavior exchange and communication/problem-solving training. *Journal of Consulting and Clinical Psychology, 52,* 295–305.

Jacobson, N.S. (Ed.). (1988). Defining clinically significant change [Special issue]. *Behavioral Assessment, 10*(2).

Jacobson, N.S., & Revenstorf, D. (1988). Statistics for assessing the clinical significance of psychotherapy techniques: Issues, problems, and new developments. *Behavioral Assessment, 10,* 133–145.

Johnson, R.F.Q. (1976). The experimenter attributes effect: A methodological analysis. *Psychological Record, 26,* 67–68.

Johnston, J.M., & Pennypacker, H.S. (1980). *Strategies and tactics of human behavioral research.* Hillsdale, NJ: Lawrence Erlbaum & Associates.

Jones, M.C. (1924a). A laboratory study of fear: The case of Peter. *Pedagogical Seminary, 31,* 308–315.

Jones, M.C. (1924b). The elimination of children's fears. *Journal of Experimental Psychology, 7,* 382–390.

Julnes, G., & Mohr, L.B. (1989). Evaluation of no-difference findings in evaluation research. *Evaluation Review, 13,* 628–655.

Kadden, R.M., Cooney, N.L., Getter, H., & Litt, M.D. (1989). Matching alcoholics to coping skills or interactional therapies: Posttreatment results. *Journal of Consulting and Clinical Psychology, 57,* 698–704.

Kaimowitz v. Michigan Department of Mental Health, 42 U.S.L. Week 2063 (Michigan Circuit Court, Wayne City. July 10, 1973).

Kazdin, A.E. (1977). Assessing the clinical or applied significance of behavior change through social validation. *Behavior Modification, 1,* 427–452.

Kazdin, A.E. (1978). Evaluating the generality of findings in analogue therapy research. *Journal of Consulting and Clinical Psychology, 46,* 673–686.

Kazdin, A.E. (1981). Drawing valid inferences from case studies. *Journal of Consulting and Clinical Psychology, 49,* 183–192.

Kazdin, A.E. (1982a). Symptom substitution, generalization, and response covariation: Implications for psychotherapy outcome. *Psychological Bulletin, 91,* 349–365.

Kazdin, A.E. (1982b). *Single-case research designs: Methods for clinical and applied settings.* New York: Oxford University Press.

Kazdin, A.E. (1982c). Observer effects: Reactivity of direct observation. In D.P. Hartmann (Ed.), *Using observers to study behavior.* San Francisco: Jossey-Bass.

Kazdin, A.E. (1984a). Statistical analyses for single-case experimental designs. In D.H. Barlow & M. Hersen (Eds.), *Single-case experimental designs: Strategies for studying behavior change* (2nd ed.). Elmsford, NY: Pergamon Press.

Kazdin, A.E. (1984b). Acceptability of aversive procedures and medication as treatment alternatives for deviant child behavior. *Journal of Abnormal Child Psychology, 12,* 289–302.

Kazdin, A.E. (1985). *Treatment of antisocial behavior in children and adolescents.* Pacific Grove, CA:Brooks/Cole.

Kazdin, A.E. (1986a). Comparative outcome studies of psychotherapy: Methodological issues and strategies. *Journal of Consulting and Clinical Psychology, 54,* 95–105.

Kazdin, A.E. (1986b). Acceptability of psychotherapy and hospitalization for disturbed children: Parent and child perspectives. *Journal of Clinical Child Psychology, 15,* 333–340.

Kazdin, A.E. (1987). Treatment of antisocial behavior in children: Current status and future directions. *Psychological Bulletin, 102,* 187–203.

Kazdin, A.E. (1988). *Child psychotherapy: Developing and identifying effective treatments.* Elmsford, NY: Pergamon Press.

Kazdin, A.E. (1989a). Identifying depression in children: A comparison of alternative selection criteria. *Journal of Abnormal Child Psychology, 17,* 437–455.

Kazdin, A.E. (1989b). Hospitalization of antisocial children: Clinical course, follow-up status, and predictors of outcome. *Advances in Behaviour Research and Therapy, 11,* 1–67.

Kazdin, A.E. (1989c). *Behavior modification in applied settings* (4th ed.). Pacific Grove, CA: Brooks/Cole.

Kazdin, A.E. (1990). Premature termination from treatment among children referred for antisocial behavior. *Journal of Child Psychology and Psychiatry, 31,* 415–425.

Kazdin, A.E., & Bass, D. (1989). Power to detect differences between alternative treatments in comparative psychotherapy outcome research. *Journal of Consulting and Clinical Psychology, 57,* 138–147.

Kazdin, A.E., Bass, D., Ayers, W.A., & Rodgers, A. (1990). The empirical and clinical focus of child and adolescent psychotherapy research. *Journal of Consulting and Clinical Psychology, 58,* 729–740.

Kazdin, A.E., Bass, D., Siegel, T., & Thomas, C. (1989). Cognitive-behavioral treatment and relationship therapy in the treatment of children referred for antisocial behavior. *Journal of Consulting and Clinical Psychology, 57,* 522–535.

Kazdin, A.E., & Esveldt-Dawson, K. (1986). The Interview for Antisocial Behavior: Psychometric characteristics and concurrent validity with child psychiatric inpatients. *Journal of Psychopathology and Behavioral Assessment, 8,* 289–303.

Kazdin, A.E., Esveldt-Dawson, K., French, N.H., & Unis, A.S. (1987). Problem-solving skills training and relationship therapy in the treatment of antisocial child behavior. *Journal of Consulting and Clinical Psychology, 55,* 76–85.

Kazdin, A.E., Esveldt-Dawson, K., Unis, A.S., & Rancurello, M.D. (1983). Child and parent evaluations of depression and aggression in psychiatric inpatient children. *Journal of Abnormal Child Psychology, 11,* 401–413.

Kazdin, A.E., French, N.H., & Sherick, R.B. (1981). Acceptability of alternative treatments for children: Evaluations by inpatient children, parents, and staff. *Journal of Consulting and Clinical Psychology, 49,* 900–907.

Kazdin, A.E., French, N.H., & Unis, A.S. (1983). Child, mother, and father evaluations of depression in psychiatric inpatient children. *Journal of Abnormal Child Psychology, 11,* 167–180.

Kazdin, A.E., French, N.H., Unis, A.S., Esveldt-Dawson, K., & Sherick, R.B. (1983). Hopelessness, depression, and suicidal intent among psychiatrically disturbed inpatient children. *Journal of Consulting and Clinical Psychology, 51,* 504–510.

Kazdin, A.E., & Hartmann, D.P. (1978). The simultaneous-treatment design. *Behavior Therapy, 9,* 912–922.

Kazdin, A.E., Kratochwill, T.M., & VandenBos, G.R. (1986). Beyond clinical trials: Generalizing from research to practice. *Professional Psychology: Research and Practice, 17,* 391–398.

Kazdin, A.E., Rodgers, A., & Colbus, D. (1986). The Hopelessness Scale for Children: Psychometric characteristics and concurrent validity. *Journal of Consulting and Clinical Psychology, 54,* 241–245.

Kazdin, A.E., Siegel, T., & Bass, D. (1990). Drawing on clinical practice to inform research on child and adolescent psychotherapy: Survey of practitioners. *Professional Psychology: Research and Practice, 21,* 189–198.

Kazdin, A.E., & Tuma, A.H. (Eds.). (1982). *New directions for methodology of social and behavioral sciences: Single-case research designs.* San Francisco: Jossey-Bass.

Kazdin, A.E., & Wilcoxon, L.A. (1976). Systematic desensitization and nonspecific treatment effects: A methodological evaluation. *Psychological Bulletin, 83,* 729–758.

Kazdin, A.E., & Wilson, G.T. (1978). Criteria for evaluating psychotherapy. *Archives of General Psychiatry, 35,* 407–416.

Kelman, H.C. (1972). The rights of the subject in social research: An analysis in terms of relative power and legitimacy. *American Psychologist, 27,* 989–1016.

Kendall, P.C., & Butcher, J.N. (Eds.). (1982). *Handbook of research methods in clinical psychology.* New York: John Wiley & Sons.

Kendall, P.C., & Grove, W.M. (1988). Normative comparisons in therapy outcome. *Behavioral Assessment, 10,* 147–158.

Kendall, P.C., & Norton-Ford, J.D. (1982). Therapy outcome research methods. In P.C. Kendall & J.N. Butcher (Eds.), *Handbook of research methods in clinical psychology.* New York: John Wiley & Sons.

Kent, R.N., O'Leary, K.D., Diament, C., & Dietz, A. (1974). Expectation biases in observational evaluation of therapeutic change. *Journal of Consulting and Clinical Psychology, 42,* 774–780.

Kidder, L.H., & Judd, C.M. (1986). *Research methods in social relations* (5th ed.). New York: Holt, Rinehart & Winston.

Kiesler, D.J. (1971). Experimental designs in psychotherapy research. In A.E. Bergin & S.L. Garfield (Eds.), *Handbook of psychotherapy and behavior change: An empirical analysis.* New York: John Wiley & Sons.

Kingsley, R.G., & Wilson, G.T. (1977). Behavior therapy for obesity: A comparative investigation of long-term efficacy. *Journal of Consulting and Clinical Psychology, 45,* 288–298.

Kirk, R.E. (1968). *Experimental design: Procedures for the behavioral sciences.* Belmont, CA: Brooks/Cole.

Kline, P. (1986). *A handbook of test construction: Introduction to psychometric design.* London: Methuen.

Klopfer, W.G., & Taulbee, E.S. (1976). Projective tests. *Annual Review of Psychology, 27,* 543–567.

Klosko, J.S., Barlow, D.H., Tassinari, R., & Cerny, J.A. (1990). A comparison of Alprazolam and behavior therapy in the treatment of panic disorder. *Journal of Consulting and Clinical Psychology, 58,* 77–84.

Klusman, L.E. (1975). Reduction of pain in childbirth by the alleviation of anxiety during pregnancy. *Journal of Consulting and Clinical Psychology, 43,* 162–165.

Korchin, S.J. (1976). *Modern clinical psychology.* New York: Basic Books.

Kohn, A. (1988). *False profits: Fraud and error in science and medicine.* New York: Basil Blackwell.

Kolvin, I., Garside, R.F., Nicol, A.E., MacMillan, A., Wolstenholme, F., & Leitch, I.M. (1981). *Help starts here: The maladjusted child in the ordinary school.* London: Tavistock.

Kraemer, H.C., & Thiemann, S. (1987). *How many subjects? Statistical power analysis in research.* Newbury Park, CA: Sage.

Krathwohl, D.R. (1985). *Social and behavioral science research.* San Francisco: Jossey-Bass.

Krause, M.S., & Howard, K.I. (1976). Program evaluation in the public interest: A new research methodology. *Community Mental Health Journal, 12,* 291–300.

Kruglanski, A. W. (1975). The human subject in the psychology experiment: Fact and artifact. In L. Berkowitz (Ed.), *Advances in experimental social psychology* (Vol. 8). Orlando, FL: Academic Press.

Kupfersmid, J. (1988). Improving what is published: A model in search of an editor. *American Psychologist, 43,* 635–642.

Kutner, B., Wilkins, C., & Yarrow, P.R. (1952). Verbal attitudes and overt behavior involving racial prejudice. *Journal of Abnormal and Social Psychology, 47,* 649–652.

Lacey, J.I., & Lacey, B.C. (1958). Verification and extension of the principle of autonomic response-stereotypy. *American Journal of Psychology, 71,* 51–73.

Lakatos, I. (1978). *The methodology of scientific research programmes.* Cambridge, England: Cambridge University Press.

Lally, R., Mangione, P.L., & Honig, A.S. (1988). The Syracuse University Family Development Research Program: Long-range impact on an early intervention with low-income children and their families. In D. Powell (Ed.), *Parent education as early childhood intervention: Emerging directions in theory, research, and practice.* Norwood, NJ: Ablex.

Lambert, M.J. (1983). Introduction to assessment of psychotherapy outcome: Historical perspective and current issues. In M.J. Lambert, E.R. Christensen, & S.S. DeJulio (Eds.), *The assessment of psychotherapy outcome.* New York: John Wiley & Sons.

Lambert, M.J., Christensen, E.R., & DeJulio, S.S. (eds.). (1983). *The assessment of psychotherapy outcome.* New York: John Wiley & Sons.

Lambert, M.J., & Ogles, B.M. (1988). Treatment manuals: Problems and promise. *Journal of Integrative and Eclectic Psychotherapy, 7,* 187–204.

La Piere, R.T. (1934). Attitudes vs. action. *Social Forces, 13,* 230–237.

Last, C.G., Hersen, M., Kazdin, A.E., Francis, G., & Grubb, H.J. (1987). Psychiatric illness in the mothers of anxious children. *American Journal of Psychiatry, 144,* 1580–1583.

Laudan, L. (1984). *Science and values.* Berkeley: University of California Press.

Lawson, D.M., Wilson, G.T., Briddell, D.W., & Ives, C.C. (1976). Assessment and modification of alcoholics' drinking behavior in controlled laboratory settings: A cautionary note. *Addictive Behavior, 1,* 299–303.

Lazarus, A.A. (1961). Group therapy of phobic disorders by systematic desensitization. *Journal of Abnormal and Social Psychology, 63,* 504–510.

Lazlo, J.P., & Rosenthal, R. (1971). Subject dogmatism, experimenter status, and experimenter expectancy effects. *Personality, 1,* 11–23.

Lidz, C.W., Meisel, A., Zerubavel, E., Carter, M., Sestak, R.M., & Roth, L.H. (1984). *Informed consent: A study of decision making in psychiatry.* New York: Guilford Press.

Lipsey, M.W. (1990). *Design sensitivity: Statistical power for experimental research.* Newbury Park, CA: Sage Publications.

Little, R.J.A., & Rubin, D.B. (1987). *Statistical analysis with missing data.* New York: John Wiley & Sons.

Lochman, J.E. (1985). Effects of different treatment lengths in cognitive behavioral interventions with aggressive boys. *Child Psychiatry and Human Development, 16,* 45–56.

Longo, D.J., Clum, G.A., & Yaeger, N.J. (1988). Psychosocial treatment of recurrent genital herpes. *Journal of Consulting and Clinical Psychology, 56,* 61–66.

Luborsky, L., & DeRubeis, R.J. (1984). The use of psychotherapy treatment manuals: A small revolution in psychotherapy research style. *Clinical Psychology Review, 4,* 5–14.

Lykken, D.T. (1968). Statistical significance in psychological research. *Psychological Bulletin, 70,* 151–159.

MacFarlane, J.W., Allen, L., & Honzik, M.P. (1954). *A developmental study of the behavior problems of normal children between 21 months and 14 years.* Berkeley: University of California Press.

Magnusson, D. (Ed.). (1981). *Toward a psychology of situations: An interactional perspective.* Hillsdale, NJ: Lawrence Erlbaum Associates.

Maher, B.A. (1978a). Stimulus sampling in clinical research: Representative design reviewed. *Journal of Consulting and Clinical Psychology, 46,* 643–647.

Maher, B.A. (1978b). A reader's, writer's, and reviewer's guide to assessing research reports in clinical psychology. *Journal of Consulting and Clinical Psychology, 46,* 835–838.

Mahoney, M.J. (1976). *Scientist as subject: The psychological imperative.* Cambridge, MA: Ballinger.

Manicas, P.T., & Secord, P.F. (1983). Implications for psychology of the new philosophy of science. *American Psychologist, 38,* 399–413.

Manson, S.M. (Ed.). (1989). *American Indian and Alaska Native Mental Health Research, 2* (Whole No. 3).

Marks, I.M. (1987). *Fears, phobias, and rituals.* New York: Oxford University Press.

Marks, I.M., Marset, P., Boulougouris, J., & Huson, J. (1971). Physiological accompaniments of neutral and phobic imagery. *Psychological Medicine, 1,* 299–307.

Martin, J.E., & Sachs, D.A. (1973). The effects of a self-control weight loss program on an obese woman. *Journal of Behavior Therapy and Experimental Psychiatry, 4,* 155–159.

Masling, J.M. (1960). The influence of situational and interpersonal variables in projective testing. *Psychological Bulletin, 57,* 65–85.

Matthews, D.B. (1986). Discipline: Can it be improved with relaxation training? *Elementary School Guidance and Counseling, 20,* 194–200.

Matthys, W. Walterbos, W., Njio, L., & van Engeland, H. (1989). Person perception in children with conduct disorders. *Journal of Child Psychology and Psychiatry, 30,* 439–448.

McGuire, W.J. (1969). Suspiciousness of experimenter's intent. In R. Rosenthal & R.L. Rosnow (Eds.), *Artifact in behavioral research.* New York: Academic Press.

Meehl, P. (1978). Theoretical risks and tabular asterisks: Sir Karl, Sir Ronald, and the slow progress of soft psychology. *Journal of Consulting and Clinical Psychology, 46,* 806–834.

Meinart, C.T. (1986). *Clinical trials: Design, conduct, and analysis.* New York: Oxford University Press.

Meltzoff, J., & Kornreich, M. (1970). *Research in psychotherapy.* New York: Aldine-Atherton.

Meyer, V. (1957). The treatment of two phobic patients on the basis of learning principles. *Journal of Abnormal and Social Psychology, 55,* 261–266.

Miers, M.L. (1985). Current NIH perspectives on misconduct in science. *American Psychologist, 40,* 831–835.

Miller, L.C. (1977). *School Behavior Checklist manual.* Los Angeles: Western Psychological Services.

Mook, D.G. (1983). In defense of external invalidity. *American Psychologist, 38,* 379–387.

Miller, S.B. (1972). The contribution of therapeutic instructions to systematic desensitization. *Behaviour Research and Therapy, 10,* 159–170.

Mohr, L.B. (1990). *Understanding significance testing.* Newbury Park, CA: Sage Publications.

Murray, E.J. (1989). Measurement issues in the evaluation of psychopharmacological therapy. In S. Fisher & R.P. Greenberg (Eds.), *The limits of biological treatments for psychological distress: Comparisons with psychotherapy and placebo.* Hillsdale, NJ: Lawrence Erlbaum Associates.

Murray, L.W., & Dosser, D.A. Jr. (1987). How significant is a significant difference? Problems with the measurement of magnitude of effect. *Journal of Counseling Psychology, 34,* 68–72.

National Academy of Sciences, Committee on the Conduct of Science. (1989). *On being a scientist.* Washington, DC: National Academy Press.

Needleman, H.L., & Bellinger, D., (1984). The developmental consequences of childhood exposure to lead: Recent studies and methodological issues. In B.B. Lahey & A.E. Kazdin (Eds.), *Advances in clinical child psychology* (Vol. 7). New York: Plenum Press.

Needleman, H.L., Schell, A.S., Bellinger, D., Leviton, A., & Alldred, E.N. (1990). The long-term effects of exposure to low doses of lead in childhood: An 11-year follow-up report. *New England Journal of Medicine, 322,* 83–88.

Newcomb, M.D., & Bentler, P.M. (1988). *Consequences of adolescent drug use: Impact on the lives of young adults.* Newbury Park, CA: Sage Publications.

Nezu, A.M. & Perri, M.G. (1989). Social problem-solving therapy for unipolar depression: An initial dismantling investigation. *Journal of Consulting and Clinical Psychology, 57,* 408–413.

Nicholson, R.A., & Berman, J.S. (1983). Is follow-up necessary in evaluating psychotherapy? *Psychological Bulletin, 93,* 555–565.

Nittany Motor Club (AAA). (1978, May–June). High mounted brake lights prove safer. *The Motorist,* p. 2

Nunnally, J. (1960). The place of statistics in psychology. *Educational and Psychological Measurement, 20,* 641–650.

O'Grady, K.E. (1982). Measures of explained variance: Cautions and limitations. *Psychological Bulletin, 92,* 766–777.

O'Leary, K.D., & Borkovec, T.D. (1987). Conceptual, methodological, and ethical problems of placebo groups in psychotherapy research. *American Psychologist, 33,* 821–830.

Ollendick, T.H., Shapiro, E.S., & Barrett, R.P. (1981). Reducing stereotypic behaviors: An analysis of treatment procedures using an alternating-treatments design. *Behavior Therapy, 12,* 570–577.

Orne, M.T. (1962). On the social psychology of the psychological experiment: With particular reference to demand characteristics and their implications. *American Psychologist, 17,* 776–783.

Orne, M.T. (1969). Demand characteristics and the concept of quasi-controls. In R. Rosenthal & R.L. Rosnow (Eds.), *Artifact in behavioral research.* New York: Academic Press.

Orne, M.T., & Scheibe, K.E. (1964). The contribution of nondeprivation factors in the production of sensory deprivation effects: The psychology of the "panic button." *Journal of Abnormal and Social Psychology, 68,* 3–12.

Palmer, A.B., & Wohl, J. (1972). Voluntary-admission forms: Does the patient know what he's signing? *Hospital and Community Psychiatry, 23,* 250–252.

Parloff, M.B. (1986). Placebo controls in psychotherapy research: A sine qua non or a placebo for research problems? *Journal of Consulting and Clinical Psychology, 54,* 79–87.

Patterson, G.R. (1982). *Coercive family process.* Eugene, OR: Castalia.

Patterson, G.R. (1986). Performance models for antisocial boys. *American Psychologist, 41,* 432–444.

Patterson, G.R., Chamberlain, P., & Reid, J.B. (1982). A comparative evaluation of a parent-training program. *Behavior Therapy, 13,* 638–650.

Paul, G.L. (1966). *Insight versus desensitization in psychotherapy: An experiment in anxiety reduction.* Stanford, CA: Stanford University Press.

Paul, G.L. (1967). Outcome research in psychotherapy. *Journal of Consulting Psychology, 31,* 109–118.

Paul, G.L., & Lentz, R.J. (1977). *Psychosocial treatment of chronic mental patients: Milieu versus social learning program.* Cambridge, MA: Harvard University Press.

Pekarik, G., & Stephenson, L.A. (1988). Adult and child client differences in therapy dropout research. *Journal of Clinical Child Psychology, 17,* 316–321.

Penk, W.E., Charles, H.L., & Van Hoose, T.A. (1978). Comparative effectiveness of day hospital and inpatient psychiatric treatment. *Journal of Consulting and Clinical Psychology, 46,* 94–101.

Perri, M.G., Nezu, A.M., Patti, E.T., & McCann, K.L. (1989). Effect of length of treatment on weight loss. *Journal of Consulting and Clinical Psychology, 57,* 450–452.

Rachman, S., & Hodgson, R.I. (1974). Synchrony and desynchrony in fear and avoidance. *Behaviour Research and Therapy, 12,* 311–318.

Reichardt, C.S., & Gollob, H.F. (1989). Ruling out threats to validity. *Evaluation Review, 13,* 3–17.

Resnick, J.H., & Schwartz, T. (1973). Ethical standards as an independent variable in psychological research. *American Psychologist, 28,* 134–139.

Rezmovic, E.L. (1984). Assessing treatment implementation amid the slings and arrows of reality. *Evaluation Review, 8,* 187–204.

Rogers, C., & Dymond, R. (Eds.). (1954). *Psychotherapy and personality change.* Chicago: University of Chicago Press.

Rosen, G.M. (1974). Therapy set: Its effects on subjects' involvement in systematic desensitization and treatment outcome. *Journal of Abnormal Psychology, 83,* 291–300.

Rosen, G.M., Glasgow, R.E., & Barrera, M., Jr. (1976). A controlled study to assess the clinical efficacy of totally self-administered systematic desensitization. *Journal of Consulting and Clinical Psychology, 44,* 208–217.

Rosenberg, M.J. (1969). The conditions and consequences of evaluation apprehension. In R. Rosenthal & R.L. Rosnow (Eds.), *Artifact in behavioral research.* New York: Academic Press.

Rosenthal, R. (1966). *Experimenter effects in behavioral research.* New York: Appleton-Century-Crofts.

Rosenthal, R. (1969). Interpersonal expectations: Effects of the experimenter's hypothesis. In R. Rosenthal & R.L. Rosnow (Eds.), *Artifact in behavioral research.* New York: Academic Press.

Rosenthal, R. (1976). *Experimenter effects in behavioral research* (enlarged edition). New York: Irvington.

Rosenthal, R. (1979). The "file drawer problem" and tolerance for null results. *Psychological Bulletin, 86,* 638–641.

Rosenthal, R. (1984). *Meta-analytic procedures for social research.* Beverly Hills, CA: Sage Publications.

Rosenthal, R., & Rosnow, R.L. (1975). *The volunteer subject.* New York: John Wiley & Sons.

Rosnow, R.L., & Rosenthal, R. (1989). Definition and interpretation of interaction effects. *Psychological Bulletin, 105,* 143–146.

Ross, J.A. (1975). Parents modify thumbsucking: A case study. *Journal of Behavior Therapy and Experimental Psychiatry, 6,* 248–249.

Ross, L., Lepper, M.R., & Hubbard, M. (1975). Perseverance in self-perception and perception: Biased attributional processes in the debriefing paradigm. *Journal of Personality and Social Psychology, 32,* 800–892.

Rossi, J.S. (1990). Statistical power of psychological research: What have we gained in 20 years? *Journal of Consulting and Clinical Psychology, 58,* 646–656.

Roth, L.H., Meisel, A., & Lidz, C.W. (1977). Tests of competency to consent to treatment. *American Journal of Psychiatry, 134,* 279–288.

Rounsaville, B.J., Chevron, E.S., Prusoff, B.A., Elkin, I., Imber, S., Stosky, S., & Watkins, J. (1986). The relation between specific and general dimensions of the psychotherapy process in interpersonal psychotherapy of depression. *Journal of Consulting and Clinical Psychology, 55,* 379–394.

Rusch, F.R., Walker, H.M., & Greenwood, C.R. (1975). Experimenter calculation errors: A potential factor affecting interpretation of results. *Journal of Applied Behavior Analysis, 8,* 460.

Rush, A.J., Beck, A.T., Kovacs, M., & Hollon, S. (1977). Comparative efficacy of cognitive therapy and pharmacotherapy in the treatment of depressed outpatients. *Cognitive Therapy and Research, 1,* 17–37.

Saigh, P.A. (1986). In vitro flooding in the treatment of a 6-year-old boy's posttraumatic stress disorder. *Behaviour Research and Therapy, 24,* 685–688.

Schaffer, N.D. (1983). Methodological issues of measuring the skillfulness of therapeutic techniques. *Psychotherapy: Theory, Research and Practice, 20,* 486–493.

Scheffler, I. (1967). *Science and subjectivity.* Indianapolis: Bobbs-Merrill.

Schuler, H. (Ed.). (1982). *Ethical problems in psychological research.* New York: Academic Press.

Schweinhart, L.J., & Weikart, D.P. (1988). The High/Scope Perry preschool program. In R.H. Price, E.L. Cowen, R.P. Lorion, & J. Ramos-McKay (Eds.), *Fourteen ounces of prevention: A casebook for practitioners.* Washington, DC: American Psychological Association.

Sears, R.R. (1963). Dependency motivation. In M.R. Jones (Ed.), *Nebraska Symposium on Motivation.* Lincoln, NE: University of Nebraska Press.

Sechrest, L., White, S. O., & Brown, E. D. (Eds.). (1979). *The rehabilitation of criminal offenders: Problems and prospects.* Washington, DC: National Academy of Sciences.

Sedlmeier, P., & Gigerenzer, G. (1989). Do studies of statistical power have an effect on the power of studies? *Psychological Bulletin, 105,* 309–316.

Seitz, V., Rosenbaum, L.K., & Apfel, N.H. (1985). Effects of family support intervention: A ten-year follow-up. *Child Development, 56,* 376–391.

Serlin, R.C. (1987). Hypothesis testing, theory building, and the philosophy of science. *Journal of Counseling Psychology, 34,* 365–371.

Serlin, R.C., & Lapsley, D.K. (1985). Rationality in psychological research: The good-enough principle. *American Psychologist, 40,* 73–83.

Shakow, D. (1982). Perspectives on research in clinical psychology. In P.C. Kendall & J.N. Butcher (Eds.), *Handbook of research methods in clinical psychology.* New York: John Wiley & Sons.

Shapiro, A.K., & Morris, L.A. (1978). The placebo effect in medical and psychological therapies. In S.L. Garfield & A.E. Bergin (Eds.), *Handbook of psychotherapy and behavior change: An empirical analysis* (2nd ed.). New York: John Wiley & Sons.

Shapiro, D.A., & Shapiro, D. (1983). Comparative therapy outcome research: Methodological implications of meta-analysis. *Journal of Consulting and Clinical Psychology, 51,* 42–53.

Shapiro, M.B. (1966). The single case in clinical-psychological research. *Journal of Genetic Psychology, 74,* 3–23.

Sidman, M. (1960). *Tactics of scientific research.* New York: Basic Books.

Simes, R.J. (1986). An improved Bonferroni procedure for multiple tests of significance. *Biometrika, 74,* 751–754.

Sindermann, C.J. (1982). *Winning the games scientists play.* New York: Plenum Press.

Skinner, B.F. (1957). The experimental analysis of behavior. *American Scientist, 45,* 343–371.

Skoloda, T.E., Alterman, A.I., Cornelison, F.S., & Gottheil, F. (1975). Treatment outcome in a drinking decision program. *Journal of Studies on Alcohol, 36,* 365–380.

Sloane, R.B., Staples, F.R., Cristol, A.H., Yorkston, N.J., & Whipple, K. (1975). *Psychotherapy versus behavior therapy.* Cambridge, MA: Harvard University Press.

Sobell, M.B., Schaefer, H.H., & Mills, K.C. (1972). Differences in baseline drinking behavior between alcoholics and normal drinkers. *Behaviour Research and Therapy, 10,* 257–267.

Solomon, R.L. (1949). An extension of control group design. *Psychological Bulletin, 46,* 137–150.

Spirito, A., Overholser, J., Ashworth, S., Morgan, J., & Benedict-Drew, C. (1988). Evaluation of a suicide awareness curriculum for high school students. *Journal of the American Academy of Child and Adolescent Psychiatry, 27,* 705–711.

Spirito, A., Williams, C.A., Stark, L.J., & Hart, K.J. (1988). The Hopelessness Scale for Children: Psychometric properties with normal and emotionally disturbed adolescents. *Journal of Abnormal Child Psychology, 16,* 445–458.

Stahl, J.R., Thomson, L.E., Leitenberg, H., & Hasazi, J.E. (1974). Establishment of praise as a conditioned reinforcer in socially unresponsive psychiatric patients. *Journal of Abnormal Psychology, 83,* 488–496.

Staudt, V.M., & Zubin, J. (1957). A biometric evaluation of the somatotherapies in schizophrenia. *Psychological Bulletin, 54,* 171–196.

Stevens, J. (1986). *Applied multivariate statistics for the social sciences.* Hillsdale, NJ: Lawrence Erlbaum Associates.

Striker, G., & Healey, B.J. (1990). Projective assessment of object relations: A review of the empirical literature. *Psychological Assessment, 2,* 219–230.

Strupp, H.H., & Hadley, S.W. (1977). A tripartite model of mental health and therapeutic outcomes. *American Psychologist, 32,* 187–196.

Sushinsky, L., & Bootzin, R. (1970). Cognitive desensitization as a model of systematic desensitization. *Behaviour Research and Therapy, 8,* 29–34.

Szapocznik, J., Perez-Vidal, A., Brickman, A.L., Foote, F.H., Santisteban, D., Hervis, O., & Kurtines, W.M. (1988). Engaging adolescent drug abusers and their families into treatment: A strategic structural systems approach. *Journal of Consulting and Clinical Psychology, 56,* 552–557.

Szapocznik, J., Rio, A., Murray, E., Cohen, R., Scopetta, M., Rivas-Vazquez, A., Hervis, O., Posada, V., & Kurtines, W. (1989). Structural family versus psychodynamic child therapy for problematic Hispanic boys. *Journal of Consulting and Clinical Psychology, 57,* 571–578.

Thigpen, C.H., & Cleckley, H.M. (1954). A case of multiple personality. *Journal of Abnormal and Social Psychology, 49,* 135–151.

Thigpen, C.H., & Cleckley, H.M. (1957). *Three faces of Eve.* New York: McGraw-Hill.

Tversky, A., & Kahneman, D. (1971). Belief in the law of small numbers. *Psychological Bulletin, 76,* 105–110.

United States Congress, Committee on Government Operations. (1990). *Are scientific misconduct and conflicts of interest hazardous to our health?* (House Report 101–688). Washington, DC: US Government Printing Office.

United States Department of Health and Human Services, National Institutes of Health, Office for Protection from Research Risks. (1983). *Code of federal regulations: Part 46: Protection of human subjects.* Washington DC: U.S. Government Printing Office.

Vaile-Val, G., Rosenthal, R.H., Curtiss, G., & Marohn, R.C. (1984). Dropout from adolescent psychotherapy: A preliminary study. *Journal of the American Academy of Child Psychiatry, 23,* 562–568.

Valins, S., & Ray, A. (1967). Effects of cognitive desensitization on avoidance behavior. *Journal of Personality and Social Psychology, 7,* 345–350.

Van Houten, R., Malenfant, L., & Rolider, A. (1985). Increasing driver yielding and pedestrian signaling with prompting, feedback, and enforcement. *Journal of Applied Behavior Analysis, 18,* 103–110.

Vermilyea, B.B., Barlow, D.H., & O'Brien, G.T. (1984). The importance of assessing treatment integrity: An example in the anxiety disorders. *Journal of Behavioral Assessment, 6,* 1–11.

Wainer, H., & Braun, H.I. (Eds.). (1988). *Test validity.* Hillsdale, NJ: Lawrence Erlbaum Associates.

Wallerstein, R.S. (1986). *Forty-two lives in treatment: A study of psychoanalysis and psychotherapy.* New York: Guilford Press.

Walster, E., Berscheid, E., Abrahams, D., & Aronson, V. (1967). Effectiveness of debriefing following deception experiments. *Journal of Personality and Social Psychology, 6,* 371–380.

Wampold, B.E., Davis, B., & Good, R.H., III. (1990). Hypothesis validity of clinical research. *Journal of Consulting and Clinical Psychology, 58,* 360–367.

Watson, J.B., & Rayner, R. (1920). Conditioned emotional reactions. *Journal of Experimental Psychology, 3,* 1–14.

Watson, R.I. (1951). *The clinical method in psychology.* New York: Harper & Row.

Webb, E.J., Campbell, D.T., Schwartz, R.D., Sechrest, L., & Grove, J.B. (1981). *Noncreative measures in the social sciences* (2nd ed.). Boston: Houghton Mifflin.

Weber, S.J., & Cook, T.D. (1972). Subject effects in laboratory research: An examination of subject roles, demand characteristics, and valid inference. *Psychological Bulletin, 77,* 273–295.

Weiner, I.B. (1983). Theoretical foundations of clinical psychology. In M. Hersen, A.E. Kazdin, & A.S. Bellack (Eds.), *The clinical psychology handbook.* Elmsford, NY: Pergamon Press.

Weiss, G., Minde, K., Douglas, V., Werry, J., & Sykes, D. (1971). Comparison of the effects of chlorpromazine, dextroamphetamine and methylphenidate on the behaviour and intellectual functioning of hyperactive children. *Canadian Medical Association Journal, 104,* 20–25.

Weisz, J.R., Walter, B.R., Weiss, B., Fernandez, G.A., & Mikow, V.A. (1990). Arrests among emotionally disturbed violent and assaultive individuals following minimal versus lengthy intervention through North Carolina's Willie M. Program. *Journal of Consulting and Clinical Psychology, 58,* 720–728.

Wells, K.B., Burnam, M.A., Leake, B., & Robins, L.N. (1988). Agreement between face-to-face and telephone-administered versions of the depression section of the NIMH Diagnostic Interview Schedule. *Journal of Psychiatric Research, 22,* 207–220.

Werner, E.E. (1987). Vulnerability and resiliency in children at risk for delinquency: A longitudinal study from birth to young adulthood. In J.D. Burchard & S.N. Burchard (Eds.), *Prevention of delinquent behavior.* Newbury Park, CA: Sage Publications.

White, G.D., Nielson, G., & Johnson, S.M. (1972). Timeout duration and the suppression of deviant behavior in children. *Journal of Applied Behavior Analysis, 5,* 111–120.

White, L., Tursky, B., & Schwartz, G.E. (Eds.). (1985). *Placebo: Theory, research, and mechanisms.* New York: Guilford Press.

Wicker, A. W. (1985). Getting out of our conceptual ruts: Strategies for expanding conceptual frameworks. *American Psychologist, 40,* 1094–1103.

Wilson, G.T. (1989). Behavior therapy. In American Psychiatric Association Task Force on Treatments of Psychiatric Disorders, *Treatments of psychiatric disorders* (Vol. 3). Washington, DC: American Psychiatric Association.

Wimsatt, W.C. (1981). Robustness, reliability, and multiple determination in science. In M.B. Brewer & B.E. Collins (Eds.), *Scientific inquiry and the social sciences: A volume in honor of Donald T. Campbell.* San Francisco: Jossey-Bass.

Windle, C. (1954). Test-retest effect on personality questionnaires. *Educational and Psychological Measurement, 14,* 617–633.

Wolf, M.M. (1978). Social validity: The case of subjective measurement or how applied behavior analysis is finding its heart. *Journal of Applied Behavior Analysis, 11,* 203–214.

Wright, D.M., Moelis, I., & Pollack, L.J. (1976). The outcome of individual child psychotherapy: Increments at follow-up. *Journal of Child Psychology and Psychiatry, 17,* 275–285.

Wright, K.M., & Miltenberger, R.G. (1987). Awareness training in the treatment of head and facial tics. *Journal of Behavior Therapy and Experimental Psychiatry, 18,* 269–274.

Yates, B.T. (1985). Cost-effectiveness analysis and cost-benefit analysis: An introduction. *Behavioral Assessment, 7,* 207–234.

Yeaton, W.H., & Sechrest, L. (1981). Critical dimensions in the choice and maintenance of successful treatments: Strength, integrity, and effectiveness. *Journal of Consulting and Clinical Psychology, 49,* 156–167.

Yeaton, W.H., & Sechrest, L. (1986). Use and misuse of no-difference findings in eliminating threats to validity. *Evaluation Review, 10,* 836–852.

Yin, R.K. (1984). *Case study research: Design and methods.* Beverly Hills, CA: Sage Publications.

Zilborg, G., & Henry, G. (1941). *A history of medical psychology.* New York: WW Norton.

AUTHOR INDEX

461

SUBJECT INDEX

ABOUT THE AUTHOR

Alan E. Kazdin is Professor of Psychology and Professor in the Child Study Center at Yale University. He is also Director of the Child Conduct Clinic, an outpatient treatment clinic for children and their families. He received his PhD at Northwestern University (1970). Prior to coming to Yale, he was on the faculty at The Pennsylvania State University and the University of Pittsburgh School of Medicine. Currently his work focuses on assessment, diagnosis, and treatment, particularly antisocial behavior and depression in children, and on psychotherapy outcome. He has been the editor of the *Journal of Consulting and Clinical Psychology, Psychological Assessment,* and *Behavior Therapy,* a Fellow at the Center for Advanced Study in the Behavioral Sciences, and President of the Association for Advancement of Behavior Therapy. He is a Fellow of the American Psychological Association and editor of the Sage Book Series on Developmental Clinical Psychology and Psychiatry.

His other books include:

Single-Case Research Designs: Methods for Clinical and Applied Settings
Child Psychotherapy: Developing and Identifying Effective Treatments
Behavior Modification in Applied Settings
History of Behavior Modification: Experimental Foundations of Contemporary Research
The Token Economy
Treatment of Antisocial Behavior in Children and Adolescents,
Conduct Disorder in Childhood and Adolescence
The Clinical Psychology Handbook (with A.S. Bellack & M. Hersen)
New Perspectives in Abnormal Psychology (with A.S. Bellack & M. Hersen)
Evaluation of Behavior Therapy: Issues, Evidence, and Research Strategies (with G.T. Wilson)
Behavior Therapy: Toward an Applied Clinical Science (with W.S. Agras & G.T. Wilson)
Single-Case Research Designs (with A.H. Tuma)
International Handbook of Behavior Modification and Therapy (with M. Hersen & A.S. Bellack)
Social Skills Assessment and Training with Children (with L. Michelson, D.P. Sugai, & R.P. Wood)
Cognitive-Behavior Modification (with L. Craighead, W.E. Craighead, & M. Mahoney)
Handbook of Clinical Behavior Therapy with Children (with P. Bornstein)
Advances in Clinical Child Psychology (with B.B. Lahey)

General Psychology Series

Editors: **Arnold P. Goldstein,** Syracuse University
Leonard Krasner, Stanford University &
SUNY at Stony Brook

*Out of print in original format. Available in custom reprint edition.